DRAMA
for Students

National Advisory Board

DRAMA for Students

Presenting Analysis, Context, and Criticism on Commonly Studied Dramas

Volume 16

David Galens, Project Editor

Foreword by Carole L. Hamilton

Detroit • New York • San Diego • San Francisco • Cleveland • New Haven, Conn. • Waterville, Maine • London • Munich

Drama for Students, Volume 16

Project Editor
David Galens

Editorial
Anne Marie Hacht, Michelle Kazensky, Ira Mark Milne, Pam Revitzer, Kathy Sauer, Timothy J. Sisler, Jennifer Smith, Carol Ullmann

Research
Sarah Genik

Permissions
Kim Davis, Debra Freitas

Manufacturing
Stacy Melson

Imaging and Multimedia
Lezlie Light, Dave Oblender, Kelly A. Quin, Luke Rademacher

Product Design
Pamela A. E. Galbreath, Michael Logusz

For more information, contact
The Gale Group, Inc.
27500 Drake Rd.
Farmington Hills, MI 48331-3535
Or you can visit our Internet site at
http://www.gale.com

ISBN 0-7876-6031-0

Printed in the United States of America
10 9 8 7 6 5 4 3 2 1

Table of Contents

The Study of Drama

We study drama in order to learn what meaning others have made of life, to comprehend what it takes to produce a work of art, and to glean some understanding of ourselves. Drama produces in a separate, aesthetic world, a moment of being for the audience to experience, while maintaining the detachment of a reflective observer.

Drama is a representational art, a visible and audible narrative presenting virtual, fictional characters within a virtual, fictional universe. Dramatic realizations may pretend to approximate reality or else stubbornly defy, distort, and deform reality into an artistic statement. From this separate universe that is obviously not "real life" we expect a valid reflection upon reality, yet drama never is mistaken for reality—the methods of theater are integral to its form and meaning. Theater is art, and art's appeal lies in its ability both to approximate life and to depart from it. For in intruding its distorted version of life into our consciousness, art gives us a new perspective and appreciation of life and reality. Although all aesthetic experiences perform this service, theater does it most effectively by creating a separate, cohesive universe that freely acknowledges its status as an art form.

And what is the purpose of the aesthetic universe of drama? The potential answers to such a question are nearly as many and varied as there are plays written, performed, and enjoyed. Dramatic texts can be problems posed, answers asserted, or moments portrayed. Dramas (tragedies as well as comedies) may serve strictly "to ease the anguish of a torturing hour" (as stated in William Shakespeare's *A Midsummer Night's Dream*)—to divert and entertain–or aspire to move the viewer to action with social issues. Whether to entertain or to instruct, affirm or influence, pacify or shock, dramatic art wraps us in the spell of its imaginary world for the length of the work and then dispenses us back to the real world, entertained, purged, as Aristotle said, of pity and fear, and edified—or at least weary enough to sleep peacefully.

It is commonly thought that theater, being an art of performance, must be experienced—seen—in order to be appreciated fully. However, to view a production of a dramatic text is to be limited to a single interpretation of that text—all other interpretations are for the moment closed off, inaccessible. In the process of producing a play, the director, stage designer, and performers interpret and transform the script into a work of art that always departs in some measure from the author's original conception. Novelist and critic Umberto Eco, in his *The Role of the Reader: Explorations in the Semiotics of Texts* (Indiana University Press, 1979), explained, "In short, we can say that every performance offers us a complete and satisfying version of the work, but at the same time makes it incomplete for us, because it cannot simultaneously give all the other artistic solutions which the work may admit."

Thus Laurence Olivier's coldly formal and neurotic film presentation of Shakespeare's *Hamlet* (in which he played the title character as well as directed) shows marked differences from subsequent adaptations. While Olivier's Hamlet is clearly entangled in a Freudian relationship with his mother Gertrude, he would be incapable of shushing her with the impassioned kiss that Mel Gibson's mercurial Hamlet (in director Franco Zeffirelli's 1990 film) does. Although each of performances rings true to Shakespeare's text, each is also a mutually exclusive work of art. Also important to consider are the time periods in which each of these films was produced: Olivier made his film in 1948, a time in which overt references to sexuality (especially incest) were frowned upon. Gibson and Zeffirelli made their film in a culture more relaxed and comfortable with these issues. Just as actors and directors can influence the presentation of drama, so too can the time period of the production affect what the audience will see.

A play script is an open text from which an infinity of specific realizations may be derived. Dramatic scripts that are more open to interpretive creativity (such as those of Ntozake Shange and Tomson Highway) actually require the creative improvisation of the production troupe in order to complete the text. Even the most prescriptive scripts (those of Neil Simon, Lillian Hellman, and Robert Bolt, for example), can never fully control the actualization of live performance, and circumstantial events, including the attitude and receptivity of the audience, make every performance a unique event. Thus, while it is important to view a production of a dramatic piece, if one wants to understand a drama fully it is equally important to read the original dramatic text.

The reader of a dramatic text or script is not limited by either the specific interpretation of a given production or by the unstoppable action of a moving spectacle. The reader of a dramatic text may discover the nuances of the play's language, structure, and events at their own pace. Yet studied alone, the author's blueprint for artistic production does not tell the whole story of a play's life and significance. One also needs to assess the play's critical reviews to discover how it resonated to cultural themes at the time of its debut and how the shifting tides of cultural interest have revised its interpretation and impact on audiences. And to do this, one needs to know a little about the culture of the times which produced the play as well as the author who penned it.

Drama for Students supplies this material in a useful compendium for the student of dramatic theater. Covering a range of dramatic works that span from 442 BC to the 1990s, this book focuses on significant theatrical works whose themes and form transcend the uncertainty of dramatic fads. These are plays that have proven to be both memorable and teachable. *Drama for Students* seeks to enhance appreciation of these dramatic texts by providing scholarly materials written with the secondary and college/university student in mind. It provides for each play a concise summary of the plot and characters as well as a detailed explanation of its themes. In addition, background material on the historical context of the play, its critical reception, and the author's life help the student to understand the work's position in the chronicle of dramatic history. For each play entry a new work of scholarly criticism is also included, as well as segments of other significant critical works for handy reference. A thorough bibliography provides a starting point for further research.

This series offers comprehensive educational resources for students of drama. *Drama for Students* is a vital book for dramatic interpretation and a valuable addition to any reference library.

Source: Eco, Umberto, *The Role of the Reader: Explorations in the Semiotics of Texts,* Indiana University Press, 1979.

Carole L. Hamilton
Author and Instructor of English
Cary Academy
Cary, North Carolina

Introduction

Purpose of the Book

The purpose of *Drama for Students* (*DfS*) is to provide readers with a guide to understanding, enjoying, and studying dramas by giving them easy access to information about the work. Part of Gale's "For Students" literature line, *DfS* is specifically designed to meet the curricular needs of high school and undergraduate college students and their teachers, as well as the interests of general readers and researchers considering specific plays. While each volume contains entries on "classic" dramas frequently studied in classrooms, there are also entries containing hard-to-find information on contemporary plays, including works by multicultural, international, and women playwrights.

The information covered in each entry includes an introduction to the play and the work's author; a plot summary, to help readers unravel and understand the events in a drama; descriptions of important characters, including explanation of a given character's role in the drama as well as discussion about that character's relationship to other characters in the play; analysis of important themes in the drama; and an explanation of important literary techniques and movements as they are demonstrated in the play.

In addition to this material, which helps the readers analyze the play itself, students are also provided with important information on the literary and historical background informing each work. This includes a historical context essay, a box comparing the time or place the drama was written to modern Western culture, a critical essay, and excerpts from critical essays on the play. A unique feature of *DfS* is a specially commissioned critical essay on each drama, targeted toward the student reader.

To further aid the student in studying and enjoying each play, information on media adaptations is provided (if available), as well as reading suggestions for works of fiction and nonfiction on similar themes and topics. Classroom aids include ideas for research papers and lists of critical sources that provide additional material on each drama.

Selection Criteria

The titles for each volume of *DfS* were selected by surveying numerous sources on teaching literature and analyzing course curricula for various school districts. Some of the sources surveyed included: literature anthologies; *Reading Lists for College-Bound Students: The Books Most Recommended by America's Top Colleges*; textbooks on teaching dramas; a College Board survey of plays commonly studied in high schools; a National Council of Teachers of English (NCTE) survey of plays commonly studied in high schools; St. James Press's *International Dictionary of Theatre*; and Arthur Applebee's 1993 study *Literature in the Secondary School: Studies of Curriculum and Instruction in the United States*.

Input was also solicited from our advisory board, as well as from educators from various areas. From these discussions, it was determined that each volume should have a mix of "classic" dramas (those works commonly taught in literature classes) and contemporary dramas for which information is often hard to find. Because of the interest in expanding the canon of literature, an emphasis was also placed on including works by international, multicultural, and women playwrights. Our advisory board members—educational professionals—helped pare down the list for each volume. If a work was not selected for the present volume, it was often noted as a possibility for a future volume. As always, the editor welcomes suggestions for titles to be included in future volumes.

How Each Entry Is Organized

Each entry, or chapter, in *DfS* focuses on one play. Each entry heading lists the full name of the play, the author's name, and the date of the play's publication. The following elements are contained in each entry:

- **Introduction:** a brief overview of the drama which provides information about its first appearance, its literary standing, any controversies surrounding the work, and major conflicts or themes within the work.
- **Author Biography:** this section includes basic facts about the author's life, and focuses on events and times in the author's life that inspired the drama in question.
- **Plot Summary:** a description of the major events in the play. Subheads demarcate the play's various acts or scenes.
- **Characters:** an alphabetical listing of major characters in the play. Each character name is followed by a brief to an extensive description of the character's role in the play, as well as discussion of the character's actions, relationships, and possible motivation.

  Characters are listed alphabetically by last name. If a character is unnamed—for instance, the Stage Manager in *Our Town*—the character is listed as "The Stage Manager" and alphabetized as "Stage Manager." If a character's first name is the only one given, the name will appear alphabetically by the name. Variant names are also included for each character. Thus, the nickname "Babe" would head the listing for a character in *Crimes of the Heart,* but below that listing would be her less-mentioned married name "Rebecca Botrelle."
- **Themes:** a thorough overview of how the major topics, themes, and issues are addressed within the play. Each theme discussed appears in a separate subhead, and is easily accessed through the boldface entries in the Subject/Theme Index.
- **Style:** this section addresses important style elements of the drama, such as setting, point of view, and narration; important literary devices used, such as imagery, foreshadowing, symbolism; and, if applicable, genres to which the work might have belonged, such as Gothicism or Romanticism. Literary terms are explained within the entry, but can also be found in the Glossary.
- **Historical Context:** this section outlines the social, political, and cultural climate *in which the author lived and the play was created.* This section may include descriptions of related historical events, pertinent aspects of daily life in the culture, and the artistic and literary sensibilities of the time in which the work was written. If the play is a historical work, information regarding the time in which the play is set is also included. Each section is broken down with helpful subheads.
- **Critical Overview:** this section provides background on the critical reputation of the play, including bannings or any other public controversies surrounding the work. For older plays, this section includes a history of how the drama was first received and how perceptions of it may have changed over the years; for more recent plays, direct quotes from early reviews may also be included.
- **Criticism:** an essay commissioned by *DfS* which specifically deals with the play and is written specifically for the student audience, as well as excerpts from previously published criticism on the work (if available).
- **Sources:** an alphabetical list of critical material used in compiling the entry, with full bibliographical information.
- **Further Reading:** an alphabetical list of other critical sources which may prove useful for the student. It includes full bibliographical information and a brief annotation.

In addition, each entry contains the following highlighted sections, set apart from the main text as sidebars:

- **Media Adaptations:** if available, a list of important film and television adaptations of the play, including source information. The list may also include such variations on the work as audio recordings, musical adaptations, and other stage interpretations.
- **Topics for Further Study:** a list of potential study questions or research topics dealing with the play. This section includes questions related to other disciplines the student may be studying, such as American history, world history, science, math, government, business, geography, economics, psychology, etc.
- **Compare and Contrast:** an "at-a-glance" comparison of the cultural and historical differences between the author's time and culture and late twentieth century or early twenty-first century Western culture. This box includes pertinent parallels between the major scientific, political, and cultural movements of the time or place the drama was written, the time or place the play was set (if a historical work), and modern Western culture. Works written after 1990 may not have this box.
- **What Do I Read Next?:** a list of works that might complement the featured play or serve as a contrast to it. This includes works by the same author and others, works of fiction and nonfiction, and works from various genres, cultures, and eras.

Other Features

DfS includes "The Study of Drama," a foreword by Carole Hamilton, an educator and author who specializes in dramatic works. This essay examines the basis for drama in societies and what drives people to study such work. The essay also discusses how *Drama for Students* can help teachers show students how to enrich their own reading/viewing experiences.

A Cumulative Author/Title Index lists the authors and titles covered in each volume of the *DfS* series.

A Cumulative Nationality/Ethnicity Index breaks down the authors and titles covered in each volume of the *DfS* series by nationality and ethnicity.

A Subject/Theme Index, specific to each volume, provides easy reference for users who may be studying a particular subject or theme rather than a single work. Significant subjects from events to broad themes are included, and the entries pointing to the specific theme discussions in each entry are indicated in **boldface**.

Each entry may include illustrations, including photo of the author, stills from stage productions, and stills from film adaptations, if available.

Citing Drama for Students

When writing papers, students who quote directly from any volume of *Drama for Students* may use the following general forms. These examples are based on MLA style; teachers may request that students adhere to a different style, so the following examples may be adapted as needed.

When citing text from *DfS* that is not attributed to a particular author (i.e., the Themes, Style, Historical Context sections, etc.), the following format should be used in the bibliography section:

"*Our Town.*" *Drama for Students.* Eds. David Galens and Lynn Spampinato. Vol. 1. Detroit: Gale, 1998. 227–30.

When quoting the specially commissioned essay from *DfS* (usually the first piece under the "Criticism" subhead), the following format should be used:

Fiero, John. Critical Essay on *Twilight: Los Angeles, 1992. Drama for Students.* Eds. David Galens and Lynn Spampinato. Vol. 2. Detroit: Gale, 1998. 247–49.

When quoting a journal or newspaper essay that is reprinted in a volume of *DfS*, the following form may be used:

Rich, Frank. "Theatre: A Mamet Play, *Glengarry Glen Ross.*" *New York Theatre Critics' Review* Vol. 45, No. 4 (March 5, 1984), 5–7; excerpted and reprinted in *Drama for Students*, Vol. 2, eds. David Galens and Lynn Spampinato (Detroit: Gale, 1998), pp. 51–53.

When quoting material reprinted from a book that appears in a volume of *DfS*, the following form may be used:

Kerr, Walter. "*The Miracle Worker,*" in *The Theatre in Spite of Itself.* Simon & Schuster, 1963. 255–57; excerpted and reprinted in *Drama for Students*, Vol. 2, eds. David Galens and Lynn Spampinato (Detroit: Gale, 1998), pp. 123–24.

We Welcome Your Suggestions

The editor of *Drama for Students* welcomes your comments and ideas. Readers who wish to suggest dramas to appear in future volumes, or who have other suggestions, are cordially invited to contact the editor. You may contact the editor via E-mail at: **ForStudentsEditors@gale.com.** Or write to the editor at:

Editor, *Drama for Students*
The Gale Group
27500 Drake Rd.
Farmington Hills, MI 48331–3535

Literary Chronology

1640: Aphra Behn is born in Kent, England.

1677: Aphra Behn's *The Rover* is published.

1689: Aphra Behn dies in April.

1732: Pierre-Augustin Caron de Beaumarchais is born on January 24 in Paris, France.

1775: Pierre-Augustin de Beaumarchais's *The Barber of Seville* is published.

1799: Pierre-Augustin de Beaumarchais dies of a stroke in Paris on May 18.

1828: Henrik Ibsen is born on March 20 in Skien, Norway.

1866: Henrik Ibsen's *Brand* is published.

1888: Eugene O'Neill is born on October 16 in New York City.

1888: Maxwell Anderson is born on December 15 in Atlantic, Pennsylvania.

1897: Thornton Wilder is born on April 17 in Madison, Wisconsin.

1906: Henrik Ibsen dies on May 23 in Oslo, Norway.

1915: Jerome Lawrence is born on July 14 in Cleveland, Ohio.

1918: Robert E. Lee is born on October 15 in Elyria, Ohio.

1920: Eugene O'Neill's *Beyond the Horizon* is published.

1920: Eugene O'Neill receives the Pulitzer Prize in drama for *Beyond the Horizon*.

1922: Eugene O'Neill receives the Pulitzer Prize in drama for *Anna Christie*.

1928: Eugene O'Neill receives the Pulitzer Prize in drama for *Strange Interlude*.

1928: Thornton Wilder receives the Pulitzer Prize in drama for *The Bridge of San Luis Rey*.

1933: Maxwell Anderson's *Both Your Houses* is published.

1933: Maxwell Anderson receives the Pulitzer Prize in drama for *Both Your Houses*.

1934: Amiri Baraka (born Everett LeRoy Jones) is born on October 7 in Newark, New Jersey.

1936: Eugene O'Neill receives the Nobel Prize in literature.

1937: Tom Stoppard (born Tomas Straussler) is born on July 3 in Zlin, Czechoslovakia.

1937: Lanford Wilson is born on April 13 in Lebanon, Missouri.

1938: Caryl Churchill is born on September 3 in London, England.

1938: Thornton Wilder receives the Pulitzer Prize in drama for *Our Town.*

1939: Terrence McNally is born on November 3 in Saint Petersburg, Florida.

1943: Thornton Wilder receives the Pulitzer Prize in drama for *The Skin of Our Teeth* .

1947: David Hare is born on June 5 in St. Leonard's-on-Sea in Sussex, on the southeastern coast of England.

1948: Pearl Cleage is born on December 7 in Springfield, Massachusetts.

1953: Eugene O'Neill dies on November 27 in Boston, Massachusetts.

1954: Eugene O'Neill receives the Pulitzer Prize in drama posthumously for *Long Day's Journey into Night* .

1954: Thornton Wilder's *The Matchmaker* is published.

1959: Maxwell Anderson dies from a stroke in Stamford, Connecticut.

1964: Amiri Baraka's *The Baptism* is published.

1971: Jerome Lawrence and Robert E. Lee's *The Night Thoreau Spent in Jail* is published.

1975: Thornton Wilder dies in December in the house in Connecticut, where he had lived for years with his sister, who served him as secretary, literary advisor, and business manager.

1975: Lanford Wilson's *The Mound Builders* is published.

1979: Caryl Churchill's *Cloud Nine* is published.

1979: Tom Stoppard's *Dogg's Hamlet, Cahoot's Macbeth* is published.

1980: Lanford Wilson receives the Pulitzer Prize in drama for *Talley's Folly.*

1988: David Hare's *The Secret Rapture* is published.

1995: Pearl Cleage's *Flyin' West* is published.

1995: Terrence McNally's *Master Class* is published.

1994: Robert E. Lee dies on July 8 in Los Angeles, California, shortly before the publication of *The Selected Plays of Jerome Lawrence and Robert E. Lee*, the final collaborative work with Lawrence in over fifty-two years of working together.

Acknowledgments

The editors wish to thank the copyright holders of the excerpted criticism included in this volume and the permissions managers of many book and magazine publishing companies for assisting us in securing reproduction rights. We are also grateful to the staffs of the Detroit Public Library, the Library of Congress, the University of Detroit Mercy Library, Wayne State University Purdy/Kresge Library Complex, and the University of Michigan Libraries for making their resources available to us. Following is a list of the copyright holders who have granted us permission to reproduce material in this volume of ***Drama for Students (DfS)***. Every effort has been made to trace copyright, but if omissions have been made, please let us know.

COPYRIGHTED MATERIALS IN *DfS*, VOLUME 16, WERE REPRODUCED FROM THE FOLLOWING PERIODICALS:

African American Review, v. 31, Winter, 1997 for "The Motion of Herstory: Three Plays by Pearl Cleage," by Freda Scott Giles. Reproduced by permission of the author.—***Costerus 76: New Essays on American Drama***, 1989. © Editions Rodopi NV, 1989. Reprinted by permission of Humanities Press International, Inc.—***ELH***, v. 56, Fall, 1989. © The Johns Hopkins University Press. Reproduced by permission.—***English Studies in Canada***, v. 13, June 1987 for "America's First Tragedy," by Stephen A. Black. © Association of Canadian University Teachers of English 1987. Reproduced by Permission of the publisher and the author.—***Modern Drama***, v. 33, December, 1990; v. 42, Spring, 1999. Both reproduced by permission.

COPYRIGHTED MATERIALS IN *DfS*, VOLUME 16, WERE REPRODUCED FROM THE FOLLOWING BOOKS:

Billington, Michael. From ***Stoppard: The Playwright***. Methuen Publishing Company, 1987. Copyright © 1987 by Michael Billington. Reproduced by permission.—Brustein, Robert. An excerpt from "Henrik Ibsen" in ***The Theatre of Revolt***. Little, Brown, and Company, 1962. Reproduced by permission.—Burbank, Rex. From ***Thornton Wilder***. Twayne Publishers, Inc., 1961. Copyright © 1961 by Twayne Publishers, Inc. Reproduced by permission.—Lomax, Marion. From ***The Rover***. W.W. Norton, 1985. © 1995 A&C Black (Publishers) Limited. Reproduced by permission.—Mazer, Cary M. From "*Master Class* and the Paradox of the Diva," in ***Terrence McNally: A Casebook***. Edited by Toby Silverman Zinman. Garland Publishing Inc., 1997. Copyright © 1997 by Toby Silverman Zinman. Reproduced by permission of Routledge, Inc., part of The Taylor & Francis Group.—Miliora, Maria T. From "Loss of Sense of Home, Family, Belonging: Narcissism, Alienation and Madness," in ***Narcissism, the Family, and Madness: A Self-Psychological Study of Eugene O'Neil and His Plays***. Peter Lang Publishing, 2000. © 2000 Peter Lang Publishing, Inc., New York. Reproduced by permission.—Sammels, Neil. From ***Tom Stoppard: The Artist as Critic***. Macmillan, 1988. © Neil Sammells 1988. Reproduced by permission.—Shivers, Alfred. "Of Sceptred and Elected Races," in ***Maxwell Anderson***. Twayne Publishers, 1976. The Gale Group.—Voglino, Barbara. "Unsettling Ambiguity in *Beyond the Horizon*," in ***"Perverse Mind:" Eugene O'Neil's Struggle with Closure***. Associated University Presses, 1999. © 1999 by Associated University Presses, Inc. Reproduced by permission.—Woods, Alan. From "*The Night Thoreau Spent in Jail*: Introduction," in ***Selected Plays of Jerome Lawrence and Robert E. Lee***. Ohio State University Press, 1995. Copyright © 1995 by the Ohio State University Press. Reproduced by permission of the author.

PHOTOGRAPHS AND ILLUSTRATIONS APPEARING IN *DfS*, VOLUME 16, WERE RECEIVED FROM THE FOLLOWING SOURCES:

Anderson, Maxwell, photograph. The Library of Congress.—Baraka, Amiri, photograph. AP/Wide World Photos. Reproduced by permission.—Beaumarchais, Pierre-Augustin Caron de, engraving. Hulton/Archive. Reproduced by permission.—Behn, Aphra, engraving.—Bryant, Michael as Brand, holding walking stick and wearing backpack, standing on broken ice while Lynn Farleigh as Agnes looks on, scene from a 1978 production of ***Brand***, written by Henrik Ibsen, directed by Christopher Morahan, performed at the Olivier Theatre, London, photograph. © Donald Cooper/Photostage. Reproduced by permission.—Carter, Helena Bonham as Rosine, speaking while Lee Cornes as Figaro looks on, scene from a 1992 production of ***The Barber of Seville***, written by Pierre-Augustin Caron de Beaumarchais, directed by Lou Stein, performed at the Palace Theatre, photograph. © Donald Cooper/Photostage. Reproduced by permission.—Churchill, Caryl, photograph. © Jerry Bauer. Reproduced by permission.—Cleage, Pearl, photograph. © Barry Forbus. Reproduced by permission of Pearl Cleage.—Cover of *Playbill*, from the theatrical production of ***The Matchmaker***, written by Thornton Wilder, directed by Tyrone Guthrie, photograph. PLAYBILL ® is a registered trademark of Playbill Incorporated, N.Y.C. All rights reserved. Reproduced by permission.—Cover of *Playbill*, from the theatrical production of ***The Secret Rapture***, written and directed by David Hare, photograph. PLAYBILL ® is a registered trademark of Playbill Incorporated, N.Y.C. All rights reserved. Reproduced by permission.—Cover of *Showbill*, from the theatrical production of ***Brand***, written by Henrik Ibsen, directed by Craig D. Kinzer, photograph. PLAYBILL ® is a registered trademark of Playbill Incorporated, N.Y.C. All rights reserved. Reproduced by permission.—Frontispiece for the 1775 edition of ***Le Barbier de Seville***, written by Pierre-Augustin Caron de Beaumarchais, photograph. © Gianni Dagli Orti/Corbis. Reproduced by permission.—Hare, David, photograph. AP/Wide World Photos. Reproduced by permission.—Ibsen, Henrik, photograph. AP/Wide World Photos. Reproduced by permission.—(Left to right) Hugh Quarshie as Belvile, Jeremy Irons as Willmore and Peter Guinness as Frederick, all smiling as Willmore rests his head on Belvile's shoulder, scene from a Royal Shakespeare Company production of ***The Rover***, written by Aphra Behn, directed by John Barton, photograph. © Donald Cooper/Photostage. Reproduced by permission.—(Left to right) Paul Shelley as Tom French, Penelope Wilton as Marion French and Jill Baker (sitting) as Isobel Glass, gathered near rattan chairs and table, scene from a 1988 production of ***The Secret Rapture***, performed at Lyttelton Theatre, written by David Hare, directed by Howard Davies, photograph. © Donald Cooper/Photostage. Reproduced by permission.—(Left to right) Walter C. Kelly as Solomon Fitzmaurice, looking at his pocketwatch, Shepperd Strudwick as Alan McClean, sitting in chair, and Mary Philips as Bus, staring at Kelly with stern look on her face, on cover of *Playbill*, from Maxwell Anderson production of ***Both Your Houses***, directed by Worthington Miner, photograph. PLAYBILL ® is a registered trademark of Playbill Incorporated, N.Y.C. All rights reserved. Reproduced by permission.—(Left to right) William Hoyland as Harry Bagley, Jim Hooper as Betty, Antony Sher as Clive, Miriam Margolyes as Maud and Julie Covington as Edward, all standing together with glasses raised in a toast, scene from a 1979 production of ***Cloud Nine***, written by Caryl Churchill, directed by Max Stafford-Clark, photograph. © Donald Cooper/Photostage. Reproduced by permission.—LuPone, Patti as Maria Callas, standing with her right index finger pointed upward, facing David Maxwell Anderson as Tony, scene from a 1997 production of ***Master Class***, performed at Queen's Theatre, written by Terrance McNally, photograph. © Donald Cooper/Photostage. Reproduced by permission.—Matthau, Walter as Horace Vandergelder, Barbra Streisand as Dolly Levi, and Marianne McAndrew as Irene Molloy, in a scene from the 1969 film ***Hello Dolly***, directed by Gene Kelly, photograph. The Kobal Collection. Reproduced by permission.—McInnerny, Tim as Clive, on knees embracing

Marion Bailey as Mrs. Saunders, stuffed leopard in background, scene from a 1997 production of ***Cloud Nine***, performed at Old Vic Theatre, written by Caryl Churchill, photograph. © Donald Cooper/ Photostage. Reproduced by permission.—McNally, Terrence, photograph. AP/Wide World Photos. Reproduced by permission.—O'Neill, Eugene, photograph. © Horace Bristol/Corbis. Reproduced by permission.—*Playbill* title page from theatrical production of Maxwell Anderson's ***Both Your Houses***, directed by Worthington Miner, at Ethel Barrymore Theatre, photograph. PLAYBILL ® is a registered trademark of Playbill Incorporated, N.Y.C. All rights reserved. Reproduced by permission.—Side profile of Zoe Caldwell as Maria Callas, superimposed over face of Maria Callas, on cover of *Playbill*, from theatrical production of ***Master Class***, written by Terrence McNally, directed by Leonard Foglia, photograph. PLAYBILL ® is a registered trademark of Playbill Incorporated, N.Y.C. All rights reserved.—Stoppard, Tom, photograph. © Jerry Bauer. Reproduced by permission.—Thoreau, Henry David, age 44, photograph. The Library of Congress.—Wilder, Thornton, photograph. AP/Wide World Photos. Reproduced by permission.—Wilson, Lanford, photograph. Hulton/Archive. Reproduced by permission.

Contributors

Bryan Aubrey: Aubrey holds a Ph.D. in English and has published many articles on twentieth-century literature. Entries on *Cloud Nine* and *Master Class*. Original essays on *Cloud Nine* and *Master Class*.

Cynthia A. Bily: Bily teaches English at Adrian College in Adrian, Michigan. Entry on *The Mound Builders*. Original essay on *The Mound Builders*.

Jennifer Bussey: Bussey holds a master's degree in interdisciplinary studies and a bachelor's degree in English literature. She is an independent writer specializing in literature. Entry on *Flyin' West*. Original essay on *Flyin' West*.

Lane A. Glenn: Glenn has a Ph.D. and specializes in theatre history and literature. Entry on *The Secret Rapture*. Original essay on *The Secret Rapture*.

Curt Guyette: Guyette holds a bachelor of arts degree in English writing from the University of Pittsburgh. Original essay on *The Night Thoreau Spent in Jail*.

Carole Hamilton: Hamilton is an English teacher at Cary Academy, a private college preparatory school in Cary, North Carolina. Entry on *The Rover*. Original essay on *The Rover*.

David Kelly: Kelly teaches creative writing and literature at Oakton Community College in Illinois. Entries on *Both Your Houses* and *The Matchmaker*. Original essays on *Both Your Houses* and *The Matchmaker*.

Rena Korb: Korb has a master's degree in English literature and creative writing and has written for a wide variety of educational publishers. Entry on *The Barber of Seville*. Original essay on *The Barber of Seville*.

Laura Kryhoski: Kryhoski is currently working as a freelance writer. She has also taught English Literature in addition to English as a Second Language overseas. Original essay on *Flyin' West*.

Kevin O'Sullivan: O'Sullivan writes for both film and stage. Original essay on *Both Your Houses*.

Ryan D. Poquette: Poquette has a bachelor's degree in English and specializes in writing about literature. Entries on *Beyond the Horizon*, *Brand*, *Dogg's Hamlet, Cahoot's Macbeth*, and *The Night Thoreau Spent in Jail*. Original essays on *Beyond the Horizon*, *Brand*, *Dogg's Hamlet, Cahoot's Macbeth*, and *The Night Thoreau Spent in Jail*.

Susan Sanderson: Sanderson holds a master of fine arts degree in fiction writing and is an independent writer. Entry on *The Baptism*. Original essay on *The Baptism*.

The Baptism

AMIRI BARAKA

1964

In 1964, the Writers' Stage Theatre in New York City staged the first production of Amiri Baraka's satirical one-act play about religion, *The Baptism.* The play was presented and published under Baraka's given name, LeRoi Jones. According to Tish Dace and Andrew O. Jones in the *Reference Guide to American Literature,* the play ''jarred and amused its spectators'' but also ''drew charges of both obscenity and blasphemy.'' That year, Baraka began garnering attention as a major playwright, with a number of his other plays also opening, including the Obie Award-winning *Dutchman. The Baptism* was also published in 1967, together with an earlier Baraka play, under the title *The Baptism and The Toilet.*

The Baptism is a challenging play on a number of levels. For example, some of the language and subject matter is of an adult nature and offensive to some. In addition, the characters are less individuals than they are representations of particular groups or ideas. The play begins with a minister's attempts to encourage a homosexual to change his ways. A boy comes to the church to be baptized, but his sins become a heated topic of discussion, launching angry accusations and a violent end. Throughout the play, the boy's identity remains a question and a source of strife for the other characters—is he simply a clever teenager, skilled at deception, or is he actually some sort of deity, maybe even Christ?

AUTHOR BIOGRAPHY

Amiri Baraka was born Everett LeRoy Jones on October 7, 1934, in Newark, New Jersey. (He changed LeRoy to LeRoi in the early 1950s.) His family was solidly middle class; his father, Coyette Leroy Jones, was a postal worker and an elevator operator, and his mother, Anna Lois Russ Jones, was a social worker. He was one of the few black students at his high school.

Jones started college at Rutgers University on a science scholarship but later transferred to the predominantly black Howard University in Washington, D.C., where he studied philosophy, religion, German, and English literature. While Jones gained a broad understanding of literature and art from his studies at Howard under the tutelage of such prominent African-American intellectuals as Sterling Brown and E. Franklin Frazier, he would later accuse the university of encouraging limited and bourgeois thinking among African Americans. During college and in later years, he was a voracious reader of such poets as William Carlos Williams, Walt Whitman, and T. S. Eliot. In 1954, Jones enlisted in the United States Air Force and served, primarily in Puerto Rico and Germany, as a weatherman and B-36 gunner.

Jones's return to civilian life in 1957 occurred at a time when many artists were experimenting with new ideas and forms as well as challenging traditional political thinking and social institutions. He moved to the bohemian neighborhood of Greenwich Village in New York City, where he started the literary journal *Yugen* and the Totem Press with his Jewish wife, Hettie Cohen Jones. Through this work, Baraka encountered such radically experimental writers as Allen Ginsberg, Gregory Corso, Jack Kerouac, and William S. Burroughs—often referred to as the Beat poets. Baraka began hosting informal gatherings in his home where these and others would come to drink, argue, and listen to jazz played by such musicians as Ornette Coleman and Don Cherry. During this period, Jones wrote extensively and contributed to numerous journals and magazines on a wide variety of topics. One of the first works for he which received widespread attention was his 1961 poetry collection entitled *Preface to a Twenty-Volume Suicide Note.* The book established Jones as a new voice in American poetry, expressing his discontent with the political and racial climate in the United States through jazz-influenced verses.

The Writers' Stage Theatre in New York City first produced Jones's play *The Baptism* in 1964, the same year in which his much-praised play *Dutchman* was staged. During the mid-1960s, Jones broke philosophically with his fellow Greenwich Village artists as he emerged as a leader in the black arts movement. In 1965, he moved to Harlem, and soon thereafter he returned to Newark, leaving his wife.

In 1966, Jones married Sylvia Robinson, an African-American woman. In 1968, he took the African name Imamu (''spiritual leader'') Ameer (''blessed'') Baraka (''prince''), prompted by his conversion to the Kawaida sect of Islam, his growing sense of black nationalism, and his appreciation of the messages of Black Muslim leader Malcolm X. He later modified ''Ameer'' to ''Amiri.'' Sylvia Robinson took the name Amina Baraka.

Throughout his life, Baraka has been involved in numerous political causes and movements, and many of his critics have pointed to his shifting allegiances. He has been a Marxist, positioned himself as a mediator between black and white intellectuals, and professed a militant anti-white stance. He has also worked in nearly every form of writing: poetry, fiction, drama, essay, autobiography, screenwriting, and literary and social criticism. Baraka's life has also been marked by a number of confrontations with legal authorities. His first imbroglio was over a copy of his 1961 play, *The Eighth Ditch,* mailed to a prisoner but intercepted by prison authorities; as a result, federal authorities raided Baraka's apartment and charged him with sending obscenity through the mail.

Baraka has taught at various institutions, including the State University of New York at Stony Brook, Columbia University, and the New School for Social Research. He has received numerous awards for his work, including an Obie Award in 1964 for *Dutchman.*

PLOT SUMMARY

The Baptism is a one-act play that takes place inside a Baptist church in New York City during the early 1960s. The play opens with the Minister and the Homosexual speaking to each other and running in place. The Minister wants to save the Homosexual's soul, but the Homosexual is making cynical comments about the Minister and religion in general.

The Boy enters the church carrying a bag. The Minister sees him as an innocent child interested in being baptized, and the Homosexual sees him as "rough trade," a slang term for a male prostitute who engages in violent sex acts. The Boy admits that he has committed some sins. The Homosexual attempts to distract the Boy by dropping his trousers, revealing that he is wearing red leotards. This angers the Minister, who rushes at the Homosexual. The Homosexual defends himself by saying that he is "the Son of Man" and has "done nothing not accounted for in the book of days." These are both biblical references, and the latter may also indicate that the Homosexual believes that any act he has committed is not new or different and should therefore be acceptable. The Homosexual indicates that the Boy should not trust the Minister.

Amiri Baraka

The Old Woman rushes into the church as the Homosexual and the Minister are exchanging insults, and she claims that the Boy is an "agent of the devil." A lively discussion ensues among the Minister, the Old Woman, the Boy, and the Homosexual. The Old Woman insists that the Boy is an evil sinner and then nearly passes out in religious ecstasy; the Minister wants to forgive him; the Boy insists that he has done nothing wrong; and the Homosexual, while suggesting that the Boy could serve as his secretary, sings, dances, and throws confetti. Eventually, the Boy admits that the Old Woman must have seen him masturbating while he was praying, and he defends himself saying, "thinking of God always gives me a hard-on."

The Homosexual tries to get the Boy to dance with him, but the Boy refuses. This refusal wins the Boy praise from the Minister, who says to the Homosexual, "This is a gifted lad. You cannot sway him with your cant about religion or the evil pleasures of the flesh." The Old Woman starts singing an old gospel song, and the Homosexual derides her. The Minister declares the Homosexual's words blasphemous, and they exchange insults. The Boy asks if he is now saved, but the Homosexual mocks the idea that he could be saved from anything, let alone Satan. The Homosexual sings a song about wanting to experience everything possible and again asks the Boy to dance with him. The Minister intervenes, arguing that the Boy "can yet be saved." The Homosexual laughs at the idea, responding sarcastically that the Boy "can yet be made sterile. Can yet be taught that blank walls yodel the crazy name of salvation."

A chorus of about six young Women of various sizes and ethnicities enters the church singing. They wear numbers pinned to their gauzy dresses. The Old Woman is enlivened, shakes her hips, and asks the Boy to dance with her. The Boy is shocked, as is the Minister, but the Homosexual jumps in and again asks the Boy to dance with him. The Boy refuses, saying that he has already sinned and should not sin again by dancing in a church. The Homosexual laughs at his seriousness and makes fun of how upset he is for having masturbated. He asks the Boy how often he masturbates; the Boy admits that he does so each time he prays, which is three times a day. The Homosexual considers this figure and praises the Boy for his regularity.

The Minister is outraged by the Boy's admission, but the Homosexual calls him an "old hypocrite" and accuses him of having masturbated at least as often. The Minister states that God will strike the Homosexual dead, but this only encourages the Homosexual, who begins to sing a song about how exciting it would be to get "drilled with holy lightning.'' The Boy is confused at this point and asks, ''What shall I do?'' The Homosexual responds, ''Become a Christian so you can understand the symbolism.'' The Boy asks to be baptized. The Homosexual thinks that baptism ''might not be such a bad idea'' for himself, as he could finally see God.

The Boy demands that he be baptized immediately. Suddenly, one of the Women shouts at the Boy, ''He's the one,'' and they all begin to call him ''The Christ child come back. . . . the Son of God. . . . Chief Religious jelly roll of the universe.'' They moan ecstatically and begin praying. The Minister and the Old Woman sink to their knees and praise the Boy, but the Homosexual is not convinced. He demands that the Boy prove he is Christ by turning the church into the White House, ''or something cool like that.''

The Boy next admits that he has lied in the past to the Women about his relation to God so that they would have sex with him, but he never meant for them to think he was Christ. The Homosexual is very impressed with the Boy's deceit, but no one else hears the admission of the trickery. Finally, the Minister realizes that the Boy has ''lied merely to further [his] lust.'' This angers the Minister, the Old Woman, and the Women, who now call for his punishment. Intent on killing him, the group moves toward the Boy. The Homosexual tries to block them and is kicked down to the ground unconscious. ''You must be sacrificed to cleanse the soul of man,'' the Minister cries out to the Boy. The Boy begs for mercy but none is offered. He pulls a sword out of the bag he has with him and kills the Women, the Minister, and the Old Woman.

Suddenly, the Messenger enters the church on a motorcycle. He is dressed in a leather jacket with the words ''The Man'' and a crown stenciled on the back. He asks what has happened, and the Boy answers, ''I have slain these sinners. . . . I am the Son of Man. The Christ.'' The Messenger says that he has come to retrieve the Boy, sent by ''the man. Your father.'' He dances a mambo step through most of the rest of the play. The Boy argues with the Messenger, noting that he was sent to save people on ''this earth.'' The Messenger tells the Boy that his father is angry that he has failed in his assignment and that ''the man is destroying the whole works tonight. With a grenade.'' The Messenger and the Boy argue over whether the Boy should be forced to leave, with the Messenger calling the Boy by the name Percy.

The Messenger finally gets tired of arguing with the Boy, hits him over the head with a tire iron, and throws him over the back of his motorcycle. After they leave, the Homosexual rises from the pile of bodies on the stage and speculates on what has happened. ''Damn, it looks like some really uninteresting kind of orgy went on in here,'' he says, and again suggests that the Minister should not have catered to ''rough trade.'' As he leaves the church, thinking about getting a drink before the bars close for the evening, he wonders, ''[W]hat happened to that cute little religious fanatic?''

CHARACTERS

Boy

The Boy is described in the play's list of characters as handsome and about fifteen years old, with a ''martyr-like shyness.'' He appears at the church as an innocent, asking the Minister to baptize him, but then admits to having sinned. The Homosexual is sexually interested in the Boy, and he and the Minister struggle for the Boy's attentions. The Boy begins the play with a timid manner, but by the play's end he is convinced that he is ''the Son of Man'' and ''the Christ.''

Homosexual

The Homosexual is in his forties and (according to the list of characters) ''elegant'' but gaining a bit of a belly and ''conscious of it.'' He seems to delight in taunting the Minister with lewd suggestions and dismisses everyone in the play except the Boy, whom he finds sexually attractive. Under his trousers the Homosexual wears red leotards, which he reveals when the Boy admits to sinning. The Homosexual is an outsider and a cynic who comments under his breath about what is going on around him.

Messenger

The Messenger rides a motorcycle into the church to pick up the Boy and take him away. He serves as a sort of *deus ex machina*—an improbable character suddenly introduced into the plot of a play, who extricates another character from a difficult situation. According to the list of characters, the

Messenger is a gaunt Spaniard or looks like the actor Lee Marvin. He wears leather pants and a jacket with a gold crown and the words ''The Man'' printed on the back. The Messenger is no-nonsense and does not care to listen to the Boy's reasons as to why he should not come with him. He inexplicably calls the Boy by the name Percy a few times.

Minister

According to the play's list of characters, the Minister is ''pompous, appears well-meaning'' but is ''generally ridiculous.'' He is an image of conventional and middle-class America—white-haired and clothed in black robes. His church is ''arrogant Protestant, obviously Baptist'' and somewhat financially well-off. His sermons are probably broadcast over the radio, as his pulpit carries the sign ''WHBI Radio.'' The Minister dislikes the Homosexual and is very interested in saving the Boy's soul.

Old Woman

The Old Woman is ''strong from years of the American Matriarchy'' and screams most of her lines. She makes her entrance early in the play, rushing in to accuse the Boy of sinning. The Minister refers to her as ''devout'' and listens to her claims about the Boy, but only to a point. When the chorus of Women enters the church, she takes up their songs and performs a seductive dance during which she removes numerous skirts from her waist, layer by layer.

Women

The Women are ''young, sleek 'Village!' types,'' according to the list of characters, referring to Greenwich Village in New York City, where many intellectuals and artists lived during the 1950s and 1960s. They number approximately six and are young and of ''diverse sizes and colors.'' The Women serve primarily as a chorus, entering the church singing gospel songs and wearing numbers pinned to their gauzy dresses. The Homosexual derides them, but the Old Woman finds them comforting and sings along with them. The Women are the first to refer to the Boy as ''the Son of God.''

THEMES

Religion

The play is a satire of organized religion; that is, Baraka is making fun of organized religion and all those who are associated with it. The story centers on a boy who enters a church, sorry for his sins and asking to be forgiven, but Baraka embellishes the tale with characters behaving in ridiculous ways. Various aspects of organized religion are lampooned in a way that launches questions about the validity of religious belief.

The typical hierarchy of religion is challenged in the play, for example. The Minister, who represents church leadership, has his position reduced when the chorus of Women announces that the Boy is Christ or Jesus. The Minister drops to his knees, kissing the Boy's feet and praising him. As soon as the Boy admits that he lied about being Christ, the Minister turns on him and says, ''May the true God strike you dead.'' Confusion reigns instead of orthodoxy, and this opens up the question of what is valid and true in organized religion.

Even when the Minister and the others know that the Boy is not the true Christ, the Minister demands that he die ''to cleanse the soul of man.'' He states that the Boy must die ''so that He should not have died for nothing.'' The play then seems to turn the story of Christ's crucifixion on its head; the Boy, as a pseudo-Christ figure, slays his accusers and is whisked away on the back of a motorcycle to ''the man.''

Sexuality

Most plays that are set inside a church do not feature the themes of sex and sexuality, but Baraka's does—possibly to shock but maybe also to join together two topics, religion and sex, about which Americans have varying levels of discomfort. The tone Baraka takes also indicates that he sees hypocrisy when religious authorities comment on or proscribe certain types of sexual behavior.

The prominence of sex as a theme in the play is stressed immediately; the play opens with the Homosexual and the Minister arguing over sexual preferences and promiscuity. The Homosexual dismisses the Minister's concerns, but the Minister responds, ''When you are strapped in sin, I pray for you, dear queen. I stare with X-ray eyes into your dark room and suffer with you.'' Sexual preference is a major point of contention between the two characters throughout the play, as is sexual behavior. Whenever the Minister accuses the Homosexual of behaving improperly, the Homosexual assures him that his actions are really not that shocking and can be attributed to his humanness. At one point the Homosexual refers to himself as ''the Son of Man,''

TOPICS FOR FURTHER STUDY

- The play takes place during the early 1960s in New York City. If you were producing the play today, what changes would you make? Would you set it during contemporary times, or would you move the setting to another city? If you did change the play's time or place, how would you then change its content and language?
- If you were asked to produce the play, who would you cast in the various roles? Would Baraka's instructions in the list of characters be helpful, or would you ignore them?
- Why do you think Baraka chose to title the play as he did? Do you think *The Baptism* is a good title? Suggest three other possible titles.
- Many critics have commented on Baraka's use of profanity in the play. What is your opinion of the language? Explain whether you think it is critical to the content and message of the play, including why or why not.
- When the play debuted in 1964, many audiences were shocked not only by the profanity but by the irreverence toward Christianity and organized religion. Does it hold the same power to shock today? Explain why or why not.

underscoring his association with human desire as well as with the divine, since this title was used by Christ.

Interestingly, the Homosexual questions the sexual preference and activities of the Minister on a number of occasions, indicating that he believes the Minister is a hypocrite. When the Boy appears in the church, he asks to be forgiven of his sins and ''sprawls'' on the floor; the Minister responds by saying the word ''love'' as if it is a question. The Homosexual whispers off to the side ''You, sir, are an opportunist,'' as if he thinks the Minister may see the Boy as something more than a prospective Christian.

The character of the Boy is surrounded by sexual references. The sin for which he seeks forgiveness when he first enters the church is masturbation. Later, he admits to lying to the chorus of Women about his identity so that he could sleep with them. They had been praising the Boy for being ''the Son of God. Our holy husband,'' moaning that he had ''popped us in those various hallways of love and blessed us with the beauty of Jehovah.'' However, when they hear him say that he is not Christ, they are angry at being deceived. ''We wanted to be virgins of the Lord. He lied,'' they chant together.

The struggle to control human sexual desires and ''the flesh'' is preeminent in the play and provides the major source of hypocrisy for Baraka's characters. Only the Homosexual is uninhibited and straightforward about what he wants. He asks to experience everything and does not want to be ''saved'' from anything. ''I want it all,'' he says. ''I want to know it. See it. . . . Feel it, if it comes to that.'' The Minister and the others are not so sure. When they think that the Boy is Christ and has slept with the chorus of Women to ''save'' them, they find him acceptable. When he admits, however, to having lied to satisfy his human desires, they become enraged and attempt murder.

STYLE

Structure

The play is accomplished in one act and takes place in one scene at a Baptist church. Numerous characters enter and leave, but the action takes place in only one location.

Baraka uses a chorus, a classical technique favored by the ancient Greeks in which a group of people sing or chant important parts of a play. Often, the chorus was used to mark the parts of the play, commenting on what the audience had just seen or was about to see. In Baraka's play, the six or so Women are a chorus, singing bits of old gospel songs and praising the Boy when they think he is Christ. The Minister claims responsibility for the chorus of Women, calling them ''my usherettes.'' The use of the chorus recalls traditional forms of drama, but it also lends an almost comic air to the play.

Character Types

Baraka has created characters that are not unique individuals but are more like representations of particular groups or belief systems. The characters are given titles, not personal names that might disguise the messages Baraka wants to deliver through their actions and words. For example, the characterization of the Homosexual is rather stereotypical—as are most of the other characterizations—with Baraka describing him as ''very queenly'' and overly concerned with his and other characters' appearances. The Minister is patriarchal, with silver hair and a rigid sense of respectability. The Old Woman, according to Baraka, is ''strong from years of the American Matriarchy.'' She is accustomed to giving orders and dictating moral responsibility.

Satire and Humor

Baraka makes fun of everyone and everything in his play by satirizing religion and all those associated with it. From the opening moments of the play, Baraka sends the message that much of what his characters are saying is ridiculous; they dance, sing silly songs, jump on one leg, take a mambo step, and even drop their pants. Baraka's use of humor reflects his desire that organized religion be exposed for what he considers are its absurdities and hypocrisies.

The Homosexual's dropping his pants to expose red leotards brings the action close to slapstick. This is not the only place where Baraka uses this kind of humor. After listening to the Boy proclaim his holy mission and demand to be left on earth, the Messenger has had enough and hits him over the head with a tire iron.

Occasionally, the language in the play shifts to a kind of street talk in which the characters use obscene words or informal phrasing. Baraka's use of these techniques supports the general satiric tone of the play, encouraging a light atmosphere around subjects usually addressed in seriousness.

For example, after listening to the Minister use formal language to condemn the Boy for his deceitfulness, the Homosexual says, ''Oh, don't ham everything up,'' relieving the tension of the moment. When the Messenger explains to the Boy that they must leave immediately, the tone and pacing of his language sounds like jazz music: ''Sorry baby. Can't make it. . . . Jump on the back of the cycle and we'll split.'' The Messenger is making light of the Boy's extreme demands that he ''perish'' and ''suffer'' with those on earth that he was sent to ''save.''

HISTORICAL CONTEXT

Bohemians and the Beat Movement in New York City

Baraka's writing and thinking was influenced during the late 1950s and early 1960s by a group of artists and intellectuals often referred to as the Beats or Bohemians. While many of the movement's participants considered San Francisco their home base, a large number of these artists also spent time in New York City's Greenwich Village while Baraka lived there. Gregory Corso, Charles Olson, Frank O'Hara, and Allen Ginsberg—who electrified the literary world in 1955 with his experimental poem ''Howl'' in San Francisco—lived in and visited Greenwich Village at various times.

The Beats rebelled against typical middle-class American values through their art and rejected the conventional in all that they came across. They experimented with the form and content of poetry and prose, relying on intuition and emotions to tell them when a piece was finished. They chafed against post-World War II conformity; William S. Burroughs and Ginsberg were open about their experimental drug use, and those who were homosexual were quite candid about it.

Struggle for Civil Rights in the 1950s and 1960s

During the 1950s and early 1960s, Amiri Baraka lived and wrote in a world in which blacks were

COMPARE & CONTRAST

- **1960s:** In the early 1960s, Black Muslim leader Malcolm X breaks away from the Nation of Islam and begins to gain a following of his own, somewhat softening his previously hard stance against whites. In the mid-1960s, after Malcolm X's assassination, Baraka begins to shift his political affiliation away from white liberalism toward black nationalism.

  Today: A controversy erupts over the ownership of Malcolm X's papers. His family is able to prevent the auction of his personal writings, at least temporarily. Baraka now considers himself a "Third World Socialist."

- **1960s:** Four young black girls are murdered when a church is fire-bombed in Birmingham, Alabama, in 1963.

  Today: An average of fifteen to twenty churches suffer arson attacks each month in the United States. A majority of these are either predominantly black or multiracial churches.

- **1960s:** In the 1960s, Greenwich Village is a center for avant-garde artists and writers (those who are experimenting with new and challenging forms of art), filled with coffee houses, storefront theaters, and a small but thriving homosexual community.

  Today: The Greenwich Society for Historic Preservation works to maintain many of the significant buildings in the neighborhood. The area is considered prime real estate now, and few "starving artists" can afford to live there.

- **1960s:** In 1964, the Twenty-Fourth Amendment to the U.S. Constitution is passed. One of its primary features is a ban on poll taxes in federal elections, giving the poor and many African Americans increased access to the voting booth. In 1965, the federal Voting Rights Act is passed, temporarily suspending literacy tests intended to restrict voting of African Americans and other minorities in some states. By the end of the decade there are 1,469 African-American elected officials in the United States, according to the Joint Center for Political and Economic Studies.

  Today: The Joint Center for Political and Economic Studies reports that there are nearly nine thousand African-American elected officials in the United States.

largely considered second-class citizens and did not enjoy many of the same legal protections as whites. For example, until a number of court cases struck down segregation of the races in the United States, blacks were barred or restricted—sometimes by state law—from a variety of public venues, such as restaurants, neighborhoods, golf courses, schools, and movie theaters. In the second half of the 1950s, the Supreme Court handed down a series of decisions invalidating the segregation of golf courses, swimming pools, and beaches.

From the late 1950s through the 1960s, some African Americans and supportive whites engaged in civil rights demonstrations, often risking their lives in the effort. Many of the demonstrations were met with violence, such as the 1963 confrontation between police and activists in Birmingham, Alabama. The local police commissioner responded to the largely peaceful demonstration by releasing dogs and using cattle prods against the civil rights protesters.

One of the largest civil rights demonstrations of that era was the 1963 March on Washington for Jobs and Freedom, led by Dr. Martin Luther King, Jr. Nearly a quarter-million Americans of varying backgrounds gathered in front of the Washington Monument to hear King deliver his now-famous "I Have a Dream" speech.

While the civil rights movement grew, and after a 1960 trip to Fidel Castro's Cuba, Baraka became increasingly more politically radical. During the early 1960s, Baraka became disillusioned with the apolitical attitude of the white experimental artists he worked with in Greenwich Village. He finally broke with them in 1965, after the assassination of Malcolm X. He moved to Harlem and then Newark, declaring that he was interested primarily in black cultural efforts such as jazz and theater written for black audiences. In Newark, he launched the Black Arts Repertory Theater-School.

CRITICAL OVERVIEW

Critical reception of Baraka's work varies widely from enthusiastic praise to equally enthusiastic condemnation. William J. Harris, in the introduction to *The LeRoi Jones/Amiri Baraka Reader,* suggests that the reason for this disparity may lie in the various modes and influences of the writer's energy and creativity. According to Harris, Baraka "is an avant-garde writer whose variety of forms . . . makes him difficult to categorize, while his stormy history clouds critical objectivity."

To get a handle on Baraka's efforts, many critics have divided his work into three or four periods. Harris sees Baraka's work falling into four periods: the "Beat Period," from 1957 to 1962, during which he was influenced by white avant-garde artists such as Allen Ginsberg; the "Transitional Period," from 1963 to 1965, during which Baraka wrote *The Baptism* and became increasingly disillusioned with white society; the "Black Nationalist Period," from 1965 to 1974, during which Baraka argued that blacks in America constituted a distinct nation; and the "Third World Marxist Period," from 1974 through today, during which the author has embraced international socialism and rejected black nationalism.

While freely admitting that classifying Baraka is difficult, Theodore C. Hudson refers to Baraka as a romantic in his *From LeRoi Jones to Amiri Baraka.* Baraka "places great faith in intuition, in feelings" and also believes that "man is divine," argues Hudson, who also writes that Baraka's romantic approach to art shows itself when he is "disdainful of the organized and orthodox religion of the majority"—a thematic element that defines *The Baptism.*

Like most of Baraka's work, *The Baptism* has received mixed responses. Tish Dace and Andrew O. Jones, writing in the *Reference Guide to American Literature,* note that the play garnered charges of "obscenity and blasphemy" while it "jarred and amused" those who went to see its opening in 1964. James A. Miller, writing in the *Dictionary of Literary Biography* Volume 16: *The Beats,* criticizes the play for its incomplete structure and substance. He argues that the play "lacks a clear dramatic focus and is heavily dependant upon the shock value of irreverent attitudes for its effects." Miller also notes, however, that Baraka was "clearly indebted" to the writings of French playwright Jean Genet and to others who wrote in the style of the "theater of the absurd." Absurdist theater typically abandons traditional dramatic devices, such as logical plot development and dialogue, and replaces them with a sense of confusion and unreality.

Praise for the play centers on its challenging message. According to Catherine Daniels Hurst in the *Dictionary of Literary Biography* Volume 7: *Twentieth-Century American Dramatists, The Baptism* is a prime example of Baraka's concern with the themes of "personal identity, self-actualization, and appearance versus reality." Hurst also asserts that Baraka has effectively interwoven "setting, character, and theme" in the play. She calls it a "modern fable" and a "satirical indictment of religious perversion." Beyond her general praise for the play, however, Hurst questions Baraka's use of profanity and obscenity and doubts whether Baraka's message can be interpreted properly when it is in "such an unpalatable form." C. W. E. Bigsby echoes this concern in his *Confrontation and Commitment: A Study of Contemporary American Drama,* noting, "it is precisely his failure to communicate which ironically constitutes the greatest weakness of his work."

Critics have noted Baraka's innovative use of language; this technique appears throughout *The Baptism.* Dace and Jones see in his early work "techniques analogous to black music—jazz and the blues." Hudson observes that Baraka uses humor and satire as a major technique—a method very broadly used in *The Baptism.* Baraka's satire is "informed by a certain hip, or superior, sensibility, by an urbane sensibility developed in street lore, [and] by a contempt born of too much perception," according to Hudson.

While Baraka has received his fair share of negative press for his shifting views and his sometimes extreme political statements, most critics agree that he is an important twentieth-century writer. ''Although he has often expressed disdain for the literary establishment,'' notes Miller, ''[Baraka's] work has clearly defined him as a major intellectual presence.''

CRITICISM

Susan Sanderson

Sanderson holds a master of fine arts degree in fiction writing and is an independent writer. In this essay, Sanderson examines the role of the Homosexual in Amiri Baraka's play The Baptism.

Amiri Baraka wrote *The Baptism* when he was still known as LeRoi Jones and was immersed in the bohemian life of New York City's Greenwich Village. All around him were artists, intellectuals, and members of the beat movement—primarily young white men, who rejected the values of middle-class American society; experimented with nontraditional artistic forms, mind-altering drugs, and Eastern religions; and openly challenged traditional sexual sensibilities. The play definitely shows evidence of Baraka's exposure to other avant-garde writers: its language is peppered with street lingo and profanity, social institutions are lampooned, and the very content and meaning of the story are in question. Who is the Boy? Is he really Christ or just a clever street punk? Why are all of these people at the church? Why does the Messenger inexplicably arrive at the end of the play to take the Boy away—and where is he taken?

While these questions cannot be completely answered without directly querying the author, an examination of the character of the Homosexual can help reveal some of the intent of the play. This must be done, however, with extreme caution, as Theodore C. Hudson advises in his book *From LeRoi Jones to Amiri Baraka.* ''To look only for rational, conscious, and ordered style in Jones's work is to subvert explication and to beg for a misreading or a nonreading,'' he warns. Nevertheless, the character of the Homosexual is a compelling one. He opens the play, deeply involved in an argument about sexual preference and sin with the Minister, and he has the final say in the play, rising from the pile of bodies on the stage to head off to a bar. ''What ever happened to that cute little religious fanatic?'' he wonders aloud, pausing for a moment to think about the Boy.

Like all of the other characters, the Homosexual is a stock character, the stereotype of a homosexual. He strikes effeminate poses throughout the play and works to attract the Boy's attention. The other characters also stand for ideas or groups and do not have any unique qualities that make them individuals. They have no names or personal histories. The Minister, for example, with his gray hair, black robes, and stern demeanor, is the image of authority. The Old Woman similarly projects authority with her loud voice and advanced age, but she also represents, as Baraka conveniently mentions in the list of characters, ''the American Matriarchy.'' The Women are, according to the list of characters, ''sleek 'Village!' types,'' probably representative of many of the women Baraka met while living in Greenwich Village—highly educated and smart but very focused on the next popular trend. In Baraka's eyes, they must have been as similar to one another as are the Women in the play, who are distinguished only by the numbers pinned on their chests.

While Hudson's warnings about ''ordered style'' in Baraka's work are valuable, he misses his own point when it comes to interpreting the message behind homosexual characters in Baraka's work—at least within this play. Hudson argues that in Baraka's work, ''homosexuality . . . may be considered as broadly symbolic of misuse of creative energies, as a deliberate turning from what is natural and good . . . as an avoidance of reality.'' In *The Baptism,* though, the Homosexual, however stereotypical Baraka has made him, has something the rest of the characters do not have: a keen sense of humor. This, along with his ability to survey a situation and call it as he sees it, sets him apart from the rest of the characters. Contrary to Hudson's assertions, the Homosexual is the character most connected to reality and most open to creative energy.

The Homosexual is the outsider, literally and figuratively. He is outside the mainstream of American life by his sexual choices and preferences. The Minister accuses the Homosexual of being ''less selective'' than he himself is when it comes to sexual partners, and at one point he calls upon God to punish the Homosexual. The Homosexual is also often outside of the play's action and in a position where he can comment about what is going on without being heard. When the Boy appears in the church, for example, the Homosexual makes a side comment that the Minister is ''an opportunist.'' Numerous times he asks another character a question or makes a demand but gets no answer, as if he is not there. When the Boy is declared to be Christ,

WHAT DO I READ NEXT?

- Baraka's *The Autobiography of LeRoi Jones* was originally published in a severely edited form in 1984. The 1997 edition restores the cuts made by the publisher and tells the story of the black literary leader and political activist through his fortieth birthday in 1974.
- Baraka won the Obie Award in 1964 for his play *Dutchman,* which relates the violence and hatred that ensues when a white woman picks up a black man on the subway in New York City. It was originally published in 1964 with another one of his plays in the book *Dutchman and The Slave: Two Plays.*
- *The LeRoi Jones/Amiri Baraka Reader* (1991), edited by William J. Harris, is a good introduction to the wide variety of works authored by Baraka between 1957 and 1990. The volume includes poetry, plays, social essays, novel excerpts, and music criticism.
- Poet Allen Ginsberg was a leader of the Beat movement, a group of avant-garde writers who influenced Baraka early in his career. *Howl and Other Poems,* originally published in 1956 with an introduction by the poet William Carlos Williams, propelled Ginsberg into the limelight. In 1996, a fortieth anniversary edition was released.
- Ntozake Shange first began publishing her plays about a decade after Baraka became well known. Her revolutionary play *for colored girls who have considered suicide/when the rainbow is enuf: a choreopoem,* originally published and produced in 1975, is an exploration of how black women are twice challenged by living in a world controlled by white men.

---

the Homosexual asks him to prove it by turning the church "into the White House or something cool like that," but no one responds to this challenge.

In his position as an outsider, the Homosexual can make sharp and perceptive comments about what he sees happening in the church. This is something no one else is able to do, as they are all busy either condemning the Boy for his sins or praising him when they think he is Christ. In fact, throughout most of the play, the tone of the other characters is often hysterical and fanatical. The Homosexual, on the other hand, is able to stand back and provide an analysis of the situation while remaining in touch with his sense of humor. When the Old Woman finishes her rant about the Boy's masturbation, she falls to the ground. The Minister sees her actions through the lens of his religious beliefs, stating, "She has swooned in the service of the Lord. A holy ecstasy has entered her soul." The Homosexual is not so sure about the Minister's interpretation. He turns over her limp body with his toe and muses to himself, "Hmm, I think maybe she's had a bit too much to drink."

The Homosexual reconsiders nearly everything he sees in the church, and no experience is closed to him—except, of course, the experience of true belief. He reacts quickly when the Minister and the Boy speak of being saved from sin, inquiring of himself why he should want to be saved. "And miss something? No, not me. I want it all," he says, and notes that he wants to feel, see, and know whatever is possible. If rejecting Satan means he will have to pass up an experience, count him out. When the Minister threatens to have his Lord strike the Homosexual dead, the Homosexual is even open to the possibility of that experience. "That's okay. It never happened before. It might be a gas. I mean drilled with the holy lightning," he says, and begins singing, "Drill me baby. Drill me so I don't need to be drilled no more."

Contrary to Hudson's general interpretation of Baraka's use of homosexuals in his work, the Homosexual in *The Baptism* is a perceptive outsider who questions all that he sees but is open to nearly every encounter and experience. He suspects hypocrisy but is flexible enough to admit that lies are

THE HOMOSEXUAL RECONSIDERS NEARLY EVERYTHING HE SEES IN THE CHURCH, AND NO EXPERIENCE IS CLOSED TO HIM—EXCEPT, OF COURSE, THE EXPERIENCE OF TRUE BELIEF."

sometimes desirable—especially when they possible more physical experiences. In addition, he delivers his evaluation of society and its participants with a sense of humor and a sharp wit. Far from drawing a negative character, Baraka has, in fact, depicted the Homosexual as the idealized Village bohemian or avant-garde artist.

Like the Homosexual, Baraka's fellow Greenwich Village residents saw it as their job to persistently challenge social institutions, such as organized religion. They purposely placed themselves outside of middle-class America to have a better view of its hypocrisy. Humor and absurdity were tools they could use to poke fun at what they perceived as Middle America's mindless rigidity and unwillingness to experience all of life.

Granted, Baraka would soon reject much of bohemian and beat philosophy in favor of a more radical black activism, but for the time being he sought to praise what he saw as the obvious solution to a mindless, cookie-cutter existence. The Homosexual, representing bohemian ideals, is, after all, the last man standing in the play. Its apocalyptic climax has been, for him, simply one more experience.

Source: Susan Sanderson, Critical Essay on *The Baptism,* in *Drama for Students,* The Gale Group, 2003.

SOURCES

Bigsby, C. W. E., "LeRoi Jones," in *Confrontation and Commitment: A Study of Contemporary American Drama, 1959–1966,* University of Missouri Press, 1968, pp. 138–55.

Dace, Tish, and Andrew O. Jones, "Baraka, Amiri," in *Reference Guide to American Literature,* 3d ed., edited by Jim Kamp, St. James Press, 1994.

Harris, William J., "Introduction," in *The LeRoi Jones/Amiri Baraka Reader,* edited by William J. Harris, Thunder's Mouth Press, 1991, pp. xvii–xxx.

Hudson, Theodore C., *From LeRoi Jones to Amiri Baraka: The Literary Works,* Duke University Press, 1973, pp. 59, 65–66, 178–80.

Hurst, Catherine Daniels, "Amiri Baraka," in *Dictionary of Literary Biography,* Vol. 7: *Twentieth-Century American Dramatists,* edited by John MacNichols, Gale Research, 1981, pp. 49–56.

Jones, LeRoi, *The Baptism and the Toilet,* Grove Press, New York, 1967.

Miller, James A., "Amiri Baraka," in *Dictionary of Literary Biography,* Vol. 16: *The Beats: Literary Bohemians in Postwar America,* edited by Ann Charters, The Gale Group, 1983, pp. 3–24.

FURTHER READING

Bigsby, C. W. E., *A Critical Introduction to Twentieth Century American Drama: Beyond Broadway,* Vol. 3, Cambridge University Press, 1985.

This book covers the period in American drama immediately after Baraka's productions of *The Baptism* and *Dutchman* and serves as an introduction to how American theater changed dramatically during the 1960s and 1970s. The author focuses on the work that was being done in the smaller, less mainstream theaters commonly referred to as off-Broadway, as well as the ground-breaking work accomplished by playwrights such as Sam Shepard and David Mamet.

Jones, Hettie, *How I Became Hettie Jones,* E. P. Dutton, 1990.

Hettie Jones, Amiri Baraka's wife when he was LeRoi Jones, remembers her interracial marriage to the famous writer. She also writes about the beginnings of her life as a child in a middle-class Jewish household in the Queens section of New York City, and about the various members of the Beat movement whom she and her ex-husband called friends in the 1950s and 1960s.

Oliver, Clinton F., and Stephanie Sills, *Contemporary Black Drama: From "A Raisin in the Sun" to "No Place to Be Somebody,"* Charles Schribner's Sons, 1971.

This volume features plays from many of the leading black playwrights of the late 1950s through the late 1960s, including Lorraine Hansberry, Adrienne Kennedy, James Baldwin, and LeRoi Jones. Each play is preceded by an introductory essay to the playwright and the play.

Watts, Jerry Gafio, *Amiri Baraka: The Politics and Art of a Black Intellectual,* New York University Press, 2001.

The author dissects the intellectual and artistic journey taken by Baraka from the late 1950s through the 1980s, covering the controversial writer's life from his Beat movement days to his more recent Marxist period.

The Barber of Seville

PIERRE-AUGUSTIN DE BEAUMARCHAIS

1775

The Barber of Seville was Pierre-Augustin Caron de Beaumarchais's first comic work and first successful play. Beaumarchais drew on age-old themes and comic types to create a work that dazzled the audience with its humorous wordplay, irreverent activity, and lively characterization. The use of archetypal characters allowed viewers to readily relate to Figaro and company. However, Beaumarchais imbues his characters with traits of particular importance to his original pre-Revolutionary audience. Thus does *The Barber of Seville* successfully take on weightier issues than do most comedies.

Figaro easily emerges as the star of *The Barber of Seville*. So popular was he that Beaumarchais brought Figaro back a few years later in *The Marriage of Figaro*. In addition, the radical cry that Beaumarchais raises, the condemnation of the prevailing social system, is most apparent through Figaro. As Geoffrey Brereton points out in *French Comic Drama from the Sixteenth to the Eighteenth Century,* "Figaro's self-confidence, rooted in the conviction that inherently he is as good as any other man, is the basis of the social criticism already apparent, though muted, in this play." Figaro also is a successful character because of his joyful yet irrepressible behavior. He survives in contemporary times as the epitome of the roguish figure, endowed with cleverness, wit, and restrained insolence.

AUTHOR BIOGRAPHY

Beaumarchais was born in Paris, France, on January 24, 1732. He attended school until the age of thirteen and then went to work as an apprentice for his father, a clockmaker. In 1753, Beaumarchais devised a mechanism for watches. He was presented at the court of Louis XV in 1754, and he soon became the royal watchmaker as well as music instructor to the king's daughters. Upon marrying Madeleine-Catherine Aubertin Franquet, a widow, he became Clerk Controller and gained her husband's property, called the property of Beaumarchais, from which he took his name. He became wealthy through business associations and purchased the title of Secretary of the King, which gave him noble status.

Beaumarchais's first literary efforts were *parades,* short comedic plays. Beaumarchais's *parades* were performed privately among the nobility, but they were not published until long after his death. They contain many of the themes, situations, and stylistic characteristics that Beaumarchais would more fully develop in his later dramas.

Beaumarchais became a serious playwright after a visit to Spain in 1764. This trip gave him the opportunity to observe Spanish life and culture, including the wastefulness of the nobility and the abuses of the government. He returned to Paris in 1767 to present his play *Eugénie*, which made use of these experiences. His next play, *Two Friends*, appeared three years later. Neither of these plays, however, was a critical success. Also in 1770, Beaumarchais became involved in a highly controversial series of court cases. Although he eventually won his case, he was stripped of his civil rights.

With the ascension of Louis XVI to the throne in 1774, however, Beaumarchais's civil rights were reinstated. The king also hired Beaumarchais as a secret government agent operating out of London. He became interested in the cause of American independence, and, with the support of the French government, helped provide money and arms to the American colonists.

He continued to work on his writings, and *The Barber of Seville*, which some critics believed derived from one of his *parades,* was produced in 1775. His *Marriage of Figaro*, which reintroduced the members of Count Almaviva's household, was produced four years later, in 1784. The libretto *Tarare* was staged 1787; it was reproduced in 1790 with a new ending adapted to the political changes brought about by the French Revolution. His final play, *A Mother's Guilt*, was presented in 1792 and culminates the Figaro trilogy.

Beaumarchais pursued other important work as well. In 1777, he founded the Society of Dramatic Authors, one of the first organizations that protected authors' rights and gave them copyrights to their works. Between 1783 and 1790, he published a complete seventy-volume edition of the works of the French writer Voltaire.

Throughout this busy period, Beaumarchais also continued to pursue his business interests. On behalf of the French revolutionary government, he undertook arms negotiations in 1792 but was imprisoned on suspicion of hiding guns. Freed in 1794, Beaumarchais fled to England and then to Hamburg, Germany. In response, the French government declared him an émigré (a French noble living abroad who wanted to overturn the Revolution) and barred his return to France, imprisoned his family, and seized his property. Beaumarchais remained in exile in Germany until 1796, when the new government, under pressure from Beaumarchais's family, finally allowed him to return. He died of a stroke in Paris on May 18, 1799.

PLOT SUMMARY

Act 1

Beaumarchais explains the plot of *The Barber of Seville* in his foreword: ''An amorous old man intends to marry his ward on the following day; a young man who is more clever forestalls him, and on that very day, captures the girl in the guardian's house, right under his nose, and makes her his wife.'' The play opens on a street in Seville, where Count Almaviva waits under a window for Rosine to appear. After seeing and falling in love with Rosine in Madrid, he has tracked her down and now is determined to make contact with her. While he is waiting, Figaro, his former servant, appears. The Count explains his predicament, and Figaro promises to help him.

Soon, Rosine and her guardian, Bartholo, appear at the window. He is angry with her for reading a modern play that he finds foolish. Dropping a note into the street, she asks the Count to identify himself. Bartholo sees that she drops a piece of paper, but she claims it is only song lyrics. Bartholo, however, suspects trouble and resolves to marry

Rosine as soon as possible. He sends his servant Bazile to a notary to make arrangements for the wedding to take place the following day.

Meanwhile, Figaro urges the Count to identify himself to Rosine in song. The Count claims to be an undistinguished young man named Lindor. After Rosine is forced to retire into the house, Figaro and the Count plot. Figaro comes up with the idea of getting the Count into the house disguised as a soldier who has billeting orders.

Act 2

To make his plot work, Figaro incapacitates the household staff with medications. Then he goes to Rosine's room and tells her that Lindor does love her. Rosine, who has been writing Lindor a letter, gives it to Figaro to deliver. When Bartholo enters, he is immediately suspicious. His suspicions are further aroused when Bazile arrives with the news that the Count has been seen in Seville, looking for Rosine. Again, Bartholo resolves to marry Rosine the following day. Figaro, hiding in the closet, learns of this plan. Once Bartholo and Bazile leave, Figaro tells Rosine of Bartholo's intention. He also tells her that he and Lindor will prevent the planned wedding.

Bartholo returns to Rosine and demands to know if Figaro brought her a reply to the note she dropped earlier. Just then, the Count appears, disguised as a drunken soldier. Although he manages to pass Rosine a letter, Bartholo sees him. After the Count has been ejected from the house, Bartholo demands to read the letter. While at first Rosine refuses, she manages to switch the letter with a letter she received from her cousin. After Bartholo leaves, Rosine reads the Count's letter.

Act 3

The Count returns to Bartholo's home, this time disguised as Alonzo, an assistant of Bazile. He says that Bazile is ill and that he will give Rosine her singing lesson. To gain Bartholo's trust, Alonzo hands him Rosine's letter, saying it was written to the Count. Bartholo determines to foil the Count's plan. Alonzo gives Rosine her singing lesson and manages to tell her about the plan that he and Figaro have devised to get her out of Bartholo's household that evening. Bazile shows up unexpectedly during the lesson, but Figaro and the Count prevent him from unmasking Alonzo. However, Bartholo realizes that something is amiss, and they all argue. Rosine announces that she will not marry Bartholo—

Pierre-Augustin de Beaumarchais

instead, she will marry whoever rescues her from him. Bartholo chases the Count and Figaro from his house.

Act 4

After Bazile informs Bartholo that he does not know Alonzo and was not sick, Bartholo grows even more upset. He sends Bazile to bring the notary immediately. He then confronts Rosine with her letter, claiming that he got it from another woman who is involved with the Count. Rosine is confused because she does not know who the Count is, and Bartholo convinces her that Lindor is not in love with her but rather is wooing Rosine on behalf of the Count. Believing that she has been betrayed, Rosine agrees to marry Bartholo. She also tells him that the Count and Figaro are planning to return to the house that night.

Figaro and the Count arrive as planned. At first, Rosine rebuffs the Count, but when he explains his true identity, she realizes that she has not been betrayed. The three try to leave the house only to discover that they have been locked in. Then Bazile arrives with the notary. Bribed, he serves as a witness to the marriage of Rosine and the Count. Then Bartholo returns. He had gone to fetch a justice of the peace to arrest the Count. However, the couple is already married, and the magistrate refuses to make the arrest. The play ends with Figaro remarking that when love and youth conspire against an old man, anything he does to stop the romance will be a useless precaution.

CHARACTERS

Count Almaviva

Count Almaviva is a young nobleman with one thought on his mind: to woo the beautiful Rosine. Having fallen in love with her at first sight in Madrid, by time the play opens, his continual presence under her window has made Rosine fall in love with him as well. The Count's desire to wed Rosine forms the intrigue of the play. The Count manages to achieve his goal of winning Rosine only through the help of the clever Figaro.

To win Rosine, the Count takes on numerous roles. Because his interest in Rosine is known to her guardian, Bartholo, he disguises himself to get into the older man's household. He dresses up as a drunken soldier demanding to be billeted, and later he masquerades as Alonzo, a music teacher and assistant to Bazile. Through both of these disguises, he is able to communicate important information to Rosine. However, he also disguises his true identity to his love. He claims to be an undistinguished, penniless man named Lindor because he wants to be sure that she, unlike the other women he knows, loves him instead of his wealth and position. He finally reveals his true identity to Rosine, once he is certain of her sincerity.

Alonzo

See Count Almaviva

Bartholo

Bartholo is an old man and the guardian of Rosine, whom he plans to marry. The crotchety, curmudgeonly Bartholo is far from an ideal match for Rosine. He despises any sign of modernity, treats Rosine like property, and tries to rule his household with absolute authority. He is constantly suspicious of Rosine's actions as well as of the actions of Figaro and the Count (in his numerous disguises). To this end, he tries to keep Rosine isolated in his household. Fearful that he will lose Rosine, he arranges for the notary to come to his home and perform the marriage ceremony. His machinations to wed Rosine are foiled, and, at the end of the play, even the law will do nothing to help him. Thus, he must accept the loss of Rosine to his rival.

Bazile

Bazile is Rosine's music teacher, but he also performs numerous duties and favors for Bartholo. However, Bazile awards his loyalty to whoever can pay the highest fee for it, which, in two important instances, is the Count. Because of this characteristic, Bazile does not tell Bartholo the truth about Alonzo, which likely would make Bartholo even more vigilant in guarding Rosine from the Count. He also fails to stop the notary from performing the ceremony.

Figaro

Figaro is a former servant of the Count. He is a sort of jack-of-all-trades; since leaving the Count's service, he has worked at many jobs, including as a writer. His personality is an unexpected mix of tenacity and laxity. He currently is employed as a traveling barber, serving Bartholo's household, but he willingly puts his job at risk to help the Count. Figaro has long proven his ability to survive and to take care of himself under any circumstances.

The clever, quick-thinking Figaro agrees to help the Count win Rosine. He masterminds the complicated series of events that lead to the union between the lovers. He devises the plan to get the Count into the house to speak with Rosine, passes letters between the two, and tries to thwart Bartholo and his mounting suspicions. He performs these services for twofold reasons. He initially agreed to do the favor for the Count, but then the Count also added a financial incentive.

Despite the aid he renders the Count, Figaro is always aware that the Count treats him condescendingly because he is a member of the lower class. However, while he does not refuse to help the Count as a result of this behavior, he continually speaks out—usually with subtlety but occasionally not—and points out this poor treatment. His comments are a statement on the inequities of the social system that prevailed in France during Beaumarchais's time as well as on the smugness of the French aristocracy.

Lindor

See Count Almaviva

Rosine

Rosine is the young ward of Bartholo. She knows Bartholo intends to marry her very soon, and when the Count, as Lindor, makes his interest known, she quickly falls in love with him. Thus, she wholeheartedly goes along with Figaro's plans. She takes chances to bring about her union with Lindor and acts obstinately toward Bartholo. To keep her affairs secret, she tells Bartholo many lies and refuses to accede to his demands. However, when she believes that Lindor has deceived her, she agrees to marry Bartholo. Upon learning that Lindor is the Count and is not merely attempting to woo her for the Count, she forgives and marries him.

THEMES

Useless Precaution

The subtitle of *The Barber of Seville* is "The Useless Precaution." The useless precaution theme in drama focuses on an old man trying to isolate his young wife or intended wife, and it harkens back to the days of Roman theater. By the 1770s, the useless precaution premise was a stock element of French literature, found in countless plays and stories, and while Beaumarchais's theme was highly derivative, his treatment of it was wholly original. As Frédéric Grendel wrote in *Beaumarchais: The Man Who Was Figaro,* "The thing that matters is that Beaumarchais made the theme his own. No one before him, not even Molière, had used the devices of ellipsis and punning so freely and so naturally." John Dunkley concurred, writing in the *Reference Guide to World Literature,* "Beaumarchais infuses it [the theme] with new life through memorable characters and a brilliantly honed dialogue."

Beaumarchais emphasizes the theme when the audience is first introduction to Rosine in act I. She claims to drop a lyric sheet from a new comedy entitled *The Useless Precaution.* Her interest in this play indicates her distaste for a marriage to the antiquated Bartholo, who assesses the play as "modern rubbish" that represents a "barbarous century." He refutes the accomplishments of the contemporary world, railing against it as filled with "Every kind of stupidity: freedom of thought, the law of gravity, electricity, religious tolerance, inoculation, quinine, the encyclopedia." Thus does Beaumarchais make clear that Bartholo is far too old and set in his ways to be an appropriate spouse to Rosine.

MEDIA ADAPTATIONS

- *The Barber of Seville* was adapted to a four-act opera, *Il barbiere de Saviglia,* in 1782. Giovanni Paisiello wrote the music, and Giuseppe Petrosellini wrote the libretto. A three-act comica opera, also entitled *Il barbiere de Saviglia,* was performed in 1816, with music composed by Gioacchino Rossini and a libretto written by Cesare Sterbine. While it was initially unfavorably received, partially because Paisiello's opera was so popular, it has since been recognized as one of Rossini's masterpieces. Numerous recordings of it are available. By the early twentieth century, at least nine more operatic versions of *The Barber of Seville* were written and performed.

Verses from *The Useless Precaution* continue to appear throughout the play. In act III, Rosine sings a song that celebrates the coming of spring and youthful love. Her paraphrasing of the song is more telling, however. She describes the disappearance of winter—which, like Bartholo, has kept people shuttered inside—and compares herself to the "slave who has been locked up for a long time and then appreciates his liberty more than ever." The play ends by invoking the theme. As Figaro reminds Bartholo—and the audience—"when love and youth unite to deceive an old man, anything he does to try and stop them can only be called a useless precaution."

Disguises

Figaro's plot to keep Bartholo from marrying Rosine and to bring about her marriage to the Count relies on a series of disguises. In order to get close to Rosine, the Count takes on several roles and costumes. Figaro first comes across the Count as the latter lurks outside Rosine's window, dressed in the long brown cloak and broad-brimmed hat of a priest. Though he has donned the clothing of a priest, however, the Count is unable to cover up other qualities that indicate his true station in life; as

TOPICS FOR FURTHER STUDY

- Learn more about the hypothesis that Figaro was Beaumarchais's stand-in on the stage and in the eyes of French society. Do you think this hypothesis is true? Write a persuasive essay supporting or disagreeing with this theory.
- What do you think will happen next with the Count and Rosine. Write a short summary explaining what course you believe their relationship will take.
- Some critics believe that Figaro's monologue in act V, in which he chronicles the nobility's abuses of the lower classes, forecasts the French Revolution and the end of the French aristocracy. Write a persuasive essay supporting or disagreeing with this theory.
- Read *The Marriage of Figaro*. Compare and contrast Beaumarchais's characterizations of the Count, the Countess (Rosine), and Figaro in the two works.
- Research the social classes of Beaumarchais's time. Does Beaumarchais portray them accurately? Explain your answer.
- Find out more about Beaumarchais's life. In what ways do you think his own experiences affected the creation of *The Barber of Seville*?
- Conduct research on the historical development of the comedic play. Comment on the importance of Beaumarchais's contribution to this genre.

Figaro remarks to himself upon first seeing the Count, ''No, he isn't a reverend. That haughtiness, that nobility. . . . I wasn't wrong: it's Count Almaviva.''

The Count is physically introduced into Bartholo's household—where he is able to communicate his love as well as important messages to Rosine—in the guise of a drunken soldier who demands that Bartholo give him quarters for the evening. He next enters Bartholo's house in the guise of a music teacher. Bartholo comments upon the inefficacy of the Count's disguise: ''You look more like a disguised lover than an official friend.'' However, even the suspicious Bartholo does not realize that he has hit upon the truth.

The Count uses disguises for other purposes as well. He refuses to reveal his true identity to Rosine. Instead, he claims to be a penniless young man named Lindor. As he explains to Figaro, ''Since she's already interested in me without knowing who I am, I'll keep this name Lindor; it'll be better to hide my title until I've won her.'' The Count wants to be sure that he is loved for himself, not for his wealth or social station.

Music

Music provides an underpinning for the play's structure and plot. Viewed in that light, it is not surprising that Figaro's introduction upon the stage takes place while he composes a song for a comic opera. Additionally, Rosine claims to carry a song sheet as she is introduced to the audience, though the sheet in her hand is actually a letter for the Count. Bazile, her music teacher—notably the only person outside Bartholo's household with whom Rosine is allowed contact—gives her verses from a new comedy entitled *The Useless Precaution.* Thus, the audience realizes immediately that music has an important role in the play and that music will reiterate the overarching theme.

The lyrics that the characters sing are important to the advancement of the plot. They give the lovers voice to ''speak'' with each other and express their feelings. The song the Count sings to Rosine in act I allows him to introduce himself—albeit disguised as Lindor—and declare his love. When the Count masquerades as a music instructor, he gains access to Rosine, who then communicates her dislike of the idea of a marriage to Bartholo by singing lyrics from *The Useless Precaution* that specifically celebrate young love. In marked contrast to their verses are those of Bartholo, who vulgarly sings a verse alluding to sexual relations between an older man and a younger wife: ''I may not be handsome, yet/I know how to play. When the night gets dark as jet/Every cat looks grey.''

Lyrics also allow characters to impugn others. For instance, in act II, the Count describes Bartholo impudently in song as ''Greedy and destructive and as vicious as a stoat. A scraggy old, baggy old, cheap minded churl'' and as a doctor who ''eliminate[s] not merely pain and disease. But also your patients.'' Bartholo readily recognizes the insult and throws the Count out of his house.

STYLE

Comedy

In his two earliest plays, Beaumarchais tried to uphold the dramatic theory known as the bourgeois drama, which was an attempt to replace the neoclassical forms of drama with subject matter and method more suited to contemporary times. Bourgeois drama was serious drama written in simple prose that emphasized moral instruction in modern social contexts. However, Beaumarchais's bourgeois dramas were generally critical failures, and, with *The Barber of Seville*, Beaumarchais abandoned the bourgeois drama and embraced pure comedy. The essential plot derives from comedies stretching back to the Greek New Comedy circa 300 B.C.E. However, as John Richetti writes in *European Writers,* ''what made his [Beaumarchais's] play much more than popular farce is . . . the irrepressible wit and cascading linguistic vivacity.'' The comic tone of the play is embodied in Figaro, who, Beaumarchais writes in his foreword to the play, is ''a comic, happy-go-lucky fellow who laughs equally at the success and failure of his enterprises.''

Characterization

The characters in *The Barber of Seville* are stock characters; they represent archetypes dating back to ancient Greek drama. Figaro derives from the wily slave or servant; the Count and Rosine represent the young lovers; Bartholo is the aging man who attempts to thwart the relationship; Bazile is the fool who possesses hardly an ounce of common sense. Beaumarchais also makes use of two character types popular in Spanish *entremeses,* which were after-dinner entertainments held in private homes: the itinerant Spanish barber, represented by Figaro, and the comic sacristan, whom Beaumarchais has transformed into Bazile.

Autobiography

Many critics have pointed out the parallels between Figaro's adventures and those of his creator, Beaumarchais. John Wells writes in his introduction to *The Figaro Plays,* ''Figaro became Beaumarchais's spokesman on stage, and the three plays represent a kind of autobiography.'' Both Figaro and Beaumarchais began their careers as dramatists in Spain. Both men dreamed of a more liberal future, in which a person's social class mattered less than his personal ability.

Figaro is introduced to the audience while he is composing a comic opera. It is in his monologues, however, that the resemblance is more substantial, as Figaro refers to life experiences that often match those of Beaumarchais. For example, like Beaumarchais, Figaro has become an author, one of those ''beset by . . . their critics, their booksellers, their censors, the people who envied them, and the people who imitated them.'' Figaro's recitation of traveling ''philosophically through the two Castiles, La Mancha, Estremadura, Sierra Morena, and the Andalusia, being acclaimed in one town, jailed in another, but always on top of events; praised by these people, denounced by those people . . . laughing at my misfortune'' evokes Beaumarchais's own travels around Europe. While today's audiences generally are ignorant of such allusions, Beaumarchais's audience understood the subtle attacks on those who attempted to stand in the dramatist's way.

Trilogy

Beaumarchais's Figaro plays, *The Barber of Seville*, *The Marriage of Figaro*, and *A Mother's Guilt*, make up a trilogy. *The Barber of Seville*, the first play, focuses on Figaro's successful plan to win the hand of Rosine for the Count. *The Marriage of Figaro* places former conspirators Count Almaviva and Figaro at odds, as Figaro must use his resourcefulness to protect his fiancée from the amorous yearnings of the Count. The final play in the trilogy, *A Mother's Guilt*, finds the Count and Countess and their loyal servants, Figaro and his wife, living in France.

Although the plays form a trilogy, several inconsistencies appear among them. Notable is the shift in the Count's character. In *The Barber of*

Seville, he is a smitten young lover devoted to Rosine, but in *The Marriage of Figaro*, he is a lecherous husband who attempts to exercise his legal rights as lord of the manor to deflower his vassal's wife on her wedding night. Another significant inconsistency is the setting. The first two plays of the trilogy take place in Old Spain, while *A Mother's Guilt* takes place in Revolutionary France.

HISTORICAL CONTEXT

France on the Brink of Revolution

Though France was the largest and most powerful nation in Europe during the 1700s, it experienced serious domestic discord by the middle of the century. French society had long been stratified. French people belonged to one of three legal, social, and political classes, called estates. The First Estate consisted of members of the Roman Catholic clergy, who made up less than one percent of the population. The Second Estate consisted of members of French nobility, who made up less than two percent of the population. People were born into the Second Estate, but they also could purchase titles, as did Beaumarchais. The Third Estate consisted of everyone else in France, from the peasants to the bourgeoisie, and constituted about ninety-seven percent of the French population. Neither the First nor the Second Estate paid any significant taxes, thrusting France's growing financial burden upon those who could least afford it.

In the aftermath of the Seven Years' War (1756–1763), France was left with huge debts. King Louis XV, who ruled France from 1715 to 1774, raised taxes, borrowed money from bankers, and refused to economize. Under his successor, Louis XVI, France's debts continued to rise as the country aided the colonists in the American Revolution. While Louis's financial advisers advocated taxing the First and Second Estates, the nobles protested, refused to cooperate, and even rioted when such taxes were proposed.

Throughout this period, France's Third Estate also experienced growing discontent. Peasants were forced to pay higher rents, and laborers' wages did not match the rising cost of food. The bourgeoisie—the urban middle-class—wanted a rise in their status equal to their economic strength. They wanted greater political power, less governmental interference in business dealings, and important positions in the church, government, and army for their sons. The Third Estate also resented being the only group to pay taxes. All these factors forced France to the edge of financial ruin in 1787, when bankers refused to lend the government any more money.

Having little choice, Louis XVI called representatives of all three estates to the Estates General, a meeting at the Palace of Versailles in May 1789. He hoped that the group would approve his new plan of imposing taxes upon the wealthy. However, the Third Estate refused to follow the old custom that called for each of the three representative bodies to cast a single collective vote. This custom had long allowed the top two estates to outvote the Third Estate. When the king closed the meeting with no action being taken, the Third Estate, on July 17, 1789, declared itself the National Assembly. This action began the French Revolution, which brought an end to the French monarchy.

The French Theater

French drama developed greatly in the 1600s. France's neoclassical period dominated the seventeenth century. Pierre Corneille wrote more than thirty plays. While most of his plays followed Aristotle's precept of unity of time, place, and action, Jean Racine introduced a simpler style with more realistic characters and plot structures. Molière, a comic genius, explored social, psychological, and metaphysical questions. The works of these playwrights remain mainstays of French and world theater. Other playwrights who contributed to the development of French drama during this period include the romantic playwright Pierre Marivaux and the absurd comic Paul Scarron. Beaumarchais drew his subtitle for *The Barber of Seville* from a Scarron short story.

The 1700s ushered in fewer great developments; however, Beaumarchais introduced exciting changes into French comedy, such as social discourse, rapid action, lively dialogue, and complex intrigue. While his plays were explicitly comedies, with fun-filled plots and schemes, they implicitly underscored and critiqued social abuses of contemporary society.

Enlightenment

In the 1700s, many educated Europeans began to question traditional rules and mores that had long guided society and politics. This change of ideas and attitudes was known as the Enlightenment, and

COMPARE & CONTRAST

- **1770s:** France is a monarchy ruled by King Louis XVI, who holds absolute power. Throughout the eighteenth century, Enlightenment philosophers increasingly call for new governmental institutions.

  Today: France is a republic headed by a president who is elected by popular vote to a seven-year term.

- **1770s:** Only about one-third of the population is literate, and the vast majority of those who can read are male. Outside the aristocratic and upper bourgeoisie classes, few women can read and write.

  Today: France has a literacy rate of 99 percent.

- **1770s:** French women lack the rights afforded to men. For instance, the father is the absolute authority of the family, and males usually supersede females in inheritance rights.

  Today: Laws guarantee women political, economic, and social rights equal to those of men. However, French women still earn less money than men and hold fewer high-level jobs and, at home, they complete about 80 percent of the domestic tasks.

- **1770s:** The nobility, who make up less than two percent of the population, enjoy special privileges such as the right to collect feudal dues from peasants. Nobles hold the highest positions in the army and government. Members of the Third Estate, however, may purchase titles and thus enter the aristocratic class.

  Today: A French aristocratic class still exists, but many members of this class work for a living. Class distinctions are generally accepted in France, and many class divisions remain rigid, even though children of all classes attend state schools.

its great thinkers were called *philosophes* (French for philosophers). The *philosophes* wanted to perfect themselves and society, and, to this end, they inspired a growing sense of individualism and personal freedom. Significantly, they also believed in the basic equality of all people, which stood at odds with governmental and social systems throughout Europe.

France was an important location for the development of Enlightenment thinking. Many political ideas that are still current today, such as separation of powers and popular sovereignty, came from French Enlightenment thinkers. The Baron de Montesquieu published *The Spirit of Laws* in 1748, in which he defined the perfect government as one in which powers are separated among different branches to prevent any single branch from becoming too powerful. Jean-Jacques Rousseau believed in the inherent goodness of all humans; he thought that society was what corrupted people. In *The Social Contract* (1762), Rousseau described his perfect society as one composed of free citizens who created their own government, according to their will.

CRITICAL OVERVIEW

In 1772, Beaumarchais wrote his first version of *The Barber of Seville* as a comic opera, complete with Spanish airs, or melodies, he had collected on his trip to Spain. When the play was rejected by the Comédie-Italienne, a group of Italian actors playing in France, Beaumarchais decided to transform it into a play for the Comédie Français, France's national theater. The play was set to be staged in early 1774 when rumors started that it included allusions to earlier legal run-ins Beaumarchais had had with a French judge. The production was forbidden. Finally, in February 1775, the play was mounted as a comedy in five acts. To

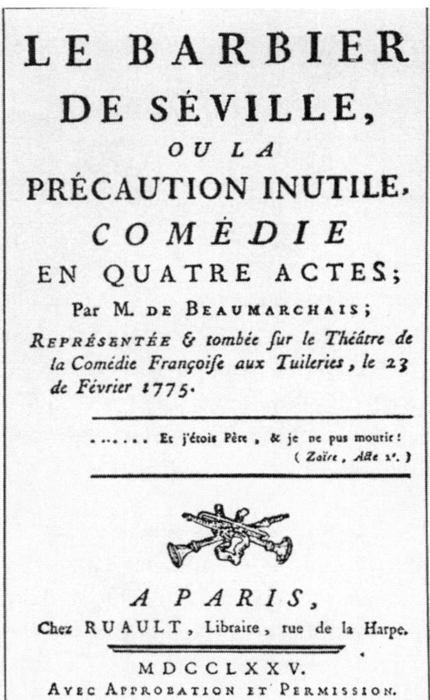

LE BARBIER
DE SÉVILLE,
OU LA
PRÉCAUTION INUTILE,
COMÉDIE
EN QUATRE ACTES;
Par M. DE BEAUMARCHAIS;
Représentée & tombée ſur le Théâtre de la Comédie Françoiſe aux Tuileries, le 23 de Février 1775.

...... Et j'étois Père, & je ne pus mourir!
(*Zaïre, Acte 2.*)

A PARIS,
Chez RUAULT, Libraire, rue de la Harpe.

MDCCLXXV.
AVEC APPROBATION ET PERMISSION.

Frontispiece for the 1775 edition of Le Barbier de Seville, *written by Pierre-Augustin de Beaumarchais*

the delight of Beaumarchais's numerous enemies, the French audience found the play too long and drawn out. Beaumarchais's friend Gudin de la Brunellerie (quoted in John Richetti's ''Pierre-Augustin Caron de Beaumarchais'') explained part of the problem: ''The comedy that enchanted us when we read it was too long for the theater. Its superabundance of wit surfeited and fatigued the audience.'' Beaumarchais revamped his play swiftly, editing it down to four acts and producing it again a scant two days later. This abbreviated play enjoyed instant success. Madame du Deffand was at both performances and recalled (quoted in Richetti's ''Pierre-Augustin Caron de Beaumarchais''), ''At first it was hissed, yesterday it had an extravagant success. It was exalted to the clouds, and applauded beyond all bounds.''

Within a year, *The Barber of Seville* had been translated into English and performed on stage in England; over time, it was translated into most European languages. In 1785, the royal court at France's Palace of Versailles even performed the play, with Marie Antoinette acting the role of Rosine and the Comte d'Artois, King Louis XVI's brother, acting the role of Figaro. Today, along with *The Marriage of Figaro*, it remains one of the only French eighteenth-century comedies to survive as part of the modern comedic theater.

Despite its great success, some critics nevertheless attacked the play, along with the stylistic devices employed by its creator. Some of Beaumarchais's contemporaries disliked his manner of allowing his characters to speak directly and without affectation. These critics believed that by allowing his characters to attack French mores he violated the overruling decorum that prevailed upon the French stage. The critic for the *Journal de Bouillon* lodged numerous criticisms against the play, which he found to be ''low comedy,'' alleging that it had no plot, that its action was implausible, and that Rosine was a ''badly brought-up daughter'' (as quoted by John Wells in an introduction to Beaumarchais's *The Figaro Plays*). One of Beaumarchais's main impetuses for writing the foreword to his play was to contradict such public statements.

Beaumarchais has consistently enjoyed a high critical reputation in France, where he is seen as instrumental in transforming comedy by emphasizing social discourse over formal style. However, his writings have received far less attention in the English-speaking world.

CRITICISM

Rena Korb

Korb has a master's degree in English literature and creative writing and has written for a wide variety of educational publishers. In the following essay, Korb discusses the disparity between social classes as seen in The Barber of Seville.

Despite its comedic situations, clever word play, and inane posturing, *The Barber of Seville* carried social messages of great importance to its earliest audiences. One of these messages was the irrationality and arbitrariness of the division of social classes. This issue was of rising interest in a society in which the majority of members, the exception being clergy and nobility, held few legal, political, or economic rights. To a self-made man such as Beaumarchais, a system that honored wealth and birth, as opposed to ingenuity, was absurd; thus,

Helena Bonham Carter, as Rosine, and Lee Cornes, as Figaro, in a scene from the 1992 theatrical production of The Barber of Seville

Beaumarchais created Figaro, a servant who is smarter and more capable than people with greater wealth and higher social standing. Indeed, Figaro's triumph was an example of a theme to which he would return more definitively and more bitingly in the play's sequel, *The Marriage of Figaro*.

The role of the social classes emerges as a major theme in this play. While the Count and Figaro work together to achieve a common goal—notably, one that serves to benefit only the Count—each individual is acutely aware of the social chasm between them. Their social roles are manifest from their first reintroduction on the street in front of Rosine's window. The Count alternately calls Figaro a rogue and a fool, while the former servant benignly acknowledges the Count's ill manners. He ironically comments, ''You always honored me with that kind of friendly greeting,'' and his audience understands his tacit criticism. The Count proceeds to further insult Figaro, telling him, ''When you were in my employ, you were a pretty slovenly character. . . . Lazy, disorganized.'' Figaro responds to the Count's numerous remarks calmly yet wittily. Notably, when the Count discovers that Figaro is his key to getting close to Rosine, his attitude quickly changes: ''Figaro, you are my friend, my guardian angel, my liberator, my savior,'' he says, embracing his former servant. Figaro accurately notes that ''Now I'm useful to you we're close friends.''

Also significant is Figaro's immediate recognition of his former master, even though the Count is dressed as a priest. For despite this humble disguise, the Count's ''haughtiness'' and ''nobility''—traits inherent to the Count's nature, as will be proven by his actions over the next twenty-four hours—are apparent in his very stance and bearing. Even though the Count is attempting to conceal his true self, he is unable to alter his innate sense of superiority, which he wears as clearly as any article of clothing. His air of superiority—cultivated by his social class and life experiences—is key in his dealings with Figaro. Although the Count is no longer Figaro's master and therefore has no real authority over him, the current relationship between the two men recalls their former relationship of master and servant. (Indeed, as seen in *The Marriage of Figaro*, after his chance encounter, Figaro once again returns to work in the household of the Count.)

Being superior is second nature to the Count, as is evident in the smallest details of the play. For example, he is unable to recognize the ''fat'' and ''flabby'' Figaro upon their first meeting because

- Beaumarchais's *The Marriage of Figaro,* first produced in 1784, reintroduces many of the characters from *The Barber of Seville.* In this play, Figaro, now manservant to Count Almaviva, is betrothed to Suzanne, maid to the Countess. However, Almaviva attempts to thwart these plans out of his own desire for Suzanne.
- Many of the plays of Molière, the great French comedic dramatist, share similar themes with *The Barber of Seville.* His *Don Juan* (1665) features the universal symbol of libertinism (a state of unrestraint or freethinking). Molière's Don Juan is particularly rebellious, disclaiming all types of obligation, while his servant is portrayed as his opposite and as one who passes judgment on Don Juan privately. *The School for Wives* (1662) concerns a pedant who decides to marry his ward, Agnes. These plans are thwarted when a young man falls in love with Agnes at first sight. Molière's *The Imaginary Invalid* (1673) features a foolish would-be doctor contrasted against young, sensible lovers.
- French writer Victor Hugo's play *Ruy Blas* (1838) centers on a valet Ruy Blas who is in love with his queen. On the orders of his master, who has been banished by the queen, Ruy Blas takes on a new identity with orders to take revenge upon the queen.
- Jean Racine, a French dramatist and contemporary of Molière, produced his play *The Litigants* in 1668. This satire attacks the Parisian legal system as a pair of young lovers obtain consent for their marriage through a trick. Like *The Barber of Seville, The Litigants* is filled with verbal dexterity, wit, and farcical elements.
- *Twelfth Night,* a comedy by William Shakespeare, was first performed in 1601. This play makes use of mistaken and disguised identities to reveal the folly of lovers.

---

poor people, or members of the servant class, are supposed to be thin. The Count's attempt to enter Bartholo's household as a drunken soldier is even more telling. Figaro coaches the Count to act more intoxicated, but the Count rejects this advice, saying, ''No, that's how commoners get drunk.'' His words imply that there is a great difference between men of low rank and men of high rank, even in such basic behaviors as becoming intoxicated. When the Count does enter the household, thusly disguised, he is impertinent, rude, and even obnoxious to Bartholo. As befits a man accustomed to getting his way, he knocks Bartholo's papers on the floor, demands to see his exemption from quartering soldiers, and sings a song describing the older man in the most unflattering terms.

Bartholo, as well, is not impervious to social rank. When the Count, disguised as Alonzo, offers the letter that Rosine wrote him, tell Bartholo that it was for the Count, Bartholo reads aloud the words, ''Since you have told me your name and rank,'' and immediately throws the letter down. Not knowing that the Count withheld the truth about his social position, Bartholo grows angry, recognizing that the Count's social position will make him infinitely more attractive to Rosine—as well as better suited to her. However, when dealing with Figaro, a member of a lower class, he treats him as shabbily as the Count (disguised as the soldier) had previously treated Bartholo. He calls Figaro a fool, accuses him of saying ''idiotic things,'' and impugns his honesty. ''You are so rude to the lower classes,'' Figaro succinctly concludes.

The importance of social rank in all aspects of daily life is made apparent, not only in the relationship between Figaro and his former master, but throughout the play. The Count's status is the reason that Bartholo and his assistant Bazile are unable to vanquish the young rival. ''We could soon frighten him away if he were an ordinary citizen,'' Bazile muses, and Bartholo agrees that if the Count were not a Count, they would be able to attack him, thus scaring him away from Madrid. Bazile instead strikes upon the idea of spreading rumors about the Count. However, this strategy is bound to fail, for Bazile is completely unsuited for slandering the much more highly placed Count. As Figaro points out, ''You need an estate, a family, a name, a rank, in other words, quality, if you want to become a professional scandalmonger.'' His words also tacitly impugn these men of ''quality,'' implying that they spread rumors—and perhaps spread them often.

By contrast, in his budding relationship with Rosine, the Count is so aware of his appeal as a member of the noble class that he refuses to reveal his true identity. He tells Figaro, ''I am bored with these unending conquests of women whose motives are self-interest, social climbing, or vanity. It is sweet to be loved for oneself,'' and he determines to see if Rosine loves him and not his money and power. From his first communication with Rosine, the Count takes on the identity of a man lacking social distinction and even a modicum of wealth. His song of introduction emphasizes his ''low birth'' and the ''simple, sincere'' pledge that a poor man is making to a woman of noble rank. He sings, ''I wish I could offer my dear one/ High rank and estates of great birth.''

Rosine, who happens to possess a fortune of her own, cares for Lindor despite his impoverished circumstances. As she points out once the Count has revealed himself (both in words and in ''magnificent'' dress), ''Fortune, birth! These are things that come by chance.'' Her words show that even in a world ordered by social stratification, some people are able to see beyond class implications and restrictions. Bartholo's reaction, upon learning Lindor's, or the Count's, true identity, warrants mention as well. ''Anywhere else, my lord, I am your humble servant, but in my house, rank does not mean anything, and I ask you to leave,'' he says. The insincerity of his words is manifest—he has already shown himself as rude and condescending to the lower classes—and they are predicated merely by his desire to keep Rosine for himself.

To Bartholo's words, the Count responds with the noble sentiment, ''No, rank doesn't mean anything here; I have nothing over you except Rosine's preference.'' Interestingly, however, once the Count admits his true identity to Rosine, he no longer hesitates to make use of his status. The arrogant Count Almaviva who emerges in the final moments of the play is a far cry from the mild, hopeful Lindor. His sense of his own grandeur is most apparent when Bartholo opposes the marriage that has just taken place between the Count and Rosine on the grounds that she is not of legal age to enter into a legal contract. ''The young lady is noble and beautiful. I am now a man of rank, and I am young and rich,'' the Count declares. ''She is my wife. Is anybody prepared to dispute this marriage which honors us both?'' No one present will speak against the Count's ''honorable marriage.''

> "THE IMPORTANCE OF SOCIAL RANK IN ALL ASPECTS OF DAILY LIFE IS MADE APPARENT, NOT ONLY IN THE RELATIONSHIP BETWEEN FIGARO AND HIS FORMER MASTER, BUT THROUGHOUT THE PLAY."

Though *The Barber of Seville* focuses on the intrigue surrounding Count Almaviva's efforts to woo and win Rosine, at the heart of the play is the relationship between Figaro and his former master. These two characters bring to life the issue of social classes brewing in France at the time in which Beaumarchais wrote his play. However, critics hold differing views on this relationship. Joseph G. Reish writes in ''Revolution: Three Changing Faces of Figaro,'' ''Neither Figaro nor the Count is guided by social role playing; class distinctions are set aside.'' By contrast, John Richetti asserts in *European Writers* that the play upholds ''the social and moral positions of man and master.'' He also believes that ''Figaro recognizes in Count Almaviva a noble dignity that deserves his service as well as a power that he needs to placate in order to survive and prosper.'' Frédéric Grendel holds yet another view of the relationship between the two men. Writing in *Beaumarchais: The Man Who Was Figaro,* he states, ''Figaro may still call his master 'Your Excellency' or 'My lord,' but he does so only to conform with custom.'' Perhaps at the time of writing, the conflict between social groups was not as pressing a topic as it would become. For, a scant few years later, Beaumarchais produced *The Marriage of Figaro*, which bitingly and archly demonstrates the rising conflict in pre-Revolutionary France.

Source: Rena Korb, Critical Essay on *The Barber of Seville,* in *Drama for Students,* The Gale Group, 2003.

SOURCES

Brereton, Geoffrey, *French Comic Drama from the Sixteenth to the Eighteenth Century,* Metheun & Co. Ltd., 1977, pp. 237–55.

Dunkley, John, ''*The Barber of Seville:* Overview'' in *Reference Guide to World Literature,* 2d ed., edited by Lesley Henderson, St. James Press, 1995.

Grendel, Frédéric, ''*The Barber of Seville,*'' in *Beaumarchais: The Man Who Was Figaro,* translated by Roger Greaves, Thomas Y. Crowell Company, 1977, pp. 134–45.

Reish, Joseph G., ''Revolution: Three Changing Faces of Figaro,'' in the *Michigan Academician,* Vol. IX, No. 2, Fall 1976, pp. 135–46.

Richetti, John, ''Pierre-Augustin Caron de Beaumarchais,'' in *European Writers,* Vol. 4, Charles Scribner's Sons, 1984, pp. 563–85.

Wells, John, ''Introduction (I),'' in *The Figaro Plays,* by Pierre-Augustin Caron de Beaumarchais, translated by John Wells and edited by John Leigh, J. M. Dent, 1997, pp. xvii–xxii.

FURTHER READING

Hayes, Julie C., *The Age of Theatre in France,* edited by David Trott and Nicole Boursier, Academic Printing & Publishing, 1988.

This volume collects essays about the French theater in the seventeenth and eighteenth centuries.

Howarth, William D., *Beaumarchais and the Theatre,* Routledge, 1995.

Howarth analyzes Beaumarchais's plays and their critical reception in the context of the political and theatrical events of the period.

McDonald, Christie, ''The Anxiety of Change: Reconfiguring Family Relations in Beaumarchais's Trilogy,'' in *Modern Language Quarterly,* March 1994, p. 47.

McDonald discusses the depiction of familial relations in *The Barber of Seville, The Marriage of Figaro,* and *A Mother's Guilt.*

Sungolowsky, Joseph, *Beaumarchais,* Twayne, 1974.

Sungolowsky presents a good overview of Beaumarchais's life and literary accomplishments.

Beyond the Horizon

EUGENE O'NEILL

1920

Eugene O'Neill's seminal, Pulitzer Prize-winning play, *Beyond the Horizon*, was written in 1918 but not produced or published until 1920, when it made its debut in New York. *Beyond the Horizon* was O'Neill's first successful full-length play, and it signaled a change in American drama. Critics and audiences responded favorably to O'Neill's dark, tragic vision, which contrasted sharply with the unrealistic, melodramatic plays of the day. The play drew heavily on O'Neill's own experiences, including his tuberculosis and his sea voyages. During one of these sea trips, he met a Norwegian sailor who criticized his choice of going to sea as opposed to staying on his family's farm. Taking this idea as a starting point, O'Neill crafted a tale of missed opportunities and failed dreams, involving two brothers. Robert, a poetic but sickly dreamer, wants to go to sea to strengthen his health and see the world. His brother, Andrew, is a born farmer who wants nothing more than to work on his family's farm. Because they love the same woman, both brothers choose to go against their natures. Robert stays on the farm, and Andrew goes to sea.

While some critics have interpreted the play's tragic ending to mean that one should follow his or her own dreams, others have seen a darker message: it does not matter what choice one makes because even dreams that come true are not fulfilling. Although O'Neill's later autobiographical tragedies, namely *The Iceman Cometh* and *Long Day's Journey into Night*, have surpassed *Beyond the*

Horizon in many critics' eyes, most still acknowledge the earlier play as the first success in O'Neill's career and one that had a strong influence on his early development as a playwright. The play has been widely anthologized and is available in *Four Plays by Eugene O'Neill*, published by Signet Classic in 1998.

AUTHOR BIOGRAPHY

Eugene O'Neill was born on October 16, 1888, in New York City, into a dysfunctional family. O'Neill's mother, Mary, became addicted to morphine as a result of pain suffered during Eugene's birth. O'Neill's father, James, was a famous actor and was so obsessed with his poor background that he only acted in plays that were surefire financial successes, such as *The Count of Monte Cristo.* As a result, critics widely proclaimed the waste of James's talent.

O'Neill lived his early life on the road; his family accompanied James on acting tours. In 1902, when he was fourteen, O'Neill learned of his mother's addiction when she ran out of morphine and tried to drown herself. As a result, the boy renounced his mother's Catholic faith. O'Neill's education took place in several different boarding schools while he was on the road with his father, and later the future playwright flunked out of Princeton. He eloped, in the first of three ill-fated marriages, with Kathleen Jenkins. Unable to deal with the responsibility of marriage or fatherhood, O'Neill did not live with his first wife and instead devoted his energies to a string of odd jobs that his father found for him, including assistant stage manager (1910), actor (1912), and sailor.

O'Neill found new strength at sea, and when he returned, he arranged to be caught with a prostitute so that he could legally get a divorce from his first wife. He then attempted suicide, and when he recovered, he found out that he had the lung disease tuberculosis. In 1914, while recuperating in a sanitarium, O'Neill decided to become a playwright and spent a year at Harvard taking a playwriting course. His first plays were short, one-act productions, many of which drew on his experiences at sea. These short plays led to some success. In 1918, O'Neill wrote his first full-length play that went into production, *Beyond the Horizon.* The play marked his debut on Broadway, in 1920, and won the Pulitzer Prize the same year. O'Neill received many other awards for his plays, including Pulitzer Prizes for *Anna Christie* (1922) and *Strange Interlude* (1928).

Although he received the Nobel Prize in literature in 1936, O'Neill's tragedies were no longer enjoyed by an America that was, at this point, in the grips of the Great Depression. *Days Without End* (1933), for example, was not received well. O'Neill shunned theater production for the rest of his life and concentrated on writing distinctly autobiographical plays, including *The Iceman Cometh* (1946) and *Long Day's Journey into Night* (1957), a painful play that was so close to O'Neill's experiences that he delayed publication until after his death. O'Neill died on November 27, 1953, in Boston, Massachusetts.

PLOT SUMMARY

Act 1, Scene 1

Beyond the Horizon begins on a country road that runs through the bustling Mayo family farm, where the entire play takes place. Robert, a delicate, poetic young man, sits on a fence by the road, reading a book. His hardy older brother, Andrew, whom most people call Andy, comes in from working in the fields and stops to talk to Robert, who is leaving the next morning to go away on a sea voyage for three years with their uncle. Andy says that everybody will miss him, including Andy, who, as a farmer, does not understand Robert's dream to see the world.

It is obvious from the behavior of the two brothers that they are both in love with Ruth Atkins, who is coming to Robert's farewell dinner with her mother. Andy leaves to wash up before dinner, and Ruth stops by to talk to Robert. She tells him that her widowed, invalid mother nags at her constantly. Ruth says she will miss Robert while he is on his trip. He tells her that the trip has been a dream of his ever since he was a sickly child, but he also says that he is going because he loves her and does not want to interfere with her future with Andy. Ruth is shocked and says that she loves Robert, not Andy. She talks him into canceling his voyage, but he looks wistfully over his shoulder at the horizon.

Act 1, Scene 2

Later that night, Andy sits with his father James, his mother Kate, and her brother Captain

Dick Scott, who is telling an old sea story. Everybody else is distracted and sad over the thought of Robert's leaving. Robert, meanwhile, has gone with Ruth to wheel her mother home. Andy leaves to check on one of the cows, and Mr. Mayo tells the others he hopes that Andy and Ruth get married, since the Atkins farm is next door to the Mayo farm, and Andy could manage both. Mrs. Mayo says that she does not think Ruth loves Andy. Robert walks in and announces that he is canceling his voyage, since Ruth has told him she loves him. Everybody is glad except Scott, who is losing a shipmate, and Andy, who has been quietly listening from the doorway. Andy forces a smile and congratulates Robert, then says that he is going to take Robert's place on the voyage. Scott is overjoyed, but Mr. Mayo is shocked and accuses Andy of running away because Ruth did not choose him. Andy lies, saying that he hates the farm and wants to get away. His father disowns him and storms out. Robert knows Andy's decision is because of Ruth but says that if he were in Andy's place, he would do the same thing.

Eugene O'Neill

Act 2, Scene 1

Three years later, the signs of neglect on the farm are evident from the condition of the farmhouse. Mrs. Mayo and Mrs. Atkins sit at the table, talking about Robert's mismanagement of both farms, Andy's expected arrival, and whether or not Mr. Mayo forgave Andy before he died. Both women agree that Ruth and Andy would have made a better match. Ruth, who looks much older after three years, comes in with Mary, her sickly child. All three women talk about Andy, whom they expect will stay to help renovate the farm. Mrs. Atkins and Mrs. Mayo go outside to escape the heat of the farmhouse. Robert comes in, and they argue about Robert not eating dinner, Ruth's pining over Andy's letters, Mary not taking a nap, and Robert's preference for books instead of work. Ben, the farmhand, comes in, announcing that he is quitting because he is embarrassed to work on such a poor farm. Robert and Ruth have a vicious fight, telling each other that their marriage has been a mistake. Robert says he wishes he had gone to sea, and Ruth says that she loves Andy and wishes Robert would leave. Andy arrives.

Act 2, Scene 2

Later that day, Robert sits on a boulder on the farm, gazing off toward the horizon. Andy comes up and says he is giving up his career at sea to move to Argentina and invest in the lucrative grain business in Buenos Aires. Robert is dismayed that Andy is not staying on at the Mayo farm, and they talk about the farm's bad condition. Andy offers to give his savings to Robert to save the farm, but Robert refuses and becomes infuriated. Ruth stops by and it is evident that she has put on makeup and gotten dressed up for Andy. Ruth sends Robert and Mary away on a work task and tells Andy that she cannot wait until he takes over. Andy tells Ruth that he is leaving but that he is going to hire some help to run the farm. He also tells Ruth that he loves her like a sister. Ruth is distraught over Andy's unexpected leaving as well as over the fact that he no longer loves her, and she rebukes him. Andy is confused at these outbursts and thinks he is not wanted. They are interrupted by Captain Scott, who tells Andy a ship is ready to leave for Argentina the next morning. This is the only ship that is going to Argentina for months, so Andy decides to take it. Andy and Captain Scott leave to walk toward the Mayo farmhouse, and Ruth breaks down crying.

Act 3, Scene 1

Five years later, the farmhouse is in total decay. Robert, who is obviously sick, talks with Ruth about Andy's imminent arrival, Mary's death, his sickness, and their money problems. Ruth puts Robert back to bed and talks to her mother about Jake, the hired hand who has just quit because Robert owed him money. Andy and a medical specialist, Doctor Fawcett, arrive. While the doctor examines Robert, Andy and Ruth talk about Robert's condition. Ruth says they could not afford to contact Andy sooner and that Robert has steadily lost interest in everything since Mary and his mother died. Andy says he needs to go away again, because he has lost most of his money on speculative investments, but that there is enough left over in his savings to fix the farm. Doctor Fawcett comes out of the room and says that Robert is dying. Robert says that his dying wish is to have Andy marry Ruth, then he goes to lie down again. Andy is confused over this request until Ruth tells Andy about the fight she and Robert had over Andy five years ago. Ruth goes to the bedroom to tell Robert that she does not love Andy and cannot marry him, but Robert has climbed out the window.

Act 3, Scene 2

A few minutes later, Robert stumbles into the same section of country road where the play started, although the fields are no longer healthy. Andy and Ruth rush up to Robert, who tells them he wants to die outside. Robert is happy because with his death, he says, he will finally be able to journey beyond the horizon. Robert dies, saying once again that Andy needs to take care of Ruth. Andy looks at Ruth, telling her they have both screwed things up but that perhaps in the future, things will be better, suggesting that maybe they will get married. Ruth, however, is exhausted and gives no sign that she agrees.

CHARACTERS

Mrs. Atkins

Mrs. Atkins is Ruth's widowed, invalid mother, who never forgives her daughter for marrying Robert Mayo instead of Andy. Mrs. Atkins criticizes Robert's inefficiency in running both the Mayo farm and her farm. She also complains about Ruth and Robert's sickly child, Mary, who often cries to her mother. Mrs. Atkins is an extremely religious person and says cruelly to Kate Mayo that her husband died early because he was a sinner and that the ill-fated marriage between Robert and Ruth was also a result of God's will. Although Mrs. Atkins claims in the second act that she is about to die, she outlives many of the other characters and survives until the end of the play. At this point, she is sneaking money to Ruth behind Robert's back to help pay the bills, since Robert is having a hard time keeping the farm running on his own.

Ruth Atkins

Ruth Atkins is Mrs. Atkins's daughter and the wife of Robert Mayo. In the beginning, she dates Andy, but she falls in love with Robert when he speaks about his dream of going on a sea voyage. As a result, she tells him she does not love Andy and convinces Robert not to go on his voyage. Her choice influences Andy to leave the Mayo farm and take Robert's place on the voyage, since he cannot bear to see Ruth with another man, especially his brother. As the play goes on, Ruth's happiness and her ability to love slowly wane. Three years later, Ruth has aged considerably. She and Robert hate each other, and Ruth says she loves Andy. They both agree that if it were not for Mary (their small, sickly child) they would leave each other. Ruth tries to rekindle the flame with Andy when he comes home for a visit, but before she can tell him her feelings, he lets her know that he does not love her anymore. Ruth is hurt and is rude to Andy, who assumes she does not want him around.

When Andy comes home again five years later, Mary has died, and Ruth is a broken woman. Like the Mayo farm, her life is in decay, and she sits around while Robert's health quickly declines. She accepts money from her mother, behind Robert's back, to help pay the bills. When Robert shows some renewed energy in his feverish state and says that they should move to the city and start over, Ruth is frightened. When Andy comes in with a medical specialist, who tells them that Robert is dying, and Andy blames Ruth, she is too exhausted to fight back. Robert's dying wish is to have Andy marry Ruth, which Andy suggests at the end of the play. But, Ruth is too exhausted to care and does not indicate whether she will be willing to do this.

Ben

Ben is the farmhand who quits working for Robert because he is ashamed to work for such a poor farm.

Doctor Fawcett

Doctor Fawcett is the specialist that Andy brings to see Robert. Fawcett tells Andy and Ruth that Robert is dying of tuberculosis and that if Robert had gotten to a better climate six months earlier, he might have survived.

Andrew Mayo

Andrew Mayo, or Andy, as most of his family calls him, is the son who is expected to take over the Mayo farm. He shocks everybody when he leaves the farm to go on a sea voyage with his uncle, Captain Scott. In the beginning, Andy is in love with Ruth Atkins and is looking forward to taking over the farm. He is distraught when his brother, Robert, whom he loves dearly, decides to cancel his sea voyage to marry Ruth and stay on the farm. Andy's decision to go to sea creates a permanent rift between him and his father, James, who dies while Andy is at sea. During Andy's three years at sea, Captain Scott trains him to become a naval officer, a career that he decides to abandon after his first voyage. The first time he comes home to visit, he makes it a point to tell both Robert and Ruth that he does not love Ruth anymore, thinking that it will remove the awkwardness between them. Instead, he hurts Ruth, who was preparing to declare her love for him.

Before Andy arrives home for his first visit, everybody places their hopes on him, thinking from his letters that he will stay to work on the farm and undo the damage that Robert has done. However, Andy lets everybody know that he is shipping out to Buenos Aires, where he plans to get rich in the grain business and send money home to help everybody. When he comes home five years later, he has gotten rich but lost almost all of his fortune through speculative investing. Andy brings a medical specialist with him, who tells Andy and Ruth that Robert is dying. Andy is angry at first and takes it out on Ruth for not contacting him sooner, until he realizes that Ruth and Robert were too poor, and Robert was too proud, to contact him. Although Andy plans to go back to Buenos Aires to make another fortune, Robert's dying wish is to have Andy marry Ruth and take care of her. Andy suggests to Ruth at the end of the play that maybe this plan would work out all right, but Ruth is exhausted from her disastrous marriage to Robert and shows no sign of agreement.

Mr. James Mayo

James Mayo is the father of Andrew and Robert. He dies while Andy is at sea. In the beginning, Andy is planning on working on his father's farm for the rest of his life, and James's love and respect for his son and his son's skills are evident. However, after Robert announces that he is staying home to marry Ruth, and Andy responds by saying he will take Robert's place on the voyage, James accuses Andy of evasion. They get into a big fight, and Andy lies, saying that he hates the farm and wants to see the world. James is shocked and hurt, and he disowns his son. Several of the characters later discuss whether James ever forgave Andy for leaving. Most think he did not.

MEDIA ADAPTATIONS

- *Beyond the Horizon* was adapted as a television movie by the Public Broadcasting Service (PBS) in 1975. The film, directed by Rick Hauser and Michael Kahn IV, features Richard Backus as Robert Mayo and Maria Tucci as Ruth Atkins. It is available on video from the Broadway Theatre Archive.

Mrs. Kate Mayo

Kate Mayo is the mother of Andrew and Robert. She also dies while Andy is at sea. Kate is the one who realizes that Ruth is not in love with Andy and is overjoyed when Robert decides to cancel his sea voyage. She tries to smooth over the fight between James and Andy, and after James's death, she is the only one who believes that, in his heart, her husband did forgive Andy. Kate sits by silently while Robert's marriage and the farm are in trouble, trusting that Robert can handle himself, although she agrees with Mrs. Atkins that Andy and Ruth would have made a better match. When Andy comes home three years after going to sea, she, like everybody else, thinks he is coming home to stay. She plans a big dinner for him. Her death is one of the factors that leads to Robert's decline in health.

Mary Mayo

Mary Mayo is the sickly child of Robert and Ruth. She dies sometime between Andy's first and second visits home. Her death is one of the factors that leads to Robert's steady decline in health.

Robert Mayo

Robert Mayo is Andrew's brother, who cancels his sea voyage to stay on the Mayo farm and marry Ruth Atkins. His decision influences Andy to take Robert's place, since Andy also loves Ruth and cannot stand to see somebody else with her. Robert's marriage is ill-fated, since he is not a farmer like Andy and does not know how to properly manage a farm; his situation gets even worse after his father dies. Robert spends a lot of time daydreaming about the voyage he never took, and as a result he loses farmhands and barely makes enough money to pay the bills. Without his knowledge, Ruth accepts money from her mother to help pay the bills. When Andy comes home after his first voyage, Robert, like everybody else, hopes that Andy will take over the farm once again and is distraught when he finds out that Andy is leaving again.

Robert's marriage to Ruth deteriorates while Andy is at sea, and the only thing that keeps them together is their daughter, Mary. When Robert's mother and Mary die, Robert's health rapidly declines. Robert becomes confined to a sickbed. At one point, sick with fever, Robert gets a burst of energy and tells Ruth they should move to the city and start over. Ruth sends an urgent message to Andy, who comes home. Andy brings a medical specialist with him, who tells them that Robert is dying of a lung disease and that if they had taken Robert away to a better climate six months earlier, he might have lived. Andy is distraught, but Ruth accepts this as just one more tragedy in her life. Robert, meanwhile, is overjoyed, because he sees his death as his opportunity to finally leave the farm and travel "beyond the horizon." Robert's dying wish is to have Andy marry Ruth and take care of her.

Ruth Mayo

See Ruth Atkins

Captain Dick Scott

Captain Dick Scott is Kate Mayo's brother and the uncle of Robert and Andrew. In the beginning of the play, Scott has made plans for Robert to accompany him on a sea voyage. When Robert backs out to stay on the farm and marry Ruth, Scott is distraught, because he wanted somebody to talk to and train on the voyage. He is also concerned that his shipmates will think that Robert's empty bunk was meant for a woman who jilted their captain and that he will take a lot of teasing for this. As a result, he is overjoyed when Andy decides to take Robert's place and tells Andy that he will make a better seaman than his sickly brother, anyway. Scott trains Andy to be an officer and gives him the tip that a ship is leaving for Buenos Aires, where Andy works for five years trying to make a fortune in the grain business.

THEMES

Dreams

Dreams provide the main theme of the play. Every one of the characters has dreams. Ruth dreams of having a husband. James dreams of having a bigger farm and hopes that his son, Andy, will marry Ruth Atkins so that they can take over the adjoining Atkins farm. Says James, "Joined together they'd make a jim-dandy of a place, with plenty o' room to work in." However, the biggest dreamers in the story are Robert and Andy, who have opposite dreams. Robert is a poet and has the romantic dream of going "beyond the horizon" to experience the world. Andy, on the other hand, is a born farmer and dreams of nothing more than marrying Ruth and taking care of the Mayo farm. They acknowledge this to each other in the first scene, when Andy says to Robert, "Farming ain't your nature," and Robert says to Andy, "You're wedded to the soil." Neither of them understands the other's dreams, but they support each other.

Ruth is the key character that interrupts these dreams. She gets caught up in Robert's romantic vision of the sea, and when he admits that he is also leaving because he loves her, she renounces her love for Andy and asks Robert to stay: "Please tell me you won't go!" Ruth's request and Robert's decision to stay set everybody's lives on a tragic course, leading to the early deaths of most of the characters and the possible ruination of Andy and Ruth. James predicts that this will happen when he declares that only bad things happen when people give up their natural dreams: "You're runnin' against your own nature, and you're goin' to be a'mighty sorry for it if you do."

Responsibility

For both Robert and Andy, dreams are also responsibilities. Robert has signed up with his uncle, Captain Scott, to work on the sea voyage. When he backs out, he neglects his responsibility, a fact that irks Captain Scott, who has gone to great lengths to accommodate Robert. Says Scott, "Ain't I made all arrangements with the owners and stocked

TOPICS FOR FURTHER STUDY

- O'Neill gives his play an ambiguous ending, leaving the audience to wonder what happens to Ruth and Andy. Write a plot summary for a fourth act to the play. Discuss whether Andy and Ruth get married, where they live (together or separately), and how their lives end. Use elements from the first three acts of the play to support your ideas.
- Research what the life of a farmer was like in the late 1910s and what life is like for today's farmers. Using this information, plot a typical day in the life of a farmer from each era, scheduling each major task. How did the hours, work environment, and lifestyle of a farmer in the early twentieth century compare to those of a modern farmer?
- Research what life at sea was like for a young, untrained man in his twenties during this time period, including his shipboard duties and the steps he followed to advance through the ranks. Using this information, write a short job description—in the style of a modern employment ad—for an entry-level sailor position, incorporating a specific description of duties as well as the advancement potential of the job.
- Robert is a chronically sick person who eventually dies of tuberculosis, although the doctor says that he could have possibly restored his health by going to a better climate. Research health-related travel, sanitariums, and other methods that people used in the early twentieth century to combat tuberculosis and other serious illnesses. How successful were these measures? How do you think Robert's health would have fared if he had taken the sea voyage as he had initially planned?

up with some special grub all on Robert's account?'' Meanwhile, Andy has trained since he was a boy to manage the Mayo farm, and when he backs out of this responsibility, his father challenges him on it: ''The farm is your'n as well as mine . . . and what you're sayin' you intend doin' is just skulking out o' your rightful responsibility.''

As the play progresses, O'Neill gives other examples of neglected responsibilities. Robert prefers reading books and daydreaming to working on the farm, a fact that Ruth notes: ''And besides, you've got your own work that's got to be done. . . . Work you'll never get done by reading books all the time.'' However, Ruth is also guilty of neglected responsibilities. Ruth has a responsibility to Mary to be a good mother, but she instead takes out her feelings of anger on the child, trying to force her roughly to take a nap—terrifying the child with threats of ''good spankings.'' This is contrasted sharply with Robert's caring treatment of Mary, as shown by the stage directions: ''*He gathers her up in his arms carefully and carries her into the bedroom. His voice can be heard faintly as he lulls the child to sleep.*'' In the end, Robert appeals to Andy's sense of responsibility when he voices his dying wish to have Andy marry Ruth and take care of her. Andy notes to Ruth that he cannot ignore this wish by promising his brother he will marry Ruth and then not following through: ''What? Lie to him now—when he's dying?''

Choices

At various points along the way, the characters have choices. When Andy returns after three years at sea, he has the choice of leaving again or of staying at the Mayo farm. The latter is a logical choice, since the main reason he left—his love for Ruth—is no longer an issue. However, Andy says to Robert, ''I'm certain now I never was in love.'' He chooses to go to Buenos Aires to make money speculating in grain instead of staying at the farm that he used to love. In the end, Robert notes that this choice has made Andy the biggest failure of them all: ''You—a farmer—to gamble in a wheat pit with scraps of paper.'' Robert's choices also increase his unhappiness, however. His biggest choice, and the one which, as noted above, sets the play on its tragic course, is the choice to stay on the farm.

However, three years later, when Robert has a chance to change things during Andy's return, he makes the disastrous choices to not tell Andy about his failed marriage and to not accept Andy's offer of financial assistance. ''No. You need that for your start in Buenos Aires,'' Robert tells Andy. Although Andy tries to argue with Robert on this point, Robert refuses to listen. He also does not try to convince Andy to stay. This point is noted angrily by Ruth when she is speaking to Andy. ''And didn't he try to stop you from going?'' Robert's pride in not asking for money or asking his brother to stay and help contributes directly to his death at the end. If he had appealed to his rich brother earlier, Andy and Ruth could have gotten Robert to a better climate and perhaps saved his life. As Doctor Fawcett says, ''That might have prolonged his life six months ago. (Andrew *groans.*) But now—. (*He shrugs his shoulders significantly.*)''

Happiness

The play also causes the reader or viewer to question what really makes people happy. In the beginning, everybody is going along on what seems to be his or her true path. Robert is going to sea, while Ruth will most likely marry Andy, who will take over the Mayo farm. When Robert, Ruth, and Andy deviate from their intended paths, however, they all become unhappy. But there is some question as to whether they would have found true happiness if they had stayed on their original paths. Although Ruth says later that she has always loved Andy, she initially says that she is in love with Robert: ''I don't! I don't love Andy! I don't.'' This is the exact opposite of her later comment to Robert, ''I do love Andy. I do! I do! I always loved him.'' This leads one to believe that Ruth would not be happy with either man. If Robert had gone away to sea and Ruth had married Andy out of necessity and not love, she may not have been any happier than she was with Robert. In other words, without marrying Robert and seeing that he was not the right one for her, she might never have realized that she loved Andy.

Similarly, there is some question as to whether Robert would have been truly happy at sea. Andy's experiences in the Far East that Robert has dreamed of are not enjoyable, as he notes to Robert on his first trip home: ''One walk down one of their filthy narrow streets with the tropic sun beating on it would sicken you for life with the 'wonder and mystery' you used to dream of.'' It is unclear whether Robert would have had a different experience. Even the ending is ambiguous. Andy says everything may work out in the end, but Ruth's reaction of hopelessness leaves the audience to question whether true happiness is possible for these two characters: ''*She remains silent, gazing at him dully with the sad humility of exhaustion, her mind already sinking back into that spent calm beyond the further troubling of any hope.*''

STYLE

Tragedy

O'Neill's *Beyond the Horizon* was a striking departure from most of the melodramatic dramas of the day. The play featured real tragedy, which became a hallmark of many twentieth-century dramas in America. Tragedy has a long literary history, dating back to the plays of the ancient Greeks, when tragic events were depicted as a result of a character flaw or defect. Although the definitions and uses of tragedy have changed in many ways since then, most tragedies still hinge on a bad decision by a character or characters. In O'Neill's play, these decisions are influenced by love. It is Robert's love for Ruth that causes him to make his impulsive but important life decision, as the stage directions note: ''ROBERT (*face to face with a definite, final decision, betrays the conflict going on within him*): 'But—Ruth—I—Uncle Dick—.''' Ruth is adamant, however, and finally breaks down crying, the final step that influences his decision: ''ROBERT (*conquered by this appeal—an irrevocable decision in his voice*): 'I won't go, Ruth. I promise you.'''

Robert's decision influences Andy to make his own tragic decision to go to sea. Says Andrew, ''You've made your decision, Rob, and now I've made mine.'' Andy also making his decision out of love. He cannot stand to see Ruth with another man, least of all his brother: ''I've got to get away and try to forget, if I can.''Mr. Mayo exposes Andy's choice as a brash defense against heartache, ''You're runnin' away 'cause you're put out and riled 'cause your own brother's got Ruth 'stead o' you.'' These two tragic decisions ultimately lead to many tragic consequences, including the deaths of most of the characters. James dies while Andy is at sea, and Mrs. Mayo notes that his death was a result of her husband's inability to publicly forgive Andy for his decision: "It was that brought on his death—breaking his heart just on account of his stubborn pride." Mrs. Mayo is in turn affected by her husband's death as well as by the decay of the farm and her son's unhappy marriage, as the stage directions indicate: "MRS. MAYO'S *face has lost all character, disintegrated, become a weak mask wearing a helpless, doleful expression of being constantly on the verge of comfortless tears.*" In addition, Mary is chronically ill. Says Mrs. Atkins, "She gets it right from her Pa—being sickly all the time. . . . It was a crazy mistake for them two to get married." Eventually, Mary dies, too, and in the end, Robert himself dies, both tragic events brought on by the decisions of Robert and Andy to go against their respective natures.

Irony

The play has a strong sense of dramatic irony, a feeling produced in audience members when they are led to believe that one situation will unfold, while in reality, the opposite becomes true. At the end of the play, the audience, like the characters, is struck with the bitter irony of the main characters' wasted lives. All three of them—Robert, Ruth, and Andy—have gotten the exact opposite of what they wanted. Andy ran away from his farming dreams, thinking it would be worse to stay and witness his brother and Ruth together. Ruth wanted a happy marriage with a man she loved, but as she notes to Andy at the end, "You see I'd found out I'd made a mistake about Rob soon after we were married—when it was too late." So, Andy runs away out of his jealousy over the relationship between Ruth and Robert, which ironically fails shortly after he leaves to go to sea, when Ruth realizes that Andy is the one for her. Meanwhile, Robert stays on the farm, thinking he will find true happiness with Ruth. Instead, he finds only misery and death, constantly yearning for the life at sea that Andy hates.

Even worse, Ruth's failed marriage has drained her so much that, as she tells Robert, "I don't love anyone." She has lost the ability to love. The tragic irony of this situation is multiplied when Robert pushes Ruth and Andy together at the end of the play, asking them to get married and honor his dying wish. At this point, Andy is willing to give it a try out of duty to his brother: "We must try to help each other—and—in time—we'll come to know what's right." But the damage is irreversible. The situation has changed since Andy left eight years ago, and even if they do get married as Andy had originally hoped, things will never be the same.

Mood

O'Neill's play calls for several staging techniques that are intended to evoke a mood in the audience. One of these, the change in seasons, is particularly effective. When the play begins, the stage directions note the following: "*The hushed twilight of a day in May is just beginning.*" This spring day in the first act progresses to "*a hot, sunbaked day in mid-summer*" in the second act. Finally, in the last act, it is "*a day toward the end of October.*" The gradual move from spring—associated with youth and hope—to late fall—a time of fading life before the death of winter sets in—mirrors the tragic action of the play and helps to darken the mood.

HISTORICAL CONTEXT

Although O'Neill wrote the tragic *Beyond the Horizon* in 1918, it features no reference to the biggest tragedy of the time, World War I, which ended the same year. This may be because O'Neill intended his story to take place in the years before World War I started. Or, it may be because the play features enough tragedy without mentioning the war. In any case, farmers and some merchant seamen—two occupations represented in the play by the Mayo brothers—were greatly affected by the war.

Even before the United States officially entered the war in 1917, American farms were helping to provide food supplies to the Allied forces. These exports, along with the exportation of munitions, helped aid the war effort and led to greater economic prosperity in the United States during the first few years of the war. As J. M. Roberts notes in his *Twentieth Century: The History of the World, 1901 to 2000:* "The Allies were the main customers of American industry and farmers; Allied spending fuelled an economic boom in the United States." However, the American merchant ships that delivered these goods were increasingly in danger from German submarines. In January 1917, Germany declared that it would sink any ship that attempted to deliver supplies to Allied forces, including neutral American ships. In March, German submarines made good on this promise when they sank some American merchant ships, sparking a national move-

COMPARE & CONTRAST

- **Late 1910s–Late 1920s:** Because of technological advances in farming, many farm workers lose their jobs, while many farms experience crop surpluses. However, the surpluses lead to lower crop prices, which cause many farms to struggle financially. Displaced farm workers and farmers head to already crowded cities to seek their fortunes there.

  Today: The majority of people continue to live in cities or in the large suburban areas that surround them. Farming is one of the least popular vocations, and many tasks traditionally performed by the farmer are now handled by machines.

- **Late 1910s–Late 1920s:** Following World War I, the New York Stock Exchange experiences a surge in speculative investing by ordinary Americans, prompting inflated stock prices and making many Americans wealthy. Many people borrow their investment money on margin, intending to pay it back with their stock profits. When the stock market crashes in 1929, many stocks become worthless, and investors are unable to pay their debts. The resulting financial disaster leads to the Great Depression.

  Today: The United States experiences an economic downturn following the crash of inflated technology stocks, many associated with newly popular Internet companies.

- **Late 1910s–Late 1920s:** The Panama Canal, a waterway connecting the Atlantic and Pacific oceans in Central America, is built by the United States, which also has complete ownership of and responsibility for the canal. Panama quickly becomes an international shipping and trade center.

  Today: After nearly a century of control by the United States, the Panama Canal is now under the full jurisdiction of Panama as a result of 1970s treaties between the two nations. For the first time in its history as an independent nation, Panama has full control of all of its land.

---

ment that advocated the United States's entry into the war. America declared war on Germany on April 6, 1917.

While the United States's neutral status had helped to produce an economic boom through the increased production of food and other supplies for Allied Forces, America's entry into the war threatened to diminish this production. In May 1917, Wilson signed the Selective Service Act, forcing many young men to register for military service. Many farmers and farm workers were drafted to fight in the war, which left gaps in the nation's workforce. The loss of workers on farms—and in factories—threatened to compromise America's ability to maintain the high production rates that it had enjoyed since the beginning of the war. In an effort to standardize production and ensure that none of the nation's supplies would be secretly transported to German forces, Wilson announced in July that he was taking official control over America's necessities. This included the pricing and transportation of food and other essential war supplies. Wheat prices were fixed and the railroads—as well as some merchant ships—were requisitioned for use by the government.

At the same time, at least one notable private effort was underway to help farmers maintain their high production levels. In October 1917, automaker Henry Ford, who had made history with his mass-produced Model T automobile (introduced in 1908), began producing the world's first mass-produced tractors. In fact, for Ford, who grew up on a farm and who was a champion for farmers, this was the realization of a dream. As Robert Lacey notes in his book, *Ford: The Men and the Machine:* "Almost as soon as the Ford Motor Company started making money, Henry Ford had started trying to develop a tractor." Since the executives in the Ford Motor

Company had little interest in this agricultural venture, in 1916, Ford founded a new company, Henry Ford & Son, to produce his ''Fordson'' tractors. Although tractors had been in limited use for years, they were too heavy and expensive for most farms. The gasoline-engine Fordson tractor, however, was lighter and much less expensive than other tractors. Fordsons were mass-produced on the same type of assembly line that Ford had implemented in 1913 for the production of his Model Ts, and became a viable option for farmers looking to replace farmhands who were off fighting the war.

At the end of the war, American farms remained a crucial industry, and one that was increasingly aided by the tractor. Tractors brought power that revolutionized farming, and helped to replace horses as the method used to plow the fields. As Roberts notes, ''power did more than perform traditional tasks more efficiently: it broke in new land.'' With their greater power, tractors gave farmers the ability to plow tough land that had previously been useless for crops. Tractors helped farmers increase their crop yields, which in turn helped to meet the increased food demands during the final months of the war. Even after the war ended in November 1918, these increased crop yields went to good use, as the United States pledged itself to helping combat food shortages in much of Europe—where resources had been severely depleted during the war.

CRITICAL OVERVIEW

Beyond the Horizon is one of Eugene O'Neill's most famous plays, although it started from humble origins. In 1918, after writing several unsuccessful and unproduced longer plays, O'Neill wrote *Beyond the Horizon*, which was bought by actor and producer John Williams. Two years later, in 1920, the play was finally produced. However, Williams made the choice to start it off as a matinee, using actors borrowed from his other current productions instead of giving the play its own billing. The play soon proved worthy of a run on Broadway.

Overall, the critics praised the play. Says J. Rankin Towse in his 1920 review of the play for the *New York Post,* ''There can be no question that it is a work of uncommon merit and definite ability, distinguished by general superiority from the great bulk of contemporaneous productions.'' However, Towse also notes that the play ''is not quite a masterpiece,'' although ''it is exceedingly promising juvenile work.'' Towse, like many critics, found fault with the play's original length; it was much longer than other plays of the day. Part of this length was due to the set changes in between scenes. As Ronald H. Wainscott notes in his 1988 book, *Staging O'Neill: The Experimental Years, 1920–1934,* ''four complete set changes were required, and each shift was time consuming.'' As Wainscott says, reviewers also noted that the shabby sets were themselves ''both inappropriate for the play and far beneath the usual standard for a Broadway production.'' In addition, many critics noted that O'Neill's call for a very young child to play Mary was unrealistic. As Wainscott notes, ''O'Neill complicated the predicament by including the toddler in two scenes and by giving her important dialogue and stage business.''

Despite critics' issues with the physical presentation, most agreed that the play was something new and that O'Neill was a new type of playwright. However, when *Beyond the Horizon* won the Pulitzer Prize in 1920, many, including O'Neill, were surprised. O'Neill proved that he was not a passing fad when he again won the Pulitzer Prize in 1922 and 1928. In 1936, after reviewing O'Neill's body of work, Lionel Trilling notes in his *New Republic* article ''Eugene O'Neill,'' ''Whatever is unclear about Eugene O'Neill, one thing is certainly clear—his genius.'' However, at this point, not all critics or audiences agreed, and many of O'Neill's plays of the time were not received well by depression-era audiences, who probably had enough tragedy in their own lives already.

O'Neill became popular again in the years following World War II, and his popularity has only increased since. While *Beyond the Horizon* is regarded as one of O'Neill's most important and seminal plays, it has rarely seen revival productions, unlike O'Neill's other plays, which have enjoyed many stage reproductions. The meaning of the play has changed for critics throughout the years. While early critics saw O'Neill's play as a message that people should follow their dreams and not go against their natures, later critics, like Linda Ben-Zvi, in her 1988 *Modern Drama* article ''Freedom and Fixity in the Plays of Eugene O'Neill,'' think the opposite. Says Ben-Zvi: ''In almost all O'Neill's works, when characters do actually get 'beyond the horizon,' what they find is far less than what they expected.''

Critics throughout the years have also noted the autobiographical quality of the play, particularly in the character of Robert. Says Virginia Floyd in her 1985 book, *The Plays of Eugene O'Neill: A New Assessment,* ''Robert is obviously a self-portrait. He is given not only O'Neill's physical characteristics but also some of his biographical background, having spent a year at college and experienced a long illness.''

Today, O'Neill is widely regarded as one of America's greatest playwrights, and many point to *Beyond the Horizon* as the seminal success that started him on his path to greatness.

CRITICISM

Ryan D. Poquette

Poquette has a bachelor's degree in English and specializes in writing about literature. In the following essay, Poquette discusses O'Neill's use of staging techniques to underscore and amplify the tragic mood of his play.

In his essay ''O'Neill and the Cult of Sincerity,'' Ronald H. Wikander notes the response of O'Neill's father, James, when he saw *Beyond the Horizon*: ''Are you trying to send the audience home to commit suicide?'' This reaction underscores the fact that O'Neill's play is impressively tragic. O'Neill increases the level of tragedy in his play through his detailed stage requirements. Through the use of stage techniques such as lighting, the use of interior and exterior sets, costumes, and makeup, O'Neill amplifies the already dark mood of the play as it progresses.

O'Neill considered his play an experiment in which he could break many of the conventions of the day. The play was widely regarded as too long, and it contained a number of specific set requirements that many thought complicated the production. One of the simpler stage techniques that O'Neill employed was the use of lighting. In the first act, O'Neill's stage directions talk about the sky, which ''*glows with the crimson flush of the sunset. This fades gradually as the action of the scene progresses.*'' The gradual darkening of the light mirrors the change in mood, which starts out light but gets tense as soon as the two brothers start talking about Ruth, whom they both obviously love. Says Andrew, ''I'd better run along. I've got to wash up some as long as Ruth's Ma is coming over for supper.'' Robert replies, ''(*pointedly—almost bitterly*): And Ruth.'' Robert is jealous that Andy has Ruth's love, and his dark mood is reflected in the fading light of day. This negative feeling culminates in Robert's obvious regret, later in the play, over his decision to forgo the sea voyage and marry Ruth. As Robert and Ruth are walking off at the end of the scene, Robert stops to focus ''*on the horizon*'' and finally ''*shakes his head impatiently, as though he were throwing off some disturbing thought.*'' Robert is not the only one who is disturbed. Thanks to the tension of the first scene, which is underscored by the diminishing lighting, the audience starts to feel a little uneasy, too.

In addition to lighting, O'Neill makes use of contrasting interior and exterior scenes that emphasize the tragic mistakes the characters have made. In the beginning of the first act, Robert sits on a fence ''*reading a book by the fading sunset light. He shuts this . . . and turns his head toward the horizon, gazing out over the fields and hills.*'' Robert is happy, looking forward to the future that he has dreamed about, when he will finally get to travel abroad and see the world beyond the horizon, which symbolizes the freedom that Robert yearns for. In the next scene, as Robert and the others are inside ''*the small sitting room of the Mayo farmhouse.*'' The farmhouse is neat and tidy, the sign ''*of the orderly comfort of a simple, hard-earned prosperity.*'' This is the type of life that Andy plans to live and Robert dreads. However, when the two brothers make their fateful decisions, Robert confines himself to the ''simple'' life of a farmer, while Andy chooses the life of freedom outdoors, a freedom that has never appealed to him. This sharp contrast between interior and exterior is evident in the remaining two acts, both of which start in the farmhouse and end outdoors with the horizon in view. In his 1979 book, *Eugene O'Neill,* Frederic I. Carpenter notes this fact: ''The structure of the play emphasizes the conflict of the two opposing ideals of adventure and security; of the two brothers who embody them.''

As the play progresses, both the interior and exterior sets degrade noticeably, signifying the neglect and decay that has come about as a result of the two brothers' tragic decisions. At the beginning of the second act, the farmhouse ''*gives evidence of carelessness,*'' as O'Neill's stage directions indicate. ''*The chairs appear shabby from lack of paint; the table cover is spotted and askew; holes show in the curtains.*'' At the beginning of the third act, the damage is even worse: ''*The curtains at the windows are torn and dirty and one of them is missing.*

WHAT DO I READ NEXT?

- In *Beyond the Horizon,* Robert offers to take Ruth with him on his three-year voyage; in addition, Captain Dick Scott is worried that his crew will think Robert's empty cabin was intended for a lover who jilted him. Wives and mistresses are two of the many roles that women have held in naval history. Women also served as nurses and in some cases disguised themselves as male sailors. In his *Women Sailors and Sailors' Women: An Untold Maritime History* (2001), noted nautical historian David Cordingly examines the rich history of women at sea, focusing mainly on the eighteenth and nineteenth centuries.
- In the play, life on the Mayo farm becomes a prison for Robert and Ruth. However, as Michael Dregni shows in his nostalgic collection *This Old Farm: A Treasury of Family Farm Memories* (1999), family life on farms in both the United States and Canada was enjoyable for many. The essays, fiction, photography, and artwork detail the various aspects of the farming life and include everything from a radio monologue by noted commentator Garrison Keillor to a commentary on tractor repair.
- Arthur Miller's classic play *Death of a Salesman* (1949) features the story of Willy Loman, a salesman who dreams of being successful. Through the examination of one day in Loman's life, Miller exposes the American dream that many people have and the tragedy that can result when this dream is not achievable.
- O'Neill's *The Iceman Cometh,* first published in 1946, is considered by many to be his best play. The story, which drew heavily on the tragedies in O'Neill's own life, details life in a skid row saloon in 1912, where society's losers—including drifters, prostitutes, and con artists—drown their failures in alcohol and talk about the successes they plan to have in the future. The one highlight in their lives is the annual visit of Hickey, a salesman who normally brings good times. However, this year, Hickey is a changed man who attempts to get the bar patrons to give up their unrealistic dreams and get their lives back on track.
- O'Neill's Pulitzer Prize–winning autobiographical play, *Long Day's Journey into Night,* was written in 1940, but the playwright was so concerned about the stark depictions of his dysfunctional family that he originally intended it to be published twenty-five years after his death. However, since the members of the O'Neill family portrayed in the play had already died, O'Neill's widow authorized the publication of the play in 1956. This harrowing play features one day in the life of the Tyrone family. The youngest son Edmond suffers from tuberculosis and hates his father, the mother is addicted to drugs, and the older son is an alcoholic.
- Before he wrote *Beyond the Horizon,* which only refers to the sea, O'Neill wrote a number of one-act plays that take place on a steamship at sea. *The Long Voyage Home and Other Plays,* published in 1995, contains four of these plays, including the title work, first published in 1917; *Bound East for Cardiff* (1916); *The Moon of the Caribbees* (1918); and *In the Zone* (1919).
- O'Neill wrote letters to various people in his life, but none are more telling than those he wrote to his second wife, Agnes Boulton. In *A Wind Is Rising: The Correspondence of Agnes Boulton and Eugene O'Neill* (2000), editor William Davies King collects these letters, which detail O'Neill's personal view of life in the spotlight. The book also includes a brief background of the lives of Boulton and O'Neill.
- Tennessee Williams's Pulitzer Prize–winning play *A Streetcar Named Desire* (1947) details the relations among Blanche DuBois; her sister, Stella Kowalski; and Stella's husband, Stanley. When Blanche, an aging southern belle, comes to stay with the Kowalskis, her idealistic dream world clashes with Stanley's brutish realism, which threatens to destroy her.

"DURING THE COURSE OF THE PLAY, DREAMS ARE CRUSHED, ALMOST ALL OF THE CHARACTERS DIE, AND THE SURVIVING CHARACTERS ARE IRREVERSIBLY CHANGED. BUT THESE FACTORS ARE NOT THE ONLY ONES THAT INVOKE A DARK MOOD IN O'NEILL'S AUDIENCE."

The closed desk is gray with accumulated dust as if it had not been used in years.'' The damage is not limited to the interior. The farm itself, depicted in the exterior scenes, also degrades from the healthy, robust farm in the first act, which has ''*rolling hills with their freshly plowed fields clearly divided from each other, checkerboard fashion, by the lines of stone walls and rough snake-fences.*'' By the last scene of the play, the farm is showing obvious signs of the neglect that Robert, Ruth, and Andrew have all been referring to in the second act: ''*The field in the foreground has an uncultivated appearance as if it had been allowed to remain fallow the preceding summer.*'' And the apple tree, which in the first scene was ''*just budding into leaf,*'' now ''*is leafless and seems dead.*'' Everything about the interior and exterior sets has been designed to signify the decay in the main characters' lives and to amplify the dark, tragic mood that the characters and plot create for the audience.

Some early critics did not appreciate what O'Neill was trying to do with the interior and exterior sets, and they focused only on the delays the set changes caused for the audience. Writes A. R. Fulton in his 1946 book, *Drama and Theatre Illustrated by Seven Modern Plays,* ''The critics objected to this arrangement, contending that no purpose was thereby served which could not have been served by staging the entire play in the single interior set.''

O'Neill's play also required extensive attention to detail in makeup and costume, another way that he indicated the regression of the characters' lives. In the case of Robert and Ruth, the signs of degradation are obvious in their appearances, which get excessively dirtier as the play goes on. In the beginning of the play, Robert is described as ''*delicate and refined, leaning to weakness in the mouth and chin.*'' He is wearing ''*gray corduroy trousers pushed into high laced boots, and a blue flannel shirt with a bright colored tie.*'' All in all, Robert is the ideal image of the cultured student. However, in the beginning of the second act, Robert is described as depressed and filthy: ''*His eyes are dull and lifeless, his face burned by the sun and unshaven for days. Streaks of sweat have smudged the layer of dust on his cheeks.*'' Just as Robert has been unable to take care of the farm, he has given up taking care of himself, letting his once-neat appearance decay. By the last act, Robert is depleted: ''*His hair is long and unkempt, his face and body emaciated.*''

Ruth's appearance also changes. In the beginning, she is described as ''*a healthy, blonde, out-of-doors girl of twenty, with a graceful, slender figure.*'' Ruth is a naturally beautiful, vibrant young woman, full of vitality, and she easily commands the attention of both Robert and Andy. However, three years later, at the beginning of the second act, she ''*has aged appreciably. Her face has lost its youth and freshness. There is a trace in her expression of something hard and spiteful.*'' Also, in the beginning of the play, ''She wears a simple white dress,'' while in the second act, her attire has changed to ''*a gingham dress with a soiled apron tied around her waist.*'' Finally, in the last act, a mere five years later, Ruth ''*has aged horribly. Her pale, deeply-lined face has the stony lack of expression of one to whom nothing more can ever happen.*'' In addition, her dress is in ''*negligent disorder,*'' her hair is ''*slovenly*'' and ''*streaked with gray,*'' and she wears black mourning clothes. Her clothes have steadily darkened just as the mood of the play has darkened. The fresh-faced young woman of twenty becomes an old woman at only twenty-eight, a tragic transformation that is depicted through costumes and makeup as the tragedy enveloping all the characters develops.

Andy's countenance changes throughout the play, but in different ways than Robert and Ruth. In the beginning, Andy is the consummate farmer, dressing in ''*overalls, leather boots, a gray flannel shirt open at the neck, and a soft, mud-stained hat pushed back on his head.*'' While the other characters get more unkempt and dirty as the play progresses, Andy gets progressively more business-like and professional. In the second act, when Andy comes home for the first time, the description in the stage directions note that, although he has not changed much, "*there is a decided change in his manner. The old easy-going good nature seems to have been partly lost in a breezy, business-like briskness of voice and gesture.*" In addition, he has traded his comfortable and slightly messy farm clothes for "*the simple blue uniform and cap of a merchant ship's officer.*" In the last act, Andy's transformation from good-natured farmer to ruthless businessman is complete, as his appearance indicates: "*His face seems to have grown highstrung, hardened. . . . His eyes are keener and more alert. There is even a suggestion of ruthless cunning about them*"; he is "*dressed in an expensive business suit and appears stouter.*" When the story starts, Andy is a muscular farmer who loves nothing better than to spend time, working the earth. By the end of the story, Andy has been transformed into a high-strung businessman who makes his living trading the grain he once loved to create. The changes in his attire and makeup amplify the tragedy of his transformation as he betrays his love and talent for farming by evading heartache.

O'Neill's play is noted for its gritty, tragic qualities. During the course of the play, dreams are crushed, almost all of the characters die, and the surviving characters are irreversibly changed. But these factors are not the only ones that invoke a dark mood in O'Neill's audience. O'Neill increases the level of tragedy in his play through his detailed stage requirements. Even without the extremely descriptive stage directions, O'Neill's *Beyond the Horizon* is a tragic play. However, through the use of special techniques in lighting, set design, costuming, and makeup, O'Neill amplifies the tragic mood the play induces in the audience. In the end, every element in this carefully designed play works to magnify the overwhelming sense of despair.

Source: Ryan D. Poquette, Critical Essay on *Beyond the Horizon,* in *Drama for Students,* The Gale Group, 2003.

Maria T. Miliora

In the following essay excerpt, Miliora analyzes the Mayo family psychologically, focusing on the narcissistic dreams of Robert and Andy.

Beyond the Horizon depicts the Mayos, a farming family. The major characters are the two brothers, Andrew, who is older, and Robert; their parents, James and Kate Mayo; Captain Dick Scott, who is Kate's brother; Ruth Atkins and her mother, Mrs. Atkins; and Mary, the child of Robert and Ruth. The drama turns on the relationship of the two brothers to Ruth and the ensuing dynamics among family members. Both Andrew and Robert are in love with Ruth, but at the play's opening, Robert has kept secret his feelings about Ruth. The family assumes that Andrew and Ruth will marry.

Robert is planning to leave the farm the following morning and begin a three-year sea journey on his Uncle Scott's ship. When he says goodbye to Ruth, he confesses that he loves her. Ruth is overjoyed and acknowledges that she loves him, rather than Andy. Robert decides that he will marry Ruth and remain on the farm. He and Ruth inform the Mayo family that evening. The news shocks and injures Andrew, but he tries to hide his feelings. He congratulates Robert, but tells his uncle that he will take Robert's place on the ship the following morning. Andy's unexpected decision precipitates a quarrel between him and his father.

The hostility that develops between father and son is the key to an appreciation of the play from the perspective of home and family. O'Neill's description of the Mayo home in the opening act indicates that the family is a cohesive unit. The two brothers are very close and the parents appear to have a warm relationship with each other and with their sons. Each of the brothers has been affirmed to do what he is most inclined to do. In short, the Mayos seemingly constitute a supportive selfobject milieu.

James Mayo had assumed that his elder son, Andy, would marry Ruth and that the two farms would merge. The news that Ruth loves Robert, rather than Andy, is disruptive to the family's cohesiveness. Andy, who loves Ruth, is very disappointed, narcissistically injured, and humiliated. His emotional reaction is apparent later in the scene when he tells Robert that, after all the plans he has made, he can not bear to remain on the farm and watch Robert and Ruth live together. This indicates that he feels foolish, demeaned in front of his family. Understandably, Andy seizes the opportunity to take his brother's place on the ship, feeling that this would allow him to get away from the humiliation that he feels at home.

James does not deal with Andy in an empathic way. He and Andy had been united in working the farm and he feels Andy's leaving as a loss. He becomes angry and confronts Andy about Ruth's rejection of him. He refers to his leaving as running away because Robert "got Ruth 'stead o' you. . . ." Andy's sense of humiliation is exacerbated by this statement made before the family. He becomes

"WITH HIS DEPICTIONS OF THE TWO BROTHERS, O'NEILL SUGGESTS THAT INDIVIDUALS CANNOT EXPERIENCE BOTH FAMILIAL LOVE AND INDIVIDUAL FREEDOM."

enraged and, in retaliation, he declares that he hates the farm. This retort fuels the cycle of hurt and rage, and the quarrel between father and son escalates into bitter antagonism. Reconciliation is seemingly impossible because both men have been narcissistically injured and both are unable to transcend their sense of injury and vehement rage. Robert's asking his father and brother, in the midst of the hostility, if they have gone mad suggests the psychotic-like level of the rage.

By the end of the first act, the supportive milieu that formerly existed within the Mayo family has been shattered. Robert feels responsible for the enmity and he is saddened. He knows that his brother wanted Ruth and he wishes that he had never told Ruth that he loved her.

The second act is set three years later. James Mayo has died and Mrs. Mayo states that his ''stubborn pride . . . brought on his death.'' This statement indicates that his quarrel with Andy and the rage that was provoked that night continued to affect him as well as the family as a whole. The description of the sitting room, which indicates carelessness and inefficiency, suggests that the family members are depressed. There is antagonism, complaining, and blaming among them. It is apparent that the family is no longer a cohesive or supportive unit. Robert seems to be particularly depressed. He is not doing well as a farmer and hears, on a consistent basis, that he is a failure. His inefficiency (as a farmer) and depression derive, at least in part, from the lack of a supportive family milieu that he needs to sustain him.

A violent quarrel erupts between Ruth and Robert. This shatters the bond between them as well as whatever illusions Robert had that Ruth loves him. As a result, he feels even more alone and in despair. When Andy returns for a visit, both Ruth and Robert are distressed to learn that he will not remain on the farm. Robert needs his help and Ruth had imagined that he still loved her. Andy is oblivious to his family's needs. He is unempathic toward his brother, thinking only of himself and his wish for material success. He expects to be understood by the family but makes no attempt to understand their plight. Andy's departure leaves the depressed family without any hope.

Five years later, the hopelessness, resignation, and despair within the family have reached crisis proportion. The death of his child, Mary, has caused Robert to sink into a deep depression, and he has become seriously ill as well. Ruth is ''without feeling,'' that is, also in the throes of a depression and a sense of hopelessness. In the final act, Andy's greed and selfishness are acutely apparent. He has been away for five years trying to amass a fortune, and he has never concerned himself with the family or farm. Robert, on the other hand, thinks of Ruth's welfare even as he is dying.

In addition to the theme of destruction of a sense of home and family, the play depicts the importance of a dream or a narcissistic illusion in organizing one's sense of self and sustaining self-cohesion. However, because they tend to be tenuous, illusions require affirmation from one's human surround in order to maintain one's sense of self.

Robert puts aside his dream of searching for beauty ''beyond the horizon'' and substitutes an illusion of having a happy and loving life with Ruth on the farm. This illusion is not affirmed. Indeed, Robert suffers considerable repudiation of his efforts at farming and, ultimately, he discovers that Ruth's declarations of love for him were lies. The death of his little daughter—''our last hope of happiness''—shatters his illusions completely. As a result, Robert's sense of self is seriously depleted. This sense of depletion is made concrete in the play by virtue of the depression and death, that is, the laying waste of the farm as well as of the characters.

Early in the play, Andy's sense of self is organized in terms of a narcissistic fantasy of being a successful farmer. He is perceived as successful in this regard by his family and neighbors. Within this milieu that affirms him, his sense of self is cohesive. Moreover, Andy has a dream of making a life with Ruth. When Ruth announces her love for Robert, Andy's dream is shattered and he fragments under the pressure of his father's attack. He reconstitutes his sense of self in terms of new illusions of attaining material success in foreign lands. Because his narcissism is relatively immature or archaic, Andy needs to show his family that he is eminently successful. His sense of self-worth is at stake. He becomes driven by greed in order to attain unlimited wealth as if this will negate the earlier sense of humiliation that he suffered before his family.

There are two ''homes'' in the play—the farm and the sea. O'Neill dichotomizes the two and concretizes this distinction by having each of the brothers inclined toward one or the other. O'Neill suggests that it is important for each person to follow his or her true nature.

Neither of the two ''homes'' is a sustaining selfobject milieu because of the narcissistic and emotional elements inherent in each. Andy goes off to sea because of humiliation, rage, and greed. Robert stays on the farm because of the illusion that Ruth loves him. O'Neill suggests that it is not the place *per se* that creates a sense of home, but rather, it is the relational context within the family that defines a real home. When there is narcissistic injury, rage, and a lack of empathy within the family, the sense of home can be destroyed.

As in a number of his plays, O'Neill includes the themes of betrayal and greed as significant in defining the emotional climate among the members of a family. Robert believes that Ruth loves him as Andy did earlier. In this context, Ruth is cast in the role of the betrayer who intrudes into the family milieu and disturbs its peace and harmony. Using the character of Andy, we can see the relationship between greed and emotional miserliness: Andy is driven by greed and lacks a capacity for empathy.

With his depictions of the two brothers, O'Neill suggests that individuals cannot experience both familial love and individual freedom. Robert chooses love and loses freedom. Andy loses love and, seemingly, attains freedom. However, neither brother gains what he sought. As suggested by the dramatic climax, true freedom is attained only in death.

There are several autobiographical elements in the play. The hostility that erupts between father and elder son in the Mayo family is suggestive of the hostility between James and Jamie in *Long Day's Journey*. According to the Gelbs (1960,1962), James O'Neill wanted Jamie to follow him in the theatre. His disappointment about his elder son parallels that of James Mayo in *Beyond the Horizon*. Moreover, the relationship between the Mayo brothers suggests elements of the relationship between Eugene and Jamie. In the play, Andy and Robert are rivals for the same woman. In the O'Neill family, Jamie and Eugene were rivals for their mother's affection. Robert's replacing Andy on the farm is indicative of O'Neill's experience with Jamie. In O'Neill's mind, Jamie was the more talented, the one who should have become the writer, and he (Eugene) felt that he had usurped Jamie's talent.

Robert's experience of feeling foolish because he had believed Ruth's assertions of love for him is consonant with O'Neill's about his mother. As Robert felt betrayed when he realized Ruth's true feelings, so O'Neill felt betrayed when he learned what he imagined were his mother's true feelings about him.

Source: Maria T. Miliora, ''Loss of a Sense of Home, Family, Belonging: Narcissism, Alienation and Madness,'' in *Narcissism, the Family, and Madness: A Self-Psychological Study of Eugene O'Neill and His Plays,* Peter Lang Publishing, 2000, pp. 69–84.

Barbara Voglino

In the following essay, Voglino explores how the last scene of Beyond the Horizon *contrasts with the predictability of the rest of the drama, chiefly through Robert's ''theatrically heightened speeches.''*

Beyond the Horizon, completed in 1918, was O'Neill's first full-length drama to be produced (1920) and his first play to be awarded the Pulitzer Prize. Despite contemporary praise for its powerful realism, early reviewers voiced an awareness that the play was flawed. Some objected to its graphic depiction of tuberculosis; others, to what they considered its excessive length. Predictability and overexplicitness were two of the more significant faults pointed out. Early reviewers Alexander Woollcott and Heywood Broun targeted the final scene for its illusion-dispelling effect. Broun attributed the break in the impact of the drama to the lowering of the curtain before the very short final scene, which he argued ''compels a wait at a time when tension is seriously impaired.'' Although Broun's explanation seems feasible enough regarding the reaction of an audience attending a staged production, the wait for a scene change does not account for the similar discomfort experienced by readers. The illusion-dispelling quality noted by

Woollcott and Broun seems more likely attributable to the sudden change in tone, matter, and the demand placed upon the audience by the final scene, which raises questions when the audience has been prepared to expect a conclusion. More recent criticism of the play's closure has focused on its ambiguity.

Up until the last scene, however, *Beyond the Horizon*, an explicitly presented, highly predictable drama, is more remarkable for its lack of ambiguity. The play is composed of three acts, each divided into two scenes. Audience expectations regarding closure are set up in the first act. Two brothers, very different in character, exchange destinies. Young Robert Mayo, upon learning that his friend Ruth loves him, renounces his chance to fulfill his lifelong dream of exploring ''beyond the horizon'' on his uncle's ship. Instead of sailing around the world as he had intended, he remains home to marry and work the family farm, a job for which he is physically and emotionally unsuited. His brother, Andrew, who loves farmwork and had intended to marry Ruth, good-naturedly takes Robert's place on the three-year voyage. Before the end of act 1 James Mayo, the father, announces the theme of the play. He warns Andrew, ''You're runnin' against your own nature, and you're goin' to be a'mighty sorry for it if you do.''

For the next three scenes, the drama rather laboriously depicts the progressive fulfillment of the father's dire prediction—intended for Andrew—with regard to both brothers. Robert, upon whose plight the play focuses, has betrayed his poet's awareness of a higher reality by surrendering to his biological attraction to Ruth. His initial moment of decision results in seemingly endless suffering in the form of poverty, marital unhappiness, and a recurrence of the tuberculosis that causes his death. By the end of the play his character has deteriorated as well: he has become jealous and vengeful. Andrew's punishment for not remaining on the Mayo farm is more subtle. After the voyage with his uncle he undertakes a huge farming venture in Argentina and accumulates a large fortune, which he proceeds to lose through unwise speculation. As might be expected to result from his risk-fraught lifestyle, his eyes develop a look of ''*ruthless cunning,*'' and he becomes inclined to distrust people. Upon returning to the Mayo farm five years later, he discovers himself bereft of family as well as financial security. His parents having already died, and his sole sibling dying, Andrew is left with only his sister-in-law, Ruth, whom the dying Robert has requested he marry, and whom Andrew has grown to despise.

Thus far the plot has proceeded rather steadily toward its predictable end, like Hofmannsthal's arrow speeding toward its target. The spectator's ''perception of structure'' has led him to anticipate that closure will be synonymous with the ultimate fulfillment of the father's prophetic warning to his sons for ''runnin' against [their] . . . nature[s].'' Another important structural device that the audience expects to influence closure is the technique of ironic reversal established early in the play with the brothers' exchange of destinies and repeated at significant intervals throughout the drama. This pattern of reversing the expectations of the characters in *Beyond the Horizon* is, in fact, repeated so consistently as to give away the plot. As H. G. Kemelman observed (1932), ''The complete and perfect frustration of the characters destroys all suspense. The audience knows what is coming: after the first act, they can predict the rest of the play.'' For example, at the start of act 2 all the characters have their hopes pinned on Andrew's imminent return from the voyage. Ruth hopes to renew Andrew's former romantic interest in her; Robert and his mother expect Andrew to take charge of the failing farm. Their very eagerness prepares the audience for the disappointment that will ensue: Andrew sails off for Argentina the next day. A nearly identical situation occurs at the beginning of act 3, when everyone is once again waiting for Andrew's return. Ruth has telegraphed Andrew about Robert's need for medical attention. She and her mother are desperately hoping for financial assistance, since Robert has been too ill to work the farm. Robert, who deludes himself about the gravity of his illness, also hopes to borrow money from his brother so that he and Ruth can move to the city. The audience, recalling the pattern of ironic reversal that has been established in acts 1 and 2, expects a repeat performance of Andrew's first homecoming, which in fact occurs. Andrew arrives at the Mayo farm financially and spiritually broken. The specialist he brings is too late to save Robert's life.

If the play had ended at this highly foreseeable, if somewhat tedious, point, its conclusion would meet both Barbara Herrnstein Smith's requirement for closure (in poetry) that it result in a cessation of expectations for the audience and June Schlueter's condition that the production of meaning be complete. The theme ''be true to yourself'' has been hammered in relentlessly from start to finish: Robert's self-betrayal has resulted in misery for all concerned. The total sum of his life's efforts is zero—no children, no crops, no happiness, and no literary output (he speculates on his potential for writing). With Robert dying, Ruth exhausted, and Andrew at the nadir of his personal and financial fortunes, nothing more of interest can be expected to occur. The viewer is ready to accept the lamentable end toward which the structure of the play has led.

The viewer is in for a surprise, however. The "perverse mind" of Eugene O'Neill would not allow this "reasonably contented ending" for which he has meticulously prepared throughout the drama. The fact is, the very concept of "contentment" appears to have had a derogatory connotation to O'Neill, who in 1921 defined "happiness" as "an intensified feeling of the significant worth of man's being and becoming . . . not a *mere smirking contentment* with ones lot" (emphasis added). In *Beyond the Horizon*, instead of being satisfied with the ending within easy grasp, the playwright demonstrates his preference for the unattainable by introducing Robert's theatrically heightened speeches in the final scene. The spectator is startled by the change in tone, which suggests a redemption not supported by the action of the play, and which contrasts strangely with the preceding, naturalistically detailed rendition of poverty and misery. Nor is the spectator prepared for the new interpretive demand placed upon him at this late stage. Unsettled from his comfortably receptive position, he needs to rekindle his imagination, which has been smothered by the play's overexplicitness. He must first decide Robert's intent in bequeathing his wife to his brother. Is the dying Robert acting out of a spirit of forgiveness and comradery? Or is he trying to punish his brother, regarding whom he has exhibited bitter jealousy only a short time earlier in this very scene? The viewer or reader may also need to make decisions regarding his own eschatology in order to interpret the closure, which O'Neill leaves ambiguous. The dying Robert joyfully purports to have been redeemed through suffering and sacrifice, so that he may resume his earlier-abandoned quest after death. Is the audience to conclude that Robert's self-assessment is correct, or that he dies tragically self-deluded? If the viewer concludes Robert is deluded, as I believe further analysis confirms, the question becomes the nature of Robert's self-delusion. Does the play depict his irrevocable forfeiture, through marrying Ruth instead of sailing "beyond the horizon," of his right to pursue the "quest"? Or is he deluded about the very

"IS THE AUDIENCE TO CONCLUDE THAT ROBERT'S SELF-ASSESSMENT IS CORRECT, OR THAT HE DIES TRAGICALLY SELF-DELUDED? IF THE VIEWER CONCLUDES ROBERT IS DELUDED, AS I BELIEVE FURTHER ANALYSIS CONFIRMS, THE QUESTION BECOMES THE NATURE OF ROBERT'S SELF-DELUSION."

possibility of undertaking such a quest? Without an understanding of Robert's final condition, the production of meaning that ought to result from the closure is incomplete, leaving closure *en l'air.*

Modern closural theories attest to the prerogative of individuals to assist in creating their own closures for ambiguous works. Interpretation is no longer the mere act of "*construing,*" but "the art of *constructing,*" asserts Stanley Fish. The reader, says Wolfgang Iser, must "[work] things out for himself." According to Henry J. Schmidt the reader's effort to impose closure on an ambiguous work can have the propitious effect of "assuring one of the correctness of one's beliefs and of the fundamental stability of one's social and moral environment."

A number of readers and viewers have chosen to interpret the ambiguous ending affirmatively. Like Robert Mayo, who invents a gratifying fiction to ensure that his suffering not be meaningless, some readers and viewers may deliberately seek "the promise of a morally legible universe" in Robert's poetic last speeches. Thus, even so illustrious a critic as T. S. Eliot, fresh from completing his celebrated religious work, *The Waste Land* (1922), was able to perceive the ending of *Beyond the Horizon* as "magnificent." Similarly, Arthur Hobson Quinn (1927) was impressed by the "exaltation of the spirit" in Robert's dying speech: "I'm happy at last . . . free to wander on and on—eternally! . . . It isn't the end. It's a free beginning—the start of my voyage! I've won . . . the right of release—beyond the horizon!." Even some very reputable modern critics have taken Robert's final speech literally. Travis Bogard describes Robert's death as "close to a blessing, both a release from pain and a reunification with the element that is rightfully his . . . he moves through death into the mainstream of continuous life energy. In Edmund Tyrone's words, he has 'dissolved' into the secret." Still more recently Virginia Floyd has interpreted the final scene as signifying redemption through suffering.

Nevertheless, a consideration of what precedes and succeeds Robert's triumphant dying speech, as well as Robert's character and O'Neill's own comments pertaining to Robert, would seem to preclude the positive readings of the closure that O'Neill's poetic language suggests. In dying, Robert says he has been redeemed through suffering, that he has "won to [his] trip—the right of release—beyond the horizon" through the "sacrifice[s]" he has made. However, nothing in the play indicates any "sacrifice" on Robert's part. If anyone has sacrificed it is Andrew, who surrendered both Ruth and the farm to his brother. But even Andrew's sacrifice was minimal: he later realizes he never loved Ruth, and satisfies his farming instinct on a much larger scale in Argentina. As for Robert, he merely made the wrong choice and was too weak to extricate himself from the consequences. This is not "sin," for which Robert requires "redemption," but mere human frailty. His fidelity to Ruth even after the collapse of their relationship seems less attributable to "sacrifice"—particularly after their little daughter's death—than passivity coupled with illness on his part.

Far from being redeemed through suffering in any significant sense, Robert, as I have indicated, undergoes a deterioration of character as a result of his unhappy marriage and the death of his child. In acts 1 and 2 Robert is gentle and loving until his nagging wife expresses the wish she had married Andrew instead of him. In act 3 the couple's personalities seem to have reversed. Now Ruth wearily ministers to her sick husband's needs, while Robert indulges in vehement name-calling: Ruth is a "fool"; the local doctor is a "damned ignoramus." Still embittered by Ruth's "defection" of five years ago (her preference for Andrew), Robert jealously accuses his wife, who numbed with despair no longer feels love for anyone, of still waiting for Andrew as she did in act 2. Raging with fever, Robert can scarcely contain his envy of the brother he once loved: "Andy's made a big success of himself. . . . And now he's coming home to let us admire his greatness."

Although Robert still has lucid moments in which he recognizes his accountability, he deliberately sets himself up as a kind of prophet for the purpose of judging and administering punishment to his brother. Seizing upon Andrew's unfortunate financial history, Robert professes to see a "spiritual significance in [the] picture" of his brother "gambl[ing] in a wheat pit with scraps of paper." Mercilessly attacking Andrew in his most vulnerable area, he continues, "[Y]ou're the deepest-dyed failure of the three [of us], Andy. You've spent eight years running away from yourself [Robert conveniently forgets that it was his action which sent Andrew away]. . . . You used to be a creator when you loved the farm. You and life were in harmonious partnership." Yet Robert is guilty of the same self-betrayal. He, too, has lost his "harmonious partnership" with life, and now it appears, from the change in his character, that he has lost not only the life he might have had, but the very self that once dreamed of that life. After telling Andrew he must "be punished" and will "have to suffer to win back", he makes what on the surface would appear a magnanimous dying gesture were it not for the implications of "punishment" and "suffering" that immediately precede it. He orders Andrew to marry Ruth: "Remember, Andy, Ruth has suffered double her share. . . . Only through contact with suffering, Andy, will you—awaken. Listen. You must marry Ruth—afterwards." The insinuation is that the suffering involved in being wedded to Ruth will "redeem" Andrew in the same manner as it did Robert—destroy what may remain of his character and perhaps cause his death.

The final closure does not bode well for Andrew and Ruth. If Robert had deliberately set out to destroy the possibility of a meaningful relationship between them, he could scarcely have accomplished his goal any more effectively than by commanding them to marry. The closing dialogue of the play, which ought—if anything—to clarify the author's intent, decidedly undercuts an affirmative reading of Robert's death. As Andrew and Ruth face each other across Robert's corpse, Andrew is furious with Ruth for not reassuring Robert she had not meant what she once said about preferring Andrew. Gradually his anger subsides, however, as a result of Ruth's sobs and the memory of Robert's dying wish that they wed. As the play closes, Andrew falters with empty words regarding their future. Ruth, for her part, is too far "*beyond the further troubling of any hope*" even to care. Although their future relationship is left somewhat open, audience expectations regarding the possibility of happiness for them together have ceased. If they do eventually marry, their union will most likely continue the cycle of misery established in the beginning of the play with Ruth's marriage to Robert.

If Marianna Torgovnick's assertion with regard to the novel that the ending is "the single place where an author most pressingly desires to make his points" may be considered applicable to drama, it is significant that O'Neill finishes the play with this despairing tableau. Albert E. Kalson and Lisa M. Schwerdt conclude, "There is nothing ahead for the dead or the living—only repetition, never change." The hopefulness of Robert's dying speech appears effectively negated by the depiction of misery that succeeds it.

Far from being redeemed through suffering, as some critics have interpreted the closure, Robert is one of O'Neill's many self-deluded characters. He began dreaming by the window as a sickly child in order to forget his pain. Throughout his life he seems to have lived more significantly in dreams and poetry than through his actions. Like Tennyson's Lady of Shalott his perception of reality, or the outside world as it exists objectively, is clouded. He never realizes Ruth loves him until she tells him, nor does he recognize that she has stopped loving him until she tells him. Moreover, even Robert's dream of the quest is but dimly conceived: it is not powerful enough in his mind to compel him to sacrifice in order to achieve it (in the manner in which O'Neill, himself, sacrificed for his goal to create drama). Instead Robert rather lazily attempts to exchange one dream for another: "I think love must have been the secret—the secret that called to me from over the world's rim—the secret beyond every horizon." In act 3, raging with fever, he is more deluded than ever. Like the sickly child who dreamed by the window to forget his pain, he plans to start a new life in the city: "Life owes us some happiness after what we've been through. *(vehemently)* It must! Otherwise our suffering would be meaningless—and that is unthinkable." In desperate need of illusion to validate his wasted life, he goes to the window seeking confirmation of his new dream in the rising of the sun. But he is too early; the sun has not risen yet. All he sees is black and gray, which he himself concludes to be "not a very happy augury." After overhearing the specialist brought in by Andrew confirm his imminent death, Robert quickly grasps at a new dream, one less easily dispelled as illusory. He claims to be continuing his original plan to journey "beyond the horizon," having won through "sacrifice" the "right of release," and envisions himself "happy at last" and "free to wander on and on—eternally." Like Captain Bartlett in another play written the same year, *Where the Cross Is Made* (1918), who dies happy in the belief that his treasure has been restored, Robert Mayo dies as deluded as he has lived.

O'Neill did not admire this young man gifted with a poet's imagination who clipped his wings through lack of character to pursue his goal and, consequently, remained literally and figuratively bound to the soil below. Several years earlier (1914) O'Neill had defined "be[ing] true to one-self and one's highest hope" as the ultimate "good." That same year he had sent Beatrice Ashe an excerpt of writing that had impressed him as valid: "[T]he only way in this world to play for anything you want is to be willing to go after it with all you've got—to be willing to push every last chip to the middle of the table. It don't make a bit of difference what it is: if you get a hand you want, play it!" Robert Mayo was not willing to push that "last chip" to the table, and O'Neill saw him as a moral coward:

> a weaker type . . . a man who would have my Norwegian's inborn craving for the sea's unrest, only in him it would be conscious, too conscious, intellectually diluted into a vague, intangible, romantic wanderlust. His powers of resistance, both moral and physical, would also probably be correspondingly watered. He would throw away his instinctive dream and accept the thralldom of the farm for—why almost any nice little poetical craving—the romance of sex, say.

O'Neill himself could have been saddled with a wife and child as a very young man. Out of conscience he married the respectable Kathleen Jenkins, whom he had impregnated, in 1909. Immediately afterward, however, he departed on a series of adventurous voyages, only meeting the son she later bore him (Eugene O'Neill Jr.) one time before he was grown. In *Beyond the Horizon*, written nine years later, the same year as his second marriage to Agnes Boulton, O'Neill may unconsciously have been attempting to justify his desertion of Kathleen as preferable to a life of clipped wings like Robert's.

In one of his more lucid final moments, Robert Mayo condemns himself for his lack of courage regarding the pursuit of his dream. Fleeing his sickbed for the outdoor road, from which he can view his last sunrise, Robert assesses his life:

> I couldn't stand it back there in the room. It seemed as if all my life—I'd been cooped in a room. *So I thought I'd try to end as I might have—if I'd had the courage—*

> *alone*—in a ditch by the open road—watching the sun rise. (emphasis added)

He then invents an elaborate fiction concerning his death to compensate for his wasted life, thus qualifying him to take his place among the numerous men and women in the O'Neill canon who, unable to face reality, resort to the comfort of dreams. But although O'Neill sympathized with his weaker fellow men who need dreams in order to survive, he did not admire them or depict them as heroes. Robert deludes himself in his final speeches: he never attains that mystical glimpse of the ultimate that he proclaims. As William J. Scheick concludes, "Rob never crosses the threshold, never penetrates in fact, language or dream the mystery beyond the horizon of life." Through his denial of the dream he has progressed to disillusionment, suffering, bitterness, and death, and that is the extent of his journey.

Finally, although the self-deluded nature of Robert's final speeches seems clear upon closer examination, the ultimate nature of Robert's tragedy remains ambiguous. Is Robert to be pitied because, through his own admitted moral cowardice, he has failed to pursue the mystical quest that once beckoned him "beyond the horizon"? Or does Robert's tragedy involve his delusion about the very existence of such a quest in the hostile world of the play? Scheick concludes, "Everything in the play . . . implies the inability of humanity to get beyond the horizon in any sense; . . . such a quest . . . is an illusion characteristic of, perhaps crucial to human life, and defines its radical tragic nature." Although Scheick's argument has merit in consideration of O'Neill's frequent depiction of the human need for "pipe dreams" (*The Iceman Cometh*) in his plays, O'Neill himself appears to have been preoccupied with such a quest. In *Long Day's Journey into Night* (1941), Edmund Tyrone, the fictional counterpart of his youthful self, describes a moment of mystical oneness with the universe when "the veil of things" is drawn back: "For a second you see—and seeing the secret, are the secret. For a second there is meaning!" Edmund's narration of his experience at sea suggests that O'Neill's own quest for spiritual significance "beyond the horizon" was not without its occasional rewards (which explains why Robert Mayo's dying speech is so poetically rendered as to convince some viewers or readers of its truth). Furthermore, in 1922 O'Neill expressed his admiration for those who sought to soar through the pursuit of unattainable goals:

> Man wills his own defeat when he pursues the unattainable. But his *struggle* is his success! He is an example of the spiritual significance which life attains when it aims high enough. . . .

As stated earlier, O'Neill's own most ambitious endeavor to reach "beyond the horizon" is represented by his effort to attain extraordinary dramatic goals through writing plays. His choice of the word "*un*attainable" regarding his quest, however, suggests uncertainty on his part. It seems possible that O'Neill's failure to clarify the nature of Robert Mayo's tragedy and thus render the closure more meaningful is the result of the playwright's own qualms regarding the validity of such a quest, given man's limitations and the hostile universe in which he has been placed. Terry Eagleton, who defends the reader's right to construct or write his own "sub-text" for ambiguous or evasive works, maintains that "what [a work] does not say, and how it does not say it, may be as important as what it articulates; what seems absent, marginal, or ambivalent about it may provide a central clue to its meanings." The ambiguous ending of *Beyond the Horizon* may represent O'Neill's own doubts concerning his goal to create significant drama, toward which he was sacrificing and dedicating his life.

In conclusion, ambiguous endings are popular in this age, which favors "openness" in preference to those endings described by William Carlos Williams (with reference to poetry) as clicking shut like the lid of a box. It would seem that the ambiguity ought not to be merely imposed upon the play's closure, however, but ought to proceed naturally from the preceding drama. For closure to be effective in an open-ended work (which includes plays with ambiguous endings), asserts Marianna Torgovnick, the test is "the honesty and the appropriateness of the ending's relationship to beginning and middle." The problem with the ambiguity in *Beyond the Horizon* is that the change in tone and demand upon the audience occurs too suddenly (early critics noted the illusion-dispelling effect of the last scene): the audience is not prepared for openness in such an explicitly presented play. In his later plays O'Neill will make ambiguous closures more integral to the dramas, as in *The Iceman Cometh* (1940), for example, a play filled with mystery and uncertainty from the beginning.

O'Neill will undergo a similar evolution by the later plays concerning his facility to maintain suspense. In contrast to the laborious predictability or Robert's deterioration in *Beyond the Horizon*, in *A Moon for the Misbegotten* (1943) another self-betrayed character, Jim Tyrone, journeys toward his destruction. Yet in this very concentrated drama, which occupies only some eighteen hours (in contrast to the novelistic *Beyond the Horizon*, which is spread out over eight years), O'Neill structures the action so that the audience retains some hope for Jim Tyrone's salvation almost until the end.

Source: Barbara Voglino, ''Unsettling Ambiguity in *Beyond the Horizon,*'' in *Perverse Mind: Eugene O'Neill's Struggle with Closure,* Associated University Presses, 1999, pp. 25–34.

Stephen A. Black

In the following essay, Black compares Beyond the Horizon *to plays by Sophocles and Euripides in arguing that it is ''the first play by an American that can justly be called a tragedy.''*

Beyond the Horizon (1918), Eugene O'Neill's first successful long play, does not hold a very prominent place in the O'Neill canon. It deserves better. Although an obviously early work, it is the first play by an American that can justly be called a tragedy. O'Neill would not consistently reach tragic levels so high until the late 1930s. I will try to defend this large claim by drawing analogies between the meanings of the play and the tragic vision I construe in O'Neill's ancient companions, Sophocles and Euripides.

Like the Attic Greeks, O'Neill is preoccupied with the discoveries people continually make of their mortality, impotence, and unimportance, of the difference between the powers they believe themselves to have and the weaknesses circumstances reveal. O'Neill's characters may sometimes seek knowledge of themselves, but their most important discoveries tend to be of the nature of the world. The world is far from being the place human thought and institutions describe, ruled by people for the glory of God, or ruled through science and reason for the glorification of humanity. Instead, the world seems, to the Greeks and O'Neill, to consist of forces not in the least susceptible to human influence. Oedipus, an exemplary humanist, falls tragically because he believes reason and forethought can deflect the course of events already set in motion. Pentheus ridicules the ''mythical'' story of his aunt's impregnation by Zeus with a rational explanation, that she must have had a human lover. Armed with reason, and representing the law as well as the oligarchy, he assumes he cannot fail to overpower the youth who madly claims to be the god. Reason and human power make it impossible for Pentheus to avoid the god's dreadful seduction. Encounters with these forces so stun human self-esteem that people can only deny or distort memory of the event.

> "THE CHARACTERS REJECT THE LESSON OF THEIR OWN EXPERIENCE, THAT SUFFERING INESCAPABLY ACCOMPANIES GROWTH AND DEVELOPMENT, AND THAT JUSTICE OCCURS RARELY, AND EVEN THEN PERHAPS ONLY IN SOMEONE'S MIND."

Nothing should seem stranger than the popularity of an Aeschylus, a Sophocles, a Euripides, a Shakespeare, a Strindberg, an O'Neill, a Bergman. Tragedy should head the list of arts and sciences that Freud once grouped with psychoanalysis. They have in common the success of their insults to human arrogance. The Pythagoreans, Aristarchus, and Copernicus; Darwin, his followers and predecessors: they all made it difficult to believe that God so favoured those He made in His image that He put them in the centre of His universe. Psychoanalysis shows that consciousness is an exceptional, rather than usual, mental state, and that we therefore do not control our own thoughts or acts, even though we continue to be responsible for them. The latter describes the true Oedipal tragedy: not the conflicts of a young child, but the dilemma of the tyrant of Thebes, who finally knows himself to have had no control over his terrible lot, but whose self-esteem will not permit him to deny responsibility for his acts. Should he disavow responsibility, he embraces helplessness and impotence. Consciousness, reason, and reasonable action represent the height of human potential—and are of little consequence.

The historical eras that have nurtured tragic literature have generally regarded humankind as the finest work of God or life. Perhaps it is only in confident times that people can entertain notions of their own unimportance. However it may be, they occasionally rediscover the triviality of human force compared to the power of natural processes. Pentheus cannot protect himself because he cannot imagine that something within himself, his perverse sexual longing, might overpower his will and reason. Nor can Oedipus imagine that anything might circumvent his determination not to murder the kindly king of Corinth. The discovery must be even more unpleasant when the person who makes it embodies the most admired human qualities and finds that they help hardly at all at the most important moments.

Discovering one's impotence and unimportance is not in itself necessarily tragic, even for one with great gifts and powers. The pitiful or ironic may become tragic when a playwright can make it possible for a character or an audience to perceive the delusion and change with sympathy and empathy. Most often that occurs when a character can articulate the vision of the world that the play newly discovers. The change that occurs when a character or audience discovers the world anew resembles the changes that sometimes occur in the private drama of the analytic consulting room. Stanley Cavell describes the magnitude of change in a way that applies both to literary tragedy and to moments of personal insight:

> [The] problems are solved only when they disappear, and answers are arrived at only when there are no longer questions. . . . The more one learns, so to speak, the hang of oneself, and mounts one's problems, the less one is able to *say* what one has learned; not because you have *forgotten* what it was, but because nothing you said would seem like an answer or a solution: there is no longer any question or problem which your words would match. You have reached conviction, but not about a proposition; and consistency, but not in a theory. You are different, what you recognize as problems are different, your world is different. . . . And this is the sense, in which what a work of art means cannot be *said.*

Cavell conveys the exaltation that sometimes, in literary tragedy, accompanies the most terrible discoveries. We approach the essence of tragedy when we say that it calls upon our best qualities of understanding, action, reason, and sensibility in order to make us conscious that action, reason, and sensibility have little power.

Like Sophocles and Euripides, O'Neill has the fate to regard the world from a point of view which finds tragedy in the falls engendered by the very qualities civilized people most value. O'Neill selected teachers like Nietzsche, Schopenhauer, and Strindberg whose views of life opposed the modern spirit, not so much by mocking or deploring its manners and materialism, but by evoking old values and gods, by thinking along lines distant from or tangential to Judaic, Christian, or other modern traditions. Louis Sheaffer, one of the few recent writers who has tried to give *Beyond the Horizon* its due, correctly points out that despite his sympathy for experimentation and the new theatre, O'Neill swims ''against the tide'' of modernism. To any who object that O'Neill is not a poet whose English is to be compared to the Attic of Sophocles or Euripides there is an answer: that O'Neill is not less effective than the Greeks are in most translations; and for Greekless readers of several centuries, that has been quite a lot.

Beyond the Horizon concludes with the dying Robert Mayo strangely insisting that his brother Andy must marry Ruth, Robert's wife, when Robert dies: not to ensure Ruth's protection, but to ''awaken'' Andy. Ruth has known suffering, has ''suffered double her share,'' Robert reminds his brother. ''[O]nly through sacrifice,'' he says, ''only through contact with suffering, Andy, will you—awaken.'' Robert dies urging Andy to ''Remember!'' and speaking the name of the sun as it rises over the hills.

The injunction means little to Andy, but O'Neill suggests it means something to Ruth she cannot express, and it is clear he intends the audience to understand. Everything in the play has led to it. The world of the play is governed by powers impervious to human consciousness, intellect, will, or longing, powers unchanged since ancient times, unaffected by progress, science, rationalism, technology. In defiance, the characters take as their motto the rubric: I think, therefore I know what is wrong and what I deserve; I think, therefore I demand justice.

They determinedly reject the lesson of their own experience, that suffering inescapably accompanies growth and development, and that justice occurs rarely, and even then perhaps only in someone's mind. In the 1920 text Robert makes explicit a meaning latent in most of his actions when he whimsically tells his father, ''I'm never going to grow up—if I can help it.'' Although he refuses to recognize it at the time, Robert reminds us that the change he resists is relentless.

Shortly before he himself awakens, Robert tells Ruth: ''Life owes us some happiness after what we've been through. (*Vehemently*) It must! Otherwise our suffering would be meaningless—and that is unthinkable.'' The dream of meaning, reason, order, and justice occurs during the sleep of life, tortured for Robert and Ruth, vaguely restless for Andy. Tragedy exists in the awakening from the dream.

It is understandable that those the fates give the worst lot in life, like Ruth and himself, would always long hungrily for whatever comes easily to those more fortunate. Because it can be understood, it implies the existence of a world order that fits with a human sense of justice and deserving. But when someone like Andy who "belongs," someone who succeeds at whatever he tries, someone who feels at one with his work and his place in the world, still is driven to the magic of gambling, the implication of order is denied. Andy's gambling implies that satisfaction exists in human life only by chance. Now that he is about to die, Robert can deny no longer that even if the fates had been kinder to him and Ruth, neither would have been any happier, nor freer than Andy is of the vague dissatisfaction that always wants more.

The example of Andy awakens Robert by pulverizing the remaining shards of his battered romanticism. When Andy transforms himself from creating in nature, from being in harmony with life, and becomes instead an entrepreneur with both eyes on the main chance, that awakens Robert to the importance of human arrogance, his own as well as Andy's. To create from the soil may be the work of a man at one with himself and his world. "[T]o gamble in a wheat pit with scraps of paper," as Robert says, has "a spiritual significance." It reduces the edible results of one's labour as a creature in nature into mere symbols of exchangeable value. The goal of life changes from that of maintaining harmony between one's environment and one's self to that of acquiring symbols that boast of dominance and control over other people, over the natural world, and over the gods and fates.

O'Neill avoids making Andy an object of satire. He shows him having more capacity for self-discipline and hard work than either Robert or Ruth. Up to a point he understands his business failure and its causes. He sympathizes with Ruth's frustrations and forebears to judge her harshly even when she sets brother against brother. Although he has no sensibility for things that attract Robert, he respects his brother and remains loyal to him even after Robert has won away his woman. Nevertheless something is missing. His greed in itself is not wrong, only natural. But he cannot care to understand or respect himself or his world, and in the long run that makes it hard to take him seriously. He is born at one with his world and throws away his birthright without ever noticing he has had it or lost it. Andy by himself, is not a tragic figure. But his situation becomes significant through his brother's understanding.

Self-indulgent and impulsive, cursed by a taste for the poetic without being given the talent to be a poet himself, Robert seems like poor stuff to make us perceive the tragic in life. Doris Falk puts the rationalist case against Robert, and against the play's final credibility.

> The insight he suddenly achieves comes not, however, from experience, but from intuition. Robert's inner and outer experience might logically have led him to the acceptance of death as a release after long suffering, but not necessarily to a revelation that sacrifice is the secret of life. Even if his conclusion could be said to have a psychological or poetic logic of its own, Robert's sudden arrival at such a conclusion makes it seem to be a *non sequitur.*

Robert seems to reach his conclusion suddenly only if one assumes that throughout the play he futilely seeks "the secret of life." He doesn't. He spends the play trying to avoid it, while he looks for the beautiful. Robert does not arrive suddenly at his conclusion. He is, at the last, finally unable to continue denying what he has known all along. Like *Oedipus the King, Beyond the Horizon* shows its characters struggling against becoming aware of things they have always known. Like Oedipus, Robert spends most of the play trying to avoid the unthinkable.

Robert's conclusion is not precisely that "sacrifice is the secret of life." The "secret"—if it is a secret—is the thing Robert has tried so long to deny: that despite all the suffering, life has nothing to do with human notions of meaning, justice, or order. Ruth's suffering may awaken Andy, not because suffering itself is meaningful or important, but because it results from continuing to demand that life eventually repay suffering or need or want with happiness or gratification.

"I'm a failure," Robert tells Andy, "and Ruth's another—but we can both justly lay some of the blame for our stumbling on God." God has made Ruth a person whose birth causes her mother's permanent paralysis and bitterness, and made Robert always to be ill and to fail. What is worse, both are given impulses toward hopefulness, the one poetic, the other romantic, that make it almost impossible for them to accept their lots.

As Robert continues, his understanding increases. When he speaks of Andy being "the deepest-dyed failure of the three" of them, the business failure is not the failure Robert means. Robert remembers Andy being a "creator when you loved the farm. You and life were in harmonious partnership." The loss of harmony causes Robert to understand that Andy has never valued what he has had and doesn't miss it now that it is gone. Without even knowing it, he tells Andy, "You've spent eight years running away from yourself." Andy's flight is symbolized by his gambling, an act that proves he has never in the least understood or valued the nature of what he has had.

It seems to me sound to compare Robert's understanding of Andy to the situation of the young Oedipus. Upon learning his monstrous *moira,* he does everything that intelligence, courage, and action can do to avert the mated disasters. The tragedy of Oedipus lies not in his fated acts, nor in the failure of his efforts to do the impossible. The tragedy lies in his confident belief that the world is a place where human will, intelligence, courage, and energy can supersede the casual weavings of the fates. The shock of discovery comes to Oedipus when he can no longer deny that the world is a place in which human power is trivial, no matter how far-sighted, energetic, and strong-willed a person may be. The tragedy of Oedipus lies in the mistaken understanding of the world generated by the most esteemed human qualities.

So too in *Beyond the Horizon.* By the end of the play Robert can force us to consider his discomforting view of the world. In the world he knows, human thought, hopes, wishes, and actions have practically no effect except upon the feelings and longings of those who think and act. We delude ourselves, Robert believes, if we imagine that reason and knowledge permit us to control the world or our lives. They symbolize humanity gone wrong, in conflict with the world and itself. The old gods of the seas, lightning, vengeance, and hospitality are forgotten in the age of the dynamo and the stock exchange. Any such beliefs are dreams, and Robert tries to awaken his brother from his sleep.

He understands that Andy, who has received so much more from the fates than he or Ruth, fails most greatly of the three when he turns his back on his talent. Therefore Robert urges him to find himself again, to awaken to the loss of harmony with his life and world that he has unknowingly sustained. Awakening to the loss will cause Andy to suffer, and suffering is what he must do, or else remain asleep. Such is the sense of Robert's strange injunction that his brother must marry Ruth and learn from her to know suffering. Robert's recognition transforms Andy's failure from the trivial to the tragic.

Andy is O'Neill's sample American, as fortunately endowed by the fates as the American land itself. But he has no more sense of natural economy than Americans have proved to have, turning away from the gifts of forests, soil, and climate. Andy gambling in the wheat pit to win something for nothing epitomizes the new American dream. He differs hardly at all from Ruth impulsively seeking escape from suffering in romance, or Robert convincing himself that he can fulfil his wanderer's spirit without leaving home.

Robert reaches more than "self-knowledge" at the end, and through Robert, O'Neill reaches authentically tragic depths. Robert discovers that the world is not the place he, Ruth, and Andy have assumed it to be, a place in which one can attain the new without relinquishing the old. Robert's recognition forces him to see the matter of his own dying as a small affair. He sacrifices the illusion that he is important. He compels our respect, not because he has a touch of the poet but in spite of it. Robert is no more heroic than old Oedipus, come to rave and be buried in Colonos, nor Philoctetes gone quirky from his wound and isolation, nor Ajax maddened into assassinating cattle, nor Heracles maddened into murdering his woman and children, nor Medea, nor the others. Like these strange figures, Robert has wounds and madness that alert us; they warn that he may know something about the world we need to know. The recognition of his own unimportance requires that we honour Robert with our most serious attention.

O'Neill repeats and develops the figure and the dilemma of Andy throughout his writing career, in characters as diverse as Brutus Jones, Marco Polo, William Brown, and Simon Harford. In 1946, almost three decades after writing *Beyond the Horizon*, with America at its height of optimistic self-confidence and world power in the afterglow of World War II, O'Neill tells a group of reporters, "[The United States,] instead of being the most successful country in the world, is . . . the greatest failure because it was given everything, more than any other country."

The principal theme of the unfinished "cycle" of plays O'Neill calls "A Tale of Possessors Dispossessed" is the loss of one's soul caused by believing one can possess the world. He continues to see America's failure represented in the betrayal of the land, a land that rewards cultivation by giving its people the easiest and richest life of any land on earth. America fails when its nationalist ideals tempt it into competing with European lands for economic and political power to wield over other nations. To do so it must sacrifice the aim of attunement with natural forces that once inspired it and once made the imaginary ideal American the fool of God.

Beyond the Horizon shows O'Neill's affinity with the fifth-century Greeks, one that exists more deeply in the mind than could be reached by calculated imitation or by years of rereading Nietzsche or the plays. It is a sensibility always aware of the danger of neglecting necessity, that knows the force of *moira* to exceed that of the gods. As with the Ajax or old Oedipus of Sophocles, or the Iphigeneia and Polyxena of Euripides, the sense of tragic exaltation comes only at the moment of the character's dying. In his manner of dying Robert Mayo compels our respect. He wins it when we witness him renounce his claim to a special status and rejoin his fellows in mortal humiliation and the impotence of ordinary life. The renunciation gives Robert's call to "Remember!" and his vision of the sun the status of prophecy.

Source: Stephen A. Black, "America's First Tragedy," in *English Studies in Canada,* Vol. 13, No. 2, June 1987, pp. 195–203.

SOURCES

Ben-Zvi, Linda, "Freedom and Fixity in the Plays of Eugene O'Neill," in *The Critical Response to Eugene O'Neill,* edited by John H. Houchin, Greenwood Press, 1993, p. 275, originally published in *Modern Drama,* Vol. 30, March 1988, pp. 16–27.

Carpenter, Frederic I., *Eugene O'Neill,* Twayne Publishers, 1979, p. 85.

Floyd, Virginia, *The Plays of Eugene O'Neill: A New Assessment,* Frederick Ungar Publishing Co., 1985, p. 143.

Fulton, A. R., *Drama and Theatre Illustrated by Seven Modern Plays,* Henry Holt and Company, 1946, p. 119.

Lacey, Robert, *Ford: The Men and the Machine,* Ballantine Books, 1993, pp. 103, 181.

O'Neill, Eugene, *Beyond the Horizon,* in *Four Plays by Eugene O'Neill,* Signet Classic, 1998, pp. 5–12, 16–18, 20, 26, 31–32, 34–35, 40, 42–43, 47, 50, 52–54, 61, 63, 66–68, 72, 79, 80, 84, 90, 93, 95–96, 99, 101, 103, 105, 107–08.

Roberts, J. M., *Twentieth Century: The History of the World, 1901 to 2000,* Penguin Books, 1999, pp. 119, 280.

Towse, J. Rankin, Review of *Beyond the Horizon,* in *The Critical Response to Eugene O'Neill,* edited by John H. Houchin, Greenwood Press, 1993, pp. 15–16, originally published in *New York Post,* February 4, 1920.

Trilling, Lionel, "Eugene O'Neill," in *The Critical Response to Eugene O'Neill,* edited by John H. Houchin, Greenwood Press, 1993, p. 165, originally published in *New Republic,* September 23, 1936.

Wainscott, Ronald H., *Staging O'Neill: The Experimental Years, 1920–1934,* Yale University Press, 1988, pp. 18, 20–21.

Wiksander, Ronald H., "O'Neill and the Cult of Sincerity," in *The Cambridge Companion to Eugene O'Neill,* edited by Michael Manheim, Cambridge University Press, 1998, p. 219.

FURTHER READING

Black, Stephen A., *Eugene O'Neill: Beyond Mourning and Tragedy,* Yale University Press, 2002.

Black is an English professor and a psychoanalyst, and he uses both of these skills in this exhaustively researched biography of O'Neill. Starting with his mother's addiction to morphine as a result of O'Neill's birth, the playwright's life was plagued by a number of tragedies, including alcoholism, family strife, a string of unhappy marriages, many deaths, and the estrangement of his children.

Brietzke, Zander, *The Aesthetics of Failure: Dynamic Structure in the Plays of Eugene O'Neill,* McFarland & Company, 2001.

Although some of O'Neill's plays are considered great works of art, other critics have noted the lack of quality in many of his published works. Brietzke examines this fact in light of O'Neill's own theory that tragedy requires failure. The book includes a chronological listing of O'Neill's plays, including production history, characters, and plot summaries.

Finch, Christopher, *In the Market: The Illustrated History of Financial Markets,* Abbeville Press, Inc., 2001.

In *Beyond the Horizon,* Andy tries his luck at investing in the commodities market, the latest of humanity's marketplaces. Finch's engaging book details the history of financial marketplaces from 3500 B.C. to the present. The book includes a time line of historical events, a glossary of financial terms, and more than one hundred short biographies of famous and infamous men and women in the financial world.

Liu, Hai-Ping, and Lowell Swortzell, eds., *Eugene O'Neill in China: An International Centenary Celebration,* Greenwood Publishing Group, 1992.

During the centennial celebration of O'Neill's birth, O'Neill scholars from around the world met in China to present their latest findings. This book collects some of the notable papers that were presented at the conference. Topics include the influence of Taoism on O'Neill's art, O'Neill's work in relation to the work of other playwrights, O'Neill's characterizations of women, and an examination of international productions of O'Neill's plays.

Shafer, Yvonne, ed., *Performing O'Neill: Conversations with Actors and Directors,* Palgrave, 2000.

For this volume, Shafer, one of the leading O'Neill scholars, conducted interviews with eleven famous actors and directors who have interpreted O'Neill's plays during the last century. Both actors and directors discuss the challenges they faced when bringing O'Neill's gritty visions of life to the stage. The stellar list of interviewees includes James Earl Jones, Jason Robards, Theresa Wright, Theodore Mann, and Jane Alexander.

Shaughnessy, Edward L., *Down the Nights and Down the Days: Eugene O'Neill's Catholic Sensibility,* University of Notre Dame Press, 2000.

Due to O'Neill's renunciation of his Catholic faith as a teenager, most critics have ignored this aspect of the playwright's life as an influence on his work. Shaughnessy, however, argues that O'Neill's Irish-Catholic upbringing influenced the moral quality of his work and examines this idea while discussing several of O'Neill's plays.

Siebold, Thomas, ed., *Readings on Eugene O'Neill,* Greenhaven Press, 1998.

This accessible, diverse collection of O'Neill criticism includes offerings from literary analysts, psychologists, playwrights, and reviewers. The book gives a broad perspective on O'Neill's work without getting bogged down in specific critical debates.

Both Your Houses

MAXWELL ANDERSON

1933

Maxwell Anderson's *Both Your Houses* is a political satire that is as relevant today as it was when it was first performed in 1933. The title comes from Shakespeare's *Romeo and Juliet,* in which Mercutio calls in his dying speech for "a plague on both your houses," referring to two warring families, the Montagues and the Capulets. In Anderson's play, the title refers to the two houses of Congress, the Senate and the House of Representatives.

The play takes place during the Great Depression and concerns an idealistic young congressman who takes the surprising position of opposing a bill that provides money for a huge construction project in his district. Alan McClean has found out since his election that the price being charged to the taxpayers for construction of the dam in his state is much more than it needs to be; in addition, there are hundreds of other, unrelated expenditures that have been added to the dam project to buy the support of congressmen from other states. Though his fight will probably cost him future support from his peers, from his constituents, and from the woman in whom he is interested (the daughter of the Appropriations Committee chairman), McClean struggles to gather opposition to a bill he knows is wrong. Throughout the play, Anderson keeps audiences balanced between the young man's idealism and the accepted way of doing business. He questions the assumption that bribes and compromise are the only way to get anything achieved in the political arena.

AUTHOR BIOGRAPHY

From high school on, it was clear that Maxwell Anderson was destined to work with words. What was not yet clear was that he would end up being one of the most prolific and respected playwrights of his generation. He was born in Atlantic, Pennsylvania, on December 15, 1888. Because his father was a Baptist preacher with no established congregation, the Anderson family moved frequently when Maxwell was young, and his education was often interrupted; still, he maintained a passion for reading and writing. He attended the University of North Dakota, graduating in 1911.

Anderson taught high school English in San Francisco for two years after graduating from college. During that time, a prestigious national magazine, the *New Republic,* published several of his poems, and Anderson earned a graduate degree from Stanford University, which helped him become the head of the English department at Whittier College in 1917. He only held that position for a little more than a year, however. His views against war made him unpopular at a time when the United States was fighting in World War I, and they cost him his job. The *New Republic* gave him a job on its editorial staff, and for years he supported himself writing for it and for several newspapers.

To make money, Anderson taught himself how to write dramas. His first play, the war drama *What Price Glory*? (1924), was a success. Co-written with World War I veteran Laurence Stallings, it ran for 299 performances and gave Anderson the financial security to quit journalism and devote his attention entirely to playwrighting. He went on to have thirty of his works produced, winning the Pulitzer Prize for Drama for *Both Your Houses* in 1933, and the New York Critics' Circle Award for *Winterset* in 1935 and for *High Tor* in 1937. He is well remembered for his work in film, having written screenplays for such classics as *Key Largo* (1948), and the 1932 film adaptation of W. Somerset Maugham's *Rain*, as well as lyrics for the popular Broadway song "September Song" and the musical *Lost in the Stars*.

As a playwright, Anderson is best remembered for the range of his style and the compassion of his worldview. He was able to satirize the complexity of American politics in *Both Your Houses* and to explore historical drama in plays about Queen Elizabeth, Anne Boleyn, and Mary, Queen of Scots. He adapted works by Lytton Strachey and Alan Paton for the stage. He was one of the few writers who could draw significant audiences to see plays written in verse as well as in the common language.

Anderson's personal life was happy but uneven. He married his first wife, Margaret Haskett, in 1911. She died of a stroke in 1931. In 1933, he married his second wife, Gertrude Maynard; she committed suicide after twenty years of marriage, in 1953. He married Gilda Oakleaf in 1954, and she was with him until his 1959 death from a stroke in Stamford, Connecticut.

PLOT SUMMARY

Act 1

Both Your Houses takes place in the House Office Building in Washington, D.C. The first scene is set in the office of the chairman of the House Appropriations Committee. Marjorie Gray, the daughter of the chairman and also his secretary, is talking on the phone to Alan McClean, a young congressman from Nevada. She is joined by an older secretary known as Bus. Bus announces that she has been fired by her boss, Eddie Wister, who has hired a pretty, inexperienced secretary provided for him by a steel company.

Throughout the scene, various persons pass through the office discussing the upcoming vote on H. R. 2007, an appropriations bill that designates millions of dollars for a new dam in Nevada. Many congressmen have been trying to get their special interests attached to the project, either to support their own investments or to appease their voters. Marjorie's father, Simeon Gray, is struggling to keep the size of the bill reasonable without losing the votes that he will need to pass it.

Alan McClean arrives too late for an appointment with Gray. He explains that he wanted to tell Gray that he opposes the bill, even though his district would benefit from it; the contractors' estimates for building the dam are much too high, and all of the other expenditures that have been added to it make it a huge, unnecessary cost to the taxpayers.

In the second scene, in the room where the committee is meeting, Simeon Gray is rejecting one amendment to H. R. 2007 after another. His colleagues are disappointed when their pet projects are cut from the package, but they are willing to go along with their leader. One measure is explained to be necessary to keep the support of the Non-Partisan League and the Farmer-Labor contingent, but Gray strikes it from the bill as being too costly. Alan enters and explains his opposition to the bill, adding that he has found out through private investigators that some of the politicians will benefit personally from these appropriations, a statement that causes general amusement. After the meeting breaks up, Alan tells Gray that he found out from some papers mistakenly given to him by his investigators that a penitentiary to be paid for by the bill is in Gray's district. Even though Gray says he was not aware of this, he admits that his support of the bill would look like graft.

Alan explains his frustration with the committee to Bus. She tells him that his own secretary has been spying on him for other politicians, so he fires his secretary and hires her.

Maxwell Anderson

Act 2

Scene 1 of the second act takes place three days later. Sol Fitzmaurice enters and tells Marjorie that, with Alan's leadership, the independent factions that had their projects removed from H. R. 2007 are close to having enough votes to stop the bill. Congressmen Eddie Wister, Levering, and Wingblatt enter, discussing their efforts to gather support for the bill and Alan's successes with the Non-Partisan League. They ask Gray to add more money to the bill for special projects that will make the dissenters happy, but he tells them that that will only make the president more likely to veto the whole bill. When they're alone together, Eddie asks Gray for fifteen million dollars to be added for decommissioning two battleships, a move that will benefit his supporters in the steel industry. He hints that he knows about Gray's interest in a bank that will be saved from failure by the penitentiary the bill provides for his district, revealing that the information Alan got by mistake was requested by a steel company chairman. Gray is blackmailed into supporting the extra appropriation.

Alan and Bus discuss the concessions that he has had to make in order to gain opposition to H. R. 2007. He tells her he had to "pledge myself to an increased tariff on lumber and an increased tariff on wheat, a new system of landbanks, an embargo on circus animals—including Siamese cats!" He decides that it would be more direct to approach Sol, who earlier made a speech about having been an idealist in his youth, and try to get his support. Sol acts sympathetic but resists Alan. Their conversation gives Alan an idea, though; he decides to load the bill with so many special requests that the other congressmen will be embarrassed to ask for so much tax money.

The second scene of act 2 takes place in the committee room. Some representatives are complaining that special projects they favored were cut from the bill, while other projects, such as Eddie's expensive battleship appropriation, were spared. When Alan enters the room, he has a list of all of the appropriations that have been proposed for the bill throughout its history, and he recommends that they all be added, raising its cost from 40 million dollars to 475 million. The committee members each see the chance to get the appropriations they wanted, even though Gray can see that such a bloated bill will only gain them public ridicule and will be vetoed by the president.

After the meeting, Gray talks to Alan about the bank in his district, explaining that, while he does stand to profit personally, the more important thing is that the people he represents need the proposed penitentiary project to ease their poverty. After Alan leaves, Gray explains to Marjorie an even more pressing interest: the bank has lied to its auditors, and if it closes this lie will be found out. Gray, as a member of the board of directors, could go to jail.

Act 3

Scene 1 of the third act takes place three days after the previous scene. The committee members, including Wingblatt, Peebles, and Dell, discuss the work they have done to have H. R. 2007 approved by the entire House of Representatives. Joe Ebner, one of the people who is enthusiastically opposing the bill, tells them that the opposition will stand behind Alan. Sol manages to talk some members into changing their votes so that the bill has the majority that it needs to pass; however, the president has promised to veto the bill, so it needs support from at least two-thirds of the representatives. Sol talks to Alan about the way the government is run, telling him that defeating the bill will ruin his effectiveness in Congress and make it impossible for him to help anyone ever again, but Alan stands by his principles. Marjorie tells Alan about the threat her father faces if the bill fails. He considers what she says, not wanting to harm Gray, whom he admires greatly, but in the end he decides that a matter of principle is more important than any one man, and he must therefore vote against wasting the country's money.

The second scene takes place after the vote has been taken. H. R. 2007 has passed the House with more than a two-thirds majority. Passage in the Senate, after such a strong showing in the House of Representatives, is certain. Instead of stopping a forty-million-dollar expenditure, Alan has assured a waste of tax dollars that is more than ten times greater. The committee members are ebullient, singing and planning a large dinner celebration, and they thank Alan for creating a bill that serves them all. Allen is outraged. Even in defeat, he stands by his principles and threatens to go to the press with the story of how much the various congressmen stand to gain from this huge appropriation. The old established politicians do not worry, certain that the public outrage will blow over.

CHARACTERS

Bus

Bus is an older, established secretary who has worked for nine congressmen. When the play begins, she has just been fired by her boss, Eddie Wister, so that he can hire another secretary sent to him by the steel industry. As she is saying goodbye to Marjorie, she hears Alan McClean talking about his attempts to stop the Appropriations Committee from passing H. R. 2007, and she offers to help him with her experience about how the system works. Bus is sometimes hopeful that something can be done about the corrupt system, but she is usually fatalistic. It is Bus who has the last line of the play; when Sol brags that he will never be stopped, she says, ''Maybe,'' showing that she is still open to the possibility of a world without graft.

Dell

Dell is one of the members of the House Appropriations Committee and a supporter of Gray. Dell makes deals with congressmen from other states in order to get H. R. 2007 passed.

Joe Ebner

Ebner is one of the political independents in Congress who does not have the power to force the projects he supports into H. R. 2007, until McClean shows up as a leader. With McClean's guidance, he is enthusiastic about defeating the bill and creating a new system of order in American politics.

Farnum

A congressman from California, one of Farnum's pet projects is a national park at the home of Joaquin Miller, although he does not know who Miller is.

Solomon Fitzmaurice

Solomon Fitzmaurice, Sol for short, is a representative of all that is wrong with the political system. He is intelligent, but he hides his shrewdness by whining about not making much money. He is friendly to all, and pretends to empathize with both sides in a disagreement. He is more interested in drinking liquor than in working for his constituents. And his main concern is to pass legislation that will lead directly to his own financial gain. In particular, Sol is interested in getting the Atlantic Fleet to dock for the winter at Rocky Point, Long Island, so that sailors on leave will spend money at a housing project he owns. When Alan McClean decides to oppose the established politicians on the appropriations bill, he seeks out Sol as an accomplice, remembering that Sol once said he himself was an idealist when he came to Congress. Sol tells him an inspiring story but tries to persuade McClean to change his mind, offering him a particularly cynical view of politics: "The sole business of government is graft, special privilege, and corruption—with a by-product of order." Sol is fiercely dedicated to Gray and is defensive of the chairman's reputation, though he is willing to make fun of all other congresspersons, including himself.

Marjorie Gray

Marjorie is the daughter of Congressman Simeon Gray and is also his secretary. In addition, she has a budding personal relationship with Alan McClean; when Bus suggests that he seems to look at her with adoration, Marjorie answers, "I wouldn't really mind!" Her affection for the two men puts Marjorie in an awkward position. At first, she seems to be grooming McClean so that he will turn out to be as smart and principled in the business of politics as her father. When she finds out that he has information he intends to use against Gray if the bill is passed, Marjorie's sympathies are solidly with her father. When she becomes suspicious about whether her father's involvement with a potentially lucrative deal is as innocent as he has told her, he explains that losing the deal could make him susceptible to punishment, even imprisonment; and so Marjorie begs McClean to drop his opposition.

Simeon Gray

Also referred to as Sime, Gray is the most powerful politician in the play. He is the chairman of the House Appropriations Committee. One of his duties is to make sure the president will approve of all of the provisions in a bill before Congress sends it to him formally. Gray is considered one of the most honest men in the Congress—the one who is most effective in holding waste and corruption to a minimum. Alan finds out that Gray has a secret reason for wanting H. R. 2007 to pass: one of its provisions would greatly help the bank in Gray's home district, and he holds a substantial interest in the bank. Gray explains that his financial concern is secondary and that he is really looking out for the economic welfare of his constituents, but privately he explains to Marjorie that he, as a member of the board of directors, could face a jail sentence if the bank were to fail. When the bill passes the committee with a ridiculously large budget, Gray uses all of his influence to make sure that the House passes it.

Levering

An influential congressman, Levering is "the presidential mouthpiece—the official whipper-in of the administration." He has a long talk with Alan, trying gently but firmly to persuade him to vote for the legislation. Some of the other congressmen call him Dizzy or Disraeli, after Benjamin Disraeli, a nineteenth-century British prime minister known for great foreign and domestic achievements.

Mark

The clerk who delivers the mail, Mark is the voice of common people in the play. Regarding the activities going on around the House offices, he asks, "What good's all this—that's what I want to know?"

Alan McClean

McClean is the central character in this drama, a young congressman who is willing to fight to change the system. He was elected to Congress on a platform of getting a dam built so that farmers in his home state, Nevada, could irrigate their land. At first, it is assumed that McClean will naturally support H. R. 2007 because it provides money for the dam, but he withdraws support when he finds out that the dam is costing many times more than it should and that his own election was financed by construction groups who would benefit from building the dam. McClean's father was a newspaper publisher who took a stand against political corruption, and McClean is so honest that he hires a private investigative firm to examine his own campaign. He opposes the bill's passage because it will waste taxpayer money. Even when Marjorie, the woman he is interested in, begs him to stop his opposition to the bill, he feels that the interests of the majority come before his own interests.

Many experienced politicians see Alan as naïve in his idealism, but he is clever enough to change his tactics: when it appears that his campaign to kill the bill will not work, he supports it but loads it with so much obvious waste that the public cannot fail to see it. He is shrewd enough to think that politicians will shy away from the bad publicity that such waste would cause, but he underestimates their greed; most of them are so enthusiastic about voting in a huge appropriations bill that they cannot see the inevitable consequence of having to face the voters. Alan ends up still willing to fight against government waste on the behalf of the American taxpayers even though no one else believes he will be successful.

Miss Bess McMurtry

McMurtry is a congresswoman on the Appropriations Committee who supports money used to increase the number of maternity nurses, and to distribute birth control information and contraceptives.

Merton

Alan McClean's secretary at the start of the play, Merton is fired at the end of act 1 when Alan finds out that he has been keeping an eye on the young congressman's activities for other, established politicians and reporting to them on a regular basis.

Greta Nillson

See Bus

Peebles

A congressman from the South, Peebles has a defeatist attitude about appropriations, telling others who have had their pet projects cut that the South was left for decades after the Civil War with little financial support from the United States government.

Sneden

One of the congressmen who supports the bill, Sneden worries that the time spent attending to government matters is keeping him away from the golf course.

Trumper

Trumper is a congressman who does not appear on stage but is talked about. He is one of the "swing votes," willing to vote against the appropriations bill for concessions that are ridiculous, such as free seeds and free silver. (The free silver issue involves a suspicion by the common people that rich people were trying to control the government by keeping silver out of circulation.) Alan is astonished that Trumper thinks of himself as a logical candidate for the presidency.

Wingblatt

One of the members of the Appropriations Committee, Wingblatt is dedicated to seeing that the bill that is negotiated will have enough support to pass both houses of Congress.

Eddie Wister

Eddie is a deal-maker who has held up the committee's business at the beginning of the play because he has been in New York making deals with the steel industry. Bus is fired as his secretary so that he can hire Miss Corey, a pretty blonde with no experience who has been the secretary for Col. Sprague of Appalachian Steel. He supports an appropriation on behalf of The Committee of 48 on National Defense, which, despite its political-sounding name, is a group of steel companies. It later comes up that Eddie has had private detectives examine Simeon Gray in order to get information with which to blackmail him.

THEMES

Moral Corruption and Decline

In this play, Sol Fitzmaurice represents a refined form of moral corruption. Sol's only interests are drinking and increasing his own personal wealth, which indicates that any sense he may have had once of using his office to serve the public has long ago evaporated. When faced with a young idealist like Alan McClean, however, Sol is able to show his empathy, remembering his own roots as a young idealist. He acts indignant at the news that there are members of Congress who would benefit from appropriations, but Sol's corruption is so thorough that no one takes his indignation seriously. His speech to Alan about how he became "a fat crook" in order to make his constituents happy might seem tinged with remorse, but, despite any regrets he might have, Sol throws himself into the corrupt lifestyle with zeal, and makes it possible to pass the graft-laden final form of the bill.

The only area in which Sol does not show corruption is in his devotion to Simeon Gray. He accepts Gray's ruling that his pet project must be dropped from the bill without putting up a struggle, and later, when Alan tells him about the penitentiary in Gray's district, Sol is certain in his disbelief: "Simeon's never been hooked up with anything." The point seems to be that, even when the congressmen lose faith in their public mission and turn to crooked means, they still might admire others who are able to work within the system and avoid being tainted with corruption.

Absurdity

Anderson presents the legislative branch of the government as an absurd place, where a bill about a dam can only pass if it has money for battleships and tariffs against circus animals. It is shown to be a place where politicians agree about the social good of a proposal like McMurtry's call for nurses and birth control, but then vote to appropriate money for making the navy dock its ships in a port where one of the congressmen owns real estate and speakeasies.

The problem that Alan McClean encounters is that he enters this situation thinking that it will bow to the rules of logic. He makes the common sense suggestion that wasteful spending should be stopped because the taxpayers cannot afford extravagant spending, particularly not in the middle of an economic crisis like the Depression. He even fails to see the sense of supporting the people who paid for his own election, if this support will mean wasting the taxpayers' money.

This leads to the ultimate form of legislative absurdity. Attempting to draw public attention to just how bloated H. R. 2007 really is, Alan adds hundreds of irrelevant measures with the assumption that the congressmen could not vote for such a senseless bill. Instead, absurdity wins the day. The bill does in fact attract massive support. The representatives care very little about what the public will think, knowing that the whole absurd process is so complex that there is little chance of public outrage. Alan's attempt to save the taxpayer 40 million dollars ends up costing them 475 million.

TOPICS FOR FURTHER STUDY

- Research recent legislation about campaign finance reform and discuss how these measures would have affected the situation described in *Both Your Houses*.
- View Frank Capra's 1939 movie, *Mr. Smith Goes to Washington,* about an idealistic man of the people who finds corruption and dishonesty in Congress. Compare how the movie handles this subject to how Anderson handles it in the play.
- Search the Internet for stories about legal and illegal ways in which corporations have given favors to politicians. Make a chart classifying the types of graft into different categories.
- Find out the names and addresses of your congressional representatives. Write to them, asking how they handle improper offers from wealthy individuals and organizations that want to influence their votes in Congress through donations or favors.

Cynicism

The political system in this play is fueled by cynicism. When Alan arrives and points out the obvious about corrupt congressmen and the unfair ways in which the committee decides what to finance, he is laughed at and pitied. The established members of the committee do not dislike what he has to say, nor do they disagree with it. Instead, they feel that they have heard it all before, have faced similar matters of conscience, and have come to the conclusion that they cannot change the system. This is shown in Sol's speech, in which he explains that what constituents expect of their congressional representative is that "he gets what they want out of the

Treasury, and fixes the Tariff for 'em, and sees that they don't get gypped out of their share of the plunder.'' Cynicism is also seen in the way in which an overwhelming majority of the House turns away from the ordinary practices that shape a bill and stampede to pass H. R. 2007 because each is focused only on what small benefit it offers him.

Simeon Gray is an example of virtue among these cynical politicians because he has maintained a small degree of selflessness. Unlike Alan, Gray has been in Congress long enough to have had his ideals destroyed, but he still maintains enough integrity to act for the common good; Marjorie, Sol, and the others who know him do not believe that his penitentiary deal is for his own enrichment but that it is, at worst, a mistake. However, the author seems to take a more cynical view of Gray than even the cynical political operatives in the play. While they all look up to Gray's small degree of honesty, the play emphasizes the dishonesty that his job requires. Except for Alan, none of the characters in the play seem to realize how awful it is that Congress must do so many bad things and waste so much money on corrupt and useless projects in order to do even the slightest bit of good.

Progress

The reason that Alan thinks he can change the system that has corrupted so many other hopeful politicians is that he believes in progress. The other, experienced members try to convince him that he will face the same pressures they did and that he will either conform to the way things are or go back home when his term is over without having made any difference to the world. They all have stories like this; those who do not explain their personal sense of defeat at the hand of the system show it by following along with the corrupt practices unquestioningly. But Alan, who is an educated man interested in the larger scope of things, has faith that the system that crushed the spirits of the other politicians will eventually be overcome. At the moment when he has been defeated, when he is most likely to admit that there is nothing one man can do except go along and hope to do some occasional good, Alan is defiant in his optimism:

> It takes about a hundred years to tire this country of trickery—and we're fifty years overdue right now. That's my warning. And I'd feel pretty damn pitiful and lonely saying it to you, if I didn't believe there are a hundred million people who are with me, a hundred million people who are disgusted enough to turn from you to something else.

Alan's faith in progress is, of course, not shared by the other politicians, who have based their careers on the premise that the future will be like the past. Their success in passing a ridiculously bloated bill like H. R. 2007, along with their lack of concern over Alan's threat to expose them all as crooked, seem to imply that Anderson does not believe Alan to be very astute. Still, the play ends with the faintest hint that progress is possible; when Sol, the old-time politician, brags that he does not expect the system to change in his lifetime, Bus, who is also a voice of experience, states flatly, ''Maybe.'' This is nothing like the hopeful speeches Alan makes, but it is Anderson's way of showing that Alan is not necessarily deluded in his optimism.

STYLE

Irony

Although the word ''irony'' is used often in ordinary conversation, it is not always used correctly. Irony is a literary technique in which an author uses language in such a way that it conveys the opposite of its literal meaning. Several times during *Both Your Houses*, Anderson has Sol Fitzmaurice give ironic speeches. Audiences know that Sol is corrupt; from his very first scene, he is drinking in the office and taking enjoyment from flouting the rules. His behavior is particularly corrupt in light of the fact that he is a lawmaker during Prohibition, the time in American history when drinking alcohol was illegal. ''On my soul, I haven't touched liquor since before breakfast,'' Sol says, in a sentence that is formulated as if he were taking a pledge of virtue. When he is concerned about his thinly disguised bid for public money, he expresses his concern like a naughty boy pouting: ''Everyone in Washington has tacked something onto the bill except yours truly,'' he whines, ''and I'm the one man that deserves it.'' The item he wants ''tacked on'' is the diversion of the navy so that its ships dock at the town where he owns real estate and speakeasies, because this will raise the value of his investments.

When Sol talks to Alan, his words are especially convincing. Taken out of context, his explanations of how the system made him corrupt could seem almost remorseful, provided that audiences fail to remember who is talking and the character traits that Sol has presented previously. Similarly, when he tells Alan that he has to be involved with dirty politics because ''you can't compete . . . without being a viper,'' his speech is almost believable if one ignores the corruption in which Sol has already been involved. Anderson does not give stage directions that tell the actor who plays Sol whether the character is being insincere when he speaks dejectedly and humbly about his own part in political corruption, but he does indicate Sol's insincerity by making his words contradict his behavior.

Verisimilitude

Verisimilitude is a literary technique in which an author creates situations that are so lifelike that the audience believes they are factual. Anderson achieves verisimilitude by peppering his dialogue with political jargon that one might hear in a congressional office. In addition, he keeps the pace of the drama moving briskly, imitating the pandemonium that might go on around the Appropriations Committee before a major bill is brought to a vote. He also convinces his audience of the reality of the situation by including unexpected touches of realism. For instance, when Eddie enlists Marjorie to help his new secretary, he offers her anything she wants, and her response is that she will do it for a cigarette. While women smoking tobacco was not unheard of in 1933, still many audience members would have been unprepared to see the modern office woman being so casual about a traditionally male vice. This would lead them to feel that the play was teaching them about the way the world really works. The same effect holds true for Miss McMurty's request for an appropriation for birth control and contraceptives, a controversial issue that was not discussed as publicly in 1933 as it is today. At the time, federal obscenity laws were used to prosecute physicians who prescribed birth control, although strong opposition from women's health advocates served to change the law by the end of the decade. Audiences may have been aware of the issues, but those familiar with the debate about birth control would probably not have thought that their elected representatives would dismiss the matter so lightly.

Didactic

Didactic works are produced to teach some moral, spiritual, or practical lesson. While all works have a moral perspective, didactic ones put teaching a lesson to the front, making it the main goal. This is often done at the expense of artistry, which is why the word ''didactic'' is usually applied negatively. Such works can be unsuccessful because audiences tune out their messages once they realize that the writer is preaching to them.

The charge of didacticism could be leveled against *Both Your Houses*. Maxwell Anderson clearly has a political agenda that he wants audiences to agree with. The question of whether the play is merely a way to broadcast his political views depends on whether he has broken rules of reality in order to control his audience's thoughts. For instance: *Could* Congress start out with a forty-million-dollar appropriations bill and end up with one more than ten times that? *Could* a major economic force like the steel industry have the Appropriations Committee chairman investigated and use what it learns to have a senseless, fifteen-million dollar appropriation added to the budget? If audiences feel that Anderson is stretching reality too far in order to make them agree with his position, then he is guilty of didacticism. On the other hand, if such things are possible, however unlikely, then the play is simply exercising creative license with its material. The basic issue is one of fairness: it would be unfair for a writer to win audiences to his point of view by warning them about a situation that does not actually exist.

HISTORICAL CONTEXT

The Great Depression

America experienced a time of great economic prosperity in the 1920s; World War I, from 1914 to 1918, decimated European manufacturing facilities and reorganized much of the Western world in such a way that America was in a position of unusual stability when it was over. Throughout the twenties, unemployment and inflation were both low, which meant that people had money, lived comfortably,

COMPARE & CONTRAST

- **1933:** The workings of Congress take place behind closed doors. Newspapers cover important stories when they can get information from members.

  Today: There are cable television stations devoted to covering Congress. Although some meetings still occur in secret, there are many more educated reporters examining the fine details of bills as well as many more congressional staffers and lobbyists willing to provide background information.

- **1933:** America is in the midst of the Great Depression. The year that *Both Your Houses* is first performed, the Roosevelt administration passes the Federal Emergency Relief Act, granting $500 million to the states in order to help ease unemployment.

  Today: The economy is fine-tuned, to a degree, by the Federal Reserve Board, which uses its power to raise and lower interest rates to try to keep the economy growing and stable.

- **1933:** Steel is one of America's most powerful industries, and people are concerned that the steel companies have unfair influence with the government.

  Today: Many of America's steel companies have closed their U.S. plants, as production has shifted to cheaper overseas locations. Energy and telecommunications are the industries that spend the most lobbying for government influence.

- **1933:** There have only been two women in the Senate and four in the House of Representatives, three of whom have taken office within the past year.

  Today: Thirty-one women have served in the Senate, with thirteen of these serving currently. One hundred and eighty-four women have served in the House of Representatives.

and were able to invest. Many invested in speculative ventures, which continued to raise profits through sales to other investors even when they were not connected to any actual products. The phrase ''Roaring Twenties'' was coined to capture the sense of excitement and fun that characterized the decade.

The fun stopped on October 29, 1929, one of the most significant dates in American history. This was the date of the stock market crash. In that one day, the Dow Jones Industrial Average, which had been slowly losing its momentum, dropped sharply, creating a rush to sell off stocks quickly, at a loss. By the end of the year, the United States economy had lost fifteen billion dollars, a number that eventually rose to fifty billion—about the entire cost of World War I.

People who had started the year with secure investment portfolios ended it looking for any low-wage jobs that became available. The sudden loss of investment capital had a rippling effect throughout the economy. People could not repay loans, and banks closed; companies could not borrow from banks and went out of business; when businesses closed, they left their workers without any incomes, and when workers could not pay the mortgages on their houses, it hurt the banks that had survived the first wave of the Depression.

The president at the time was Herbert Hoover, who had come into office in April of 1929, when the economy was strong. After the crash, he resisted calls to use federal funds to ease unemployment, insisting that the situation would correct itself. He eventually used money to aid endangered banks, but his refusal to create new jobs made him immensely unpopular. In 1933, Franklin Delano Roosevelt took over the presidency. His economic program, dubbed the ''New Deal,'' included billions of dollars to provide jobs for Americans through such agencies as the Tennessee Valley Authority, responsible for, among other things, building and managing Wilson Dam; the Civilian Conservation Corps, which employed about three million young men to tend the nation's resources; and the Works Progress Administration, which employed unskilled laborers as well as talented artists. Unemployed Americans who did not pay taxes—that is, the vast majority—appreciated Roosevelt's efforts and did not mind the huge expenditures from the treasury. Roosevelt was the only American president to be elected to four terms.

CRITICAL OVERVIEW

As time has passed, Maxwell Anderson has been best remembered for the plays he wrote in verse, which attempted to revive a lost art. When he was writing, he was generally associated with the social focus of his plays, although his reputation as a social critic has not held up as well as the reputations of other playwrights. At one time, for example, Anderson was considered almost an equal of Eugene O'Neill, who also satirized the modern social order and drew from theater's rich history; now, O'Neill's works are performed much more often than Anderson's. Because political issues change, *Both Your Houses* could be expected to lose relevance as time goes by, but critics still consider it fondly, even though they do not write about it as one of Anderson's major works.

When it was first performed, the play was considered timely, ground-breaking material. In 1933, Barrett H. Clark gave this assessment of its importance: ''*Both Your Houses* is perhaps more important for the direction that it takes than as an actual achievement: it is, I believe, the first American play concerned exclusively and seriously with federal political intrigue.'' Whether or not Clark was right, satire of the complex government system was rare enough at that time that it deserved mention—a concept that might seem quaint to modern readers who are used to seeing the government ridiculed.

Since literary critics concentrated on Anderson's historical plays and his experiments with verse, *Both Your Houses* was generally neglected. Because Anderson was an important writer, long

Playbill cover from the 1933 theatrical production of Both Your Houses, *directed by Worthington Miner*

studies of his career were eventually published, and these usually included a few notes about the play, although they did not examine it in depth as they did works like *High Tor* and *Winterset*. Mabel Driscoll Bailey wrote in her 1957 book *Maxwell Anderson: The Playwright As Prophet* that it is an ''important'' play: ''[For] all its serious implications, the play is highly entertaining, not only in the cynical dialogue, but even in the central action in which the hero defeats his own ends by trying to beat his adversaries at their own game of clever manipulation.'' The importance of *Both Your Houses* is the aspect that most critics have attached themselves to, although many let its serious subject matter distract them from appreciating its entertainment value.

Finally, some critics have charged that the play does not actually deal with the social issues that it raises because Alan McClean does not, for all of his disgust at the system, have any better alternative to offer. Alfred S. Shivers dismissed the concerns of such critics as unfairly expecting too much of both the playwright and his character, since Anderson could not be expected

> to have figured out on short notice what has eluded for centuries the most eminent philosophers, social scien-

tists, and statesmen. Anyway, no playwright is or should be required to offer a solution to the social problems he presents: it is quite enough to lay forth the problem in an entertaining manner.

It is, in fact, the very insolubility of the situation presented in *Both Your Houses* that makes the issues outlined in the play relevant to this day.

CRITICISM

David Kelly

Kelly teaches creative writing and literature at Oakton Community College in Illinois. In this essay, Kelly explains why Anderson was right to keep Alan McClean's relationships with Congressman Gray and his daughter in the background of the play, while another writer might have made them the focus of the story.

In the earliest versions of his satirical drama *Both Your Houses*, Maxwell Anderson left his protagonist, Alan McClean, the high-minded outsider bent on reorganizing the political structure of the House of Representatives, incapable of taking any definitive action. Alan sees his deepest beliefs violated by those around him, and he knows that he can impose some measure of honesty, but he also knows that doing so will endanger Simeon Gray's career. The play was more centered around human relations in those early drafts than it is in the final, published version. McClean's bond with Gray and Gray's daughter, Marjorie, dictated his behavior then, and the complex political maneuvering that goes on before a bill is passed was used as colorful background. The earlier versions told a more traditional story, one that audiences would feel comfortable with, framing the issues with familiar dynamics. It relied on the human tendency to care that the boy loves the girl; that the young man finds out that his hero is flawed; that the youth must surpass his father-figure and replace him; and that the youth defends his vulnerable old mentor.

These are elements that appear in the version of *Both Your Houses* that was eventually published in 1933, but by the time the play had been refined and rewritten they were pushed into the background, functioning as mere plot complications rather than as crucial elements that drive the action. In many ways, this de-emphasis of the human aspect weakens the play, leaving it to hold audiences' interest solely with its depiction of bureaucratic procedures. In the broader scope, though, it was wise of Anderson to give up the traditional emphasis on interpersonal relationships. Pushing them out of the way in order to show just what actually goes on in the legislature is a move that takes some nerve, but it pays off in the end, and makes the play a more unique, unpredictable work. Anderson seems to have found what is at the heart of this situation; it is not a play about love or respect, although it does have room to include those two elements, briefly. The play's impact is gained from its disregard of human emotions; this enables it to show the inhumanity of government policies that affect the lives of all citizens.

The relationship between McClean and Marjorie is presented as being so faint and uneven that it is barely discernible. Viewers seated late, or readers who have trouble discerning who is who in the play's turbulent first pages, might understandably fail to realize that there is a relationship between them. When Bus, the older and more experienced secretary, notes that there are clear signs of interest from McClean, Marjorie hopes that Bus is right. The matter is never discussed after that. Marjorie and McClean have lunch dates, and she does hesitate before asking him to give up his crusade to defeat the appropriations bill, but aside from that the only sign of affection between them is her continuous use of his first name. Readers can sense some bond of affection between them, and audiences can have even more of a sense of this depending on how the characters are played on stage, but there is nothing in the script that indicates a love affair that is torrid or deep.

In fact, the relationship between Marjorie and McClean shows itself to be exactly what it is: the shadow of a plot device important in an earlier version but not really needed here. Marjorie worries about McClean when she is talking to the old gang around the committee room, but she is in no position to offer him any aid or comfort. She is too much a product of the political machine to be drawn in to his idealistic plan to change the way the federal govern-

WHAT DO I READ NEXT?

- This play is often referred to as an example of Depression-era political thought, pointing out how the rich feed off the labor of the poor. Perhaps the purest example of the pro-labor movement in the 1930s is Clifford Odets's 1935 play *Waiting for Lefty,* in which taxi drivers in a union hall discuss life and their place in it. It is available in the paperback *Waiting for Lefty and Other Plays,* published by Grove Press in 1993.
- Anderson was often said to be the artistic successor of Eugene O'Neill, who also wrote about sweeping historical subjects. Many people consider O'Neill's 1939 drama *The Iceman Cometh,* about an assortment of lower-class people in a run-down bar, to be his best work. It has been published by Vintage Books in a 1999 edition.
- Anderson is remembered for his experiments writing dramas in blank verse. Readers will find his best examples of this style, written between 1929 and 1939, in *Eleven Verse Plays,* published in 1968 by Harcourt, Brace and World. Included are the favorites *Winterset, Valley Forge,* and *Key Largo.*
- Anderson's daughter, Hesper, is an accomplished screenwriter. She recently published her memoir of what it was like growing up with a famous writer and associating with the greatest literary figures of the thirties and forties. *South Mountain Road: A Daughter's Journey of Discovery,* by Hesper Anderson, was published by Simon & Schuster in 2000.
- Readers can gain a sense of what Anderson was thinking when he wrote this play and of his long and varied career from *Dramatists in America: Letters of Maxwell Anderson, 1912–1958.* It was published by University of North Carolina Press in 1977.
- One of the more recent biographies of Anderson is Nancy J. Doran Hazelton's *Maxwell Anderson and the New York Stage,* published in 1991 by Library Research Associates. As the title suggests, the focus is not on Anderson's entire life but on a vibrant time in Broadway theater, the 1930s through the 1950s.
- In 1947, at the height of Anderson's career, da Capra Press compiled some of his major pieces about show business in *Off Broadway: Essays about Theater.*
- This play is just one mentioned in *Political Stage: American Drama and Theater of the Great Depression,* by Malcolm Goldstein. It was published by Oxford University Press in 1974.

ment is run. The effect of her actions on the plot is practically nonexistent, but what she does not do speaks volumes about the hypnotic control of political power. One gets the impression that the sort of person who would allow this relationship with McClean to wither on the vine before it had a chance to bloom into a full-fledged romance would be content to live a life in emotional isolation, true to no one except her father.

In most respects, McClean's relationship with Bus, the wisecracking older secretary, is more interesting than the one he shares with Marjorie. The romance between McClean and Marjorie is described and referred to but never really acted upon, while the relationship between Bus and McClean grows right before audience's eyes. She is a better foil for him: cynical when he is overly idealistic, but then surprisingly idealistic just as he is losing faith in his crusade. By contrast, Marjorie is written as a party insider, but she is not exactly corrupt enough to serve as a lesson in the seductive nature of power. Bus is used to bring out more aspects of Alan McClean, while Marjorie is used to complicate his motives.

Congressman Simeon Gray could also be a more significant figure in McClean's attempt to

"IT IS CRUCIAL TO THE PLAY, AND TO THE VIEW OF AMERICAN POLITICS ANDERSON PRESENTS THROUGH IT, THAT MCCLEAN NOT FIND ANY STRONG, DEPENDABLE ALLY IN WASHINGTON."

right the wrongs of congressional appropriations, but making him a stronger presence in *Both Your Houses* would dilute Anderson's message about the unbelievable horror of the political system. Gray functions in the final version of the play as a touchstone, as the one person who is seen the same way by people on both sides of the debate. He is considered by all of the characters, though not necessarily by the author, to be an honest man who has gotten himself into a vulnerable position by trusting his co-workers and by working so hard that he fails to keep track of his own relationship to the bill he is working on. No one in the play—not McClean or even the jaded old politico Sol Fitzmaurice—doubts Gray's claim that the provision in the bill for construction of a penitentiary in his district appeared there before he even noticed it. Also, there is no debate about whether this penitentiary is needed for the common good, unlike measures requested by the other congressmen, which clearly have no purpose but to siphon cash out of the federal coffers.

Still, audiences cannot accept Gray's innocence as blindly as his friends and acquaintances do. It is unlikely that an appropriation for a large construction project in his district would have appeared in the bill without his notice, especially when it seems to be the answer to his personal financial dilemma. An argument could be made that Col. Sprague, the steel tycoon who dug up the information about Gray's failing bank, could have manipulated the situation by having some other congressperson plant the penitentiary in the bill, tempting Gray subtly to cross the line into corruption. There is, after all, a hint that Sprague arranged for the crusading young McClean to find out about the penitentiary, and that the ''mix-up'' at the detection agency was no mix-up after all. Anderson arranges this situation so that the truth could be either that Gray was cunning or that he was duped; the author leaves the matter open to interpretation.

If McClean were more closely involved with Gray or with his daughter, there would be less room for interpretation; Gray would have to be rendered more clearly, and the answer to whether he is as innocent as he claims to be would have to come into sharper definition. Such clarity would actually defeat one of the play's main points, that of the uncertainty of trust. It is crucial to the play, and to the view of American politics Anderson presents through it, that McClean not find any strong, dependable ally in Washington. Morality is so vague in Congress that McClean asks for help in his crusade from Sol, who is painted as the most unabashedly corrupt politician of them all. *Both Your Houses* would be less confusing if Simeon Gray were clearly virtuous or corrupt, but it would not be as true to the complexity that Anderson does succeed in capturing.

One can easily see why Anderson would have originally conceived *Both Your Houses* as a story of initiation or loss of innocence; an idealistic young man finding out that the woman he loves and the man he admires are as compromised as the worst of the political hacks he is struggling against is an eternal theme. It is often repeated throughout literature because it works, holding audience's interest while presenting the opposing sides of a conflict. It takes a skillful writer to know that he does not have to frame the issue so clearly, that the situation he presents does not have to boil down to an eternal theme in order for audiences to follow it. Another story might feature McClean's relationships with Marjorie and Simeon Gray, but for this one, revealing less gives the situation more mystery, and makes the young congressman's journey into the dark corridors of the government that much more frightening.

Source: David Kelly, Critical Essay on *Both Your Houses,* in *Drama for Students,* The Gale Group, 2003.

Kevin O'Sullivan

O'Sullivan writes for both film and stage. In this essay, O'Sullivan examines the tension between message and method in Maxwell Anderson's Both Your Houses.

Maxwell Anderson's play *Both Your Houses*, winner of the Pulitzer Prize in 1933, is a hard-biting indictment of political corruption in the houses of congress. Leavening indignation with acerbic humor, it reveals the disillusionment of a high-minded but politically naïve freshman congressman who arrives in Washington determined to clean things up. Although written more than seventy years ago, the play retains a certain currency; graft and pork barrel spending are as present today as they were then, and the reformist impulse seems to be renewed during each election cycle.

Prior to beginning his long career as a playwright, Anderson worked as a teacher and journalist. He was no doubt well acquainted, through his journalism, with the culture of corruption in our nation's capital. It is easy to imagine him identifying with the idealistic protagonist of his play and sharing his dismay at what appears to be an intractable problem. The play itself is an exercise in muckraking, exposing the back room dealings and nest-feathering of a congressional committee. The intent is, no doubt, to inspire indignation and a call for reforms. In this it resembles a number of other plays, written during the 1930s, that forwarded strong social messages. There was a marked leftward tilt among a number of the leading playwrights as well as a move towards experimentation in theatrical form. The results varied from kitchen sink social realism to Wellsian spectacle. The impulse behind many of these productions was to radically transform society, sometimes through outright instruction, more often through appeal to the emotions. Anderson, although a liberal, was neither didactic nor formally inventive in his writing. In fact, *Both Your Houses* is structured along traditional lines, closely observing action, time, and place.

The journalist-turned-playwright took a scientific approach to his plays. After an initial string of dramatic failures, Anderson revisited the classics and analyzed popular contemporary plays to see what made them tick. He also returned to Aristotle's *Poetics* and developed a theory of dramatic principles that, not surprisingly, closely resembled Aristotle's. Anderson even found a way to incorporate Aristotle's notion of the "recognition scene." This is a scene wherein a character's disguise or assumed identity is uncovered and the true identity is revealed. The Greeks and Elizabethans often used this device of discovery, but the demands of realism made it increasingly difficult for modern audiences to accept. Anderson solved this dilemma by turning it into self-recognition; the hero discovers something about himself or his place in the world around him of which he was previously unaware. This is the moment in which the veil is lifted and the truth is revealed. In his book of essays, *Off Broadway*, Anderson wrote:

> “THERE IS, IN FACT, A TENSION BETWEEN ANDERSON THE EDITORIAL WRITER AND ANDERSON THE CAREFUL PLAYWRIGHT, WHICH MAKES THIS WORK OF SPECIAL INTEREST.”

> When I had once begun to make discoveries of this sort they came thick and fast. And they applied not, as is natural to suppose, to extraordinary plays only—to Shakespeare and Jonson and the Greeks—but to all plays, and to those in our modern repertory as much as any others.

While Anderson did not codify his views until after he had written *Both Your Houses*, it hews, quite closely, to the basic contours of tragedy (or drama), as first mapped by Aristotle and modified by Anderson. But one can also detect the influence of his previous profession; the dialogue has a no-nonsense, reportorial sound that is, nonetheless, stylized. More notable is the voice of the writer of liberal editorials, apparent in the character of the protagonist Alan McClean. There is, in fact, a tension between Anderson the editorial writer and Anderson the careful playwright, which makes this work of special interest.

The play is divided into three acts and takes place over the course of three days. Set in the House Office Building, Washington, D.C., it employs two locations: the office of the chairman of the appropriations committee and the committee room itself. The drama, or conflict, is centered on the contest over a spending bill, with the two opposing sides struggling to line up their votes. This compression both helps to unify the play and creates a dramatic tension: there is a deadline, the clock is, in effect, ticking, the gavel ready to fall.

The hero, or protagonist, Alan McClean is an ideal type, representative of decent middle-class American values, hostile to superfluous spending. Newly elected to congress, he is determined to root out wasteful spending. This is a place where the congressmen feather their nests—the world of the backroom deal. It is a place where the congressmen do not pay their taxes. Not a revolutionary but a reformer, McClean has impluses the same as those that will inspire the taxpayer revolts of the 1970s and '80s. He is fed up with the corruption he sees among the political classes and is determined to clean things up (hence his name).

To drive home the point of McClean's lily-white character, Anderson has him investigate his own election campaign for improprieties. McClean refuses to support a bill that contains provisions beneficial to his own constituents on the grounds that the bill is loaded with pork. He has obviously set high standards for himself; that he is willing to go against his own political interests, on principle, shows that he is serious about his efforts. His intransigence sets in motion the events that ultimately lead to his defeat. What is shown in McClean, in other words, is someone very close to a tragic hero.

McClean finds as his antagonist a character that one would assume to be a natural ally; the chairman of the appropriations committee, Simeon Gray, is known to be personally honest. The chairman occupies a gray area between idealism and realism; accepting compromise of one's ideals as a necessary condition of doing business. One might imagine that this is terrain that even the most high-minded politician must travel. It is made explicit in the play that compromises must be made to get anything done. It is, in effect, the nature of a democracy where many voices clamor to be heard and each voice must be taken into account. Anderson himself does not necessarily disagree with this but seems to find the manner in which it is done distasteful, and the way in which particular or selfish interests are served immoral.

The chairman's daughter, Marjorie, supplies the love interest. She is being wooed by the freshman congressman, which causes complications late in the play. She is one of three women in the play, the other two being a cynical, straight-talking secretary named Bus and a congresswoman named Miss McMurtry. All three are very close to being mere types; the ingenue, the "gal," and the spinster. Together, they form a feminine principle, something that is lacking from the congressmen who dominate the play. They represent a humane element, lacking in the guile, duplicity, and self-righteousness that characterizes the male characters. Bus, who joins forces with McClean in an unsuccessful coup, is motivated not by abstract principle but by concrete experience. McMurtry, who in McClean's eyes is complicit in the pork barrel he is intent on trimming, accepts her slice of the pie to fund a maternity ward. Marjorie, who dotes on her father, is there to remind readers of the potential human costs in pursuing an ideal. Her first loyalty is to her family. These characterizations are consistent with what Anderson believed an audience wanted to see (and no doubt reflect his own bias). As Charles Meister, in his book *Dramatic Criticism*, has pointed out, Anderson believed that "theatergoers admire strong conviction in the male characters and passionate faith in the female."

To add levity to the proceedings, there is a comedic character, Solomon Fitzmaurice—a dipsomaniac congressman and former idealist who aims to dock the Atlantic Fleet in his congressional district. He is almost a stock character, who functions like a clown or jester, but there is a Falstaffian quality to his fecklessness, which gives him weight. Much comedy is made in the contradiction between his words and his behavior. He, like a clown in Shakespeare, is able to say things that no one else can. As crooked as any of his cronies, he speaks the truth about their venality.

The first act begins just before an important vote on the appropriations bill. Chairman Gray is scrupulously trying to remove the excess fat, trimming the bill to a size acceptable to the president. His is a dignified presence and he stands above his colleagues. They accept that he is honest and he accepts that a degree of graft must be tolerated. A sort of moral equilibrium has been reached until it is upset by the arrival of McClean. Principle soon clashes with pragmatism.

The paternal aspects of Gray's character are brought out, and it is shown that he is not entirely unsympathetic to the young congressman; yet McClean's determination to kill a bill that Gray has worked hard to see pass, pits the two men against one another. It is a contest that McClean cannot hope to win, but the long odds increase his determination. By the end of the first act, with the seasoned Bus on his side to mentor him through the ways of congressional politicking, McClean is ready to go head to head.

As McClean tries to gather enough supporters to kill the bill, his opponents dole out more favors to garner the crucial votes. Fat, once carefully trimmed, is added back onto the bill, ensuring its passage. Recognizing his pending defeat, McClean decides that the high road is inadequate to reach his goal. He engages in some duplicity, tricking Fitzmaurice, and decides that the best way to kill the bill is to load it with so much pork barrel spending that the president will be forced to veto it.

This act represents growth in McClean's character; new to the system, he has matched wits with—and apparently bettered—his superiors. Bus has mentored him too well. The pupil has now surpassed the teacher. At the close of act 2, scene 1, she says: ''I resign, Alan. I abdicate. Take my hand and lead me. I'm a little child!'' Yet, this statement represents a moral compromise of which McClean seems insufficiently aware. He is so convinced of the righteousness of his cause that he does not properly weigh the implications of his design. The question is never raised as to whether the ends justify the means. This is the fateful decision, the one that sets in motion a chain of events that threaten to undermine the protagonist's integrity.

The contest between Gray and McClean intensifies. There will be an unintended consequence if the bill is ultimately defeated; Chairman Gray will be implicated in an impropriety for which he is only partly culpable. The gray in his character proves a shade darker, yet he remains sympathetic. The two antagonists, who, up until then, have shared a mutual respect, now square off. McClean continues to fight for a principle. Gray fights for survival.

Sympathy falls to the threatened chairman, despite his impropriety. His involvement in a potential bank scandal also occupies a gray area: he is neither wholly guilty, nor wholly innocent. His relationship with his doting daughter, and his concern for his constituents, humanize him. McClean's unwavering principles seem cold, inhumane. For a principle, people are forgotten.

McClean's strategy works well; the bill is fattened with pork, and a presidential veto seems inevitable. McClean seems to have won. Gray's only hope is to have an overwhelming majority that can override a presidential veto. Fitzmaurice appeals to McClean to release a bloc of voters he controls in order to save Gray. Marjorie tells McClean that his victory will send her father to prison. His crusade has brought about some unintended consequences. Simeon Gray appears to be collateral damage. And so, apparently, is McClean's relationship with Marjorie. He refuses to help. As he says to Marjorie, ''I'm not fighting you or your father. I'm fighting this machine!''

This is the recognition scene, where McClean realizes the human cost of what he has brought about and is either unable or unwilling to stop it. He denies Marjorie's request. ''Don't ask it of me and don't tell me what I've lost!'' he says. ''I know what I've lost from all of you. And it's not my choice to lose it—but I'm in a fight that's got to be won—and you're asking for something I've no right to give!''

In the end, McClean's stratagem proves self-defeating. The bill passes with a large majority, which makes it veto-proof. Through his efforts to correct an ill, he has only magnified it. Yet sympathy shifts towards McClean as the victors indulge in a celebration of their venality. The shift is from tragedy to satire with a biting edge. Fitzmaurice articulates the mood: ''Graft, gigantic graft brought us our prosperity in the past and will lift us out of the present depths of parsimony and despair.'' Gray's words are more to the point: ''Our system is every man for himself—and the nation be damned.'' Embittered, McClean announces his intention to resign from office and continue his fight from the outside, warning that the tide will turn against the old guard: ''Anything else but this.'' In this scene, Anderson seems to be speaking through McClean; it is the voice of the liberal editorial writer. The tension between Anderson the journalist and Anderson the playwright is not so much resolved as exhausted in this scene. The message, which may have been buried by the high drama of the penultimate scene, stands out amidst the clamor of the victory celebration. If the scene seems inconsistent with the overall tone of the piece, it is nevertheless consistent with the author's intention; *Both Your Houses* is, in essence, a political editorial in dramatic form.

Source: Kevin O'Sullivan, Critical Essay on *Both Your Houses,* in *Drama for Students,* The Gale Group, 2003.

Alfred S. Shivers

In the following essay excerpt, Shivers surveys the political terrain in Both Your Houses *and Anderson's technique in rendering it.*

Both Your Houses (note the Shakespearean echo) exists in two complete versions—the 1933 published one which we shall look at first, and the 1939 unpublished one. These two versions illustrate Anderson's changing attitude toward democracy and the possibilities of individual fulfillment. Barrett Clark and George Freedley praise. *Both Your Houses* as ''the first play of any moment written by an American that dealt exclusively or largely with political

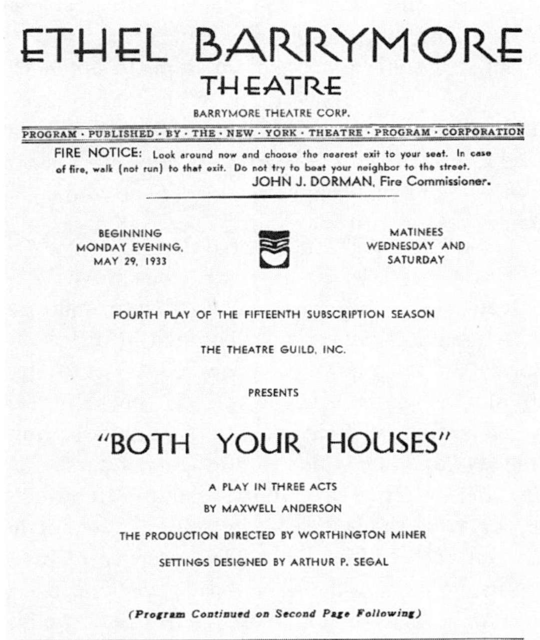

ETHEL BARRYMORE
THEATRE

BARRYMORE THEATRE CORP.

PROGRAM · PUBLISHED · BY · THE · NEW · YORK · THEATRE · PROGRAM · CORPORATION

FIRE NOTICE: Look around now and choose the nearest exit to your seat. In case of fire, walk (not run) to that exit. Do not try to beat your neighbor to the street.
JOHN J. DORMAN, Fire Commissioner.

BEGINNING
MONDAY EVENING,
MAY 29, 1933

MATINEES
WEDNESDAY AND
SATURDAY

FOURTH PLAY OF THE FIFTEENTH SUBSCRIPTION SEASON

THE THEATRE GUILD, INC.

PRESENTS

"BOTH YOUR HOUSES"

A PLAY IN THREE ACTS
BY MAXWELL ANDERSON

THE PRODUCTION DIRECTED BY WORTHINGTON MINER

SETTINGS DESIGNED BY ARTHUR P. SEGAL

(Program Continued on Second Page Following)

Playbill title page from the 1933 theatrical production of Both Your Houses, *performed at the Ethel Barrymore Theatre in New York*

crookedness in the federal government''; but its main predecessor seems to have been Harrison G. Rhodes and Thomas A. Wise's *A Gentleman from Mississippi* (1908) which was also concerned with the loading of a Congressional appropriation bill with graft.

Both Your Houses reached the stage of the Royale Theatre on March 6, 1933; but, if it had arrived when Anderson first wanted it to and if a producer had not kept delaying its presentation until the Hoover administration, the original target of the satire, was out of office, the point would have been sharper and the stage run perhaps longer than one hundred and twenty nights. There is the consolation, however, that the Pulitzer Prize committee recognized with its award for the 1932–33 season that the work had certain values which were presumably not completely dependent upon ''timeliness.'' However belated in its production, the play was not altogether useless as social criticism: it made a valuable appeal to the new federal administration, containing one hundred and twenty-seven new members, that was readying to assemble in Washington at the crisis of the Depression and correct the wrongs of the Hoover era. But whether any such politicians attended or read the play is a matter about which I have no information.

The narrative illustrates once more Anderson's stance of despair. An idealistic freshman congressman, Alan McClean, whose surname is an apt characteronym for his sterling makeup, learns that an omnibus House appropriation bill is laden with ''pork barrel'' as well as graft which will cost the already over-taxed public many millions of dollars. One of the congressmen, Sol Fitzmaurice, has even tagged on a measure that will anchor the Atlantic fleet off his private resort area rather than Hampton Roads. Alan opposes the bill despite its inclusion of funds for a dam project in his own district, for he has recently learned about the dishonest bidding for the contract, a bidding engineered by his backer and campaign manager.

Meanwhile, most of McClean's fellow congressmen have no scruples whatever in using skulduggery; in fact, dishonesty is so routine that they are surprised that Alan raises any objections. Sol, a somehow likeable old rascal and the most individualized figure in the play, candidly asserts that the processes of government absolutely depend upon graft and that this very nation was built by brigands who looted the treasury and the national resources. In Alan's research about the tainted appropriation bill, he encounters a moral dilemma: he learns that the committee chairman, Gray, an essentially honest man and the father of the girl he is courting, has innocently compromised himself by owning stock in an insolvent bank which the money in the bill would probably save. But Alan chooses to follow his conscience and try to defeat the bill, even at the risk of ruining the man he admires. Unable to block the legislation in committee, he loads onto it such flagrantly colossal riders that the whole thing will, he hopes, fail when it comes to a vote in Congress. Astonishingly, it passes anyway.

Of the various technical excellences in Anderson's construction of this play, a critic would have to concede the advantage of subordinating the love relationship to the drama of ideas: at the end, there is no forced or sentimental reconciliation between Alan and Marjorie, at least on stage; indeed, no more than two lines are devoted to the whole business. Moreover, Alan is also not portrayed as a knight in shining armor (he exposes his own campaign), otherwise he would differentiate the forces of good and evil either too neatly or too obviously. Still, he is clearly and believably a heroic figure, even though, like many of the Shaw and the Ibsen male creations, he lacks well-roundedness. John H. Lawson has sharply criticized the conception of McClean because he is not made to ask himself. "How can I live and achieve integrity under these conditions [?]"; because he has no rational solution for the dilemma of government in which he finds himself; because he admittedly has no conviction as to what the best type of government is; because, therefore, he has no specific proposal for reform; and because "the very condition against which McClean is fighting is brought about by the apathy or uncertainty of people as to 'the best kind of government.'"

In countering Lawson's first point, I contend that McClean has had, at least for the time being, his bridges burned behind him: if he stayed in, as Lawson seems to suggest, and publicly denounced his colleagues as dishonest, this legislator who had won his office under a cloud of suspicion would cut a sorry figure! But, it seems to me that Alan McClean might become more successful at winning sympathy and support for his exposure of the others as the voluntarily resigned congressman that Anderson plans him to be—providing he could write a book or afford a lecture tour. As the novice legislator that we find him to be at the end of the story, he realizes that he has already cost the country a vast amount of unnecessary money in trying to outwit the crooks; for him, then, it seems wise to choose a field of combat in which the public will not have to pay through the nose for his inexperience.

As for McClean's supposed fault of not having any rational solution to the dilemma of government. I believe that Lawson is simply unfair in asking such a newcomer, already a disastrous failure in politics, to have figured out on short notice what has eluded for centuries the most eminent philosophers, social scientists, and statesmen. Anyway, no playwright is or should be required to offer a solution to the social problems he presents; it is quite enough to lay forth the problem in an entertaining manner. Apropos Lawson's last objection, the hero in this play does *not,* I maintain, act apathetically or uncertainly about what he wants done, which is clearly a public exposure leading to reform. It would be grossly unfair to equate Alan McClean's patriotic state of mind with that of the general electorate who tolerate Sol Fitzmaurice and his hoggish breed. At worst, McClean is an idealist who is unwilling to accommodate himself to working out in the hurly-burly of "dirty politics" the kinds of rewards that Congressman Gray finds and is satisfied with.

"AT WORST, MCCLEAN IS AN IDEALIST WHO IS UNWILLING TO ACCOMMODATE HIMSELF TO WORKING OUT IN THE HURLY-BURLY OF 'DIRTY POLITICS' THE KINDS OF REWARDS THAT CONGRESSMAN GRAY FINDS AND IS SATISFIED WITH."

Though mainly a drama of ideas in which there is scant physical action, the narrative nevertheless grips the attention from the moment Alan enters in Act I to his angry exit in Act III. Unquestionably, the amusing secondary characters go far to sustain this interest; and these include Alan's fast-talking but honest secretary, Bus, and the eloquent old tippler and jovial antagonist, Sol Fitzmaurice. The dialogue is crisp throughout, and Maxwell Anderson illustrates in this dialogue his special and much-overlooked gift for lifelike vernacular in plays with contemporary settings.

Both Your Houses (1933), notwithstanding its gloom, is a shade lighter on the scale of optimism than is typical of Anderson's plays of the 1930s wherein the ideal is impossible of attainment in social institutions and human affairs. The pessimism of this published version was, incidentally, still more intense in the three preliminary drafts that now survive. These drafts start near the close of Act II to emphasize McClean's moral struggle about whether to save Gray or to remain true to the national interest; but the published version emphasizes throughout the external struggle between McClean and the sponsors of the bill. In the early drafts, McClean is unable to stay true to the national interest because, upon learning of Gray's predicament with the bank, he is so conscience-stricken about the possibility of ruining the honest Gray that he decides to endorse the bill to protect this man even at the loss of his own professional ideals. At the end, after McClean's realization that the prestigious United States House of Representatives does not by any latitude of thinking embrace the good of the nation, he resigns his post to return to teaching.

The upshot is that, as an idealist trying to make the actual world over into his own image, he had no choice but to fail one way or the other.

Consequently, the preparatory drains of *Both Your Houses* are stained with that very spirit of hopelessness which permeates other early Anderson dramaturgy. But late in rehearsals significant changes were introduced—most likely at the suggestion of other theater people engaged in the production—which sharpened the satirical point considerably. These changes allowed at least the possibility of public altruism and constructive reform despite the consuming self-interest that allegedly motivates leaders in government. As such, the published version of *Both Your Houses* is evidently a compromise, scarcely to be regretted on our part, between what Anderson felt in his heart about government and what the production staff felt was expedient in order to secure a viable drama.

Fortunately, however, the slightly revised *Both Your Houses* that Anderson prepared for a staging at the Pasadena Community Playhouse, Pasadena, California, during July of 1939, has never seen print. The new writing consists of two new speeches for McClean that are, sad to relate, inconsistent with the tone of what had gone before; but they do reflect the author's latest convictions at that time to defend democracy from the threat that Hitler's Germany was making to the free peoples of the earth. And so, after staring at the totalitarianism that was spreading like cancer over the body of Europe, Anderson now viewed our imperfect democracy as a relatively healthy system that was well worth saving.

Source: Alfred S. Shivers, ''Of Sceptred and Elected Races,'' in *Maxwell Anderson,* Twayne, 1976, pp. 101–31.

SOURCES

Anderson, Maxwell, *Off Broadway,* William Sloane Associates, Inc., 1947, pp. 24–25.

Bailey, Mabel Driscoll, *Maxwell Anderson: The Playwright as Prophet,* Harper & Row Publishers, Inc., 1957, pp. 60–61.

Clark, Barrett H., *Maxwell Anderson: The Man and His Plays,* Samuel French, Inc., 1933, p. 28.

Meister, Charles W., *Dramatic Criticism,* McFarland & Company, Inc. Publishers, 1985, p. 182.

Shivers, Alfred S., *Maxwell Anderson,* Twayne Publishers, 1978, pp. 98–99.

Wilson, Edmund, *The Triple Thinkers: Twelve Essays on Literary Subjects,* Fararr, Straus & Giroux, 1938, pp. 26–27.

FURTHER READING

Clawson, Dan, Alan Neustadtl, and Denise Scott, *Money Talks: Corporate PACs and Political Influence,* Basic Books, 1992.

This book outlines the structure and political influence of Political Action Committees.

Gassner, John, ''Introduction,'' in *20 Best Plays of the Modern American Theatre, 1930–1939,* Crown Publishers, 1939, pp. vii–xxii.

Gassner was a respected theater scholar who headed the Theater Guild's play department at the height of its glory. His summary of this decade in theater gives modern readers a fair sense of the excitement of New York theater in the thirties.

Lewis, Charles, and the Center for Public Integrity, *The Buying of Congress: How Special Interests Have Stolen Your Right to Life, Liberty, and the Pursuit of Happiness,* Avon Books, 1998.

Lewis and his investigative team take a cynical look at the political process, writing with a sense of moral outrage that Maxwell Anderson would have appreciated.

Smith, Hedrick, ''The Coalition Game: The Heart of Governing,'' in *The Power Game: How Washington Works,* Random House, 1988, pp. 451–508.

Smith, who at that time had been reporting on Washington throughout six Presidential administrations, shows that the basic rules of behavior Anderson attributed to his characters still dominate the American government.

Brand

HENRIK IBSEN

1866

Henrik Ibsen's religious drama, *Brand*, caused a huge stir when it was first published in Scandinavia in 1866. Although it was well received in Denmark, it was highly debated in Norway, Ibsen's pious homeland. Ibsen wrote the play while on a self-imposed exile in Italy, which began in 1864. Although the play's sources of inspiration have been interpreted in many different ways, it is likely that the work—like Ibsen's exile—was a statement on Norway's failure to join with its Danish neighbors in preventing Germany from taking two of Denmark's duchies in 1864. The play was the first commercial and critical success of Ibsen's and paved the way for his future successes, starting with *Peer Gynt*, which he published a year after *Brand*. Both plays are verse dramas—plays written in the style of a poem—a more literary but less common type of modern drama.

Brand was a cathartic writing experience for Ibsen, who never intended the play to be staged. Like the inspiration for the play, the meaning in the work has also been interpreted in many different ways. The main character, Brand, is a pastor who holds himself and all of his followers, including his wife, to the rigid command of ''Naught or All!'' This essentially means that people must be willing to risk their lives and all earthly attachments if they wish to find eternal salvation. Brand is tested on this faith, and even though he falters a few times, he nevertheless goes the distance, sacrificing his mother, son, and wife in an attempt to adhere to his beliefs. The ambiguous ending has been interpreted in many

contradictory ways, including that Brand's life is either meaningful or worthless. Although this is one of Ibsen's major works, it is currently out of print. Various translations can often be found in libraries. One such translation is the 1960 Doubleday edition, translated by Michael Meyer.

AUTHOR BIOGRAPHY

Ibsen was born on March 20, 1828, in Skien, Norway, to a wealthy family. However, in 1834, Ibsen's family lost its money when the family business failed. When he was fifteen, Ibsen left school to work as a pharmacist's assistant, although he eventually tried to get admitted to Christiania University. When he failed the entrance exams, Ibsen turned his attention to writing and wrote his first play, *Cataline*, in 1850. At this point, Ibsen's work was relatively unknown, so he became assistant stage manager at the Norwegian Theater in Bergen, where he was expected to write and produce one drama each year. These early plays were not well received, and in 1862 Ibsen petitioned the government for a pension that would allow him to travel while he wrote. He was eventually given a small stipend in 1864.

The same year, Ibsen began a self-imposed exile from Norway that would last for the majority of his adult life. Although many critics say that Ibsen left his country to get away from bad memories of his father's failed business and Ibsen's own failure as a stage manager, the playwright himself said that he needed to leave his homeland to write drama that accurately reflected Norwegian life. While in Italy during the first few years of his exile, Ibsen published *Brand* (1866) and *Peer Gynt* (1867), two plays that made him famous. From this point on, Ibsen's works were more popular, but in some cases, such as 1879's *A Doll's House*, which addressed the oppression of women, his plays dealt with controversial topics.

In 1891, Ibsen returned to Norway from his twenty-seven-year exile and continued to write major plays, including *The Master Builder* (1892) and *John Gabriel Borkman* (1896). Shortly after completing *When We Dead Awaken* (1899), a highly autobiographical play in which Ibsen questions his own life as an artist, Ibsen suffered several strokes, which rendered him an invalid until his death several years later. Ibsen died on May 23, 1906, in Oslo, Norway.

PLOT SUMMARY

Act 1

Brand begins in the frigid mountains of Norway in the mid-eighteenth century. Brand, a pastor, strides confidently through the dangerous and disorienting mountain mist, while a peasant—crossing the mountains with his son to be with his dying daughter—turns back and tries to convince Brand to do the same. Brand is unshakable in his will, however, and challenges the peasant to risk his life for the daughter he loves. The weather clears, and Brand comes across a young couple—Einar, an artist, and Agnes. Although the couple is happy, Brand is grim and says he is on his way to the funeral of the false God that people have been worshipping. Although Einar is defiant and brushes off Brand's speeches, which he sees as religious fanaticism that belongs to an earlier age, Agnes is affected and is no longer carefree. Brand meets Gerd, a mad girl, who throws stones at a hawk that only she can see and tells him about the Ice-Church, a natural, church-like formation of ice in the mountains. Brand tells Gerd to stay away from the church because the formation is unstable and could come crashing down in an avalanche. Gerd invites Brand to come with her, then screams when she sees the imaginary hawk again. She runs away. Brand reflects on all of the travelers he has seen thus far and concludes that none of them is living life the way it should be lived. Brand goes down into the valley.

Act 2

By the fiord—a narrow inlet of water surrounded by mountains, which leads to the sea—Brand comes upon a group of peasants begging the town's sheriff for food. Brand offers sermons instead of money, and the hungry peasants move in to beat Brand. They are interrupted by a woman who begs Brand to come across the stormy bay to her house to perform last rites for her husband who has killed their starving child out of mercy and has mortally wounded himself out of shame for the act. Brand prepares to brave the stormy boat ride to the woman's house. He asks for help from the woman, but she is afraid for her life and will not go; neither will most of the crowd. Only Agnes, the bride of Einar, decides to leave her new husband to help Brand. Together, they make it in time to perform the last rites. The crowd arrives much later, impressed by Brand's courage. A man asks him to stay on as their pastor. Brand refuses at first, not wishing to waste his life in this small village when he could do greater good in the world at large. Brand's mother walks up and attempts to bequeath her fortune to him, as long as he agrees to hoard it and to give his mother her last rites on her deathbed. Brand says that he will not give her last rites unless she gives her entire fortune away to charity. His mother initially refuses to do this, although she leaves the possibility that she may change her mind. Einar comes up and asks Agnes to return to him, but Agnes chooses to align herself with Brand and his rigid demand of ''Naught or All,'' meaning that she must give herself totally to God without attachments to safety, either personal or financial, and other earthly aspects.

Act 3

Three years later, Brand and Agnes are married and living in the little village by the fiord where Brand has decided to serve as pastor. Brand's mother is on her deathbed, and he waits for her summons, refusing to go serve her last rites until she agrees to give her fortune up to charity. At the same time, Brand and Agnes discuss the fact that their son, Alf, is becoming sick. Various messengers come to Brand, telling him that his mother is willing to give up half of her fortune, then nine-tenths, but she is unwilling to give up all of it. Although other characters accuse Brand of being too hard, including Agnes, he sticks to his pledge and refuses to administer last rites to his mother. The sheriff comes up and says that, since Brand is rich from his inheritance, he should use the money to move away. The sheriff is worried that Brand's depressing sermons are affecting the townspeople and disturbing a sense of peace and harmony. Brand refuses to leave and declares war on the sheriff. The doctor comes up to tell Brand that his mother is dead and accuses him of being too hard on her. At Agnes's frantic request, the doctor looks at Alf and says that if they do not move to a warmer climate, the boy will die. In a panic, Brand says he will leave, until the doctor points out Brand's hypocrisy. At this point, Gerd, a mad little girl, arrives. Brand takes her ravings as a sign that he should stay, and although Agnes is crushed that they have to sacrifice their son's health to do it, she agrees to stay with Brand.

Act 4

It is Christmas Eve, and Agnes is mourning their dead child. Brand asks his wife not to cry over Alf, as grief is a worldly attachment. Although it takes a while, Agnes finally dries her tears and tries to continue with the Christmas celebration, honoring Jesus instead of mourning her child. The sheriff arrives and says that Brand has won his war, as the majority of the townspeople are following his sermons. The sheriff offers a truce and asks if Brand will donate his inheritance to build a multipurpose building that can be used as a poor house and jail. However, Brand has other plans, which are to build a new church, an idea that the sheriff does not like when he thinks the townspeople will have to pay for it. However, when Brand says he will cover the expense, the sheriff suddenly supports the idea. The sheriff mentions that gypsies have come to town. He also says that, in the past, Brand's mother had spurned the advances of a gypsy man, who instead married another gypsy and had a number of children—including the mad girl, Gerd, for whom the townspeople have been providing food and clothes. The sheriff leaves, and Agnes looks out at Alf's grave, daydreaming about her dead son. Brand catches her doing this, then catches her taking out Alf's old clothes. A gypsy woman comes to the door, begging for clothes for her freezing child. At Brand's request, Agnes eventually gives the gypsy woman Alf's clothes, the last remnant that she has

Henrik Ibsen

to commemorate her dead son. However, this act is not good enough for Brand; Agnes must avow that she has given the clothes willingly.

Act 5

A year and a half later, the new church is completed, and the town is ready to throw a big celebration. The clerk and schoolmaster talk about the church and about how Brand's grim teachings interfere with the harmony of the village. They hear Brand playing a mournful tune on an organ, and they talk about Agnes's death. They momentarily lose their composure and talk about the possibility that they themselves might follow Brand's grim teachings. The sheriff comes up to Brand, who is unhappy about the grand church he has built, seeing it as yet another abstraction from God. The sheriff talks about the celebration, in which Brand is to be made a knight. Brand is mortified that they are going to try to make him a celebrity, which he sees as being even farther removed from God. Brand leaves, running into the dean, who echoes the sheriff's sentiments and tells Brand that, with this new church, he now serves the government and that he wants Brand to give lighter sermons. Einar, the former artist, comes up to Brand. Einar has had a revelation, has given up his prideful dependence on willpower, and has sacrificed his life to God. He condemns Brand for his own pride.

The crowd starts getting rowdy, wanting the celebration to start. Brand addresses them, inciting them to follow him. The majority follows Brand into the mountains, but the followers have doubts and begin to stone Brand, thinking he has tricked them. The dean and sheriff follow the crowd. When the crowd turns on Brand, because he cannot offer them anything but a rough life, the dean and the sheriff coax them back to town with the lie that an abundance of fish has come into the bay. Wounded, Brand continues on into the mountains, where he sees a vision of his wife, Agnes, who tells him to give up his strict policy of "Naught or All." Brand refuses, and the vision vanishes. Gerd appears with a rifle, sees Brand's wounds, and equates him with Christ. Gerd tells Brand that they are in the Ice-Church, and when she thinks she sees the hawk of Compromise, she fires, killing them both in an avalanche. As he dies, Brand calls out to God, asking him how to achieve salvation. A voice responds: "God is Love!"

CHARACTERS

Agnes

Agnes is, first, wife to Einar, then to Brand, whom she obeys until the end of her life, even when it means losing her life and the life of her son. At the beginning of the play, Agnes is a carefree, young woman, recently engaged to Einar. Brand gives them a sermon, which falls on Einar's deaf ears but impacts Agnes, so much so that when Brand asks for a volunteer to risk his or her life to help someone, Agnes leaves Einar to help Brand. Agnes decides to leave Einar for good, marries Brand, and has a child with him. Although Agnes has agreed to Brand's harsh requirement of "Naught or All!" she struggles with Brand's decision to stay in the harsh weather of the village when it means the death of their son. She follows Brand in the end, however, as she eventually does when Brand commands her to stop grieving for their dead son. When Brand tells Agnes to get rid of her last memories of their son, as well as his clothes—donating them to a needy gypsy woman—she once again falters at first but eventually adheres to Brand's strict religious requirements and gives up her earthly attachments. Agnes also dies from the harsh weather in the mountains, and her death greatly affects Brand, so much so that when he is tempted in the mountains by a vision, it takes the form of Agnes.

Brand

Brand is the unyielding title character, a priest who forces himself and his family to adhere to a strict religious life, even though it means the death of them all. Brand is driven by his strong will, which he thinks is the way to God. He believes that by having the personal strength to relinquish all of one's earthly attachments, a person can achieve eternal salvation. Brand's faith is fiery, as are the gloomy sermons that he gives to villagers. Brand repeatedly puts his life on the line for his principles, thinking that an attachment to one's life is unholy. He counts on his enormous strength of will to get him through situations, and most of the time he is successful, overcoming great odds to live through storms and in harsh climates that ultimately kill his wife, Agnes, and their son, Alf.

Brand's famous requirement for his wife or for anybody who chooses to follow him is "Naught or All!" meaning that one must be willing to give everything in order to be saved. Brand is tested in his faith on several occasions. When his mother is on her deathbed, he refuses to give her last rites because she will not give up her hard-earned fortune to charity. When his son is given the prognosis of death if Brand does not move him to a warmer climate, Brand nevertheless stays in the mountains, sacrificing his son, because he has a job to do with his parish. Although Brand's own faith wavers on occasion, he is reminded of his mission by others, such as the mad girl, Gerd, and the doctor, and is ultimately able to stick to his rigid faith. At the end, Brand's rigid faith is put in question, first by Einar, a reformed man who tells Brand that he himself was only saved when he gave up his pride and his belief in his own strength. Einar senses similar qualities in Brand and declares him damned. In the end, Brand retreats to the mountains, where he is tempted by a vision of his dead wife—who tries unsuccessfully to get Brand to compromise his ideals. He also runs into the mad girl, Gerd, who reveres him like Christ and kills them both when she shoots her own vision, the hawk of compromise, causing a massive avalanche. As Brand dies, he appeals to heaven, asking how a man can achieve salvation. A voice answers, "God is Love!" ending the play on an ambiguous note.

Brand's Mother

Brand's mother dies without receiving last rites from her son because she refuses to donate her hard-earned money to charity. Brand warns her that he will not perform last rites for her unless she gives away all of her money, but his mother has had to suffer greatly for the money, and she wants Brand to hoard it after she is gone. Although his mother ultimately offers to give nine-tenths of her money away, it is not enough for Brand, who requires her to give it all away.

A Clerk

The clerk is a normally rational person who decides to go with Brand at the end of the play, although, like others, he turns on the priest. When the clerk and the schoolmaster are talking before the dedication of the new church, they both betray a sense of emotion, which is quickly suppressed. However, when Brand gives his fiery sermon to the crowd, the clerk follows him up into the mountains. Even after he has turned on Brand, the clerk is afraid to go back to town, since he is afraid he has lost his job. He is relieved to find out that he has not.

The Dean

The dean tells Brand that since the priest has built the new church, he must now serve two masters—the people and the state. He also tells Brand that his gloomy sermons do not serve the needs of the state and that Brand needs to tone down his fiery proclamations. Brand refuses, but the dean says it is no use. Brand tries to run away to the mountains, taking many of the townspeople with him. When they turn on Brand, the dean is there with the sheriff to reclaim them, saying that they will have a much easier life in the village than with Brand. The people gladly go with the dean and the sheriff.

The Doctor

The doctor attends Brand's mother on her deathbed and, like many others, accuses Brand of being too strict in his requirements for faith. The doctor also lets Brand know that his son will die if Brand and Agnes do not move to a warmer climate. When Brand has a moment of weakness and says he will leave at once, the doctor calls him a hypocrite, although he says that most men are. This, along with the appearance of Gerd, helps to convince Brand to stand by his strict faith and stay, even though it means the death of his son.

Einar

Einar is the hedonistic artist, initially engaged to Agnes, who eventually trades his wanton ways for faith in God. When Einar is first introduced, he is a happy bridegroom, and he and Agnes look forward to their happy and carefree lives together. After Agnes leaves him to marry Brand and commit herself to Brand's harsh lifestyle, Einar commits himself to a life of sin but is saved by a few nuns and eventually becomes a missionary. He tells Brand that his salvation came from transferring his faith in his human will to prayer and says that Brand is damned—presumably because Brand still believes in the strength of human will.

Gerd

Gerd is the mad little girl who appears several times in the play when Brand is doubting himself. Gerd is the daughter of a gypsy man who was spurned by Brand's mother. The townspeople have been feeding and clothing Gerd. She has religious visions, and she inspires Brand to stick to his strict morals, such as when her presence encourages him to stay living in the fiord—even though it means the death of his son. At the end of the play, when Brand walks alone through the mountains, Gerd appears with a rifle, saying that she is hunting the hawk of compromise. For once, Brand has seen the hawk, in the vision of his dead wife, Agnes, who has tried to convince him to give up his strict beliefs. Gerd believes that Brand is Christ, since the priest's wounds from the villagers match Christ's wounds. At the end, Gerd shoots the hawk in the Ice-Church, which causes the avalanche that kills both Gerd and Brand.

The Schoolmaster

The schoolmaster of the village is a rational person who eventually succumbs to Brand's powerful preaching at the end and follows him into the mountains. He is one of many who turn on Brand when the priest cannot offer guarantees of an easy life. Even after he has turned on Brand, the schoolmaster is afraid to go back to town, since he is afraid he has lost his job. He is relieved to find out that he has not.

The Sheriff

The sheriff, Brand's nemesis, tries several times to get Brand to leave the village, since the priest's gloomy teaching disrupts orderly village life. The sheriff first meets Brand when the sheriff is giving out food to the poor. When Brand offers sermons instead of donations, the sheriff is angry. When Brand is about to receive his inheritance, the sheriff encourages Brand to take the money and leave. When Brand refuses, the sheriff threatens him, and Brand declares war. Later, the sheriff declares Brand the winner of their war, as Brand has won the support of the majority of people. The sheriff offers a truce and tries to get Brand to use his inheritance to build a new poor house, which will also serve many other functions. Brand, however, wants to build a new church, which the sheriff supports. On the day the church is to be dedicated in a big party, Brand realizes his mistake and tries to get back to the simple life once again, going into the mountains, away from the showy church, to seek the simple life. When Brand incites a number of villagers to follow him into the mountains, the sheriff is worried but bides his time. He follows the crowd, which turns on Brand after he promises them a hard life but a good afterlife. The sheriff then dupes the villagers into coming home by lying to them, saying that millions of fish have entered the fiord.

The Woman

The woman saves Brand from being beaten by the townspeople in the beginning by her frantic request for a priest to administer last rites for her husband. Although the woman is glad Brand is willing to cross the stormy bay to her house, she will not, for fear of losing her life.

THEMES

Willpower

Depending on how one looks at the ambiguous ending of the play, Brand's iron strength of will is either a curse or a blessing. If one interprets the ending statement, "God is Love!" to mean that Brand should have focused less on prideful will and more on love, then it is a curse. If, however, one takes the voice to mean that God is acknowledging Brand's hard work and welcoming him to heaven at the hour of Brand's death, then his will is a blessing. In any case, Brand's will is his personal driving force, and it becomes the driving force of the play. With rare exception, the other characters are not able to use their strength of willpower in the absolute way that Brand does. As Brand notes after the peasant and his son refuse to cross the mountains to be with the peasant's dying daughter, Brand would help people like this if he could: "But help is useless to a man / Who does not *will* save where he *can*!"

In other words, if somebody is only willing to give up items that are expendable, then it is not a true sacrifice. When it comes to giving up irreplaceable items, such as one's life, most people fail the test, as Brand says: "Much will they give with willing mind, / Leave them but Life, dear Life, behind." Brand, however, follows his own ideal, as one of the village men notes after Brand braves the stormy fiord to administer last rites to a man. Says the village man, "*You* have the strength. . . . The way you showed, you *went,* at length." In other words, Brand is not all talk; he has done exactly what he said he was going to do.

Religious Conviction

In the majority of cases, Brand's will is tied to his religious conviction. Unlike the villagers, who Brand says follow a "bald, grey, skull-cap-pated God," a meek divine being that is convenient for the villagers, Brand's God is a powerful vision from more devout times: "And He is young, like Hercules,— / No grandad in the seventies." Brand's vision of God does not allow a compromise. Instead, Brand, in serving his God, adheres to the phrase "Naught or All!" which does not give room for

- Ibsen is not the only Norwegian who left the country in the nineteenth century. Between 1815 and 1915, tens of millions of Norwegians migrated to the United States. Research the history of this mass exodus, and compare Ibsen's reasons for leaving the country with the motivations of the masses who came to America.
- Darwin's evolutionary theories instigated a debate between evolutionists and creationists that still rages in some areas today. Research a historical case, legal or otherwise, that illustrates this conflict. Write a short script for a modern-day court television episode in which the two parties argue their beliefs in front of a judge.
- Brand can be, and has been, described as a religious fanatic. Choose another religious group or cult labelled fanatical from history, and research its beliefs. Then, taking the viewpoint of one of the members, write a newspaper editorial that explains what types of conflicts or persecutions members of the group face, using your research to support your claims.
- Ibsen was in the extreme group that supported maintaining an alliance with other Scandinavian countries when it came to dealing with wars and other foreign affairs. Find another Scandinavian who held this belief, and research how this person fought for this unification. Write a journal entry from this person's point of view, detailing the struggles faced by Scandinavians of this belief.
- Compare Norway's refusal to support Denmark to the political policy of Norway, Denmark, and other Scandinavian countries during World War II, when Nazi Germany fought with much of Europe. How did the actions of Scandinavian countries affect the outcome of the war? If they did not greatly affect the war, discuss how they could have.

compromise. Throughout the story, he lives by this strict code and insists that anybody who follows him does the same. At the end of the play, a number of townspeople become inspired by Brand's impassioned sermon and follow him into the mountains.

However, it is not long before the crowd starts complaining about the harsh conditions in the mountains. ''I haven't had a crumb today,'' says one person, instigating several to ask for food and drink. Other people cry out such complaints as ''My child is sick!'' and ''My foot is sore!'' Brand admonishes them: ''The wage before the work you claim,'' saying that they need to work before they will get their salvation. Several members of the crowd take this to mean that they will get their salvation during their lives and start asking very specific questions such as ''Can I be certain of my life?'' and ''What's *my* share, when the prize is won?'' Brand tells them that they must give up their tendency to compromise and that their reward will be in heaven, and the crowd, who feels tricked, turns on Brand. The rigid religious conviction that Brand demonstrates is not inherent in most of the other characters, who do not have enough patience or faith.

Sacrifice

As part of the strength of will and the religious conviction that Brand requires of his followers, he also instructs them to make certain sacrifices other than their lives, such as giving up earthly ties like money. When Brand's mother tells him she is bequeathing the hard-earned family fortune to him, as long as he hoards it after she is dead, Brand refuses to do this. He also refuses to give his mother her last rites until she gives the money away to charity: ''That of free will you cast away / All that binds you to the clay.'' However, Brand's mother is unable to make this sacrifice and so goes to her grave without receiving her last rites. In addition to their lives and money, characters must also be willing to sacrifice the lives of other loved ones. Brand does this with his mother when he refuses her last rites. He also sacrifices his son, Alf, and calls upon his wife to perform this sacrifice willingly. Even after Alf is dead—as a result of the cold weather of the mountain parish that Brand refuses to abandon—Brand asks Agnes to give up all of her memories of the child, even to sacrifice his baby clothes. Although Agnes does this, Brand is doubtful that she has done it wholeheartedly: ''Did you with a willing heart / Face the gift, nor grudge the smart?'' In other words, in order for Agnes's sacrifice to be totally pure, she must not only willingly give away the clothes but must do so without bitterness. Although Agnes eventually succeeds, most characters in the play are not able to make this type of sacrifice.

STYLE

Verse Drama

Ibsen wrote his play as a verse drama, also known as a dramatic poem, a play that is composed entirely of lines of poetry. This more romantic, less realistic style of play is less common in modern drama. From the first conversation in the play, the exchange between Brand and the peasant man, it is evident that the play is a verse drama. The first sign is that the dialogue is arranged into lines, as opposed to paragraph style. For example, when the peasant is describing the bad weather conditions and the near invisibility of Brand in the fog, he says: ''The mist is closing in so thick, / A body's eyesight barely passes / Beyond the measure of his stick.'' This example also illustrates the second sign that marks the play as a verse drama—the rhymes. Although the rhymes continue throughout the poem, they do not follow a set pattern or scheme, as many rhyming poems do.

Symbolism

Ibsen is known for heavy use of symbolism in his plays, and this one is no different. The play incorporates a number of aspects that symbolize religious objects or ideas. For example, the mountains suggest proximity to God as the setting of the natural Ice-Church, which collapses on Brand at the ambiguous end, as the place where God answers Brand's exclamation prior to his death, and as a setting where characters retreat from the perversions of humanity, such as Brand's self-imposed exile. Believing that the church is not large enough, Brand builds another one, then realizes his mistake, telling the people, ''Out from here, where God is not! / Can He dwell in such a spot,'' and then throwing the keys to the new church into the river. Brand has realized that, no matter what kind of church he builds in the valley, it will always be tainted by humanity. As a result, Brand goes into the mountains and, ultimately, ends up at the Ice-Church.

Other religious symbols that Ibsen plants in the mountains include Brand himself, who, after being stoned by the villagers, resembles Christ. Says Gerd when she sees Brand's wounds: ''On thy brow, the red drops stand / Where the thorns' sharp teeth have caught it! / Aye 'tis *thee* the Cross did bear!'' In addition, Gerd sees the vision of a hawk, which she says is ''Compromise,'' ambiguously symbolizing either the lack of religious conviction in many of the peripheral characters or the overbearing will of Brand.

Satire

The play also makes use of satire, a technique used to depict characters or their actions in a manner that scorns and ridicules to prove a point that the playwright wishes to make. In this case, Ibsen satirizes many government or social institutions, through many general characters such as the sheriff and the dean. The sheriff is depicted as an unscrupulous person who will do what it takes to maintain harmony in the village. When the sheriff first meets Brand, he does not like the pastor, since Brand does not give comforting sermons. The sheriff makes this clear when he comes to visit Brand and encourages him to leave, letting him know that ''You've set all harmony a-jangle.'' At the end of the play, when the villagers follow Brand into the mountains, the sheriff is not worried and uses a lie to win the villagers back: ''Because a shoal of fish / Has come into the fiord—by millions!'' When the sheriff and the dean are discussing this miracle later on, the sheriff admits that there are no fish:

> Besides, a day or two days hence,
> When folk have found their common sense,
> Who'll care a rap if victory
> Was won by truth or by a lie?

This comment satirizes government officials who are willing to lie or to perform other dishonest deeds in order to get their way. The dean is also a morally suspect character, who gives Brand all sorts of advice about how to tone down his sermons and serve two masters—the people and the state: ''Our working days you know, are six; / We save the seventh for emotion.'' The dean has relegated religion to one day a week so that the majority of the week can be devoted to work activities, which more directly benefit the state. This type of mentality contradicts Brand's entire style of life and satirizes the government institutions that hold this same view.

HISTORICAL CONTEXT

Charles Darwin

In November 1859, the English naturalist Charles Darwin published his book, *On the Origin of Species,* and the world was never the same again. Darwin's theory of evolution, based on his plant and animal research from a five-year voyage around the world on the H.M.S. *Beagle,* posed the idea that all species had evolved from a limited number of common ancestors through a process known as natural selection. Through natural selection, only those animals that possessed the random mutations necessary to adapt to changing environments were able to reproduce often enough to pass on their genes successfully. Viewed over a long timescale, these mutations could cause one species to evolve into a totally new species. Darwin's theory had horrible implications for the religion. If humans had evolved, they said, it challenged the idea of a human creation by God and, some said, the very existence of God.

Land Disputes in Northern Europe

In the mid-1800s, two wars broke out in connection with the administration of two duchies, Schleswig and Holbein. Although the lands had been under Danish rule for centuries, the inhabitants were mostly German. In 1863, when the Danish King, Frederick VII, tried to formally annex Schleswig, the German inhabitants revolted. The neighboring Germanic country of Prussia got involved and encouraged Austria to support its war against Denmark for control of the duchies. In 1864, the Norwegian parliament voted not to back Denmark in its fight against Prussia, a decision that disgusted Ibsen and others who supported a united Scandinavia. The Danish army was easily defeated by Prussian forces later that year, and Denmark turned over control of the two duchies to Prussia and Austria.

Prussia and Austria split the administration of the territories between them—Austria controlled Holstein, and Prussia controlled Schleswig. This arrangement led to tensions between the two countries, which then took up arms against each other in 1865 in the Austro-Prussian War, also known as the Seven Weeks' War. Prussian troops, making use of railroads and using newer breech-loading rifles, easily conquered the Austrian and other Germanic forces, which were still using older, muzzle-loading guns. In addition to annexing the combined Schleswig-Holstein, Prussia's win also led to its annexation of five of Austria's six allies, instantly changing the political landscape of Germany.

Alfred Nobel's Discovery of Dynamite

While the breech-loading rifle represented a major advance in the design of guns, at the same time, a Swedish pacifist, Alfred Nobel, was working on an invention that would eventually change the face of explosives—and battles—forever. In 1866, Nobel, who was manufacturing and performing dangerous experiments on nitroglycerin—an explosive liquid—set off an accidental explosion that ruined his factory and killed his brother and workers. Although the Swedish government refused Nobel's request to rebuild his factory after the explosion, the next year, Nobel, whom some called a mad scientist, was able to perfect his discovery, combining the liquid nitroglycerin with sand to create portable explosive sticks known as dynamite.

CRITICAL OVERVIEW

Brand has always been a work that invites many interpretations, beginning with its stormy reception in Norway in 1866. In F. L. Lucas's 1962 book, *The Drama of Ibsen and Strindberg,* Lucas notes that ''its effect on Norwegian pietism was like pitching a millstone into a small pond.'' Likewise, in his 1969 book, *Ibsen: A Portrait of the Artist,* Hans Heiberg notes that ''all over Norway the controversy raged, becoming the subject of sermons from pulpits, as well as social debate.'' However, while many Norwegians took Ibsen's attacks personally, in Denmark, Heiberg says that the book was considered by critics ''a sensational break-through of Norwegian

COMPARE & CONTRAST

- **Late 1850s—Mid-1860s:** Denmark and Norway face unification issues, which eventually factor into the two wars in Northern Europe over the duchies of Schleswig and Holstein. At the same time, the United States faces its own unification issues, which erupt in a vicious civil war.

  Today: The United States stands unified against a common enemy—terrorism—following vicious attacks by terrorist groups on the World Trade Center in New York and the Pentagon in Washington, D.C.

- **Late 1850s–Mid-1860s:** Swedish pacifist Alfred Nobel performs a number of experiments on explosives. These experiments lead to the creation of nitroglycerine, which ultimately takes the portable form of dynamite. This powerful explosive is sometimes employed as a weapon.

  Today: Terrorists make isolated attacks using bacteriological weapons like anthrax, and there is some concern that terrorists may resort to other, newer forms of warfare.

- **Late 1850s–Mid-1860s:** Charles Darwin publishes his landmark argument about evolution, *On the Origin of Species,* which shakes up the religious and educational worlds, igniting a controversy between creationists and evolutionists.

  Today: Most public schools teach evolution, which is a respected scientific discipline. Academia explores the links between science and religion and identifies some potential bridges between the formerly contradictory disciplines.

---

literature.'' The book was a popular success, and Heiberg notes that it was reprinted three times within the same year, ''an almost unheard-of sales success.''

With the success of *Brand*, which he wrote while on a self-imposed exile in Italy, Ibsen also achieved financial freedom. Though early reactions were mixed, the play is generally been received well now, although interpretations throughout the years have differed greatly. In 1889, Edmund Gosse of the *Fortnightly Review* called the play a ''beautiful Puritan opera,'' whereas, in 1931, in his book, *The Life of Ibsen, Vol. 2,* Halvdan Koht says that Ibsen's intended meaning of the play ''was that it was not honest or worthy of a human being to do anything else than to stand alone, to be one's self.'' There was a massive amount of scholarship on Ibsen and his works in the 1960s, when critics focused on many different aspects of the play. In his 1961 article in *The Lock Haven Bulletin,* Irving Deer identified a sharply divided critical argument that had sprung up by that point: ''Simply stated, the controversy boils down to whether Ibsen intended him to be a hero or a villain.''

Likewise, a year later, in 1962, Lucas notes only one aspect of the play, the ambiguous voice at the end of the work, spawned at least five different interpretations by critics, including that ''this voice is the Devil's,'' it is ''the voice of God'' either condemning or welcoming Brand as a result of his adherence to his rigid faith, it is the ''real or imagined'' voice ''of the dead Agnes,'' it is ''the voice of Brand's own soul,'' and it ''is what Ibsen says it is—simply a voice.'' This assessment is representative of other aspects in the play, which have also been debated endlessly.

One of the other aspects that academics in the 1960s focused on was the connection between *Brand* and the writings of the philosopher, Søren Kierkegaard. As Heiberg notes, ''Kierkegaard was undoubtedly one of the godparents of the fundamental ideas behind *Brand.*'' In her 1966 book, *Ibsen, The Norwegian: A Revaluation,* M. C. Bradbrook also notes this, saying that ''Kierkegaard too demanded that a man should give his All.'' Heiberg notes one other idea about the play, that it ''is first and foremost Ibsen's settlement with himself,'' a sentiment that has been echoed by other critics. As biographical and critical studies have illustrated, and as Ibsen's own comments verified, *Brand* was a cathartic experience for the playwright, in which he explored his own views about life and religion.

Debates over the play's meaning continue today. However, regardless of how people interpret the play, there is no doubt that *Brand*, along with his next play, *Peer Gynt*, is considered one of Ibsen's major works—and the seminal work that helped lead to his immense critical and popular success both in Scandinavia and around the world.

Showbill cover from the theatrical production of Brand, *written by Henrik Ibsen and directed by Craig D. Kinzer*

CRITICISM

Ryan D. Poquette

Poquette has a bachelor's degree in English and specializes in writing about literature. In the following essay, Poquette discusses Brand's conflicting desires, which ultimately drive him mad and lead him to death.

In Ibsen's *Brand*, the title character has such strength of conviction that he sacrifices everything, including his family, to stick to his beliefs. On the surface, this appears to be a noble thing to do. In fact, many critics, like Edmund Gosse, who in the 1889 *Fortnightly Review* notes that the play is a ''beautiful Puritan opera,'' have seen Brand as a hero. However, as Irving Deer states in his 1961 article, ''Ibsen's *Brand:* Paradox and the Symbolic Hero,'' this is not a foregone conclusion with all critics. Wrote Deer, ''Simply stated, the controversy boils down to whether Ibsen intended him to be a hero or a villain.'' By studying Brand's spiritual journey, however, it appears that Ibsen meant to show Brand as a man who ultimately goes mad from the strain of trying to reconcile the contradictory ends of religious fanaticism and humanity.

At the beginning of the play, the audience is led to believe, as are the peasant and his son, that Brand is not a normal human. He claims himself to be ''a Great One's messenger'' and shows little concern for the bad weather in the mountains, which the peasant fears will kill them all if they continue on. Brand says he is willing to make the ultimate sacrifice if God requires it: ''If of my life the Lord hath need / Then welcome precipice and flood!'' The peasants think that Brand is crazy and do not follow him. Brand notes that these peasants, like most others in the world, are unwilling to make ultimate sacrifices: ''Much will they give with willing mind, / Leave them but Life, dear Life, behind.'' With this thought, Brand suddenly remembers his childhood and ''two fancies of the brain'' that he had. He describes these states of mind as ''An Owl that dreads the dark, a fish / With water-fright.'' In other words, as a child, he had a fear of living the life that he was meant to live. Just as an owl is meant to live at night and a fish is meant to live in water, Brand felt that he was ''bound to bear'' a burden and, as a child, had a moment of weakness about this fact.

This passage introduces the idea that Brand is not invincible, as audience members might first believe after seeing him risk his life and survive harsh mountain weather whereas normal mortals turn back. It also underscores the idea that Brand is different from many other humans, who live in fear

WHAT DO I READ NEXT?

- Anton Chekhov, along with Ibsen and August Strindberg, is widely considered to be one of the three most influential playwrights in early modern drama. Like Ibsen's *Brand,* Chekhov's *The Seagull,* originally published in 1895, deliberately goes against the stage conventions of the day. Instead of building the dramatic action as the play goes on, Chekhov reduces it. Instead of introducing one major protagonist, Chekhov introduces several. The play also borrows the type of overt symbolism recognized in Ibsen's plays.
- Ibsen's *A Doll House,* originally published in Norwegian in 1879 and translated into English in 1889 as *A Doll's House,* is one of Ibsen's most famous and most controversial plays. The story concerns the oppression and liberation of a woman in a middle-class marriage and was ahead of its time in its promotion of women's rights.
- *Peer Gynt* (1867), the play Ibsen wrote directly after *Brand,* is in many ways exactly the opposite of the earlier play, as evidenced by their respective title characters. Brand is a devout pastor, while Peer Gynt is a storyteller and liar. *Peer Gynt* also employs a much lighter tone than the heavy-handed religious feeling in *Brand.* The latter play is considered by many to be the single most definitive work that represents life in Norway at the time.
- In the late 1300s, a poet named William Langland wrote three versions of a Middle English poem, "The Vision of Piers Plowman." In modern translations, the title of the poem has often been shortened to "Piers Plowman." The poem features a title character who has many religious experiences—through the form of several dream visions—and who ultimately rebels against the corruption that he finds in both the religion and politics of his time.
- C. S. Lewis, an Oxford professor and English man of letters in the twentieth century, experienced a profound conversion to Christianity. After this, he was extremely outspoken and gave a number of radio addresses on various aspects of Christianity. *Mere Christianity,* originally published in 1952, collects and expands on three of Lewis's radio lectures—"The Case for Christianity," "Christian Behaviour," and "Beyond Personality." Together, these three talks outline the primary beliefs of Christianity, in an informal and conversational argument.
- August Strindberg, along with Ibsen and Chekhov, is widely considered to be one of the three most influential playwrights in early modern drama. One of Strindberg's most famous plays, *Miss Julie,* originally published in Swedish in 1888 and translated into English in 1912, was written without act divisions—a departure from nineteenth-century stage conventions.

most of their lives, as other characters show. Brand is so strong in his mission for God that the fears only appear to have plagued him when he was a child. At this point, the audience gets another glimpse into Brand's past, when he runs into Agnes and Einar—a boy with whom he went to school. Einar describes Brand's childhood as follows: "Aye, the same solitary elf / Whom, still sufficient to himself / No games could ever draw away." Brand, with his philosophical thoughts and fears about the meaning of his life and his greater mission, chose to isolate himself from the other schoolchildren. This is an important idea that Ibsen plants in the beginning because it foreshadows what will eventually happen to Brand as he alienates himself from the human race as a whole.

It is appropriate, then, that after Brand meets Einar in the mountains, he runs into Gerd, a mad little gypsy girl who has visions. She questions Brand: "You saw the hawk just now?" Brand is not mad, however, and so cannot see the visions that

Gerd speaks of. Gerd is not deterred. When they start to talk about the church in the valley where Brand is headed, Gerd makes mention of a much more impressive one, ''A church built out of ice and snow!'' Brand recognizes that Gerd is talking about the Ice-Church, a natural, chapel-shaped structure that exists in the mountains, but he warns Gerd that she should not go there, for fear of an avalanche: ''A sudden lurch / Of wind may break the hanging ice: / A shout, a rifle-shot, suffice—.'' The rifle-shot foreshadows the avalanche at the end that kills both Brand and Gerd, but more important, this reference to the Ice-Church helps to illustrate Brand's mentality at the beginning of the play. While he is willing to face any danger and give his life for his mission to God, he does not see the Ice-Church as a worthy spiritual endeavor, and so he cautions against going there.

"ALTHOUGH ALF'S DEATH AFFECTS BRAND GREATLY, HE SUPPRESSES HIS GRIEF, THOUGH BARELY, AND REQUIRES AGNES TO DO THE SAME. BUT WHEN AGNES DIES, BRAND CAN NO LONGER SUPPRESS HIS HUMANITY, AND THE STRAIN OF TRYING TO FOLLOW HIS MISSION WHILE IGNORING HIS HUMANITY IS APPARENT."

When Brand's mother arrives, the audience gets one more example of Brand's self-imposed exclusion from humanity: says Brand to his mother, ''I've gone against you from my youth; / You've been no mother, I no son, / Till you are grey and I am grown.'' Brand is disgusted with his mother's materialistic behavior, which first manifests itself after his mother dies. Unseen by his mother, Brand watches as she loots his father's dead body, searching for money, then expands her search to the rest of the room: ''Finding, she seized with falcon's pounce / 'Twixt tears and glee, each several ounce.'' This base materialism horrified the young Brand and shaped his disparaging view of humanity: ''Barely one in thousands sees / How mere life is one immense / Towering mountain of offence!'' Instead of living an offensive life with other humans, Brand devotes himself to what he believes is a higher cause, setting the ultimately unachievable goal of suppressing his humanity through sheer will. When the doctor accuses Brand of being inhumane, since he would not give his mother last rites after her failure to give up material goods, Brand states his view of humanity:

> Humane! That word's relaxing whine
> Is now the whole world's countersign!
> It serves the weakling to conceal
> The abdication of his will;

However, even though Brand tries to suppress his humanity, this is impossible, a fact that gradually becomes clear. Although Brand is not interested in preserving his money, his power, or his physical health, as others are, he does have an obsession with his mission—something that he is initially unwilling to give up. One of the peasant men points this hypocrisy out to Brand when he is trying to talk Brand into abandoning his grander plans and do a good service by helping their village: ''This Call of yours, this holy strife / You yearn for and will not let drop—/ It is then dear to you?'' Brand is emphatic, letting the man know that ''It is my life to me!'' At this point, the man turns Brand's words back on himself, saying that, as Brand has counseled others to be willing to give up things that are dear to them, such as their lives, Brand should be willing to give up his own ''life.'' Brand recognizes this and decides to stay.

Even though he stays in the village, Brand tries to maintain his seclusion from humanity. Says Brand: ''Of what the paltering world calls love, / I will not know, I cannot speak; / I know but His who reigns above.'' This, however, is not true, because he falls in love with Agnes, his wife, and loves their son, Alf. These attachments threaten to compromise Brand's mission, starting with his son, Alf. Brand and Agnes are unsure whether or not Alf will be able to survive the harsh weather in the fiord, but Brand is convinced that the sacrifices he has already made for God mean that he will not be called upon to sacrifice Alf, too: ''He will not take away our joy . . . / My little lad in time will grow / As big and strong as can be found.'' However, as he starts to dwell on this idea, he realizes the immensity of such a sacrifice, questioning the possibility of it along with his strength of will: ''But if He dared demand?'' When the doctor tells Brand and Agnes that their son will die if they do not leave, Brand immediately says he will go, even though it will mean abandoning his parish and his mission. Here, he is responding to his human emotions, which want to preserve the life of his son. However, he is eventually able to suppress these emotions once again, and through the strength of his will, he stays at the parish, sacrificing his son for his mission.

Although Alf's death affects Brand greatly, he suppresses his grief, though barely, and requires Agnes to do the same. But when Agnes dies, Brand can no longer suppress his humanity, and the strain of trying to follow his mission while ignoring his humanity is apparent. Says the clerk: "Aye, he's not quite right: / He's felt a lonely, gnawing tooth / Since he became a widower." The clerk notes that Brand expresses his grief by playing the organ and that "Each note's as wild / As if he wept for wife and child." The musical notes are not the only thing that is wild about Brand at this point. When the townspeople try to make him a hero, idolizing him and the new church he has built, Brand is once again disgusted with the materialism of humanity, which now has intruded into his vocation. He gives an impassioned speech to the crowd about "the flaw, in me and you," and the impressed crowd follows Brand into the mountains.

The dean is worried that Brand is stealing their villagers, but the sheriff says: "Who would butt against a bull? / Let him have his craze out full!" The sheriff can see that Brand has gone mad from the strain of trying unsuccessfully to suppress his humanity, and he knows that the villagers will eventually turn on Brand when he offers them gloomy sermons instead of comfort. When this inevitably happens, the clerk, echoing the sentiment of many others, says: "Let be the lunatic!" Brand retreats into the upper reaches of the mountains. He is distraught, searching for the strength of will he once had, and at this point totally mad from his grief:

> Alf and Agnes! O come back
> Where the peaks are bleak and black
> Lone I sit, the wind blows through me
> Chilled by visions weary and gloomy—

At this point, in his despair, Brand sees a vision of his dead wife, Agnes, tempting him to compromise and give up his mission. Brand fights the vision, however, and refuses to give up his mission, saying: "Wandering dreams no more are rife: / No, the horror now is . . . life!" Having exiled himself from humanity, Brand now turns his back on his life and the memory of his wife. As the vision disappears, Gerd, the mad girl, comes up to him. She asks him if he has seen the hawk of compromise, her vision from before, and he admits: "Aye! For once I saw him true." Although Brand shied away from Gerd before, now he finds in her the only human company he can have, since, in her madness, she has set herself on a similar mission as Brand—hunting down and killing the spirit of compromise. Unlike in the beginning of the play, Brand now willingly allows Gerd to lead him to the Ice-Church, where she sees the hawk and shoots him with her rifle. The resulting avalanche buries them both but not before Brand calls out to God asking if human will is enough to achieve salvation. Brand hears a voice cry out, "God is Love!" Although there are several interpretations of this, the most likely, given Brand's steady breakdown into madness, is that he is hearing a voice that does not exist.

Since he was a child, Brand has attempted to adhere to an impossible ideal, which was easy enough for him to do when he had no attachments. However, by falling in love with Agnes and loving their son, Alf, he succumbed to one of the human material weaknesses that he has despised since his childhood. Over the course of the play, Brand's attempt to suppress this weakness fails, and the strain, coupled with the grief over his dead family, slowly drives him mad.

Source: Ryan D. Poquette, Critical Essay on *Brand,* in *Drama for Students,* The Gale Group, 2003.

Robert Brustein

In the following essay excerpt, Brustein explores connections between Ibsen's leaving his native Norway and the rich inspiration present in Brand, *calling the drama "a sudden revelation from the depths of an original mind."*

Any discussion of Ibsen's mature art must start with *Brand*, since this monolithic masterpiece is not only the first play he completed after leaving his native country, but his first, and possibly his greatest, work of enduring power. Nothing in Ibsen's previous writings prepares us for a play of this scope, not even the substantial talent he displays in *The Vikings at Helgeland* and *The Pretenders*, for *Brand* is like a sudden revelation from the depths of an original mind. It is highly probable that Ibsen's achievement in *Brand* was intimately connected with his departure from Norway, for he seemed to find an important source of creative power in his self-imposed exile: "I had to escape the swinishness up there to feel fully cleansed,'' he wrote to his mother-in-law from Rome. ''I could never lead a consistent spiritual life there. I was one man in my work and another outside—and for that reason my work failed in consistency too.'' Ibsen's desire for creative consistency was certainly fulfilled during his sojourn in Rome. Besides filling him with admiration for the ''indescribable harmony'' of his new surroundings (''beautiful, wonderful, magical,'' he called them), Ibsen's *Italienische Reise*, like Goethe's before him, seems to have opened him up to an expansive romanticism. Ibsen himself was quite conscious of the influence of Rome on his art, for in describing to a friend how *Brand* had come to be written, he said: ''Add to this Rome with its ideal peace, association with the carefree artist community, an existence in an atmosphere which can only be compared with that of Shakespeare's *As You Like It*—and you have the conditions productive of *Brand*.'' It was a period of the most exquisite freedom Ibsen had ever known, and his nostalgia for these years was later to find expression in Oswald's enthusiastic descriptions of the buoyant *livsglaede* (joy of life) to be found in the Paris artist community.

On the surface, *Brand*—an epic of snow and ice with a glacial Northern atmosphere and a forbidding central figure—would seem to have little in common with this warm, sunny Italian world. Yet the sense of abandon which Ibsen was experiencing is reflected in the play's openness of form and richness of inspiration (''May I not . . . point to *Brand* and *Peer Gynt*,'' wrote Ibsen later, ''and say: 'See, the wine cup has done this!'''). Though it was originally conceived as a narrative poem, Ibsen soon reworked *Brand* into a five-act poetic drama, a work so conscientiously long and unstageable that Ibsen was astonished when a Scandinavian company decided to produce it. For Ibsen, exulting in the luxury of pure self-expression, had written the work unmindful of the limiting demands of an audience or the restricting requirements of a theatre. Having finally freed his imagination from its frozen Northern vaults, Ibsen had at last discovered how to make his work an integral part of his spiritual life. The solution was simple enough; he had to be the same person *in* his work as outside it. Although in *The Pretenders* Ibsen had dramatized the conflicts in his own soul through a fictional external action, *Brand* has the most thoroughgoing revelation of his rebellious interior life that Ibsen had yet attempted, an act of total purgation, in which he exorcised the troll battle within his heart and mind by transforming it into art. With *Brand*, Ibsen confronted for the first time and in combination the great subjects which were to occupy him successively during the course of his career: the state of man in the universe, the state of modern society, and the state of his own feverish, divided soul.

"THE ENDING OF *BRAND,* NEVERTHELESS, LIKE THE ENDING OF SO MANY OF IBSEN'S PLAYS, IS INCONCLUSIVE, AN EARLY EXAMPLE OF IBSEN'S FAILURE TO INTEGRATE HIS DRAMA OF IDEAS WITH HIS DRAMA OF ACTION. . . ."

The play, a storage house for all of Ibsen's future themes and conflicts, is constructed like a series of interlocking arches, each ascending higher than the last. The lowest arch is a domestic drama, in which Ibsen examines the relationship of the idealist to his family (the basis for later plays like *The Wild Duck*); the middle arch is a social-political drama, in which he analyzes the effect of the aristocratic individual on a democratic community (the basis for plays like *An Enemy of the People*); and the highest arch is a religious drama, in which he shows the rivalry between the messianic rebel and the nineteenth-century God (the basis for plays like *The Master Builder*). Pastor Brand—a reforming minister of extraordinary zeal (his very name means ''sword and fire'')—is the hero of all three dramas, and Ibsen's supreme idealist, individualist, and rebel. In the tradition of the Old Testament prophets, and those apostles of religious purification who arise in human history to change the course of the world, Brand is remorselessly dedicated to his cause. Like Luther, he has elected to be the ''chastiser of the age,'' scourging the excesses of individuals and institutions; like Moses, he is determined to bring new codes of spiritual purity to a generation of idlers, appeasers, and dreamers; and like Christ, he is committed to the salvation of all mankind through a complete transformation of human character. Brand, however, is a very peculiar Christian, if indeed he can be called Christian at all. Intensely masculine, patristic, strict, and unyielding, he rejects the compassionate side of Christianity in his determination to close the gap between what is and what should be by making human practice conform to spiritual ideals. Actually, Brand is more extreme than the most apocalyptic Puritan reformers, a Savonarola of the will who brings Protestant individualism to the furthest reaches of its own implications. For, as Brand develops his theology, he demands not only that each man become his own Church, but—so strict are the extremes of his ideal—*even his own God.*

Man becomes a god by imitating God, but Brand's God—not a ''gentle wind'' but a ''storm''—is almost inimitable, being the purest and most uncompromising of celestial beings. He is identified with the Ideal itself, to be attained through the unlimited striving of the human will. Because of his emphasis on will, the mortal sin for Brand is cowardice and half-heartedness. Like Kierkegaard before him, and Nietzsche after, Brand is disposed towards the great saint or the great sinner—the man who lives his life extremely with a purpose either good or evil—but he cannot abide the will-less mediocrities who fail to be anything fully. Brand's Devil, therefore, is the spirit of compromise, while his concept of evil is identified with the middle way of moderation, accommodation, luxury, ease, and moral laziness. Taking ''All or nothing'' as his rebellious credo, he has resolved to make ''heirs of heaven'' out of the dull and cloddish inhabitants of the modern world, fashioning a new race of heroes to match the heroic figures of the past.

Brand, who follows his own precepts with uncompromising integrity, is himself one of these heroes—but at a terrific cost. Struggling painfully to conquer any emotions which might lead him from the path of righteousness, he becomes contemptuous of any but the hardest virtues: for him, love is merely a smirch of lies (''Faced by his generation / Which is lax and slothful, the best love is hate''), while charity and humanitarianism are the encouragement of human weakness (''Was God humane when Jesus died?''). Thus, Brand finally succeeds in suppressing his own human feelings, an ambiguous victory which makes him at the same time both wholly admirable and wholly impossible. Like most monastic, disciplinary types, he has something forbidding and inhuman in his nature. Ibsen usually associates him with images of cold and hardness (snow, steel, iron, stone); even the conditions of his birth (he was ''born by a cold fjord in the shadow of a barren mountain'') suggest his icelike qualities. By comparison, the beauty-loving painter Ejnar and his lovely fiancée Agnes are identified with ''mountain air, the sunshine, the dew, and the scent of pines,'' and their pursuit of Southern pleasures is a striking contrast to Brand's singleminded pursuit of the ideal.

Yet, such is Brand's heroic stature, fierce courage, and charismatic power that by the end of Act II Agnes has been converted to his religion of ''grayness,'' leaving Ejnar to take up her duties by Brand's side. It is in the domestic scenes that follow (Acts III and IV) that Brand's defective humanity is most strongly dramatized, for his fanatic ideals of moral purity succeed in destroying his entire family; first his mother, who dies unshriven when Brand refuses to visit her unless she freely gives away her fortune; then his young son Alf, a victim of the Northern cold who has been refused the Southern warmth (an Ibsenist image for love); and finally Agnes herself, forced into dreadful choices and ultimately deprived of even the relics of her mother love. All this while, Brand has been engaged in a terrific struggle with himself, torn between his ideal and his love for Agnes and Alf. Yet his decision to be a god has left him with no real choice; and when Agnes warns him ''He dies who sees Jehovah face to face,'' he can only accept the terrible implications of his Godhead and let her die. When she abdicates her painful life with an ecstatic cry (''I am free Brand! I am free!''), Brand has achieved a moral victory only through the sacrifice of everything he loved in the world—as Shaw put in through ''having caused more intense suffering by his saintliness that the most talented sinner could possibly have done with twice his opportunities.''

Yet it is only in the domestic portions of the play that Brand emerges as a villain-idealist; like all great reformers (even Christ treated his family with scant respect), he has no time or capacity for a happy private life. When he plays a public role, in the social-political scenes, he is a bright contrast to the citizenry he has come to reform. Here, Brand, a typical *Sturm-und-Drang* hero, is the individual at war with society, denouncing its worm-eaten conventions, its limited aspirations, its corrupt institutions. His antagonist, in this drama, is the Mayor, society's elected representative—like Mayor Peter Stockmann and Peter Mortensgard, a ''typical man of the people,'' and therefore Brand's instinctive enemy. The conflict between them arises from their conflicting expectations from their constituents. Brand, appealing to spiritual man, seeks the salvation of the individual through a revolution in his moral consciousness; the Mayor, appealing to social man, seeks the pacification of the community through attention to its material needs. Wishing to make life easier, the Mayor wants to construct public buildings; Brand, wishing to make life harder, wants to construct a new Church. This conflict—in which Brand obviously expresses Ibsen's own predisposition in favor of the individual against the community, the moral against the social, the spiritual against the material, radical revolution against moderation and compromise—is ultimately irreconcilable. But since Brand's following has increased, the Mayor, pulling his sheets to the wind, capitulates, following the desires of the compact majority by helping Brand with his plans. The Mayor, however, has not lost the battle. He has merely made a strategic retreat in order to assimilate his enemy. And, as for Brand, his temporary success has made him unwittingly betray his own ideal.

In Act V, which forms the climax of the religious drama and the heart of the play, Brand becomes what Ibsen really intended him to be—neither a villain-idealist nor a hero-reformer but a tragic sufferer existing independently of moral judgments. At the beginning of the act, Brand is seen as a fashionable preacher, a popular commercial personality like Billy Graham. His new Church is about to open and Brand himself is to be decorated by the State for his services to the community. Multitudes have gathered for the event—vaguely sensing that the destruction of the old Church was some form of sacrilege and trembling with apprehension "as though they had been summoned to elect a new God." Brand himself is very morose; he cannot pray and his soul is full of discords. His mood grows blacker when the Provost—the theological counterpart of the Mayor—begins to inform him that religion is merely an instrument of the State to insure itself against unrest. When he warns Brand to concern himself with the needs of the community rather than the salvation of the individual, Brand suddenly becomes aware that the Church is a lie and that he has become a corrupt institution himself. Ignoring the Provost's contention that "the man who fights alone will never achieve anything of a lasting nature," he tells his enthusiastic followers that the only true Church is the wild and natural world of the fjords and moorlands, not yet tainted by human compromise, hypocrisy, and evil: "God is not here! / His kingdom is perfect freedom."

Like Moses leading his people towards the beautiful promised land, Brand makes his way upwards to the freedom and purity of the cliffs and mountains. But like Moses' followers, the people begin to slacken and grumble when the way grows hard. The Grand Inquisitor, in Dostoyevsky's *The Brothers Karamazov,* had told the resurrected Christ that the common man seeks not Godhead, but miracle, mystery, and authority. And now it is Brand's turn to learn of human limitation, as his followers clamor for water, bread, prophecies, security, and miracles in place of the spiritual victory he promises. When he offers them no more than "a new will," "a new faith," and "a crown of thorns," they feel betrayed and begin to stone their Messiah. And when the Mayor arrives with the Provost to reclaim the sheeplike flock with a promise of food and safety, they repudiate Brand's salvation altogether, meekly returning to their secular lives below.

Brand is left alone on the moorlands, torn and bleeding, to meditate upon his mistakes. In putting vengeance, justice, and retribution before forgiveness, charity, and compassion; in repudiating the "God of every dull and earthbound slave," Brand has pursued Godhead through the pursuit of an incorruptible ideal. But while making him Godlike, this quest has also made him a rebel against the very Deity he had tried to serve. Brand's messianism has turned him into something harder and crueler than God, and it has broken the backs of his all-too-human followers. Now Brand must learn that man cannot be God; that he must live with the Devil if he is to live at all; and that even the freedom of the will is limited by the inexorable determinism of inherited sin. Now, like Moses on Mount Nebo, Brand is denied the promised land, and must await retribution himself. Yet, still he adheres to his ideal. When a specter appears, in the shape of Agnes, offering him warmth, love, and forgiveness if he will only renounce the awful words *"All or nothing,"* Brand refuses; and when the spirit is transformed into a hawk flying across the moorlands, Brand recognizes his ancient enemy, the Devil of Compromise.

Still struggling upwards, Brand finally reaches the Ice Church, a mighty chasm between peaks and summits where "cataract and avalanche sing Mass." It is Brand's true parish, for there, in the ideal habitat of the extreme Romantic, Brand may preach his gospel of the absolute, free from the human world and its compromising influences. When Gerd—the wild gypsy girl who has accompanied him—suddenly has a half-ironic, half-sincere vision of Brand as the incarnation of Christ and begins worshiping him as a God, Brand, at last, gives way to human feeling:

> Until today I sought to be a tablet
> On which God could write. Now my life
> Shall flow rich and warm. The mist is breaking.

Michael Bryant, as Brand, and Lynn Farleigh, as Agnes, in a 1978 production of Brand, *directed by Christopher Morahan and performed at Olivier Theatre in London*

I can weep! I can kneel! I can pray!

But it is too late. Shooting at the devil-hawk with her rifle, Gerd has started an avalanche, and Brand is about to be buried in the snow. At the last minute, Brand asks a final tortured question of God: ''If not by Will, how can man be redeemed?'' And the answer comes from the heavens in booming tones: *Han er deus caritatis*—''He is the God of charity, mercy, love.''

It is an answer which completes the play, but denies its philosophical basis. For if Brand's severe demands have all been wrong, and man is redeemed only through love, then the whole intellectual structure of the work collapses; and Brand's relentless attacks on compromise and accommodation are all superfluous. We must remember, however, that Ibsen is not rejecting Brand's revolt as an idea; he is merely rejecting it as a form of action. And since Brand's judge is a God of love, even Brand, we must assume, is forgiven at the last. The ending of *Brand*, nevertheless, like the ending of so many of Ibsen's plays, is inconclusive, an early example of Ibsen's failure to integrate his drama of ideas with his drama of action—and this itself is the result of his refusal to adopt a positive synthetic doctrine. Up until the ending, we can regard Brand *both* as a great hero-saint-reformer with a redeeming message of salvation *and* as a flawed, repressed, and ice-cold being whose ruthless dedication to an impossible ideal causes untold suffering and needless deaths. Up until the ending, we can admire Ibsen's extraordinary capacity for keeping two antithetical attitudes in his mind at the same time, so that he is able to exalt messianic rebellion as an idea, while condemning it in practice. But the ending demands a synthesis which the author cannot provide; instead, he chooses to invalidate the intellectual hypothesis of his play. Still, even in this vaguely unsatisfying ending, one is filled with admiration for this defeated, yet triumphantly Godlike hero whose eternal struggle upwards has somehow enlarged the spiritual boundaries of man.

We must conclude, then, that both the success and failure of the play stem from the unreconciled conflicts of the playwright. For Ibsen's split attitude towards his hero reflects the clash in his own soul between the twin poles of his temperament—the Romantic idealism of the reforming rebel and the Classical detachment of the objective artist. This dualism—fatal to a man of action but invaluable to a dramatist—is present whenever Ibsen examines the effect of absolute idealism on private happiness, a subject that is to obsess him all his life. But though he will treat this delicate theme again and again in the future, he will never make a presentation of such compelling power and grandeur.

Source: Robert Brustein, ''Henrik Ibsen,'' in *The Theatre of Revolt,* Little, Brown and Company, 1962, pp. 35–84.

SOURCES

Bradbrook, M. C., *Ibsen, The Norwegian: A Revaluation,* Archon Books, 1966, p. 43.

Deer, Irving, ''Ibsen's *Brand:* Paradox and the Symbolic Hero,'' in *Ibsen: A Collection of Critical Essays,* edited by Rolf Fjelde, Prentice-Hall, 1965, p. 52, originally published in *The Lock Haven Bulletin,* Series 1, No. 3, 1961, pp. 7–18.

Gosse, Edmund, ''Ibsen's Social Dramas,'' in *Fortnightly Review,* Vol. XLV, No. CCLXV, January 1, 1889, pp. 107–21.

Heiberg, Hans, *Ibsen: A Portrait of the Artist,* translated by Joan Tate, University of Miami Press, 1969, pp. 125, 129, 132, 134–35.

Ibsen, Henrik, *Brand,* translated by F. E. Garrett, J. M. Dent & Sons Ltd., 1960.

Koht, Halvdan, *The Life of Ibsen,* translated by Ruth Lima McMahon and Hanna Astrup Larsen, Vol. 2, W. W. Norton & Company, 1931.

Lucas, F. L., *The Drama of Ibsen and Strindberg,* Cassell, 1962, pp. 62, 66–67.

FURTHER READING

Adler, Stella, *Stella Adler on Ibsen, Strindberg, and Chekhov,* edited by Barry Paris, Vintage Books, 2000.

This book offers an engaging way for actors and non-actors alike to approach works by the three playwrights. Adler, a famous actress and acting instructor, discusses the best way for actors to approach roles in the plays, while giving an academic analysis of the major works.

Donnelly, Marian C., *Architecture in the Scandinavian Countries,* MIT Press, 1991.

Donnelly's book gives a detailed account of Nordic building, starting with the remains of structures that date back to 7,500 B.C. and continuing through to the 1970s. The book covers structures and the architects who created them, from Norway, Sweden, Denmark, Finland, Iceland, and the Faroes.

Goldman, Michael, *Ibsen,* Columbia University Press, 1998.

Goldman explores the often-overlooked connection between Ibsen's dramatic art and the effects that specific dramatic techniques have on audiences who experience the plays. The book offers a thorough discussion of many of Ibsen's major plays, including *Peer Gynt, The Master Builder, A Doll's House,* and *The Wild Duck.*

Kierkegaard, Søren, *The Essential Kierkegaard,* edited by Howard V. Hong and Edna H. Hong, Princeton University Press, 2000.

Most critics acknowledge the profound influence that Kierkegaard had on Ibsen's beliefs and on his dramatic works. This comprehensive anthology collects the major works of the nineteenth-century Danish philosopher.

Marker, Frederick J., and Lise-Lone Marker, *Ibsen's Lively Art: A Performance Study of the Major Plays,* Cambridge University Press, 1989.

In this production study of six of Ibsen's major plays, the Markers explore non-English theatrical productions from other countries, including Germany, Russia, France, and Scandinavia. The book covers early productions from Ibsen's life up to more modern and unconventional interpretations of the plays in the twentieth century.

Roesdahl, Else, *The Vikings,* Penguin USA, 1999.

Brand mentions the legendary exploits of the Vikings, the Nordic conquerors who initially inhabited the Scandinavian countries. Traditionally, Vikings have been largely viewed as lawless pirates who plundered at will. In her extensive study, Roesdahl digs underneath the legends, incorporating the latest archaeological research to provide an accurate description of the geography, culture, and lifestyle of the Vikings. The book also includes a section on how the Vikings have influenced modern culture.

Cloud Nine

CARYL CHURCHILL

1979

Cloud Nine, by British playwright Caryl Churchill, was first performed at Dartington College of Arts in February 1979 by the Joint Stock Theatre Group. It was then performed on tour at the Royal Court Theatre in London and was first staged in New York in 1981.

Cloud Nine, which can be found in Churchill's *Plays One* (London and New York, 1985), was a popular and critical success. In addition to frequently being very amusing, the play highlights colonial and gender oppression. The first act is set in the nineteenth century in an African country ruled by Britain, and Churchill satirizes the repressive nature of the Victorian family, the rigidity of narrowly prescribed gender roles, and the phenomenon whereby oppressed peoples in colonized countries take on the identity of the colonizers. Act two takes place in London one hundred years later with mostly the same characters, who have aged only twenty-five years. In this act, Churchill explores such topics as women's liberation, gay liberation, and the sexual revolution, all of which were prominent social movements in Britain, as well as the United States, in the 1970s.

AUTHOR BIOGRAPHY

Caryl Churchill was born on September 3, 1938, in London, England. She spent most of her early childhood in and near London before her family moved in 1948 to Montreal, Canada, where Churchill attended the Trafalgar School until 1955. Churchill began to write as a young girl, and she also developed an early interest in the theater. She continued these interests during her undergraduate years, which began in 1957 when she enrolled at Lady Margaret Hall, Oxford, in England. She graduated with a Bachelor of Arts in English in 1960. During her university years, two of her plays received student productions, and in 1962, *The Ants*, her first professional radio play, was broadcast.

In 1961, she married David Harter, a barrister, and from 1963 to 1969 the couple had three sons. During this period Churchill continued to write radio plays, including *Identical Twins* (1968), and to develop a socialist and feminist approach to drama. Churchill's first professional stage production was *Owners*, performed at the Royal Court Theatre Upstairs in London in 1972. The play premiered in New York the following year. During the 1970s, Churchill wrote a number of plays that were broadcast on BBC television, including *Turkish Delight* (1974) and *The After-Dinner Joke* (1978). Her two stage plays, *Objections to Sex and Violence* (1975) and *Light Shining in Buckinghamshire* (1976), brought her critical attention. The latter play was the result of Churchill's involvement in London's experimental Joint Stock Theatre Group. Another play written for Joint Stock was *Cloud Nine*, which in 1979 became Churchill's first big success. It was also a hit in the United States, where it opened off-Broadway in New York at the Theatre de Lys in May 1981 to positive reviews and large audiences. *Cloud Nine* won the Obie Award in 1982.

Churchill followed this success with *Top Girls*, a play that portrays women achieving success by imitating the worst of male behaviors. It was staged at Royal Court Theatre in 1982 and transferred to New York later that year. It also won an Obie Award. In 1983, Churchill wrote *Fen*, which was the result of a group of Joint Stock actors and playwrights living for two weeks in a hard-pressed farming community in the Fens of England. *Fen* was a critical and popular success in London and New York, and it won the 1984 Susan Smith Blackburn Prize.

After *Softcops* (1984), which was performed by the Royal Shakespeare Company in London, and *A Mouthful of Birds* (1986), co-written with David Lan, Churchill wrote *Serious Money* (1987), a play about greed and financial scandal on London's stock exchange. Two short plays followed, *Ice Cream* and *Hot Fudge* (1989), and then *Mad Forest* (1990), in which Churchill examined life in Romania before, during, and after the downfall of the dictator Nicolae Ceausescu. During the 1990s, Churchill wrote *Lives of the Great Poisoners* (1991); the surreal and mythic *The Skriker* (1994); *Thyestes* (1994), a translation of a play by Seneca; *Hotel* (1997), in which all the parts are sung; and *This Is a Chair* (1999).

Caryl Churchill

PLOT SUMMARY

Act 1, Scene 1

Act 1 of *Cloud Nine* is set in a British African colony in the nineteenth century. The first scene takes place on the verandah of a house. After an opening song introduces the characters, Clive tells his wife, Betty, that he is expecting a visitor, Harry Bagley, an explorer. Betty tells Clive that their black servant, Joshua, insulted her, and Clive makes Joshua apologize. Then the family gathers: their children Victoria and Edward; the governess, Ellen; and Betty's mother, Maud. Edward is looking after Victoria's doll, which annoys his father because he thinks this is unmasculine. Betty is nervous at the thought of entertaining a guest. Mrs. Saunders, a widowed neighbor, arrives to take shelter; the local tribes are preparing for war, and she is afraid to stay in her own house. Harry arrives, and he and Clive speak about the dangerous situation, exhibiting a disdainful view of the indigenous people. Harry and Betty are left alone; they are romantically attracted to each other. The scene ends as Harry, who is bisexual, propositions Joshua for sex.

Act 1, Scene 2

A couple of nights later, in an open space some distance from the house, Mrs. Saunders meets with Clive. It is revealed that Clive has already seduced her and has a sexual passion for her, which she goes along with even though she does not like him.

The family gathers for a Christmas picnic. They play a ball game, but the men monopolize it, claiming that the women cannot catch. Then everyone plays hide and seek. Joshua warns Clive that the stable boys are not reliable and are carrying knives. Harry and Betty exchange endearments, and Betty bemoans the fact that they can never be alone. Edward says he loves Harry, and it is clear that they have on former occasions had sex with each other. Betty confides in Ellen that she loves Harry, and Ellen reveals that she is in love with Betty.

Act 1, Scene 3

In the house, the women discuss the fact that the stable boys are being flogged, and Mrs. Saunders goes to investigate the situation. Edward is still fond of Victoria's doll, but Betty takes it away from him and slaps him, and Ellen slaps him also. Edward confesses to the returning Clive that he said bad things about his father, but Clive forgives him because he owned up. Clive reveals that he knows of Betty's feelings for Harry and is ready to forgive her, but he says she must resist her lustful feelings or they will destroy their marriage.

Act 1, Scene 4

On the verandah, Clive tells of a raid by British soldiers on a nearby village. Edward pleads with Harry to stay, while Ellen says she only wants to be with Betty forever. Clive tells Harry that he values male friendship; Harry misinterprets this and makes a sexual advance, which disgusts Clive, who tells Harry that he must save himself by marrying. Mrs. Saunders informs Clive that Joshua's parents were killed in the British raid, but when Clive offers him a day off, Joshua sides with the British, saying his parents were bad people. Harry proposes marriage to Mrs. Saunders, who is not interested, and then to Ellen.

Act 1, Scene 5

On the verandah, there is a wedding reception for Harry and Ellen. Ellen confesses to Betty that she knows nothing about lovemaking, but Betty says there is nothing to it. Mrs. Saunders announces that she is leaving the next day, and Clive kisses her, which prompts Betty to lunge at her in a jealous assault. Clive blames Mrs. Saunders and says she must leave instantly. After her departure, Harry makes a speech, the wedding cake is cut, and then Clive makes a speech also, congratulating the couple and saying that all is well. But at that moment, Joshua readies himself to shoot Clive. Edward sees this but does nothing to alert the others.

Act 2, Scene 1

This scene takes place one hundred years later on a winter afternoon in a London park. Some of the characters from act one reappear, but they are only twenty-five years older. Victoria is married to Martin, and they have a son, Tommy. Victoria's friend Lin, who is divorced, has a four-year-old girl, Cathy. Cathy plays with a gun as the two women talk about the problems of parenting; Lin says that she is a lesbian and hates men. Edward, who is a gardener at the park, arrives and tells Victoria that their mother is walking there. This is not good news for Victoria, since she does not like her mother. Betty appears with Tommy, who has a bruise from playing rough games. Betty announces that she is going to leave Clive. When Betty leaves, Edward and Victoria express their surprise and consternation, believing that now, both their parents will need a lot of attention. As the scene ends, Lin propositions Victoria for sex.

Act 2, Scene 2

In the spring, Edward and his gay lover Gerry are outside in the open air. Edward seeks an explanation of where Gerry was the previous night, but Gerry is evasive. After Edward leaves, Gerry tells of his sexual adventures in a soliloquy. Victoria and Betty talk. Betty says she is worried that she will not be able to manage on her own, now that she has left Clive. She is frightened. Martin tries to offer Victoria support in her dilemma about whether to accept a job in Manchester, but his advice is not much use to her because he is more concerned with demonstrating how good and understanding he is than with helping her. Lin is in love with Victoria and asks her to live with her. Then Lin reveals that her brother, a British soldier, has been killed that morning in Belfast, Northern Ireland. Gerry tells Edward he is bored with their relationship, which is too much like that between husband and wife. Gerry says he is moving out of the apartment they share. Edward expresses amorous interest in his sister, touching her breasts, and she does not object.

Act 2, Scene 3

In the park on a summer night, Victoria, Lin, and Edward are drunk. They perform a farcical ceremony in preparation for a sexual orgy. Martin arrives, and the three of them jump on him and try to make love to him. They are interrupted by a stranger who turns out to be Lin's dead brother, Bill, who is there because he wants sex. As the others leave, Gerry arrives on his own and tells the audience how he picks up lovers in the park. Then all the characters sing a song called Cloud Nine, which is an expression for sexual ecstasy.

Act 2, Scene 4

It is an afternoon in late summer. Lin, Edward, and Victoria now live together along with the two children. Betty arrives and announces that she has a job as a doctor's receptionist and enjoys it. When Betty, Lin, and Victoria leave, Gerry arrives. Edward tells him that he is now unemployed and that in his new domestic situation, he does the housework. Gerry tells him of another sexual adventure; they arrange to meet for a meal. When they leave, Betty returns and tells of her sexual awakening. Victoria reveals that she has decided to go to Manchester. After she leaves, Betty befriends Gerry and invites him to dinner. She says she knows that both her son and Gerry are gay and that this does not distress her. Then Clive appears for the first time since act one and says that he does not feel the same way about Betty that he used to. He also bemoans the loss of the British Empire. Finally, Betty from act one enters, and she and Betty from act two embrace.

CHARACTERS

Harry Bagley

Harry Bagley is an explorer and a friend of Clive. Clive regards him as an eccentric—a bit of a poet as well as a hothead. Betty says he is a bore and a heavy drinker, but when Harry visits Clive and his family, she falls in love with him because he kisses her and says he needs her. However, Harry is bisexual, and his main interest appears to be males of any description. It is revealed that on a previous visit he seduced Edward, and he also propositions Joshua and Clive. Clive is horrified by this and tells Harry he must marry. So, to keep up the appearance of propriety, Harry marries Ellen.

Betty

Betty is Clive's wife and is played by a man. Betty accepts her role as the dutiful Victorian wife, living only for her husband. But she finds her life monotonous and boring. When Harry arrives, she allows herself to develop a passion for him, which Clive, who finds out about it through Joshua, tells her she must overcome. Betty's unfaithfulness, however, does not prevent her from becoming jealous when Clive kisses Mrs. Saunders.

In act two, Betty reappears and is twenty-five years older. This time she is played by a woman. She has decided to leave her husband, and at first she has difficulty building an independent life for herself. But she finds her feet when she gets a job as a receptionist in a doctor's office. She also learns to explore her own sexuality through masturbation. She no longer lives entirely for and through a man.

Cathy

Cathy is the four-year-old daughter of Lin. She is played by a man. In the park, Cathy amuses herself by painting and playing with guns, and she also likes to play with a group of boys called the Dead Hand Gang. But she has refused to wear jeans at school since the other children called her a boy. She now wears only dresses.

Clive

Clive is a British colonial administrator, married to Betty. He is a loyal, patriotic servant of the British Empire, and he has a patronizing and sometimes brutal attitude toward the local Africans, whom he does not trust. Clive is soaked in Victorian moral values. He takes great pride in presiding over his family and has rigid ideas about the way each member should behave. He believes that his son Edward should not play with dolls, for example, and he would take any show of independence by a woman as an insult. He is also shocked by homosexuality, as is seen when his friend misinterprets his comments about male friendship and makes a sexual advance. But Clive is also a hypocrite because he wastes no time in seducing Mrs. Saunders and constantly lusts after her. Clive returns briefly at the end of act two to say that he does not feel the same about Betty as he once did.

Edward

Edward is the nine-year-old son of Clive and Betty, and he is played by a woman. Edward likes dolls, although this displeases both his parents. His father wants him to act like a man, and his mother instructs him not to tell anyone at school that he likes dolls, because then they will not speak to him or let him play cricket. Edward may harbor a secret hatred of his father, because he does nothing to intervene in the last moment of act one, when Joshua is about to shoot Clive.

In act two, Edward is shown as a man in his thirties. He is gay and lives with Gerry. But their relationship breaks up, and he moves in with Lin, Victoria, and Cathy. He is happy doing housework.

Ellen

Ellen is the young governess in charge of Edward and Victoria. She is a lesbian and falls in love with Betty.

Gerry

Gerry is a gay man who lives with Edward. He boasts a lot about his sexual life and conquests. After a disagreement with Edward about the terms of their relationship, he moves out of the apartment they share. Gerry is later befriended by Betty.

Joshua

Joshua is a black African who is the servant in Clive and Betty's home. He is played by a white man. Joshua has internalized the values of his employers; he hates his own tribe and does not condemn the killing of his parents by the British. He serves his master, Clive, informing him that the stable boys are not to be trusted and then whipping them as Clive instructs. Joshua also reports to Clive on the illicit attraction between Harry and Betty and on Ellen's sexual love for Betty. But he also harbors resentment about his subordinate position, which is suggested by his insulting Betty on two occasions. And in the last moment of act one, Joshua points a gun at Clive and is ready to shoot.

Lin

Lin appears only in act two. A working-class friend of Victoria, she is a divorced mother (of Cathy) and is also a lesbian. Her husband used to beat her, and she says she hates men. Lin is sexually attracted to Victoria, and eventually the two of them live together along with Edward.

Martin

Martin is Victoria's husband in act two. He is a novelist who claims to be writing a novel about women from the woman's point of view. He prides himself on being in favor of women's liberation and believes that he goes out of the way to make his wife happy, but in fact he gets impatient with her indecisiveness and only serves to confuse her. Victoria believes that she is more intelligent than he is, but she is still dominated by him.

Maud

Maud is Betty's mother, and she enjoys giving Betty old-fashioned advice about life and love.

Mrs. Saunders

Mrs. Saunders is an independent-minded widow who comes to the home of Clive and his family for safety after the local Africans become threatening. She is seduced by Clive, though she does not like him. She does, however, enjoy the pleasures of sex.

Victoria

Victoria is the daughter of Clive and Betty. In act one, she is two years old and is represented only by a doll. In act two, she is married to Martin and has a child, Tommy. Victoria, who reads widely and likes to offer her intellectual insights to her less educated friend Lin, is in a dilemma about whether she should accept a job as a teacher in Manchester that would separate her from her husband. Since she is beginning to assert herself and not be so subordinate to Martin, she eventually decides to take the job. She also experiments with bisexuality, embarking on a sexual affair with Lin. Victoria does not get along with her mother, remarking that after a ten-minute conversation with Betty she needs to take a two-hour bath to get over it.

THEMES

Colonialism and Sexism

Churchill wrote in her introduction to the play that she wanted to show "the parallel between colonial and sexual oppression." She meant that it is the same mentality of the colonial power, reflecting male values, that also results in the oppression of women.

The colonial attitude can be seen in Clive, who has contempt for those he refers to as the "natives." His attitude is paternalistic. He thinks of himself as a father to the natives, just as he is a father to his family. He also has a low opinion of the natives' capabilities. After praising his black servant, Joshua, as a jewel, he adds, "You'd hardly notice that the fellow's black." Clive regards the local African population as little better than savages, commenting that he knows three different tribal leaders who "would all gladly chop off each other's heads and wear them round their waists." He exerts harsh discipline on the black stable boys when he learns that they cannot be trusted to be loyal servants of his interests.

The point Churchill wishes to make is that Joshua, the only black man in the play, has internalized the values of his white colonial masters and therefore cooperates in his own oppression. As he says at the beginning of the play, "My skin is black but oh my soul is white." His goal is to become what white men want him to be; he says he lives only for his master, a comment that clearly echoes the way Clive's wife Betty regards her own life.

Betty's own attitude contributes to a sexism that pervades the play, especially in act one. Men such as Clive and Harry Bagley go out and have adventures, but the women (Betty, Maud, Ellen) lead dull, monotonous lives. Betty's place is in the home, reading poetry, playing the piano, and waiting for Clive, around whom her life revolves, to return. Gender roles are clearly defined, and the women accept them as part of the nature of things. "The men have their duties and we have ours," says Maud, and Betty regards her own loneliness as a form of service not only to her husband but also to the British Empire. She believes that she is perfectly happy, although she has little understanding of what her true nature and capabilities might be. She has allowed herself to be formed entirely to fit a male image of what a woman should be.

The men have very patronizing ideas about women. Clive regards his wife, and most likely all women, as delicate, sensitive creatures given to fainting and hysteria. But he may prefer things this way, since the weakness of women enables him to feel strong and chivalrous. He regards any sign of independence in a woman as an insult; it is he who must be the protector. Similarly, Harry, when he declares his love for Betty, reserves for himself the active life and allocates to her a purely passive role: "I need you, and I need you where you are, I need you to be Clive's wife. I need to go up rivers and know you are sitting here thinking of me."

The sexism of the men extends to other areas. In act one, scene two, Ellen and Betty begin to play catch, and the men express surprise and congratulations whenever the women manage to catch the ball. Obviously, women are not expected to possess such an ability. Then Edward, who is only nine years old but has learned well from his father, tells his mother, and then Ellen, that they shouldn't play ball because they cannot catch. It is a judgment that Betty is all too ready to agree with. Then the men take over. Edward cannot catch and is mocked by Harry and Clive; it appears that this is a test of masculinity. And when Betty informs Clive that he has hurt

TOPICS FOR FURTHER STUDY

- Are there innate differences between men and women, in terms of their interest in or aptitude for certain careers or leisure pursuits, or are most differences a result of social conditioning? Do research to learn what experts have to say on this question. What are some of the ways in which social conditioning is changing today?
- To what extent is being gay considered acceptable in America today and to what extent is there still prejudice and discrimination against gays? What forms does that discrimination take? Should laws be passed to make discrimination against gays illegal?
- Is homosexuality innate, or is it a learned behavior? In other words, are people born gay, or do they choose to be gay? Investigate the current research on this question.
- In order to succeed and be accepted in American society, do blacks have to "act white" (like Joshua in the play)? Explain your answer.

Edward's feelings, Clive reveals another of his unconscious gender stereotypes: "A boy has no business having feelings."

The aim of the play is to deconstruct these gender stereotypes. Edward, for example, although a boy, likes to play with dolls, even though he is told by his elders that such behavior is not considered masculine. The playwright invites the audience to question this and other assumptions, such as the passivity of women. Mrs. Saunders, for example, shows that a woman can enjoy sex for its own sake, just as a man may, and this is in contrast to Betty's dreamy, romantic notions of love.

The theme of liberation from the false, socially induced constraints of gender becomes even more pronounced in act two, which shows how the characters, especially Betty and Edward, break free of the rigid roles that were formerly prescribed for them. Society has changed, too, making it easier for them to do so. Betty is able to acquire a real job of her own, and she also relearns the pleasures of autoeroticism, initially as an act of rebellion against her husband and her mother. Betty's discovery shows how women are now more able to accept their bodies and sexual desires as natural, not something to be ashamed of or repressed. This theme is also apparent in act two, scene three, when Victoria and Lin chant in praise of ancient female goddesses.

In addition to the liberation of women, in the world portrayed in act two, homosexuality is not the shameful thing it was to Clive or Harry. Edward and Gerry can live as an openly gay couple, and Betty is not distressed at her knowledge that her son is gay or that her daughter is involved in a sexual relationship with her girlfriend, Lin.

There are changes in the way the family is constructed, too. If act one is a satire on the Victorian family, in which desires and sexual orientation are repressed in order to present a false appearance, act two shows the forming of alternative family structures. For example, a gay man, Edward, lives with two women and their two children. One of the women, Lin, is a confirmed lesbian, while the other, Victoria, is experimenting with bisexuality. This is a long way from the image of the family that Clive presents in the first scene of the play.

Churchill also sets out to undermine the ideology of colonialism. Since such a system is based on exploitation, violence, and the belief in the inferiority of the colonized people, it can only result in resentment and, ultimately, violence, as is apparent several times in the play. Joshua, for example, for all his dutiful attempts to act as his master wants him to, brazenly defies Betty's orders (which also reveals the powerless position of women). When Joshua aims a gun at Clive's head in the final scene in act one, it hardly comes as a surprise. Whatever surface appearances might suggest, Joshua will never wholly succeed in becoming "white." (The specter of colonialism returns in act two, when Lin's brother, Bill, a British soldier, is killed in Northern Ireland, where the British are fighting a guerrilla war against Irish nationalists. This time the emphasis is on the dispiriting life led by the soldiers who serve in the British army, which the Irish nationalists believe to be the arm of a colonizing, oppressive power.)

STYLE

Gender Reversals

The play uses a number of unconventional techniques to create its effects. One of these is for some of the characters to be played by actors of the opposite gender. This reinforces the theme of undermining gender stereotyping. For example, Edward as a nine-year-old boy is played by a woman, which visually reinforces for the audience the notion that Edward does not behave in the way his Victorian family believes a boy should. Betty is played by a man because, as Churchill states in her introduction to the play, "she wants to be what men want her to be." She does not value herself as a woman. Her true nature is therefore hidden from herself and others. Joshua is played by a white man, to reinforce the idea that he has embraced the values of white culture and behaves as his white employers expect of him.

In act two, the characters are played for the most part by members of their own gender. Betty is now played by a woman, which visually reinforces for the audience the fact that for the first time she is discovering who she really is. Edward is played by a man, to show that he has found his own identity and is comfortable with being gay.

The only exception to this is that four-year-old Cathy is played by a man. This has the same effect as the playing of Edward by a woman in act one. It subverts traditional expectations of how a girl should behave and what interests she should have. Cathy, for example, likes to play rough games with the boys, and she also plays with a toy gun. The other reason for having Cathy played by a man is, as Churchill writes, ''because the size and presence of a man on stage seemed appropriate to the emotional force of young children.''

Structure

Another unconventional technique in the play is the use in act two of many of the same characters from act one, even though the action takes place one hundred years later. Churchill managed this by having the characters age only twenty-five years from act one to act two.

The two acts are different in other ways, too. The first is dominated by men, especially Clive, who tries hard to keep everything under control, arranged the way he believes things should be. But the second act is dominated more by the women and the gays, who show a capacity for change and a willingness to entertain new ways of being and living. Those who were powerless earlier—Betty in particular—now grow into positions in which they feel more in control of their destinies. The fact that when the play was first staged the actor who played Clive in act one also played the child Cathy in act two reinforces this idea of the reversals that have taken place—the powerlessness of the old ideals in a new world. (Churchill wrote the play for seven actors, which means that some parts must be doubled. It is not essential, however, that Clive be doubled with Cathy; other combinations are possible.) In act two it is the man, Martin, the equivalent of Clive in act one, who must struggle to come to terms with the new feminist consciousness rather than have everything his own way.

Another way in which the structure of the play allows the playwright to convey her themes occurs at the end of act one. The final scene appears to have the form of a typical romantic comedy. Enemies are banished, order is restored, love triumphs, and there is a wedding celebration for the happy couple. Clive appears to sum things up when he makes a speech in neatly rhymed verse that ends, ''All murmuring of discontent is stilled. / Long may you live in peace and joy and bliss.'' But, of course, the reality is somewhat different. Not only is there a nasty little quarrel about the doll, as a result of which Clive hits his son, but there is also the more fundamental fact that all the words in praise of the marriage and in celebration of the ending of discontent are false. Nothing is what it appears, since Ellen and Harry are in fact gay and are marrying merely to shore up appearances, and a drunken Joshua is about to take a shot at Clive. The ostensibly comic form is belied by the reality of the situation.

HISTORICAL CONTEXT

Women's Liberation Movement

Britain in the 1970s was marked by vigorous and politically effective campaigns for women's rights and gay rights. The First National Women's Liberation Conference was held in Oxford in 1970. The goals it decided upon were equal pay for women, equal opportunity in education and employment, abortion rights, day care, and free contraception. The women's liberation movement aimed to raise women's consciousness about social issues and encouraged them to challenge some of the basic underpinnings of a male-dominated society—the assumption that women should always be secondary to men, for example, or that women are important only through their relationships with men. Women increasingly challenged the traditional division of labor in the family and in the workplace. They rejected the idea that certain roles, such as child-rearing and housekeeping, were suited only to women, and they fought for the right to pursue careers in areas traditionally open only to men. They argued that traditional gender roles had been constructed by a male-dominated society rather than being inherent in the nature of human life. And what had been socially constructed could also be changed.

During this time, there was a feeling of excitement among many women that a new era was dawning. Gillian Hanna, one of the founders of the feminist theatre company Monstrous Regiment, recollected:

> We wanted to change the world. At the time, this didn't seem like such an outrageous project. All around us, women in every area of the world we knew were doing the same thing. It seemed as natural as breathing.

The women's movement made a measurable impact on 1970s British society. The Equal Pay Act of 1970, which was implemented in 1975, established the principle of equal pay for equal work. In 1975, the Sex Discrimination Act banned discrimination on the grounds of gender or marital status and established the Equal Opportunities Commission. Women also gained the right to maternity leave.

COMPARE & CONTRAST

- **1880:** The British Empire is at the height of its power. More than a quarter of the world's landmass is under British rule, including large portions of Africa.

  1980: Britain has long since renounced its empire and is now a middle-sized European power and a member of the European Community (EC). There is an ongoing debate in Britain about how much national sovereignty should be surrendered to an EC bureaucracy.

  Today: Britain's colonial legacy is apparent in the sometimes troubled relations between the races in what is now a multi-ethnic nation. The majority of non-white Britons are descendents of Asian or West Indian immigrants (former subjects of the British Empire) who were admitted to Britain beginning in the 1950s. In 2001, race riots erupt in three northern English cities.

- **1880:** In Britain, women are not allowed to vote, and educational opportunities are limited. In the better-off families, a woman's place is in the home, supervising the large household and entertaining visitors. Only working-class women take paid employment, in the textile industry, for example, or as domestic help.

  1980: The women's movement is a powerful force in British society, and discrimination by gender or marital status is illegal. Britain has its first woman prime minister, Margaret Thatcher, and the number of women in the professions increases, as does the number of women in the workforce as a whole. But women's earnings still lag behind those of men.

  Today: Economic inequalities between men and women remain. In Britain, women's earnings are only 81 percent of men's. Women still face obstacles to career success, including the so-called glass ceiling (a barrier that is invisible but is nonetheless there), which make it difficult for women to be promoted to the highest levels in business.

- **1880:** The growing suffragette movement, with its aim of securing voting rights for women and access to the professions, helps to bring more women into work in the theater. Many actresses play important roles in producing and performing plays.

  1980: As a result of the women's liberation movement of the 1970s, an impressive number of plays are written and produced by women, many of which dramatize issues that are important in the lives of women.

  Today: Young women playwrights now start writing, confident of their equal status with men. But women involved in British theater also say that women need to have greater access to money and resources, that there should be more women in positions of power in theater management, and that more plays by women should be produced in large theaters.

Gay Liberation Movement

A major landmark in the acceptance of homosexuality in Britain was the Sexual Offences Act of 1967, which decriminalized homosexuality between consenting adults in private. The age of consent was fixed at twenty-one, five years older than the age of consent for heterosexual acts. (In 1994, the age of consent for homosexual acts was lowered to eighteen.) But gay people still faced discrimination, such as being fired from their jobs or denied custody of their children. In 1970, the Gay Liberation Front (GLF) was formed. That year, the first gay rights demonstration in Britain took place in London. More than one hundred members of the GLF protested police harassment and intimidation. The first Gay Pride march was held in London in 1972, and a newspaper, *Gay News,* was published from 1972 to 1983. Adapting a slogan from the American civil rights movement (''black is beautiful''), gays proclaimed that ''gay is good.'' They rejected the shame and guilt that had often accompanied gay life in the past, due to disapproval of homosexuality by church and state and to almost universally negative portrayals of gays in the media.

The GLF also organized radical protests involving sit-ins at pubs (the British equivalent of a bar) that refused to serve gays, and GLF activists disrupted a lecture by noted psychiatrist Professor Hans Eysenck after he advocated electric-shock aversion therapy to "cure" homosexuality. The increasing visibility of gay people encouraged many to "come out" and live openly (as Edward and Gerry do in *Cloud Nine*), without having to disguise the fact that they were gay. Many gays (as well as feminists) linked their oppression to the structure of the traditional family. By learning to form nontraditional family structures, many gays declared that they had rejected the masculine and feminine roles that society had designed for them. During this period, gays became freer in discussing the ways in which a masculine identity had been imposed on them in their upbringing although such an identity did not correspond to what they felt themselves to be (just as in the play, Edward comes to realize that the kind of man his father expected him to become was not who he was).

Women's and Gay Theater

The 1970s saw the emergence of feminist and gay theater in Britain. Cultural historian Michelene Wandor, in *Carry On, Understudies,* divides this period into four phases. From 1969 to 1973, avant-garde and experimental writing flourished, and street theater companies performed plays that probed social issues from a socialist and feminist viewpoint. Theater was viewed as a means of raising women's social consciousness. Phase two was from 1973 to 1977, during which alternative theater gained some stability as a result of receiving state subsidies. This was the period when women's professional theater companies, dedicated to producing work by women or emphasizing women's issues, began to spring up. The most prominent of these were the Women's Theatre Group (1974) and Monstrous Regiment (1975–76). Churchill became involved in Monstrous Regiment and wrote her play *Vinegar Tom* for the company. During the same period, Gay Sweatshop, a theater company made up of lesbians and gay men, was also formed. Phase three, from 1977 onward, was a period of contraction for alternative theater groups, as the Arts Council reduced its subsidies. Phase four, according to Wandor, was from 1979 onward, when numerous female and gay playwrights came to prominence. These were either new writers with confident voices as a result of the work done by others over the previous decade or experienced writers who had worked through the previous stages and developed a stronger theatrical voice. These writers included, in addition to Churchill and Wandor herself, Pam Gems, Mary O'Malley, Nell Dunn, and Claire Luckham.

CRITICAL OVERVIEW

When *Cloud Nine* was first produced in England in 1979, it was a commercial success, establishing Churchill as a leading British playwright. However, critics were divided as to the merits of the play. Robert Cushman in the *Observer* (quoted in *Plays in Review*) described the second act as "almost the best thing to arrive in the London theatre this young and dismal year." And John Barber's verdict in the *Daily Telegraph* (quoted by Erica Beth Weintraub in *Dictionary of Literary Biography*) was also positive; Barber described it as "cheerfully entangling itself in the problems of fitting complex human instincts into workable social patterns." But a different view was taken by J. C. Trewin of the *Birmingham Post,* who expressed puzzlement about the play's themes. Whether the play was "a treatise on bisexuality" or "a view of parents and children," Trewin regarded it as "superfluous." He argued that the satirical approach to the British Empire in the first act was a hackneyed theme, and he dubbed the second act a "wholly muddled fantasy." Peter Jenkins, in the *Spectator* (quoted in *Plays in Review*), was also less than enthusiastic, writing that the play's "most constant danger is degeneration into a mere sequence of acting exercises, or cabaret turns, loosely plotted together."

When the play reached New York in 1981, critics were lavish with their praise. Rex Reed, in the *New York Times,* called it "the most rewarding surprise of the theatrical season," and Clive Barnes in the *New York Post* wrote that it is "a play that has something to say about kindness, affection, perversion, and most of all love" (both reviews quoted by Weintraub).

Scholars of the theater continue to write about the themes and techniques of the play, which has acquired a permanent place in the history of British theater.

Tim McInnerny, as Clive, and Marion Bailey, as Mrs. Saunders, in a 1997 production of Cloud Nine, *performed at the Old Vic Theatre in London*

CRITICISM

Bryan Aubrey

Aubrey holds a Ph.D. in English and has published many articles on twentieth-century literature. In this essay, Aubrey discusses how two books, Kate Millet's Sexual Politics *and Frantz Fanon's* Black Skin, White Masks, *influenced Churchill as she developed the main themes of* Cloud Nine.

Churchill has stated in interviews that two of the books that influenced her writing of *Cloud Nine* were Kate Millet's *Sexual Politics* and Frantz Fanon's *Black Skin, White Masks.* Millett's book was published in 1970 and became something of a bible for the emerging women's movement. Although today *Sexual Politics* is less well known than the work of other feminists of the period, such as Germaine Greer and Gloria Steinem, it was in its time a revolutionary work that awakened many American and European women to an awareness of the nature of the patriarchal society in which they lived.

Fanon was a black psychiatrist from Martinique, a French colony, who wrote about his own experience of how the psychology of black people had been warped by the culture of the white colonizers. Churchill had already used Fanon's work as a basis for her play *The Hospital at the Time of the Revolution* (first published in *Churchill: Shorts: Short Plays* in 1990), in which Fanon himself appears as a character. The two books together (*Sexual Politics* and *Black Skin, White Masks*) helped Churchill make the link between colonial oppression and gender oppression, a connection that she noticed had also been made by the French playwright Jean Genet, who called it "the colonial or feminine mentality of interiorised repression" (quoted by Churchill in her introduction to *Cloud Nine*).

Fanon's study was first published half a century ago, in 1952. He wrote of the various ways in which the colonizing white man treated the black man as inferior. He noticed this operating in his own profession: the doctors in the public health service usually spoke pidgin English to their black or Arab patients in a way that was demeaning. They did not treat people of color as equals. This kind of attitude on the part of whites led blacks to a mentality that accepted their own inferiority. They believed that if they were to become fully human, they had to bring themselves as quickly as possible into step with the white world. Fanon characterizes the typical thought process: "I will quite simply try to make myself white: that is, I will compel the white man to acknowledge that I am human." Fanon describes a dream reported by one of his black patients who was having problems in his career. The man dreamed that he was in a roomful of white men, and he too was white. Fanon concluded that this was simply wish fulfillment; the man wanted to be white. This was because "he lives in a society that makes his inferiority complex possible, in a society that derives its stability from the perpetuation of this complex, in a society that proclaims the superiority of one race." The black man in the colonized world thus is faced with a choice: "turn white or disappear."

In the play, Joshua, the black servant, has chosen to "turn white" rather than disappear. Those who choose the opposite are either flogged (like the stable boys) or run the risk of being the victims of a punitive raid by British soldiers, their lives considered of no importance. Joshua's words, "My skin is black but oh my soul is white" are an allusion to "The Little Black Boy," a poem by William Blake that carries the same theme:

My mother bore me in the southern wild,

WHAT DO I READ NEXT?

- *Rites* (1970), by British playwright Maureen Duffy, is an imaginative recasting of *The Bacchae,* a play by the ancient Greek dramatist Euripides. Like *Cloud Nine,* it is a feminist play that brings traditional gender roles into question.
- Wendy Wasserstein is a leading American playwright; her play *The Heidi Chronicles* (1988) is a satirical approach to the successes and failures of two decades of the feminist movement.
- Churchill's *Plays Two* (1990) contains four of her best plays: *Softcops, Top Girls, Fen,* and *Serious Money.* Churchill's introduction and her notes on each play provide an illuminating commentary.
- Elaine Aston's *An Introduction to Feminism and Theatre* (1994) is a lucid introduction that explains difficult theoretical issues in a way that a reader new to the field can understand.

> And I am black, but O! my soul is white.
> White as an angel is the English child:
> But I am black as if bereav'd of light.

In "turning white," Joshua renounces his own parents and regards Clive as both his mother and father, an illustration of the paternalism at the heart of the colonial exploitation of indigenous peoples. Joshua is treated as a dependent; he is regarded as being like a child—Clive refers to him as his "boy"—or a woman.

The legacy of colonialism also appears in act two, in the reference to Lin's brother Bill, a British soldier who is killed in Northern Ireland. The struggle in Northern Ireland was the legacy of centuries of British rule. From the 1970s through the 1990s, many British soldiers were killed by the Irish Republican Army, a terrorist organization fighting to free Northern Ireland from British rule. Churchill noted that when the actors in *Cloud Nine* conducted workshops about the play, they suggested that Britain's relations with Ireland were much the same as a stereotypical male/female relationship. "The traditional view of the Irish is that they're charming, irresponsible, close to nature, all the things that people tend to think about women," said Churchill (quoted in Aston).

Thus the link is made between colonial and gender oppression. It is also interesting that Joshua, although obsequious toward Clive, feels relatively free to insult Clive's wife, Betty. He refuses to fetch her book when she asks for it, and later, when she asks him to fetch some thread from her sewing box, he tells her that she has "legs under that skirt" (and so can do it herself) and then adds the lewd remark, "And more than legs." Joshua is able to defy Betty because he perceives that as a woman in the white, British family, she has no authority. It is likely that he believes waiting on a woman to be against the natural order of things. It is, after all, the job of women to wait on men.

For her critique of this kind of gender stereotyping, Churchill turned to Millett's *Sexual Politics.* Millett's argument is simple in its outlines but carried through with relentless conviction and intellectual power. It is a sustained attack on patriarchy, the universal system by which males rule over females simply by virtue of being male. According to Millett, patriarchy as a means of perpetuating and justifying the rule of a particular group is more uniform and enduring than any class system or any other form of segregation in history. Each sex is socialized into the system at the psychological, sociological, and political levels. Personality is formed along stereotypical lines based on what the dominant group finds acceptable: aggression, intelligence, force, and efficacy are assigned to the male, while passivity, ignorance, docility, and "virtue" are given to the female. This is reinforced by the roles society assigns, in terms of codes of conduct, attitudes, and approved activities. Domestic service and the raising of infants are allocated to the woman; everything else, such as achievement and ambition,

> "IT IS SEX AND SEXUAL ORIENTATION THAT LOOM LARGE IN *CLOUD NINE,* THE VERY TITLE OF WHICH IS A REFERENCE TO SEXUAL ECSTASY (AS THE SONG THAT CLOSES ACT TWO, SCENE THREE MAKES CLEAR)."

is reserved for the man. At the political level, this is reflected in huge disparities in status and power; in many societies women are considered little more than the property of men.

Underpinning all this is the assumption that such arrangements rest on a biological basis. They are "natural." Against this, Millett argues that such patriarchal structures do not originate in human nature at all but are a result of human culture. She suggests that there are no significant inherent differences between male and female beyond the obvious ones relating to the physical body. There is no evidence of any mental or emotional difference; the studies that purport to show otherwise merely reflect the biases of their authors. Gender is in fact an arbitrary notion and may even run counter to biological fact, so ruthlessly is gender identity ("I am a girl," or "I am a boy") instilled in the first eighteen months of childhood. According to Millett, gender, as opposed to physical sex, is a learned behavior.

Sexual Politics was at once a scholarly examination of the origins and nature of patriarchy and a revolutionary manifesto. Millett called for the end of the institution of the family as well as of the notion of monogamous marriage that accompanied it, since the family was the chief enforcer of patriarchal values. Millett also derided the concept of romantic love, which she claimed was a form of "emotional manipulation" on the part of the male and which was useful to patriarchy because it obscured the woman's low social status and economic dependence.

Millett's argument formed the core beliefs of the women's movement in the 1970s. Today, many (not all) of her views may not sound so radical—a sign of how successful the women's movement has been in changing deep-seated attitudes in America and Europe, although few would dispute that Western societies today remain patriarchal in most important respects.

Cloud Nine is Churchill's Millett-inspired attack on patriarchy, using the theatrical weapon of comedy. The family structure that Clive values so highly ("the family is all important") is clearly unworkable because it is essentially unnatural, not conforming to the facts of the matter as they appear. Edward will not grow up into the man Clive wants him to be, whatever his parents do or say to him, and Betty's denial of her own sexuality is a denial of the truth of her being. "You just keep still" is the best advice she can offer to Ellen about sex, and when Ellen asks whether it is enjoyable, Betty replies, "You're not getting married to enjoy yourself." Millett pointed out in *Sexual Politics* that one of the consequences of Victorian patriarchy was that "the vast inherent potential of female sexuality had come . . . to be nearly totally obscured through cultural restraints." The assumption was, as Betty clearly also believes, that "sex is for the man." Underlying this suppression of female sexuality are the male fear of women and the association of women, sex, and sin that goes all the way back, as Millett points out, to the Genesis story of Eve leading Adam into sin. This belief is expressed by Clive after he has praised male friendship to Harry. "There is something dark about women, that threatens what is best in us," he says. This is one reason why Mrs. Saunders, who is an independent woman who likes sex and expects to get pleasure from it (something that fails to happen in her encounter with Clive), has to be expelled from the wedding party. She does not fit in the world that Clive chooses to believe he lives in, even though he has been quite willing to use her for his own sexual pleasure.

It is sex and sexual orientation that loom large in *Cloud Nine*, the very title of which is a reference to sexual ecstasy (as the song that closes act two, scene three makes clear). And it is the repressing of the sexual instinct, particularly same-sex attraction, that leads the characters into the lies and cover-ups that feature in act one. The infinitely varied nature of human sexuality simply cannot forever be squeezed into the narrow heterosexual and monogamous channels that patriarchy decrees. This seems to be the message of the play. Although the sexually liberated world of act two may also have its problems—Victoria's struggles to break free of Martin's dominance and the failure of the gay relationship between Gerry and Edward—it is at least a world in which the characters' relationships start to have a closer resemblance to who they really are.

Source: Bryan Aubrey, Critical Essay on *Cloud Nine,* in *Drama for Students,* The Gale Group, 2003.

Apollo Amoko

In the following essay, Amoko examines the text of Cloud Nine *and criticisms of the drama, identifying in both a lack of attention paid to acts of colonial violence and the generalization of white women in Africa to represent the experience of all women.*

> . . . colonialism has long served as a metaphor for a wide range of dominations, collapsing the specific hierarchies of time and place into a seamless whole. In this scenario, "to colonize" is an evocative and active verb accounting for a range of inequities and exclusions—that may have little to do with colonialism at all. As a morality tale of the present the metaphor of colonialism has enormous force but it can also eclipse how varied the subjects are created by different colonialisms.

A certain personal ambivalence defines my response to *Cloud Nine*, Caryl Churchill's drama in two acts featuring an audacious attempt to parallel sexual and gender oppression with colonial and racial oppression. While the attempt to enact the interrelated nature of these oppressions remains attractive, the apparent ease with which a playwright and company drawn exclusively from and implicated by racial and colonial privilege make direct comparisons and equivalencies between gender/sexual and colonialist oppressions is disturbing. These comparisons and equivalencies are made despite critical material differences in the history of gender and sexual oppression within specific cultural contexts, and the history of colonialism and the peculiar history of gender and sexual oppression within colonialism. As a consequence, certain oppressed identities, for example white women, may have been provided with the prospect of empowering representation at the cost of consigning certain other identities, specifically African women, to further subjection and invisibility.

In a bid to trace a certain coherence of effects in Western feminist practices of writing and reading, this examination of *Cloud Nine* concerns itself as much with the playtext as with its critical reception. Critical reaction to the play has focused disproportionately on what are perceived to be its "feminist accomplishments" to the near total exclusion of any in-depth or sustained examination of race and colonialism. Where passing review of colonialism has been made, it has been merely to point out how racism and sexism occasionally interpenetrate or how racism, the play's "other" concern, illustrates sexism, the play's "central" or "ideal" concern. Critical discourses generated by *Cloud Nine* seem to imitate the structure of racialized omission inadvertently reproduced in the play. Acts of colonial occupation, mass murder, arson, and violent repression by colonial settlers in Africa depicted in passing in the first act of the play have attracted little critical attention. Visually no attempt has been made in the critical writing on this play to investigate the manner in which the peculiar experience of African women under British colonial occupation has been effaced in *Cloud Nine*. Nor has any attempt been made to investigate the ways in which the experiences and struggles of white settler women (complicit, however contradictorily, in the colonial project) have been generalized, in a play set substantially in colonial Africa, to represent the plight of all women in a manner comparable to the way men were historically generalized to represent all humanity.

> "IT IS VITAL, HOWEVER, TO SITUATE THIS PLAY WITHIN THE CONTEXT OF THE WESTERN CREATIVE AND CRITICAL PRACTICES FROM WHICH IT EMERGED AND WITHIN WHICH IT HAS CIRCULATED IN THE LAST SIXTEEN YEARS TO WIDESPREAD ACCLAIM."

One article, Elin Diamond's "Closing No Gaps: Aphra Behn, Caryl Churchill and Empire," appears to question the impact of the "foregrounding" by these two feminist playwrights of gender critique at the expense of race and colonization. Diamond concludes that "unacceptable gaps" exist in the examination of race and imperialism in the works of the two playwrights, and attributes these "gaps" to their imperialist (British) background. However, despite noting in passing that women make up half the population of colonized nations, Diamond does not proceed to examine specifically the inherent differences between the respective histories of "colo-

A scene from the 1979 production of Cloud Nine, *written by Caryl Churchill and directed by Max Stafford-Clark*

nized'' and ''colonizing'' women. In two separate studies that examine *Cloud Nine*, Diamond herself foregrounds racially marked feminist concerns and almost entirely ignores race and colonialism. She seems to exempt feminist critics from critical review at precisely the same instant that she indicts the two playwrights for their implication in imperial ideology, leaving unexplored the sources of her own feminist authority even as she challenges the sources of Churchill's authority.

Against this background of existing feminist examinations of *Cloud Nine*, it is instructive to trace the ruses of power (both institutional and discursive) that foster the appearance of mutual exclusiveness between the two intertwined economies of white supremacy and phallotocracy. The phallotocratic economy and the colonial economy enacted in *Cloud Nine* are neither mutually exclusive sites of power that can be used to illustrate each other, nor entirely separable sites of power that occasionally collude and/or collide; rather, they represent interrelated structures of gender, racial, and sexual domination. Churchill's attempt to investigate these two economies therefore enacts (in the theatrical sense of that term) the complicated and contradictory mechanics through which power is (re)produced and exercised. It is vital, however, to situate this play within the context of the Western creative and critical practices from which it emerged and within which it has circulated in the last sixteen years to widespread acclaim. These creative and critical practices, even in their deconstructive and/or feminist configurations, continue to be implicated in colonial discourses and the contemporary exercise of global power.

Claims regarding the interrelatedness of structures of domination ought not, then, to preclude the posing of what Homi K. Bhabha has termed ''the colonial question, the 'other' question.'' In his essay ''The Other Question: Difference, Discrimination and the Discourse of Colonialism,'' Bhabha asserts:

> To pose the colonial question is to realize that the problematic representation of cultural and racial difference cannot be read off from the signs and designs of social authority that are produced in the analyses of class and gender differentiation. As I was writing in 1982 the conceptual boundaries of the west were being busily reinscribed in a clamor of texts—transgressive, semiotic, semanalytic, deconstructionist—none of which pushed those boundaries to their colonial periphery; to that limit where the west must face a peculiarly displaced and

decentered image of itself in "double duty bound," at once a civilizing mission and a subjugating force.

Bhabha's insights enable a reconsideration of the ways in which Churchill and her critics may have reproduced an undifferentiated African landscape as the limit text of their critiques of gender and sexual differentiation. They allow, as well, for an examination of the ways in which various empowering white subjectivities seem to materialize against the dark reflection of a generic and stereotypic African man (Joshua). Churchill's feminist critics appear to use colonial and racial difference to produce social and critical authority for Westernized notions of gender and sexual difference.

Cloud Nine enacts a multiple and highly differentiated structure of oppression that constructs the prevailing gender, sexual, and racial definitions. Churchill demonstrates, as much by her silences and contradictions as by effective and self-conscious dramatization, that these categories are not mutually exclusive; rather, they are inextricably interconnected. While patriarchy forms the foundational basis for this structure. Churchill deploys a number of dramatic devices in attempts to disclose and then dispute these oppressive categories and their informing ideology. These include instances of cross- casting, the destabilization of racial, gender, and sexual identities as discrete categories in character development, and Brechtian alienation attained through a non-linear dramatic structure and a historicized plot. As a result of the complex dynamics of power ceaselessly and contradictorily at play, the disruption of these categories is simultaneously facilitated and invalidated throughout the play.

Churchill identifies white patriarchy as the philosophical basis of the multiple structure of social organization early in the play. In his opening statement, Clive, a senior administrator in the colonial Empire in (undifferentiated) Africa, says:

This is my family. Though far from home
We serve the queen wherever we may roam.
I am a father to the natives here.
And a father to my family so dear.

This statement exposes not only a multiply oppressive structure, but also the interrelation between the colonization of Africa (and of African bodies) and (metaphorically) that of white women and children within a patriarchal structure. The social order constructed reveals itself to be white in its dominant racial ideology, masculinist in its dominant gender ideology, and heterosexist and monogamous in its dominant sexual ideology.

Churchill's exposition of the prevailing social hierarchies is enacted most powerfully, in my view, in Act One, scene three, during which scene Clive and Harry (both white colonial settlers and both males) are supervising the flogging of their native domestic servants. Joshua, Clive's senior domestic servant and trusted ally, flogs the other African workers—"the stable boys"—for not being "trustworthy," for "whispering," for "visiting their people," for "going out at night," and for "carrying knives." While the men are administering this punishment the white women are kept indoors; under patriarchy, acts such as flogging (and violent components of colonial empire-building) are constructed as male acts from whose rigors the women and children are shielded. Significantly, the women embody and reinforce their oppression by performing and embodying their apportioned gendered roles: "The men will do it [the flogging] in the right way. . . . We have our own part to play." "Luckily this house has a head, I am squeamish myself but Clive is not." The "part" the domesticated women have to "play" is the consistent reproduction, in a deeply theatrical sense, of docile, obedient bodies useful in support of the colonial economy. Churchill specifies that the role of Betty be played by a male actor during the first act of the play. This casting choice physicalizes and concretizes the occupation of her body and that of other women by patriarchy. She says in self-introduction: "I am a man's creation as you can see. And what men want is what I want to be." She displays (as, indeed, do all the other women in this scene) a crucial facet of "colonial occupation" as she seems to consent to her oppression, a consent at once authorized and undermined by the glaring inequalities in power. Embodiment and enactment are dramatized early in the play as the principal ways through which an oppressed identity, "woman," is normalized in a colonial setting. The history of colonialism (both of territories and of bodies) is replete with instances in which it entrenches itself through the materialization of subjects as "oppressed bodies."

The introduction of Edward into this scene presents the final facet of social construction portrayed in the play—the "colonization" of (white) children by a patriarchal family structure that seeks to script onto their bodies a "natural" bipolar gender identity and a "natural" heterosexual disposition. Edward reveals the ways in which the colonial margin functions as a space for the cultivation of the ideal (white, male) subject. He is beaten for playing with a doll because, as he has been told before, ''dolls are for girls.'' In a powerful illustration of the intersection of the discourses of race, gender, and class in the colonial arena, Churchill parallels the flogging suffered by the colonized Africans for their ''misbehaviour'' with the beating suffered by Edward for transgressing prescribed gender roles. The on-stage beating occurs concurrently with the beatings suffered by the Africans off-stage. *Cloud Nine* demonstrates the nonvoluntary manner in which bodies are forcefully compelled to materialize within prescribed gender, racial, and sexual forms. At the very outset of her play, Churchill illustrates some of the multiple but inter-related sites of white patriarchal oppression: the colonization of Africa and the enslavement of African bodies, and the metaphorical colonization of women and children.

A critical facet of social organization that is consigned to invisibility in *Cloud Nine*—and, more pointedly, in *Cloud Nine* criticism—is the unique deprivation suffered by African women and children, who are not featured at all in the play. Unlike the gendered materialization of the settler women, which was mitigated (at least in part) by complicity in racial and economic privilege, and that of African men, which was mitigated in some degree by male privilege, the experience of African women under both autogenous and colonial misogyny deserves but fails to receive specific and separate reenactment. One could argue that in the world of *Cloud Nine* black women do not matter—which is to say, black women fail to materialize. The exclusion of African women, especially in *Cloud Nine* criticism, seems to presume a trans-historical and universal patriarchy and elides important distinctions between women in terms of race and colonial history. The construction and/or disruption of womanhood in *Cloud Nine* must be understood from a standpoint that takes into account the at once contradictory and complementary discourses of race, gender, and sexuality. This erasure of black women illustrates the problems (as pointed out in the epigraph to this essay) that arise in the use of colonialism as a metaphor for understanding other forms of inequality and exclusion. The erasure of black women from both the creative and critical universes of *Cloud Nine* seems to constitute a condition of the play's feminist possibilities.

As she exposes—but also replicates—the multiple modes through which a white patriarchal structure variously manifests itself, Churchill deploys a number of dramatic strategies to disrupt the categories inherent in this epistemic regime, including what Diamond and Reinelt classify as ''cross-racial'' and ''cross-gender'' casting. The elaborate use of ''cross-casting'' in *Cloud Nine* anticipated and in some instances seems to have triggered debates over gender identity in contemporary Western culture and in Western theatre theory. Such debates would include, for example, the works of Diamond and Butler. In an uncanny sense, Churchill's enactment of gender constitution seems to anticipate Butler's contentions regarding the performativity of gender. In ''Performative Acts and Gender Constitution: An Essay in Phenomenology and Feminist Theory'' (as well as in her book *Gender Trouble: Feminism and The Subversion of Identity),* Butler adopts the philosophical doctrine of constituting acts from the phenomenological tradition in order to demonstrate the performativity of gender. (The analysis of the ways bodies materialized as various racialized, sexual, and gendered subjects in *Cloud Nine* undertaken above drew much of its implicit authority from Butler's work). Basing her argument on Simone de Beauvoir's claim that ''one is not born a woman, but, rather, one becomes a woman.'' Butler explores the potential for deconstructing and subverting the gender script. She argues:

> . . . gender is in no way a stable identity or locus of agency from which various acts proceede [*sic*]; rather, it is an identity tenuously instituted through time—an identity instituted through a *stylized repetition of acts.* Further, gender is instituted through the stylization of the body and, hence, must be understood as the mundane way in which bodily gestures, movements, and enactments of various kinds constitute the illusion of an abiding gendered self.

Butler's conception of gender affirms de Beauvoir's assertion that ''woman'' is a historical construction and not a natural fact. Butler makes a firm distinction between ''sex as biological facticity and gender as the cultural interpretation or signification of that facticity,'' even as she contests the given-ness of sex as a natural fact. She argues that discrete and polar gender identities are punitively regulated cultural fictions whose reproduction sustains a system of compulsory heterosexuality based on a notion of opposing ''natural'' sexes with ''natural'' attractions for each other. This argument is forcefully enacted throughout *Cloud Nine*, particularly in the scene examined above (Act One, scene three). In that scene, such mundane acts as bodily comportment, floggings, playing with dolls, and speech acts are coded in race- and gender-specific ways. These race- and gender-inflected bodily codes are violently enforced in order to ensure that bodies materialize in very specific ways.

Butler's project aims beyond providing women, as oppressed subjects, with the capacity to effect social change. It points to the ontological insufficiency of the falsely essentializing and oppressive category "woman." It seeks to disrupt the reification of sexual difference as the founding moment of Western culture and calls, in conclusion, for contestation of the gender script, for a different sort of stylized repetition of acts to be accomplished through "performances out of turn" and/or "unwarranted improvisations." Although the play predates Butler's arguments by nearly a decade, the casting choices and character realizations in *Cloud Nine* enact Butler's call for contestation of the gender script through myriad gender performances out of turn and unwarranted improvisations.

In a separate attempt to deploy the notion of performance in order to grapple with the problematics of female identity and representation in Western culture, Diamond embarks on an insightful intertextual reading of Brechtian theory and feminist theory in "Brechtian Theory/Feminist Theory: Towards A Gestic Feminist Criticism." This essay seeks "the recovery of the radical potential of the Brechtian critique and a discovery, for feminist theory, of the specificity of the theatre." Diamond envisions the site of performance as simultaneously a site of feminist resistance. She appropriates key Brechtian concepts—*Verfremdungseffekt,* the "not, but" historicization, and *Gestus*—and reinterprets them using feminist concepts. Emerging from this intertextual reading is a theatre-specific aesthetic—gestic criticism—that seeks to use the theatre as a site for enactments of feminist resistance. Diamond suggests, for example, that the Brechtian concept of *Verfremdung*—the defamiliarization, in performance, of words, ideas or gestures in order to provoke fresh appreciation and insights—be deployed to critique gender differentiation. She provides as an example of this feminist *Verfremdung* the "cross-dressing" (a rather erroneous description) that occurs in *Cloud Nine*.

The construction of character and the casting choices directed in *Cloud Nine* ought then to be apprehended against the background of the disparate theorizing outlined above. The use of cross-casting and of other theatrical strategies to demonstrate and subvert the oppressive performativity of racial, gender, and sexual identities would seem to enjoy a fundamental, though admittedly limited, feasibility. Butler writes on the limits of the theatre metaphor and on the susceptibility of theatrical acts of gender subversion to being innocuously (indeed pleasurably) contained within the spectacle of dramatic illusion. Such pleasurable containments may have the reactionary effect of reinforcing the naturalness of real life identities. But perhaps the ultimate limit of the purportedly subversive re-enactments is the ontological status and stability of the notion of the West in the contestations of naturalized subject positions. In *Cloud Nine*, the attempted destabilization of normative gender and sexual subjectivities may disclose a creative and critical desire, to adopt Gayatri Spivak's argument, to conserve the West as the ideal subject of discourse or, alternately, to conserve the subject of the West. The specific efficacy of the casting choices made by Churchill to denaturalize oppressive modes of identity formation is undermined by the Western-ness of these identities.

Cross-racial casting is introduced in *Cloud Nine* through the character of Joshua. In her cast list Churchill describes Joshua as Clive's black servant who is played by a white actor. This description presents the first level of cross-casting, at which level the concurrent process of facilitation and invalidation of coherent racial subjectivity and an eventual reification of a white episteme is dramatized. Cross-casting challenges the conflation of skin colour and racial identity by dominant ideology and seeks, by portraying a white-skinned actor performing a black racial identity, to destabilize and problematize this conflation. Butler's argument for a different sort of gender performance, a different stylization, can be adopted here with a racial difference. This apparent cross-casting is, however, seemingly invalidated by the very process that facilitates it. In order to disaffirm, in performance, the notion of racial identities immutably defined by skin colour, it must first be stabilized and reified during casting as well as in the perception of the audience. It seems, therefore, to be a strategy that cannot resist containment in the process of its own materialization. Further, the playwright seems to be trapped within dominant racial configurations. She unproblematically describes Joshua as a "black [man]" and the actor playing him as a "white [man]" in her cast list and in her introduction to the play (I discuss the introduction in some detail below), thereby re-conflating skin colour and racial identity and reiterating the existence of discrete and stable polar racial categories.

Confining analysis of the problematization of racial identity to the casting of Joshua would be misleading. Joshua's character construction and development appear to contradict any apparent cross-casting. For cross-casting to occur the racial identity of both the actor and the character in question must, paradoxically, be perceived as stable and clearly defined. This is not quite the case with Joshua. ''Cross-casting'' is problematic as a description to the extent that Joshua's skin color and his performed racial identity are stricken with indeterminacy. As a result, racial identification has been complicated or made ambivalent; this ambivalence authorizes but also potentially threatens the discourses of colonialism. In Churchill's account of events Joshua, at least in the original production, was played by a white-skinned actor as a matter of practical necessity, there being ''no black member of the company [the Joint Stock Company].'' This led at a deeper level to ''the idea of Joshua being so alienated from himself and so much wanting to be what the white man wants him to be that he is played by a white man.'' Considering the emphasis that has been placed on the fact that the company in the play's first production consisted of actors of ''plural sexualities and sexual experiences,'' this racial and colonial exclusivity seems odd—or perhaps is instructive.

The character of Joshua goes beyond obsequiousness and develops an active desire to be white, effectively renouncing claims to a black identity. In his disruptive construction Joshua purports to become a white man with a black skin—black skin, white masks ?! He seems to embody that form of subjectification that Homi Bhabha classifies as ''colonial mimicry.'' Bhabha defines colonial mimicry as ''the desire for a reformed recognizable Other, *as a subject of difference that is almost the same, but not quite.* Which is to say, that the discourse of mimicry is constructed around an *ambivalence;* in order to be effective, mimicry must continually produce its slippage.'' Churchill seems to construct Joshua as a ''mimic man'': almost the same but not quite; almost white, but not quite; anglicized, but not English. He says in self-description:

> My skin is black but oh my soul is white.
> I hate my tribe. My master is my light.
> I only live for him. As you can see.
> What white men want is what I want to be.

He regards Clive as his father and mother, disowning his own parents after their murder by the forces of colonial occupation during an arsonist raid on his native village. He asserts that black people are bad people, that they are not his people and that he does not visit them. He flogs his African coworkers as part of his duties—this punishment is in fact administered at his instigation. He has been Christianized (he prays to Jesus) and is domesticated. Despite being black, he seems to enjoy considerable power over Betty, Clive's wife. He continually spies on her, reporting her ''misbehaviour'' (just like that of ''the stable boys'') to a grateful Clive. He defies Betty's orders with misogynous insolence and a degree of impunity, with the none-too-subtle connivance of his master. He has become an ingratiating subordinate enforcer—concurrently a target and an instrument of power—of white patriarchy in conspiracy with white men.

Crucially, both Betty and Joshua lend legitimacy to Clive's superiority over them and expend their respective energies battling each other to determine who takes second place and oppresses the other. Any prospect of cooperative struggle is rendered unlikely by the differences in their oppression and in the power they wield. By playing the subjects of colonial occupation against each other, using offers of limited and discriminatory power, Clive entrenches his authority. Churchill dramatizes in this instance a central feature of colonial power—the racialized and gendered diffusion of power—a feature to which her feminist critics appear to fall prey by reifying a white epistemic regime even as they assault a universalized patriarchy.

Through Joshua (not unproblematically), racial identification is presented as a mutable performative, capable of being cast aside or reconfigured. Bhabha contends that the mimic figure, as a crystallization of the exercise of colonial power, marks the discourses of colonialism with their inevitable discursive failure by dramatizing the inability of these discourses to contain difference: ''mimicry is at once resemblance and menace.'' Joshua, in spite of his obsequious conduct in Clive's presence, seems to embody the threat or menace of mimicry in his conduct in Clive's absence. A potent instance of the menace of mimicry is presented when Joshua secretly narrates to Edward (the young ''idealizable'' white subject) a creation story that directly contradicts the Christian creation story they are both required to proclaim. Asked by Edward to narrate, in the secrecy of early morning, another ''bad story,'' Joshua replies. ''First there was nothing and then there was the great goddess. She was very large and she had golden eyes and she made the sun and the earth. But soon she became miserable and lonely and she cried like a great waterfall and her tears made all the rivers in the world. . .'' At the conclusion of the lengthy recitation of this unauthorized creation story, Edward says, ''It is not true, though.'' Joshua concedes, ''Of course it is not true. It is a bad story. Adam and Eve is true. God made man white like him and gave him the bad woman who liked the snake and gave us all trouble.'' Although Joshua and Edward end their encounter with a reaffirmation of the official creation story, ''the bad story'' they conspiratorially indulge in powerfully illustrates the menace of mimicry. In Bhabha's terms, Joshua as a mimic figure can be seen simultaneously to cohere to the dominant strategic function of colonial power and to pose an immanent danger to normalized knowledge and disciplinary power.

As if to contain the menace latent in mimicry, Joshua's final and dramatic act in the play (an act that concludes the first act) is a decontextualized act of violence. He unexpectedly shoots at Clive, his erstwhile master. Rather than elaborating the menace of mimicry, this decontextualized act appears to be a contrived re-enactment of the stereotype of the randomly violent and murderous African. A colonial stereotype is seemingly evoked to finally erase the menace immanent in mimicry. Churchill may have intended Joshua's violence at the end of the first act to represent a belated act of native resistance. Indeed, my analysis above of the menace in Joshua's mimicry lends some credence to this reading. However, the completely decontextualized nature of the shooting undermines its dissident potential. In its unexpectedness and unexplainedness, Joshua's shooting of Clive seems to hark back to white supremacist stereotypes that assign a tendency for atavistic violence and incorrigible duplicity to the black character. In its belatedness—and it is not so much the belatedness, as such, as the unexplainedness that is importantly at issue here—this act of native violence seems to legitimate the paranoia that colored many of the actions of the white settlers earlier in the play. These acts of white paranoia include an arsonist raid on a native village, Mrs. Saunders's flight from her home to Clive's, and the racial diatribes of Clive and Harry. This reading may seem unfair and one-sided until one considers the fact that Joshua's shooting of Clive has attracted very little critical attention; as a singular act, this eruption of native violence seems in harmony with the surbordination of race and colonial history to gender and sexuality in the world of the play and its interlocutors.

It is instructive that the one black character portrayed on stage in *Cloud Nine* does not seek to disrupt the fundamental assumptions of hierarchical racial identification. Joshua self-denigratingly affirms the existence of a racial bipolarity in colonial Africa and idolizes whiteness. It is also instructive that the other Africans in this drama—the ''stable boys'' as well as the invisible African women and children—who have, presumably, not mimicked whiteness in quite the same fashion as Joshua, are denied representation except on the periphery: offstage, being flogged. The antithetical (re)production of the colonial subject—the absent but always already criminalized ''stable boys''/ native villagers in contrast to the obedient and obsequious Joshua—authorize the reproduction of the discourses of colonialism. Further, in view of Diamond's elaborate analysis of the potential in Churchill's plays to remove women from historical and conventional invisibility, it is instructive that, while seeming to offer white women the prospect of non-romanticized representation, *Cloud Nine*, as if in conspiracy with colonizing white power, has sustained the continued invisibility and entrapment of African women. Not only does this play seem to be trapped within an ambivalent bipolar racial identification, it ultimately reifies whiteness as the Ideal Subject and casts blackness as the Other, at best the mimic, even in the heart of Africa. It is instructive that, in an act set in colonial Africa, white existence occupies center stage and black deprivation is stereotyped (on stage), marginalized (off stage), or erased.

Further attesting to the location of this drama in a white epistemic regime is the fact that Churchill, in her cast list and throughout the play, does not feel impelled to specify the racial identities of the (other) characters in the play, with the exception of Joshua, whom she pointedly identifies as ''black.'' Whiteness, as if by irresistible inference, is the given circumstance to which Joshua provides the lone (in)visible exception of a mimicking inferior. Is the generally laudatory critical reaction to the play's contestation of gender and sexual difference similarly located in a white epistemic regime? Is whiteness, for instance, (in)visibly inscribed on the female bodies purporting, as Diamond puts it, to refuse the romanticism of identity?

Race and colonialism are not as centrally at issue in the second act of the play. The comparison between sexual or gender oppression in contemporary Britain and British colonial settlement in Africa in the nineteenth century is abandoned at the end of the first act, following the uncontextualized and unexplained end of the colonial presence in Africa.

The treatment of race and colonialism seems to serve primarily as a backdrop (in Bhabha's terms, as a limit text) that underwrites and sustains a critique of Western gender and sexual difference. *Cloud Nine* features a sustained attempt to use cross-casting to critique Western gender and sexual ideology. The actors (whose race we know by omission) involved in the out-of-turn gender performances or unwarranted improvisations are all white. The whiteness of all these characters and actors is at once presumed and effaced by Churchill and especially by her critics, who generalize these racially exclusive gender or sexual reconfigurations. An implicit assumption of the West as a primary referent underwrites these readings.

At the level of casting, by assigning ''men,'' as perceived sexed bodies, to play ''female'' roles, and ''women,'' as perceived sexed bodies, to play ''male'' roles (Betty is, in the first act, played by an actor identified as a ''man''; Cathy as a young child is, in the second act, played by a grown actor described as a ''man''; and Edward, as a young child, is, in the first act, played by an adult actor identified as a ''woman''), Churchill uncouples gender and sexual identities and appears to fulfill Butler's call for disruptive gender performances, for a different sort of stylization of acts. This is accomplished by the presentation of images of actors, as perceived sexed bodies, playing gender roles or repeating performative acts in conflict with the genders that dominant ideology ''naturally'' and unalterably assigns them—''women'' acting ''masculine'' and ''men'' acting ''feminine.'' The uncoupling of gender and sexual identity is reiterated by doubling, where an actor plays more than one role in the course of a performance, in some instances across the boundaries of biological sex. In the first production of the play the following roles, among others, were doubled: the same actor, identified as a ''woman,'' played Edward in the first act and Betty in the second; and the same actor, identified as a ''man,'' played Clive in the first act and Cathy in the second. This demonstration of the performativity of gender and the possibility of transformation through gender performances out of turn is contained by its specific theatrical setting. The actors ''real'' sex and ''real'' gender cannot altogether be subverted in the theatre. As in cross-racial casting, the scheme to illustrate theatrically the performativity of gender (and consequently to undermine it) is simultaneously invalidated by the same means that set it in motion. The stability of ''masculinity'' and ''femininity'' as discrete and polar categories must first be affirmed and reified, before the seeming disruptiveness of cross-casting can be achieved and appreciated in performance.

Toward the conclusion of *Cloud Nine* Africa makes an abrupt return into the world of the play. Clive's authority as father to his family has by this point been seriously undermined. In his final failure, his newly liberated wife, Betty, divorces him and begins a life of sexual exploration and self-fulfillment. Clive's empire seems to be crumbling. Conceding this, a despairing Clive remarks at the end of the play: ''You are not that sort of woman, Betty. I can't believe that you are. And Africa is to be communist, I suppose. I used to be proud to be British. There was a high ideal. I came out of the verandah and looked at the stars.'' The irony in Clive's remark is that the discourses of empire in the play's imagination and in its critical reception continue to be everywhere foundational.

Source: Apollo Amoko, ''Casting Aside Colonial Occupation: Intersections of Race, Sex, and Gender in *Cloud Nine* and *Cloud Nine* Criticism,'' in *Modern Drama,* Vol. 42, No. 1, Spring 1999, pp. 45–58.

SOURCES

Aston, Elaine, *Caryl Churchill,* Northcote House, 1997, pp. 31–37.

Churchill, Caryl, *Cloud Nine,* in *Plays,* Methuen, 1985, pp. 245–320.

Fanon, Frantz, *Black Skins, White Masks,* Grove Press, 1967.

Lloyd Evans, Gareth, and Barbara Lloyd Evans, *Plays in Review, 1956–1980: British Drama and the Critics,* Batsford Academic and Educational, 1985, pp. 235–36.

Millett, Kate, *Sexual Politics,* Virago, 1977.

Wandor, Michelene, *Carry On, Understudies: Theatre and Sexual Politics,* Routledge & Kegan Paul, 1986.

Weintraub, Erica Beth, ''Caryl Churchill,'' in *Dictionary of Literary Biography,* Vol. 13: *British Dramatists Since World War II,* edited by Stanley Weintraub, Gale Research, 1982, pp. 118–24.

FURTHER READING

Betsko, Kathleen, and Rachel Koenig, *Interviews with Contemporary Women Playwrights,* William Morrow, 1987, pp. 75–84.

In this interview, Churchill talks about her work, including *Cloud Nine, Top Girls, Fen,* and other plays.

Gray, Francis, ''Mirrors of Utopia: Caryl Churchill and Joint Stock,'' in *British and Irish Drama since 1960,* edited by James Acheson, St. Martin's, 1993, pp. 47–59.

Gray examines the far-reaching consequences of the plays that emerged from Churchill's work with the Joint Stock Company, which added a political dimension to her work. He includes an analysis of *Cloud Nine.*

Itzin, Catherine, *Stages in the Revolution: Political Theatre in Britain since 1968,* Eyre Methuen, 1980.

This is a year-by-year account of the development of what Itzen calls the theater of political change from 1968 to 1978. She includes sections on Churchill and the important women's companies of the period as well as other companies that gave opportunities to women writers and performers.

Wandor, Michelene, *Drama Today: A Critical Guide to British Drama, 1970–1990,* Longman, 1993.

This is a concise guide to themes, writers, and works in contemporary British drama. Wandor discusses Churchill along with Nell Dunn, Harold Pinter, Edward Bond, Alan Ayckbourn, and others.

Dogg's Hamlet, Cahoot's Macbeth

TOM STOPPARD

1979

Dogg's Hamlet and *Cahoot's Macbeth* are two one-act plays by Tom Stoppard, which are often performed together as *Dogg's Hamlet, Cahoot's Macbeth.* First published together in England in 1979, the two plays were inspired by separate sources. *Dogg's Hamlet* is an expanded version of two earlier, similar plays. The play is based on a section of the philosophical investigations by Ludwig Wittgenstein, who explored how people use language to communicate. The play introduces an alternate language, called Dogg, which uses English words that have different meanings in Dogg. This inconsistency leads to confusion on the part of the play's characters, who try to communicate in their respective languages, English and Dogg. By the end of this first play, the English-speaking character, Easy, is speaking Dogg.

Cahoot's Macbeth, which is more political in nature, was dedicated to a Czechoslovakian playwright, Pavel Kohout. Because censorship in his country prevented public theatrical productions, Kohout wrote an abbreviated version of Shakespeare's *Macbeth,* which he performed in people's living rooms. Stoppard's play features a similar living-room theatre production of *Macbeth,* which gets broken up by an inspector, who threatens to arrest the actors and audience members for breaking the censorship rules. However, Easy, the English-speaking character from the first play, arrives and teaches the actors Dogg. When the inspector comes back a second time and catches them speaking

entirely in Dogg, he cannot arrest them because he does not understand what they are saying. Both plays are united in their use of a common invented language, but they also explore how manipulations of language—a characteristic technique of Stoppard's drama—can be used in various political and nonpolitical ways. A current copy of *Dogg's Hamlet, Cahoot's Macbeth* can be found in *The Real Inspector Hound and Other Plays*, which was published by Grove Press in 1998.

AUTHOR BIOGRAPHY

Stoppard was born as Tomas Straussler on July 3, 1937, in Zlin, Czechoslovakia. In 1939, just prior to the Nazi invasion of Czechoslovakia during World War II, the Strausslers, who had at least some Jewish heritage and feared persecution, fled the country to Singapore. In 1942, the playwright's mother moved the playwright and his brother to India to escape the Japanese. The playwright's father, a doctor, stayed behind in Singapore, where he was killed. Mrs. Straussler married Major Kenneth Stoppard in 1946, and the family moved to England, where the young Stoppard received a traditional preparatory education and became a naturalized English citizen.

In 1954, Stoppard began his career as a journalist in Bristol, England, writing for the *Western Daily Press,* where he stayed until 1958, when he began writing for the *Evening World* in Bristol. In 1962, Stoppard moved to London, where he wrote theater criticism, radio plays, and his first stage play, *A Walk on the Water*, which was shown on television in 1963. However, it was not until 1966's *Rosencrantz and Guildenstern Are Dead* that Stoppard achieved his first critical and popular success. Although some of his next plays explored political issues, it was not until the late 1970s that Stoppard wrote four plays that are commonly referred to as his dissident comedies. Among these was 1979's *Dogg's Hamlet, Cahoot's Macbeth*, two one-act plays linked through their use of a common invented language.

Stoppard is regarded as one of the preeminent post-World War II dramatists, and, as such, his plays have received several awards from the dramatic community, including Antoinette Perry (''Tony'') Awards for *Rosencrantz and Guildenstern Are Dead* (1968), *Travesties* (1976), and *The Real Thing* (1984). In addition, Stoppard has been recognized by the film community for his screenwriting work. He was nominated (along with Terry Gilliam and Charles McKeown) for an Academy Award in 1985 for *Brazil*. In 1998, Stoppard received the Academy Award (along with Marc Norman) for best screenplay written directly for the screen, for *Shakespeare in Love*.

Tom Stoppard

Stoppard continues to live and work in London, England, and his latest plays include *Arcadia* (1993), *Indian Ink* (1995), and *The Invention of Love* (1997).

PLOT SUMMARY

Dogg's Hamlet

Dogg's Hamlet begins on an empty stage when Baker, a schoolboy, says, ''Here,'' asking another boy to throw him a football. However, since he says it in ''Dogg,'' a language that uses English words with unconventional meanings, what he really says is ''Brick.'' From this point on, most of the characters in *Dogg's Hamlet* speak Dogg, which, to anybody who does not know it, sounds like gibberish.

For the reader, Stoppard initially provides translations from Dogg to English in brackets, but audience members have no such aid and must learn Dogg as the play goes on. Baker joins Abel on the stage, and together they test the microphone, which is dead. Charlie and Abel fight over the football, and Dogg, the headmaster, arrives and takes it from them, hitting Abel in the process.

They make idle conversation with Dogg, who tells them that a lorry, or truck, is about to arrive. Dogg leaves, and the three boys eat their lunches, then Abel and Baker start rehearsing their lines for *Hamlet,* the school play they are acting in later that day. The play is in English, and the boys say their lines tonelessly, as if they are speaking a foreign language they do not quite understand. The lorry-driver, Easy, arrives with the materials needed to build the stage for the school play. He speaks in English, and the boys are confused. Baker tries to communicate by reciting one of the English lines from *Hamlet,* but it does not work. Dogg enters, and Easy wishes him a good afternoon, which is an insult in Dogg. Dogg threatens Easy, who is now very confused. Dogg looks at Easy's construction plans and positions everybody to start building the stage. Dogg starts off the construction by calling out ''Plank,'' a word that means ''Ready.'' Easy notes that the boys throw Dogg a plank, the first item they need to start building the stage, and he thinks everybody is finally speaking English. Easy calls for two more planks, and they are thrown to him. Dogg leaves, and the next time Easy calls for a plank, a block is thrown instead.

Easy is confused and passes the block back. This happens several times; then Easy walks offstage and hits Abel, thinking Abel is giving him a hard time. The language confusion continues as they build the stage, and the audience hears Easy hit Abel again. Charlie has a radio, which broadcasts sports scores in Dogg. Dogg comes by when the platform is finished, and looks at the wall that the boys have built. Easy stands admiring the wall, which is composed of lettered blocks that spell out the words, ''MATHS OLD EGG,'' three seemingly harmless words. Dogg reads the words and knocks Easy through the wall, offended. The words the boys have spelled out are an insult, written in Dogg, although Easy does not know this. The boys rebuild the wall twice more, each time creating seemingly harmless words that are actually insults in Dogg. Each time, Dogg takes offense at the words and throws Easy into the wall, knocking it down, although Easy dutifully throws himself through the wall the last time.

Finally, the letters on the wall are arranged correctly, reading ''Dogg's Hamlet.'' Easy introduces the play, speaking Dogg, and Dogg's fifteen-minute version of *Hamlet* begins, with the three boys acting their parts and several others acting the other standard parts of *Hamlet,* in this highly abbreviated version of the play. Although the play is shortened, the lines are still borrowed directly from Shakespeare's original play. At the conclusion of the play, the actors come out for an encore, in which they act out the play again using Shakespeare's lines, although this time the play is cut down even more, and the actors fly through the dialogue in only a couple of minutes. Easy thanks the audience, in Dogg, and walks out.

Cahoot's Macbeth

Cahoot's Macbeth takes place in a living room across town, although when the play starts, there is such little light on the stage that the audience does not know this. Unlike the previous play, this play starts out in English, with several actors acting out an abbreviated performance of Shakespeare's *Macbeth.* As in the earlier play, the lines are borrowed directly from Shakespeare's play. At a certain point in the play, a police siren is heard in the background, followed by a knocking noise at the door. These disturbances are incorporated into the dialogue of the play. The hostess goes offstage and lets a police inspector in to what is now an empty living room. He is surprised to find that the hostess is hosting a play in the living room of her home and references the audience—the audience who is watching Stoppard's play. Landovsky, the actor playing Macbeth, comes back into the room. The actors and the inspector talk about how public acting has been censored, and the inspector takes a seat in the audience, intending to watch the rest of the *Macbeth* production. The actors are wary, however, because they do not want to be arrested by the inspector for breaking censorship laws, which forbid acting.

The inspector tells them that they had better continue their acting for his pleasure and that if he does not like it, he is going to arrest them. The nervous actors reluctantly finish acting out the interrupted scene from their abbreviated version of *Macbeth,* and the inspector is not impressed, saying that the police do not like Shakespeare. The inspector says that the police would rather have people say that there is no freedom outright, instead of acting it out in cryptic plays. One of the actors, Cahoot, a banned writer, suddenly falls to his hands and knees and acts like a dog. The inspector asks him to make a statement, and Cahoot speaks in Shakespearean language. The inspector tells him that he cannot get around the law by quoting verse at him, then lists the various freedom-fighting organizations he has persecuted. Cahoot growls, which Macbeth says is due to the fact that he has been made a nonperson.

The inspector leaves, telling everybody else to go as well. However, the actors resume their play as soon as he is gone. After the play has progressed somewhat, Easy, the lorry-driver from the first play, arrives on stage, speaking Dogg. The actors continue to speak their lines from *Macbeth,* while Easy appears at various places on and around the stage, trying to get their attention. Macbeth starts to incorporate these appearances into the play, as if Easy were a ghostly apparition. Finally, the hostess stops the production so they can talk to Easy. In Dogg, he tries to tell them that he has a load of materials for them. He opens the shutters and shows them his truck, and they start to understand him. The actors resume their acting.

Once again, the inspector arrives. Easy tries to talk to him in Dogg, and the hostess explains that Easy does not understand English. Cahoot enters and starts to speak to Easy in Dogg. Cahoot tells the others that Easy only speaks Dogg, a language that is caught, not learned. Easy starts speaking Dogg to the other actors, who are picking up on the language. The hostess tells the inspector to leave the stage so they can perform the final act of *Macbeth,* and the inspector warns her that the place is bugged and that the recording will be used against the actors at their trial. The actors resume acting *Macbeth,* although now they say all of their lines in Dogg. The phone rings, and the inspector answers it. His partner outside says that they cannot understand the words on the recording. The inspector is flustered and gets more so as the actors continue acting in Dogg, while Easy and some of the actors build steps on the stage, talking in Dogg as they work. The inspector finally blows up and calls in other policemen, who use the building materials to start walling up the stage—hiding the actors from the audience. The phone rings, and Easy answers it. As he talks into the mouthpiece to somebody, his language slowly changes from Dogg back into English. His last line is completely in English, and he says that it has been a funny week but that he expects he will be back by Tuesday.

CHARACTERS

Abel

In *Dogg's Hamlet,* Abel is one of three schoolboys who helps set up the production of *Hamlet* and acts in it. Abel is the boy who receives the most abuse in the play. In the beginning, the headmaster, Dogg, catches Abel playing with a football while they are setting up for their play and hits him for goofing off. When Easy, the lorry-driver, arrives, Abel and the others do not understand Easy's English and respond to him in Dogg. As a result of this language confusion, Abel does not hand Easy the right building materials when they are constructing the platform on the stage, and Easy takes his frustration out on Abel by hitting him. In the *Hamlet* production, Abel and Baker play guards.

Baker

In *Dogg's Hamlet,* Baker is one of three schoolboys who helps set up the production of *Hamlet* and acts in it. With Abel's help, Baker helps set up the microphone on the stage. When the boys do not understand Easy's English, Baker tries to speak to Easy in Shakespearean English, borrowing one of the lines from their production of *Hamlet.* Baker and Charlie are the ones who initially build the letter-block wall on stage, spelling out insulting words in Dogg, which gets Easy in trouble. In the *Hamlet* production, Abel and Baker play guards.

Cahoot

In *Cahoot's Macbeth,* Cahoot is a censored writer and the only one of the *Macbeth* actors who initially speaks Dogg. When the inspector confronts the actors, Cahoot, who has, up until that point, played Banquo in their production of *Macbeth,* now acts like he has turned into a dog. He barks at the inspector and then speaks to him in Shakespearean language, but the inspector tells him to talk straight.

When Easy arrives speaking in Dogg, Cahoot is the only one who can translate. Although the play was dedicated to the censored writer, Pavel Kohout, Stoppard claims that Cahoot is not Kohout.

Charlie

In *Dogg's Hamlet*, Charlie is one of three schoolboys who helps set up the production of *Hamlet* and acts in it. Baker and Charlie are the ones who initially build the letter-block wall on stage, spelling out insulting words in Dogg, which gets Easy in trouble. In the *Hamlet* production, Charlie plays Ophelia and wears a dress over his shorts.

Dogg

In *Dogg's Hamlet*, Dogg is the school's headmaster, who oversees the setup for the school's play, *Dogg's Hamlet*. When Easy first meets Dogg, Easy wishes him good afternoon, which is an insult in Dogg, the language named after the headmaster. As the play progresses, Easy inadvertently gets on the bad side of Dogg several more times when Baker and Charlie create a wall of letter-blocks, which spell out insults in Dogg. However, Easy does not realize these words, which are harmless in English, are insults. As a result, he is very surprised when Dogg repeatedly throws Easy into the wall, knocking it down and prompting the students to use the letter blocks to create new insults. In the *Hamlet* production, Dogg speaks the prologue. *Dogg's Hamlet* is dedicated to Ed Berman and Inter-Action Productions, a play group that performed many of Stoppard's plays. In the play, Berman is represented by Dogg.

Easy

The lorry-driver, Easy, is the only character who is present in both *Dogg's Hamlet* and *Cahoot's Macbeth*. In the former play, Easy, who works for Buxton's Deliveries, delivers a load of building materials to the school where the headmaster, Dogg, and three of his students, Abel, Charlie, and Baker, are getting ready to put on a play. Easy tries to speak to them in English, but they only speak Dogg, so he becomes very confused. Dogg sets them all to work building a platform on the stage. Easy gives instructions in English, which the schoolboys take for their Dogg equivalent, so Easy gets very confused when the building does not go the way he has planned. In addition, the schoolboys play a prank, rearranging the letter blocks of the play's title to say insulting things in Dogg—which happen to be normal, non-insulting words in English—and Dogg blames Easy for the insults. By the end of the first play, Easy has started to pick up on Dogg.

By the time Easy arrives at the living-room theater in *Cahoot's Macbeth*, he can only speak in Dogg and can no longer understand English. Unfortunately, most of the actors who are performing their illegal production of *Macbeth* can only understand English, so Easy is once again confused, although this time the situation is reversed. Easy finally makes them understand that he has brought building materials for their stage. At the same time, the inspector—who has come to shut down the production of *Macbeth* and arrest the actors and audience—gets very confused when he hears Easy speak in Dogg. When one of the other actors, Cahoot, comes in and sees Easy, he begins speaking to him in Dogg and explains to the other actors that this is what he is doing. Although the inspector does not catch on to Dogg language, the rest of the actors do, and for the rest of the play, they perform *Macbeth* completely in Dogg, while Easy and some of the actors build steps in the background. At the end of the play, Easy answers the phone and talks to the person on the other end, slowly switching back to talking in English.

The Hostess

In *Cahoot's Macbeth*, the hostess owns the private residence where the actors are staging their abbreviated production of *Macbeth*. The hostess refers to members of her audience—which is actually Stoppard's audience—and tries to convince the inspector that the audience members are all personal friends of hers. In this way, she hopes to avoid being arrested. However, the inspector warns her that she is still liable for the acting, which is against censorship rules. When Easy arrives speaking Dogg, she thinks he might be crazy, although, like the other actors, she soon picks up the language.

The Inspector

In *Cahoot's Macbeth*, the inspector is the policeman who has been staking out the hostess's home and who tries unsuccessfully to arrest the actors. When the inspector first arrives, he is lighthearted, referencing the odd jobs the actors have worked—such as working in newspaper kiosks—where he has admired their ''acting.'' For the inspector and the police force, selling newspapers and working other non-acting jobs is the only form of artistic expression allowed. The inspector talks about the censorship that prevents the actors from acting. However, he still insists on seeing the actors perform their play and threatens them with legal action if they do not act for him.

However, at the end of the scene, the inspector says that he and the police do not like Shakespeare because his language is covert. Instead, they prefer a straightforward protest. He leaves, telling them they had better stop the play or he will arrest them. While he is gone, the actors resume their play, and Easy arrives speaking Dogg. The inspector comes back amidst all of this confusion, and lets them know he is recording everything that is being said, to use against them in court. The actors, who at this point have picked up Dogg, perform the rest of the play in Dogg, and the inspector is unable to arrest them as a result. In retaliation, the inspector uses Easy's building materials to construct a wall across the stage, cutting off the actors from the audience as the actors complete their production of *Macbeth.*

Landovsky

In *Cahoot's Macbeth*, Landovsky is the actor who plays Macbeth. Landovsky is Pavel Landovsky, the actual Czechoslovakian actor who was banned from acting in public. The inspector has seen and enjoyed Landovsky's other ''performances'' in the odd jobs that the actor has been forced to take in place of acting.

THEMES

Communication

Communication is the central theme of *Dogg's Hamlet*, and it provides a means for connecting this play to *Cahoot's Macbeth*. When the play begins, the schoolboys speak, using English words such as ''Brick!'' and ''Cube,'' but they use them in ways that are unconventional for the presumably English-speaking audience. For example, when Abel tests the microphone, he says, ''Breakfast, breakfast . . . sun—dock—trog . . . ,'' a phrase that, in English, means ''Testing, testing . . . one—two—three. . .'' For Stoppard's readers, he includes translations in brackets, converting these Dogg words into English. Stoppard's audience, however, does not receive these translations and so must pick up the meaning in context.

This is also true for the character Easy, who becomes a representative for the audience. When Easy first arrives at the school to deliver building supplies and to help construct a platform for the stage, he only knows how to communicate in English. Like the audience members, who are also confused at first, Easy tries to understand what the schoolboys and Dogg, the headmaster, are saying. The schoolboys, who only understand Dogg, are equally as confused at the English. However, they have experienced at least one form of English—the Elizabethan English found in Shakespeare's plays—when practicing for their abbreviated version of *Hamlet.* Because of this, Baker tries to communicate with Easy at one point by quoting a line from Shakespeare: ''By heaven I charge thee speak!'' When they start building the platform, Easy is relieved to find that the schoolboys are using words in a context that he can understand—or so he thinks. When Dogg calls out ''Plank!'' a word that means ''Ready'' in Dogg, Easy notices that Abel throws in a plank from the truck. When Dogg leaves and has Easy take over, he then naturally starts to call out the names of the building materials he needs—in English—and so is frustrated and surprised when he does not always receive what he asks for.

However, by the end of *Dogg's Hamlet*, Easy has picked up on Dogg and no longer speaks English, as he demonstrates when he says, ''Cube . . .'' (''Thank You'') to the audience and walks off. However, even at this point, Stoppard tricks the audience somewhat, because he has Easy say ''Cube'' while he is holding a cube, so the audience is left to wonder if he is speaking Dogg or English.

Censorship

In *Cahoot's Macbeth*, the ability to communicate in Dogg eventually becomes a tool for fighting censorship. The play is set in a woman's living room—a supposedly nonpublic location where the actors can perform their plays, without having to

TOPICS FOR FURTHER STUDY

- Stoppard devoted *Cahoot's Macbeth* to his Czechoslovakian friend, Pavel Kohout, whose own plays were censored during the 1970s. Read one of Kohout's censored plays, and compare it to *Cahoot's Macbeth*, paying particular attention to how each play acts as political commentary.
- Choose another era in history when a region experienced literary censorship for political reasons. Research the history and outcome of this dispute, and write a short biography about one of the literary leaders who was censored.
- Research the history behind Czechoslovakia's split into the Czech and Slovak Republics. How did both cultures react to this political divide? Compare the two cultures as they exist today, paying particular attention to any artistic and political issues.
- Trace the history of communism back to its origins. Using your research, create a timeline that details the major events in the history of communism, and explain how these events affected the world at large.
- In the play, Stoppard creates an entirely new language, Dogg, which is derived from English words that have different meanings. Stoppard gives most of the English translations for the words in brackets throughout both plays. Using these, and any other sources mentioned in the play—such as the lyrics to the song ''My Way''—create a Dogg-English phrasebook. Include a short introductory page that talks about any common patterns you find between the two languages.

worry about being arrested. However, while the actors are performing their abbreviated version of *Macbeth,* a police inspector arrives and looks for reasons to arrest the actors and hostess. He walks around the room, saying, ''Testing, testing—one, two, three . . . ,'' which is, as Stoppard notes in the stage directions, an obvious sign that ''*the room is bugged for sound.*'' Stoppard provides other clues that the inspector is trying to set up an ambush, as when he talks to the ceiling, giving the phone number of the apartment to his partner who is recording the conversation: ''Six seven eight one double one.'' Shortly after this, the phone rings, and the inspector answers it, acting like he does not know who it is: ''Six seven eight one double one? Clear as a bell.'' This is an obvious test to see if the phone works so the inspector can communicate to his other officers outside, if necessary.

While the inspector acts like he is trying to hide his ambush at the beginning, as the play progresses, he becomes increasingly more vocal about the fact that he is there to arrest them for breaking the censorship rules, although he is willing to be lenient at first: ''I don't want to spend all day taking statements. It's frankly not worth the candle for three years' maximum and I know you've been having a run of bad luck all round.'' At this point, the inspector gives a laundry list of ways that artists have been persecuted: ''jobs lost, children failing exams, letters undelivered, driving licenses withdrawn, passports indefinitely postponed—and nothing on paper.''

Subversion

Later on in the same long speech about censorship, the inspector says that the police do not like Shakespeare's plays, which can have hidden meanings and be used as a protest—in the same way that Stoppard is using *this* play as a protest. Says the inspector: ''The chief says he'd rather you stood up and said, 'There is no freedom in this country,' then there's nothing underhand and we all know where we stand.'' However, later, the inspector lets them know what happens to people who speak out: ''I arrested the Committee to Defend the Unjustly Persecuted for saying I unjustly persecuted the Committee for Free Expression, which I arrested for saying there wasn't any.''

In the end, the actors are able to use subversive methods—the same type of subversion for which the inspector wants to arrest them—to defeat the inspector. When Easy, from the first play, arrives, he can at this point only understand Dogg, which he uses to tell them that he is delivering building materials. Says Easy, ''Useless . . . useless . . . Buxtons cake hops . . . artichoke almost Leamington Spa . . .'' The translation in English—''Afternoon . . . afternoon . . . Buxtons blocks and that . . . lorry from Leamington Spa''—is lost on most of the actors, who do not know how to speak Dogg. However, when Cahoot, one of the actors, comes in and hears Easy speaking in Dogg, he explains this fact to everybody, including the inspector. Pretty soon, all of the actors are speaking in Dogg, and even though the inspector knows that this is being used as a subversive language, he cannot do much about it. He and his officers are unable to understand Dogg. Says the inspector into the phone to the man recording the actors' language: ''How the hell do I know? But if it's not free expression, I don't know what is!'' In the end, the inspector cannot prosecute the actors for speaking what sounds like gibberish.

STYLE

Language

Stoppard's obvious technique in both plays is his manipulation of language, something for which he is known. In this play, however, he creates an entirely new language, Dogg. Although at first it seems like the language is random, as Stoppard shows through his characters' interactions, he has chosen many of his words very carefully. For example, in some cases, harmless English words translate into insults or inappropriate slang in Dogg. In *Dogg's Hamlet*, Easy tries to say ''Afternoon, squire'' to Dogg, the supervisor on the job. However, as Stoppard notes in the translation brackets: ''[This means in Dogg, *Get stuffed, you b——.]'' Dogg is offended, and ''*grabs EASY by the lapels in a threatening manner.*'' Easy is confused at this behavior and only gets more confused when, later in the play, Dogg looks over the wall that Baker and Abel have built from letter blocks. The letters spell out ''MATHS OLD EGG,'' which Easy thinks is harmless enough. However, Dogg's violent reaction—which he repeats—indicates that these harmless English words are actually insulting in Dogg:

> EASY *looks at the wall.* EASY *looks at Dogg.* EASY *smiles.* DOGG *slaps* EASY *lightly on the cheek.* EASY *opens his mouth to protest.* DOGG *cuffs him heavily on the other cheek and knocks* EASY *through the wall which disintegrates.*

Humor

As demonstrated above, Stoppard places his characters in situations where their lack of understanding of each other's language leads to humorous effects. He repeats this pattern throughout *Dogg's Hamlet*. Humor is expressed in other ways in the first play, namely in the abbreviated version of *Hamlet,* the play within the play. Although these plays use lines that are taken verbatim from Shakespeare's *Hamlet,* the normally tragic play itself is abbreviated, and it is acted by people who do not speak the language, so the normally tragic performance becomes humorous. For example, when Baker and Abel—who play guards in the play—are practicing their lines, Stoppard notes in the stage directions that ''*They are not acting these lines at all, merely uttering them, tonelessly.*'' In addition, since the *Hamlet* scene is speeded up, it leads to some comic effects. Abel says, '''Tis there. (*Pointing stage left*),'' while Baker says, '''Tis there. (*Pointing stage right, their arms crossing awkwardly*).'' This technique achieves its maximum effect during the encore, when the already condensed version of *Hamlet* is condensed even more, and the entire play takes place in only a few minutes. At this speed, the play becomes even funnier, because it no longer has any context and becomes merely a disembodied set of tragic quotes and events: ''GERTRUDE: I am poisoned! (*Dies*) / LAERTES: Hamlet, thou art slain! (*Dies*) / HAMLET: Then venom to thy work! . . . *Kills* CLAUDIUS.''

In *Cahoot's Macbeth*, the humor is expressed in different ways, most notably in the dialogue of the inspector, who unintentionally says humorous things when he misunderstands the other characters.

When the inspector asks Cahoot if he would like to make a statement, Cahoot quotes a line from Shakespeare's *Macbeth:* ''Thou hast it now: King, Cawdor, Glamis, all / As the weird sisters promised.'' The inspector, responding to the ''weird sisters'' part, says, ''Kindly leave my wife's family out of this.'' In another instance, the inspector blows up at the actors, telling them they had better act for him. Right after this, ''(*He goes back to his seat and says genially to audience*) / So sorry to interrupt.''

Juxtaposition

Stoppard's two plays are filled with juxtapositions, starting with the structure. The first play is an instructional play, which teaches Easy and the audience how to understand the second play, a political play. Likewise, Stoppard's plays follow the style of prose dialogue found in most modern dramas, but this is juxtaposed next to the highly elevated Shakespearean language in *Hamlet* and *Macbeth,* which are both in verse. In addition, as noted above, Dogg language is juxtaposed next to English. Their differences and the miscommunications that these differences inspire lead to much of the humor in the first play.

HISTORICAL CONTEXT

Czechoslovakia Under Communist Rule

Following the death of Soviet communist dictator Josef Stalin in 1953, many European communist countries like Hungary and Poland breathed a sigh of relief and set about undoing the damage that the Soviet leader had caused during his reign of terror. Unfortunately, in Czechoslovakia, following the death of President Antonín Zápotocký, Antonín Novotný, a devoted Stalinist, became president in 1957. For the next decade, the Czech economy steadily declined, and political protests—often in the form of subversive plays—increased, in spite of censorship efforts.

Alexander Dubcek and Prague Spring

In January 1968, Novotný resigned from office and was replaced by Alexander Dubcek, a liberal communist leader who offered Czech citizens hope for a better life. Dubcek introduced widespread reforms in the communist system, opened lines of communication and trade with the West, encouraged complaints and suggestions from Czech citizens, and ended censorship in the arts. The resulting liberalization of Czechoslovakia was referred to by many as ''Prague Spring,'' symbolizing the birth of a new way of life.

However, Leonid Brezhnev, the Soviet leader in the Kremlin who had chosen Dubcek to rule Czechoslovakia—still technically a satellite Soviet country—was nervous about these reforms. Brezhnev feared that other satellite countries under Soviet rule would also try to liberate themselves and might rebel against the Soviet Union. In May 1968, Ludvík Vaculík, a Czech writer, published *The 2,000 Words,* a manifesto that denounced the Communist Party for its past behavior and current corruption. Brezhnev ordered Dubcek to condemn the manifesto, but Dubcek refused and assumed that Brezhnev would drop the issue.

Soviet Invasion of Czechoslovakia

On August 21, 1968, Prague Spring ended when troops from the Soviet Union and its allies invaded Czechoslovakia in warplanes and tanks, killing and wounding hundreds of citizens, who tried to fight back with everything from guns to sticks. Dubcek was arrested and dragged to Moscow in handcuffs. When he was returned to Czechoslovakia after a few days, his liberal spirit was defeated, and he no longer tried to institute any reforms. Dubcek was soon replaced by Gustav Husák, and Czechoslovakian citizens lost their freedom once again.

Censorship and the Artistic Resistance

Following the Soviet invasion, censorship was instituted once more. Some artists, like playwright, Václav Havel—whose plays had savagely criticized the communist system during the 1960s—were forbidden to publish or perform their works. In his 1997 book, *The Czech Republic,* Steven Otfinofski wrote: ''Overnight, Czechoslovakia's most prominent playwright was a non-person.'' In *Cahoot's Macbeth,* Stoppard symbolizes this by having the writer, Cahoot, suddenly start acting like a dog. The inspector asks Macbeth (played by real-life actor Pavel Landovsky, another banned artist): ''What is the matter with him?'' Macbeth replies: ''He's been made a non-person.'' Throughout the 1970s, Václev Havel—a playwright—and other dissidents were routinely arrested for their subversive efforts. In 1977, Havel, Landovsky, Pavel Kohout and other

COMPARE & CONTRAST

- **Late 1960s–Late 1970s:** Many eastern European countries are under communist rule by the Soviet Union, including Czechoslovakia.

  Today: China is the only major communist power in the world.

- **Late 1960s–Late 1970s:** Prague Spring—a brief period of artistic and social revitalization in Czechoslovakia after decades of communist repression—is quickly suppressed by a Soviet invasion. Following the invasion, the works of many Czech writers and artists are censored.

  Today: The former country of Czechoslovakia is now the Czech Republic and the Slovak Republic. In both republics, people enjoy increased artistic freedom.

- **Late 1960s–Late 1970s:** The United States engages in a war in Vietnam to try to stop the spread of Communism in Asia.

  Today: The United States engages in a war in Afghanistan to try to stop the spread of terrorism in the world.

artists formed Charter 77, a human rights organization that opposed communism. Havel—who would eventually become the first president of the Czech Republic in the 1980s—was sentenced in 1979 to several years of hard labor as the result of his subversive efforts.

CRITICAL OVERVIEW

Stoppard's quirky *Dogg's Hamlet, Cahoot's Macbeth* has an even more quirky creation history. The play began as a one-act play, entitled *Dogg's Our Pet*, which was performed in 1971 in London. In 1976, Stoppard wrote a different play, *The 15 Minute Dogg's Troupe Hamlet*. In 1979, this play was combined with *Dogg's Our Pet*, and the two plays were revised to create *Dogg's Hamlet*. In the same year, *Dogg's Hamlet* was combined with *Cahoot's Macbeth*, and the two have usually been performed together ever since.

Critical reaction to this set of plays has generally been mixed. In 1979, Brendan Gill noted in the *New Yorker* that Stoppard is an ''ingenious author'' and that the audience is ''amused and instructed.'' However, he also stated that the plays lack substance: ''The Master Juggler has left us nothing to do but laugh, and that is a welcome but insufficient activity.'' In a 1980 review in the *Theatre Journal*, however, Gerlad M. Berkowitz found little fault with the two plays, calling the first ''a delightful curtain-raiser'' and commenting that the second demonstrates that ''an artist's imagination is itself his greatest weapon against tyranny.''

Critics have generally commented on the language of the plays. Wrote Felicia Hardison Londré in her 1993 entry on Stoppard for *Contemporary Dramatists:* ''Stoppard makes fun of the arbitrariness of language by having some of his characters speak Dogg's language, which is composed of English words used to mean different things.'' On a similar note, in her 1993 essay, ''Stoppard's Theatre of Unknowing,'' Mary A. Doll noted that the two plays juxtapose ''traditional theatre with its expectations of top-down authority and elevated blank verse alongside post-Absurdist theatre with its confusion in rank ordering and idiomatic speech.'' In other words, Shakespeare, traditional theater that is considered high-brow for its formal conventions, is in this set of plays performed alongside more modern theater—which does not always adhere to these traditional artistic conventions.

When discussing *Cahoot's Macbeth*, most critics have noted Stoppard's obvious political commentary. Stated Benedict Nightingale, in his 1979 review for the *New Statesman, Cahoot's Macbeth* is ''fresh evidence that its author is becoming a sort of one-man Amnesty International, with a special interest in his native Czechoslovakia.'' Still, as in other mixed reviews, Nightingale noted that the play degrades into a sort of ''nuthouse lingo.'' Similarly, in her 1999 chapter on Stoppard's minor stage plays in *Twayne's English Authors Series Online,* Susan Rusinko noted that in both plays ''plot mechanisms and ideas vie equally with each other for audience attention, sometimes distractingly.''

CRITICISM

Ryan D. Poquette

Poquette has a bachelor's degree in English and specializes in writing about literature. In the following essay, Poquette discusses the inspector's inability to learn Dogg in Stoppard's play.

In *Dogg's Hamlet, Cahoot's Macbeth*, most of the characters who do not speak Dogg at the beginning have picked it up by the end, just by listening to others speak it. This mirrors the audience's experience as they learn Dogg along with the characters. However, there is one major character who does not understand Dogg—the inspector. In her 1999 chapter on Stoppard's political plays in *Twayne's English Authors Series Online,* Susan Rusinko noted of the inspector that ''Without realizing it he has picked up some Dogg, thus illustrating the . . . earlier comment that one doesn't learn Dogg, but only catches it.'' Why is the inspector able to catch the Dogg language enough to repeat it but not understand it? Two of the inspector's characteristics prevent him from being able to ultimately understand Dogg—his confusion over how his own language works and his desire for normalcy.

When the inspector arrives at the hostess's apartment partway through *Cahoot's Macbeth*, it is instantly apparent that he is a little confused, as Stoppard notes in the stage directions: ''*He seems surprised to find himself where he is.*'' The inspector asks if he is at one of two different theaters and is surprised when he finds out it is neither theater. Says the inspector, ''I'm utterly nonplussed. I must have got my wires crossed somewhere.'' As the play continues, the audience gets a view of how utterly confused this individual is. In fact, it is ironic that at one point in the play, the inspector, threatening the hostess with potential legal action, tells her that ''Words can be your friend or your enemy, depending on who's throwing the book, so watch your language.'' In *Cahoot's Macbeth,* words become the friend of the actors and the enemy of the inspector.

The inspector is a likely target to dupe through the use of words, because he does not have a good command of English as it is. He is constantly offering contradictory words or phrases in the same sentence and, on certain occasions, seems to search for the meaning even as he says them. For example, after the inspector has started examining the audience, he warns the hostess that ''If there isn't a catch I'll put you up as a heroine of the revolution. I mean, the counter-revolution. No, I tell a lie, I mean the normalization—Yes, I know.'' Revolution and counter-revolution are contradictory terms, and normalization is another word for the type of censorship that Czechoslovakia imposed on its citizens in the 1970s. So, he could not very well arrest the hostess for being a heroine of the conformity that he is trying to enforce. In statements like these, the inspector shows himself to be something of a confused person when it comes to using and understanding words. Another example is when he congratulates one of the actors on the performance, saying, ''Stunning! Incredible! Absolutely fair to middling.'' The first two are legitimate compliments, while the last statement can be viewed as an insult and definitely does not belong with the other two.

Still, it seems as if the inspector tries to flaunt his linguistic knowledge—or lack thereof. He often mixes foreign language fragments in with his statements, and they do not always make sense or belong in the sentence. For example, after he says that his initial assessment of *Macbeth* is good, he soon says that he was lying, because he is following the creed ''when in Rome *parlezvous* as the natives do.'' This statement mixes Rome as a location, the French phrase *parlez vous,* and the word ''natives,'' which implies Native Americans or some other form of tribal culture. In another instance, at the end of the play, after he gives a cue to Roger, the man running the tape recorder, the inspector is ready to try to

WHAT DO I READ NEXT?

- Like the schoolboys in *Dogg's Hamlet,* the young gang members in Anthony Burgess's novel *A Clockwork Orange* (1963) talk in a different language. After wreaking havoc on their community, their leader is eventually caught and entered into a criminal rehabilitation program, where even thinking of criminal activities makes him sick.
- Stoppard dedicated *Cahoot's Macbeth* to the Czechoslovakian playwright Pavel Kohout, who faced censorship during communist rule in his homeland. Kohout's novel, *The Widow Killer,* published in 2000, takes place during World War II in Nazi-occupied Czechoslovakia. This detective story concerns the events surrounding the assassination of a baroness and pairs a Gestapo agent and a Czech detective to solve the crime.
- Stoppard is famous for his interest in both Shakespeare and language, which he explores in many of his plays. In *Coined by the Shakespeare: Words and Meanings First Used by the Bard* (1998), Jeffrey McQuain and Stanley Malless explore the enormous impact that Shakespeare has had on language.
- In addition to plays, Stoppard has also worked on screenplays, such as his Academy Award–winning script *Shakespeare in Love* (1999), which he wrote with Marc Norman. This script incorporates many aspects from Shakespeare's life and uses poetic license to fill in the rest, creating an engaging story that utilizes the language skills of both Shakespeare and Stoppard.
- Shakespeare's *Hamlet,* first published in the early 1600s, is considered by many to be the playwright's best work. The tragedy concerns the title character, the Danish prince who sees a ghost of his murdered father, who commands Hamlet to avenge him.
- Shakespeare's *Macbeth,* first published in 1623, concerns the tragedy of the title character, who commits many murders. When three witches prophesy that he cannot be killed by any man who was born of a woman, Macbeth becomes overconfident, and, as a result, dies at the hand of a man who was removed from his mother's womb by cesarian section.
- Stoppard's *Arcadia,* first published in 1993, explores complex mathematical and scientific concepts such as chaos theory. The play involves major characters from two different time periods in the same house, who are involved in a mystery that takes place in both eras.
- Stoppard's *Rosencrantz and Guildenstern Are Dead,* first published in 1967, is the play that made Stoppard famous. The play concerns Rosencrantz and Guildenstern, minor characters from Shakespeare's *Hamlet,* who talk about the play, tell jokes, and reflect on reality while they wait for their inevitable deaths.

---

arrest everybody. At this point he incorporates a couple of foreign languages along with English: ''Right—that's it (*To ceiling.*) Roger! (*To the audience.*) Put your hands on your heads. Put your—placay manos—per capita . . . nix toiletto!'' He also speaks in accents, such as when he hears a Scottish line from the Macbeth play and tries to mimic it: ''Och aye, it's a braw bricht moonlicht nicked, and so are you, you haggis-headed dumbwits, hoots mon ye must think I was born yesterday.''

In addition to creating strange foreign language concoctions, the inspector tends to mix his metaphors and other sayings. In one threat, he warns, ''I'm the cream in your coffee, the sugar in your tank, and the breeze blowing down your neck.'' The first description is a positive one, whereas ''sugar in your tank''—if Stoppard means it to refer to the prank of pouring sugar into someone's gas tank to incapacitate it—is definitely less pleasant than the first. And a ''breeze blowing down your neck'' is a

"ENGLISH WORDS THAT THE INSPECTOR USES ALL HAVE A HEATED TONE TO THEM AND SOUND LIKE A THREAT. HOWEVER, IN DOGG, APPARENTLY THE INSPECTOR HAS MADE A GREAT SPEECH, BECAUSE EVERYBODY RESPONDS FAVORABLY TO IT, CLAPPING AND SHOWING THEIR PRAISE."

neutral statement that is not inherently good or bad. The best example of the inspector mixing up his metaphors happens when he is discussing why artists are being censored:

> A few years ago, you suddenly had it on toast, but when they gave you an inch you overplayed your hand and rocked the boat so they pulled the rug out from under you, and now you're in the doghouse . . . I mean, that is pure fact. Metaphorically speaking. It describes what happened to you in a way that anybody can understand.

By the end of the play, the inspector is speaking Dogg, but he does not know it. Unwittingly, he gives a long speech in Dogg: ''Scabs! Stinking slobs—crooks. You're nicked, Jock. Punks make me puke. Kick back, I'll break necks, smack chops, put yobs in padlocks and fix facts. Clamp down on poncy gits like a ton of bricks.'' The English words that the inspector uses all have a heated tone to them and sound like a threat. However, in Dogg, apparently the inspector has made a great speech, because everybody responds favorably to it, clapping and showing their praise.

In addition to not understanding the rules of his own language, which is often the precursor to effectively learning a new language, the inspector also has a lack of open-mindedness to anything that is not normal. When he first arrives, the inspector gives his view of artists. He tells the hostess: ''I can see you're not at the bottom of the social heap. What do you do?'' When the hostess tells him, ''I'm an artist,'' the inspector notes: ''Well it's not the first time I've been wrong.'' In other words, he sees artists as being at the bottom of the social heap. When it comes to art, the inspector is only able to see and approve of art that adheres to the censorship laws, which is not art in the conventional sense. The inspector tells Landovsky (who plays Macbeth in the play) that he is a big fan of his, but Landovsky says he has not worked for years, meaning that the censorship laws have kept him from acting.

However, the inspector persists and asks him where he was the previous year. Landovsky says, ''I was selling papers in—'' Here, the inspector excitedly finishes Landovsky's sentence: ''—the newspaper kiosk at the tram terminus, and you were wonderful! I said to my wife, that's Landovsky—the actor—isn't he great?'' To the inspector, high art is the mundane task of selling newspapers and watching great acting is observing Landovsky saying ''Getcha paper!'' at his job. In fact, when faced with normal acting, the inspector does not always understand it. For example, after watching a part of *Macbeth,* a tragedy, he says, ''Very good. Very good! And so nice to have a play with a happy ending for a change.''

The inspector is so against uniqueness that he considers his barely educated coworkers a potential threat: ''Yes, one of them can read and the other one can write. That's why we have to go around in threes—I have to keep an eye on those bloody intellectuals.'' The inspector prefers the normalization that Czechoslovakia is under, which keeps everybody at a certain intelligence level and discourages freedom of thought. When somebody asks him about their rights in the Constitution, he says: ''Personally I can't read that stuff. Nobody talks like that so it's not reasonable to expect them to live like it.'' Even the Constitution falls outside the normalization that the inspector adheres to.

In the end, this dependency on normalcy, coupled with the inspector's inability to master the English language, prevents the inspector from understanding Dogg, an abnormal language. As a result, the very thing that terrifies him—freedom of expression—is performed right in front of him, and he is not able to do anything about it except try to wall off the stage so that the audience cannot see the show anymore.

Source: Ryan D. Poquette, Critical Essay on *Dogg's Hamlet, Cahoot's Macbeth,* in *Drama for Students,* The Gale Group, 2003.

Neil Sammells

In the following essay excerpt, Sammells explores the "spontaneous" language of dissent utilized by Stoppard in Dogg's Hamlet, Cahoot's Macbeth.

In *Dogg's Hamlet, Cahoot's Macbeth,* however, Stoppard returns to the formal exuberance of the earlier stage plays. In the first half of the play, by staging a language-game from Wittgenstein's *Philosophical Investigations,* Stoppard attempts to teach a new language to the audience. This element of engagement is heightened in the second half when the bizarre proceedings (which have included crude slapstick and the staging of a ravaged Shakespearean text) are suddenly transposed into a new and menacing context. Philosophical parlour-game and mildly diverting stage-business are given a critically new aspect. *Dogg's Hamlet, Cahoot's Macbeth* evinces, in this sense, the same intention as *Travesties;* both show Stoppard's desire to ambush his audience's assumptions about the kind of play they are watching.

"BY TEACHING HIS AUDIENCE DOGG-LANGUAGE STOPPARD HAS IMPLICATED THEM IN AN ACT OF COLLECTIVE AND EFFECTIVE DISSENT, COMPLETING THE TRAIN OF DEVELOPMENT WHICH SUCCESSIVELY DIMINISHES THE ISOLATION OF HIS CHARACTERS WHO CRITICISE THE PREMISES AND PROCEDURES OF THE COMMUNIST STATE."

The opening section (a conflation of two plays previously written for Ed Berman's Inter-Action Group, *The Fifteen Minute Hamlet* and *Dogg's Our Pet*) is a demonstration of the central tenet of *Philosophical Investigations*—that language is not a calculus logically inferred from the grid-pattern of reality but a form of life, a communal activity capable of change and growth. Indeed, the play shows Stoppard's discovery in *Philosophical Investigations* of ideas and tools which meet his needs as a dramatist, as well as some which deny them. First, the form of language analysis that is practised and recommended in *Philosophical Investigations* is an advance from that of *Tractatus Logico-Philosophicus.* Language is no longer to be analysed back, through a hierarchy of forms, to the reality it transposes. Language is now itself the primal reality; because it has no external support language is not reduced in analysis but laid bare. Analysis displays the manifold language-forms which have become so entwined and knotted that the whole has acquired a prodigious internal strength. Meaning, for the later Wittgenstein, is defined not by an appeal beyond language: it is identified quite squarely with use. Language is a public activity and understanding is defined accordingly as the applicational knowledge of certain operative conventions. Wittgenstein insists, as a consequence, that language can never be private, that it exists solely by virtue of its public presence. Such conclusions would appear to deny the strivings of the spiritual loner or dissident in their attempt to make language susceptible to private initiative: private intention and conviction are ever smothered by the public form of language.

There are, however, other implications to *Philosophical Investigations.* Wittgenstein claims that no discourse is inherently 'realistic' in the sense of being a simple transposition of a state of affairs beyond it. Indeed, freed from any obligation to exterior supports, language becomes alive, capable of change. *Philosophical Investigations* is full of reminders of this obvious fact about language—that it is a continual process of renewal and formation. There are, Wittgenstein tells us, *countless* different kinds of sentences, and 'this multiplicity is not something fixed, given once for all; but new types of language, new language-games, as we may say, come into existence, and others become obsolete and get forgotten.' Pursuing this analogy between language-forms and the games we play he points to the case where we make up the rules as we go along, and 'there is even one where we can alter them—as we go along.'

Wittgenstein's insistence that no single language-form, or collection of rules, is guaranteed by external support parallels Stoppard's that language can be appropriated as a means of criticism. The possibility of dissent as a way of life with its own language—making up the rules, perhaps, as it goes along—becomes real. From this angle Wittgenstein's declaration of the impossibility of a private language looks rather different. When he says this he means that no language is necessarily *unteachable,* that no language is learnt simply by a process of introspection matched with ostensive definition. The language of dissent must, then, be a group activity: a form of life and a means of expression capable of being learned by others. (Just, in fact, as it is learnt by Anderson.) Language as dissent can be caught, learnt in a flash: 'And this is just what we say we do. That is to say: we sometimes describe what we do in these words. But there is nothing astonishing, nothing queer, about what happens.' *Dogg's Hamlet, Cahoot's Macbeth* is about learning in a flash, about spontaneous dissent and the fitting of words to the requirements of a form of life.

The second half of the play presents us with the attempts of a group of dissident actors to perform a truncated version of *Macbeth* which, for the assembled audience, in portraying a brutal and illegal seizure of power, is a reflection of what has happened in Czechoslovakia. For the dissidents the crowning of Malcolm is both an assertion of hope and an affirmation of faith in the efficacy of criticism. The proceedings are constantly interrupted by the Inspector (a sinister development of Stoppard's earlier comic detectives, owing much to Orton's Truscott) who attempts to appropriate both the text and the performance by ending it at the crowning of Macbeth and lauding it with his ominous banalities: 'Very good. Very good! And so nice to have a play with a happy ending for a change.' Stoppard's audience have already picked up some Dogg-language before the interval as they follow the attempts of the lorry-driver, Easy, to make sense of the strange world he has wandered into. In the end, Easy learns Dogg for the specific purpose of abusing the authoritarian headmaster of the boys' school. His entrance in the second half, as he blunders into the action and confuses himself with Banquo's ghost, gives the troupe the chance to use Dogg to finish their performance of *Macbeth* in spite of the Inspector's intrusive presence.

The Inspector is a further demonstration of Stoppard's abiding claim that politically repressive systems are linguistically repressive also. The problem for the actors is that, like the jumpers, he can do with language what he will. 'I've got the penal code tattooed on my whistle,' he assures Landovsky, 'and there's a lot about you in it. Section 98, subversion—anyone acting out of hostility to the state. . .Section 100, incitement, anyone acting out of hostility to the state. . .I could nick you just for acting—and the sentence is double for an organised group, which I can make stick on Robinson Crusoe and his man any day of the week'. The pun, for the Inspector, is an offensive tactic, a means of making us listen in a certain way: 'You know as well as I do that this performance of yours goes right against the spirit of normalization. When you clean out the stables, Cahoot, the muck is supposed to go into the gutter, not find its way back into the stalls'. 'Words,' he announces, happily, 'can be your friend or your enemy, depending on who's throwing the book, so watch your language.'

However, the inventiveness of the Inspector is matched, indeed surpassed, by that of the dissidents. Cahoot (who has earlier howled on all-fours and been accused by the Inspector of being in the 'doghouse') starts to abuse him, reminding the audience that 'Afternoon, squire,' means, in Dogg, 'Get stuffed, you bastard.' The Inspector asks where Easy learnt Dogg: 'You don't learn it,' replies Cahoot, 'you catch it'. This riposte is a triumphant reapplication of the formulaic identification of disease with dissent which is at the centre of *Every Good Boy Deserves Favour*, and evidence of Stoppard's appropriation of Wittgenstein's claim that we can learn in a flash. (Compare the Inspector's 'She's making it up as she goes along' when 'Lady Macbeth' starts to translate Shakespeare into Dogg, which is a similar reflection on Wittgenstein—this time on his remarks about the way we evolve rules for new language-games.) The performance of *Macbeth,* and that of Stoppard's own play, now speed to a climax. Dogg becomes a means of repelling the Inspector (his announcement that anything they say will be taken down and played back at the trial meets with the response, 'Bicycles! Plank!' and of completing *Macbeth* before he realises what is happening. He is at a complete loss as language is wrested from his control. In fact, it is now the Inspector who appears to be spouting nonsense: 'Wilco zebra over,' he bellows into his walkie-talkie, 'Green Charlie Angels 15 out'. By teaching his audience Dogg-language Stoppard has implicated them in an act of collective and effective dissent, completing the train of development which successively diminishes the isolation of his characters who criticise the premises and procedures of the Communist state.

In *Dogg's Hamlet, Cahoot's Macbeth,* the jokes, claimed Michael Billington in reviewing the first production, 'are too relentless and by the end the fun has become diagrammatic rather than, in any sense, spontaneous.' The remark reminds us of Stoppard's own praise of Muriel Spark in *Scene,* his claim that, at its best, her work does not so much promulgate a thesis as toy with it, and have fun with it. Although the emphasis on spontaneity is something of a red herring (we have seen how the 'playfulness' of Stoppard's drama is deliberate and pointed rather than simply high-spirited and diverting) Billington has located a problem with *Dogg's Hamlet, Cahoot's Macbeth.* The play protests too much: the slapstick and hectic confusion of the finale are the work of the guilty conscience, abashed by its own earnestness. In *Every Good Boy Deserves Favour, Professional Foul* and *Dogg's Hamlet, Cahoot's Macbeth* Stoppard is on the attack against the iniquities of Communist governments in general, and that of Czechoslovakia in particular. Between the two latter, however, comes *Night and Day* and here, as in *The Real Thing*, his most recent stage play, he is on the defensive: both plays attempt to promulgate a thesis, mounting apologies for the political status quo in Britain. An examination of certain contradictions and confusions in Stoppard's thinking on the relationship of politics and art (and that of drama to the problems it addresses) will prepare the way for an understanding of how *Night and Day* and *The Real Thing* betray his distinctive gifts as a dramatist and how, in the name of freedom, they seek to deny to their audience the possibility of dissent.

Source: Neil Sammells, "The Dissidents," in *Tom Stoppard: The Artist as Critic,* Macmillan Press, 1988, pp. 111–22.

Michael Billington

In the following essay excerpt, Billington examines the truncation of Shakespeare and the word games found in Dogg's Hamlet, Cahoot's Macbeth.

At the same time as *Night and Day* was running at the Phoenix and *Undiscovered Country* at the Olivier (both plays deriving from mainstream European naturalism), Stoppard also had performed in London two linked one-act plays, *Dogg's Hamlet, Cahoot's Macbeth* that were anti-naturalistic in style and cerebral. They brought together several of Stoppard's prime concerns: Shakespeare, Wittgenstein, language-games, and the heavy-handed persecution of artists (and many others) in Czechoslovakia. *Dogg's Hamlet, Cahoot's Macbeth* were written for BARC: the British American Repertory Company which was devised by Ed Berman as a means of allowing non-star actors to function on either side of the Atlantic. It was a useful, if short-lived, idea. And it encouraged Stoppard to conceive an entertainment that was playful and serious at the same time, but, one is bound to say, nowhere near as successful as a naturalistic masterpiece like *Professional Foul* in plunging our noses into the Czech situation or achieving what Benedict Nightingale called a 'committed hilarity'.

Dogg's Hamlet (an extension of the earlier *Dogg's Our Pet*) was based partly on Wittgenstein's notion of language as an assemblage of games as various in their nature as hopscotch, polo and chess. Stoppard himself says, 'The appeal to me consisted in the possibility of writing a play which had to teach the audience the language the play was written in.' So we see a group of schoolboys, with names like Able, Baker, Charlie, erecting a platform for a prize-giving and speaking a nonsenselingo (Dogg) in which words often have the opposite meaning from their familiar associations. Thus when a schoolboy says to his headmaster 'Cretinous pig-faced git?' he is actually enquiring 'Have you got the time please, sir?' What complicates the situation is that the boys are also rehearsing the school play and lapse into Shakespearian English and that a lorry-driver, Easy, arrives with a load of blocks from Leamington Spa and also speaks received English. When he cries matily to the headmaster, 'Afternoon, Squire' he doesn't realise that translates in Dogg as 'Get stuffed, you bastard.' And when the headmaster says to him 'Moronic creep' his natural instinct is to grab him by the lapels not realising he is referring to the maroon carpet. Stoppard's point is perfectly clear: that language is an arbitrary means of signification. It also leads to some good jokes such as a figure of imperturbable regality beginning her speech to the assembled pupils with 'Scabs, slobs, yobs, yids, spicks, wops . . .' But although Stoppard proves to his, and our, satisfaction that language is a form of game and that we can very quickly become attuned to the new rules (Easy soon becomes conversant with Dogg), one is secretly rather glad when the joke is over and the letters spelling out 'Dogg's Hamlet' appear on the assembled blocks.

After this slightly dogged opening what follows is, in theatrical terms, hilarious: a potted 15-minute version of *Hamlet* as performed by Stoppard's students to whom Shakespeare is clearly a foreign language. Stoppard is by no means the first person to appreciate both the laughs you can get and the shock effects you can create by chopping up Shakespeare and even transposing the lines. Many years ago in *Punch,* Paul Dehn came up with a potted *Macbeth* that boasted the memorable couplet, 'The devil damn thee black, thou cream-faced loon,/ Whom we invite to see us crowned at Scone.' And,

"THE GOOD THING ABOUT *CAHOOT'S MACBETH* IS THAT IT BRINGS HOME TO SPECTATORS IN PRIVILEGED BRITAIN AND AMERICA A GLIMMER OF WHAT IT MUST BE LIKE TO LIVE IN A COUNTRY WHERE THE SIMPLE ACT OF PUTTING ON A PLAY MAY LAND YOU IN GAOL."

on a marginally higher level, Charles Marowitz has offered his own collage versions of *Hamlet, Macbeth* and *Othello.*

Marowitz's collage-effects are, for me, less theatrical than Stoppard's collegiate humour which both makes the point that you can preserve the salient points of *Hamlet* in a boiled-down version and also says something about the modern world's impatient hunger for compression and its short-circuiting of human sensibility. First Stoppard brings on Shakespeare himself who, in an opening Prologue, confirms the opinion of the lady who said that *Hamlet* was full of quotations by offering us all the best-known lines ending with 'Cat will mew and Dogg will have his day'. We then launch into what Jack Kroll in *Newsweek* called 'transistorized Shakespeare'. No sooner, for instance, has Hamlet said 'To be or not to be that is the question' than Ophelia rushes in crying 'My lord' and is peremptorily told 'Get thee to a nunnery'. On stage, the effect is of watching Hamlet played at lightning speed by the Keystone Cops. The joke is not at the expense of Shakespeare but of a modern society that has little time for philosophical digressions or teased-out dilemmas, and craves incessant action executed by moral ciphers. Spurred to an encore, the cast then do a 90-second repeat of the whole play that leaves one helpless with laughter.

Cahoot's Macbeth, in the second half of the evening, also plays on the idea of truncated Shakespeare and the power of words to take on new meanings depending on the context in which they are used. The purpose here is anything but frivolous since it is to draw attention to the iniquities of the Czech regime and the fact that an acclaimed actor, Pavel Landovsky, (who was driving the car on the day in January, 1977 when police stopped him and his friend's car and seized the document that became known as Charter '77) had been driven from his profession in the theatre and obliged to take Living-Room Theatre into people's homes. Interestingly, there is a similar company in Britain that, on request, will come and perform *A Streetcar Named Desire* or *The Servant* in your home; but what for us is bourgeois titillation is in Czechoslovakia the only means of self-expression for outlawed actors.

Stoppard imagines such a troupe performing *Macbeth* in a private sitting-room with us, the theatre audience, becoming the assembled playgoers. The performance is then interrupted by a grotesque Inspector (a favourite Stoppard character) who is both more theatrical than the actors and a sinister-comic agent of repression. The play works on several levels: on one, it is a reminder of the horrific modern applicability of Shakespeare's tragedy with its theme of the illegal usurpation of power; on another, it is a jokey farce that uses (like *Rosencrantz and Guildenstern* and *The Real Inspector Hound*) the intrusion of reality into theatrical artifice.

It is a dangerous, tightrope-walking play because it makes us laugh at a situation that in real life is anything but funny. Stoppard gets away with it partly because of his own impeccable credentials as a human-rights campaigner, partly because there is nothing tentative or apologetic about his jokes, and partly because the laughs all point up the gravity of the situation. Discovering a telephone under a tea-cosy, the Inspector is perturbed:

> INSPECTOR: You've even got a telephone. I can see you're not at the bottom of the social heap. What do you do?
>
> HOSTESS: I'm an artist.
>
> INSPECTOR: Well it's not the first time I've been wrong.

In a country where, as Stoppard recorded in the *New York Review of Books,* you can find boilers stoked by economists, streets swept by men reading Henry James in English, where filing-clerks rise early to write articles for learned journals abroad and where third-rate time-servers are chauffeured around in black, bulbous Tatra 603s, the Inspector's response is all too apt. What Stoppard does in the play is depict the upside-down nature of a society in which a fine actor like Landovsky is acclaimed by the coarse-grained Inspector for his work as a factory floor-cleaner or a newspaper seller and in which language itself is corrupted. George Orwell in *1984* and *Animal Farm* reminded us that language and liberty are intertwined and that when words are perverted or repressed so is freedom. Stoppard makes the same point through brutal, quick-fire comedy:

> INSPECTOR (*to* HOSTESS): Which one were you?
>
> HOSTESS: I'm not in it.
>
> INSPECTOR: You're in it, up to here. It's pretty clear to me that this flat is being used for entertaining men. There is a law about that you know.
>
> HOSTESS: I don't think MacBeth is what was meant.
>
> INSPECTOR: Who's to say what was meant? Words can be your friend or your enemy depending on who's throwing the book, so watch your language.

Maybe there is something too direct and upfront about the way Stoppard sends a figure like Orton's Inspector Truscott from *Loot* crashing around pointing out the way artists are degraded, rooms are bugged, language is twisted and Shakespeare becomes a reckless subversive in a police-state: the play lacks the subtlety of *Professional Foul*. But it gets its point across through a mixture of unashamed farce and clear statement; and never more so than when the Inspector points out that Shakespeare—Old Bill as he is known to the force—becomes all too contemporary in politically explosive situations:

> 'The fact is that when you get a universal and timeless writer like Shakespeare there's a strong feeling that he could be spitting in the eyes of the beholder when he should be keeping his mind on Verona—hanging around the ''gents.'' You know what I mean. Unwittingly, of course. He didn't know what he was doing, at least you couldn't prove he did, which is what makes the chief so prejudiced against him.'

I am reminded of Ian McKellen's account in the book, *A Night at the Theatre,* of playing Richard II in Bratislava in 1969 after the Russian invasion of Czechoslovakia. During the scene where Richard weeps for joy to stand upon his kingdom once again, as McKellen spoke the familiar lines, 'Dear earth, I do salute thee with my hand' he became aware of a collective mewing, grieving, crying sound from the audience: a token of their recognition of the earth as their only symbol of a future freedom and a continuing past. Stoppard also never lets us forget the relevance of *Macbeth* to modern Czechoslovakia even to the point of having a police-siren wail as Macduff cries 'Bleed, bleed, poor country.'

The good thing about *Cahoot's Macbeth* is that it brings home to spectators in privileged Britain and America a glimmer of what it must be like to live in a country where the simple act of putting on a play may land you in gaol. It is affirmative, committed, political: all those things one has always wished Stoppard to be. My only real cavil is that Stoppard's love of diagrammatic neatness slightly runs away with him and he rounds off the play by bringing back the Dogg-speaking lorry-driver, Easy, with a load of timber for Birnam Wood, the actors tune in to Dogg themselves and deliver the final speeches of *Macbeth* in this alternative language. It's a clever way of bringing the evening full circle and of harnessing Stoppard's fascination with word-games and Shakespeare to the uncontainability of the Czech situation as Malcolm takes the crown off Macbeth's head and places it on his own. The implication is that change is inevitable. But, lively as *Dogg's Hamlet, Cahoot's Macbeth* is, you feel at the end of the evening you haven't quite seen Stoppard stretching his talent to his fullest; and that his true direction for the future lies away from theatre-as-game and towards the excavation of true feeling. It wouldn't be fair to say that this generously-donated double-bill shows Stoppard BARC-ing up the wrong tree but it seems a digression from his exploration of a refined and heightened naturalism.

Source: Michael Billington, ''Cricket Bats and Passion,'' in *Stoppard: The Playwright,* Methuen, 1987, pp. 132–68.

SOURCES

Berkowitz, Gerald M., Review of *Dogg's Hamlet, Cahoot's Macbeth,* in *Theatre Journal,* Vol. 32, No. 1, March 1980, pp. 117–18.

Doll, Mary A., ''Stoppard's Theatre of Unknowing,'' in *British and Irish Drama since 1960,* edited by James Acheson, Macmillan Press, 1993, pp. 117–29.

Gill, Brendan, ''Stoppard's Shakespeherian Rag,'' in *New Yorker,* Vol. LV, No. 35, October 15, 1979, pp. 147–48.

Londré, Felicia Hardison, ''Stoppard, Tom,'' in *Contemporary Dramatists,* 5th ed., edited by K. A. Berney, St. James Press, 1993, pp. 636–40.

Nightingale, Benedict, ''Git Away,'' in *New Statesman,* Vol. 98, No. 2522, July 20, 1979, pp. 104–05.

Otfinowski, Steven, *The Czech Republic,* Facts on File, Inc., 1997, p. 37.

Rusinko, Susan, ''Chapter 10: Minor Stage Plays,'' in *Tom Stoppard,* Twayne's English Authors Series, Twayne, 1986.

———, ''Chapter 11: Political Plays,'' in *Tom Stoppard,* Twayne's English Authors Series, Twayne, 1986.

Stoppard, Tom, *Dogg's Hamlet, Cahoot's Macbeth,* in *The Real Inspector Hound and Other Plays,* Grove Press, 1998.

FURTHER READING

Fleming, John, *Stoppard's Theatre: Finding Order amid Chaos,* University of Texas Press, 2001.

Fleming offers the first book-length analysis of Stoppard's plays in almost a decade, taking an extensive look at Stoppard's three newest plays—*Arcadia, Indian Ink,* and *The Invention of Love.* In addition, the book gives a thorough overview of Stoppard's career and studies some of Stoppard's previously unpublished works.

Havel, Václev, and Karel Hvizdala, *Disturbing the Peace: A Conversation with Karel Hvizdala,* Vintage Books, 1991.

Havel, a former playwright, helped lead the struggle against Communism in Czechoslovakia and became president of the Czech republic. This book collects a series of interviews that Hvizdala conducted with Havel and offers an in-depth perspective of his experiences.

Kipfer, Barbara Ann, *The Order of Things: How Everything in the World Is Organized into Hierarchies, Structures & Pecking Orders,* Random House Reference, 1998.

Although technically a reference book, this eclectic and comprehensive information guide offers an engaging look into how everything in the world follows a specific order or structure. Kipfer is a language guru known for her thesauruses.

McCrum, Robert, William Cran, and Robert MacNeil, *The Story of English,* Penguin USA, 1993.

This highly accessible book, the companion to the PBS series of the same name, offers an in-depth, illustrated view of how English evolved into the language it is today. It is a great overview for those interested in the rich linguistic history of English.

Wittgenstein, Ludwig, *Philosophical Investigations: The English Text of the Third Edition,* translated by G. E. M. Anscombe, Prentice Hall, 1999.

Wittgenstein's philosophical writings influenced a number of writers and academics, including Stoppard, who based *Dogg's Hamlet* on one of Wittgenstein's investigations. In addition to language, Wittgenstein investigates the concepts behind objects, categories, symbols, sensations, and other aspects of the human experience.

Flyin' West

PEARL CLEAGE

1995

Pearl Cleage's *Flyin' West* is the story of a small group of African-American women whose lives changed when the West was opened up for people willing to settle in a harsh and untested region. The backgrounds, actions, and feelings of the play's four women and two men reflect themes of determination, racism, miscegenation (intermarriage between races), feminism, pride, and freedom. These themes are evident in much of Cleage's work, which includes plays, novels, and essays.

Flyin' West was published in 1995 by Dramatists Play Service but was performed in Atlanta prior to publication. The play was originally commissioned in 1992 by the Alliance Theatre Company and was produced with the support of AT&T and the Lila Wallace-Reader's Digest Fund Resident Theatre Initiative. Critical response was favorable, and audiences were pleasantly surprised at the play's bold content. Besides portraying strong black women in late nineteenth-century America, the play serves as a reminder that the West was settled by a diverse population. Cleage seeks to inform audiences that the Homestead Act enabled people from all races and genders to own land and to use that land to support themselves, or to develop it and sell it for a profit. The women in the play have left the oppressive South in hopes of enjoying the freedom that they have so long been denied. *Flyin' West* remains one of Cleage's most admired works.

AUTHOR BIOGRAPHY

Pearl Cleage (pronounced "cleg") was born December 7, 1948, in Springfield, Massachusetts, to Doris and Reverend Albert B. Cleage, Jr. She was reared in Detroit, where her father's ministry allowed her to hear speakers such as Malcolm X and Martin Luther King, Jr. Cleage graduated from high school and, during the turbulent 1960s, went to Howard University in Washington, D.C., where she stayed for three years. She went to Yale University in 1969, then the University of the West Indies in 1971, and finally transferred to Spelman College in Atlanta, where she graduated in 1971 with a degree in drama. She also did graduate work at Atlanta University.

In 1969, Cleage married Michael Lomax, a politician. The marriage lasted ten years and produced a daughter named Deignan. Cleage remarried in 1994. Her second husband, Zaron Burnett, Jr., is a writer and producing director of Just Us Theatre Company in Atlanta, Georgia, where the couple met. Cleage was the theater's first playwright-in-residence, and she and Burnett collaborated on several works after she became the artistic director in 1987. Another Atlanta theater, The Alliance Theater, is responsible for debuting some of Cleage's most notable plays. Among these is *Flyin' West* (1992), the play credited with gaining Cleage a widespread audience. The success of this play led to the production of *Blues for an Alabama Sky* in 1995.

Cleage is regarded as an important contemporary African-American writer and feminist. Her work includes plays, poetry, essays, and novels. She has contributed to magazines such as *Ms.* and *Essence,* and she is the founding editor of the literary magazine *Catalyst.* Her work is unique in that it portrays an overlooked chapter in history, the migration of black women to the West. She also addresses modern issues such as racism, sexism, and AIDS. In her first novel, *What Looks Like Crazy on an Ordinary Day*, Cleage depicts the life of a modern African-American woman struggling with her positive HIV status. When this novel was selected for talk-show host Oprah Winfrey's book club, Cleage reached a wide and diverse audience. The book stayed on the *New York Times* best-seller list for almost ten weeks in 1998, and Cleage's writing in general attracted a great deal of interest. Today, Cleage continues to write fiction, essays, poetry, and drama from her home in Atlanta.

PLOT SUMMARY

Act 1

As *Flyin' West* opens, Sophie and Miss Leah are at home drinking coffee and talking about land acquisition for African Americans. They are homesteaders who came to Kansas (their farm is outside the all-black town of Nicodemus) to accept free land for cultivation. Miss Leah is a feisty elderly woman who demands respect, and Sophie is a good-natured but strong-willed woman who takes care of Miss Leah without making her feel dependent. The two women discuss the emergence of all-black communities; they resent threats to such communities by white speculators who want to buy their land. Sophie expresses her determination to get a school for the town by the spring. Outside, Fannie and Wil talk about acquaintances they have in common, as well as Wil's travels in Mexico and Fannie's love of wildflowers.

Fannie's younger sister Minnie arrives by train with her husband, Frank. Frank is fifteen years Minnie's senior, and he is clearly in control of the relationship. The couple lives in London and enjoys a wealthy lifestyle. Frank is of mixed heritage and has little in common with his wife's black family. He acts superior, an attitude that carries over into his marriage; he is physically abusive toward Minnie, although she lies to hide it from her family.

Minnie and Frank talk about their life in London, where they rarely see other black people. This saddens Minnie but suits Frank. He is condescending toward black people in general and is clearly trying to suppress that aspect of his heritage. That night, Fannie, Minnie, and Sophie gather outside to hold hands and perform a ritual that they first performed when they left Memphis to be free in the West. The ritual consists of Sophie leading the other two in declaring their intentions to be free and to honor themselves and the women who came before them.

The next morning, Minnie and Miss Leah talk about children. Miss Leah reveals that she had her first child at the age of thirteen, and over the years, she lost all ten to the slave trade. When she and her husband, James, were finally free, they lost five more children to illness. Miss Leah tells how this destroyed James, who desperately wanted to see a son grow into a man. Minnie tells Miss Leah that she misses being around other black people, and

Miss Leah braids Minnie's hair the way she did long ago. Frank reproaches Minnie for making herself look that way.

That night, Frank is gone and Sophie is showing Minnie her plans for the town of Nicodemus. She has drawn a map of the town, complete with a school, library, and everything a self-supporting town needs. While Sophie is out checking the horses, Frank returns drunk and finds Minnie in the guest room in which they are staying. He tells Minnie that he was out gambling with white men and lost all his money, and he blames her for being bad luck. He also tells her that he heard that the land Sophie and Fannie have is worth a fortune to the white speculators who have shown up looking to buy land. Minnie insists that they will never sell the land because it is their home. Frank becomes enraged and pushes her to the floor. Sophie charges in with her shotgun, pointing it at Frank and getting ready to shoot. Minnie yells for her not to do it because she is pregnant. Presumably, Minnie is afraid that if Frank is killed, she will have no way to support herself and the baby.

Pearl Cleage

Act 2

The next morning, the women are talking about Frank. Sophie is caustic in her remarks, Fannie wants the marriage to work, and Minnie insists that Frank is a good man who has been pushed too far by circumstances. Frank had been receiving money from his white father, but upon the man's recent death, Frank's white brothers stopped sending him money.

The next day is Sunday, but before Fannie, Sophie, and Miss Leah leave for church, they have a birthday present for Minnie. Sophie hands her an envelope containing the deed to her portion of the land. Because she is turning twenty-one, she is able to own land. Frank talks about how much the land is worth and tries to convince the women that they should sell the land, which would fetch fifty thousand dollars per portion. The women insist that they are not interested in the money; they prefer the freedom and self-sufficiency of owning the land.

Wil arrives to escort the ladies to church and to deliver a telegram for Frank. It states that he has been cut off from his family, which now denies him completely. He is angry and feels trapped in the rustic West among people he loathes. After everyone else leaves for church, Minnie and Frank argue about the deed. He insists that they sell the land so that they can resume their former lifestyle, but the land and her family are more important to Minnie. He threatens and demeans her.

On their way back from church, the group meets Frank. He says that Minnie is resting at the house and that he has some business in town. When they get to the house, they discover that Frank has severely beaten Minnie to force her to add his name to the deed so he can go to town and find a buyer for the land. Outraged, they come up with a plan. Wil goes after Frank and convinces him to return to the house. Although Sophie wants to kill him with her shotgun when he gets back, Miss Leah has a better idea. She tells them about a friend of hers who was threatened by the overseer at the plantation where they used to live. Her friend baked him a poisoned apple pie, and nobody ever knew why he died. Miss Leah, rolling out a pie crust, tells them that she has the recipe.

Frank returns and Fannie tells him that they do not like what he did to Minnie, but they forgive him. She also tells him that they have enough money to buy the land. He agrees to sell to them and also sits down to enjoy a piece of apple pie. After a few bites, he starts choking and gasping for breath but realizes too late what is happening. As his body is being removed from the house, Minnie takes the deed out of his pocket.

The final scene takes place seven months later. Miss Leah is rocking the baby while the others get ready to attend a dance. Wil and Fannie are finally engaged, and everyone is happy. Alone with the baby in the final moments of the play, Miss Leah tells the baby (a girl) about all the "fine colored women" who came before her and have made a place for her.

CHARACTERS

Frank Charles

Frank is Minnie's thirty-six-year-old domineering and abusive husband. He is a man of mixed heritage whose mother was a slave owned by his father. Because of his light skin, he is often mistaken for a white man. Frank romanticizes his parents' relationship, claiming that they were in love and that his father wanted to marry his mother, despite the fact that he would not free her. Frank and Minnie live in London, enjoying a wealthy lifestyle because of the money Frank receives from his father. When his father dies, however, the family disowns him, leaving him penniless and desperate. It is this desperation that drives him to the sell Minnie's portion of the homestead. His intentions are discovered by the others, however, and he is killed.

Frank has a superior attitude and looks down on Minnie's family. He regards himself as sophisticated and elite, and he has no respect for the difficult life on the western plains. His duplicity is evident in the way he speaks with false sweetness in the presence of Minnie's family and then beats Minnie behind closed doors.

Minnie Dove Charles

Minnie turns twenty-one years old during the play and is married to Frank, who is fifteen years her senior. While Minnie loves her family very much, she is not strong enough to stand up to her abusive husband. As a result, she rarely sees her family because she lives in London, where she is not happy. Minnie left Memphis with Fannie and Sophie so that they could claim free land in Kansas and make a new life together. When she attends a conservatory (she has a beautiful voice), she meets Frank.

During the course of the play, Minnie reveals that she is pregnant, and when Frank beats her, she is most afraid for her child. When Frank is killed, Minnie does not cry but merely takes the deed to her land from his pocket.

Fannie Dove

Fannie is thirty-two years old and unmarried. She lives with Sophie and Miss Leah outside the all-black town of Nicodemus, Kansas. She and the other women run a wheat farm and have achieved self-sufficiency.

Fannie enjoys the outdoors and is especially fond of flowers. Although she and Wil are very close to each other, it is not until the end of the play that they make plans to wed. In family matters, Fannie is a peacemaker. She believes in love and family, and she encourages Minnie to work out her marital problems with Frank. Still, she realizes that Frank must be stopped, so she participates in the plot to kill him.

Miss Leah

Miss Leah is a seventy-three-year-old woman who spent most of her life in slavery. She gave birth to ten children while she was a slave, and she lost them all to the trade. After she became free, she and her husband had five more children together, but they were all lost to illness. When her husband died, she buried him and headed west in hope of a better life. When her new life is threatened by Frank, she bakes him a poisoned apple pie and serves it to him without remorse.

Miss Leah now lives with Sophie and Fannie. She is a feisty woman who demands respect, speaks her mind, and believes strongly in the oral tradition. Although Fannie wants to preserve Miss Leah's stories in writing, Miss Leah insists that some stories can only be preserved by being told. At the end of the play, she continues the oral tradition by telling stories to Minnie's baby girl.

Wil Parish

Wil is a forty-year-old man who was born into slavery. He is a trusted and loyal friend of the women, but he has a special relationship with Fannie. At the end of the play, they are finally engaged.

Wil is diligent in work and protective in relationships. He offers to "take care of" Frank when the women discuss the problems he poses. When the women ask him to be part of their scheme to get Frank back to the cabin, Wil is more than happy to help. He is respectful of all of the women, and his character provides a contrast to Frank.

Sophie Washington

Sophie is a thirty-six-year-old woman who was born into slavery and is now determined to make the most of her chance at independence. She is strong, both physically and emotionally, and she performs her responsibilities without complaining. She is also a visionary with a plan for what Nicodemus can become in the future. She envisions an all-black town complete with schools, churches, and libraries.

Sophie is not actually a sister of Fannie and Minnie, although the relationship among the three women has developed as if they were all related. Sophie originally joined the family when, in Memphis, she was doing laundry to support herself. She did laundry for Fannie and Minnie, and she eventually became like a sister to them. Sophie is supportive and protective of her friends and family, and she has no tolerance for condescension.

THEMES

Ethnic Pride

The characters (with the exception of Frank) take pride in their ethnicity and the obstacles they have overcome to seize opportunities in the West. They believe that their black heritage is a fundamental part of their individual and collective identities and should affect everything they do. Sophie criticizes Frank's poems because anyone reading them ''couldn't even tell a Negro wrote them,'' adding, ''We have to see everything differently because we're Negroes.''

Having land of their own is important to them because it offers freedom to the characters individually and provides a foundation for emerging all-black communities in which members can share common experiences, foster their unique culture, and support one another's efforts at establishing new lives. At the same time, characters such as Fannie and Miss Leah recognize the importance of remembering the past. Fannie strives to preserve the past by recording Miss Leah's stories. Miss Leah prefers to pass on the past by way of the oral tradition. At the end of the play, she is seen telling her stories to Minnie's baby. She believes strongly that African Americans must recall the past accurately, as she explains in the first scene: ''Colored folks can't forget the plantation any more than they can forget their own names. If we forget that, we ain't got no history past last week.'' This is why she begins to tell the baby about all the strong black women who went before her. She wants the baby girl to grow up knowing how hard her ancestors worked on her behalf.

Frank provides an important contrast to the theme of ethnic pride. Although his mother was African American, he distances himself from that part of his heritage. He strongly prefers to live in London, where his black ancestry matters much less to the English than it does to Americans. He does not miss seeing or speaking with blacks and is more comfortable with his white friends. His denial of his black heritage goes very deep, and he is emotionally disconnected with the experiences of his mother and her contemporaries. He makes inappropriate jokes, such as when Sophie tells him there are not many mulattos in Nicodemus, and he responds, ''I can understand why. This is a lot closer to the field than most of us ever want to get! *(Laughs.)*'' While Sophie is committed to keeping Nicodemus out of the hands of white speculators, Frank seeks to make a profit by selling his wife's portion of the homestead to those same speculators. Cleage uses Frank as a contrast to add emphasis to the ethnic pride felt by the other characters, whose pride is as hard-earned as it is deep.

Freedom

At the heart of the play is the theme of freedom, specifically newly won freedom. Most of the characters in the play were born into slavery and remember that way of life. Although the idea of heading west on the promise of land was scary, they understood that doing so was their best chance to enjoy a better life and establish new homes and communities for future generations. The sisters connect their freedom with the distant past of their ancestors in the ritual they performed when they left the South, a ritual they continue to perform in the West. They hold hands and say:

> Because we are free Negro women, born of free Negro women, back as far as time began, we choose this day to leave a place where our lives, our honor, and our very souls are not our own. We choose this day to declare our lives to be our own and no one else's. And we promise to always remember the day

TOPICS FOR FURTHER STUDY

- The land given away by the Homestead Act of 1862 was originally settled by Native Americans. Research how and when the Native Americans lost their land to colonists and pioneers. Write an essay about this land, addressing what the land meant to the Native Americans and what it meant to the homesteaders. Do you feel that one group was more deserving of the land than the other?
- Why do you think Cleage chose *Flyin' West* as the title of this play, and do you think it is a good title? Explain your answer, and also suggest three other titles for the play.
- Read Fannie Flagg's *Fried Green Tomatoes at the Whistle Stop Cafe* or watch the 1991 movie version, *Fried Green Tomatoes.* Write an essay as if you are a film critic comparing and contrasting Flagg's story and *Flyin' West.*
- Sophie describes the negative reactions of many of the other African Americans in Memphis when the sisters headed for the West. Imagine you are one of those doubtful people who chose to stay in the South, and write a one-week journal from that point of view. Be sure to include the day Sophie, Minnie, and Fannie left.
- Research the beginnings of feminism in the United States. What were some of the original issues that inspired the first feminists, and at what point did African-American women become involved in the movement? How do the characters in *Flyin' West* reflect and/or negate the basic principles of feminism?

> we left Memphis and went west together to be free women as a sacred bond between us with all our trust.

Miss Leah is fiercely protective of the opportunity to own and keep land. She feels that despite the insurmountable gap in power between the races in the South, the rules are more equitable in the West. In the first scene, Sophie tells Miss Leah that some of the black settlements have made rules against selling their land to white speculators. Miss Leah responds, "Ain't nobody gonna give you the right to tell them when and how to sell their land. No point in ownin' it if you can't do what you want to with it." Freedom is even more valuable to her than a strong sense of community.

Sophie and Miss Leah are committed to securing freedom not just for themselves but for future generations. Sophie makes plans for the future of Nicodemus because it is important to her that future black generations have a community that nurtures them. This is especially evident in her focus on getting a teacher so that the school can open. Miss Leah knows better than any other character what it is like to live without freedom, having lived the longest as a slave. She lost ten children to the slave trade, and she continues to feel the depth of her loss. In a discussion with Minnie, Miss Leah says, "None of this makes any sense without the children."

STYLE

Symbolism

Cleage introduces symbolism by using well-chosen objects to convey meaning. She introduces flower symbolism first. Flowers are beautiful products of nature, and they represent new life and strength. They also represent a lifestyle above simple survival; having fresh flowers in the house is a cheerful indulgence. Fannie brings flowers from outside and places them in water throughout the house, an act that demonstrates her natural tendency to bring the life and vitality of nature indoors. Different flowers express different ideas. For example, Sophie considers sunflowers too large to be displayed inside. This expresses the idea that not everything about the external world is appropriate or comfortable in the women's domestic setting. Roses symbolize independence. Fannie tells the story of her father telling her mother that "colored women ain't got no time to be foolin' with roses," to which her mother responded that if he had time to worry about how she spent her time, she was entitled to grow roses.

Another example of symbolism is Fannie's china, which represents a better way of life than the slave existence endured by the other characters. The china also represents the importance of the past to Fannie. Sophie wanted to leave it behind when they packed up to head out West, but Fannie refused to leave without it because it was her mother's china. The china is significant to Fannie, just as Miss Leah's stories are significant to her, and Fannie wants to preserve both to preserve the past.

Irony

Irony refers to a difference between what appears to be true and what is actually true. It is a complex literary technique that requires contrasts and opposing forces or perceptions. That Cleage uses Frank, a mulatto, as a tool of irony, is therefore appropriate. Despite his cool demeanor, he is deeply conflicted about his mixed parentage. He chooses to believe the romantic notion that his white father and his black mother were genuinely in love and that his father wanted to marry his mother. In reality, his father would not give his mother her freedom. Frank needs to believe that he was the result of a loving and dignified union, when the truth is that he was the product of an imbalance of power and, in all likelihood, of violence. The irony is extended when he recreates the same dynamic with his own wife. He asserts his control over her and dominates her with physical and emotional abuse. The marriage is characterized by an imbalance of power, and he does not recognize that he is recreating the truth of the past. To make the parallel especially clear to the reader, Frank is very light-skinned (like his father), and Minnie is dark (like his mother); he reveals to her that he led some white men to believe that Minnie was his "black whore," not his wife. His blindness toward his own hypocrisy is equally apparent in his desire to return to London, where blacks are treated better; he fails to realize that he is guilty of mistreating his own people, both individually and collectively.

Frank's character is also ironic in the way he tries to impress Minnie's family. He believes that he can demonstrate his superiority to them by pointing out how civilized his way of life is compared to their rustic lifestyle. Because he believes that European civilization is superior in every way to that of the American West, he assumes that everyone else will agree. This renders him incapable of earning the respect of Fannie, Sophie, Miss Leah, or Wil, all of whom see Frank's "finer things" as frivolous and meaningless. They respect hard work, integrity, and freedom. As a result, the more Frank tries to command their respect on his terms, the less likely he is to get it.

HISTORICAL CONTEXT

The Homestead Act of 1862

The notion of free land in the United States existed from the nation's formative years, but it was not until the Civil War that the idea became reality. During the mid-1840s, the entire United States experienced significant growth, but growth in the West outpaced that of other regions. Despite its expansion, the West consisted of territories that had not yet become states. As a result, they did not have representation in Congress and thus did not enjoy the government programs afforded the older areas of the North and the South. The issue of free land was supported by Westerners, who knew that it would attract more people, and by Northerners, who wanted the newly settled land to become a productive market for manufactured goods. On the other the hand, the South opposed free land, as it would result in agricultural competition and entice many Southerners, especially slaves and other laborers, to leave the South.

In 1860, however, Southern states began seceding, making it easier for the remaining states to pass legislation in favor of free land. Congress passed The Homestead Act, and President Abraham Lincoln signed it in 1862. This Act enabled any citizen who was the head of the household, twenty-one years of age, or a veteran of at least fourteen days of active service to claim a piece of public land equal to 160 acres. Land was available everywhere except in the original thirteen states, as well as Maine, Vermont, West Virginia, Kentucky, Tennessee, and Texas. Once a homesteader had lived on and cultivated the land for five years, he or she got the title to it. The Homestead Act provided a strong incentive to settle the West, and the result was that pioneers settled and developed the region more quickly than it would have been settled otherwise.

COMPARE & CONTRAST

- **1898:** The people of Nicodemus are determined to create a strong community, despite the fact that their petition to have the new railroad come through their town has been denied. Railroads bring growth and progress, so the people of Nicodemus are disappointed that the railroad is bypassing them.

  Today: Nicodemus is an important historical site but no longer a thriving town, due in part to the fact that the railroad bypassed it.

- **1898:** Homesteaders in Kansas receive 160 acres each to cultivate, although the average farmer can only cultivate 40 acres at a time.

  Today: The average farm size in Kansas is over five hundred acres. With modern equipment and technology, farmers are able to farm hundreds of acres, although issues such as soil erosion and depletion complicate production.

- **1898:** The face of agriculture is the family farm. Farms are run by families who live on the land—often for many generations—and have a deep tie to it.

  Today: The family farm is the most rapidly declining business in America. The face of agriculture is corporate farms run by large agricultural businesses that oversee large tracts of land, to which they have no tie beyond the financial.

Nicodemus, Kansas

In the 1870s, a white man named W. R. Hill, a black homesteader named W. H. Smith, and five black ministers founded the Nicodemus Town Company and recruited settlers to build an all-black community. The town's name is significant, although accounts differ. Some sources say that Nicodemus was the name of a slave who predicted the Civil War, but other sources say he was the first slave to buy his freedom in America.

In September 1877, a group of 350 settlers arrived from Kentucky. Their optimism soon met the harsh realities of the flat landscape, the difficulties of farming, and dwindling supplies. Although about sixty families returned to Kentucky, the others were assisted during the winter by a group of Osage Indians, who provided food.

More settlers joined the homesteaders after the hardships of the first year, and by 1885, Nicodemus had a population of almost seven hundred people. Nicodemus had also become a proper town, complete with two newspapers, livery stables, a post office, a store, a physician, hotels, restaurants, schools, and churches. The town lost some momentum when the railroads that brought expansion to the West bypassed Nicodemus, but it continued to be a viable town until the Great Depression in the 1930s. At that time, many residents left in hopes of finding better opportunities elsewhere. Although its population dropped, Nicodemus remained a center for African-American culture and achievement.

Today, Nicodemus hosts an annual Emancipation Celebration on the last weekend of July. Descendants of the original settlers gather from all over the country to celebrate the courage and fortitude of their ancestors.

Jim Crow Laws

Jim Crow laws established a legal foundation for racial segregation in the South. The legalized racism of these laws was what many African Americans fled to the West to escape. Jim Crow laws got their nickname from a black minstrel-type character who often appeared in stage entertainments of the time and who remained completely ignorant and happy despite being cruelly treated by whites. They were first enacted in 1865 to provide for racial separation in public transportation, but the attitudes behind the laws soon led to separation in virtually every aspect of Southern society. While the laws began by addressing railroads, they soon called for segregation in schools, hospitals, theaters, hotels, streetcars, residences, and cemeteries.

CRITICAL OVERVIEW

Critical reception of *Flyin' West* has been overwhelmingly positive. Critics commend Cleage for portraying a forgotten chapter in history and for doing so in a way that empowers women. Jane T. Peterson and Suzanne Bennett in *Women Playwrights of Diversity: A Bio-Bibliographical Sourcebook* wrote that this play ''provides a new and unique perspective on the traditional telling of how the West was won.'' Similarly, Cathy Madison of *American Theatre* wrote, ''Frank's fate is ultimately decided by the women themselves. Unwilling as they are to relinquish their land and freedom, they manage to offer a searing new testament to how the West was won.'' Addressing the importance of Cleage's focus on history in several of her plays (including *Flyin' West*), Freda Scott Giles observed in *African American Review:*

> Cleage seeks to bring us to grips with our American past and to help us understand and acknowledge its impact on present conditions, especially with regard to issues of race and gender. She examines great historical events and movements not through the eyes of leaders and celebrities but through the experiences of the ordinary people who lived them.

Other critics agree that the female characters are admirable and the themes are relevant today. As a feminist, Cleage introduces themes of female power, relationships, and injustice in her plays, and *Flyin' West* is no exception. In *Significant Contemporary American Feminists: A Biographical Sourcebook,* editor Jennifer Scanlon described the play as blending ''serious feminist concerns with melodrama, balancing motifs of sexism, rape, wife-battering, miscegenation and racism, betrayal, and murder.'' The characters in the play face unique challenges, and critics find their courage inspiring. Steve Monroe of *American Visions* found that the characters ''entertain audiences with passion and humor, anger and wit, idealism and dignity.'' Scanlon noted that the story ''pivots around a primarily female cast whose efforts to establish, protect, and defend each other and their property withstand attacks not only from outside (whites encroaching upon their territory) but also from inside (one of their own men betrays them).''

Giles was particularly taken with the ways in which Cleage juxtaposed her characters. She remarks, ''*Flyin' West* is primarily a study in character contrasts.'' The starkest contrasts are between Frank and the other characters. Reviewing a performance of the play in *North American Review,* theater critic Robert L. King commended Cleage for making ''him deserve the death that the audience vigorously applauded.''

Giles concluded her critical analysis of Cleage's historical plays with the comment that the playwright ''demands that we air the festering wounds of our history, as black and white Americans and as men and women, so that we can begin to clean and heal them.'' King gave Cleage credit for an original and important premise that ''allows her to raise questions of race, history, and gender—indirectly for the most part—and to introduce humor with the casual comfort that a true community enjoys.''

CRITICISM

Jennifer Bussey

Bussey holds a master's degree in interdisciplinary studies and a bachelor's degree in English literature. She is an independent writer specializing in literature. In the following essay, Bussey explains the power, security, risks, and opportunities represented by the indoors and the outdoors in Flyin' West.

Most of the action of Pearl Cleage's *Flyin' West* takes place in and around the home of Fannie, Sophie, and Miss Leah. Their home is a frontier cabin, and although it is rustic and humble, it is priceless in its worth to them. Throughout the play, Cleage portrays the indoors and the outdoors as distinct realities. For the female characters, the indoors represents domestic comfort, immediate security, the familiar, and female power and wisdom. On the other hand, the outdoors represents opportunity, risk, challenges, and future security. As women in 1898, the characters are accustomed to the traditional view of women as keepers of the hearth; their tasks are cooking, cleaning, rearing children, caring for family members, and providing an inviting home atmosphere. The outdoors is where men traditionally work, especially in the context of the women's African-American heritage; slavery

WHAT DO I READ NEXT?

- Cleage's *Bourbon at the Border* (1997) explores many of the same themes as *Flyin' West,* including racism, determination, and suffering. The story is about a black voter registration drive in the South in 1964. In the wake of the violence and killing that results, the two main characters struggle to make sense of it and long to run away to start a new life.
- Zora Neale Hurston's classic *Their Eyes Were Watching God* (1937) is about an African-American woman who was tried and acquitted for the murder of the last of her three husbands. This novel is known for its use of dialect and its themes of identity, female bonding, and gender relations in the black community.
- Written by Lawrence Bacon Lee and edited by Stuart Bruchey, *Kansas and the Homestead Act, 1862–1905* (1979) offers students an in-depth look at the Homestead Act and the factors that influenced its passage and its effects on the opening of the West.
- Anna Quindlen's *Black and Blue* (1998) explores the issue of domestic violence in a contemporary setting. Having finally escaped her abusive husband, Fran Benedetto takes her son to start a new life, but lives in constant fear that her husband will find them. Quindlen reveals the psychological struggles of women in abusive situations and how Fran is compelled by her love for her son to change her life.

has only recently been abolished, and most African-Americans endured its hardships. Farming, ranching, caring for livestock, cutting wood, and hunting and trapping are all activities that take place outside and are associated with men.

For Fannie, Sophie, and Miss Leah, however, there are no men, so it is they who must see that all tasks are performed, indoors and outdoors. Although the outdoor tasks are difficult and physically demanding, the women are glad to take them on because the outdoors represents something new to them: freedom and opportunity. They are responsible for the land because it is theirs, and although traveling west to cultivate land was risky, they did it because they saw it as an opportunity too precious to refuse. The land offers them freedom in the present and in the future because, as owners, they become the decision-makers.

Each character's entrance reveals something about the character and the significance to her of the indoors and the outdoors. First, the audience meets Sophie. She enters the cabin from the outside, rushed, tired, and relieved to sit down for a moment. Sophie is tired from running errands in town and returns home for respite. Her freedom both enables and requires her to carry out duties among the townsfolk, but it is inside the cabin that she feels restored. Once she gets comfortable in a chair, however, she turns to a window and opens it. Relaxing indoors, she gazes appreciatively outdoors. Her sentiment toward the wide open spaces of the West is evident in her recollection of the day she, Minnie, and Fannie left to go west. She says:

> The day our group left Memphis, there were at least two hundred other Negroes standing around, rolling their eyes and trying to tell us we didn't know what it was going to be like out here in the wilderness. I kept trying to tell them it doesn't matter what it's like. Any place is better than here!

Sophie's entrance tells the reader that Sophie is equally comfortable indoors and outdoors, and she appreciates her responsibilities in both contexts. Next, Miss Leah appears from within the house. With the exception of going to church, Miss Leah is always seen indoors. When she enters the audience's view, she sees the open window and is annoyed. As the oldest character, Miss Leah lived the longest as a slave. She worked in the fields, so the outdoors represents hard labor with no reward. The audience should hardly be surprised that she strongly prefers the indoors.

Next, Fannie and Wil make their entrance together. They are first seen outdoors, strolling and chatting. Wil is in work clothes and Fannie is gathering flowers. These characters recognize opportunities in the outdoors. To Wil, the outdoors is where he now works for himself and has the chance to take charge of his destiny. Talking about whether there is room for both flowers and vegetables to grow, Wil tells Fannie, "There's room for everything to grow out here. If there ain't nothing else out here, there's plenty of room." Wil recognizes that just as there is room for all kinds of plants to grow outdoors, there is also room and opportunity for him to grow. For Fannie, the outdoors is a source of beauty and simple luxuries such as flowers. Fannie brings the flowers indoors, which demonstrates her comfort in either setting.

Although Fannie is of the same generation as Sophie (Fannie is only four years her junior), she was not born into slavery, so her perceptions of the indoors and outdoors differ from those of Sophie and Miss Leah. While both Fannie and Sophie appreciate the outdoors, the opportunity they perceive outdoors is quite different. Sophie sees opportunity to work her own land and build a future with her own hands, and she is satisfied to sit inside, relax, and appreciate the outdoors. On the other hand, Fannie recognizes the beauty of the outdoors, and she prefers to bring its elements indoors, as when she puts flowers in water and sets them all over the cabin. Because Fannie appreciates the tangible in the outdoors, she can bring it inside and enjoy it, but Sophie appreciates an intangible aspect of the outdoors—the opportunity to work for herself.

The entrance of Minnie and Frank takes place at a train station. This is significant to the discussion of the indoors and outdoors because their placement in either is less clear. A train station is neither a household nor outdoors. The train on which they have arrived possesses beds, a dining car, seating, and places to relax—an "indoors" that crosses the vast outdoors without acknowledging it. Their lifestyle is quite different from the frontier lifestyle of the other four characters, and they maintain the comforts of a comfortable domestic setting even in the middle of the wilderness. Their divergent perceptions of domestic comfort become clear when they arrive at the cabin. Minnie is right at home, but Frank is miserable. The indoors represents the female realm and the source of female power and wisdom, so this reaction is perfectly consistent with his character. Minnie values family, simple comforts, and fellowship, but Frank is demeaning and cruel toward everything Minnie values. In the cabin, he is out of his element, both physically and emotionally.

"THE GROUP OF WOMEN HAVE LEARNED TO TRUST AND EMBRACE THE INDOORS AND THE OUTDOORS AND EVERYTHING THAT BOTH REPRESENT—TO REALIZE A LIFE THAT THE GENERATION BEFORE THEM COULD ONLY IMAGINE."

Besides their entrances, the orientations of the characters continue to reveal what kind of women they are. Miss Leah is most comfortable indoors, and she is the character most closely bonded to everything the indoors represents. Sophie and Fannie pass from the indoors to the outdoors and back again with ease throughout the play, but the ways in which they interact with the outdoors differ. Sophie goes outside for practical purposes; she has duties such as bringing in wood for the fire, checking on the horses, and bringing in laundry. Fannie goes outside for pleasure. She loves flowers and walking outdoors because she appreciates nature not for its tangible offerings but for its spiritual ones. When Minnie arrives at the cabin, she spends most of her time inside. The cabin is her real home, and she misses it terribly. The outdoors and what it represents—risk and independence—frighten her.

The manner of Frank's death at the end of the play is fitting given the indoor/outdoor significance. His plan to betray the women becomes clear, and it is so offensive to them that they can not allow him to go through with it. Further, their anger is fueled by his abusive treatment of Minnie. Sophie remarks, "All the dreams we have for Nicodemus, all the churches and schools and libraries we can build don't mean a thing if a colored woman isn't safe in her own house." The women lure Frank back to *their* circle of power when he is on his way to his realm of control. He is going to town to make a business deal, but the women trick him into coming back to the cabin. Once there, he does not realize that he is under their control. Appropriately, Miss

Leah uses an apple pie to kill him. An apple pie symbolizes domestic tasks, female duties, and the comforts of home. The women use this decidedly feminine object as a deadly weapon to kill the man who threatens everything they have worked to secure for themselves. Sophie initially wants to kill Frank outside with her shotgun, but Miss Leah's plan is much more fitting. In his final moments, Frank is forced to realize that for all his abuse (physical, verbal, and emotional) of women, his fate is to become their victim.

The final scene of the play serves to emphasize the importance of both the indoors and the outdoors to the group of frontier women. It is seven months after Frank's murder, and Miss Leah is watching Minnie's baby as the others prepare to go to a dance. As the scene closes, the group has left for the dance, which demonstrates the burgeoning community growing strong beyond the domestic confines of the cabin. This community represents the future, a future that will nurture the family as it continues to grow. Inside the cabin, Miss Leah begins to tell the infant girl about the past and all the women who have worked to make the world better for her. Earlier in the play, Miss Leah and Minnie discuss the importance of children and the pain of having them taken away. Miss Leah says to Minnie:

> They broke the chain, Baby Sister. But we have to build it back. And build it back strong so the next time nobody can break it. Not from the outside and not from the inside. We can't let nobody take our babies. We've given up all the babies we can afford to lose.

The cabin represents the culmination of the past in the present as the elderly Miss Leah instructs and supports the tiny infant. Beyond the cabin, a community gathers to dance, and in doing so suggests the future. The group of women have learned to trust and embrace the indoors and the outdoors and everything that both represent—to realize a life that the generation before them could only imagine.

Source: Jennifer Bussey, Critical Essay on *Flyin' West,* in *Drama for Students,* The Gale Group, 2003.

Laura Kryhoski

Kryhoski is currently working as a freelance writer. She has also taught English Literature in addition to English as a Second Language overseas. In this essay, Kryhoski considers the power of race to define perceptions of freedom.

Pearl Cleage, in her work *Flyin' West*, examines the concept of freedom through careful character exploration along colorful lines. Cleage contrasts the character of Sophie to that of Roland, in her consideration of the attempts these characters make to realize freedom. Both take different approaches, based on their own sense of cultural identity. Specifically, Sophie sides with the African side of her biracial past while Frank chooses to identify with the white aspect of his. While there is a clear moral victory at the play's end, it is never clear that either of the characters have formulated an appropriate response to the racism dictating their lives. The result is an illumination by Cleage of the moral ambiguities inherent in racial struggles, ambiguities that not only pit white against black, but also tear families apart.

Besides sharing a common ancestry, Frank and Sophie also share a desire for personal autonomy in their surroundings. Early in the text, the desires of both are to distance themselves as far from the constraints of racial bias as possible. Sophie divulges that she was motivated to move West because ''Memphis was full of crazy white men acting like when it came to colored people, they didn't have to be bound by law or common decency.'' She elaborates, saying that whites were above the law, making living conditions unbearable, adding ''I heard there were Negroes going West.'' Her vision for the future of Nicodemus is one that stretches beyond ''just one more place where colored people couldn't figure out how to be free.'' On some level, both Sophie and Frank clearly recognize the value of personal freedom unadulterated by discrimination.

As coarse as Frank may seem conversationally, his motivations mirror Sophie's. He has moved to England to avoid similarly oppressive forces. Both Minnie and Frank can walk down English streets, people of color among whites, in a world without reprisal and devoid of Jim Crow laws. Minnie shares with her sisters that as a couple, she and Frank even have white friends. In contrast, as an American resident, Frank claims that both he and his wife are ''just ordinary niggers,'' that he'll be reduced to stepping off the street to let ''every ignorant white man'' pass. Clearly, Sophie and Frank's plights are the same, as are their personal desires for freedom. Yet the terms by which they choose to define freedom and the paths they choose to take to realize freedom are completely different.

Freedom for Sophie is defined at the outset of the play. She claims she'll ''have enough'' when as far as she can see ''there'll be nothing but land that belongs to me and my sisters.'' What does land ownership mean? It means that Sophie and her sisters have control over their own surroundings, and by doing so, they can effect change in their lives. The type of change Sophie hopes for is one free of whites, consequently, one free of the oppressive forces that have added up to a life of mistreatment, persecution, and savage abuse. She has a vision of "colored folks farms and colored folks wheat fields and colored folks cattle everywhere you look." Sophie's vision is a noble one, demonstrated in her own wishes:

> I want this town to be a place where a colored woman can be free to live her life like a human being. I want this town to be a place where a colored man can work as hard for himself as we used to work for white folks. I want a town where a colored child can go to anybody's door and be treated like they belong there.

"FRANK IS A PRODUCT OF A SOCIETY WHERE BOTH SUCCESS AND FREEDOM ARE MEASURED BY THE FAIRNESS OF ONE'S SKIN. BUT UNLIKE SOPHIE, HE PROFITS FROM HIS ANCESTRY BY DENYING AND BETRAYING HIS OWN FAMILY."

A black community based on self-sufficiency fuels Sophie's vision for the future. Similarly, her personal experiences as a land owner have shaped her dreams. Sophie looks to the task of farming with a sense of accomplishment, as demonstrated in a conversation with Miss Leah. Miss Leah tells Sophie of her initial experience, stating that "Every other wagon pull in here nowadays got a bunch of colored women on it call themselves homesteadin' and can't even make a decent cup of coffee, much less bring a crop in!" Homesteading is an avenue by which both Sophie and Miss Leah not only experience a sense of personal achievement but, relative to their accomplishments, can realize a profit, an experience made even more uniquely personal to them. In a world dominated by whites, the prospect of owning a plot of land runs profoundly deeper than the soil comprising it.

Sophie is determined to see nothing but acres of farmland owned by color folks. It is her personal charge to awaken this idea, this spirit in her neighbors. Miss Leah warns that folks don't necessarily see it that way. While the place is a refuge for them, a way to get away from the torment of white folks settling on land where they are largely ignored, Miss Leah recognizes the dangers in expecting her fellow African American neighbors to side with her. She says, "The thing you gotta remember about colored folks all the stuff they don't say when they want to, they just gonna say it double-time later." The privilege of land ownership is the ability to sell one's property at will as well, and no rules will prevent these property owners from selling. To ask her neighbors to see beyond the realm of self-interest, to build a sense of community in order to realize freedom, is an arduous or difficult task. Miss Leah warns of a situation in which Sophie is seeing things from her perspective without hearing the underlying tensions or problems that may face Sophie in her efforts to keep the land.

Frank's aspirations for freedom run along racial lines as well and are framed by his perceptions of people of color. Sophie goes so far as to admit to Minnie she is unnerved by Frank's hatred of all things colored, and with good reason. Her credibility is solidified by exchanges between her and Frank, occurring throughout the play. In his attempts to get to know Sophie, Frank unexpectedly turns to her and says, "Min tells me you're a mulatto." Sophie is startled, and in response Frank qualifies his comments by way of apology for being so obviously personal. He also shares with her that he is a mulatto himself "interested to know if there are many of us this far West." This response proves to be particularly telling as the events of the play unfold. Frank's manner remains characteristically course and ungracious. He seems to be particularly haughty and self-serving in his conversations concerning race. In a discussion of England, Frank is quick to comment that the only people of color he encounters are those of Eastern Indian decent. Miss Leah is perplexed and asks him if he gets lonely for colored people, to which he responds, "To tell you the truth, I've seen about all the Negroes I need to see in this life," and laughs. This inspires Miss Leah to excuse herself immediately for bed, to avoid being detained by the "long-winded" member of the group. He is also callous enough to speak of a lynching a week in New Orleans, that it's "the same as it's always been" with a chuckle. He's cut off by Sophie when he claims that the victim brought it on himself due to his own crimes. She responds, "I don't care what he was involved in. . . . Whatever it was, he doesn't deserve to die like that." Cleage makes effective use of Sophie repeatedly in the text as a foil, or a character whose qualities strongly contrast those of Frank's, to shed light on the moral forces shaping Frank's conversations. The affront Frank's comments have on Sophie, as well as the audience, proves to be more disturbing still when examined in the spirit of the social dictates driving them.

Yet even more disturbing is his formula for success—to capitalize on his white heritage in order to realize freedom. At the outset of the play, Frank pins his hopes on the inheritance of his white father, only to have his hopes dashed when he discovers he has no claim to such assets. His vision for success in and of itself is a fallacy—what plagues him is something that runs much deeper than whiteness; it is a fact of heritage. He was born to a slaveholder who ultimately denies Frank by leaving his son out of his will. Yet Frank persists by clinging to his Caucasian ancestry rather than embracing his African roots, as explained by Minnie: ''Frank says he doesn't see why he only has to be with Negroes since he has as much white blood in him as colored.'' But to Sophie, the reality of Frank's background is no different from hers. When Minnie tells Sophie that although Frank's father was a slave owner, he loved and planned to marry Frank's African mother, Sophie points out that without evidence of a marriage, his father's love is a sham. By extension, so are his illusions of being ''white,'' i.e., moving in society with the same freedoms as other white men. To Sophie, Frank is betraying the memory of his mother and, by extension, of his race.

Frank does consistently disappoint Minnie and her family, despite their efforts to receive him. He showers a rain of abuse upon his wife, in one instance calling her a ''pickanninny'' for plaiting her hair, in another, beating her for causing his luck to change during the course of a card game. Of the card game, he emphasizes that all was well until he was asked about ''that nigger woman that kept following [him] on the train.'' He doesn't share the same perspective on what land ownership could mean for Minnie and her family. He instead blatantly disregards the attempts of his family to keep the land by seizing the deed from his wife with threats of physical harm. In Frank's shortsightedness, he only sees a hefty cash return and assured passage to England. In the process, he violates his wife's trust in a brutal assault on her property, willing to desecrate Minnie's dreams in favor of his own. However deluded the idea may seem, Frank is mentally tied to this idea of freedom from persecution as a function of his appearance and his willing embrace of his ''whiteness.'' He is a product of a society where both success and freedom are measured by the fairness of one's skin. But unlike Sophie, he profits from his ancestry by denying and betraying his own family. The irony of this situation is that he was deluded into believing he is somehow exempt from the problems of and obligations to his own people, that he is somehow above the fray, even after he is rejected by his blood relations.

It could be argued that there is no greater wisdom in the choice of Sophie versus that of Frank—both are based on nepotism (family favoritism). In Frank's case, there is ample evidence in the play to suggest that until recently, his movement in such circles is attributable to his relationship to a white person. Until his father's death, it is alleged that Frank has been supported solely by the good fortune of a white father. He has enjoyed the benefits of money and privilege. By reaping such rewards, he is able to move in circles unheard of in Sophie's present circumstances. Money has sheltered Frank from the unpleasantries of the discrimination Sophie faces in America. He has been able to act as if he is a free man. His expectations are perfectly reasonable given his history. Frank is a victim of more than just his own naivete, he is victim of the forces which shape both his social and emotional life. On some level, he feels just as betrayed by the white brothers who choose to deny him his inheritance on the basis of color rather than on the wishes of their own father as does Sophie when she discovers Frank plans to intercede in her own dreams of freedom. Can it be argued that Frank is any less adroit under pressing conditions than Sophie in his decision to pose as a white man by moving in primarily white circles?

The illusion of choice and of freewill is a repeated theme with Cleage. Her characters attempt to step outside of their boundaries, which are unforgiving and imposed upon them, in favor of freedom that is seemingly tangible but is often impossibly unrealistic. Frank's discovery that he is no more exempt from societal boundaries drawn by color than is Sophie leads to his eventual demise. Although Sophie and her counterparts triumph in the end, a contemporary audience is left knowing history will render these landowners helpless against the advances of their white neighbors. In this way, racial atrocities are brought to light again and again by Cleage, the emotional dance played out as we see hopes rise and fall. There is no permanent solace or restitution for any of the characters; there is only the delusion that they will somehow be granted amnesty from the prejudice and injustice dictating their lives. In this way the audience becomes part of this deeply human drama. After all, it is a human tendency to believe in the idea of justice prevailing, of rules being followed, of wrongs being righted, even in the most tragic of circumstances, and Pearl Cleage demonstrates this beautifully in *Flyin' West*.

Source: Laura Kryhoski, Critical Essay on *Flyin' West,* in *Drama for Students,* The Gale Group, 2003.

Freda Scott Giles

In the following essay, Giles explores the family unit and characters Cleage presents in Flyin' West, *calling the drama "a study in character contrasts."*

Pearl Cleage, highly regarded poet and essayist, first gained widespread recognition as a playwright with the production of *puppetplay* by the Negro Ensemble Company in 1983. The chronicle of a failed marriage, *puppetplay* expressed the divided consciousness and ambivalent emotions of the wife through the use of two female actors to portray her, while expressing the perceptual gulf between marital partners by representing the husband as a seven-foot marionette. Though *puppetplay* was moderately successful, and though several of her other works have been produced outside of the Just Us Theater and Club Zebra, performance venues which she helped to found in her home city, Atlanta, Georgia, it is through an artistic partnership forged with Atlanta's Alliance Theatre and its Artistic Director, Kenny Leon, who commissioned Cleage to write *Flyin' West* (1992), *Blues for an Alabama Sky* (1995), and *Bourbon at the Border* (1997) that Cleage has realized a rare achievement for African-American playwrights: consistent professional production in regional theatres. Each production has further distilled her exploration of essential thematic elements which fuel her dramatic vision.

Through these three plays, Cleage seeks to bring us to grips with our American past and to help us understand and acknowledge its impact on present conditions, especially with regard to issues of race and gender. She examines great historical events and movements not through the eyes of leaders and celebrities but through the experiences of the ordinary people who lived them. The issue at hand and its relationship to our actions remains the focus, rather than the impersonation of an iconic figure. Cleage's interest is in helping us face our responsibility for being part of the flow of history (interview). Describing herself as "a third[-]generation black nationalist and a radical feminist," Cleage defines her task as a dramatist as creation of dialectic and political/social action:

> My response to the oppression I face is to name it, describe it, analyze it, protest it, and propose solutions to it as loud[ly] as I possibly can every time I get the chance. I purposely people my plays with fast-talking, quick-thinking black women since the theater is, for me, one of the few places where we have a chance to get an uninterrupted word in edgewise.

"CLEAGE IS A RESISTANT READER OF HISTORY, TURNING HER AUDIENCE TOWARD INTERROGATION OF 'STANDARD' INTERPRETATIONS . . . AND IS NOT HESITANT TO FORCE THE AUDIENCE INTO THE UNCOMFORTABLE PSYCHOLOGICAL AND EMOTIONAL AREAS INTO WHICH AN HONEST DIALOGUE ON RACE AND GENDER RELATIONS MUST VENTURE."

Cleage has turned to the familiar structure of the well-made play, subtly subverting what appear to be stock situations and characters to invoke new ideas. She is a resistant reader of history, turning her audience toward interrogation of "standard" interpretations, be they from black or white perspectives, and is not hesitant to force the audience into the uncomfortable psychological and emotional areas into which an honest dialogue on race and gender relations must venture.

Flyin' West, for example, turns domestic melodrama into a polemic against domestic violence while it addresses the issues of what constitutes and defines a family, and whether black nationalism will hold together the community of Nicodemus, Kansas, founded by the Exodusters who "flew" West to escape racist oppression during the late nineteenth century. A family of homesteading sisters—Fannie, Minnie, and adopted sister Sophie—augmented by Miss Leah, a survivor of slavery who has passed the long winter on their farm, not only persevere but thrive on the products of their labors. As Minnie approaches her twenty-first birthday, they prepare to turn over her portion of the homestead to her. However, her new husband, Frank, through his verbally and physically abusive behavior, threatens not only Minnie's life, but the homestead itself, since he plans to sell Minnie's share to white land speculators who are attempting to buy out Nicodemus and the surrounding area. Empowered by his legal position as male and husband, Frank feels he can act with impunity, and he can only be stopped by a family conspiracy which leads to his death.

Flyin' West primarily a study in character contrasts. Sophie, oldest sister and head of the family, like Frank, is of mixed race. Frank follows the tragic mulatto pattern of internal conflict and hatred of his black heritage, while Sophie embraces her black identity and the idea of nationalistic autonomy that Nicodemus represents. In defense of the things she loves and believes in, she finds her voice as a woman and a community leader, while Frank plots the course of his own destruction. Another male character, Wil, appears as a suitor for Fannie and contrasting foil for Frank, but it is the struggle for the direction of the family and the community, represented through the struggle Sophie leads against Frank, which is paramount. Despite his painful past and his stature as a recognized poet, Frank is held accountable; his violent acts bring violent retribution. In one of her most well-known essays, *''Mad at Miles,''* Cleage explains that no artist, no matter how brilliant the art, is excused from responsible behavior toward family and community, and that the creations by artists who refuse this responsibility is tainted and should be rejected by the community. Even the creations of a Miles Davis must be rejected in light of his documented abuses of women.

In a similar vein, Angel, the pivotal character in *Blues for an Alabama Sky*, is called to account for her refusal to take responsibility for her actions. Angel, an entertainer riding the last wave of the Harlem Renaissance, must survive in Depression-era Harlem. Through Angel's relationships with Guy, her resolutely un-closeted gay friend and protector; Delia, an idealistic social worker; Sam, a world-weary black doctor; and Leland, a suitor freshly arrived in Harlem from Alabama, Cleage gives us a view of a Harlem embroiled in controversy over the issue of reproductive rights. Using historical fact, she dramatizes the conflict between Margaret Sanger, who opened a family-planning clinic in Harlem with the support of Adam Clayton Powell, Jr., and the remnants of Marcus Garvey's followers and others, who viewed Sanger as an agent of genocide.

To relieve their anxiety over their economic survival, Guy shares with Angel his tenement apartment and his dream of designing costumes in Paris for the legendary Josephine Baker, who ''laughs like a free woman.'' Angel, however, can only see her destiny in terms of the economic and emotional support of a man, and uses her body as the commodity through which she will achieve this support. Her myopic pursuit of self-interest strains her relationship with Guy to the breaking point and leads her to ignore the dangerous ground she treads in her relationship with Leland, who tries to recast her in the mold of his deceased wife, who died in childbirth. The disastrous results of Leland's obsession with Angel culminate in a crime of passion which costs Sam his life. In a final act of poetic justice, Guy leaves for Paris, taking Delia, Sam's grieving lover, with him and leaving Angel alone to contemplate her next move.

The action of *Bourbon at the Border* is set in 1995, but actually pivots around the events of Freedom Summer, the black voter registration drive which took place in Mississippi in 1964. Murdered volunteer workers Andrew Goodman, Michael Schwerner, and James Cheney were only three among the casualties of that effort. Two who survived, physically if not emotionally, Charlie and May, are the protagonists of *Bourbon*. Their antagonists are wounds that cannot heal, outrage that cannot be quelled, and guilt over their inability to protect each other from suffering. They share a small apartment near the Ambassador Bridge which connects Detroit, Michigan, with Windsor, Ontario. Their odyssey to escape their pain has led them there, ''like desperadoes drinking bourbon at the border and planning our getaway.'' May's dream, like the dreams of runaway slaves, is to find peace in the Canadian wilderness; she and Charlie cling to the memory of a few happy days they once spent there.

May walks an emotional tightrope as she struggles to negotiate the couple's material and emotional survival, trying to help Charlie regain his balance without losing her own. When Charlie enters the apartment, returning from another in a series of confinements in a psychiatric hospital, he vows to make one more attempt to overcome his despair. Hope arrives in the form of Rosa, their downstairs neighbor, and her latest paramour, Tyrone, a truck driver who helps Charlie get a job where he works. Left with a permanent limp from wounds he received in Viet Nam, Tyrone bonds with Charlie in the realization that they are in actuality casualties of the same war.

At first Rosa and Tyrone appear to be comic relief, bruised but hearty survivors of hard times, dancing to Johnnie Taylor's blues and Motown oldies. Rosa's employment-seeking ventures, including an audition for a job as a phone sex operator, provoke empathetic laughter. However, Cleage makes them much more. Rosa and Tyrone have tried to skate on top of the system, while May and Charlie have paid dearly for trying to change it. They have received nothing but indifference or hostility in return. In an explosive second-act confrontation with Rosa, May recounts the traumatic events of Freedom Summer which inexorably shaped her future and drove Charlie to madness. Through May, Cleage demands that we examine our own positions on the borders between white and black experiences as well as the lines of demarcation of our perceptions of the events, and the ramifications of those events, which surrounded the Civil Rights Movement during the 1960s.

The violence of the past, violence our nation has yet to come to terms with, is eventually manifested in the present, directly and indirectly, and death ensues. May's efforts to endure the unendurable and to fight to the end a losing battle to regain for herself and for Charlie what was brutally taken from them in Mississippi raise her to tragic stature. She is the most complete and ultimately heroic of the women at the core of Cleage's three "history plays." Through *Flyin' West, Blues for an Alabama Sky*, and *Bourbon at the Border*, Cleage demands that we air the festering wounds of our history, as black and white Americans and as men and women, so that we can begin to clean and heal them.

Source: Freda Scott Giles, "The Motion of Herstory: Three Plays by Pearl Cleage," in *African American Review,* Vol. 31, No. 4, Winter 1997, pp. 709–12.

SOURCES

Bennett, Suzanne, and Jane T. Peterson, "Pearl Cleage," in *Women Playwrights of Diversity: A Bio-Bibliographical Sourcebook,* Greenwood Press, 1997, p. 91.

Giles, Freda Scott, "The Motion of Herstory: Three Plays by Pearl Cleage," in *African American Review,* Vol. 31, No. 4, Winter 1997, pp. 709–12.

King, Robert L., "Flyin' West," in the *North American Review,* Vol. 279, No. 6, November–December 1994, pp. 51–52.

Madison, Cathy, "Home Sweet Homestead," in *American Theatre,* Vol. 9, No. 8, December 1992, p. 11.

Monroe, Steve, "Black Women as Pioneers," in *American Visions,* Vol. 9, No. 5, October–November 1994, p. 31.

Scanlon, Jennifer, ed., "Pearl Cleage," in *Significant Contemporary American Feminists: A Biographical Sourcebook,* Greenwood Press, 1999, p. 71.

FURTHER READING

Braxton, Joanne M., ed., *The Collected Poetry of Paul Laurence Dunbar,* University Press of Virginia, 1993.

Dunbar is considered among the most important early African-American poets, and his poetry reflects the emotional spectrum and unique experiences of late nineteenth-century African Americans. Frank and Minnie refer to his poetry in *Flyin' West.*

Chafe, William Henry, Raymond Gavins, and Robert Korstad, eds., *Remembering Jim Crow: African Americans Tell about Life in the Segregated South,* New Press, 2001.

This volume contains the first-hand experiences of African-Americans during the racial segregation of the Jim Crow years. Interviewees include individuals of various economic, social, and geographic backgrounds. The book comes with an audio disk that allows readers to hear some of the interviewees telling their stories.

Painter, Nell Irvin, *Exodusters: Black Migration to Kansas after Reconstruction,* Random House, 1977.

This review relates the events leading up to the migration of many African Americans in the post-Civil War years. Painter also reveals what life in Kansas was like for black homesteaders and factors of their successes and failures.

Spelman College Museum of Fine Art, *Bearing Witness: Contemporary Works by African American Women Artists,* Vol. 1, Rizzoli International, 1996.

This volume captures the art on display during the title exhibition. Various media were included in the exhibit, and twenty-five notable artists contributed work. The photos of the art are complemented by relevant essays written by such prominent African-American women as Cleage and Maya Angelou.

Master Class

TERRENCE MCNALLY

1995

Terrence McNally's *Master Class* was first produced by the Philadelphia Theatre Company in March 1995; it opened at the Golden Theatre in New York City in November of the same year. The play is based on a series of master classes given by the renowned opera singer Maria Callas at the Juilliard School of Music in New York in 1971 and 1972. Callas (1923–77), was the greatest dramatic soprano of her generation and also a controversial figure. Her restless and tempestuous personality often led her into disputes with opera managements and feuds with rival singers. However, she was adored by her fans and was the subject of constant media attention, including gossip about her jet-set life with the wealthy Greek shipowner Aristotle Onassis.

Although *Master Class* does delve into the triumphs and tragedies of Callas's life, its primary focus is the art of dramatic singing. As McNally's fictional version of Callas teaches her class, she explains to her students, two sopranos and a tenor, just what it takes to invest the music with real feeling, revealing as she does so how demanding the profession of opera singing is. She also reveals her own contradictory personality—proud and egotistical yet also vulnerable and self-pitying. In spite of all the flaws of its main character, however, *Master Class*, written by a man who has been a Callas fan since he was a teenager in high school, is a tribute to the dedication of a great singer and actress to her chosen art.

AUTHOR BIOGRAPHY

Terrence McNally was born in Saint Petersburg, Florida, on November 3, 1939, the son of Hubert Arthur and Dorothy Rapp McNally. McNally grew up in Corpus Christi, Texas, where he was introduced to the theater at the age of seven when his parents took him to see *Annie Get Your Gun.* McNally graduated from high school in 1956, after which he attended Columbia University in New York. After graduating Phi Beta Kappa in 1960 with a bachelor's degree in journalism, he went to Mexico on a Henry Evans Traveling Fellowship. In Mexico, he wrote a one-act play, which he sent to the Actors Studio in New York, and in 1961, the Actors Studio offered him a job as stage manager. Later that year, McNally began touring the world as a private tutor for the children of John Steinbeck. When he returned to New York in 1962, he received the Stanley Award for his play *This Side of the Door.* After revisions, this play became *And Things That Go Bump in the Night*, which was produced in New York in 1965.

The play was a failure, and McNally briefly changed careers, becoming assistant editor for *Columbia College Today.* But he soon returned to playwriting, and he won a Guggenheim Fellowship in 1966. Over the next few years, McNally wrote a number of one-act plays, many of which were later produced off-Broadway or on television. The most successful of these was *Next* (1968), a comedy about the indignities suffered by an overweight man at a military induction center. *Where Has Tommy Flowers Gone*? (1971) and *Whiskey* (1973) were less successful. *Bad Habits* (1974), made up of two one-act plays that satirize the treatment of the mentally ill, was a box-office success and won the Hull-Warriner Award and an Obie Award. *The Ritz* (1975) was also a box-office hit.

After the failure of *Broadway, Broadway* in 1978, it was six years before McNally returned to the Broadway stage as the creator of the book for the musical *The Rink.* His next play, *The Lisbon Traviata,* about a gay playwright and opera fan who attempts to revive his career and preserve his relationship with his lover, opened off-Broadway in 1985. *Frankie and Johnny in the Clair de Lune* (1987), a drama about romance in the age of AIDS, was a critical and commercial success that was later adapted for film, with the screenplay written by McNally.

During the 1990s, McNally continued to write many plays, including *Lips Together, Teeth Apart* (1991), *A Perfect Ganesh* (1993), *Love! Valour! Compassion*! (1993; winner of a Tony Award), *Master Class* (1995; also a Tony Award winner), and *Dusk* (1996). McNally also wrote the books for the musicals *Kiss of the Spider Woman* (1993) and *Ragtime* (1996), for both of which he received Tony awards, and the libretto for *Dead Man Walking*, an opera by Jake Heggie that premiered in San Francisco in 2000.

Terrence McNally

McNally has been a member of the Dramatists Guild Council since 1970 and its vice president since 1981.

PLOT SUMMARY

Act 1

As *Master Class* begins, the house lights are still up. An accompanist seats himself at a piano, after which Maria enters, wearing expensive clothes. She announces that there is to be no applause, because everyone is there to work. She makes some remarks about music as a discipline and says that the singer must serve the composer. In the first of many anecdotes about her life, she tells how, during

World War II, she used to walk to the conservatory and back every day, even though she had no proper shoes.

She calls for the house lights to be turned off, and addresses some remarks to the accompanist, telling him that all performers must have a distinctive appearance. The accompanist becomes the butt of her somewhat cruel humor, and she pays tribute to her own teacher, Elvira de Hidalgo.

The first student, a young soprano named Sophie de Palma, enters. Maria criticizes her appearance and tells her to get over her nerves. Sophie says she is going to sing an aria from *La Sonnambula* (*The Sleepwalker*), an opera by the Italian composer Bellini. It is a difficult aria in which the heroine, Amina, bemoans her loss of love.

After a bored stagehand brings out the footstool that Maria has requested, the accompanist plays the introduction to the aria, but Sophie only manages to sing the first word before Maria interrupts. She tells Sophie that she is not really listening to the music and shows her how to do it. Sophie tries again, but again Maria interrupts her after the first word. She tells the soprano that she is not feeling the true emotions of the character.

Following another interruption from the stagehand, who brings a cushion for Maria, Sophie sings again. Maria gives instructions as her student sings. Then Maria asks the singer to translate from the Italian, and Maria instructs her on the passion behind the words. She also draws her attention to the stage direction, which calls for the singer to fall on her knees, which Maria demonstrates. Then she talks Sophie through the emotions that are being expressed in the aria and berates Sophie for not having a pencil handy to take notes. Maria recalls that her teacher never had to ask her if she had a pencil and adds that that was during the war, when there were shortages of everything. Having a pencil meant going without an orange. She made notes on everything, so she could continue the tradition built up over centuries of opera. She berates Sophie for not knowing the names of all the great sopranos, such as Giudetta Pasta (1797–1865), Zinka Milanov (1906–89), Rosa Ponselle (1897–1981), and Lotte Lehmann (1888–1976).

Sophie begins to sing, and Maria hears in her mind her own performance as a recording of Maria Callas is played. Her mind goes back to her relationship with the wealthy Greek businessman Aristotle Onassis, whose companion she was for many years. As she reminisces, she imitates Onassis's voice and his crude way of speaking. She has him say that he bought her with his wealth and that she gave him class, allowing him to acquire the respect that had not formerly been given to him. He tells her how wealthy he is and that she can have everything she wants. He wants her to stop her singing career and sing only for him, and he also asks her to have his child.

The aria ends, and on the recording the audience applauds. Maria thinks back to when she was on the stage at La Scala, the famous opera house in Milan. The last part of the aria, known as a caballeta, plays. It is also the end of the opera. She thinks back to an early disappointment, when another girl was chosen to sing the role of Amina at a student recital. Then she proudly relates how she, who was fat and ugly with bad skin, succeeded. She listens to the musical embellishments that the real Callas is singing on the recording and imagines the way the house lights used to come up while she was still singing. It thrills her to see everyone watching her; her triumph is complete as she listens to the ovation.

Then the lights come back up, and the setting is once more the master class. Maria thanks the soprano and leaves the stage.

Act 2

Maria speaks about the sacredness of her art. She notices that there is a bouquet of flowers for her on the piano, but she does not seem to appreciate them. The next student to come out is another young soprano, Sharon Graham, who is to sing one of Lady Macbeth's arias from Verdi's opera *Macbeth.* Maria tells her to go off the stage and re-enter in character. She also mentions that Sharon's gown, although gorgeous, is inappropriate for the occasion. Sharon goes off and does not reappear. Maria realizes that she has hurt the student's feelings but is unrepentant, saying that one cannot be sensitive in a tough business.

A tenor named Anthony Candolino is the next student. Maria asks him some questions, and he says his ambition is to be a great singer, rich and famous. He has chosen to sing an aria from Puccini's opera *Tosca.* He sings the first phrase, and Maria stops him. She is dissatisfied with him, and after a short exchange, she tries to send him home, but he refuses to go. Maria relents and gives him instructions about voice technique and the expression of feeling. Anthony sings, and Maria is enraptured.

The next student is Sharon, who has decided to return, claiming that she has been sick. She starts Lady Macbeth's aria once more, but again Maria is displeased. Maria takes over, entering as Lady Macbeth, reading a letter. She sings the first few lines, but her voice is cracked and terrible. Sharon takes over as Maria coaches and cajoles, urging her to get the feelings right, to sing with passion, and to take her cues from the music. After this, she sends Sharon backstage and then summons her again to repeat the scene. But this time, the audience hears not Sharon but a recording of Maria Callas singing the same piece in a live performance from 1952. Maria adds comments as she listens. Her mind goes back to her debut at La Scala, and she imitates the voice of her husband Battista Meneghini. Battista asks whether she loves him, but the question, which he asks often, only irritates her. After giving expression to her resentments and her past difficulties, she boasts that she is now beautiful and had thirty-seven curtain calls that night. Then she breaks some bad news to her husband: she will be marrying Onassis. She apologizes. Then she starts speaking to Onassis, saying that all the years she spent perfecting her art were for him, even though he dislikes opera. She tells him she is pregnant with his child. He bullies her into having an abortion. She tells him that she was fired at La Scala but that in the last performance, she was defiant. She kneels and asks him to marry her.

The recording of Callas ends. Maria tells Sharon she should work on some music more appropriate to her limitations. Sharon bursts into tears and lashes out at Maria, telling her she cannot sing anymore and is envious of anyone younger who can. She leaves.

Maria says that if she has been harsh, it is because she has been harsh with herself, but she has tried to communicate something of what she feels about what an artist and musician does. She concludes with advice to the singer: think of the expression of the words, good diction, and your own deep feelings. She gathers her things and leaves.

CHARACTERS

Accompanist

Manny the accompanist rehearses with Maria the day before the master class, but she cannot remember him since he is now wearing a different sweater. She tells him that he does not have a distinctive look and that he must acquire one. Manny is an admirer of Maria and does not react badly to her rather rough treatment of him in act one. In act two, he wins her praise.

Anthony Candolini

See Tenor

Sophie de Palma

See First Soprano

First Soprano

Sophie de Palma is Maria's first student. She tries to sing an aria from Bellini's *La Sonnambula* but does not get past the first word before Maria interrupts her. Maria tells her that she is not listening to the music; she is singing but not really feeling the emotions of the character. Maria's relentless criticism, although meant to be constructive, makes Sophie cry. Maria even tells her that her skirt is too short.

Sharon Graham

See Second Soprano

Maria

Maria is a woman of deep feeling and passion who has had many triumphs and tragedies in her life. Having suffered greatly, she believes this is the key to capturing the tragic emotions of the characters whose roles she sings. She is deeply proud of her achievements because through hard work and persistence she was able to overcome many obstacles. Even as a young woman during World War II, she did not allow hunger and other adversities to interfere with her studies. Her recollection of how a fat and ugly (in her own estimation) adolescent later became a beautiful woman on the stage at La Scala is tinged with pride and pain. There is also a hint of self-pity when she recalls that no one cared about the times she cried herself to sleep at night. It was only her performance on stage that people cared about. Totally dedicated to her art, Maria views a performance as a struggle for domination. She regards the audience as an enemy that she must conquer; she must win listeners over by convincing them that she is right in her singing and in her interpretation of the role. She believes that her musical art makes a difference in the world if practiced with dedication.

Maria reveals herself as a courageous, restless, tempestuous woman, much as the real-life Maria Callas was. Her anecdotes show that she was always ready to face her enemies, to relish her triumphs, and even to turn her disasters into triumphs. In her conduction of the master class, which she takes as seriously as her own performances, she is totally confident, even arrogant, regarding the rightness of her opinions about acting and singing. She is therefore an intimidating presence for the young students who have come to learn from her. She can be domineering and contemptuous, with an acerbic, mocking sense of humor. She is impatient with interruptions, browbeating the stagehand and using the accompanist as the butt of her humor. She is also ruthless in her appraisal of her students' efforts. Although she is sincere in wanting to pass on her knowledge, she lacks patience, humility, and grace. She tells her students to forget about her presence, while making it impossible for them to do so. She is also always ready to disparage other singers, and she has withering put-downs for some of the great figures of the operatic world, such as Joan Sutherland, Renata Scotto, and Zinka Milanov.

Second Soprano

Sharon Graham is Maria's second student, who comes on in act two. She elects to sing Lady Macbeth's entrance aria, known as the Letter Scene. Maria tells her that her beautiful gown is inappropriate for the occasion and then sends her off to make a more forceful entrance. But Sharon does not return, and Maria assumes that she has hurt her feelings. Later, Sharon does return, with the excuse that she was taken ill. She begins reading the text of the letter and then starts on the aria, as Maria aggressively coaches her. But when Maria tells her that she should attempt something less difficult, Sharon bursts into tears and says that she does not like Maria, adding that Maria can no longer sing and is envious of anyone who is young and can.

Stagehand

The stagehand, dressed in jeans and a tee-shirt, brings Maria a footstool and later a cushion. He is clearly uninterested in his work, and he arouses Maria's contempt.

Tenor

Anthony Candolini is the student tenor who has a session with Maria in act two. He has two music degrees and has performed some minor roles. His ambition is to be a great singer and to become rich and famous. He sings an aria from Puccini's *Tosca,* and after some coaching from Maria he wins her enthusiastic approval.

Manny Weinstock

See Accompanist

THEMES

Creating Art

Although the play touches on many of the main events of Maria Callas's life, it is not in essence a biographical portrait. Rather, it is an exploration of the nature of artistic creation, as applied to operatic singing and acting. Maria makes clear that art is serious business that cannot be done by half measures; it demands total commitment on the part of the singer/actress. Being an opera singer can never be an easy career; the singer must give everything to the demands of her craft. This means intense discipline over a lifetime.

In addition to total commitment, the singer must be able to call on resources within herself that will enable her to fully inhabit whatever role she is playing. Since the essence of opera is raw emotion, she must be able to fully experience all the emotions felt by the character—joy, sadness, love, hate, jealousy, rage. It is not enough merely to sing the words and get the notes right. ''It's not a note we're after here,'' says Maria to her student Sophie, ''It's a stab of pain.''

Since Maria emphasizes again and again that her art consists not only of vocal technique but of ''Feeling, feeling, feeling,'' the question arises of how an artist can capture the feeling, say, of a character like Amina in *La Sonnambula,* who has lost the man she loves. Maria makes clear that the singer must have some life experience behind her before she can successfully create the role. She must have experienced the same emotions herself, in her own circumstances. Maria constantly nags the students about whether they really know what they are singing about, and she is not inquiring merely about their knowledge of Italian. She asks Sophie whether she has ever had her heart broken, as Amina has, because no one to whom this experience is foreign could express the passion required in the role.

It is the same when Maria coaches Sharon. Is there anything, Maria quizzes her, she would kill for—a man, perhaps, or a career? She asks because that is exactly what Lady Macbeth is contemplating in the aria that Sharon is about to sing. If Sharon has not felt such desire herself, how can she sing about it? When Sharon replies that she has never really thought about such matters, Maria says that is because she is young. Life will eventually teach her, although in Maria's view, art is even harder to master than life. The point Maria wishes to make is that the singer must reach down into the depths of her psyche to access those times in her life when she felt similar emotions. ''You have to listen to something in yourself to sing this difficult music,'' she tells Sharon. What she is alluding to, whether consciously or not, is a concept developed by acting teacher Lee Strasberg, known as ''emotional memory,'' based on the work of Konstantin Stanislavski (1863–1938) and his ''method'' system of acting. The technique of emotional memory focuses on recalling the sensory atmosphere of a past activity in order to recapture the emotion associated with it. That recovered emotion can then be used by the actor as the equivalent of the emotion being experienced by the character in the play. This is one reason why, for example, Maria sets the scene of the tenor's aria in praise of Tosca, telling him that it is ten o'clock on a beautiful spring morning and that he made love all night to Tosca, the most beautiful woman in Rome. When the tenor points out that the score says nothing about such things, Maria replies, ''It should say it in your imagination. Otherwise you have notes, nothing but notes.''

At the heart of this is a paradox. By digging deeper into herself, the singer can in fact transcend herself. The artistic imagination transforms the singer into a kind of spiritual medium who can identify absolutely with the fictional character she is portraying. ''When I sang Medea I could feel the stones of Epidaurus beneath the wooden floorboards at La Scala,'' says Maria. She found for herself a ''direct line'' to the character, as if the woman she was portraying were a real person. It is not a matter of acting, a word that Maria dislikes, but of *being.* (*Medea* is an opera by Italian composer Luigi Cherubini based on a play by the Greek dramatist Euripides. Callas was famous for her performances as Medea.)

- Near the end of the play, Sharon says to Maria, ''I don't like you.'' What is your reaction to Maria? Do you like her or dislike her? Is she a good teacher or is her manner too harsh?
- Describe a moment in theater, opera, musical, or film in which you have been emotionally moved by the performance of a particular actor or singer. Who was the performer, and how did he or she create the effect that moved you?
- Music has power to touch the emotions in ways that the spoken word cannot. Why should this be so? Analyze some music that you know well, either instrumental or vocal, and try to account for why it has the effects it does. Describe some of the many effects music can have on people. Why for many centuries did soldiers march into battle to the sound of music?
- Maria Callas's life was full of emotional turmoil. Is there a link between suffering and creativity? If not, why have people often thought that there is? In what ways is the artist different from other men and women? What are the essential qualities that a creative artist, whether musician, singer, painter, or writer, must have?

STYLE

Structure

Both acts share the same basic structure. In its essentials, act one consists of Maria's interaction with the first student, the soprano Sophie de Palma, followed by a long monologue in which Maria recalls events from her life. In the original New York production, Zoe Caldwell, who played Maria, stood alone in the light on a darkened stage for this reminiscence, which includes her relationship with Aristotle Onassis, during which he asks her to bear his child, and one of her great triumphs at La Scala. As La Scala is recalled, the interior of the famous opera house is projected on the back of the stage.

The entire reminiscence is accompanied by a recording of the historical Maria Callas singing the same aria (Amina's from *La Sonnambula*) that Sophie has been attempting. Act two contains Maria's session with the second young soprano, Sharon Graham, which is split into two sections, before and after her session with the tenor, Anthony Candolino. This act reaches its climax with the same device that was used in act one. It is an even longer monologue this time, as Maria imagines herself in an earlier period of her life, in her first marriage, then again with Onassis, and finally once more at La Scala, although in different circumstances. Continuing the parallelism with act one, she recalls how she became pregnant with Onassis's child (just as he had asked her to in act one). The final parallel is that, as in act one, a recording of Callas plays, and again she is singing the same aria (Lady Macbeth's) that the student had been attempting. The transition is effected through a change in lighting.

The Leading Role

Since the play is virtually a one-woman show, with the other characters brought in mostly as foils so that Maria can reveal her artistic personality and her views about singing and acting, the success of the production rests on the ability of the actress who plays Maria to capture the imperious, querulous, and tragic essence of the character. Not only this, she also needs to impersonate convincingly various figures from Maria's life, such as her first husband, her lover Onassis, and her teacher, Elvira de Hidalgo. The actress must also be able to speak the small amount of Italian in the play in a convincing and accurate manner.

Music

Obviously, in a play about a legendary opera diva, music is of central importance. Not only are two Callas recordings played, but the tenor and soprano sing arias on stage (the latter does not complete hers). The centrality of singing, and the tragedy of Callas, whose voice deserted her at a comparatively young age, is forcefully made in the only line of music that Maria herself sings in the entire play. This comes midway through act two, and it is the opening of Lady Macbeth's aria, after she has read the letter. The stage directions read, "What comes out is a cracked and broken thing. A voice in ruins. It is a terrible moment." The audience is thus given a contrast to the glorious voice on the recordings and so becomes aware of its fragility—as well as the tragic vulnerability of the character on stage to whom the voice belongs.

HISTORICAL CONTEXT

Maria Callas

Maria Callas was by common consent the greatest dramatic soprano of her generation, excelling in the Italian *bel canto* repertoire. She had a mesmerizing stage presence, and although many regarded her voice as flawed, she could communicate intensity and emotion as no other soprano could. Her personal life was scarcely less dramatic than the operatic roles she played, and there were well publicized incidents involving her legendary fiery temperament, her feuds with opera managements, her rivalries with other singers, and her love affairs.

Callas was born in New York in 1923. She was American by birth and early upbringing, but her parents were Greek, and in 1937 she and her mother left the United States for Greece. Callas was also Italian by virtue of her marriage to Giovanni Battista Meneghini, which lasted from 1949 to 1959.

In Greece, Callas became a pupil of the soprano Elvira de Hidalgo at the Athens Conservatory. She made her operatic debut as Tosca at the Athens Opera in 1941, and she took on other roles over the next three years. In 1945, Callas returned to New York, where she was engaged by Giovanni Zenatello for Ponchielli's opera *La Gioconda* at Verona in 1947. This appearance was in effect the beginning of Callas's career, and in Italy she was soon singing major roles in operas by Wagner, Verdi, and Puccini. Gradually, under the guidance of Italian conductor Tullio Serafin, she began to concentrate on earlier Italian opera. She made a name for herself singing Violetta in *La Traviata,* Gilda in *Rigoletto,* Lucia in *Lucia di Lammermoor,* Amina in *La Sonnambula,* and Norma in Bellini's opera of that name, as well as in *Tosca.* She made her debut at La Scala in *Aida* in 1950; her first appearances in London (1952), Chicago (1954), and New York (1956) were in *Norma.*

By this time, Callas was world famous and had become an extremely controversial figure, known for her great triumphs on the stage but also for her explosive, sometimes quarrelsome personality and her backstage disputes. She was the center of media attention wherever she went, and her rivalry with fellow soprano Renata Tebaldi kept the gossip columnists busy. Callas once said that the difference between her and Tebaldi was the difference between champagne and Coca-Cola. She was known for withdrawing from performances at the last minute, and on many occasions there were factions of the audience that were openly hostile to her. Callas caused one of the greatest scandals in operatic history in January 1958, when she attempted to sing Norma in Rome while suffering from bronchitis. In the audience were the Italian president and other dignitaries. Heckled by the audience, Callas struggled through the first act and then abandoned her performance. The debacle produced an avalanche of negative publicity.

In 1959, Callas left her elderly husband for Aristotle Onassis, but in the mid-1960s Onassis abandoned her for Jacqueline Kennedy, whom he married in 1968.

Troubled by difficulties with her voice, Callas withdrew gradually from the operatic stage. She gave her final performance as Tosca at Covent Garden in 1965. In 1971–72, she gave a series of master classes in New York, and in 1973 and 1974 she emerged from retirement to make a concert tour with her former colleague, Giuseppe di Stefano.

Callas died in Paris in 1977 at the age of fifty-three.

Callas's Master Classes at Juilliard

Callas conducted twenty-three two-hour opera master classes at the Juilliard School of Music in New York from October 1971 to March 1972. She had not sung in public for six years, and her voice was not the great instrument it once had been. Doing the master classes was a way of overcoming her terror of performing by incorporating singing as part of her teaching.

There were twenty-five students in the master class and a paying audience that included some of the great names in opera. Callas did not allow applause from the audience, saying on one occasion (captured in the play), ''None of that. We are here to work.'' Callas scholar John Ardoin writes in ''Callas and the Juilliard Master Classes,'' ''And work she did—serious concentrated, dedicated work that placed her, her voice, her personality, and her ideas squarely at the service of her students. . . . This was no ego trip.'' In the real-life master class, Callas did not offer insulting comments about other singers or indulge in personal reminiscences or displays of ill temper, as she does in McNally's play, although she did on one occasion tell a student that she was inappropriately dressed. However, much of the advice she gave conformed to the sentiments McNally gives her in *Master Class*. Arianna Stassinopoulos, in her biography of the singer, reports that Callas said to a soprano who had just sung one of Gilda's arias from Verdi's *Rigoletto,* ''Gilda is a passionate girl, you know; you must convey to the audience all her palpitating emotion before you even begin to sing.'' Only one of the three arias that figure in *Master Class* was on Callas's syllabus at Juilliard, and that was the tenor aria from *Tosca.* In the play, Maria says she never really listened to that aria, but the master class shows clearly that the real-life Callas knew it extremely well.

Callas was always well prepared for her class, having sung earlier in the day, with her accompanist, all the arias that were to be covered in the session. Sometimes she would sing during the class. On some days, the voice was only a shadow of what it had been, but (unlike the dramatic moment in the play when Maria's voice fails her), Callas would simply say, as Ardoin reports, ''I'm not in voice today'' and move on without fuss. At other times, her voice would attain its characteristic splendor.

At her last class, Callas said good-bye in almost exactly the words that McNally gives her in the final paragraph of her last speech in *Master Class.* In his early version of the script in 1994, the entire farewell speech was virtually word for word what Callas had said, but McNally altered the speech in his revisions.

CRITICAL OVERVIEW

Master Class was a resounding commercial success. It ran from November 1995 to June 1997 on Broadway, recording over six hundred performances. By 1997, there also had been about forty productions abroad, including those in Argentina, Estonia, Germany, Israel, Italy, Hungary, Japan, Korea, New Zealand, and Turkey.

Zoe Caldwell received high praise for her performance as Callas, whom she played from opening night until June 28, 1996, and for which she won a Tony Award. Brad Leithauser, in *Time,* wrote that

Playbill cover from the 1996 theatrical production of Master Class, *directed by Leonard Foglia*

''you don't doubt that if [Caldwell] could only transfer what's inside her to her pupils, they would sing like angels.'' However, Caldwell's strong performance tended to obscure, according to Leithauser, the shortcomings of the play. He questioned the division of the play into two acts, since ''the second act doesn't deepen, it merely extends.'' He also declared that McNally's attempt to ''drive [the play] toward an old-fashioned theatrical climax (one of the students ultimately mutinies against Callas' bullying) feels contrived.'' These alleged shortcomings, however, did not stop the play from winning the number six slot in *Time's* end of year list of the best plays of 1995.

Nancy Franklin in the *New Yorker* also remarked on Caldwell's outstanding performance (''Caldwell plays Callas with . . . steely force and conviction'') but felt that the play did not serve the historical Callas well. She argued that the recordings available of Callas's master classes make it clear that ''as a teacher Callas was a consummate professional . . . . she was unfailingly attentive to her students, and didn't use the audience as a foil for her egomania,'' unlike the Callas in the play. Franklin's conclusion was that because of McNally's desire to present Callas as an ''artistic personality''—complete with haughty, sardonic manner—and to discover what it was in Callas that so moved her audiences, the play ''says more about its author than about its subject . . . . *Master Class* doesn't get us any closer to Callas.''

When Patti Lupone took over from Caldwell on Broadway in the summer of 1996, Vincent Canby, reviewing the production for the *New York Times,* commented that the play was more ''complex and difficult than it first seemed.'' He was referring to the way *Master Class* goes back and forth between Callas's memories and her interactions with her students. Canby described the Callas of the play as ''a spectacular pousse-café of gallantry, [b——]iness, dedication and impatience with the second-rate.'' Lupone, who played the original title role in the musical *Evita,* did not quite convince Canby with her performance, which he described as possessing ''more power than control'':

> Under Leonard Foglia's direction, she makes all the right moves, but she doesn't execute them with the innate grace of the woman who was possibly the twentieth century's most dazzling opera star. There's something slightly crude about this Callas when she should be cleanly, imperially demanding.

Later actresses who have taken on the role of Callas include Faye Dunaway, who plays Callas in the film version of the play. Dunaway appeared in a touring production of *Master Class* at the Shubert Performing Arts Center in New Haven, Connecticut, in 1997. Alvin Klein, reviewing the production for the *New York Times,* found some weak spots in her interpretation of the role and argued that she did not own it as completely as Caldwell and Lupone had. He pointed in particular to her veiling of her emotions in the crucial section when the tenor moves Callas deeply with his rendition of an aria from Puccini's *Tosca:* ''Ms. Dunaway's reaction to his splendid performance is guarded. She masks her tears, turning away from the audience, after he leaves.'' Although Klein acknowledged that there may be some merits to the choice Dunaway made, he adds, ''yet Ms. Dunaway's reserve narrows the performance and works against much of the role as Mr. McNally crafted it.'' Since Klein regarded the play as ''little more than a sketch for an actress of largesse to fill in with heartbreak and transcendence,'' he claimed that a less than perfect performance in the leading role merely exposed the relative weakness of the script.

WHAT DO I READ NEXT?

- McNally's play *Love! Valour! Compassion*! (1994) arose from McNally's desire to write about what it was like to be a gay man in America in the 1990s. The play received laudatory reviews and won several awards, including a Tony Award for best play.
- *Greek Fire: The Story of Maria Callas and Aristotle Onassis* (2001), by Nicholas Gage, sympathetically documents the tempestuous nine-year affair between Callas and the Greek shipping tycoon. Relevant for students of *Master Class* is Gage's claim that Callas gave birth to Onassis's son in 1960 and that the baby died within hours.
- *Maria Callas: An Intimate Biography* (2001), by Anne Edwards, is the latest of more than thirty biographies of Callas. Edwards is at pains to search for the facts behind all the myths about Callas, and she produces evidence to refute Gage's assertion in *Greek Fire* that Callas had a son by Onassis. In addition to the riveting tale of Callas's ultimately tragic life, Edwards also provides many descriptions of opera plots, costumes, and sceneries.
- *Diva: Great Sopranos and Mezzos Discuss Their Art* (1991), by Helena Matheopoulos, covers twenty-six leading female opera singers, who discuss topics such as their vocal development, the roles for which they are best known, and their personal lives. Many offer advice to young singers.

CRITICISM

Bryan Aubrey

Aubrey holds a Ph.D. in English and has published many articles on twentieth-century literature. In this essay, Aubrey discusses some outstanding moments in Maria Callas's singing that have been captured on audio and videotape and how these reflect the themes of Master Class. *He also discusses the changes Callas brought to opera singing.*

Playwright McNally is a lifelong fan of Maria Callas. He first heard her when he was a fifteen-year-old high school student in Texas in 1953. The recording was of Callas singing in Donizetti's opera *Lucia di Lammermoor,* and McNally felt that she was singing just for him. He later wrote, "Listening to Callas is not a passive experience. It is a conversation with her and finally, ourselves. . . . She tells us her secrets—her pains, her joys—and we tell her ours right back" (quoted by John Ardoin, author of "Callas and the Juilliard Master Classes," in *Terrence McNally: A Casebook*).

McNally was fortunate enough to have heard Callas sing live twenty-five to thirty times, something that few other people in the United States can match. Callas's career was short, and not many people younger than fifty are likely to have heard her live on the operatic stage, since her last performance, as Tosca at London's Covent Garden, was in July 1965. (Many determined operagoers waited in line for five nights to get tickets.) Her last performance in the United States was at New York's Metropolitan Opera a few months earlier. At the Met, the audience gave Callas a tumultuous reception, and the long bouts of applause at her entrance and during the acts extended the performance an hour longer than scheduled. "The stage presence shown by Callas in her performance would have raised the hackles on a deaf man" was only one among the torrent of accolades that the critics bestowed on her in the morning newspapers the following day (quoted by Arianna Stassinopoulos in her *Maria Callas: The Woman Behind the Legend*).

However, despite the legendary status Callas attained in her lifetime, for today's reader or playgoer who has little knowledge of opera, the name

"SO GREAT WAS CALLAS'S IMPACT THAT SCHOLARS ROUTINELY REFER TO THE 'CALLAS REVOLUTION' WHEN THEY DISCUSS THE CHANGES THAT SHE BROUGHT TO OPERA SINGING."

Maria Callas may be scarcely more than a name from the distant past. Perhaps for the non-opera fan, the most vivid moments that capture what Callas meant and still means to many people occur in the 1993 film *Philadelphia,* for which Tom Hanks won an Oscar. Hanks plays Andrew Beckett, a gay lawyer who has AIDS and who is illegally fired from his job because of it. He fights back against the law firm as he also battles the deadly disease. In a key scene Andy listens at home, with his lawyer Joe Miller (Denzel Washington), to a 1954 recording of Callas singing Maddalena's aria, ''La Mamma Morta,'' from Umberto Giordano's opera *Andrea Chenier.* Andy, whose favorite aria this is, is transported in ecstasy and pain as Callas sings the story of Maddalena's tragic life. Translating the words over her voice as he listens, he asks Joe, ''Can you hear the heartache in her voice? Can you feel it, Joe?'' Joe, who knows nothing of opera and is stunned by what is going on, nods his head earnestly. The aria reaches its climax when Maddalena tells how Love came to her and urged her, in spite of her despair, to live: ''Sorridi espera! lo son l'amore! . . . lo son divino'' (''Smile and hope! I am Love! . . . I am divine''). As Callas's top notes ring out in affirmation and triumph—an ecstasy emerging from bitterest pain—Andy feels the same inspiration, ready heroically to affirm life even as he faces a cruel death. It is Callas's disembodied voice that creates the intense drama of this scene, which is so pivotal to the movie. It perfectly illustrates McNally's comment quoted above, to which he added an imaginary snatch of dialogue between diva and devotee: '''I have felt such despair and happiness,' Callas confesses. 'So have I, so have I,' we answer.'' McNally suggests that what we see and hear in the characters that Callas brings to such vivid life is a reflection of ourselves, of our own hopes and disappointments, sorrows and joys, just as the aria from *Andrea Chenier* mirrors the deepest emotions of Andy in *Philadelphia.*

It is fortunate that all the great roles Callas sung have been preserved on audio recordings so that present and future generations will be able to enjoy and learn from her. However, many people who heard her sing in person say that audio recordings do not convey everything that Callas brought to the roles. In addition to her expressive voice, with its distinctive dark timbre, she was also a dramatic actress of astonishing gifts. She had an electrifying stage presence, as this comment by London critic Bernard Levin (quoted in Nigel Douglas's book, *More Legendary Voices*) makes clear: ''We all tingled when she entered as though we had touched a live wire.''

Although Callas's career ended before the age of video had fully arrived, several of her performances have been preserved on videotape in black and white. Although they cannot convey the full force of what it must have been like to hear and see her in the flesh, they do preserve something of Callas's magnetic presence, the passion and emotional power she brought to her singing, and the adoration she evoked from her fans. Two of the videos are concert performances given in Hamburg, one in 1959, in which she sings the letter-reading aria from Verdi's *Macbeth* that is featured in *Master Class*, and the other in 1962. Two of the arias in that 1962 video recording (which is still commercially available) perfectly illustrate the themes of *Master Class* that Maria labors to instill in her students: they must fully inhabit the roles they are singing, they must summon up from somewhere within themselves the emotions that are required, they must *become* the characters they are representing.

In the videotape from Hamburg on that long-ago night in 1962, Callas makes her entrance with dignity and basks in the applause, smiling radiantly and offering a regal wave of the hand. Not for nothing does Maria in *Master Class* instruct Sharon Graham to make a *real* entrance, not just come out on stage: ''You're on a stage. Use it. Own it. This is opera, not a voice recital. Anyone can stand there and sing. An artist enters and *is.*'' In the Hamburg recording, Callas then accepts a rose from a middle-aged admirer, breaks off the stem, and with a spontaneous flourish inserts the flower into her cleavage. (''Never miss an opportunity to theatricalize,'' says Maria in *Master Class.*) Callas is now fully the diva, lapping up the adoration of her fans. But then it is time for business. As the orchestra begins the introduction to ''Pleurez, mes yieux,'' Chimène's aria from act 3 of Jules Massenet's opera *Le Cid,* Callas closes her eyes, and a contemplative look appears on her face. It is as if we are watching the moment of metamorphosis, in which the diva turns into the character Chimène (a transition that is never seen in the opera house, since the singer is in character all the time she is on stage). Callas then opens her eyes and glances upwards. Now she *is* her character, and is ready to expresses the conflict in Chimène's mind and heart: the man she is in love with is also the man who killed her father, and she knows that whatever happens in the future, there will be great sorrow for her. Callas closes her eyes again, tilting her head to the left as an expression of anguish crosses her face. She has taken her cue from the agitation that appears in the music. It is just as Maria in *Master Class* urges her students: listen to the music, because the music tells the singer all she needs to know. And as Callas begins to sing the aria, one senses that nothing in that concert hall exists for her at that moment other than the music and the emotions that it summons forth in her. ''Very few people can weep in song,'' Maria says to her student Sophie, and this aria reminds us that Callas was one of them.

It is a similar story for the final aria on this recording, ''O don fatale,'' from Verdi's *Don Carlos.* (The aria is mentioned in passing in *Master Class.*) Callas's singing here is so dramatic that it is likely to give anyone goosebumps. There is little buildup—a moment of inner contemplation, a sudden glance upward like a stab of pain or a moment of shock, and then Callas tears into the aria, with all its twists and turns of deeply felt emotion, holding nothing back. It is a testament to her fictional counterpart in *Master Class,* who says over and over that the singer must *feel* the music she is singing: her art is all about ''Feeling, feeling, feeling.''

It is also, of course, about technique. All the passionate intensity in the world is of no use unless it can be channeled through the confines of the art form in which it is expressed. As Callas herself said in one of her real-life master classes, advising a student to study a difficult aria meticulously and slowly, ''Do not try to add exterior passion until you are confident with the aria's internal demands. In opera, passion without intellect is no good; you will be a wild animal and not an artist'' (quoted in John Ardoin's *Callas at Juilliard: The Master Classes*). No one who studies the transcripts of Callas's master classes could fail to appreciate her deep knowledge of the minutiae of the vocal music, even in arias for voices other than soprano.

It was this combination of technical mastery, emotional expressiveness, and dramatic skill that made Callas the preeminent artist she was. Although vocal technique was something that Callas, throughout her life a perfectionist, labored hard to perfect—her voice had flaws that she never succeeded in eradicating—the dramatic, expressive power that could so electrify an audience seemed to be a natural ability. As Ardoin puts it in *The Callas Legacy,* ''Callas seemed incapable of being inexpressive; even a simple scale sung by her implied a dramatic attitude or feeling. This capacity to communicate was something she was born with.''

So great was Callas's impact that scholars routinely refer to the ''Callas revolution'' when they discuss the changes that she brought to opera singing. No longer was the Italian *bel canto* (literally ''beautiful singing'') repertoire, such as Bellini's *Norma* or Donizetti's *Lucia di Lammermoor,* merely an opportunity for a beautiful vocal performance, with dramatic considerations secondary. Callas interpreted the roles with such feeling and dramatic intensity that the heroines of these operas became believable characters. Since her career, which spanned the 1950s and early 1960s, came at a time when the increasing popularity of film and television was beginning to condition audiences to expect greater realism from operatic performances, Callas played a vital role in maintaining opera as a viable form of entertainment.

There is no doubt also that Callas paid a price for her gifts. The underlying suggestion in *Master Class* is that the artist, as a consequence of being able to feel deeply, must also suffer deeply. She must know not only the heights of human experience but also its depths, the extremes of anger, grief, despair, and isolation. Callas in her personal life knew all these emotions intimately. It is to her lasting credit that she was able to harness her pain and send it out in the service of great art.

Source: Bryan Aubrey, Critical Essay on *Master Class,* in *Drama for Students,* The Gale Group, 2003.

Cary M. Mazer

In the following essay, Mazer examines how the character of Maria Callas in Master Class *evinces the paradoxical nature of the diva as performer and self.*

Master Class begins with a double untruth. Maria Callas (or, more accurately, the actress playing Maria Callas) strides on stage, almost certainly to the accompaniment of the audience's applause, looks directly at the audience, and announces, ''No applause. We're here to work. You're not in a theatre. This is a classroom.''

The first untruth is the statement that we are not in a theatre, since we in fact are in a theatre, both outside of and within the fictional world of the play. In *Master Class*, the stage of the theatre represents the stage of a theatre—the recital hall at the Juilliard School, where Maria Callas gave a series of master classes in 1971 and 1972 before a full house of students and spectators. In the theatre, when *Master Class* is performed, it is, of course, not really 1971 but the present; it is not Juilliard but (for the play's Broadway run) the Golden Theatre; and the audience is comprised of paying theatregoers, not advanced voice students. But the audience is *there,* as an audience, in both the reality of the theatrical event and the fiction of the play. The actor may be (in the original production) Zoe Caldwell and not the ''real'' Maria Callas, but the response of the audience to Caldwell—applause—is the same response that the 1971 Juilliard audience (the fictional audience that the real audience pretends to be) has for Callas. For Caldwell/Callas to tell us that we are not in a theatre flies in the face of what we know to be true, both in life and in the fiction of the play.

The other untruth is that Maria Callas does not want applause. Maria Callas, we soon see, lives for applause, and thrives on having an audience, alternately revealing and concealing herself from it, pandering for its affection and sympathy and holding it in contempt. Later in the play she will even deny that she had asked the audience not to applaud. Maria's attitude and her philosophical pronouncements are filled with such contradictions: that we cannot know what she suffered in Greece during the war and that we have to know it; that one can only create art if one has suffered and that one must not bring one's private suffering to one's art; that singers sing for the sheer joy of it and that singers must never give away their talent except for sufficient pay, etc., etc. The paradox of the audience's simultaneous presence and absence, of the fiction's theatricality and non-theatricality, is mirrored by Maria Callas's opinions—at best paradoxical and at worst contradictory and mutually exclusive—about life, art, performance, and their relationship. And at the heart of these paradoxes is the real subject of the play, what one might call ''the Paradox of the Diva.''

Terrence McNally has dramatized the phenomenology of the diva before, most notably in what might be considered the ultimate play about ''opera queens,'' *The Lisbon Traviata*. But there the focus is not on the diva but on her fans, the homosexual protagonists who project onto the diva their own identity, desires, and suffering. In *The Lisbon Traviata* the opera queen's identification is both with the singer and with the operatic role she plays: both with Maria Callas, the self-consuming performer who makes her private suffering transcendently public through her performances, and with Violetta, the consumptive courtesan in *La Traviata*, who sacrifices her happiness and her health for love.

McNally is not interested in the phenomenon of the opera queen in *Master Class* (though in one of the flashback sequences, Maria ventriloquizes the voice of her lover Aristotle Onassis, who observes ''The fags just want to be you.'' Instead he shifts his focus to the object of the opera queen's emulation, the diva herself. But the way he views the diva is clearly in line with the paradoxes and contradictions in the way opera queens admire and emulate the diva, a phenomenon most recently articulated in Wayne Koestenbaum's autobiographical polemic, *The Queen's Throat: Opera, Homosexuality, and the Mystery of Desire*. The opera queen, Koestenbaum argues, admires both the diva's persona—her arrogance, grandeur, and self-fashioned hauteur and sublime bitchiness—and the roles that the diva plays. Indeed, the opera queen's identification with the roles the diva plays magnifies the opera queen's emulation of the diva, for the diva, the opera queen believes, identifies with the character even more closely than the opera queen ever can and so becomes the opera queen's emotionally expressive, sacrificial surrogate. As Stephen, one of the two opera queens in *The Lisbon Traviata*, explains, ''Opera is about us, our life-and-death passions—we all love, we're all going to die. Maria understood that. That's where the voice came from, the heart, the soul, I'm tempted to say from some even more intimate place.'' At the end of the play, Stephen, having failed to enact Don Jose to his departing lover's Carmen, throws his head back in a silent scream of heartbreak while Callas's Violetta plays on the stereo, the diva's voice expressing a pain that is simultaneously the singer's, the character's, and the listener's.

The diva, the subject of the opera queen's emulation, is simultaneously present and absent, playing a distilled and self-fashioned version of herself in every role she plays and dissolving herself into the music and the dramatic situation of the character she acts and sings, rendering herself transparent to the character and the composer (and librettist) behind the character. The difference between the actor and the character she is playing is erased in the eyes of the opera queen: the diva is both transcendently herself and transubstantially the character; indeed, that is to a great extent the source of her glory.

But the relation of an actor to the character he or she is playing is, in the theatre as well as in opera, much more complicated and more paradoxical than the opera queen imagines. And this complicated relationship of actor to role—the paradoxical complementarity of the consummately self-effacing actor and the transcendently-herself diva—is the real subject of *Master Class*, a play in which the opera-singer-as-lecturer is not "in character" ("You're not in a theatre. This is a classroom") and yet is never, strictly speaking, "out" of character, in which theatrical performances draw upon the performer's true "self" and yet the "self" is itself always performative.

The salient biographical facts about Maria Callas's life are all made reference to in *Master Class*, her American and Greek upbringing, her training, the patronage of Battista Meneghini, her debut, her radical physical transformation and weight loss, her affair with Onassis, her conflicts with tenors, managers, directors, and rival sopranos, the hirings and firings, and the precipitate decay of her voice. But the play is less a biography of the artist than it is a play about the nature of artistry, the relation of a particular artist's life to her art. The paradoxes of this relationship are both the play's subject and dictate the play's form, and these paradoxes ultimately lead to a shift in the play's focus that muddies the play's focus and, as we shall see, finally undoes the play's otherwise pristine structure.

The play's action, such as it is, consists of three consecutive coaching sessions in real time: Sophie de Palma, a soprano, who sings Adina's "Ah, non credea mirarti" from Bellini's *La Somnambula;* Anthony Candolino, a tenor, who sings "Ricondita armonia" from Puccini's *Tosca;* (and soprano Sharon Graham, who is driven from the stage by Callas's brow-beating but returns to be coached in Lady Macbeth's entrance aria, "Vieni! t'afretta" from Verdi's *Macbeth.* In each of these sessions, Callas is rude, condescending, dismissive, and egocentric. And in all three sessions she is a brilliant teacher.

"WE SEE WHAT SHE HAS BECOME AND WE LEARN THE PROCESS BY WHICH SHE BECAME THIS WAY. . . . WHAT WE DO NOT KNOW . . . IS THE LIFE LIVED, THE NATURE OF THE ACTUAL SUFFERINGS THAT THE SINGER TRANSMUTES INTO HER PERFORMANCES."

And there emerges from her teaching, however obnoxious, a coherent, if complex, philosophical position about the relationship of the singing actor to the operatic role.

Callas interrupts the first note that Sophie de Palma sings in the Bellini aria: "I want to talk to you about your 'Oh!'" The student answers, "I sang it, didn't I?" Callas explains:

> *That's just it. You sang it. You didn't feel it. It's not a note we're after here. It's a sob of pain. The pain of loss. Surely you understand loss. If not of another person, then maybe a pet. A puppy. A goldfish.*

Mixed with Callas's patronizing examples ("a puppy. A goldfish") is a stereotypical "Stanislavski Method" acting exercise—Lee Strasberg's "emotional memory"—in which the actor substitutes an experience from his or her own life to generate an emotional response equivalent to the emotions of the character that are called for in the dramatic situation of the script. Callas repeatedly rejects "just singing" ("You were *just* singing," she tells the tenor, "which equals nothing"). Instead she calls for acting, in the twentieth-century Stanislavskian tradition: feeling "real" emotions based on the "given circumstances" of the script and embellished or translated in the imagination of the actor (when the tenor complains that "It doesn't say anything about ten A.M. or spring or Tosca's body in the score," Callas responds, "It should say it in your imagination. Otherwise you have notes, nothing but notes."

The emotions that Callas calls for are not "realistic"; they are channeled through the artifice

Patti LuPone, as Maria Callas, and David Maxwell Anderson, as Tony, in a scene from the 1997 production of Master Class, *performed at Queen's Theatre in London*

of the operatic medium (''Anyone can walk in their sleep,'' she tells Sophie, singing a somnambulist's aria; ''Very few people can weep in song''). Each successive level of expression in opera is more artificial: speech is more active and demands more actively channeled emotional energy and a more intense revelation of one's own more intense emotions than silence; recitative calls for more energy and emotion than speech (''When you can no longer bear to speak, when the words aren't enough, that's when he [Bellini] asks you to sing''; aria more than recitative; and a cabaletta more than its preceding aria.

''This is not a film studio,'' she explains, ''where anyone can get up there and act. I hate that word. 'Act.' No! Feel. Be. That's what we're doing here.'' And she later tells Sharon, helping her ''make an entrance'' for her Lady Macbeth entrance aria, ''This is opera, not a voice recital. Anyone can stand there and sing. An artist enters and *is.*'' What Callas means by ''be'' and ''is'' is clearly something more than passive existence or inexpressive emotion and is rather a grand, artificial, projected distillation of one's identity and emotional truth: as she tells Sophie, ''This is the theatre, darling. We wear our hearts on our sleeves here.'' When she tells Sophie ''I'm not getting any juice from you, Sophie. I want juice. I want passion. I want you'', she clearly means that the ''you'' that an opera singer needs to ''be,'' the being that breathes and feels and sings on stage, is something grand, extreme, distilled, and directed. Callas doubts whether Sophie has that magnitude of experience or the magnitude of expressiveness: ''He's broken her heart. Have you ever had your heart broken?'' she asks. When Sophie answers, ''Yes,'' Callas adds, snidely, ''You could have fooled me''; and Sophie herself concludes, ruefully, ''I'm not that sort of singer. . . . I'm not that sort of person either.''

What ''sort of person'' does it take to be an opera singer? Here again there are both paradoxes and contradictions in what Callas teaches. On the one hand, she claims on her first entrance, the diva must practice complete self-effacement: ''If you want to have a career, as I did—and I'm not boasting now, I am not one to boast—you must be willing to subjugate yourself—is that a word?—subjugate yourself to music.'' But, paradoxically, the singer both erases herself and is completely herself. For subjugation involves sacrifice, and what is being sacrificed is the singer's own self. The diva must be a supreme egotist in order to make the supreme sacrifice of her ego to her audiences. And, she argues, you must be well paid for your pains. ''Never give anything away. There's no more where it came from. We give the audience everything and when it's gone, *c'est ca, c'est tout. Basta, finito.* We're the ones who end up empty.'' She invokes Medea's line to Jason in Cherubini's *Medea*—''I gave everything for you. Everything''—to explain this: ''That's what we artists do for people. Where would you be without us? Eh? Think about that. Just think about it while you're counting your millions or leading your boring lives with your boring wives.'' The sacrifice of the self is too great to be wasted on psychotherapy: ''Feelings like Sharon's''—who has run off stage to vomit and has not yet returned—''We use them. We don't give them away on some voodoo witch doctor's couch.'' Instead, they should be saved for the stage, where they are distilled and delivered, at great personal pain, to the audience.

Callas's relation to her audience—both the audience of her operatic past and the current audience in the classroom/recital hall—is fraught with contradictions. ''The audience is the enemy,'' she says, quoting Medea's line to Jason; ''Dominate them. . . . Art is domination. It's making people think for that precise moment in time there is only one way, one voice. Yours. Eh.?'' At times (including the flashback sequences, in which Callas recalls singing only for Meneghini or only for Onassis), the audience is worthy of the singer's self-immolation and sacrifice. At other times the audience is passive, unappreciative, and unworthy: she talks scornfully of an acquaintance whose favorite part of the operas are the intervals; and we see her hold in contempt the stagehand in the recital hall, who neither knows nor cares about the art being created on the stage within earshot.

McNally best dramatizes the capacity of an audience to be moved by the artificially distilled expressive powers of the singer's voice and emotions channeled through the composer's music when Callas herself listens to Tony Candolino sing ''Ricondita armonia.'' To the tenor's disappointment, after he has finished singing, she says only ''That was beautiful. I have nothing more to say. That was beautiful.'' Being an audience member, being the recipient of the imagined emotions of Cavaradossi for Tosca as channeled through the voice and soul of the tenor as she never was when she played Tosca herself (''I was always backstage preparing for my entrance''), Callas is, for one of the rare moments in the play, left speechless. And she stumbles awkwardly from that moment—a moment that demonstrates why, from an audience's point of view, the singer's art is worthwhile—to the unexpected admission that ''It's a terrible career, actually. I don't know why I bothered.''

Through her pedagogical encounters with Sophie and Tony, Callas teaches both the students and the audience what it takes to become an effective singing actor. One must have suffered sufficiently to provide the emotional raw material for embodying the character's emotion. One must be willing to re-experience the most difficult times of one's life over and over again, with all of the focused and distilled intensity of the first experience. One must be willing to display one's most private feelings and experiences in public, both to an uncaring and ungrateful audience (personified, in *Master Class*, by the stagehand) and to an attentive and appreciative public that demands that each performance be yet another self-consuming and self-consumed display of re-experienced emotional agonies. And, finally, becoming a singing actor requires the singer to turn him- or herself into an artificial being, in part because the medium of musical and theatrical expression is so highly conventionalized and artificial and in part because of the cutthroat world of the operatic profession. One must, in short, play the part of the diva to be a diva; one must become a monster of egotism, selfishness, competitiveness, and vindictiveness, capable of cutting a swathe for oneself in the world of managers, conductors, directors, claques, and other divas, in order to get the opportunity to practice one's art. And, by practicing one's art, by dredging up every life experience and emotion in the service of the drama, and the dramatic character, and the music, one self-destructs, consuming irreversibly the raw material of the art in the very act of making the art. Becoming the diva leaves little more than dry tinder; singing sets the tinder alight, burning with a brilliant flame before the audience, until all that is left are ashes, thorns, and nails.

And so we see Maria Callas through the play: a brilliant actress still, still wearing her all-too-public life's pain on her sleeve, still grabbing the spotlight, indulging her ego, destroying with a glance or a quip everyone around her. And when she finally sings, the stage directions record, ''What comes out is a cracked and broken thing.''

By the middle of the second act, after Callas has coached two singers and driven a third from the stage, we have learned about the paradoxes of acting contained within the diva's craft, and we have come to some understanding of how this craft calls upon the singer to create a particular performative persona and to put that persona to the service of the self-consuming art of singing. Callas, in her roundabout and often contradictory way, explains these principles to us as she coaches Sophie and Tony, and she demonstrates, in her abominably egotistical behavior, what she has become in service of this art. But it not until the final third of the play, when she coaches Sharon Graham, that we see the means by which a younger singer can put these principles into practice, that we see a singer who can become, potentially at least, another Callas and, in this instance, chooses not to.

Sharon has returned to the recital stage after vomiting in fear and humiliation, determined now to prove herself. Callas humiliates her and browbeats her into acting and not just singing the aria, as she did with Sophie and Tony. But here, as we watch, the Stanislavskian exercises and the Strasbergian emotional memory substitutions begin to work. Callas insists that everything be concrete, specific: the letter from Macbeth that Lady Macbeth reads, in unsung speech before the recitative, must be real, and not imagined ("I don't want pretending. You're not good enough. I want truth; the news of Duncan's imminent arrival comes not from 'someone' but from 'a servant'." When Sharon hesitates between the recitative and the aria, Callas, swept up in the flow of the drama and encouraging Sharon to be swept up too, insists "don't even think of stopping! You are Lady Macbeth!." After the aria, with the news of Duncan's arrival, the emotional identification of Sharon with Lady Macbeth is, with Callas's coaching, nearly complete:

Maria: How does that make her feel?

Soprano: Happy?

Maria: Don't keep looking at me for answers, Sharon. Tell me, show me. Vite, vite!

Soprano: Really happy.

Maria: Love happy? Christmas morning happy?

Soprano: Murder happy!

Maria: Ah! And what is she going to do about it?

Soprano: She's going to sing a cabaletta!

Maria: She's going to kill the king! Do you know what that means?

Soprano: Yes, it's terrible.

Maria: Not to her! Do you believe women can have balls, Sharon?

Soprano: Some women. Yes, I do!

Maria: Verdi is daring you to show us yours, Sharon. Will you do it?

Soprano: Yes!

The stakes of the scene, the stakes of the act of performing itself, have become, for Sharon, nearly like those for Callas. "This isn't just an opera. This is your life," Callas insists. "Is there anything you would kill for, Sharon," she asks her, suggesting "A man, a career?" "You have to listen to something in yourself to sing this difficult music," she insists, suggesting that the characters she has sung, and the characters of the classical tragedies of her native Greece—Medea, Electra, Klytemnestra—were real people, to whom she has a real connection:

Maria: These people really existed. Medea, Lady Macbeth. Or don't you believe that? Eh? This is all make-believe to you?

Soprano: I've never really thought about it.

Maria: That's because you're young. You will. In time. Know how much suffering there can be in store for a woman.

As Sharon sings, she feels in her soul, her body, and her voice the connection that Callas insists is the true art of the diva. And she is told, and undoubtedly understands, the life, emotions, and experience to which the singing actor's art must be connected: one in which she is capable of feeling that she *could* kill for a man or a career, where in time she will know how much suffering is in store for her, where she can not only believe in Medea or Lady Macbeth but can feel so strong a kinship with them that she can *become* them, emotionally and viscerally. Sharon, unlike Sophie and Tony, is capable of learning the lessons that Callas has to teach.

After Sharon finishes singing the complete aria and cabaletta, Callas, coming out of her reverie/flashback sequence, dismisses Sharon's professional prospects, damning her with the faint praise:

I think you should work on something more appropriate for your limitations. Mimi or Micaela maybe. But Lady Macbeth, Norma, I don't think so. These roles require something else. Something. How shall I say this? Something special. Something that can't be taught or passed on or copied or even talked about. Genius. Inspiration. A gift of god. Some recompense for everything else.

Sharon, in tears, responds:

I wish I'd never done this. I don't like you. You can't sing anymore and you're envious of anyone younger who can. You just want us to sing like you, recklessly, and lose our voices in ten years like you did. Well, I won't do it. I don't want to. I don't want to sing like you. I hate people like you. You want to make the world dangerous for everyone just because it was for you.

Sharon clearly wants to get back at Callas for her condescension. But there is more to her response than this. Sharon sees in Callas's cruelty the more important truth of the diva's art: that this type of art exacts too high a price, that one would not wish upon oneself the experiences and suffering that could generate such art, and that creating art from such personal and emotional raw materials is self-consuming, and ultimately destroys the medium of the art—the singer's voice. Sharon leaves the stage; Callas brushes off the confrontation, withdraws into the shell of her professional persona, utters a few platitudes about art and, saying "well, that's that", brings both the master class and *Master Class* to a close.

Throughout the play, McNally has been putting forth as his hypothesis the myth of Callas the diva: she so channels her own life and emotions into her singing and acting; she so fully becomes a conduit for her own sorrows and the object of projection for the fantasies and emotions of her audiences that she has ruined her voice and withered into a cruel and egotistical if magnificent monster, a *monstre sacre.* Sharon's defection at the end only confirms the hypothesis and elevates the diva to an even-greater level: a figure of sublime loneliness, shunned as a pariah, so monstrous that she can be watched in awe but is too horrifying to be emulated.

The dramaturgical mastery of *Master Class* lies in its twin strategies for representing Callas as a dramatic character. For, in watching her teach, we see the monster she has become; and in learning *what* she teaches—the practices of personal, emotional-based acting that she teaches unsuccessfully to Sophie and Tony and successfully if Pyrrhically to Sharon—we learn how she has become that person. We see less the genuine person and more the persona that Callas has created for herself and that has been created for her: the diva. From the moment that Callas singles out a member of the audience to demonstrate how ''It's important to have a look'', we see the theatricality, the performativity of the diva's persona. ''This isn't a freak show. I'm not a performing seal,'' she tells Sophie, explaining that her fabled fieriness is not a performance but an ingrained part of her identity: ''My fire comes from here, Sophie. It's mine. It's not for sale. It's not for me to give away. Even if I could, I wouldn't. It's who I am. Find out who you are. That's what this is all about. Eh?'' And yet Callas *is* a freak, a performing seal. Within Callas's talents as a self-creator, within the persona that she has forged from her status as diva (''Never miss an opportunity to theatricalize,'' she tells Sharon), everything is a performance. Acting, even when acting means surrendering to a character and effectively becoming that character, never entails the loss of self; indeed, it is where the performative self is created and articulated. As the stage director Visconti tells her (in the first-act flashback sequence), ''You are not a village girl. You are Maria Callas playing a village girl.'' Callas's ''performance'' as teacher of a master class *is* Callas. The diva uses herself to perform; consequently she only *is* when she performs.

And so it is—or should be—with McNally's drama: We see what she has become and we learn the process by which she became this way. But this is, of course, not the entire play, nor is the master class, despite the play's title, the only narrative and dramaturgical means by which the playwright shows us Callas's character. McNally has demonstrated for us what she has become and taught us the process of acting that has made her this way—one that demands that she wear her emotions on her sleeve and transmit her own life and suffering into her performances through her body and voice on stage. What we do not know—and what opera queens cannot know about a diva, except through gossip columns and the fanciful projections of their own imaginations—is the life lived, the nature of the actual sufferings that the singer transmutes into her performances.

The genius of *Master Class* is that, once we have seen what Callas has become and learned how she used (and used up) her life to get this way, we don't actually *need* to know the life that she lived. But this is precisely what McNally gives us, in the most theatrically stunning sequences of the play: the flashback fantasy sequences, to the accompaniment of Callas's live recordings of the arias that the student singers are singing. These sequences—brilliant as they are in performance, affording an opportunity for the actor to jump back and forth between Callas's student years and her triumphant debuts and between her public and private lives—belong to two other genres of play entirely. One genre is the autobiographical one-hander (such as the Lillian Hellman vehicle that Zoe Caldwell played a few years before she created the role of Callas in *Master Class*), in which the historical figure, through some theatrical pretense (Emily Dickinson inviting us in as neighbors to share her recipes, Truman Capote speaking into a tape recorder for the benefit of a journalist) retells and relives formative events from his or her life.

The other genre to which the flashback sequences of *Master Class* belongs is, arguably, the largest segment of American twentieth-century dramatic writing, what might best be called the ''psychotherapeutic whodunit.'' In such plays, a protagonist's tragic agony or a family's crippling dysfunction can be traced, as in the Freudian psychoanalytical model, to a single, traumatic event, real or imagined, that is concealed from several of the characters and the audience until late in the play: Biff sees Willy with a prostitute in a cheap hotel in Boston; Mary Tyrone regresses to a point in her life before she discovered her husband to be an alcoholic and, more significantly, before the infant Eugene died of the infection given to him by his older brother Jamie; George and Martha ''kill off'' the child which the audience and Nick discover to have been invented by them; Dodge and Bradley narrate the story of the child buried in the backyard.

The flashback sequences in *Master Class* satisfy the whodunit energies generated by the theories of acting taught and practiced by Callas in the real-time framework of the play. If Callas is indeed transforming her real-life suffering, to which she casually alludes repeatedly in her teaching, then the audience naturally desires to learn more about these traumatic experiences: Callas proving herself to her teacher, Callas's La Scala debut, her final performances at La Scala in defiance of the general manager who was firing her, the patronage of Battista Meneghini, and her abusive relationship with Onassis. Moreover, the flashback sequences confirm the ways that Callas's personal emotions—shame, desire, vindictiveness, revenge—are channeled into her singing. Just as Lady Macbeth invites the unholy spirit to enter her body, Callas invites the voices of her own life to enter her, through Verdi's "infernal music," to "Come, fill me with your malevolence". As the house lights in La Scala come up as Callas finishes her *La Somnambula* aria on the stage of La Scala, she is able to reverse the audience's vampiric gaze, to see the eyes of the viewers devouring her performance, and can declare, "My revenge, my triumph are complete."

The logic of the standard American dramaturgical master narrative demands that the audience know the biographical causes of characterological effects. For an audience, to understand the formative traumas is to know the character; for a character, to face the cause is to begin to heal; and, for character and audience alike, theatrically reliving these traumas is both a form of purgation and a fulfillment of the play's dramaturgical logic. In *Master Class*, the traumatic event to which the whodunit logic of the play points turns out to be a familiar one in American drama: Callas, having been told by Onassis that the greatest gift she can give him is a child, announces that she is pregnant and is now told by him that she must get rid of the child. As in *Long Day's Journey into Night, Desire Under the Elms, Who's Afraid of Virginia Woolf, The American Dream, Buried Child, Talley's Folly,* and countless lesser American plays, the central hidden trauma of the play turns out to be female fertility; the missing center of the play and its character turns out to be, as it is in so many plays, the missing, dead, murdered, unconceived, or aborted baby. Underneath a fascinating metatheatrical drama about art lies a far more conventional American "dead baby" drama. We discover that Callas, the object of the opera queen's emulation and envy, is herself consumed with envy; and the object of her envy is something common both to American drama and to the mythology of male homosexuality: the womb.

In exploring the phenomenon of the diva, the play's own logic asks us to resist such easy answers. Callas was willing to create art from the material of her life at great cost. We learn how she did so, and we see the cost. If *Master Class* is indeed about art and its making out of life, then, ironically, we need to see the life *only* through the art. But in the flashback sequences and in their reversion to the traditional dead-baby trope, the playwright gives us too much. The sequences are arguably more than just a violation of the playwright's own metatheatrical fiction and more than just a deviation from his chosen dramaturgical structure in favor of a return to the more traditional structural conventions of the psychotherapeutic whodunit: they are a violation of the theories of art explored in the play. The flashbacks effectively turn the playwright, and the audience, into opera queens: they not only allow us, like the opera queen, to imagine that the person's real pain can be heard in the diva's voice; they materially confirm that the pain and its origins is everything we imagine it to be. In narrating and reenacting her life to sounds of her own voice singing Adina or Lady Macbeth on a recording, Callas is effectively lip-synching her own life, just as Stephen lip-synchs to Callas's Violetta at the end of *The Lisbon Traviata* Callas not only fulfills the opera queen's myth of the diva; in *Master Class* the queen of opera demonstrably becomes an opera queen herself.

Source: Cary M. Mazer, "*Master Class* and the Paradox of the Diva," in *Terrence McNally: A Casebook,* edited by Toby Silverman Zinman, Garland Publishing, 1997, pp. 165–80.

SOURCES

Ardoin, John, "Callas and the Juilliard Master Classes," in *Terrence McNally: A Casebook,* edited by Toby Silverman Zinman, Garland Publishing, Inc., 1997, pp. 157–63.

———, *Callas at Juilliard: The Master Classes,* Amadeus Press, 1998, p. 39.

———, *The Callas Legacy: A Biography of a Career,* rev. ed., Charles Scribner's Sons, p. 210.

Canby, Vincent, "Patti LuPone's Arrival Changes the Effect of McNally's Script," in the *New York Times,* July 26, 1996, Section C, Column 1, p. 3.

Douglas, Nigel, *More Legendary Voices,* Andre Deutsch, 1990, p. 22.

Franklin, Nancy, ''Goddesses,'' in the *New Yorker,* November 27, 1995, pp. 109–11.

Gurewitsch, Matthew, ''Maria, Not Callas,'' in *Atlantic Monthly,* October 1997, pp. 102–07.

Klein, Alvin, ''The Teacher as Star of the Class,'' in the *New York Times,* October 19, 1997, Section 14CN, Column 4, p. 8.

Leithauser, Brad, ''Legends of the Fall'' in *Time,* November 20, 1995, p. 121.

Stassinopoulos, Arianna, *Maria Callas: The Woman behind the Legend,* Simon and Schuster, 1981, pp. 268, 314.

FURTHER READING

Brustein, Robert, ''*Master Class,*'' in the *New Republic,* February 5, 1996, pp. 27–28.

Brustein's review was one of the few negative reviews of the play. Brustein regards it as capably written, but forgettable, although it does have some value as a tribute to Callas.

Christianssen, Rupert, *Prima Donna,* Pimlico, 1995, pp. 266–98.

Calling Callas a ''naïve genius,'' Christianssen analyzes the Callas revolution in terms of the singing tradition she inherited, the changes she wrought, and her influence on sopranos who followed.

Kroll, Jack, ''*Master Class,*'' in *Newsweek,* November 13, 1995, p. 85.

Kroll's review is a laudatory review that describes the play as a profile in courage, with Zoe Caldwell, as Callas, putting on a virtuoso performance to remember.

Torrens, James S., ''*Master Class,*'' in *America,* February 17, 1996, p. 30.

Another review that is full of praise for what Torrens calls the most exciting play of the Broadway season. McNally's love of opera finds its perfect vehicle.

Zinman, Toby Silverman, ed., *Terrence McNally: A Casebook,* Garland Publishing, Inc., 1997.

This text contains interviews with Zoe Caldwell and McNally, as well as Cary M. Mazer's article, ''Master Class and the Paradox of the Diva,'' in which he discusses what he sees as paradoxes and contradictions in what Maria teaches her students.

The Matchmaker

THORNTON WILDER

1954

Thornton Wilder's play *The Matchmaker* is a farce in the old-fashioned sense. It uses such time-honored conventions as characters hidden under tables and in closets, men disguised as women, a complex conspiracy to bring young lovers together, and a happy ending in which three couples are united with plans to marry. The traditional aspects of the play should come as no surprise: Wilder himself was the first to acknowledge the sources that it was based upon. The character of Dolly Levi came from French playwright Molière's comedy *L'avare,* or *The Miser,* from which Wilder lifted some scenes directly. A closer influence was Johann Nestroy's *Einen Jux will er sich Machen,* performed in Vienna in 1842. Wilder referred to his play as a "free adaptation" of Nestroy's, which itself was adapted from British playwright John Oxenham's 1835 comedy *A Day Well Spent.* Wilder's first adaptation was called *The Merchant of Yonkers*, which failed on Broadway in 1938, running for only twenty-eight performances. *The Matchmaker* was itself adapted as *Hello, Dolly!,* which began in 1963 and ran for years, ranking as one of Broadway's longest-running musicals.

In all of these permutations, the basic plot has been the same as it is in *The Matchmaker*. In Wilder's version, an irascible, penny-pinching store owner, Horace Vandergelder, refuses to let his niece marry the poor artist she loves, although he himself plans to remarry. Dolly Levi, the matchmaker of the title, pretends that she is helping Vandergelder find a suitable bride, but she actually schemes to marry him herself, and she works to help the young lovers gain his approval. Vandergelder's beleaguered clerk, who is longing for excitement, also meets the woman of his dreams, although she happens to be the one Vandergelder intends to marry. In the end, everyone is happy and just a little smarter.

AUTHOR BIOGRAPHY

Thornton Niven Wilder was born in Madison, Wisconsin, on April 17, 1897, the only survivor of twin brothers. His mother, the daughter of a minister, and his father, a strict, moody newspaper editor, both had a strong influence on the view of the world that he would eventually develop. In 1906, his father joined the foreign service as a consular general to Hong Kong. The entire family moved there with him, but after six months Wilder's mother took the children and moved back to the United States, living in Berkeley, California. When his father transferred to Shanghai, Wilder returned to Asia and attended German and Chinese schools before returning to the United States once more to finish high school in Berkeley.

When his father enrolled Wilder in Oberlin College in Ohio, Wilder was disappointed, having hoped to attend Yale. He found that the small college atmosphere suited him, however. Several of his works were published in the student magazine, and he came to know professors on a personal level. He transferred to Yale for his last two years, which were interrupted by a short tour of service in the Coast Artillery Corps, the only branch that would accept him because he was severely nearsighted. Returning to Yale, he had his first full-length play published in serial form in the *Yale Literary Review* before graduating in 1920. He received his master's degree in French literature from Princeton in 1926.

In 1926, his first novel, *The Cabala*, was published, and his first play, *The Trumpet Shall Sound*, was produced. The following year, his life was changed forever when his second novel, *The Bridge of San Luis Rey*, became a sensation, selling millions of copies and winning the Pulitzer Prize. After that, he taught part-time, taking visiting professorships at Harvard, the University of Chicago, and the University of Hawaii; and he wrote, alternating between novels and dramas.

In 1938, Wilder won a second Pulitzer Prize for his play *Our Town*, making him the only American to ever win Pulitzers for both fiction and drama. Every year, *Our Town* is still one of the most often-produced plays. He won a third Pulitzer, in drama, for 1942's *The Skin of Our Teeth*.

Thornton Wilder

Wilder served in the Air Force during World War II, earning the Legion of Merit and the Bronze Star. After the war, he wrote less, and his new works were greeted with less enthusiasm by critics, but his place in American literature was already firmly established. He died in December 1975, in the house in Connecticut where he had lived for years with his sister, who served him as secretary, literary advisor, and business manager.

PLOT SUMMARY

Act 1

The Matchmaker is set in the 1880s and begins in the cluttered living room of Horace Vandergelder, a wealthy old widower living above his prosperous hay, feed, and provisions store in Yonkers, New York. His bags are packed, and he is being shaved by a barber. Ambrose Kemper, an artist, is trying to get Vandergelder to allow him to marry Vandergelder's niece, Ermengarde. Vandergelder does not approve because Ambrose does not make a steady income, and the old man is too practical to consider either love or the promise of future earnings as significant reasons to change his mind. Ambrose points out that Ermengarde is twenty-four and old enough to do what she wants. Vandergelder says that he is sending Ermengarde away to a secret place to prevent the wedding, but then his housekeeper, Gertrude, comes in and announces out loud the address where Ermengarde's luggage is being sent.

Vandergelder sends for his chief clerk, Cornelius Hackl, and explains to him that he is going away for a few days to be married. He says that he is promoting the thirty-three-year-old Cornelius to the position of chief clerk, even though, as Cornelius tells the junior clerk later, it is a position he has held for several years already.

When no other clerks are in the room, Malachi Stack enters with a letter of recommendation from a past associate. Vandergelder agrees to hire him and sends him away immediately to catch a train to New York City so that he can prepare for Vandergelder's arrival after his marriage.

Vandergelder is out of the room when Dolly Levi arrives. She is an old friend of his late wife, a matchmaker who is supposed to be finding a suitable wife for Vandergelder. She hears Ermengarde and Ambrose complaining that he is obstructing their wedding plans, and she agrees to help them, arranging to meet them at a restaurant in New York that night.

Vandergelder arrives and tells Mrs. Levi his plans to marry Irene Molloy. She makes up a story about a woman who is wealthy, socially connected, and interested in him, and so he agrees to put off proposing to Mrs. Molloy.

Left alone, Cornelius complains to the other clerk, Barnaby Tucker, that they never get time off to go out and experience life. He goes downstairs to the store and heats some cans of tomatoes until they explode, creating a foul smell that forces them to close the store, and they take off to New York, planning to have an adventure.

Act 2

In the hat shop that she owns, Irene Molloy tells her assistant, Minnie Fay, that she will marry Vandergelder if he asks, in order to get out of the hat business. She feels trapped by the reputation that milliners have, with her every move being watched by people who expect her to be a woman of low virtue. Minnie objects that Mrs. Molloy should not marry if she does not love Vandergelder.

They are in the back room when Cornelius and Barnaby come into the shop to hide, having seen Vandergelder on the street. When the women enter, the two clerks pretend to be wealthy men who are shopping for a hat—actually, ''five or six''—for a friend. Cornelius falls in love with Mrs. Molloy immediately.

Seeing Vandergelder and Mrs. Levi approaching the shop, Cornelius and Barnaby hide in a closet and under the table, respectively. Mrs. Molloy suspects what is going on and leads Vandergelder to the back room to give them a chance to escape, but Cornelius decides to stay so that he can get to know Mrs. Molloy. Dolly Levi finds out about their situation and decides to help them. When Vandergelder and Mrs. Molloy come back, the conversation turns to Cornelius. Mrs. Molloy is under the impression that he is wealthy, and Vandergelder says he is just a clerk. Mrs. Levi explains that Cornelius is actually a well-known socialite, a prankster who comes from a wealthy family and works at the shop in Yonkers to amuse himself. The clerks sneeze and are found out; Vandergelder walks out, indignant, taking Mrs. Levi with him. Mrs. Molloy, thinking that Cornelius really is wealthy, insists that he and Barnaby take Minnie and her to an expensive restaurant for dinner.

Act 3

At the Harmonia Gardens Restaurant, Vandergelder plans to meet Mrs. Levi and the mysterious woman whom she said admires him. He sees Ermengarde and Ambrose enter. He pays Malachi and the cabdriver who brought them to abduct the young couple when they leave and take them to the house of Miss Van Huysen.

The two clerks arrive with Mrs. Molloy and her assistant. As she orders food and champagne, Cornelius worries about how they will pay the bill at such an expensive restaurant. The waiter sets up another table and puts up a screen between the two, for privacy; at the other table he seats Vandergelder, who is waiting for his date. Malachi finds a wallet on the floor and, not seeing that it has dropped out of

Vandergelder's pocket, takes it around the screen and gives it to Cornelius, whom he has never met. No longer worried about the bill, Cornelius confesses to Mrs. Molloy that he is not rich and is just a clerk. She suggests that they just have a good time.

Mrs. Levi joins Vandergelder and explains that the woman she told him about has run away and gotten married. During their conversation, he discusses how difficult Mrs. Levi can be, and she pretends that he is flirting with her and hinting at marriage, in order to plant the idea in his head.

To get out of the restaurant without being seen by Vandergelder, Cornelius and Barnaby put on the ladies' coats and veils. Before leaving, they take time to dance. Vandergelder, dancing with Mrs. Levi, bumps into Cornelius and recognizes him. He fires both clerks, and Mrs. Molloy breaks up with him. Ermengarde enters and faints, to be carried out by Ambrose. Mrs. Levi points out the sorry situation of Vandergelder's life: ''Without niece—without clerks—without bride—and without your purse. Will you marry me now?'' He still refuses.

Act 4

The cab driver and Malachi arrive at Miss Van Huysen's house with Cornelius and Barnaby, who is still disguised as a woman; they have mistaken them for Ermengarde and Ambrose. Miss Van Huysen explains that she has no intention of interfering with young love as Vandergelder expects her to.

The real Ermengarde and Ambrose show up. Expecting Miss Van Huysen to object to their relationship, they tell her that Ambrose is Cornelius Hackl.

Dolly Levi arrives with Mrs. Molloy and Minnie. She pays off the cabdriver with money from Vandergelder's wallet, which Cornelius gave to her.

When Vandergelder arrives, Mrs. Van Huysen insists that he let the young lovers marry. Everyone goes to the kitchen, and Dolly Levi, addressing her dead husband Ephraim, explains that she intends to marry Vandergelder in order to spread his money around, creating happiness. When Vandergelder comes back, he does in fact propose to Mrs. Levi. Barnaby comes in and says that the other two couples are going to marry, too, and Mrs. Levi has Barnaby, as the youngest member of the cast, give a final speech to the audience about the importance of having enough adventure in one's life.

MEDIA ADAPTATIONS

- *The Matchmaker* was made into a film by Paramount Pictures in 1958, starring Shirley Booth as Dolly Levi, Anthony Perkins as Cornelius, and Shirley MacLaine as Irene Molloy. John Michael Hayes wrote the adaptation, which was directed by Joseph Anthony.
- In 1963, this play was adapted as a Broadway musical, *Hello, Dolly!,* with a book by Michael Stewart and music and lyrics by Jerry Herman. Carol Channing played Dolly, in a career-defining performance. *Hello, Dolly!* ran on Broadway for 2,844 performances.

CHARACTERS

August

August is the younger waiter at the Harmonia Gardens Restaurant. He is so nervous that he bursts into tears at the slightest provocation.

Cabman

When Vandergelder finds out that his niece Ermengarde is at the Harmonia Gardens Restaurant with the man whom he has forbidden her to see, he hires a cabdriver named Joe to take them to Miss Van Huysen's house and keep them there, by force if necessary. The Cabman has a few drinks with Malachi, and they end up kidnapping the wrong couple.

Cook

Miss Van Huysen's cook has waited all day with her for Ermengarde to arrive. She watches out the window and reports to Miss Van Huysen whenever anyone approaches the house.

Ermengarde

Ermengarde is the niece of Horace Vandergelder. She is twenty-four and intends to marry Ambrose Kemper, an artist, even though he does not make a good salary. When Vandergelder forbids her marriage and sends her to live in New York to keep her away from Ambrose, she goes along with him. She is rebellious enough to plan marriage to a man her uncle does not approve of, but she is also very concerned about her standing in society: when Ambrose suggests that they elope, she is not only against the idea but is shocked that he would even mention such a scandalous word.

Minnie Fay

Minnie works in Mrs. Molloy's hat shop. She is amazed that the older woman would even consider marrying a man whom she does not love. Minnie is not very worldly and has to ask if the Harmonia Gardens Restaurant is "what they call a 'cafe.'"

Gertrude

Gertrude is Vandergelder's housekeeper. She is described as "eighty; deaf; half blind; and very pleased with herself." When arrangements are made to send Ermengarde away so that she cannot marry Ambrose, Gertrude spoils the plan by mentioning the address that Ermengarde is going to in Ambrose's presence.

Cornelius Hackl

Cornelius is the thirty-three-year-old chief clerk at Horace Vandergelder's store. Early in the play, Vandergelder announces to him that, after much consideration, he has decided to promote Cornelius to the position of chief clerk. The announcement that he has been promoted to the position he already holds makes him realize that he is in a rut, so he convinces Barnaby to join him for a night on the town in New York. There, he runs into Irene Molloy in her hat shop while he is pretending to be a wealthy socialite shopping for a hat, and he falls in love with her.

To keep Mrs. Molloy from finding out that Cornelius is just a clerk, Dolly Levi concocts an extravagant story about him being one of the most sought-after bachelors in New York, explaining that he comes from a wealthy family and that he only works in Vandergelder's store because he wants to. When Mrs. Molloy sees him next, she insists that he and Barnaby take her and her assistant to an expensive restaurant. Cornelius goes along, not wanting to tell her the truth, but he is frightened about being arrested when he cannot pay the bill until a stranger finds Vandergelder's wallet filled with money and gives it to Cornelius, assuming that he dropped it. A series of mistaken identities causes Miss Van Huysen to spend most of act IV thinking that Cornelius is Ambrose Kemper and that Ambrose is Cornelius, but in the end Cornelius and Mrs. Molloy plan to marry.

Ambrose Kemper

Ambrose is an artist who wants to marry Vandergelder's niece, Ermengarde. Because he is an artist, he does not have a secure economic future, and for this reason Vandergelder objects to the marriage. Ambrose tries to convince Ermengarde to elope with him, an idea which she finds scandalous, forcing him to accept Dolly Levi's help. In the end, he and Ermengarde are engaged.

Dolly Levi

Dolly is one of the play's central characters and the one after whom it is named. She is a manipulator and schemer who does not mind making up stories to get the results she wants. Her business cards claim skills in reducing varicose veins and in giving instruction on guitar and mandolin, but she states her principal occupation as "a woman who arranges things." Although she plans to marry Vandergelder for his money, her intentions are good; as she says to the audience in the last act, she plans to spread his money around to make the world a better place.

Mrs. Levi is a widow, an old friend of Vandergelder's late wife. As she points out later in the play, she and Vandergelder danced together at each other's weddings. Vandergelder brings her into the situation because he wants her to chaperone Ermengarde, whom he plans to send to New York while he goes to marry Mrs. Molloy. Mrs. Levi starts planning against him almost immediately. She works to help Ermengarde and Ambrose get together, and she disrupts Vandergelder's intention to propose to Mrs. Molloy by making up a fabulously wealthy, sophisticated woman whom she says is interested in him. When she finds Cornelius in Mrs. Molloy's shop, she helps him hide from Vandergelder, and she makes up a ridiculous story so that Mrs. Molloy will not realize that he is a lowly clerk. This serves two purposes: she wants to help the lovers, and she wants to keep Mrs. Molloy from Vandergelder. At dinner with Vandergelder, she carefully but obliquely states the case for his marrying her so that he will think that the idea was his own. Her strategy works, in part because he is a willing victim, which becomes obvious when he announces that she has agreed to become his wife and she has him change his announcement to "*finally* agreed," as if he had been begging her for a long time.

Irene Molloy

At the beginning of the play, Vandergelder intends to marry Mrs. Molloy. She has no personal interest in him, but she is interested in being married in order to get out of the hat business. As she explains to her assistant, people think of women in the millinery trade as being wicked, and she has had to limit her social life in order to keep up an air of respectability. She cannot go out to restaurants, balls, or the theater, because it would hurt her reputation. The only men she meets are feather merchants. In addition, she is interested in marrying Vandergelder because she thinks he would be a good fighter, which she thinks an attractive trait in a husband.

When Cornelius ducks into her shop to hide from Vandergelder, he falls in love with her, and she is just as quickly attracted to him. Part of her attraction comes from the fact that he is pretending to be a wealthy man, an impression that Dolly Levi later promotes when she makes up a story about him being the famous Cornelius Hackl, a millionaire rogue who is well-known in the highest reaches of society. At the Harmonia Gardens Restaurant, she finds out the truth, but by then she is so in love with Cornelius that it does not matter. In the end, they are engaged to be married.

Rudolph

The senior waiter at the Harmonia Gardens Restaurant, Rudolph is a snob who tries to maintain dignity when dealing with the antics of the play's main characters. He speaks with a German accent.

Joe Scanlon

Joe is the barber who is grooming Vandergelder in the first act as he prepares to go off to get married. As a barber, Joe has ethics: when Vandergelder offers him fifty cents to do "something a little special" for his looks, Joe is horrified, as if he had been offered a bribe for something improper. "All I know is fifteen cents' worth, like usual, Mr. Vandergelder," he explains, "and that includes everything that's decent to do to a man." The attempted bribe that Joe refuses turns out to be for hair dying.

Malachi Stack

Malachi arrives at the store in Yonkers with a stack of letters of recommendation from employers in different trades, including a letter from one of Vandergelder's friends named Joshua Van Tuyl. Vandergelder hires him and sends him to New York on a train that is leaving immediately, so that he does not meet the other clerks. Therefore, when he runs into Cornelius and Barnaby at the Harmonia Gardens Restaurant, he does not know them, and he gives Cornelius the wallet he finds on the floor, which is Vandergelder's. Malachi explains his honesty in trying to return a wallet full of money to its rightful owner: he used to be a thief, then took to drink, and has found that a person can only handle one vice well, so he drinks but doesn't steal. Later, his drinking clouds his judgment, and he and the Cabman abduct Cornelius and Barnaby instead of Ermengarde and Ambrose.

Barnaby Tucker

Barnaby is seventeen, the junior clerk at Vandergelder's store. He is naive about the world, which makes him inclined to follow after whatever Cornelius does, even when Cornelius leads him off on an adventure that gets them both into trouble. At the Harmonia Gardens Restaurant, Mrs. Molloy rewards Barnaby for his sweetness by kissing him, and he is so overwhelmed with his first kiss that he falls to the floor.

To get out of the Harmonia Gardens without being spotted by Vandergelder, Barnaby dresses up in a woman's hat and coat, which gets him mistaken for Ermengarde, a disguise that he has to maintain throughout the fourth act.

At the end of the play, when harmony is restored and everybody is happy, Dolly Levi says to the audience, "I think the youngest person here ought to tell us what the moral of the play is." Barnaby makes a speech then about the need for "just the right amount" of adventure in life.

Flora Van Huysen

An old friend of Ermengarde's deceased mother, Miss Van Huysen is a very old spinster who lives with her servants at 8 Jackson Street, New York. Vandergelder sends Ermengarde to live with her so that she cannot marry Ambrose, but they follow Miss Levi's advice and go to the restaurant instead, leaving Miss Van Huysen to wait in vain all day for

Ermengarde's arrival. When they do arrive, it turns out that Miss Van Huysen has no intention of keeping them apart. She considers herself "a friend of all young lovers," hinting that her own love life was ruined by "obstacles and disappointments." She is easily confused, fooled into thinking that Barnaby is Ermengarde, but her good intentions are essential to everything coming out all right in the end.

Horace Vandergelder

Vandergelder is the play's central character. He is sixty years old and is described in the stage notes as "choleric, vain, and sly." He is stingy with money and rude to everyone he talks to. He is displeased with practically everything around him. He does not approve of the man his twenty-four-year-old niece intends to marry and so sends her away to ruin the engagement. He does not like the clerks who work at his hay, feed, and provisions store because he thinks that they should work more than fifteen hours a day, six days a week.

Vandergelder, a widower, plans to marry again, explaining to the audience in a soliloquy that a woman who marries into a household will keep house better than one who is hired to do so. He originally plans to marry Mrs. Molloy, but his interest in her is so feeble that he is willing to postpone his proposal when Dolly Levi tells him another woman is interested in him.

Throughout the play, other characters spend their time either trying to avoid Vandergelder because of his fearsome temper or plotting to get their hands on the money that he has hoarded by living a miserly existence. In the end, though, he becomes a warmer person. Dolly Levi tricks him into marrying her, and he goes along with it good-naturedly; he consents to the marriage of Ermengarde and Ambrose, which he had violently opposed in the first scene; and he agrees to make Barnaby a partner in his business. The sudden transformation implies that Vandergelder was a good-natured person all along but just did not know how to show his softer side.

THEMES

Gender Roles

Wilder uses the different expectations that society has for males and females to twist the comic situation of *The Matchmaker* into a tighter knot than the events would otherwise permit. The first and most obvious example of this is the way in which Horace Vandergelder attempts to control his niece's life, dictating whom she may or may not marry, and the way in which Ermengarde accepts his authority. At the same time that he is trying to control Ermengarde's love life, Vandergelder is also planning on marrying someone—he is not very concerned about whom—in order to get an efficient housekeeper. Keeping house is a task for women, he explains, but the women who do it for hire do not do it well. "In order to run a house well," he tells the audience, "a woman must have the feeling she owns it. Marriage is a bribe to make a housekeeper think she's a householder." Throughout the play, Vandergelder is presented as an example of prejudice and ignorance, so blind to reality that he cannot see how his clerks think of him or how Dolly Levi is manipulating him into marriage. His view of gender roles is therefore not necessarily one that audiences are expected to accept.

A more realistic view of gender roles is the one held by Irene Molloy. She owns her own business, a hat shop in New York, and so has financial independence. Still, she wants to get out of the hat business because of the stereotype that "all millineresses are suspected of being wicked women." She is not able to go to public events because people will think that her behavior is improper for a lady. This knowledge of unwritten social conventions and of how people would punish her if she broke them is more telling of gender roles in this society than Vandergelder's skewed notions. Even so, the play probably gives its female characters more freedom than they would actually have enjoyed in the 1880s, reflecting more about the time when it was written than the time when it is set.

Money

One of the keys to the social situation in *The Matchmaker* is the uneven way in which wealth is distributed among the characters. Vandergelder is clearly the wealthiest character, and how he spends money helps audiences gauge what he considers important. He usually pays fifteen cents for a haircut, but for the occasion of proposing to Mrs. Molloy he is willing to go up to fifty cents. (The barber, Joe Scanlon, will not accept more than three times his regular fee for something as improper as dying a man's hair.) The wages he pays his workers for ninety hours of work per week leave them with about three dollars each in their pockets. Yet Vandergelder is willing to pay the Cabman fifteen dollars to help him keep Ermengarde and Ambrose apart. He carries a purse that is stuffed full of twenty dollar bills, and he is only willing to consider the adventure of remarrying because he has half a million dollars in the bank.

The plot revolves around Vandergelder's insistence on holding onto his money. His objection to Ambrose is based solely on Ambrose's poor financial prospects and has nothing to do with the young man's character. Ermengarde, on the other hand, thinks nothing about money whatsoever. Dolly Levi represents a compromise between the two: though she says that she wants Vandergelder's fortune, her affection for him is clear. His theory is that money should not be spent, and hers is that it should. Once Vandergelder learns to trust Dolly, he lets his money go, and once he does that he can have open relationships with his niece and clerks.

Love

Like many comedies, *The Matchmaker* takes advantage of the mysteries of love in order to put its characters into complex situations. Vandergelder may be cheap and rude, but it is when he denies having ever heard of such a thing as a broken heart that audiences know he will get his comeuppance, just as surely as they know that Ermengarde, who thinks of nothing but love, will be satisfied in the end. Vandergelder fools himself into thinking that he is interested in women for all sorts of reasons that are not love. He tells himself that he wants a housekeeper and falls for Dolly Levi's idealized portrait of a woman who is a great cook, wealthy, infatuated with him, and a third his age. In the end, though, he cannot keep himself from falling for Dolly, even though she is none of the things that he was looking for.

The play would end in the second act if Cornelius and Barnaby simply hid out at Mrs. Molloy's hat shop for a while and then went away. What keeps them engaged in the action, and therefore involved with the main characters, is that Cornelius falls instantly, hopelessly in love with Mrs. Molloy. A realistic play would not have a character lose control of himself so quickly after their first meeting, but then, a realistic play is not trying to make audiences laugh. Without faith in love at first sight, the various plot threads of *The Matchmaker* would spin out in different directions. Without faith in a love that is more powerful than sound thinking, the play would leave Horace Vandergelder unpunished for his stinginess and his plotting, which would not make it a very satisfactory comedy at all.

TOPICS FOR FURTHER STUDY

- Find a character on television who reminds you of Horace Vandergelder. Explain what the two have in common and what you think each would do if put in the other's place.
- A marriage is often thought of as a beginning, though it often comes as a happy ending in comedies. Write a short story that shows what life is like for one of this play's couples a year after they are married.
- Vandergelder's shop sells hay in Yonkers in the 1880s, a time when New York City already had elevated trains. Research your town, and report on the period from when the first automobiles arrived through when the last horses left.
- Instead of matchmakers, the modern world has dating services. What kind of business would Dolly Levi consider herself to be in today? Design an ad that she might run in the newspaper, on the Internet, or on television to promote her services.
- Write an explanation, with illustrations, showing why, in the 1880s, canned tomatoes heated with a match would explode.

Adventure

When the play is over, and all of its extraordinary events are through, Dolly Levi has the youngest character tell the moral of the play to the audience. The speech that Barnaby gives talks about the need for adventure in life. In the most direct sense, this is the lesson that he and Cornelius have learned throughout the play: they were reluctant about leaving their posts as clerks at the store in Yonkers and end up happier for having interrupted their routine. In a broader sense, it is the lesson that nearly all of the characters learn. Vandergelder, certainly, starts the play thinking only of safe prospects and ends it happier because things that he would not have wanted have had their effect on him. Irene Molloy, who has been waiting for a rich man to take her from the job she hates, falls in love instead, which she apparently finds better. Minnie goes to the kind of restaurant that she would never have thought existed; Barnaby receives his first kiss; Ermengarde and Ambrose find a solution to the problems that kept them from getting married. All of these characters are better off at the end because they went through a frightening situation that was out of their control and were willing to enter into an adventure for its own sake.

The only character who does not really have an adventure is Dolly Levi. She is, as she explains to Ambrose early in the play, ''a woman who arranges things.'' Throughout the course of *The Matchmaker*, she is not someone who has adventures but someone who causes adventure to happen to others. She is, however, open to the unexpected; in her speech in act IV, she describes how she was shut away from life after her husband's death until one night when ''I decided to rejoin the human race.'' Because of Vandergelder's overbearing personality, the end of the play suggests that Dolly Levi's adventure is just beginning.

STYLE

Soliloquy

A soliloquy is the speech a character gives directly to the audience, either when alone on the stage or else ignoring the other characters, who cannot hear it. Wilder has several characters give soliloquies in *The Matchmaker*. In the first act, after everyone else has gone and left him alone, Vandergelder talks at length about why he wants to be married now. These are personal thoughts that he would not share with any of the other characters; he may explain his theory of marriage as a way to get a decent housekeeper, but the idea that he is willing to take a chance is too personal, and sharing it would leave him too vulnerable. He ends his soliloquy by acknowledging that he is talking to an audience, telling them, ''Think it over.''

Cornelius gives a soliloquy in act II, when he and Barnaby are supposed to be hiding. His speech explains how wonderful he feels, having fallen in love. These are ideas that Barnaby has shown himself unable to understand, and Cornelius certainly could not tell them to anyone else.

In act III, Malachi tells the audience his theory about the need to have one vice but no more than one. His ideas are relevant to the play in general, but, again, they would not fit into the dramatic scene because they represent things that Malachi, a relative newcomer, would not explain to anyone else there.

Dolly Levi's soliloquy in the final act is addressed to the memory of her dead husband rather than to the audience. Since the subject is remarriage, she would naturally think of him, but as a dramatic technique this is handled in the same way as the other soliloquies.

Barnaby's speech at the end takes off from the earlier soliloquies. In them, characters talked to the audience, but they never acknowledged the audience to one another. In the play's final moments, though, Mrs. Levi drops the pretense that usually separates players from audiences, acting like a mutual friend who is introducing Barnaby to the audience and vice versa.

Subplot

If this play's main plot is the strange courtship between Horace Vandergelder and Dolly Levi, then the other two romances would have to be considered subplots. Either one could be removed without substantially changing the whole play. Ermengarde and Ambrose do give Vandergelder a chance to show off his intolerance and autocratic nature in the beginning, but that could have been handled in any number of other ways. For most of the play, the young lovers are gone, signifying their relative unimportance. On the other hand, the blossoming romance between Cornelius Hackl and Irene Molloy takes up most of acts II and III, at times becoming more important than Vandergelder's story, Still, all that this romance really adds to the plot is that it removes Mrs. Molloy from the pool of available wives and gives Cornelius a chance to expound upon how good it is to take a chance.

Another way to look at it, however, is that these are not subplots at all. They are only subplots if the story of Vandergelder and Mrs. Levi is considered the one main plot. *The Matchmaker* is not necessarily their story, though. It is a story about love, and as such each of the three variations on the theme of love is as important as the others, regardless of how colorful the characters are or how much time they spend onstage.

Denouement

Denouement is a French word that means "the unraveling." In literature, it is used to describe the action that happens after the story has reached its climax. In *The Matchmaker*, the final few pages clearly are there to tie up loose ends. The play does not end with action but with Barnaby coming in from the kitchen bringing news. Before that comes Vandergelder's proposal to Mrs. Levy, but even that seems to be a necessary but minor afterthought: from the fact that he calls Dolly "wonderful woman" and lets her keep his purse, audiences can tell that he has already changed his character. Even Dolly Levi's speech to her dead husband does not represent any advance in the plot but just a clarification of the principles she has been following all along.

A good case can be made for the idea that the climax of the play occurs when Vandergelder's pretensions are finally put to rest at the end of act III. Mrs. Levi explains very clearly that he has lost everything: his niece, his bride, his clerks, and even his money. This seems to have no effect on Vandergelder, as he still refuses to marry her, but the next time he shows up on stage he is humbled. He allows Mrs. Van Huysen and Mrs. Levi to give him orders and behaves civilly at their request. Once Horace Vandergelder allows others to tell him what to do, the rest of the play is just a matter of clearing away leftover plot elements.

HISTORICAL CONTEXT

The Gilded Age

The phrase "Gilded Age" comes from the title of an 1873 book by Mark Twain and Charles Dudley Warner. The book was an exposé of corruption in politics and business after the end of the Civil War in 1865, but the phrase is used today to describe the American situation throughout the last third of the century.

Economically, the era was notable for the rise of industry. The population was in the process of shifting from rural to urban, and the growth of cities provided the workforce to create larger production facilities. Railroads expanded across the country—the transcontinental railroad was completed at Promontory, Utah, in 1869—making it possible to move materials for production and to ship manufactured products nearly anywhere on the continent. From 1870 to 1900, the use of bituminous coal, which powered industry, rose tenfold, and the use of rolled iron and steel increased to twelve times what it had been. The country's gross national product multiplied six times over in those years. Out of this situation arose the businessmen who made giant fortunes from this economic growth, usually by controlling an entire industry, as John D. Rockefeller controlled the oil industry, Andrew Carnegie controlled steel, and J.P. Morgan controlled banking. At the same time that a few individuals were amassing incredible fortunes, there was terrible poverty and illness among the common laborers who worked in the factories.

Although *The Matchmaker* takes place among shops and not factories, the economic situation of the times can still be seen in the disparity between the characters' finances. Horace Vandergelder, a store owner, comes off as a miserly tyrant who carries stacks of twenty dollar bills in his wallet, while his clerks, who are forced to work from six in the morning to nine at night six days a week, have to scrounge for train money. And while class differences will always be present, this play portrays the restaurant as being a particularly unsafe place for those of the lower classes. By contemporary standards, Vandergelder is a heartless, petty tyrant, and the Harmonia Gardens Restaurant is too snobby, but the 1880s were a time of extreme wealth and poverty.

Nostalgia

The time when *The Matchmaker* was produced was a particularly trying time in American history. After the tumultuous decades of the 1930s, which saw the worst economic depression in the nation's history, and the 1940s, which were defined by the second world war, the 1950s were peaceful and prosperous. Still, even as external conflict was lacking, there were social forces that served as continuous reminders of life in the modern world.

One defining characteristic was the awareness of the potential for nuclear destruction. World War II ended after the United States dropped the first nuclear bomb ever used on August 5, 1945, killing

COMPARE & CONTRAST

- **1880s:** People going from Yonkers, which is adjacent to the Bronx, into Manhattan, which is also adjacent to the Bronx, most often take a train or ride a horse. (In the play, Vandergelder's shop sells horse supplies.)

  1954: The trip from Yonkers to Manhattan is often made by automobile.

  Today: Because of traffic congestion and a shortage of in-town parking, the trip from Yonkers to Manhattan is often made by train.

- **1880s:** The American economy is prospering during the Industrial Revolution.

  1954: The American economy is secure, but many in the audience for this play remember the Great Depression (1929 through 1941) clearly.

  Today: America has just experienced a period of unprecedented economic growth due to the technology revolution.

- **1880s:** Energy production is a growing industry. Gasoline and oil are just starting to be in demand for combustion engines, and the newly-invented electric light bulb creates the need for power lines to spread electricity from municipal generators into homes.

  1954: The first nuclear power station starts up in the Soviet Union. In the United States, Bell Laboratories creates a solar cell to convert sunlight into energy.

  Today: Most of the world is still committed to using non-renewable fossil fuels, which are in greater demand than ever due to the growing demand for electricity and gasoline.

- **1880s:** Millinery shops are common in all cities, because women do not think of going with their heads uncovered.

  1954: Hats are still popular but are considered optional.

  Today: It is rare to see either a woman or a man wearing a formal hat.

almost 130,000 people with one blast. The second bomb was dropped on Nagasaki on August 9, 1945. In the 1950s, people were aware of the devastation of the bombs and uncertain of the ability of politicians to refrain from using them. People at that time practiced disaster drills to prepare for nuclear attacks. Homeowners built bomb shelters and stocked them with food, preparing for the time, that could come any day, when civilization would be wiped away in an instant.

The other defining element of the 1950s was the Cold War. During World War II, the Soviet Union and America were allies in the fight against German aggression. After the war, though, their different political ideologies led them to be fierce competitors. The Soviet Union pursued a policy of spreading communism around the globe, leading to an American foreign policy based on containing communism. There were hearings, led by Senator Joseph McCarthy of Wisconsin, aimed at identifying communists who had infiltrated the U.S. government and the entertainment industry in order to spread communist ideas. (McCarthy was later censured by the Senate, and his name has come to be associated with systematized fear mongering.) The United States became involved in wars in South Korea and Vietnam with the goal of stopping the growth of communism in those places.

In a time of constant worry about sudden annihilation, of suspicion that treacherous spies were trying to overthrow the government from within and to control American minds, *The Matchmaker* offered reassuring, light entertainment. It was set in a time in the nation's history when there were no great disturbances, no war or imminent danger. Racial issues are not approached in the play, and genders are equal, with a female-owned shop in New York balancing a male-owned shop in Yonkers. Unlike comedies with contemporary settings, the historical setting of *The Matchmaker* allowed audiences to forget the problems of the day and to bask in the warm feeling of nostalgia for a simpler time.

CRITICAL OVERVIEW

Thornton Wilder is considered one of America's most important authors, although *The Matchmaker* is not generally thought of as one of his most important works. Taken as an evening's entertainment, the play has always been well-respected by critics. Negative views have only come when critics have thought the work of such an important author should do more.

Wilder's place in American literature is secure, if only because he is the only writer to have won Pulitzer Prizes for both fiction (for *The Bridge of San Luis Rey*) and drama (for both *Our Town* and *The Skin of Our Teeth*). Overall, his reputation as a dramatist has held up better than that as a novelist. *The Bridge of San Luis Rey* is still required reading in literature classes, but it is seldom read outside of schools, and his other novels have disappeared. *Our Town*, on the other hand, remains one of the most enduring and most frequently performed works in America, performed by over four hundred amateur groups each year.

Wilder's first critical and popular success came with *The Bridge of San Luis Rey* in 1927. Not only did it win the Pulitzer, but it sold millions of copies. Just three years later, though, a critical backlash began with a 1930 article by Michael Gold for the *New Republic* and a second article he wrote later that year for *New Masses,* in which he said, "Yes, Wilder writes perfect English. But he has nothing to say in that perfect English. He is a beautiful, rouged, well-dressed corpse, lying among the sacred candles and lilies of the past, sure to stink if exposed to the sunlight." His criticism struck a chord with other reviewers, who began taking Wilder to task for his failure to address complex social problems. As Jackson Bryer explained the critics' complaints in his essay commemorating Wilder's one-hundredth birthday, "What these critics were saying was that Wilder was not sufficiently attuned to the problems of his day, that by setting his novels in remote times and places, he was ignoring the present." Bryer went on to explain that it had to be that

Playbill cover from the 1957 theatrical production of The Matchmaker, *directed by Tyrone Guthrie*

way. Unlike other major writers of the day, such as Faulkner or Hemingway, Wilder grew up in different places on different continents, and so he had no place that he could feel deep in his heart was his own. It was natural for him to set his fictions in different times and places, even though some critics took this as a sign of aloofness.

It was not long after the critical backlash against his fiction began to arise that Wilder experienced his first success in the theater with *The Long Christmas Dinner* in 1931. Divided into three acts, it is, like most of his works (except, notably, *The Matchmaker*), experimental in form. This fragmented structure carried on in his works throughout the 1930s, reaching its high point in *Our Town* in 1938. Even more than *Bridge of San Luis Rey*, *Our Town* was hailed by critics and by audiences. A fairly representative example is John Mason Brown, who wrote that *Our Town* "is a remarkable play; one if the sagest, warmest, and most deeply human scripts to have come out of our theatre."

The first version of *The Matchmaker*, named *The Merchant of Yonkers*, was produced the year following *Our Town*. Reviews are difficult to find because it had an extremely short run, fewer than thirty performances. Most critics attribute its failure to the direction of Max Reinhardt. Though Wilder wrote it for him, Reinhardt was German and probably did not understand the pacing of comedy suitable for American audiences. The evidence of this is that *The Matchmaker* was a success ten years later, even though the script is not substantially different.

Because Wilder had, by the time *The Matchmaker* was produced, won two Pulitzers and established himself as a fixture of the American literary scene, reviewers had to lower their expectations in order to think of the play in the right sense. As Rex Burbank was to put it in his overview of Wilder's career in 1961, "There is less claim to serious attention and contemplation in this play than in any of Wilder's other full-length works; and it should be enjoyed for what it is—a farce." The lack of social insight that became a rallying cry against Wilder in the 1930s helps readers understand the spirit of *The Matchmaker*, according to Burbank: "one enjoys laughing at Vandergelder's absurdities but is not constrained to give much thought to their social or ethical significance."

CRITICISM

David Kelly

Kelly teaches creative writing and literature at Oakton Community College in Illinois. In this essay, Kelly examines elements of The Matchmaker *that make it function as a parody, as Wilder intended.*

As an old show business adage puts it, tragedy is what happens to you, while comedy is what happens to someone else. This explains, in one sentence, the complex problem Thornton Wilder examines in the famous preface to his collection *Three Plays*. He discusses how, starting in the 1920s, he found himself growing increasingly bored with the theater, which he had loved all his life. The plays were competent enough, but they did not affect him on a personal level, the way that good art should. At length, Wilder traced the problem to the rise of the middle class in the nineteenth century. His explanation went like this: the middle class, then a new social phenomenon, did not want the sharp discomfort that art can cause when it makes one face reality and instead supported art that was soothing. One result was that writers began producing characters as broad types, which audiences could then distance themselves from, telling themselves that the concerns of the character on the stage were nothing like the ones they faced themselves. Another, related way to make drama soothing was to use the stage itself as a frame to separate "their" world from "ours"—the stage becomes, as Wilder puts it, a "box set."

At the end of his preface, Wilder applied this artistic theory to the book's three plays—*Our Town*, *The Skin of Our Teeth* and *The Matchmaker*—and explained how each one represents his stand against soothing art. The misfit of the group is *The Matchmaker*, his romantic comedy that whips up complications and misunderstandings that come out all right for everyone in the end, as do the bloodless plays that Wilder said bored him. In the preface, he explained that he wrote the play as a parody of plays he saw in his youth, taking a sharp-witted German comedy of manners (*Ein Jux es sich Machen,* by Johann Nestroy) and flattening it to meet American standards. "One way to shake off the nonsense of the nineteenth-century staging," he explained, "is to make fun of it." The problem with theater was that people no longer came away from plays feeling, "This is the way things are." In *The Matchmaker*, he addressed art's relationship to reality by presenting a situation so contrived that audiences would *have* to be aware of its falsity.

The Matchmaker is meant to be such an extreme example of middle-class art that it forces those who experience it to notice how little it resembles true art. To accomplish this goal, Wilder had to distance the audience from the action and make them aware of the distance while at the same time creating a play that is so cold and impersonal as to be unwatchable.

The play is certainly made to be felt at a distance. The characters are meant to be understood at a theoretical level, but their problems are not felt, which is exactly the feeling Wilder described having plagued him about other plays that did not claim to be parodies. He uses several techniques to make audiences feel that "they" on stage are different than "us" beyond the footlights.

The most obvious distancing mechanism is the surly personality of the play's main character, Horace Vandergelder. Certainly, there are elements to his character that anyone can relate to, but just as certainly there are not people coming away from the theater telling themselves, "He's like me." He is a curmudgeon, a crank, and a tightwad, too money-

WHAT DO I READ NEXT?

- Wilder's most famous work of fiction is *The Bridge of San Luis Rey,* his 1927 best-selling novel about the collapse of a bridge in Peru. It won the Pulitzer Prize in 1928. It is available in a 1998 edition from Harper Perennial.
- Wilder's most popular play is *Our Town,* a heartwarming view of small-town American life. It won the Pulitzer Prize in 1938, the year it was produced. It is available along with *The Matchmaker* and *The Skin of Our Teeth* in *Three Plays,* published in paperback by Harper Perennial in 1998.
- Bernard Malamud's 1954 short story "The Magic Barrel" is one of the most famous literary works about matchmaking. Drawing on New York Yiddish culture, Malamud weaves a tale about a mysterious stranger who promises to find a wife for a busy rabbi. It is available in Malamud's *The Complete Stories,* published by Farrar, Straus & Gireaux in 1997.
- Gertrude Stein was one of the greatest writers of the twentieth century and a close friend of Wilder. *The Letters of Gertrude Stein and Thornton Wilder,* published by Yale University Press in 1996, helps readers get to know both authors through the correspondence they had over the course of twenty years.
- The spirit of the farce in *The Matchmaker* is indebted to the seventeenth-century French playwright Jean Baptiste Poquelin Molière. In fact, Wilder uses two passages that he adapted directly from Molière's *L'Avare,* which translates into English as *The Miser.* Two versions if it are available in *Molière: Four Plays,* published in 1999 by Branden Publishing Co.
- A series of interviews with Wilder concerning his views of the world and theories about writing was collected by University of Mississippi Press in the 1992 book *Conversations with Thornton Wilder,* edited by Jackson R. Bryer.

conscious to recognize true love and too stingy to let his employees have one evening off out of the week. He distrusts the young, but he also has no respect for the law. He parts with cash sparingly, a few dollars here and there, but he carries a huge amount in his purse, which he is surprisingly careless enough to lose. In short, he is a compilation of unpleasant human traits, which would make him a fine secondary character. As the lead, he serves to remind audiences of the extremist nature of comic characters. Putting Horace Vandergelder in the middle of the play is like focusing a movie camera so tightly on a science-fiction monster that a zipper in the back of the suit eventually shows.

The play's other main character, Dolly Levi, is just as artificial, but in the other direction: she is too good, too knowing, to be from the world ordinary humans inhabit. Her chosen mission as a "woman who arranges things" comes with supernatural powers. She can tell the two young lovers to go to a certain restaurant at a certain time, and everything will come out all right for them. She can tell outrageous stories, such as the one about Vandergelder's clerk being an undercover millionaire, and have them accepted if not quite believed. The only way audiences can accept Dolly's abilities is by distancing the world onstage from their own and accepting that things happen there that could never happen here.

Wilder uses other theatrical conventions, or, rather, overuses them, to keep his comedy at arm's length. Inside the box set, people do not realize that a character wearing a woman's coat and a veil could be a man. They do not hear what is being said on the other side of a screen. They find men hiding in cupboards and under tables, and the proper response is to walk away in a jealous snit. These stage conventions make theatrical sense, because they allow the playwright to put different characters onstage and move them in and out without having to

> "THE MATCHMAKER SATIRIZED HOW MODERN CULTURE FLATTENS THE REALNESS OF THE THEATRICAL EXPERIENCE, BUT MODERN CULTURE HAS ABSORBED WILDER'S SATIRIC METHOD AND FOR THE LAST FORTY YEARS HAS BEEN JOYOUSLY SATIRIZING ITSELF."

constantly change sets; and they are funny, too, drawing from the human capacity to be fooled. They are exactly what is to be expected from a comedy that means to be there just to make people laugh. At the same time that they chide the characters for their intellectual nearsightedness, though, they openly mock the play for having wandered so far from meaningfulness.

Whenever audiences come close to accepting the world onstage as its own separate place, with its own physical, psychological, and moral rules, Wilder reminds them, through the use of soliloquies, that the actors are present in a common reality after all. When it works, the objectified theater does so by presenting events for audiences to scrutinize like grasshoppers in a jar. The open area facing the audience is referred to as "the fourth wall," an invisible barrier between the two worlds. Soliloquies break that fourth wall. When characters step out into the footlights to talk to the audiences directly, the spell of watching a separate reality is broken. This technique comes up just a little short of having actors introduce themselves and announce that they know they are just people in makeup pretending to be other people who never existed. Audiences made aware of theater's artifice experience the feeling that Wilder describes in his preface, that modern theater has "shut the play off in a museum showcase."

Having determined Wilder's intention to satirize modern theater and examined some of the methods he used to do this, the question that then arises is how effective is he at making audiences reconsider comedies. The answer is almost certainly different for today's audiences than it was for those who saw the play in its first run. At that time, it was rare for a Broadway playwright to take an ironic look at his material, which is why Wilder seemed to feel that doing so was necessary. He wanted his audiences to become aware of what is happening to them when they are in the presence of a play, and to do that he had to draw attention to technique. Today, however, irony is done to death. Comedians give hammy exaggerations of what it is like to be a comedian; serious artists scrutinize advertising art; television shows are about people making television shows, with the interior show being the sort of static product that Wilder sought to lampoon. *The Matchmaker* satirized how modern culture flattens the realness of the theatrical experience, but modern culture has absorbed Wilder's satiric method and for the last forty years has been joyously satirizing itself. With so much irony going around, the earliest attempt looks primitive.

One more aspect to the weakening of *The Matchmaker*'s satiric strength is that it was turned into the sort of consumer-friendly, "soothing" entertainment product that it was supposed to unmask, as the musical *Hello, Dolly*! Musicals in general are meant to entertain, not to provoke thought; musical adaptations usually end up cutting out any challenging ideas to make room for songs. Because the world of musical theater is, by its nature, farcical (audiences are not supposed to *really* think that a band just suddenly appeared and that everyone improvised lyrics and dance steps in unison), any satiric sense is lost.

Why should *Hello, Dolly*! influence how people interpret the ironic stance of *The Matchmaker*? It shouldn't, but it does. *Hello, Dolly*! was the more popular of the two, with a title song that has become a standard of pop music. When *The Matchmaker* is mentioned, you can count the seconds until someone mentions that it was the basis for *Hello, Dolly!,* with as much certainty as counting the seconds between a lightning flash and thunder. If the satiric element of *The Matchmaker* had been stronger, it could stand alone, as the nasty little piece that was declawed and made into a feel-good musical. But the satire is actually so quiet that it has to be explained, and so it is often missed.

The problem with satirizing pop art is that one is halfway into the pop art world already, and it is easy to be accepted by the mainstream. Songs by the Who and Janis Joplin, once emblems of the counterculture, are catchy enough to use in car ads, if the lyrics are left out. "Born in the U.S.A.," an angry song about betrayal and disappointment, is found suitable background music for political rallies if no one listens to anything it says besides the title and refrain. And *The Matchmaker*, which Wilder meant as an examination of theatrical conventions, reads like just another comedy of manners today, because modern audiences are more accustomed to satire that is sharper and more obvious.

Source: David Kelly, Critical Essay on *The Matchmaker,* in *Drama for Students,* The Gale Group, 2003.

Rex Burbank

In the following essay excerpt, Burbank provides a thematic overview of The Matchmaker, *finding it belongs to Wilder's pre-World War II phase, rather than the later period in which it achieved hit status.*

The Merchant of Yonkers was a plea for a freer stage and a freer and fuller participation in life. Its first performance was at the Colonial Theatre in Boston on December 12, 1938, a little less than eleven months after the first production of *Our Town* at Princeton, New Jersey. On December 28, 1938, it opened in New York, where it had a short run of twenty-eight performances. It lay unused until Wilder revised it slightly, changed the title to *The Matchmaker*, and brought it out again in August, 1954, in Edinburgh. From Edinburgh it went to London, where it began a successful run the following November 4. In October, 1955, it was brought to Philadelphia, where it also succeeded; and when taken to New York, it engaged a run long enough to win ''hit'' status.

The Matchmaker doesn't differ materially from *The Merchant of Yonkers;* and it belongs, therefore, with the work of this earlier period of Wilder's career rather than with that after World War II. As Harold Clurman pointed out in his review of *The Matchmaker*, the failure of the earlier version and the success of the latter were probably owing to the difference in directors. *The Merchant* was directed by Max Reinhardt, for whom Wilder wrote it; and it failed, probably, because of what Clurman called the director's ''unfamiliarity with American theatre custom.'' *The Matchmaker* was directed by Tyrone Guthrie, who by common critical consent kept the action moving at the rapid pace it requires.

Wilder took much of the material for this play from Johann Nestroy's *Einen Jux will er sich Machen* (Vienna, 1842). He calls it a ''free adaptation'' of Nestroy's play, which was in turn based upon *A Day Well Spent* (London, 1835) by John Oxenham. ''One way to shake off the nonsense of the nineteenth-century staging is to make fun of it,'' he wrote in the preface to *Three Plays.* ''This play parodies the stock-company plays that I used to see at Ye Liberty Theatre, Oakland, California, when I was a boy.'' Much of its humor arises from the use of such old comic stage devices as mistaken identity, quick leaps for hiding places under tables, characters dressed in clothes of the opposite sex, and people caught in folding screens. It features stock characters and absurd situations that develop into a conventional complicated plot. It has a ''villain,'' for instance, in the merchant Vandergelder, who tries to prevent the marriage of a young couple—his niece Ermengarde and the impecunious young artist Ambrose Kemper.

> "THERE IS LESS CLAIM TO SERIOUS ATTENTION AND CONTEMPLATION IN THIS PLAY THAN IN ANY OF WILDER'S OTHER FULL-LENGTH WORKS; AND IT SHOULD BE ENJOYED FOR WHAT IT IS—A FARCE."

The action takes place in Yonkers during the 1880's and involves the efforts of the principal characters, whose enjoyment of life is in one way or another dependent upon Vandergelder, to ''participate'' in life. In addition to Ermengarde and Ambrose, the main characters include Vandergelder's two clerks, Cornelius and Barnaby, who go to New York in search of ''adventure,'' and Dolly Levi, the ''Matchmaker,'' who pretends to make a match for Vandergelder with a young, attractive woman (Irene Molloy) but actually makes it for herself. Vandergelder's ''sensible'' behavior and values are the obstacles in each instance to their free enjoyment of life, and the plot consists in the attempts of these people to combat his life-denying conventionality. His most formidable antagonist is Dolly Levi, who is the arranger, the artist of life who follows no doctrine except that of the full enjoyment of it and opposition to the conventional theories of ''suc-

Walter Matthau, Barbara Streisand (as Dolly), and Marianne McAndrew in a scene from the 1969 film adaptation Hello, Dolly!

cess'' held by Vandergelder to whom work and money are life's highest values. She frankly and simply wants to marry him for his money, but her ideas about wealth are in direct opposition to his. She is determined to put Vandergelder's coins into circulation so they can free others from habit, convention, and isolation—for the enjoyment of life. She explains her economic philosophy to Ambrose: ''Money should circulate like rain water. It should be flowing down among the people, through dressmakers and restaurants and cabmen, setting up a little business here, and furnishing a good time there.''

When she has conquered Vandergelder, his unconditional surrender contains assurances that his money will be spent instead of saved. Vandergelder is ''sound'' from the standpoint of conventional social values; for he has saved, worked hard, and been cautious. He is the stolid, pompous ''self-made'' man who equates the acquisition of riches and the exploitation of others with virtue and ''good sense.'' The clever Dolly turns the platitudes he lives by to her own uses in such delicious bits of dialogue as the following:

VANDERGELDER: Mrs. Molloy, I've got some advice to give you about your business.

MRS. LEVI: Oh, advice from Mr. Vandergelder! The whole city should hear this.

VANDERGELDER: In the first place, the aim of business is to make a profit.

MRS. MOLLOY: Is that so?

MRS. LEVI: I never heard it put so clearly before. Did you hear It?

VANDERGELDER: You pay those girls of yours too much. You pay them as much as men. Girls like that enjoy their work. Wages, Mrs. Molloy, are paid to make people who do work they don't enjoy

MRS. LEVI: Mr. Vandergelder thinks so ably. And that's exactly the way his business is run up in Yonkers.

Enjoyment of life requires nurturing of a vice as well as the virtues. The ne'er-do-well Malachi expresses this bit of philosophy: ''There are some people who say you shouldn't have any weaknesses at all—no vices. But if a man has no vices, he's in great danger of making vices out of his virtues, and there's a spectacle. We've all seen them: men who were monsters of philanthropy and women who were dragons of purity. We've seen people who told the truth, though the Heavens fall—and the Heavens fell. No, no—nurse one vice in your bosom. Give it the attention it deserves and let your virtues spring up modestly around it.''

The clerks Cornelius and Barnaby are also in rebellion against Vandergelder and what he stands for. Yearning for excitement and resolving to go to New York for an ''adventure,'' they blow up the tomato cans on the shelves of Vandergelder's store and leave. They are determined to have a good meal, to be ''in danger,'' almost to get arrested, to spend all their money (three dollars), and to kiss a girl. Much of the best humor of the play consists in the attempts of these two—and, later, Irene Molloy—to have a part in the excitement of life heretofore denied them by conventions that equate ''adventure'' with foolishness. It is tender humor, a bit sentimental, even a bit ''heartwarming,'' but nevertheless very enjoyable. The hilarious scene in Act III, where Dolly twists Vandergelder's exasperation with her into a hinted proposal, is one of Wilder's most comical.

It is interesting that while this play first appeared during the depression and featured a conflict between a villainous ''boss'' and his exploited employees, it was utterly unproletarian; it did not present a ''problem'' for which social amelioration or reform was needed. The play says in effect that Vandergelder is a moral rather than a social problem. Like *Heaven's My Destination*, it proposes that a vigorous, robust spirit of humanism is the answer to materialism: that effective reform should begin with the moral improvement of individuals rather than with legislation. But the play is really too good-natured to command serious consideration of its humanistic propositions; and perhaps this is one reason it failed in the thirties. Furthermore, it lacks the bite of real satire; and, while there is some ridicule aimed at conventional notions of "success," the character representing it, Vandergelder, is so candidly, absurdly, and farcically "bad" that the seriousness of what he represents does not become apparent.

There is less claim to serious attention and contemplation in this play than in any of Wilder's other full-length works; and it should be enjoyed for what it is—a farce. The laughter it evokes at Vandergelder and the conventions he embodies is that of compassion for a fellow human who is unaware of his own foolishness and not that of bitterness or contempt. Wilder often uses the phrase "makes fun of" where "satirizes" might ordinarily be expected. The difference in terminology is relevant, for he seldom *satirizes* in the sense that he holds persons up to ridicule or scorn. He takes the more gentle way of viewing his people with mild irony, and he achieves a kind of spontaneous gaiety out of his depictions of human folly instead of a laughter of superiority and contempt. The result in *The Matchmaker* is that one enjoys laughing at Vandergelder's absurdities but is not constrained to give much thought to their social or ethical significance.

Source: Rex Burbank, "Three Theatricalist Plays," in *Thornton Wilder,* Twayne, 1961, pp. 82–111.

SOURCES

Brown, John Mason, "America Speaks," in *Two on the Aisle: Ten Years of the American Theatre in Performance,* W. W. Norton & Co., Inc., 1938, pp. 133–93.

Bryer, Jackson R., "Thornton Wilder at 100: His Achievement and His Legacy," in *Thornton Wilder: New Essays,* edited by Martin Blank, Dalma Hunyadi Brunauer, and David Garrett Izzo, Locust Hill Press, 1999, pp. 3–20.

Burbank, Rex, *Thornton Wilder,* Twayne Publishers, 1961, pp. 100–01.

Gold, Michael, "Notes of the Month," in *New Masses,* April 1930, pp. 3–5.

Wilder, Thornton, "Preface," in *Three Plays,* Harper & Row, 1957, pp. viii–xiv.

FURTHER READING

Cowley, Malcolm, "Thornton Wilder: Time Abolished," in *New England Writers and Writing,* University Press of New England, 1996, pp. 232–43.

This brief essay gives readers a concise overview of Wilder's life from one of the most respected literary critics of his time.

Haberman, Donald, "Appendix," in *The Plays of Thornton Wilder: A Critical Study,* Wesleyan University Press, 1967, pp. 127–136.

At the end of his analysis of Wilder's work, Haberman includes a three-column, side-by-side comparison of a section from Molière's *L'Avare* and Wilder's rewriting of it.

Lifton, Paul, "'The Sign of Kierkegaard': Existential Aspects of Wilder's Theatre," in *Vast Encyclopedia: The Theatre of Thornton Wilder,* Greenwood Press, 1995, pp. 122–67.

Certainly one of the most scholarly treatments of this farce, Lifton's study finds the philosophical basis for the actions of Irene Molloy and Dolly Levi, placing them in the context of Wilder's plays in general.

McClatchy, J. D., "Wilder and the Marvels of the Heart," in the *New York Times Book Review,* April 15, 1997, p. 1.

This article looks with great appreciation at Wilder's comic instincts, relating biographical facts that shaped his easygoing style and attitude.

Walsh, Claudette, *Thornton Wilder: A Reference Guide, 1926–1990,* G. K. Hall & Co., 1993.

This 450-page bibliography refers readers to thousands of publications about Wilder.

Wilder, Amos Niven, "A Brother's Perspective," in *Readings on Thornton Wilder,* Greenhaven Press, 1998, pp. 145–53.

Wilder's brother Amos, himself a respected literary figure, has a unique summary of the author and his work.

The Mound Builders

LANFORD WILSON

1975

Lanford Wilson's *The Mound Builders* was first produced on February 2, 1975, in New York City at the Circle Repertory Company. It was directed by Wilson's long-time collaborator and co-founder of the ''Circle Rep,'' Marshall W. Mason. The play explores the conflicts between a team of visiting archeologists who are excavating several early Mississippian mounds and a local man who hopes to make his fortune by developing the land where the mounds are located. As the archeologists ponder and celebrate the dignity of the pre-Columbian people who built the mounds, they overlook the humanity of the people alive around them. The play is presented as a series of flashbacks, as August Howe, the chief archeologist, dictates notes about his slides from a recently ended expedition.

Wilson has said several times that *The Mound Builders* is his own favorite among his plays. It has not been his most successful play, either commercially or critically, in part because the issues and connections between the characters are so complicated and subtle that audiences miss much of what is going on. Wilson revised the play for a Circle Rep revival in 1986, deleting the character of Kirsten, August's daughter, but reviewers were still lukewarm. Readers of the published play (which is the 1975 version) have been able to better appreciate the play's richness. Though not currently in print as a separate volume, *The Mound Builders* is part of the collection *Lanford Wilson: Collected Works Volume II 1970–1983*.

AUTHOR BIOGRAPHY

Lanford Wilson was born on April 13, 1937, in Lebanon, Missouri. His father left the family when Wilson was five years old, and his mother took a job in a garment factory in Springfield. Six years later she remarried, and Wilson and his mother moved to his stepfather's farm near Ozark. As a teenager, Wilson discovered a love for the theater and acted in school plays. He also had a strong interest in art. After graduating from Ozark High School, Wilson went to California to try living with his father and to take courses in art and art history at San Diego State College. Neither the classes nor the reunion with his father went well, and he moved again a year later to Chicago to start a career as a graphic artist. He worked in an advertising agency and wrote short stories in his spare time. When he realized that the strongest part of his stories was the dialogue, he decided to try his hand at writing plays.

At twenty-five, Wilson left Chicago for Greenwich Village in New York City, determined to become a playwright. He worked at a series of odd jobs and attended the theater whenever he could, especially plays in the new off-off-Broadway movement. He met Joe Cino, founder of a coffeehouse that also staged new plays. Cino became his mentor and in 1963 staged Wilson's first production, *So Long at the Fair*, the first of ten plays by Wilson produced at the coffeehouse. By 1969, Wilson had several plays produced in New York, London, and other European cities. With three other artists, he founded the Circle Repertory Company to produce new plays. He served as a writer-in-residence, and the company produced more than a dozen of his plays over the next thirty years, while also encouraging other playwrights.

Wilson's plays have been critical as well as popular successes. He has won the New York Drama Critics' Circle Award twice, for *The Hot l Baltimore* (1973) and *Talley's Folley* (1980). *Talley's Folly* also won the Pulitzer Prize for Drama and was nominated for the Tony Award for Best Play. Wilson's own favorite of his plays, *The Mound Builders*, won the Obie Award in 1975, although it was not a popular success.

Wilson has had more than forty of his plays produced. Many of them saw their first productions at the Circle Repertory Theatre, and although he has had some success on Broadway, he has found his work with smaller repertory companies more satisfying. In 1998 and 2000, two new Wilson plays were produced at the Purple Rose Theatre in Chelsea, Michigan. One of them, *Books of Days* (1998), won the American Theatre Critics Award for best play in 1999.

Lanford Wilson

PLOT SUMMARY

Act 1

As the curtain rises on *The Mound Builders*, Professor August Howe, an archeologist, is alone in his office in Urbana, Illinois, looking at slides of ''last summer's expedition'' and dictating notes into a microphone. He shows a lake, a house, and an archeological dig. August and his slides will make frequent brief appearances throughout the play as a way to separate one scene from another. There are no breaks within the two acts; instead, short episodes merge into each other as flashbacks, illuminating and expanding August's dictated notes. In this opening scene, August shows several slides in succession as the audience hears sounds of a car stopping, and lights go up on another part of the stage to reveal the house where the archeologist lived. As August finishes his last line, Cynthia and Kirsten come down the stairs and begin the next scene.

Cynthia and Kirsten come to the door to welcome Dan and Jean, who have just arrived. Chad is finishing up a bit of maintenance, and August tells the group that his sister Delia is on her way from Cleveland. As Dan and Jean unload their car, the relationships among the characters become clear: August is married to Cynthia, and Kirsten is their daughter; Dan is August's assistant and Jean's husband; Chad, the caretaker, is the son of the man who owns the house. This will be the fourth summer that August and Dan have worked on this site, excavating mounds built by pre-Columbian people known as the Early Mississippians or the Mound Builders, who lived in great cities near the Mississippi River. This will also be their last chance to find artifacts in the mounds, because a new man-made lake and a planned interstate highway will soon cover the entire area.

Another scene follows with August showing more slides, many taken by Cynthia, the unofficial photographer for the project. He speaks mockingly of the townspeople from Blue Shoals, of the archeology students who helped with the digging, and of Cynthia and Kirsten, from whom he is now estranged. In the next series of flashbacks, the relationships between the characters are shown to be more strained than was revealed previously. Delia arrives, against her will, and meets Dan and Jean for the first time. She is angry about the care she was getting in Cleveland and angry about being sent to her brother, but she is clearly too ill to be on her own. Dan and Jean have never met Delia before, though both are familiar with her writing because Delia has published two popular books. Jean is a gynecologist and listens kindly to Delia's complaints about her health, while August mocks her. As Dan excitedly tells the women about the excavation, he makes fun of the local people and their questions but speaks admiringly of the Mound Builders. Throughout this scene and the rest of the play, Dan and Cynthia frequently use alcohol and marijuana (Jean has given up intoxicants for the duration of her pregnancy), Delia complains and sulks, and August criticizes Delia and patronizes Chad.

August's next slides show the beginning of the excavation and the screening of the first few inches of soil on the first mound. As the scenes in the present with August and his slides progress, they present a chronology of the dig over the four years, showing the most important artifacts. Toward the end of the play, they also show the rising water getting nearer the site. August's commentary becomes increasingly bitter and weary. As this third scene in the present ends, a slide of Chad standing in front of the lake merges into a flashback in which Chad tries to convince Jean to come to the courthouse to see the model of the development planned for the new lakeshore. He and his father expect to be wealthy beyond their wildest dreams when the new lake is completed and their land becomes the site of a highway interchange, new industry, resorts, and restaurants. Chad is excited about the money, and he hopes it will impress Jean enough that she will leave Dan for him; apparently Chad and Jean had a relationship the previous summer, before Jean and Dan married. But Chad is unsophisticated and uneducated, and Jean is not interested in him.

Jean has been at Blue Shoals only once before, and this is Delia's first visit, so Dan and Cynthia try to fill in the gaps in the women's knowledge. Dan provides a lesson on the ancient peoples who inhabited the area going back to A.D. 600, and Cynthia provides a spouse's eye view on what the men are looking for and recording. August and Dan can talk of nothing but the Mound Builders, while the women discuss their hopes and their lost dreams. Delia can no longer write, and Cynthia never became a professional photographer; Jean wonders whether she will have a medical career after her baby is born. Jean reveals that she was National Spelling Champion when she was twelve and that the effort led to her being institutionalized. Delia explains that her collapse was also caused by the pressure of success. Cynthia begins an affair with Chad and makes no attempt to hide it. Dan and Chad, both heavy drinkers, get drunk and go fishing together. When they return, Jean sends Chad home and Dan to bed, and she and Delia reflect on the sad roles of men and their wives.

Act 2

As the second act opens, it is evening and all of the adults are gathered and puzzling over the latest find from the dig: a man who is buried in an unexpected position. Chad tries again to connect with Jean, and August advises Jean not to socialize with Chad, whom he considers inferior. Rain falls steadily, making digging impossible and making the lake rise more quickly. Dan is frustrated. He admires a bone awl, made in approximately A.D. 1100, and imagines the nobility of the man who made it. The women discuss Chad's plans for the new development. Jean is sure Chad will soon be rich, but Cynthia believes that poor people will always be poor and that somehow Chad will be cheated out of his wealth.

As Jean and Delia sit reading one day, Dan bursts in with exciting news. The unusual burial site has turned out to be the tomb of an Early Mississippian God-King, an archeological wonder that no one has ever seen before. They have found a gold mask, a hoard of pearls and copper bracelets, and other treasures. They will be famous. Chad tries to determine the value of the artifacts, and Dan and August explain that the value is not in the worth of the gold itself but in the rarity of the find. As the men talk, several things are revealed. Chad learns that Jean is pregnant and realizes that he will never win her. He and the women discover that August and Dan arranged a year ago for the site to be protected by law. The planned highway has been moved, and Chad will not be able to sell or lease his land.

At these revelations, submerged hostilities are brought into the open. Chad leaves in anger but returns after dark to coax Dan outside. In the morning, both Chad and Dan are missing, their fishing boat found empty on the lake. The treasures from the tomb have disappeared, and Chad has driven a bulldozer over the site, ruining everything. When Cynthia deliberately destroys the film in her camera, the only record of the important find is lost. Police and volunteers arrive to drag the lake for the men's bodies, and Jean collapses into Delia's arms. As the play closes, August shows his last slide, of the house half-submerged in the still-rising lake.

MEDIA ADAPTATIONS

- *The Mound Builders* was produced for the PBS series *Theater in America (Great Performances)* in 1976, starring Trish Hawkins, Brad Dourif, and Tanya Berezin. It is available as a ninety-minute video from Insight Media.

CHARACTERS

D. K.

See Delia Eriksen

Delia Eriksen

Delia, or D. K., is August's mentally ill sister, aged thirty-eight. In her twenties, she wrote two books of fiction that made her a popular and critical success; her books were so well regarded that Dan studied them in a college literature course. Lately, however, D. K. has been known primarily for her eccentric and drunken living. She has come to Blue Shoals to stay with August because, penniless, she has suffered another in a series of breakdowns and has nowhere else to go. She and August have never approved of each other, and they seem to have spent their youth competing for their father's respect. D. K. spends most of the play bundled in a chair, physically ill and cynical about her own work and about August's project. At the end of the play, however, she is the one who most clearly sees the motives and strengths of the other characters, the one who, in Wilson's words, is "strong enough to comfort the others." She is dressed to leave for good on the morning that Dan turns up missing, and August is glad to see her leaving. Instead, however, she stays and holds onto Jean.

In an interview with Gene A. Barnett, Wilson explained that he had created the character of Delia with the actor Tanya Berezin, a member of the Circle Repertory, in mind. Berezin "had said she couldn't play a genius, and she also had a great fear of comedy, of being funny." Once he had the basic idea for Delia, Wilson shaped the character specifically to provide a comic genius to challenge Berezin.

August Howe

August is the head archeologist on the dig, the person around whom all the action revolves. Cynthia and Kirsten are his family; Dan is his assistant; Delia is his sister; Chad is his landlord, his temporary rival for Cynthia's affections, and his rival for a claim to the land on which the mounds are located. August is forty years old, a respected but not famous archeologist employed by a large university. This is his fourth summer digging near the town of Blue Shoals, Illinois, where he and his team are excavating mounds built by early Mississippian people. They have uncovered pieces of pottery and one excellent bone awl, which August carefully records in his notes.

The land on which the mounds are located will soon be along the shores of a new lake that will be created by the Blue Shoals Dam. Chad, the owner of the home where August stays in the summer, hopes to be rich when the new highway comes through, because he owns the land on which a Holiday Inn and a golf course will sit. August sees Chad as inferior to him in social class and education and treats him with determined disrespect. Secretly, August has already arranged with the State of Illinois to re-route the new highway to protect the mounds. Chad will never be rich, and August has never bothered to tell him why.

When August and his team locate the tomb of a God-King, he expects to finally have the recognition that has eluded him. In the end, however, he loses everything: his family, his artifacts, his assistant, and his job. In the scenes in his study in Urbana, Illinois, during which he looks at slides from the expedition, August is bitter and cynical. In the flashback scenes, he is generally distant, often passing silently through a room where people are talking, to head for his study. He does not share Dan's passions for archeology and for imagining the people who came before him. In fact, August is much more likely to be found in his study than out in the mud. He is impatient and even cruel with Delia, and he either does not notice or does not care that Cynthia is having an affair with Chad. But when Kirsten awakens in the night and calls for her mother, it is August who comforts her.

Cynthia Howe

Cynthia, age thirty-five, is August's wife and Kirsten's mother. When she was younger, she dreamed of a career as a photographer, but after Kirsten was born she never got back to it. She has never found something to be passionate about in place of her career. Now she takes pictures in an unofficial way for August; the slides August is looking at in the "frame" scenes were shot by Cynthia. She has learned quite a bit about the expedition over the years and passes along her knowledge and her humorous perceptions of the men to Jean and Delia. Underneath her ironic attitudes, Cynthia is restless and unhappy, especially in her marriage. She drinks too much and throws herself at Chad, but none of it helps. When she learns that August has deceived Chad about his property rights, she takes the only action she can think of to express her disdain for August: she ruins the film with the only existing photographs of the artifacts from the God-King tomb so that August will have nothing to show for his discovery. Chad rejects her anyway. After the summer's events, Cynthia divorces August and obtains custody of Kirsten.

Kirsten Howe

Kirsten is the eleven-year-old daughter of August and Cynthia. She does not have much to do in Blue Shoals or in the play. Early on, she awakens from a bad dream in which she hears voices and is comforted by August. At other times, she hovers in the background, occasionally making a bored or sullen comment. When Wilson revised the play in 1986, he deleted the character of Kirsten.

Chad Jasker

Chad, twenty-five, is the son of the man who owns the land on which the summer house and the mounds are located. He serves as a general caretaker for the archeologists, fixing windows and carrying gear. August condescends to him, but Jean and Chad were romantically involved the previous summer, Cynthia has an affair with him during the summer of the play, and Chad and Dan drink and fish together. Chad is not educated as the others are, and he both admires and despises them because of this. He dreams of the day when he will be wealthy and therefore equal or superior to them. Chad is disappointed that Jean has married Dan; he had hoped that she would share his new life. When he learns that she is pregnant and that August has arranged for the highway to bypass his land, he runs the bulldozer over the dig site and lures Dan outside. Earlier, Chad saved Dan's life, but now he takes it away. The empty fishing boat is found the next morning, but neither man is seen again.

Dr. Dan Loggins

Dan, twenty-nine years old, is August's assistant and Jean's husband. Dan has worked with August for four years, and he and Jean have gotten married since the previous summer's expedition. Dan is passionate about archeology. He loves to spend time in the mud digging for artifacts (unlike August, who prefers office work) and to spin imaginative tales of what ancient humans were like. He also likes to drink and use drugs, which he does whenever he is not on the site. Dan is open and friendly, and he has earned the nickname Pollyandy, after the eternally optimistic fictional character Pollyanna. He socializes easily with Chad, though August discourages it. The previous summer, Chad saved Dan's life, and this has created a friendly bond between them as they drink and fish together now. Dan has no suspicion that Chad carries a grudge against him, and even after the deception about the new highway is revealed, Dan willingly goes out with Chad after dark.

Dr. Jean Loggins

Jean, twenty-five, is a gynecologist married to Dan. She is bright and optimistic, a former spelling champion and a dedicated wife. The previous summer she accompanied Dan to Blue Shoals, but she was not married to him then, and she gave Chad some cause to believe that he might have a chance with her. This summer, however, she is married to Dan and pregnant again after two miscarriages. She has been working in a clinic but has taken an eighteen-month leave to have the baby and plans to spend the summer in Blue Shoals resting, reading professional journals, and typing up Dan's notes. Chad, unaware of the pregnancy, tries to rekindle their former relationship and hopes to impress her with his plans for developing the shores of the new lake, but she pushes him away. She is the only member of the party who takes Delia seriously, and it is to Delia that she turns when Dan dies.

THEMES

Betrayal

Among its other themes, *The Mound Builders* is an examination of betrayal. All of the adult characters gathered in the house in Blue Shoals are bright and capable people; what keeps them from reaching their goals is a pattern of betrayal—real and merely perceived, large and small—visited on the characters by each other.

Chad, for example, destroys the dig site and probably kills Dan and himself. From his point of view, however, Chad is more victim than criminal. He reveals that he values two things above all others: Jean ("the only thing I ever saw I really wanted") and his future riches. Both have been taken from him by the actions of others. The summer before, when he was involved with Jean, he "didn't really figure" that she would marry Dan. In his mind, Jean has betrayed him by marrying Dan and is "trying to make a fool" of him now. The betrayals by Dan, whose life Chad saved the previous summer, increase through the play: he has taken Jean away, he has gotten her pregnant, and he is part of the secret machinations to have the highway moved.

Cynthia also betrays and is betrayed. She betrays August by having an affair with Chad. When she learns that August has deceived them all about the plans for the highway, she herself feels betrayed, because her photographs were used without her knowledge to persuade the authorities to protect the dig site. She acts against August again by exposing the film that has the only photos of the God-King's artifacts.

August is at the center of the cycle of betrayal. He is the instigator of the plan to keep Chad from getting rich. He and his father have betrayed the bonds of family for many years by making a fool of Delia. August is cruel enough to tell Delia about their betrayal: "Dad never read a word you wrote. He quoted your reviews back to you verbatim and laughed behind your back because you never noticed." The only honest relationship in August's life is his friendship with Dan, and August's betrayal of Chad leads to Dan's death.

In the end, of course, betrayal leads to unhappiness and loss. Dan and Chad are dead. August and Cynthia are divorced. Delia and August will be forever estranged. The expedition has come to ruin. The play ends pessimistically; there seems to be no way to protect oneself from betrayal. In Jean's mind, Dan died because he was too innocent: "WHY DID HE TRUST PEOPLE, WHY DID HE BELIEVE IN THINGS?" Whether they are trusting or cynical, most of the characters in *The Mound Builders* hurt each other in the end.

Permanence and Impermanence

The world of *The Mound Builders* is a cruel one. Not only do people betray each other, but the simple passage of time makes everything people do turn to dust. The constant action of the universe is to destroy, yet, even knowing this, the primal urge of people is to try to build something permanent. In the introduction to *Lanford Wilson: Collected Works Volume II 1970–1983,* Wilson wrote that even in the earliest drafts of the play, he realized that "at the burning heart of the theme was: Why do we strive to achieve? To build, to make our mark? Why are we Mound Builders?"

TOPICS FOR FURTHER STUDY

- Research the early Mississippian cultures that thrived along the Mississippi River from about A.D. 600 to 1100. What is known about these cultures? What is still unknown?
- Investigate the local tensions in your area between land developers and those who resist development. What are the developers trying to create? What are their opponents trying to preserve? Which group do you support, and why?
- Interview a woman in your community who has both children and a challenging career. What challenges did she face in balancing work and family when her children were infants? How have the challenges changed as her career and/or her children have grown?
- Research the Hetch Hetchy Dam, built in California in 1913. How are the controversies surrounding the building of the dam echoed in the effects of the Blue Shoals Dam in *The Mound Builders*?
- Who was the Apache chief Cochise? In what ways is he an appropriate metaphor for the things Dan is trying to explain in his long speech about the Mound Builders? In what ways is Dan being respectful or disrespectful?

The parallels between the pre-Columbian Mound Builders and the modern characters trying to make *something* echo throughout the play. Dan makes the comparison plain early in the play, when he answers an imaginary girl's question: "Why did they build the mounds? They built the mounds for the same reason I'd build the mounds." There are frequent references to the past and records from the past. The Mound Builders lived from about A.D. 600 to 1100, and the poetry, pots, and bone awls they left behind are the foundation for what August and Dan are trying to accomplish. Delia compares the house in Blue Shoals to a painting by the Midwestern artist Grant Wood and compares her life to the Charles Dickens novel *Dombey and Son.* Chad cites local folklore, and Dan quotes Confucius (or tries to), when the two are drinking together. Jean quotes an old Chinese proverb. August compares Cynthia's work with that of famed photographer Diane Arbus. Dan's nickname, Pollyandy, is a reference to Pollyanna, a fictional character from a series of early twentieth-century novels. These references demonstrate that the past is useful in the present: people can use what others have left behind to help them live today.

All of the adult characters are trying to create something that will live on after they are gone. August and Dan are trying to build a national monument as well as careers and a reputation, "to conquer lost worlds with a doctorate in one hand and a trowel in the other." Jean wants to make a family and after two miscarriages in less than a year is cautiously optimistic about her current pregnancy. Chad plans to build a motel, a golf course, and a restaurant. Delia has written two books that will endure, and her inability to write more has driven her to alcohol and despair. Cynthia makes photographs, and although she is not as talented as the famous Diane Arbus, she is responsible for the visual record of August and Dan's work. (She is also the only one who chooses to destroy her own work.)

None of it is any good. August and Dan's work is destroyed, first by Chad and the bulldozer and then again by the floods. Jean, presumably, will deliver a healthy baby, but she will not have the family she dreamed of because her husband is dead. Chad is also dead, after being cheated out of his planned development. Delia and Cynthia may find new outlets for their art, or they may sink deeper into drink. As for the Mound Builders, their pots and bone awls and gold beads lie at the bottom of the lake, buried again as they were for nine hundred years before August came along. The cycle is complete—until another group of archeologists finds the artifacts and dreams of using them to build something permament.

STYLE

Frame

As the curtain rises on *The Mound Builders*, August Howe is in his study in Urbana, Illinois, dictating notes into a tape recorder as he looks at slides of ''the wreckage of last summer's expedition.'' The slides are projected onto a wall on the stage so the audience can see them, and the first series includes pictures of the lake, the house, the construction of the dam, the bulldozer, and the dig itself. Although most of the action of the play happens in Blue Shoals, Illinois, the Blue Shoals scenes are flashbacks, and the present time is February in Urbana. Twelve times throughout the play, scenes of August in his study are interspersed with scenes of the characters living out the events recorded in August's notes and Cynthia's slides.

This framing device has several effects. Mechanically, it enables Wilson to provide images for his audience that would not be possible to present in live action. The characters talk to each other inside the house, but much of what they talk about is outside: ''August up to his a—— in mud,'' the mounds as they are excavated and after they are flattened by a bulldozer, the rising lake. Wilson cannot have a bulldozer run over a mound on stage, but the slides enable him to show a picture of it stuck in the mud afterward. Other items, such as a pot from the excavation and the bone awl, are too small to show the audience in detail, but the slides enable the audience to gain a deeper understanding of the artifacts the team is finding.

Another important effect of the framing device is to cast doubt on everything that happens between the characters. If the Blue Shoals scenes are August's memories of events, how reliable are they? Of all the characters in the house, August is the least engaged; he spends most of his time alone in his study and hurries through the room where others are talking. He is angry with Delia for being a burden on him, and after the summer, he is angry with Cynthia and Kirsten for leaving him. He has never respected Chad and must feel even less regard for him after, it may be assumed, Chad kills Dan and himself. It is likely that these events and emotions have colored August's memories of the summer. And if he did not even notice that his wife was having an affair (and making little effort to hide it), how accurately can he remember conversations? Wilson points out in the stage directions that ''the house is seen from August's memory,'' and the same must be said of all of the flashback scenes. The frame repeatedly reminds the audience that the play is itself an artifact. It is imperfect, as all artifacts are, but it is all we have.

Foreshadowing

When a writer drops clues about what is going to happen in a story—especially clues to unhappy or evil events—those clues are said to foreshadow future events. In *The Mound Builders*, Wilson leaves no doubt from the very beginning that the play is going to end unhappily. One of August's first lines in the first scene is a reference to ''the wreckage of last summer's expedition,'' and audiences who have seen Wilson's earlier play *The Hot l Baltimore* know that the slide of the bulldozer in the first scene foreshadows future destruction.

Many of August's slides and comments refer to events before they happen on stage. In his second series of slides are pictures of Cynthia, whom he twice refers to as his ''ex-relation.'' Halfway through the play, he comments that ''by the time the lake over-ran the site, it didn't matter at all.'' He later reveals that his years of work ultimately came to ''a salvage operation from which we salvaged nothing.'' Other elements of foreshadowing include Delia looking into the future at a ''sad old world of widows'' on the shore ''looking out over the water''; Dan making Jean uncomfortable by putting on the death mask; and Cynthia telling Jean that Chad will never get rich, that he and his father will ''have the whole property extorted out from under them.'' All of these moments (some more overt than others) indicate what is going to happen before it actually occurs.

Why would an author do this? Why spoil the surprise? Wilson uses foreshadowing to shift the audience's attention from the plot and onto the underlying themes. In other words, the plot itself is not the main point in this play; the play is about ideas. Wilson is concerned less with *what* happens than with *why*. By relieving the audience from the responsibility of keeping track of the action, he makes it easier for them to focus on motivation and cause.

HISTORICAL CONTEXT

The Drug Culture of the 1970s

For readers in the twenty-first century, the casual drug use by the characters in *The Mound Builders* may seem surprising. Contrary to the stereotype today of drug users as primarily young, poor, and uneducated, the marijuana and mescaline users in the play are in their twenties and thirties, middle class, and highly educated. Dan, the heaviest drug user, has a doctoral degree and works for a major university. Jean is a medical doctor, who has a history of being a ''drughead'' but who has gone ''cold turkey'' for the duration of her pregnancy. These characters are not meant to be seen as perverse or unusual but as fairly typical young professionals for whom recreational drug use is nothing to hide. In fact, the period of the 1970s saw the highest rate of drug use in the nation's history.

Before the second world war, drugs were difficult to obtain. Working with other countries to reduce production of opium poppies and coca, the United States was able to prevent most drugs from entering the country. Drug use was scarcely recognized as a social problem. The bursting economy after the war and advances in production methods led to many benefits for the country but also led to an increase in drug use. Beginning in the 1960s and continuing through the 1970s, the United States had a large population of middle-class young people who had the money to buy drugs and a ready supply of drugs. In the 1960s, marijuana became widely available for the first time, and psychedelic drugs were said to help users ''expand their consciousness.'' In the era of Watergate and the end of the Vietnam War, drug use became a sign of rebellion for many people who needed a way to distance themselves from what they saw as an immoral society. Because many of the drug users were middle-class, use became somewhat casual and acceptable (although still illegal) in most places, which helped spread drug use even further. The 1970s saw the re-emergence of cocaine, which had virtually disappeared after the 1920s but later was now seen as a sign of power and status because of its high cost. Some celebrities made no secret of their drug use. Drugs were celebrated in movies and in music, and a comedy team named Cheech and Chong made a career of mocking and championing the drug culture.

By 1979, government figures estimated that one in ten Americans was using recreational drugs. Since that time, drug use has continued to be a major problem for the United States, but the numbers of users and the casual nature of their use has not been equaled.

The Nation's First Energy Crisis

In the early 1970s, the United States was enjoying a period of cheap energy and a growing economy. The idea of conserving energy was far from the minds of most Americans, who imagined energy to be so limitless that they never really considered it at all. Like the early settlers who could not imagine this huge country ever running low on land or on buffalo, Americans had a disturbing awakening in 1973. Suddenly, large cities found they could not meet the demand for electricity to power the air-conditioners and other electrical appliances that had multiplied faster than energy companies' capacity to produce power. This led to periods of low power over large areas, called ''brown outs,'' as utility companies simply could not produce enough power. Rates increased rapidly.

In October of 1973, the members of the Organization of Petroleum Exporting Countries (OPEC) staged an embargo, which means they intentionally reduced the amount of oil they would sell to other nations, including the United States. The effect was immediate and dramatic. In the United States, customers found long lines at gas stations, and in some areas customers were allowed to buy gasoline only on certain days. In December, the national Christmas tree went without lights as a symbol that all Americans needed to use less energy.

The price of oil rose from three dollars a barrel in 1973 to thirty dollars a barrel in 1980, leading to a worldwide recession. In the United States, it seemed important to reduce dependency on foreign oil. Federal laws called for energy conservation and encouraged the development of alternative sources of energy. Funding became available for solar, wind, and hydroelectric power development. This led directly to projects similar to Wilson's fictional Blue Shoals Dam, which would provide hydroelectric power and, incidentally, create a lake and all its accompanying tourist activity. As Jean says to Chad,

COMPARE & CONTRAST

- **1975:** The first software to operate a personal computer is developed, but personal computers are not generally available. Scientists in major universities have access to large mainframe computers, but archeologists in the field make notes with pen and paper and have them typed up on electric typewriters.

  Today: Many homes in the United States have at least one personal computer, and many people have portable laptop computers. Archeological projects sponsored by universities use computers, global positioning satellite systems, digital cameras, cellular phones, and other electronic equipment.

- **1975:** The United States remains under pressure from the energy crisis of 1973 and continuing fuel shortages. The federal government passes various energy bills to help the country become less dependent on foreign oil and encourages the production of wind farms, solar panels, and dams.

  Today: Foreign oil dependency is still a major concern for the United States. Federal policy concentrates on increased domestic production of oil.

- **1975:** Although women have nearly all the same legal rights as men and many women have active and successful careers, it is still unusual for a woman to maintain her career after she becomes a mother. Few day care centers exist, and only affluent women can afford to hire child care.

  Today: Many women pursue careers, even as physicians and photographers, after the birth of their children. Good quality child care is available to most middle- and upper-class women, although mothers with lower incomes still find it difficult to arrange child care.

- **1975:** The town of Bull Shoals, Arkansas, likely a model for Blue Shoals, Illinois, is a resort community with motels, restaurants, boat rentals, golf courses, and other attractions along the shores of Bull Shoals Lake, created by the Bull Shoals Dam in the late 1940s.

  Today: Bulls Shoals enjoys continued prosperity, as the number of tourists and permanent residents increased by more than 25 percent in the 1990s.

''The signing of an energy bill in Washington transforms rural areas into resorts—field hands into busboys.''

CRITICAL OVERVIEW

Although *The Mound Builders* is Wilson's favorite of his plays, it has not been the favorite of critics. For the most part, it is fair to say that the play has been more widely admired by those who have read it and studied it as a text than by those who have seen it performed. Both groups agree that the play is complicated and literary, even ''opaque''—just the type of play that is often more rewarding to readers, who can pause and retrace their steps to confirm connections. And most critics who have studied Wilson's career have found that Wilson did not hit his stride and produce fine, mature work until the Talley family plays a few years after *The Mound Builders*.

When the play opened off-Broadway in 1975, Wilson and the Circle Repertory were already important enough to draw the attention of New York's most influential reviewers. For Wilson, this was both good and bad. His play was reviewed in the *New York Times* and important magazines, but the reviews were not favorable. Edith Oliver, reviewer for the *New Yorker,* described an ''elaborate production of a dim and insubstantial play.'' She admired Wilson's ability to write dialogue, writing ''the lines are speakable, and there are a number of good, funny ones,'' but did not believe the characters to be ''based on any firsthand observation, or even on memory.'' Stanley Kauffmann, on the other hand, found the play's ''authentic base—in Wilson's well-known feeling for the Midwest'' to be its strongest virtue. Kauffmann's review for the *New Republic* described moments of ''real wit'' and ''genuine feeling'' but concluded that ''Wilson lacks the intellectual depth to make the schema fruitful or the art to keep it from the mere filling-out of a pattern.'' The most positive review was Harold Clurman's for the *Nation.* Clurman called the play ''Wilson's most ambitious'' and the play's idea ''provocative and unmistakably felt.'' He found himself ''strangely disturbed'' by the play's ''density as well as the pull and tear of motivations and thoughts evoked and left unresolved,'' and he concluded that the play ''is one I genuinely respect even in my dissatisfaction with it.''

The play was revived by Circle Repertory in 1986 with a slightly revised script. In this new version, the character of Kirsten was deleted, and other changes were made to sharpen the conflicts, but the critics were not much impressed. Reviewing the revival for *New York* magazine, John Simon commented, ''Even the most talented playwrights cannot score all the time.'' He found the play ''rather opaque'' and joked that the characters and their issues were so difficult to empathize with that ''It's all just making mounds out of molehills.'' John Beaufort, writing for the *Christian Science Monitor,* agreed, praising ''the gifts that have served Mr. Wilson so admirably in other works'' but finding that in this play ''the characters and their problems arouse no particular concern.''

Literary critics have focused on delineating the central conflicts of the play and on showing how the play fits into Wilson's body of work. In his Twayne overview *Lanford Wilson,* Gene A. Barnett intentionally sidesteps the play's weaknesses to focus on its strengths: ''Thematically, *The Mound Builders* is Wilson's most complicated play, and any flaw in the work does not mitigate the validity of its themes.'' Barnett examines the themes of conflict between man's dreams and reality and ''the cyclical repetition of history and culture.'' Only one scholarly article devoted entirely to *The Mound Builders* has been published, Johan Callens's ''When 'the Center Cannot Hold.''' Callens examines the play as both ''an exploration of the psychological tensions that arise when people from different professions and classes'' come together and as ''an investigation of the nature of reality and man's relation to it.'' Mark Busby, author of a brief monograph entitled *Lanford Wilson,* traces the play's themes of ''work, family, and betrayal'' through several other of Wilson's plays. He admits that reviewers did not admire the play in performance but finds that ''its complexity makes it perhaps his most satisfying play to read.''

CRITICISM

Cynthia A. Bily

Bily teaches English at Adrian College in Adrian, Michigan. In the following essay, Bily examines Wilson's uses of parallels in The Mound Builders *to show the connections between Dan and Chad, characters who seem on the surface to be dissimilar.*

Lanford Wilson's *The Mound Builders* is a play about time and human attempts to outrun it. All of the characters dig into the past—literally and figuratively—to find materials with which to build a future, and in their attempts they get in one another's way and prevent one another from achieving their goals. Since everything in the play is filtered through August's consciousness, his personality and his struggles are easy to see. As August understands it, he has lost his life's work because of his own deception and because of a conflict between two young men, one good and one evil. Wilson, however, indicates not only that August's work was perhaps doomed from the beginning but that the characters of Dan and Chad are more complex and more similar than August realizes.

The title *The Mound Builders* refers to the Temple Mound people, the early Mississippian people who built burial mounds between A.D. 600 and 1100. Wilson has written, though, that he intended the title phrase to encompass all of the characters and, in fact, all people. In his introduction to the play in *Lanford Wilson: Collected Plays Volume II 1970–1983,* he explains that ''at the burning heart of the theme was: Why do we strive to achieve? To build, to make our mark? Why are we Mound Builders?'' The ''we'' is telling here. We are all Mound Builders. Wilson has created a play whose characters ''somehow reflected that culture,'' and his challenge as a playwright is to make that reflection clear to the audience. He achieves this through

WHAT DO I READ NEXT?

- *Talley's Folly,* first produced in 1979, is Wilson's most award-winning play. Like *The Mound Builders,* it deals with uncovering secrets from the past, but in *Talley's Folly* love is attainable, people can be trusted, and the atmosphere is sweet.
- *Fifth of July,* produced in 1978, is another of Wilson's plays set in a big house near a lake in the Midwest with a small group of extended family members and friends. Ken, a wounded Vietnam War veteran, has decided to sell the family home without consulting his family or his lover and must weigh money against family to find the course of action that will make him happy.
- Michael Ondaatje's novel *Anil's Ghost,* published in 2000, is about an anthropologist and an archeologist who examine human remains found in Sri Lanka. They suspect that the bones are not ancient but are instead the bones of political prisoners tortured with the government's knowledge.
- *The Mississippian Moundbuilders and Their Artifacts* is available on the World Wide Web at http://www.mississippian-artifacts.com and features a collection of well-documented photographs. The artifacts pictured are similar to those found by August Howe and his team.
- *Cahokia: The Great Native American Metropolis,* by the writer Biloine Whiting Young and the archeologist Melvin L. Fowler, was published in 1999. It offers an overview of what is known about the site which, like the area being studied in *The Mound Builders,* was an early Mississippian city in Illinois.
- Kathleen King's novel *Cricket Sings: A Novel of Pre-Columbian Cahokia,* published in 1995, tells the story of a young woman living with her family in Cahokia.

highlighting parallels between the pre-Columbian people and the modern-day characters and between Dan Loggins and Chad Jasker. In doing so, he also makes his characters more complex, less clearly good and evil.

The most obvious parallel comes near the beginning, when Dan is making fun of the townspeople of Blue Shoals and what he perceives as their stupid questions:

> ''Why did they build the mounds?'' They built the mounds for the same reason I'd build the mounds. Because I wanted to make myself conspicuous; to sacrifice to the gods; to protect me from floods, or animals; because my grandfather built mounds; because I was sick of digging holes; because I didn't have the technology to build pyramids and a person isn't happy unless he's building something.

Dan's answer is somewhat facetious; he believes the answer to the question is so obvious that no one should even have to ask it. But his answer serves several important functions in the play.

Dan's comment that ''they built the mounds for the same reason I'd build the mounds'' states a direct connection between the prehistoric people and modern people. We are all the same kind of people. The adult characters in the play are all trying ''to leave something behind,'' to build something—reputations, books, photographic records, children, buildings, a monument. Once Wilson has established that the archeologists are in this way like their subjects and that the man who wants to build a golf course is like the man who wants to build a temple, he can help us examine how different characters manifest that similarity.

The question that Dan is mocking is a question that Wilson thinks is central to the play's theme: ''Why did they build the mounds?'' or, in Wilson's words, ''Why are we Mound Builders?'' The fact that Dan takes the question so lightly says something about his character. On the one hand, he is filled with respect for the Temple Mound people

"HOW CAN DAN NOT GO WITH CHAD? ANOTHER MAN MIGHT BE SUSPICIOUS AND REFUSE TO GO OUT IN THE DARK WITH A MAN WHOM HE HAS CHEATED AND WHOM HE HAS FOUND STEALING PRICELESS ARTIFACTS, BUT DAN DOES NOT HESITATE. HE AND CHAD SPEAK THE SAME LANGUAGE. . . ."

because they fulfilled the human need to build something. He has devoted his professional life to understanding and preserving what remains of their culture and has published a book on the subject. He speaks of his typical Mound Builder chief ''Cochise'' with awe and reverence. Why, then, can't he understand Chad's need to build? Is Chad's need so different from Dan's? Dan is like the *Peanuts* character who proclaimed, ''I love humanity; it's people I can't stand.'' Dan is an academic who loves ancient cultures but has nothing but disdain for the townspeople and the students in his life. Even as he says, ''Listen to Chad Jasker tell you about the restaurant he's going to build,'' Dan knows that Chad is never going to have the chance. Dan and August have already seen to it that the highway will be moved, and therefore Chad's land will not make him rich. Why should Chad's desire to build a restaurant be thought of as less noble than the Temple Mound people's desire to build a burial mound? Because Chad would profit from his project? Doesn't he want to build ''for the same reason'' they did? By setting the two building projects side-by-side early in the play and by putting the comparison in Dan's mouth, Wilson makes it harder for us to see Dan and August as the ''good guys'' and Chad as the bad.

Wilson will continue to show that Dan and Chad are as alike as they are different, and Dan will continue to miss the similarities. For one thing, they both love the same woman, Jean. In the scene in which the two men are drunk and fishing, Dan praises Jean's intelligence and beauty and twice tells Chad, ''you wouldn't believe it.'' Of course, Chad does believe it and loves Jean for these qualities, but Dan has no inkling of Chad's feelings.

Because of the differences in their social class and education, Chad, too, believes that he and Dan are different kinds of people. He tells Dan and August, ''I admire you people. You're really trying to make something of yourself.'' Neither archeologist steps in to say that Chad, too, is trying to ''make something'' of himself, but Cynthia does, pointing out that ''They wouldn't have the patience to bust down a transmission.'' Chad brushes her off.

But Wilson demonstrates in one more way that the instinct to build is the same in both men. They not only want to build, but they want people to know they've built. As Dan explained earlier, he can understand that a Mound Builder would build something ''Because I wanted to make myself conspicuous.'' Throughout the play, Chad urges Jean to come with him to the courthouse to see the scale model of his proposed development. He tells her, ''there's something I want you to see''; ''I want to show you''; ''you ought to look at it.'' When Chad finally realizes that he is not going to get his highway interchange, Cynthia's first reflex is to try to compensate him with something. Jean also tries to appease him by telling him, ''Chad, I went down to the courthouse; I saw the model you told me to see.'' He ignores both women; it is too late for them to help him.

The other character who repeatedly wants to show people things is Dan. He grumbles about townspeople coming out to the dig to see what they're doing, but, as Jean says, ''He loves it, of course; he performs for them like a dancing bear.'' When he stumbles home drunk after fishing with Chad, he wants Jean to come out and see the big fish he's caught. It's not enough to have caught it and not enough to just tell her about it. Even though it's late at night and cold, and Jean is barefoot, he insists, ''Come out and look. Come—Would you come out here and look?'' Later, when the team finally finds the tomb of the God-King, the archeological find of a lifetime, Dan's first urge is to show it to Jean: ''Jean, Jean, Jean, Jean—come out—come down.'' He even wants Delia to come see the tomb (''Delia, if you don't come and see this, I'll never read another word''), although she has been ill and scarcely out of bed all summer. If she can't make it to the site, he will carry her on his back.

When Chad decides to have his terrible revenge, it is Dan with whom he is most angry. He felt closer to Dan than to August. Because they shared so much in common, Dan's betrayal is the most hurtful. Chad knows just how to coax Dan outside to his death: he says, ''I got something I want to show you''; ''There's something outside I want to show you''; ''I want to show you something.'' How can Dan not go with Chad? Another man might be suspicious and refuse to go out in the dark with a man whom he has cheated and whom he has found stealing priceless artifacts, but Dan does not hesitate. He and Chad speak the same language, they think the same way, they want the same things. When Chad calls, Dan follows.

In comparing Dan and Chad, Wilson seems to be saying that the blame for the disaster falls equally on all shoulders—or at least equally on the male shoulders. The role of the women seems to be to record and admire what the men accomplish. Delia feels sorry for men, ''depressing poor bastards, breaking their balls for their families. We're their reflection, I suppose, but I don't know as they love us for it.'' When it is all over, however, it is the women who have truly made things that will outlive them: Delia's books, Cynthia's photographs, and Jean's child. They have created without fanfare or praise: August only makes fun of Cynthia's photographs; it is when Delia seeks approval from others that she finds herself unable to write; and Jean tries to keep her pregnancy a secret. It would be stretching things to say that Wilson was writing a feminist play when he created *The Mound Builders*. But it is fair to say that he took pains to show that Dan and Chad are more similar than they appear and that their similarity is wrapped up in their maleness and in their masculine approach to what it means to be a Mound Builder.

Source: Cynthia A. Bily, Critical Essay on *The Mound Builders,* in *Drama for Students,* The Gale Group, 2003.

Johan Callens

In the following essay, Callens discusses Wilson's intent, his characters, and critical response to The Mound Builders.

The Mound Builders, was first produced by New York's Circle Repertory Company on February 2, 1975, under the guidance of Marshall W. Mason, Lanford Wilson's usual director. It could have been the simple story of how ''The signing of an energy bill in Washington transforms rural areas into resorts.'' But important archeological discoveries determined it otherwise. In Wilson's play the decision to build the Blue Shoals Dam in Southern Illinois indeed interferes with the excavation of remnants from the Early Mississippian Culture. The ensuing complications are enough to expand a commonplace idea—based on the true though partial destruction of the historical site of Cahokia by encroaching civilization—into an exceptional play, given, of course, the help of a good playwright who has for the occasion sharpened his pen into an etcher's needle.

To Chad Jasker, the landowner's son, the lake created by the dam cannot fill up fast enough, the new highway and interchange should have been there already, together with the hotels, motels, restaurants, tennis courts and golf course, so that the tourists can start to enjoy themselves and the money to pour in. Chad and his father have in fact made agreements with the developers about the percentage they ought to get on every dollar spent. The archeologists, however, Prof. August Howe and his assistant, Dr. Dan Loggins, for a fourth consecutive summer down at the site with their respective wives, Cynthia and Jean, are ''racing time'' against the lake. It has been a ''sopping spring'' and the summer rains do not let up, with the result that the water level is rising fast. To make things worse, August is saddled with his ailing sister, Delia, an itinerant writer whom he flew down from a Cleveland hospital where she was stranded, broke, and briefly suffering from amnesia.

Under these conditions work is not easy, but as long as the Jasker Village proves to be typical, the archeological team has grudgingly accepted that its excavation is to be a mere salvage operation. Yet once the grave of a God-King has been discovered—for the first time ever the atmosphere becomes more hectic and desperate. For the lake brooks no resistance, in contrast to the developers whom August had little trouble in warding off by appealing to a state law against public-funded construction defacing Indian monuments: ''a brief report, a few pictures, and a phone call'' is all it had taken him two years ago to have the legislature reroute the highway to the other side of the lake. The foresighted scientist could not foresee everything, though: through August's intervention, Chad sees his life's dream wiped out in an instant. As a result, the night after the great discovery, he takes off with the few artefacts already unearthed from the tomb, followed by Dan who caught him redhandedly, and runs a bulldozer over the site. The next morning both men have disappeared. Only an oar from Chad's boat is found floating near the center of the lake. Any efforts to find the men, however, remain unsuccessful.

"WILSON'S CRITICISM OF CONTEMPORARY SOCIETY, AS WELL AS THE ALTERNATIVE HE BRIEFLY SKETCHES, PARTLY BY IMAGINATIVELY BRINGING TO LIFE A LOST AMERINDIAN CULTURE, SEEMS INSPIRED A GREAT DEAL BY EXISTENTIALISM."

These are the bare facts of a play that is presented as an extended recollection: while from his study in Urbana, Illinois, August is dictating into a tape-recorder comments on the slides from the expedition, past events materialize on stage. They do so intermittently, for every now and then the dramatic action is exchanged again for the illustrated narrative, which has the advantage of permitting jumps in time. The use of a narrator and of slides is no easy attempt on the part of a mainstream dramatist to reinforce one of his plays with Brechtian techniques and to pass it off as a docu-drama or modernist experiment. The slides certainly enliven the production and instruct the average spectator or layman about the nature of archeological fieldwork in general and about the Early Mississippian Culture in particular. Incidentally, when writing the play Wilson was assisted by Dr. Howard Winter from the Department of Anthropology of New York University. The speed with which the slides follow one another also influences the play's pace and never goes without any emotional impact: now their fast succession expresses August's anger and frustration, now the uninterrupted accumulation of shots from the lake charges it with an ominous, symbolic power. Yet, none of these is the slides' major function, which is that of leading up to the play's central problem, the mediation of reality. The frame establishes a distance between the present (February) and the layered past (immediate—the previous summer—or remote—the Mound Builders), between the nearby (Urbana) and the far away (Blue Shoals), an exemplary distance which the audience is never allowed to forget throughout the enacted sections of the play.

I say an "exemplary" distance because *The Mound Builders* is as much an exploration of the psychological tensions that arise when people from different professions and classes, and hence with different outlooks and convictions, are forced to live together under increasing pressures, as it is an investigation into the nature of reality and man's relation to it, carried out between the lines of the dialogue and through recurring metaphors. In this respect, archeology stands not just for the attempt to retrieve the past but for the quandary of reaching reality, whether past, present or future. In the highhanded jargon of philosophers, *The Mound Builders* touches upon the ontological issue (concerning the existence of reality) and the epistemological one (concerning our knowledge of reality). It is to Wilson's credit that he succeeds in translating these elevated issues into ordinary and intelligible terms without falsely and unduly simplifying them.

In Wilson's existentialist inspired portrait of contemporary life, reality is almost but not quite hopelessly fragmented, human existence alienated and devoid of a strong center that holds things together. Time is one culprit here: as soon as it has brought the future within easy reach, it carries it off again into the past. Frustrated as he is by this, man tries to hold on to present reality by reducing it to objects he can—so goes the illusion—rationally know and thus—double illusion—possess. The source of these two false assumptions lies in the early history of philosophy. It was Plato who in his allegory of the cave from the *Republic* (to which the frame alludes), turned reality into a figment of the human mind rather than something of which we are an integral part. Still, Plato never doubted the existence of the external world. By doubting even that, Descartes outstripped the Greek: his sceptical consciousness was the only thing he could be certain of. The gains of this radical exercise in critical awareness have been considerable in terms of scientific advances and man's manipulative power over the things his rational mind isolates from reality and subjects to scrutiny. Nevertheless, reason has caused a fissure between man and nature through which the essence of things may have slipped and which may have consolidated the limits of rational knowledge. Reality still holds many mysteries despite reason's grandiose claims to unveil them. Other endowments of which man is so proud are, in Wilson's view, equally problematic mediators of reality: memory is unreliable and the controversy about the relation between human language and reality is still raging. The few mechanical tools man has invented to aid him in the process of grasping or mediating reality also falter: tape-recorders and cameras distort. In the end, art, so often vilified by (abstract) scientists may prove its worth as a more intuitive and integral approach to reality. Art, Wilson is suggesting in and through this play, may help to understand the nature of the problem and offer a solution that is inspired by archeology as an empirical science, the ancient Mound Builders' way of life (as interpreted imaginatively by the playwright), and by existentialist philosophy: a Being rooted within the world. The profound pessimism of *The Mound Builders* is not due to Wilson's conviction that solutions to the alienation and disintegration of modern life do not exist, rather to his exasperation about man's refusal to see these solutions and put them into practice.

It immediately strikes the attention how alienated and divided Wilson's characters are. In this sense *The Mound Builders* satisfies the dramatist's long-standing attraction to misfits and deviants. There is, in the first place, Chad Jasker, the landowner's son. On the one hand, he is attracted to the archeologists—to the women to be sure, but also to the men for their education, intelligence and drive. On the other hand, he is repelled by their arrogance and facile breaches of trust. He admires their dedication but also annihilates their achievement. Delia, another outsider in the archeological group, represents an extreme case of modern alienation: she is a divorced woman, like a ''nomad'' always ''in motion'', and the author of a novel called *Spindrift.* Her homelessness goes back to that moment when, aged seventeen, she left the parental house. Although that was long before August sold it, the sale is nonetheless symptomatic. In this house with its ''Oak floors and old oak furniture'' and its rooms full of light Delia must have felt rooted and inspired at the same time, an organic unity before her world-wide traveling and countless misfortunes turned her into a ''dissipated'' character without any sense of time and place. She ignores, e.g., how long she was kept at the hospital.

Dan is familiar with her feeling of disorientation because of a horrible fit of drunkenness, during which he ended up with his arms wrapped around a fire-alarm box as if it were his mother. This sad and grotesque picture of loneliness ends with the ironic and revelatory message on the fire-alarm box: ''You must answer to get help.'' Had Dan known all the answers he would not have been in such dire straits. Like Delia he does not stand up well to the questions with which modern life confronts him. In search of security he retreats from reality into alcohol, joints and an archeologist's dream. Whichever he chooses, alienation is the price he pays. Take the last of the three: a hard day's work on the site leaves Dan ''dirty and mildly refractory,'' the stage directions read, i.e., tired and unresponsive, as well as ''falling apart,'' so to speak.

The general life-style of the archeologists is indeed conducive to a sense of personal fragmentation. Shuttling back and forth between home and the site, Cynthia has developed a feeling of schizophrenia. It remains to be seen, though, whether her philandering with Chad will relieve the feeling, as it leads to her divorce from August. The tensions between the members of the team prevent us from calling it the ''sort of cozily, scientific, cenobitic community'' as Delia does. It is more an ''enclave'' or ''hothouse'', an artificial environment breeding violent conflicts, death and disaster. In any case, Delia is right about the isolation in which the archeologists are operating: Jean realizes that conservators of the past are an ''anachronism'' from the viewpoint of the developers and in retrospect August compares the house at Blue Shoals to an ark tugged loose from its unstable moorings by the water flooding the valley. The drama as a whole even appears as a Platonic vision of his ''mind's eye,'' concocted from the seclusion of his study and projected onto the back wall of the stage. Thus Wilson conveys the emotional, temporal and spatial estrangement of the archeologists' task in a world devoted to progress. Yet, even the play's token devotee of progress suffers from estrangement, which brings us back to the character we started with: Chad is already living on his ''island'' within the lake, his prospective wealth is a ''fantasy'' nurturing other, more romantic ones, such as the idea that he can seduce Jean with it. Chad is not just divided but as much as the others wrapped up in dreams, and therefore isolated. The disease of alienation is widespread, a generalized condition of contemporary life.

If we step back but a little from the characters' concrete experience of disjunction and deracination, we also notice the many thematic opposition pairs interwoven into the play and polarizing its substance. The structure, in its alternation of narrative and dramatic action and in the use of separate slides instead of an ongoing film, is also manifestly discontinuous. Nowhere, however, does the play approach the ''facile scheme'' Stanley Kauffmann claims it to be, ''the mere filling-out of a pattern, step by overlong step.'' The numerous secondary oppostions need not simply align themselves with the primary ones of past and present, archeologists and developers, specifying their meaning. It may be the case, as when Delia's childhood comes to stand for rootedness and her present life for alienation. More often, new polarities transpose the terms of the original ones and shift their sense. They may latch onto one of the initial poles, further breaking it down, or draw new configurations that bridge former contrasts. Depending on the viewpoint, then, the dualisms may be apparent or real. For instance, Dan and August are idealists acting for the benefit of Mankind, sacrificing their time and energy to Science and to the promotion of man's historical consciousness, whereas Chad, living in the present, is the materialist and opportunist eager for personal profit. This multi-faceted opposition is echoed in the images of the (greedy) hand and the (disinterested) eye. And yet, Chad generously saves Dan's life twice, whereas the archeologists are not immune to the fame and money which the discovery of a royal tomb can bring them or the Department. In the end, the value scales are reversed, the initial contrasts suffused and mitigated by parallels.

This is no proof of Wilson's inability to keep things distinct, or, as John J. O'Connor argues, of Wilson's reluctance to commit himself and follow through the implications of his material. The playwright first teases the audience into establishing clear-cut oppositions, then deliberately mixes the lines, mediates the poles. Cynthia, for instance, associates her hometown with a comfortable but cluttered and stifling life in ''eleven rooms of memorabilia,'' the site with a primitive but free and sexually exciting one. So Urbana, Illinois, apparently comes to stand for modern urban civilization and the site for natural existence. However, we have already seen how artificial the situation of the archeologists on that site is. Moreover, Chad, from whom Cynthia derives her image of country life, definitely sides with the developers and urbanizers. It is no use trying the polarity of urban and natural life onto that of the present and past, either. The Mound Builders were farmers tied to their land, who also built the first permanent settlements, the precursors of modern cities. Cahokia, we are told, outstripped Paris and London at the time.

Another example of Wilson's working method is provided by the opposition of the religious past and the secular present. The Mound Builders honored the Gods in return for an abundant crop and protection against floods and wild animals. At present, the ancient gods are either dead or no longer worshipped, incapable or unwilling to protect people against floods. Science has superseded religion. Facts for faith, that, Delia insists, is our present condition. But despite the decline of religion, there remains according to Dan and to Delia a need to dream and hope. The aspiration clumsily expresses itself in the brutal defacement of the ancient mounds and the erection of new structures such as the Blue Shoals Dam and recreation facilities: shrines to the modern idols of Progress and Leisure. From this it does not follow that Wilson conceives of his Mound Builders as devout innocents in comparison to our present-day vandals and desecrators of tombs (Chad as well as the archeologists). The cycle of destruction and construction must have functioned already in the days of the Early Mississippians, since they supplanted other cultures, as Wilson tells us, when they arrived in the region now known as Southern Illinois. To think, therefore, that the shabby present is only a falling-away from the greatness of the past, is to jump to conclusions. The same holds for the reverse but equally simplistic assumption that history is the steady rise from savagery to civilization and culture, a view cherished by the rationalists.

The point of Wilson's hedging, amply illustrated in the foregoing paragraphs, is twofold: to demonstrate the complexity of reality and the ultimate failure of attempts to comprehend it through dualistic thinking. Reality defies regimentation into the straightjacket of binary sets such as idealism/materialism, city/country, religious/secular, progress/decay, or to mention the sets supplied by Delia and Cynthia: ''those who hustle and those who don't,'' ''winners and losers, givers and takers,'' ''the quick and the dead.'' These antagonistic categories offer only partial insights—hustling, for instance, is a common and appropriate enough metaphor for our mercenary world—never the whole truth. ''Chad tries to be among the quick'' but fails, Delia resembles a zombie compared to the ebullient Dan but will survive him. Dualistic thinking is in fact a manifestation of the analytical spirit which we inherited from the Greeks through Descartes and which now reigns almost unchallenged. Reason is the supreme God of our age, the computer, its idol whose artificial mind operating with zeroes and ones only, is modeled after human intelligence at its worst. Unless checked and corrected, reason's sifting and searching may lead to total fragmentation and meaninglessness.

August suffers badly from an extreme rationalism. One of his personal notes reads:

> Separate personal from professional. Discard personal. Separate separate from separate; separate personal from imaginary, illusion from family, ancient

> from contemporary, etc., if possible. Organize if possible and separate if possible from impossible. Catalogue what shards remain from the dig; celebrate separation; also, organize (a) brain, (b) photographic material, (c) letter of resignation, (d) health, (e) budget, (f) family, (f-1) family ties, (g) life. Not necessarily in that order.

This sample of rational thought is rather confusing, to say the least. It confirms that the play's formal discontinuity is partially due to August's chaotic mind. In the absence of interpretative links, taxonomies and lists of loose facts do not add up to a meaningful whole. Your "thinking machine" will tell you as much: "You feed it all into a computer," Delia tells Jean, "all the facts and fancies the doctors have printed or typed or brushed and the computer would print out NOTHING APPLIES. It doesn't scan." Reason's proper means of unification are deficient. Even the sacrosanct cause-and-effect by which Delia characterizes rational thought, may be, as Hume maintains, a matter of the reported and haphazard concurrence of separate events, rather than, of a logically necessary connection. To a rational mind like August's, reality is a collection of objects ("eleven rooms of memorabilia") or else appears muddled and uncertain, at times disturbingly so, at times ludicrously: among the eight girls assisting Dan there is one "presumed" male, all of them are "alleged" students and now that Cynthia's sleeping around has been divulged, Kirsten is an "Alleged" daughter. Of course, these qualifiers may be simply interpreted as cynical markers of August's spite or embitterment but thematically they go beyond immediate character psychology.

Jean's story of her experience as a twelve-year old spelling bee champion directly correlates excessive analysis and nagging doubts about reality. The contests taught her many new words (quantitative knowledge) and how to spell them (analytical knowledge) but too many of them caused her to have a nervous breakdown. Jean could not stop: every word that was said to her, she spelled in her head. The meaning of sentences dissolved as she reduced them to words, syllables and letters. By the same token, the familiar world rarefied into similar and equally elusive Platonic universals:

> there were days when the world and its objects separated, disintegrated into their cellular structure, molecular—worse—into their atomic structure. And nothing held its form. The air was the same as the trees and a table was no more substantial than the lady sitting at it. . .

Systematic, frontal attacks on reality such as August's and Jean's, are bound to end in failure. In *Spindrift,* Delia, too, approached reality the wrong way so that it kept retreating, never yielding its secrets. She set herself, in all reasonableness

> a simple problem and tried to solve it. Write a Chinese puzzle box. Write a Russian doll. A box within a box within a box within a box. Every time something was solved, within the solution was another problem, and within the solving of the second riddle another question arose. And when that riddle was unwound there was still a knot. And you know why I failed? For me? Because either a Chinese puzzle box must go on *ad infinitum* or there must finally be a last box. And when that box is opened, something must finally be in it. Something simple like maybe an answer. Or a fact, since we all seem to be compulsive compilers.

This is not the only occasion on which Delia vents her frustration about the limits of human knowledge. Earlier she admitted ignoring the answer to most existential problems, which explains why she hates the complacent smiles of Indian deities, looking as if they knew all the solutions. And during her stay at the hospital she briefly forgot her identity, an occurrence that symbolizes, rather bluntly, modern man's restricted self-knowledge as well as his loss of personality. Actually, Wilson instills in his audience a personal feeling of ignorance and uncertainty while making these explicit as themes. By withholding facts about his characters until late in the play and by the piecemeal giving away of historical information about the Early Mississippian Culture, he is not just keeping his plot lively enough to hold his audience, or lapsing into didacticism. Delia learns only at the end of Act I that Chad saved Dan's life. Still later Dan finds out that Delia had started, though never finished, a third novel, and both characters are surprised to hear that, around the year 1100, "Parakeets were as common in Illinois as the sparrow is now", which makes Delia conclude that there are "Some things we don't know." With this very formula Dan had initially reproached Delia for assuming that Chad "had something on him." Without complete knowledge, which we will never attain, judgments, Wilson implies, will always appear somewhat premature, a matter of suppositions that require constant revision. It is only normal then that the play leaves some questions unanswered. Did Dan try to save the excavation and retrieve the artefacts but drown in the attempt? Or was he murdered? Perhaps he caused Chad's death or else Chad killed himself? These are some of the questions that must preoccupy the audience. For Jean, shattered as she is by the immense loss, these questions have been superseded by others, such as:

> Why did [Dan] go out? Why didn't someone hear him? Why did the girls stay at the motel? WHY DID HE HAVE TO HEAR NOISES IN THE NIGHT? WHY DID HE TRUST PEOPLE? WHY DID HE BELIEVE IN THINGS?

All these questions can be summed up into the one and only ''Why did it have to happen to my husband?''

Wilson approaches the problem of the elusiveness of truth and reality not only from the angle of reason or rational knowledge but also from that of language. To some extent, this is like begging the question since logic and logos are etymologically related. Man is a being of logic and language, so the shortcomings of the one may be those of the other. Perhaps Wilson has even given us a clue to the parallel in ''Loggins,'' the family name of Dan and Jean, two scientists, the former an archeologist, the latter a gynecologist. Historically, the claims made for language have certainly been as high as those made for reason. In primitive cultures words are often invested with the power to conjure up reality. The superstition survived the advent of Christianity through the Bible, the Christian God's incarnation on earth. Does not the opening of St. John's Gospel read: ''In the beginning was the Word, and the Word was with God, and the Word was God?'' For children language has always amounted to ontological proof: the eleven-year old Kirsten considers the presences in her dream real enough—not just the ''shadows'' August calls them—because they were ''talking.'' Even Wilson's adults believe in the incantatory effect of the language. Delia fears that prophecies and especially evil curses make things happen. Although Jean has been pregnant for some time now, she and her husband still have not come up with a name. After Jean's two former miscarriages they refuse to anticipate events. Naming the unborn child would be equal to assuming its existence and suffering its eventual loss like the death of a physical presence.

The playwright here touches upon the dilemma of the chicken and the egg. Which comes first, language or reality? Are words invented to arbitrarily denote pre-existing realities or do things exist by the grace of language? The evidence in *The Mound Builders* points in opposite directions. Sometimes reality takes after words/language/literature. Dan is called Pollyandy for his naively optimistic and benevolent character, which is a generally forgotten reference to Eleanor Porter's novel *Pollyanna* (1913). Delia occasionally allows herself ''to cause a brawl or pass out in the middle of the ring because [she] knew it was good for the biographer.'' ''The signing of an energy bill in Washington [often enough] transform[s] rural areas into resorts—fieldhands into busboys'', though not in this play. Sometimes language flatly ignores reality or truth. August scornfully labels a slide of Cynthia ''Horse,'' alluding to his comment on the previous slide, bathers at the lake involved in ''Horse play.'' And Delia glibly purports to ''know all the answers'' but none ''of the questions'' because it sounds so good. She knows ''It's a lie, but it's neat.'' Words do seem to have a life and mind of their own. Unfortunately they can be trapped in their proper sphere against their will.

Writing can be a self-generating, autonomous activity of one book leading to the next without much affecting the world for all its efforts. Among intellectuals like Dr. Landau, Dan's American Literature Professor at College, Delia's novel, *Spindrift,* caused a ripple or two but the ''neat, sweet, meek'' secretary who typed the manuscript remained very composed when confronted with this chronicle of despair. She is unlike the typist in Truffaut's *L'homme qui aimait les femmes* who staunchly refused to finish the story of the protagonist's debaucheries. At the beginning of *The Mound Builders* August tests the tape-recorder with the word, ''The quick gray fox jumped over'' suddenly forgets the remainder of the line used to check the keys of a typewriter, and concludes with ''whatever it was that the quick gray fox jumped over.'' In this particular case the referential value of language is *nihil,* its circularity total. The same applies, so to speak, to dictionaries, tautological closed systems, in which words refer to other words, without coming to terms with reality. Jean's spelling bees gave her just that, the abstract knowledge of a dictionary.

Wilson's preoccupation with the ambivalent status of language with regard to reality explains, to me, the presence of aphorisms within the play and the relevance of establishing their difference from axioms. The dictionary—that flawed but handy tool—tells us an aphorism is either a ''concise statement of a principle'' or ''a terse formulation of a truth or sentiment.'' Chad calls it ''a saying that tells you how to judge.'' In other words, it has a practical value to him, derived from experience. According to the aphorism ''Beer on whiskey—Mighty risk. Whiskey on beer, never fear'' he and Dan need not worry about topping the many beers they have had with a shot of whiskey. Still, Dan is afraid it might kill them because they have already had too many beers. And he is right, the point being that aphorisms convey relative truths as opposed to the absolute truths of axioms. Chad insists that the thing he is looking for is not an axiom, i.e. ''a maxim widely accepted on its intrinsic merits'' or ''a proposition regarded as a self-evident truth, a postulate,'' namely something that foregoes the test of reality. The reason why people use aphorisms is that they provide a sense of superior wisdom and some grip on reality and its unpredictability. Those who do not heed them at all, are clearly in the wrong. The old Chinese proverb—''If you save someone from drowning you're responsible for them for the rest of their life''—should have warned Dan about Chad's prerogatives with regard to him and his life's dream. Strictly speaking aphorisms and proverbs may deceive, yet their practical knowledge at least has the advantage of bearing the stamp of reality as opposed to purely abstract knowledge. Thus, Cynthia parries Delia's reproach of dropping August in favour of Chad—''You're paying the gold of the realm for bazaar merchandise''—with the words ''All that glitters. . .[is not gold].'' She happens to know August as a husband from first-hand experience whereas Delia can only presume what he is like as a husband from having known him as a brother.

Archeology is an empirical science facing the problems of man's limited knowledge and of an uncertain, fleeting reality in acute form because it deals with the past. Most of Wilson's plays deal with the past or the passage of time and how one must cope with it in order to make the present bearable and to guarantee a future. But only in *The Mound Builders* did the playwright hit upon such a suggestive and eloquent metaphor for this concern, namely archeology. Its activity represents on a grand scale the human condition, characterized as it is by the (futile) attempt to retrieve one's personal past, to possess oneself totally. Indeed, the temporality of human existence is offering the archeologists a life task as well as thwarting it. For this reason only, and not just because the man-made lake is inundating the area and threatening excavation, *The Mound Builders* is already enacted under the sign of the ''passing'' and ''unstable'' moon, that symbol of transience which is featured on separate slides. No wonder life feels like an insubstantial dream. According to August ''We do not allow ourselves''—and Time often does not permit us—'' to dream of finding what we might find and dream every sweep of a trowel.'' Human civilizations do tend to disappear. They might not vanish entirely, ''without a trace,'' corresponding to Delia's pessimistic forebodings, yet they do tend to perish. August's fatalism with regard to his personal past surely influences his attitude towards his archeological endeavours and vice versa. The hope and joy of small discoveries and retrievals—an image or emotion, a bone awl or mask—must constantly jar with the feeling that too much has ''vanished without a trace'', like ''water under the bridge.''

So despite the fieldwork and the palpable evidence collected, archeology remains to a large extent a speculative business, as gets illustrated with the golden mask of the God-king. Says Dan, ''It's a death mask—*we guess.* It might have had feathers around it here. *We have to guess.* We've never seen anything like it before'' (italics added). Considering all the imponderabilities, some claims sound rather strange, like August's about the bone awl: ''We have no clear idea what the bone awl was actually used for, but it was undoubtedly used for something. This is a particularly good one.'' I suppose ''good'' means ''well-preserved'' and not ''good at doing whatever it was made for.'' Still, the ambiguity remains and elicits a smile. It is a disturbed smile because from August's utilitarian viewpoint, a view which weathered times remarkably well given the primitive belief that the being of a thing lies in its use, the bone awl is a dead and meaningless object. The life and soul has left the sediments of the past when archeologists find them. After the wrecked expedition, August admits with resignation that ''A great amount of work has been done on the early cultures of North America and we have found only the periphery of the culture.'' For all we know, there might no longer be a center, as with the gold-decorated beads of which the wooden core has disintegrated. The center may forever elude the archeologists. Somehow we get the feeling that exposing the royal tomb to the light of day and publicity has caused its disappearance. This reminds us of the frescoes in Fellini's *Roma.* Constant light and atmospheric conditions preserved them in a perfect state for centuries. But their exposure to the sun and fresh air during excavations for the subway has made them fade immediately. The same happens with the pictures Cynthia took of the artefacts. In an act of compassion for Chad, who had been cruelly deceived by Dan and August, she destroys the crucial evidence by exposing the film.

It is not so certain, though, that the pictures, had they been saved, would have been of much help. After all, they are only reflections of a bygone reality, unsuccessful attempts at fixing it, confirming in their function of mementoes time and reality's passing. "All photographs are *memento mori,*" says Susan Sontag. The pictures of the tomb should have served as evidence of the discovery but they would only have shown what was no longer attainable. The thousand photographs of Kirsten as a baby could not prevent her from growing up nor can they bring back the baby she used to be. The photo of Dan wearing the death mask must be a meagre consolation to his wife. In retrospect that picture may even, metaphorically speaking, have consolidated Dan's death. Remember primitives refuse to have pictures taken of them lest their souls be stolen. Photographs "trans-fix" living reality while reproducing it. The equivocal nature also explains Delia's contempt for the genius of Rank, the British inventor of the copy machine and a movie mogul, though in her eyes a peddlar in gross lies and illusions. Movies, copies and photographs give man the illusion of an objectified reality that can be appropriated and manipulated. A similar deception is worked by the slides of the expedition. Of course, August's subjectivity adds to the problem with these slides. Through the unreliability of his memory he may accidentally get a few facts wrong or personal feelings may color his comments. Thus objective and subjective comments alternate, at times even fuse, as when August moves from "slides of need" to "slides of spear points." The tape-recorder fails to neutralize the human distortion. On the contrary, it fastens and compounds it by mechanical means. To tell the truth, no matter how trustworthy August is, the dice have been loaded from the start, since the slides were taken by Cynthia. Surely he cannot always fathom the meaning certain shots had for her.

Photographs slides, movies, Xerox-copies, and audio-tapes: all these material products of inventions made by the rational mind function in *The Mound Builders* as flawed mediators of reality and truth, examples of perfunctory reproduction vastly inferior to creative visions. This is at least the opinion of Delia, the exemplary artist and visionary of Wilson's play. It is an opinion she metaphorically extends to matrimonial affairs. As long as wives are satisfied with being the trapped "reflections" of the men who have assumed the responsibility for a family, Delia believes they will be a "sad old" lot. If she briefly thinks that some "women are wonderful," we may assume it is because these come closer to Sartre's cruel but more truthful "miroir aux allouettes" than to so-called *bona fide* mirrors. As for Delia herself, once she had conquered "the anxiety to please" her husband, that "strong, hirsute, sweating, horny cocksman" selling "drilling equipment", she managed to divorce him. As a visionary she could no longer reflect the image he had of himself.

And Delia is a visionary, Cynthia's sight is impaired by a blind spot, perhaps because she ignores that August has the government reroute the highway. Dan knows all about archeology but confesses to an "absolute blind spot in folklore", which goes to show how one-sided scientists specialized in one field can be. Only Delia has enough "eyes in [her] head" to carry the honors of being an artist. She is the "Gorgon" whose glare can turn people into stone. Her illness has even given her, we are told with sarcasm, the haggard outlook of a soothsayer. After the death of her father, a physiologist who had written a book on vision, Delia's inspiration flagged and she stopped reading or writing books. Yet, like a contemporary palmist she kept reading the graffiti on the wall. Like an archeologist of the human mind she kept searching for the truth in "dreams and nightmares", chasing "that graceful, trim, and dangerous leviathan in the cold depths of some uncharted secret currents where the sun has never warmed the shadows." If artistic visions excel artificial duplications it is because they go beneath bland and glossy surfaces to reveal hidden truths, or better to forge them in the smithy of reality with the help of the imagination. Because of this revelatory and (re)creative power, artistic visions possess far more truthfulness and substantiality than mere mechanical reflections.

However, as with the contrasts mentioned earlier, the one between "reflections" and "visions" is not always as radical as might be expected from Delia's remarks. Art photography and art movies are valid forms of artistic expression, too, giving full scope to human creativity and inventiveness. At present artistic experimentation with color copiers has even begun. Incidentally, the invention of such machines requires creativity as well as rational thought. And the representational value of (post)modern art may be larger than supposed, given the fact that it imitates, to some extent, a world which is continously shifting and recreating itself. Although Wilson does not resort to these examples, he nonetheless remains true to his method of reconciling oppositions set up by his characters.

Dan wants Delia to write a "fictionalized" account of the great discovery to prove that it has not been "faked." So long as this account offers to be no more than a servile ''reflection,'' corroboration or propaganda adding to the archeologists' glory, Delia shows no interest. Once she realizes the opportunities for ingeniously exposing the intrigues behind the enterprise, she rises to the occasion. (We have every reason to believe that Wilson took over Delia's project.) Whereas an objective and factual journalistic or photographic report may ''cover'' the events (in both possible senses), a subjective literary rendition, in other words a more direct falsification may ''uncover'' the truth beneath them. Art may well be the lie that discloses the truth. The accomplished artist does not jeopardize truth by bluntly exposing it, as the archeologists do with the royal tomb in this play. He or she provides a favorable and fertile environment for deeper truths to inhabit and develop in, whereas (abstract) scientists often scare or impale them with the light of reason. Instead of tackling reality with the orderliness and directness of rational minds, great artists approach it in a stealthy, round-about and more intuitive manner. As Jerry says in Albee's *Zoo Story:* ''Sometimes it is necessary to go a long distance out of the way in order to come back a short distance correctly.'' Success is never guaranteed, though, for the artist's vision can become blurred by drugs, like Delia's when she was traveling through the exotic landscapes of ''Egypt, Lebanon, Syria, Cyprus, Metaxa, Ouzo, Grappa, Cinzano. . . . ''

August believes archeology can survive without art lending it a hand. No sooner has Delia informed him of her renewed desire to write than he advises her to leave. Irony number one: had she, the artist, been around, she could have prevented Chad from stealing the artefacts. Irony number two: many relics of the vaunted God-King are jewels and ornaments, i.e., art objects. They have long survived the person or culture they belonged to. Art, Wilson here suggests, is a substantial form of truth, whatever neo-Platonists may say to the contrary. But he subtly qualifies his claim by picking as *pièce de résistance* a fragile golden mask, the reflection or shadow of its owner's face. And he further mediates the contrast between archeology and art by having Dan ask that we use our imagination, the artistic faculty par excellence, and picture the death mask surrounded by feathers. It is symptomatic that Dan, the one to recognize the role the imagination can play in the sciences, replies to Delia's reproach of scientists for their immoderate analysis and compulsive compilation of loose facts: ''Not of themselves—in association. Where are they? Why are they there?'', for the imagination is invaluable in tying things up again. It is the faculty with which to reconstruct and interpret the past and to survive the future, the divine gift that allows man to defy mortality and restore the continuum of time: ''Not marble nor the guilded monuments/Of princes shall outlive this pow'rfull rhyme,'' etc. . . .

In any case, with regard to the art objects from the Early Mississippian Culture, August overstates the common attack against aesthetics and the brainless ''representatives of the humanities ransacking anthropological collections for pots they find pleasingly shaped and carrying them off to museums, where they lecture without content on form—and without the least anthropological information or understanding.'' His own utilitarianism has its drawbacks, too, witness the havoc it caused in the history of the West, which includes, ironically, the destruction of large parts of our archeological heritage. The one occasion on which August has recourse to the imagination, he lapses into fancifulness. In his mind's eye ''the river's currents swept the house before it as a great brown flood bears off everything in its path.'' Reality proves less spectacular: ''The lake had risen to half-cover the house. Much of the second level was above the water. The house looked more scuttled than inundated.''

As mentioned, the entire play is actually a vision originating from August's mind. Wilson's mediation here borders on confusion when we realize that Delia, the artist, shares her brother's visionary faculty. From her father's ''diagrams of the eye with the retina and rods and cones and iris and lens and those lines projected out into space indicating sight,'' it appears to Delia ''that rather than the eye being a muscle that collects light those beams indicated that the eye projects vision onto the outside.'' But unlike August, who spends most of his time in the seclusion of his study—the sight of the ''august'' Professor ''with a trowel in his hand.'' or ''up to his ass in the mud'' is rather uncommon, we are told—Delia until recently totally immersed herself in life's currents. This contrast between isolation and immersion is seen at its tightest if we compare Delia's father, an erudite man with a hatred for practising physicians, writing theoretical works on medicine in the peace and quiet of his great Victorian house, with Jean who gets her kicks from the hectic work at the university clinic. In August and Delia these two extremes of isolation and immersion are associated through the image of vision and with the purpose of stressing how detrimental and alienating both are. August's retreat into his private shell after the wrecked expedition—he divorces Cynthia and resigns from his job—is as bad as Delia's former immersion, for she ''went down'' into ''the liquid world'' to the point of ''drowning.'' For both characters the external world loses its foundation and solidity. Neither can tell in the end whether it exists outside or inside their head.

As befits the central thesis of this article, Wilson's solution to the excrescences of total isolation and immersion lies somewhere in between. In this respect the Mound Builders' way of life acquires symbolic significance. I repeat that Wilson nowhere nostalgically idealizes the past, notwithstanding Dan's childish vision of Cochise taming wild animals and of wolves gently muzzling at his thighs. From the play we learn that the Mound Builders fought, built fortifications, kept slaves and sacrificed people in honor of deceased Kings. Nevertheless, in some respects the Early Mississippian Culture, as depicted by Wilson, presents a more balanced, less alienated and fragmented life than the one modern man is leading.

We have said earlier that the Early Mississippian Culture was partly agricultural, partly urban. The land as major means of subsistence was still respected, not just possessed and exploited as real estate. The settlements in all likelihood permitted a safer life than present-day New York City. For some reason—historical or other—the Mound Builders receive the epithet ''muck-a-muck,'' muck being ''filth, manure'' as well as ''material removed in excavations.'' It is a clear indication of Wilson's intention to convey their rootedness in the earth, which did not prevent them from building mounds out of aspiration for something higher. To Dan these mounds also betray a sense of tradition or rootedness in the past and foresightedness, in other words, a sense of continuity which modern man hooked on immediacy and impermanency may have lost. The epithet ''muck-a-muck'' sounds like a permanent reminder of man's earthly origin and destination, a mark of humility contrasting sharply with today's Faustian striving. The dominant tone in the Early Mississippian Culture must have been set by the anonymous Aztec poem Dan quotes:

> Here are our precious flowers and songs
> May our friends delight in them,
> May the sadness fade out of our hearts.
> This earth is only lent to us.
> We shall have to leave our fine work.
> We shall have to leave our beautiful flowers.
> That is why I am sad as I sing for the sun.

In that remote past art still succeeded in checking blind human pride an untrammeled (scientific) progress. Like life in general art still obeyed ''the dictates of nature,'' the way Yeats wanted it to, and Wilson, too, as Gautam Dasgupta observed.

The social organization of the Natchez, the last of the Mound Builders, is also instructive. They were an ''upward-mobile'' matriarchal society in which the highest classes of the ''Suns,'' ''Nobles'' and ''Honored Men'' had to marry into the lowest one of the ''Stinkards.'' Thus the elevated and low were joined. Also, it is to be expected that in a matriarchate the female sex was better off than in our male-dominated modern western society where intelligent women are still considered exceptions to the rule: ''We're all freaks—all us bright sisters,'' says Delia. She is the militant defender of women's rights, including that of making a fool of herself, which is always better than to be exploited as a sexual object, like ''a virgin to distract the horny unicorn.'' By referring to the matriarchal organization of the Mound Builders, Wilson is not necessarily advocating a simple power transfer from men to women. Rather, he is making his audience aware of the one-sidedness and restraints of the present, patriarchal situation by confronting it with its opposite, in order to convey the possible diversity of an eventual social organization in which men *and* women can claim their rights.

Wilson's criticism of contemporary society, as well as the alternative he briefly sketches, partly by imaginatively bringing to life a lost Amerindian culture, seems inspired a great deal by existentialism. Alienation of the self from the roots of Being, the feeling of absurdity overwhelming and paralyzing man, the decline of religion, the lopsided flowering of Rationalism at the expense of more intuitive values, the destructiveness and present-orientedness of modern civilization as opposed to the awareness of human transience and death resulting in a commitment to the continuity of life: all these aspects figure prominently in existentialist analyses of modern life and in *The Mound Builders*.

With regard to the existentialist influence, Wilson drops several hints, the most obvious one being the reference to Camus' *The Plague,* which is ingeniously transformed into an extra reference to Sartre's *The Flies* by an apparently innocent realistic touch. When staying at Oran, Algeria, ''Camus's model for the *locus in quo* of *The Plague,*'' Delia was ''host to every fly on the Mediterranean.'' Like

Sartre's hero she believes in assuming the responsibility for her own existent. The perspective that her creed—"Nobody owes their life to anybody"—opens up, is severely curtailed, though, by her double assurance that spiritually speaking man "still crawls on its belly like a reptile." And that he is utterly transient. Temporality is the constitutive characteristic of human being which Heidegger has made much of in his monumental *Being and Time* (1927). In the face of death, which is to say of human finitude, one may easily lose heart, like August. His final attitude is one of total indifference and resignation: whether Dianne, his secretary, types up his comments or goes out to lunch, does not matter, for he feels like having wasted all his energy in a senseless "salvage operation from which was salvaged nothing." The word "nothing" is repeated seven times, which reminds us of Hemingway's "A Clean, Well-lighted Place" with its proliferation of "nadas." Hemingway's answer to Nothingness was a personal code of valor, the thrill and security of ritual action: fishing, hunting, or bull-fighting. Dan and Chad's fishing party—that brief, moonlit moment of male companionship and communion with nature—may well be an allusion to Hemingway, besides being, no doubt, one of the many anticipations of their deaths with which the play is studded and which color it with impending doom. It is also an indication that the play never deteriorates into cheap sentimentality as Edith Oliver claims.

Actually, the playwright's view of his subject and of contemporary life is too bleak to permit such lapses. Existentialism has frequently been accused of pessimism, even morbidity, and *The Mound Builders* seems to suffer from the same defect. There is a real demolition job going on: no dream or illusion is allowed to remain standing, whether it is Chad's dream of riches, the archeologists' hope of contributing to history or Delia's conviction that her father cared for and respected her work. Like Delia, Wilson seems to be "checking off the possibilities of the species." Her apocalyptic vision of the future, at the end of Act I, leaves little to be enthusiastic about:

> You know how the world ends? You know what the "with a whimper" is? A sad old world of widows: wizened old women, lined up on beaches along all the Southern coastlines looking out over the water and trying to keep warm. (*Beat.*) Good Lord. That sounds so horribly right I'll bet it's prophetic. The species crawls up out of the warm ocean for a few million years and crawls back to it again to die.

The prophecy is almost born out at the end of the play when the three women are sitting in the house on the border of the lake, waiting—in vain, Cynthia harshly insists—for the divers to find Chad's and Dan's bodies. And as if this visual image is not nihilistic enough, Wilson crowns it with August's weak appeal to his secretary before becoming speechless, while the tape-recorder continues to turn, and silence, as in *Krapp's Last Tape*, takes over.

The desolation of this finale is so absolute and devastating that the few positive and future-oriented notes tend to be swallowed by the void. Upon closer inspection the play—like most of Wilson's—indeed possesses a comic orientation. It may seem less open-ended than usual but some questions are left dangling. The Biblical connotations of the flood goad us into expecting a new beginning, though persevering pessimists may add that, this time, the water may never retreat to allow for such a beginning. These pessimists may have hit the mark because, according to Maturin Le Petit, the French Jesuit, those Natchez who during their life had violated the laws of the chiefdom, were chastized after death by being cast "upon lands unfruitful and entirely covered with water." Still, Jean carries Dan's baby and it is due for "December, January", a date that also suggests a rebirth. Again, our pessimist may retort that Jean's "history" of miscarriages augurs ill, together with her feeling of "blinding damnation," of having "fallen from grace" after she had told Dan about her pregnancy, as if she had "breached a covenant" between her and the baby. Still, life continues, even if it takes courage and sacrifices. Remarkably enough it is Delia who sets the example, her moral strength and resolve to write another book have revitalized her. The burden of Jean's body now feels like nothing to her. There is still hope for the two of them who believe in starting another life, if only one cares enough: Delia has a capacity for "dying" and hence being reborn and Jean doubts that one lives only once. Both women are ultimately on the side of the living: Jean as a gynecologist, Delia as a writer not much given to "In Memoriam[s]." Actually, all the women, including the bitterly realistic Cynthia, exemplify the human capacity for endurance and commitment to life. There is a definitely Chekhovian touch when August, returning from his office with Dan, interrupts Cynthia's recollection of the "miracle" of pregnancy with the words, "But that has nothing to do with us", by which Wilson seems to imply that women may be better equipped than men to apprehend the mystery of life. For all his hedging

Wilson does not escape the association, pervasive since the Greeks, of the feminine with (passive) nature and of the male with (active) reason.

In *The Mound Builders* Lanford Wilson set the stakes very high. The reviewers at the time agreed about this, except for Edith Oliver who gave the play short shrift as a ''dim and insubstantial piece.'' These reviewers also agreed about Wilson's relative failure to fulfill the expectations raised by the play. O'Connor called it Wilson's ''most ambitious'' work to date but ''also one of his more disappointing efforts.'' And Kauffmann scathingly reproached Wilson for having remained the ''ambitious undergraduate pouring out promising scripts for his professor of playwriting.'' Clurman diagnosed the main problem as follows: ''The play's idea is provocative and unmistakably felt. What weakens it is that many of its details are diffuse and ill-digested. The dialogue is heaped pellmell with sundry reflections that do not establish their relevance to the whole.'' Reflections that do not immediately establish their relevance, would have been closer to the truth, since a close reading of the play does reveal an underlying thematic unity. Actually, Clurman charges the playwright with no less than the failure to fuse the disparate elements into an organic whole. This is a serious charge, the more so since it is raised against a play about the problem of mediation: mediation between different views; between past, present and future; between abstract contemplation and sense perception, utilitarianism and aestheticism; Science and Art; between the analytical and differentiating power of Reason and the synthetic and (re)creative power of the Imagination. Truth seems better served, reality more easily apprehended in the twilight zone where these so-called opposites meet.

In this sense Wilson's view approaches the classical ideal of a balance between different faculties. With regard to Foucault's distinction between the organizing principles of thought operating in Western Culture, Wilson seems to favor a partial return to the classical ''épistème'' in which knowledge is a matter of discovering correspondences, away from the modern Cartesian one in which knowledge equals discrimination and the establishment of differences. By extension the classical ideal also calls for thinking engaged within the world, and not imposed upon a world conceived as separate from the mind. This is in keeping with Wilson's existentialist inclination. An important clue to Wilson's classical world view is his Baroque conviction that life is a text, a dream and that the world is inseparable from the words used to interpret it. That also seems to resolve the language issue of the play. If Wilson did not believe in the power of words to affect reality, there would be little use in his writing any further.

When leveling the charge of incoherence against *The Mound Builders*, critics forget one crucial point: that, as in *The Rimers of Eldritch*, Wilson may not have wanted to create a harmonious whole without further ado. He presents the drama through August's mind, a mind thoroughly disturbed by the wrecked expedition and driven by its consequences into isolation from the sensory world, into reasoning and reminiscing about the past. Even before the disaster, August proved, as we saw, an unbalanced character, dwelling in ''eleven rooms of memorabilia'' and neglecting the empirical side of his profession. The formal discontinuity due to the narrator's intervention is mirrored by the other characters' alienation and by the different views expounded. This double exemplification of fragmentation—that of the play and that within the play—demonstrates the problematic nature of mediation much more convincingly than if Wilson had merely posited it.

The other charges frequently made against *The Mound Builders* or its author—that of sententiousness, poor characterization, or lack of originality—may equally be accounted for, if not refuted. Wilson's love of language occasionally exceeds the boundaries of his realistic mode, despite the fact that, in other plays, the language has often been lyrical. But many a sententious line is uttered by Delia, the writer in residence, and is, therefore, in character. Moreover, the aphoristic quality of the writing is relevant to the opposition between practical and theoretical knowledge. The thematic burden of the play probably explains why less effort went into the characterization. With regard to Wilson's originality or lack of it the name most often dropped is that of Tennessee Williams. It may be useful to recall that Wilson adapted *Summer and Smoke* and the short story, ''One Arm,'' for the screen. He even co-authored with Williams the script for *The Migrants*. Such a collaboration may betray an affinity of both writers' ''idea of the theater'' but as might be expected in such cases, the lesser figure is bound to be accused of profiting from the greater one. I have no doubt about who the greater playwright is. For any writer working in the same mode as Williams to break away entirely from his pervasive influence on post-war American drama may nearly be impossible. The universality of

Wilson's theme in *The Mound Builders* belittles, however, criticisms about his so-called gift for ''Sincere Imitation.''

Source: Johan Callens, ''When 'The Center Cannot Hold'; or, The Problem of Mediation in Lanford Wilson's *The Mound Builders,*'' in *New Essays on American Drama,* edited by Gilbert Dubusscher and Henry Schvey, Costerus series, Vol. 76, Rodopi, 1989, pp. 201–26.

SOURCES

Barnett, Gene A., *Lanford Wilson,* Twayne, 1987, pp. 100–01.

———, ''Recreating the Magic: An Interview with Lanford Wilson,'' in *Forum,* Vol. 25, Spring 1984, p. 68.

Beaufort, John, Review of *The Mound Builders,* in the *Christian Science Monitor,* February 5, 1986, p. 29.

Busby, Mark, *Lanford Wilson,* Boise State University, 1987, p. 31.

Callens, Johan, ''When 'the Center Cannot Hold' or the Problem of Mediation in Lanford Wilson's *The Mound Builders,*'' in *New Essays on American Drama,* edited by Gilbert Debusscher and Henry I. Schvey, Rodopi, 1989, p. 203.

Clurman, Harold, ''Theatre,'' in the *Nation,* March 15, 1975, pp. 315–16.

Kauffmann, Stanley, ''Stanley Kauffmann on Theatre: Two American Plays,'' in *New Republic,* March 1, 1975, p. 22.

Oliver, Edith, ''On the Mounds,'' in the *New Yorker,* February 17, 1975, pp. 84–85.

Simon, John, ''Rum Deals Two with Coke,'' in *New York,* February 10, 1986, p. 56.

Wilson, Lanford, Introduction to *The Mound Builders,* in *Lanford Wilson: Collected Works, Volume II, 1970–1983,* Smith and Kraus, 1998, pp. 126, 128.

FURTHER READING

Barnett, Gene A., *Lanford Wilson,* Twayne, 1987.

This biography provides the best introduction to Wilson's life and work. In a full chapter devoted to *The Mound Builders,* Barnett examines the play's plot, structure, and major characters and discusses the play's origins as two imagined scenes in the writer's mind.

Bryer, Jackson R., *Lanford Wilson: A Casebook,* Garland, 1994.

Twelve critical articles, an introduction, a chronology, and an annotated bibliography of primary and secondary works comprise this volume. While *The Mound Builders* is mentioned only briefly, interviews that Bryer conducted with Wilson and his collaborator Marshall Mason illuminate Wilson's creative process.

Busby, Mark, *Lanford Wilson,* Boise State University, 1987.

This brief monograph focuses on Wilson's family history as it has influenced his writing. Busby treats *The Mound Builders,* Wilson's first play set in the Midwest, as an important stepping stone toward the playwright's Talley family plays—his greatest works.

Cooperman, Robert, ''Lanford Wilson: A Bibliography,'' in *Bulletin of Bibliography,* Vol. 48, September 1991, pp. 125–35.

Although no longer up-to-date, this bibliography is a good source for information about productions of *The Mound Builders* and other plays, including performance and publication dates, and citations for criticism and reviews. Interviews with Wilson, and performances by him, are also listed.

Ryzuk, Mary S., *The Circle Repertory Company: The First Fifteen Years,* Iowa State University Press, 1989.

This is a history of the theater company founded in 1969 in New York by playwright-in-residence Lanford Wilson and managing director Marshall W. Mason. Wilson wrote *The Mound Builders* and other plays with the ''Circle Rep'' company in mind; the character of Delia, for example, was created specifically for one of the company's actors.

The Night Thoreau Spent in Jail

JEROME LAWRENCE AND ROBERT E. LEE

1971

The Night Thoreau Spent in Jail, by Jerome Lawrence and Robert E. Lee, was first published in New York in 1971, during the Vietnam War. The play, which was a clear protest against the war, used a related incident from America's history to comment on the current war. In 1846, the writer, Henry David Thoreau, spent a night in jail for not paying his taxes. Thoreau refused to pay money that would support the war that was currently being waged against Mexico. This incident later provided the basis for Thoreau's popular essay, ''Civil Disobedience.'' Lawrence and Lee's immensely popular play, which was deliberately produced in regional theaters as opposed to on or off Broadway, struck a chord with Vietnam-era audiences. In fact, the play was so relevant to the times that it was temporarily shut down shortly after its first performances in 1970, when another anti-Vietnam protest—at Kent State University—resulted in the death of several students.

Despite the lack of critical commentary, the play continues to be one of the most popular works by Lawrence and Lee, a writing team that enjoyed a fifty-two-year collaboration, and who also wrote the immensely popular play, *Inherit the Wind*. In *The Night Thoreau Spent in Jail*, time and setting are shifted between each episodic scene without indication or explanation, forcing the audience or reader to pay close attention. These dream-like effects serve to highlight the main themes of the play—rebelling against authority and expressing one's individuality—universal themes that have appealed to many audiences, both nationally and internationally, since the play's first production.

The Night Thoreau Spent in Jail was published in a reissue edition in 1992, which is available from Bantam Books.

AUTHOR BIOGRAPHY

Jerome Lawrence was born in Cleveland, Ohio, on July 14, 1915. Robert E. Lee was born in Elyria, Ohio, on October 15, 1918. Although both men grew up in the same region of Ohio, attended Ohio universities, and worked in commercial radio, they did not meet each other until 1942, when they met in New York and immediately became writing partners with their production of *Inside a Kid's Head*, a radio play. The two men, who had already lived somewhat parallel lives, continued this trend when they both entered the armed forces that summer. They both served in the war until 1945, and together, they co-founded the Armed Forces Radio Service (1942), where they created and produced radio programs.

Following World War II, Lawrence and Lee continued to concentrate mainly on writing, producing, and directing scripts for radio shows, including *The Frank Sinatra Show* and *The Railroad Hour*. In 1955, when the advent of television reduced the amount of radio-show programming, they produced their first stage production, *Inherit the Wind*. The play, which has proved to be their most successful work, also introduced a technique that Lawrence and Lee would use in most of their plays—staging an historical incident to comment on a current situation. In the case of *Inherit the Wind*, the dramatized incident was the famous Scopes trial of 1925, in which a high-school biology teacher was put on trial for attempting to teach evolution. The play was an obvious commentary on the Communist trials instigated by Senator Joseph McCarthy in the 1950s, just as *The Night Thoreau Spent in Jail* (1971), their second most successful work, was an obvious commentary on the war in Vietnam.

Lawrence and Lee produced several more plays together from the 1970s until the 1990s, during which time they were recognized by many regional and national awards within the dramatic community. In 1990, they were both named to the Theatre Hall of Fame. Three years later, in 1993, Lawrence's Malibu home was destroyed by the fires that were raging through California. Although many of his personal literary and art collections were lost, he was able to escape with the latest draft of *Whisper in the Mind* (1994), the last play that Lawrence and Lee produced in their fifty-two-year collaboration. Lee died on July 8, 1994, in Los Angeles, California, shortly before the publication of *The Selected Plays of Jerome Lawrence and Robert E. Lee*, their final collaborative work. Lawrence currently lives in Malibu, California.

PLOT SUMMARY

Act 1

The Night Thoreau Spent in Jail takes place in Concord, Massachusetts and the surrounding area. As the stage directions note, "time and space are awash here." The play starts in one time period, and then abruptly shifts around to many other times and places. At all times throughout the play, Henry David Thoreau's jail cell can be seen in the background. The play starts at its latest point in time, during a Concord winter when Ralph Waldo Emerson is an old man, walking with his wife, Lydian. With his wife's help, Waldo remembers the name of Henry (Thoreau), who was his best friend. With this realization, the action shifts to Henry's jail cell, when the writer is a young man.

Henry's mother asks Henry why he is in jail, and he gives vague answers, a tactic that he uses throughout the play. Henry shows what his mother calls his strangeness, by questioning the order of the alphabet. Henry's brother, John, comes into the jail cell and their mother leaves. The location shifts to a sunny field at an earlier time, when Henry has just returned from Harvard. Henry and John talk about Henry's education, which Henry counts as worthless, except for hearing the lectures of Waldo, whom he says he wants to emulate. Back in the jail cell, Henry talks with his cellmate, Bailey, who has been accused of burning down a barn; Bailey has been waiting for his trial for three months, a fact that outrages Henry.

Henry tries to talk to Bailey about conformity, but Bailey is not an educated man. Henry teaches Bailey how to spell his name, then grabs a chair from the jail cell and moves to the front of the stage, shifting back in time to when he was a teacher. He is interrupted by Deacon Nehemiah Ball, the Chairman of the Concord School Committee, who criticizes Henry's deviations from the approved school textbooks. Henry gets into a theological argument with Ball, who is outraged at Henry's transcendentalist beliefs, and Henry provokes the class to laugh at Ball. John later tells Henry he should apologize to save his job, which Henry does. However, although Ball excuses him, he forces Henry to whip six of his students for laughing. Henry reluctantly does this, then quits teaching, just as Waldo quits his position as Unitarian pastor, in another time-space shift.

Henry proposes to John that they start their own unconventional school, which they do. Henry and John stand in a meadow teaching a number of students, including Ellen, a beautiful young woman who is much older than the class. Henry criticizes Ellen for trying to take notes, a method used in conventional schooling. The action shifts back to the jail cell, where Bailey has successfully learned how to write his own name. Henry encourages Bailey to unlearn it and remain uneducated. Henry pushes the jail cell's locker box to the front of the stage, where it becomes a boat by a pond. John tells Henry their school is losing all of its students. John leaves, and Ellen enters. Henry uses the opportunity to invite her for a boat ride, during which he tries to explain his transcendentalist views to her and profess his love to her; both attempts are unsuccessful, and Henry suggests that Ellen go to church with John.

Back in the jail cell again, Henry proclaims to the sleeping Bailey that they are freer in prison than the outside community, who must conform. At the front of the stage, a crowd of churchgoers files out of the church, Ellen on the arm of John. Although Lydian attempts to mask Waldo's satirical comments, it is clear from Waldo's conversation with Deacon Ball that Waldo is critical of organized religion. This belief is underscored by the appearance of Henry, who, to the dismay of his mother and Ball, is working on Sunday. Later, Henry and John talk about Ellen's refusal to marry John. John dies from blood poisoning, cutting himself with a dirty razor.

The action shifts back to the day when Henry hires on as Waldo's handyman and tutor for Edmund, Waldo's son. This is the beginning of the friendship between the two men. Waldo insists on paying Henry, but Henry will not take money, and instead asks for the future use of a portion of Waldo's wooded estate, Walden, for an experiment. Waldo also asks for Henry's occasional help in polishing his speeches. Back in the jail cell, Henry and Bailey talk about Walden, where he remains secluded from civilization, except when he has to go into town for supplies. The action shifts, and Henry walks into town to get his shoe fixed. Constable Sam Staples comes up to Henry and serves him with a bill for unpaid taxes. Henry refuses to pay, since he does not support the way the tax money is being spent. Sam reluctantly takes Henry to jail. Waldo gets a note saying that Henry is in jail and goes to see him. Sam pleads with Henry to pay his tax, but Henry, cryptic no longer, finally explains that he is not paying his tax because it is going to pay for the war against Mexico, which he does not support. The act ends with Waldo asking Henry what he is doing in jail, while Henry asks what Waldo is doing out of jail, implying that Waldo should be protesting in jail with Henry.

Act 2

Lydian sends Edward with Henry to go huckleberry hunting. Edward says he wishes Henry was his father, a sentiment he later repeats to his mother. Lydian suggests that Henry should get married, and he says nature is his chosen bride. Back in the jail cell, Bailey asks Henry to be his lawyer, but Henry refuses. The action shifts to Walden Woods, where Henry feeds an escaped slave, Henry Williams, on his way to Canada. The time shifts ahead, and Henry and Waldo argue about the fact that Waldo is not protesting the release of slaves like Williams, who has been shot. Henry accuses Waldo of not practicing what he preaches, and encourages Waldo, who has much more influence than Henry, to speak out against slavery and the war. Waldo hesitantly agrees, and Henry rushes off, ringing the town bell and announcing that Waldo is going to make a speech. Lydian comes up and tells Henry that Waldo is not coming, that he has chosen to think over the matter and write a carefully worded essay describing his position. The crowd disperses. Henry tries to get their attention again, but this time, the bell makes no sound.

Back in his jail cell, Henry is in the grips of a nightmare. The Mexican war rages around his sleeping body, and all of the major characters in the play are in the battle. Edward Emerson is a drummer boy, Sam Staples is a sergeant, Bailey is a soldier, Ball is the general, and Waldo is the president. Henry tries to talk to Waldo, but no sound comes out. When Ball asks Waldo for instructions, he says that he needs to collect his thoughts. Williams appears as a Mexican soldier. Edward is wounded, but Waldo ignores this fact, saying he needs more time to think, and write a carefully worded essay. The unseen voice of then-Congressman Abraham Lincoln advocates stopping the war. John comes on the scene in a soldier's uniform and gets killed.

Back in the jail cell, Henry wakes up from his nightmare, and finds Sam is there with breakfast. He also tells Henry that somebody paid his tax for him, and that he is free to go. Henry is outraged and forces Sam to tell him that it was his Aunt Louisa who did it. Henry leaves the cell, telling Bailey that he is leaving Walden, because he has to stop hiding in the woods and take a more active stand against society's injustices.

CHARACTERS

Bailey

Bailey is Henry's vagrant cellmate, who has landed in prison after he fell asleep in somebody's barn and burned it down by accident. Henry tries many times to talk to Bailey about his crusade against conformity, but Bailey is an uneducated man, who says he cannot even write his own name, much less understand Henry's preaching. Henry shows Bailey how to write his name, but then encourages him to unlearn it, since writing will only get him in trouble. Bailey is excited to hear about Henry's place in Walden Woods, and says that he [Henry] had a place to call home. Bailey gets panicked about the idea of a trial, and asks Henry to be his lawyer, since he is an educated man. Henry refuses, and Bailey frantically asks him what he can do. Although he does not believe in it, Henry suggests prayer, and Bailey asks Henry to help him pray. Henry is outraged when he finds out that Bailey has been waiting three months for a trial, and at the end of the play, threatens to sit in the jail cell until Sam Staples intervenes on the behalf of Bailey. Bailey is touched, since nobody has ever stuck up for him before, and says that when he gets out of jail, he may come visit Henry at Walden Woods. However, Henry says that the Walden stage of his life is over, and he needs to rejoin civilization and take a stand. In Henry's nightmare, Bailey is a civilian soldier who refuses to fight.

Deacon Nehemiah Ball

Deacon Nehemiah Ball, a religious leader who also acts as the chairman of the school board, does not like Henry. When Ball visits Henry's class, he is shocked that Henry is deviating from the authorized textbooks and considers Henry's transcendental view of God to be blasphemous. Ball is also outraged when he finds Henry working on Sunday. When Henry refuses to pay his taxes, Ball is the first to suggest throwing him in jail. In Henry's nightmare, Ball is the General, who advocates destroying the enemy and who incites the Federal forces to kill.

Edward Emerson

Edward Emerson is the son of Waldo and Lydian, and he wishes Henry was his father instead of the often absent Waldo. Edward's parents hire Henry to work as a handyman and serve as a companion and tutor to Edward. Henry takes Edward hunting for huckleberries, and Edward gets excited and drops his basket of berries. Although he is upset, Henry consoles him, saying that he is helping to fertilize the earth to make more huckleberries. Edward is delighted when Henry puts gloves on the claws of Lydian's chickens—so that they cannot trample Lydian's flowers anymore. In Henry's nightmare, Edward plays a drummer boy who is wounded in the fight. When Henry carries the wounded boy to Waldo, the president in the dream, the dream Waldo echoes his noncommittal statement from before, saying that he needs to write a carefully worded essay about the situation.

Lydian Emerson

Lydian is the wife and supporter of Waldo, and encourages Henry to settle down, get married, and conform. Although Lydian appears to agree with many of Henry's ideas, she refuses to go against her husband by supporting Henry. Lydian is a lonely wife, since Waldo is often away giving lectures. She tells Henry that Waldo cannot possibly live up to the ideal image that Henry has painted of her husband. It is Lydian who comes in place of Waldo, to tell Henry and the assembled crowd that her husband is not ready to speak yet. In Waldo's old age, Lydian helps her befuddled husband remember Henry's name, the event that starts the play.

Ralph Waldo Emerson

Ralph Waldo Emerson, one of America's greatest writers, is in this play shown to be an ineffective preacher when compared with Henry's activism. Waldo gives many lectures at Harvard outlining the beliefs of Transcendentalism, and he finds a willing acolyte in one of his audience members, Henry David Thoreau. Waldo hires Henry as a handyman and tutor for his son, Edward, in exchange for the use of a piece of Waldo's wooded estate. This arrangement later provides the location for Henry's Walden Woods project. Waldo spends much of his time writing or delivering lectures, much to the chagrin of his lonely wife, Lydian, who nevertheless supports Waldo completely. Waldo and Henry become great friends, but the friendship sours when Henry gets fed up with Waldo's lack of public protest.

Henry accuses Waldo of failing to use the whole of his massive influence to speak out against such injustices as slavery and the war in Mexico. Waldo marvels at the fact that Henry is a living, breathing example of the principles that he lectures on, but is unable to adopt an activist lifestyle of protest himself. Instead, he prefers to work within the laws, and write his lectures and essays. When Henry challenges Waldo to become a greater activist by speaking to the town, Waldo tentatively agrees, but backs out after Henry has already gathered a crowd. Waldo sends Lydian to let Henry know that Waldo will not be giving the speech. At the end of the first act, Waldo asks Henry what he is doing in jail, while Henry counters, asking Waldo why he is out of jail. In other words, if Waldo really practiced what he preached, he would refuse to pay his taxes and protest in jail as Henry is. In Henry's nightmare, Waldo is the president, who refuses to acknowledge the war tragedies that are happening around him or make any decisions; instead, he says he needs to write careful essays about them, echoing his earlier message about why he cannot speak out like Henry.

Farmer

The Farmer appears twice when Henry's actions draw a crowd, and he claims that Henry is always starting false fires, as when he says Waldo is going to give a speech and Waldo does not. In Henry's nightmare, the farmer serves as a soldier.

Henry

See Henry David Thoreau

Henry's Mother

Henry's mother does not understand why Henry always acts so strange, and wishes he would just conform like everybody else. Henry's mother calls Henry by his official name, "David Henry," even though Henry prefers to go by his middle name. She disdains Henry's working on Sunday, and prays that Ellen Sewell will accept John's marriage proposal. At John's funeral, she tries to get Henry to pray, but Henry is unable to pray to a God that felt it necessary to take John.

Ellen Sewell

Ellen Sewell is a young woman who attracts both Henry and John, and who declines John's marriage proposal. Ellen is much older than the other students in Henry's and John's school, although she asks to be able to study with them. She is intrigued, then turned off, by Henry's transcendental beliefs, and Henry suggests that she go to church with John. Although she does accompany John to church, she claims that her father is forbidding her from marrying either Henry or John. However, Henry and John both believe that she wants to have both brothers. When John dies, Ellen is out of town, so she asks Henry what has happened. Henry is very rude to her, describing John's death in very graphic terms, which shocks her at first. In the end, however, she suggests that maybe they are meant to transcend John's death, an admission that makes Henry believe Ellen is starting to understand his beliefs.

Constable Sam Staples

Sam Staples is the law enforcement officer in Concord, who reluctantly throws Henry in jail. Sam is a good-natured man, who first of all serves Henry with his bill for unpaid taxes, then offers to loan Henry the money to pay for them. Henry is outraged at this suggestion, and forces Sam to take him to jail. Sam does not understand why Henry will not just pay his taxes. At the end of the first act, Henry explains that he does not want his tax money to support the Mexican-American war. This is the first time that Henry has stated outright why he is in jail, a question that it posed at the beginning of the first act but not answered until this point. In Henry's nightmare, Sam is a Sergeant, who inspires his troops to hate, and who forces Henry and Bailey to take guns they do not want.

Henry David Thoreau

Henry David Thoreau, considered one of America's greatest writers, is the fiery protagonist who goes to jail. In the beginning of the play, Henry is in jail, but the audience does not find out until the end of the first act that it is because he does not want to pay the taxes that will support the Mexican-American war. Henry is an uncompromising believer in casting off the chains of conformity and deliberately suggests that society should do things differently, such as starting the alphabet with a different letter. Because of these ideas, his mother, and indeed many of the townspeople, find Henry strange. Henry is a Harvard-educated man, but does not believe in conventional education. He tries teaching his open-minded beliefs in the strictly censored school, and when that fails, he opens his own ill-fated school with his brother, John. He is initially attracted to Ellen Sewell, but realizes that his brother, John, would make a better match, although Ellen turns John down. After John's death, Henry's views on organized religion and his belief in a caring God deteriorate even more.

A devoted disciple and friend of Ralph Waldo Emerson, Henry spends all of his energies trying to adhere to the ideals that Waldo lectures about. At one point, Henry hires on as Waldo's handyman and the tutor of Waldo's son, Edward, in exchange for the use of part of Waldo's wooded estate, which later becomes Thoreau's Walden. Henry encounters an escaped slave, Williams, at Walden, and treats him as a free man. Henry is distraught when he hears that Williams was shot as he was trying to make his way to Canada, and uses the incident to launch an argument about Waldo's lack of activism. Henry accuses Waldo of not practicing what he preaches, even though Waldo has much more influence than Henry and could do more good. Waldo tentatively agrees to give an impromptu speech against slavery and the war in Mexico, but backs out, leaving Henry to try, unsuccessfully, to get the attention of the frustrated townspeople. In Henry's nightmare, he is initially sleeping, as the war rages around him. Sam Staples wakes Henry up within his dream, forces a gun in his hand, and forces him to join the nightmarish war. When Waldo appears as the president, Henry tries to talk to him, but Waldo cannot hear anything that he is saying, and refuses to comment on the war or make any decisions. At the end of the play, Henry wakes up to find that his tax has been paid by his Aunt Louisa, a fact that angers him. When Henry leaves the jail, he vows to leave Walden and take his activism to the next level.

John Thoreau

John Thoreau is Henry's much-loved brother, who shares many of Henry's beliefs, but does not have the same conviction as Henry. John welcomes Henry home from Harvard, and the two brothers discuss their lack of faith in conventional education. However, John convinces Henry to apologize to Deacon Ball, so that Henry can save his job. After the school founded by Henry and John fails, John goes back to his job at the pencil factory. Both John and Henry are attracted to Ellen Sewell, a young woman who asks to join their school. When Henry's attempt to win her love fails, he encourages her to see John. However, although she accompanies John to church, Ellen does not accept his marriage proposal, because her father does not like the Thoreau brothers. Also, as John and Henry discuss, it appears that she wants both brothers, not just one or the other. John dies from blood poisoning, after he cuts himself shaving with an old razor. In Henry's nightmare, John is a Federal soldier, who dies at the end of the dream.

Waldo

See Ralph Waldo Emerson

Henry Williams

Henry Williams, an escaped slave who derives his first name from Thoreau and his last name from his former owner, encounters Henry in Walden Woods. Although Williams is suspicious of Henry at first, he is soon amazed that Henry treats him as an equal. Henry gives Williams food, and is distraught when he hears that Williams has been shot while trying to escape to Canada.

THEMES

Freedom

The overriding message in the play is the struggle for freedom, which manifests itself in several ways. The idea of racial freedom is addressed through the many references to slavery. During the play, Henry meets a slave, Williams, who plans to go "North as I kin git! They say the Norther ya git, the *free-er* ya git!" However, although Henry supports Williams's escape to Canada, he warns him that men in the north are not free, either: "Every man shackled to a ten-hour-a-day is a *work*-slave. Every man who has to worry about next month's rent is a *money*-slave."

TOPICS FOR FURTHER STUDY

- Research the causes, conditions, and outcomes of the Mexican-American War, choosing one prominent military or political figure from both Mexico and the United States of America who took part in the conflict. Imagine that these two leaders have been invited to appear on a modern-day, televised debate show, to defend their viewpoints about, and actions during, the war. Write a short script or scenario that depicts what might happen during this debate.
- Research the main beliefs of transcendentalists in the mid-nineteenth century, and the beliefs of hippies in the 1960s and 1970s. Putting yourself in the place of Henry David Thoreau, imagine that he has traveled through time to the early 1970s. Incorporating your research from both major belief systems, write a journal entry that describes how he might have contributed to or been affected by the Vietnam antiwar movement.
- Freedom fighting is a common theme throughout human history. Pick a non-American, pre-1800s society that had to fight for its freedom, and research the history of the struggle, focusing especially on ways that this society fought against or protested its oppression. How do these compare to the methods used by Thoreau or the Vietnam antiwar movement? Discuss any significant figures who led the protest or fight.
- In the play, Thoreau says at the end that he cannot afford to just stay at Walden anymore, and that he needs to be more active in his fight with society. Research Thoreau's life after the jail incident and use this information to discuss whether or not his efforts to effect change society were successful.
- The expressionistic techniques that Lawrence and Lee used in their play were also prevalent in other visual arts in the twentieth century, such as painting and film. Choose a visual medium, and find an example of a work that you feel accurately represents at least one of the main themes of the play. Discuss the history behind the work, including how it was received.

This idea of being chained to institutions, even within a free society, is expressed further through Henry's individual struggle. When he is confronted by Sam Staples, the friendly constable tells Henry he has to pay his taxes, to help support the war. Henry, however, refuses to pay, on the grounds that he does not support the war and says that he does not want to be part of a society that does:

> If *one* honest man in this state of Massachusetts had the conviction and the courage to withdraw from this unholy partnership and let himself be locked up in the County Jail, it'd be the start of more true freedom than we've seen since a few farmers had the guts to block the British by the bridge up the road.

With statements like this about various social institutions, and with his resulting actions—Henry *does* have the courage to be locked up—Henry proves that he is willing to stand up against conformity, a phrase commonly referred to as ''rocking the boat.'' This phrase is given a very literal translation in the play when Henry is in a boat with Ellen Sewell, whose father has forbidden her or her brother, Edmund, to attend Henry's school. Says Henry: ''Stand up to your father! (*He stands. The boat rocks.*)'' This action terrifies Ellen, as it does society.

Finally, the lack of freedom is expressed through dialogue, specifically the words ''get along'' and ''go along,'' which are used by various characters to imply that one should just ''go along'' with whatever society dictates. When Henry wants to complain about the fact that his cellmate, Bailey, has been waiting three months for trial, Bailey stops him, saying he does not want to ''make a ruckus. I'm not a troublemaker. I just want to earn my keep, make a little tobakky money, and get along.'' As Henry says to Bailey, '''Get along'!'' Those words turn my stomach.'' At the beginning of the second act, Lydian tells Henry that ''in order to *get* along, you have to *go* along,'' a statement that enrages Henry, who responds by shouting ''GO ALONG! GO ALONG! GO ALONG!'' Shortly after that, Waldo tells Henry that ''We have to go along with the majority!'' a statement that again frustrates Henry. Finally, in Henry's nightmare, General Ball asks President Waldo if he is prepared to ''go along'' with the military's plan to ''conquer the entire territory.'' In response to this, all of the characters chant ''Go along!'' several times, emphasizing that most, in the end, will conform.

Activism

Because of his objections to various social ills like slavery and the war against Mexico, Henry becomes an activist, although in the beginning, his form of activism is very passive, rebelling against society by retreating from it and living at Walden. Waldo calls Henry on this fact during their argument about activism. Says Waldo, ''And what are you doing about it, young man? You pull the woods up over your head. You resign from the human race.'' Henry is not deterred, however, and challenges Waldo, asking him if he is really aware of what is going on in the war. Here, Henry merges his distaste for slavery and the war against Mexico into one comment. Says Henry, when describing the reasons for the war, it is ''slave-holders grasping for more slave territory? *More* slavery and less freedom, is that what you want?''

As the play progresses chronologically, Henry's activism becomes more pronounced than just retreating from society. After his heated conversation with Waldo, Henry convinces his mentor to address the issues of slavery and war in a public statement and goes to drum up a crowd for the speech. He rings Concord's town bell, and people come running. He preps the crowd, getting them excited by saying that ''Emerson is going to rile up the whole country. And you're going to hear it *first*!'' However, Waldo backs out of the speech, and when the townspeople realize it was a false alarm, they start to leave. Henry tries to get them to come back, by ringing the bell again, but this time, as the stage directions indicate, ''*THE BELL DOES NOT RING*!'' Henry wonders aloud: ''How do we make a sound? How do we break the silence?'' He is an activist who has tried to use others, like Waldo, to spread the message, but has been unsuccessful. In the end, after Henry wakes from his nightmare, he realizes that he needs to be more personally active, and tells Bailey that if he comes to find Henry at Walden, ''I may not be there.'' As the final stage directions indicate, Henry is moving to the next step in his activism: ''*He seems to grow in stature, lifted and strengthened by a greater challenge.*'' Henry realizes that he cannot count on other people like Waldo to change society, that he must leave Walden and try to change society himself.

Intellectualism

In contrast to Henry's activism, Waldo's intellectualism—thinking thoroughly about the situation but rarely acting—is shown to be ineffective. Through his lectures and writings at Harvard and elsewhere, Waldo has inspired people like Henry to '''Cast Conformity behind you.''' As a result, Waldo has become a very popular and influential public figure. Because Waldo never rocks the boat by actually achieving the ideal that he sets forth in his lectures, this is a very safe popularity. Henry, however, does attempt to follow the style of independent, transcendental life outlined in Waldo's writings. In fact, Waldo calls Henry, ''my walking ethic!'' Waldo is the type of person who cannot live up to his ideals if they compromise his personal security.

Waldo's ineffectiveness is demonstrated when he refuses to show up for the public appearance that Henry sets up. Waldo's wife, Lydian, is the one who delivers Waldo's message, saying that her husband, ''wants more time to meditate on these matters. . . . So that he can write a careful essay setting forth his position.'' This highly intellectual approach angers Henry, who wants Waldo to take action. In addition, Lydian's words haunt Henry, literally, when President Waldo speaks them in Henry's nightmare, saying variations of Lydian's quote in response to the questions of whether or not he supports total destruction of the enemy and in what he thinks about the fact that his son has been shot.

STYLE

Expressionism

Expressionism was a movement that was popular in drama and other, mainly visual, arts, beginning in Germany in the 1910s. Expressionism has never been completely defined in concrete terms, which is oddly fitting, since the main characteristic of expressionistic works is their tendency to bend concrete reality—to express emotions and ideas. In the case of *The Night Thoreau Spent in Jail*, Lawrence and Lee bend reality by staging their drama in a shifting landscape, where the main characters, especially Henry, move instantly and dream-like through time and space. The resulting dream-like episodes cause the audience to become somewhat disoriented. Ultimately, these feelings express the playwrights' message—activism is not always easy, and can in fact be uncomfortable and unpredictable, just like the respective wars that were going on in Thoreau's time (the Mexican War) and in the 1970s (the Vietnam War).

Time and Space

As noted above, the characters in the play move through time frequently. These time and space jumps all take place either in or around Henry's jail cell. Although Henry's jail cell is constantly present on stage, he leaves it often—sometimes physically, sometimes not—to travel to other times and places. An example of Henry jumping through time and space without leaving his cell occurs when John visits Henry in his jail cell, Henry is in a trance, remembering a speech that he has heard Waldo say at Harvard. John looks at Henry, who is still stuck in his memory of Harvard, and says: "Now here's a rare specimen—."

At the end of this statement, Waldo makes a remark from another part of the stage, and then, as the stage directions indicate, "*The light intensifies on Henry and John—the amber of sunny fields.*" At this point, John picks up his specimen conversation from the jail cell and continues talking until Henry notices him and comes out of his trance. With the lighting change, the time and place have shifted from the jail cell to a meadow, just after Henry has returned from Harvard. In addition to the lighting, this fact is revealed to the audience when John says, "Welcome home. How's your overstuffed brain?" Although Henry is still technically in the jail cell as far as the stage dynamics are concerned, the playwrights convey to the audience the time and place of the new location through lighting and dialogue. In some cases, Lawrence and Lee indicate the time and space change by having Henry or another character move to a different part of the stage, or by having Henry use a stage prop such as a chair or storage locker.

However, depending upon how subtle these clues are, the audience is sometimes called upon to work harder to recognize these setting shifts. For example, at the beginning of the second act, after Henry erupts at Lydian for telling him that he has to "*go* along," the stage directions indicate that "*Lydian has reached for a little straw berry-basket.*" With this small act, the setting shifts smoothly to an earlier time, using Lydian's words of "go along" as a transition from the argument to a time right before Henry takes Edward huckleberry hunting. Says Lydian in the next line, "Edward? (*The little boy comes running to her.*) Go along with Mr. Thoreau." This more subtle technique makes it harder for the audience to follow, but, once again, underscores the expressionistic and uncomfortable quality of the play. Although the entire play is dreamlike, the play achieves its ultimate expression in the actual dream at the end of the play, Henry's nightmare, which convinces Henry to take action.

Foil

In the play, the characters are all juxtaposed with Henry, and in the process become foils for him. A foil is a character who, when placed next to another character, makes the other character seem better in some way. In this case, Henry is the obvious activist, and his status as an activist is raised when Henry is compared to the other characters, who all experience a relative lack of activism. As described above, the most overt foil is Waldo, whose intellectualism prevents him from acting. However, other characters in the story also exhibit various degrees of activism, such as Henry's brother John, who agrees with Henry's ideas of unconventional schooling, saying that: "All a school needs is a mind that sends, and minds that receive." John even partners with Henry to start their own school. However, after they lose most of their students, John loses heart and leaves to go "back to the pencil factory," a conforming job that compromises the ideals that he and Henry share. Henry, on the other hand, decides to trade his intellectual pursuits for natural pursuits, eventually hiring on as Waldo's handyman, although, even then, he refuses to be paid in money, instead preferring a gift of nature: "Perhaps, some day, if my work has been useful to you, and if we remain friends, I may ask you for a bit of your woods."

Ellen Sewell is also a foil for Henry. When Ellen first comes to sit in on classes at Henry's and John's school, she is intrigued by everything Henry is saying, and takes down notes. Henry tells her: "Don't just remember what I said. Remember what I'm talking about." Although Ellen eventually stops taking notes, showing that she can follow this concept of nonconformity, she nevertheless does not fully adopt the transcendentalist ideas that Henry tries to explain to her. Says Henry: ''When you transcend the limits of yourself, you can cease merely living—and begin to BE!'' However, Ellen is ''a little bit afraid—just—to 'be!''' and as a result soon goes back to her normal life of conformity, as most of the characters do. Because of this contrast between the other characters and Henry, the only one who persists in trying to achieve the ideal that Waldo has set forth, Henry appears as the ultimate activist.

HISTORICAL CONTEXT

The American Renaissance

During the time the play takes place, America was experiencing a renaissance, or rebirth, in the arts, particularly literature. This renaissance was sparked mainly by Ralph Waldo Emerson, whose famous Harvard addresses in the 1830s inspired other contemporary New England writers, like Thoreau, to produce many great literary works. At the center of Emerson's teachings and the American Renaissance was the idea of Transcendentalism, a literary and philosophical movement that idealized self-sufficiency and freedom of individual thought and opposition to conformity, even to the point of neglecting to form a concrete definition of Transcendentalism itself. Transcendentalists were opposed to rationalism and, ultimately, believed in the potential of the human mind to transcend the physical reality and thus find the meaning in life. Along with Emerson and Thoreau, other writers of the American Renaissance formed a group that was eventually called the Transcendental Club. Members included Nathaniel Hawthorne and Bronson Alcott, both residents of Concord. Bronson was the father of Louisa May Alcott, another writer who would later incorporate the Transcendentalist beliefs she learned as a child into her own writings later in the century.

Mexican War

As Henry notes in the play, he refuses to pay taxes that will go to support the Mexican War, which was taking place at the time Thoreau was arrested. The Mexican War, also known as the Mexican-American War, took place between the United States and Mexico from April 1846 to February 1848. The war began over a dispute between the two countries about where the dividing line was between Texas—which the United States had annexed in 1845—and Mexico. In 1845, directly following this annexation, President James Polk sent an emissary to negotiate both the border dispute and to try to buy additional lands—modern-day New Mexico and California. Mexico refused to negotiate, and Polk sent General Zachary Taylor and his troops into the disputed border area, which technically belonged to Mexico. This move, in turn, instigated an attack by Mexican forces. Polk cited this attack as taking place on American territory—even though the dispute over the Mexico border territory had not been settled—and Congress authorized a war. Support for the war was largely divided. Although Polk and many southerners were ecstatic, many in the northern states viewed the war as an attempt to acquire more lands, which some believed were only for the purpose of creating more slave-holding southern states.

The war was one-sided, as United States's technologically advanced forces won consecutive battles on two fronts. Under Colonel Stephen Kearny, New Mexico and California were easily occupied, with the native populations putting up little fight. Meanwhile, in Mexico, General Taylor's forces conquered the Mexican forces in a couple of key battles, but neglected to follow the defeated forces farther into Mexico. When President Polk learned of this, he deployed a different force, under the direction of General Winfield Scott, to land at Veracruz and march inland to overtake Mexico's capital, Mexico City. On September 14, 1847, after a series of victories, Scott's forces conquered the capital. As a result of the treaty between the two nations, Mexico sold the United States much of the land in current Southwestern states such as New Mexico, Utah, Nevada, Arizona, California, Texas, and western Colorado, for $15 million.

Vietnam Antiwar Protests

When Lawrence and Lee wrote *The Night Thoreau Spent in Jail*, they used Thoreau's historical protest against the Mexican War as a form of current protest against the Vietnam War. This method of protest was more subtle than many other antiwar protests used during Vietnam. Common methods of protest during Vietnam included men burning their draft cards, which legally obligated them to report for duty in the military. Because skipping this duty was a punishable offense, some were not content with destroying their cards, and fled the country—

COMPARE & CONTRAST

- **Mid-1840s:** The United States engages in a brutal war in Mexico in an attempt to gain more land for America.

  Late 1960s–Early 1970s: The United States engages in a brutal war in Vietnam in an attempt to stop the spread of Communism in southeast Asia.

  Today: The United States engages in a war in Afghanistan, in an attempt to locate hidden terrorist groups.

- **Mid-1840s:** The U.S.–Mexican War is started by President Polk with authorization from Congress. Polk says that Mexico's attack on American soil justifies the war, but the area of the attack is a disputed borderland, not officially recognized American soil. In addition, it is Polk's placement of American forces in this disputed borderland that prompts the Mexican army to attack.

  Late 1960s–Early 1970s: Congress gives President Johnson unlimited powers to wage war in Vietnam, as the result of two alleged attacks on American naval destroyers in the region. Although one attack is later confirmed, the other is not. In addition, the ships, which Johnson claims are on routine missions in neutral waters, are actually on covert missions within enemy waters, which provokes the first attack.

  Today: The War on Terrorism starts after the World Trade Center in New York and the Pentagon in Washington, D. C., are attacked by terrorists, who crash fueled commercial jetliners into the two structures. Much of this is captured on live television, and Americans widely support the moves by President Bush and Congress to begin and escalate a war on terrorism.

- **Mid-1840s:** During the U.S.–Mexican War, many Americans in the northern states do not support the war. Thoreau is one of the notable cases of people who protest, in his case by refusing to pay taxes that help to support the fighting.

  Late 1960s–Early 1970s: Many young American men protest against the Vietnam war by refusing to fight. Common methods of protest include burning draft cards and fleeing to other countries, although demonstrations—peaceful and violent—also increase.

  Today: The American military experiences a surge in its ranks as patriotic men and women willingly join the fight against terrorism.

---

in many cases to Canada—to avoid military service or prosecution. Some chose to ignore their draft notices and stay inside the country, actively voicing their protest. Among the more famous protesters was world-champion heavyweight boxer, Mohammed Ali, who in 1967 refused to be drafted as a result of his religious beliefs. Ali's case went to court later that year, and he was sentenced to five years prison and a $10,000 fine, although he eventually appealed the case all the way to the Supreme Court, which decided three years later to reverse the decision and let Ali go free. However, Ali was not so lucky in his boxing career. When he refused to be drafted, the World Boxing Association and the New York State Athletic Commission stripped Ali of his championship boxing title and revoked his boxing license, a decision that remained in effect until the Supreme Court's decision, at which point Ali was able to box again.

Besides protesting the draft, others protested the war itself in demonstrations, many of which were meant to be nonviolent. One of the most famous, and tragic, of these protests took place on Kent State University's campus in May 1970. Following the April 30 announcement by President Richard Nixon that the United States' military forces were invading Cambodia, students at Kent State staged the first of many demonstrations that week. As the demonstrations spawned rioting and arson,

Ohio's governor called in the state's National Guard to try to maintain order. During the demonstrations on May 4, the National Guardsmen fired a number of bullets into the crowd, killing four students and injuring many others. Although many of the students on campus were protesting the war, some were merely gathering in the protest area to eat their lunch or watch what was going on. In the end, the four students that were killed were never confirmed as protesters. This tragic event ignited college campuses around the country in protest, and many campuses were temporarily closed as a result.

CRITICAL OVERVIEW

The Night Thoreau Spent in Jail is one of Lawrence and Lee's most famous plays, although it has received very little critical attention. As Alan Woods wrote in his introduction to the play in *The Selected Plays of Jerome Lawrence and Robert E. Lee*, the play was ''widely produced across North America,'' but ''was deliberately never performed either on or off Broadway.'' As Woods noted, Lawrence and Lee did this to demonstrate ''that the theatre could be born and continue to live elsewhere than on a few blocks of Manhattan real estate.'' As a result, the New York dramatic critics did not review the play. However, as Woods wrote in his general introduction to *The Selected Plays of Jerome Lawrence and Robert E. Lee*, the play ''was a landmark success in the regional theatre movement.''

This pattern of having many successful productions with little critical commentary has been repeated since the play's first productions in 1970. In fact, with rare exception, the only criticism has come from regional newspapers that reviewed local performances, such as Christopher Rowan's 1998 review in the *Pittsburgh Post-Gazette.* Rowan called the play ''charmingly artless but also clunky,'' saying that the play mixes ''family comedy'' with ''homespun philosophy and high-minded debate.'' In addition, the only major academic commentary has been from Woods, who directs the Jerome Lawrence and Robert E. Lee Theatre Research Institute at The Ohio State University—Lawrence's alma mater.

In addition to editing *The Selected Plays of Jerome Lawrence and Robert E. Lee*, Woods also wrote the entries for Lawrence and Lee for the *Dictionary of Literary Biography.* As he noted in his

Henry David Thoreau

Lawrence entry, the play ''signaled new modes of production in the American commercial theater,'' such as having ''the stage light grows brighter rather than dimmer'' at the end of the play, while ''Thoreau strides through the audience to confront the future.''

These new modes were used specifically to highlight the playwrights' anti-war message, which resonated with the Vietnam-era audiences. As Woods noted in his introduction to *The Night Thoreau Spent in Jail* in *The Selected Plays of Jerome Lawrence and Robert E. Lee*, the play ''comments on contemporaneous events, as do most of Lawrence and Lee's plays.'' Although it has still never been produced in New York, the play has achieved international fame. As Woods notes in his Lawrence entry, in 1989, the play was performed in Hong Kong as a memorial to the students killed during the anti-Communism protest in Tiananmen Square. The play is also frequently used in high school and college courses, and in one notable case, a law school course. In his 1997 article, ''Fiction Draws Students Into the Culture of Law,'' Ronald W. Eades noted how he has used the play as one of the texts in his American Legal History course, since the play provides ''a fictional account of issues that are raised in the course.''

Today, *The Night Thoreau Spent in Jail* is considered, along with *Inherit the Wind*—another play based on a historical event—to be one of the playwrights' greatest works.

CRITICISM

Ryan D. Poquette

Poquette has a bachelor's degree in English and specializes in writing about literature. In the following essay, Poquette discusses how Lawrence and Lee use changes in dialogue and plot to slowly darken the tone of their play.

When *The Night Thoreau Spent in Jail* begins, the play is very lighthearted, and many of Henry's lines are designed to elicit laughs in other characters or the audience. By the end of the play, however, when Henry has his gritty nightmare, humor is replaced by a grim sense of purpose. This change is not abrupt. Rather, over the course of the story, Lawrence and Lee use shifts in Henry's dialogue and the events in his life to induce a gradually darker tone into the play.

In the beginning of the play, Henry is very sarcastic, expressing all sorts of witticisms on various topics. When his mother tells Henry he is "getting everything backward," and wonders how he learned his alphabet, Henry uses this discussion as a transition to give his ideas about the way systems like the alphabet conform to a set pattern, and to suggest alternatives. Says Henry, "*Must* the alphabet begin with A? . . . Why not with Z? Z is a very sociable letter." Henry is equally flippant about the idea of traditional education, and when his brother asks about his Harvard diploma, he says that "They charge you a dollar. And I wouldn't pay it." John says that their mother would have liked to have the diploma to hang up, and Henry gives another witty response: "Let every sheep keep his own skin." Likewise, when Henry is in jail with Bailey in the beginning, and Bailey starts to snore—while Henry is straining to hear something outside—Henry does not just ask his cellmate to stop snoring. Instead, he uses his wit again, to say a line that is meant to make the audience laugh: "Every human being has an inalienable right to snore. *Provided* it does not interfere with the inalienable right of *other* men to snore."

In the first act of the play, Henry also uses witty and playful language to others in the community besides his family and his cellmate. He makes witty comments to his supervisor, Deacon Ball, who calls Henry an atheist. Says Henry, "I've often wondered, Deacon Ball, if atheism might even be popular with God himself." This witty retort causes the audience to think, and once again is intended to elicit a laugh, as is Henry's report to his class that, due to Ball's strict requirements, "You must not listen to a cricket or smell a flower that has not been approved by the School Committee." Henry expands on this joke, by illustrating the logistical improbabilities of doing this with only two hands: "You'd better close both ears and hold your nose—though you may have to grow an extra hand to do it." When Henry opens his own school with his brother, John, he also offers witty comments to his students, such as Ellen Sewell, who he catches taking notes. "*You* keep a notebook," she tells him. Henry's reply is quirky and witty: "I also wear a ridiculous straw hat. That doesn't mean that *you* should wear a ridiculous hat. You'd look ridiculous in it."

Although the play starts out with a lot of witty, playful comments from Henry, it starts to get more serious at this point. Henry is so committed to the idea of not conforming that he yells at Ellen: "Follow-the-leader is not the game we're playing here! Young lady, BE YOUR OWN MAN!" From this point on, Henry still makes witty comments, such as his witty banter when he is applying for a job with Waldo, and says he wants to use his hands. When Waldo asks about his head, Henry says: "It could be useful. For burrowing, perhaps. . . . I could beat it into a ploughshare." However, as the play progresses, the majority of Henry's comments become more politically charged, as opposed to just witty.

Near the end of the first act, when Sam tells Henry that he has to pay his taxes to support the war, Henry is furious, and tries to renounce his citizenship. Says Henry, "I wouldn't pay the tithe and tariff to the church, so I signed off from the church! Well, I'm ready right now, Sam, to sign off from the government. Where do I sign?" Henry's transformation in language reaches its climax at the very end of the act, in the last exchange. Waldo has come to the jail to confront Henry, and says: "Henry! *Henry*! What are you doing in jail? However, at this point, Henry is very politically charged, and does not balk from confronting his former mentor, who

WHAT DO I READ NEXT?

- *Mother Courage and Her Children,* an antiwar play by German playwright, Bertolt Brecht, was originally published in 1949 following World War II. Like *The Night Thoreau Spent in Jail,* Brecht's tragic play is set in an earlier historical era, in this case seventeenth-century Europe, during the multi-national Thirty Years' War. Brecht's play depicts the tragic figure of Mother Courage, whose attempts to make money from the war inadvertently kill all of her children. *Mother Courage and Her Children* is available in a reprint edition from 1991, translated by Eric Bentley.
- Ralph Waldo Emerson and his transcendentalist ideas were a strong influence on the life and works of Henry David Thoreau. In 2000, many of Emerson's major works were collected in *The Essential Writings of Ralph Waldo Emerson.* This book offers a great introduction to Emerson's teachings.
- Lawrence and Lee's *Inherit the Wind* is the writing team's most successful play. In 1925, the state of Tennessee filed suit against Michael Scopes, a young teacher who was teaching evolution. The play, which was first published in 1955, dramatizes this famous trial, as an obvious commentary on the Communist ''witch trials'' that were being held by Senator Joseph McCarthy and others during the 1950s.
- Harmon Smith's *My Friend, My Friend: The Story of Thoreau's Relationship with Emerson* (1999) details the historic friendship between the two writers, which lasted from Thoreau's Harvard days in the 1830s until Thoreau's death in the 1860s. Although this relationship has been explored by many scholars, Smith's engaging account, which includes many quotes from the journals of Emerson and Thoreau, offers new insights.
- Thoreau's one night in jail eventually became the basis for his essay ''Civil Disobedience,'' which was first published in 1849 as ''Resistance to Civil Government.'' Although the work received little critical or popular attention at the time, it found an audience with twentieth-century readers. The essay was reprinted with Thoreau's other major essays in 1993 in *Civil Disobedience and Other Essays.*
- Unlike ''Civil Disobedience,'' Thoreau's *Walden; or, Life in the Woods,* a collection of essays originally published in 1854, did find an audience during Thoreau's lifetime, although the book's sales did not really take off until it was reprinted shortly before Thoreau's death, at which point it was renamed, simply, *Walden.* Since then, it has sold millions of copies, achieved enormous critical success, and been translated into many different languages. *Walden* is currently available in a reprint edition from 1998.

---

he feels should be in jail protesting with him: ''(*Defiantly, pointing accusingly across Concord Square.*) Waldo! What are you doing *out* of jail?''

While the first act features some light, witty dialogue from Henry that slowly darkens, the second act is mainly serious, as evidenced by the opening scene. Lydian tells Henry that ''in order to *get* along, you have to *go* along.'' Henry is disgusted at this idea of conformity, and shouts: ''GO ALONG! GO ALONG! GO ALONG!'' to show his rage. The second act also witnesses Henry's realization that, while witty language is fun, it is not always effective. When Bailey comes to him, nervous about his upcoming trial, he asks Henry to ''Tell me what to do!'' Henry responds: ''Well, you might try getting yourself born in a more just and generous age. That's not a very practical suggestion.'' Although Henry's witty comments about alphabets and atheism worked in the beginning when the stakes were

"ALL OF THE GRADUALLY MORE SERIOUS EVENTS HAVE HARDENED HENRY'S RESOLVE, A FACT THAT IS MANIFESTED BY THE CHANGE IN HIS LANGUAGE, FROM WITTY AND PLAYFUL, TO MORE POLITICALLY ACTIVE, TO SILENT—LETTING HIS ACTIONS SPEAK LOUDER THAN HIS WORDS."

not as high, now he is dealing with a man's life, and he realizes that in such heady matters, humor does not always offer a practical solution.

In the end, after his nightmare, Henry trades in his witty dialogue for an activist's sense of purpose. The very end of the play, which is silent, offers a marked contrast to Henry's impassioned dialogue throughout the beginning of the story. The stage directions describe in detail how Henry ''*seems to grow in stature, lifted and strengthened by a greater challenge,*'' but Henry does not say anything. He has learned that actions speak louder than words, and is prepared to act.

The shift in Henry's style and frequency of speech mirrors the events in Henry's life, which also shift from the comedic and lighthearted to the tragic and purposeful. In the beginning of the play, when John asks Henry what he wants to do with his life, he says ''I want to be as much as possible like Ralph Waldo Emerson.'' Henry is fresh out of school at this point, and thinks that he will be able to live his Transcendental life without being greatly affected by other events. However, when Henry tries to pursue his vocation of teaching, he runs up against the strict requirements of the school, which include whipping the students when they misbehave. Reluctantly, Henry does this, but he is so disgusted with himself that he informs Deacon Ball he ''has administered the Sacrament of the Schoolroom; and he resigns as a 'teacher' in the Public Schools of Concord!'' Since, at this point, the audience does not know the negative circumstances surrounding Henry's imprisonment, Henry's resignation from school becomes the first event that is portrayed as negative. It is followed by a series of events, which get progressively more tragic. The Transcendentalist school established by Henry and John fails when they lose all of their students. Henry tries and fails to explain the ideas of Transcendentalism and his love to the beautiful Ellen Sewell.

Then, the first major tragic event in the play happens, the death of John, an event that profoundly affects Henry. Once again, Henry employs his wit when he talks about the details that surround John's death, but it is anything but humorous. Says Henry to Ellen: ''He had a glamorous death. Like the Knights of the Round Table who slashed at each other with rusty swords until they all died of blood poisoning.'' As Henry elaborates, he tells Ellen about the shaving accident that gave John his own blood poisoning: ''John, three mornings ago, happened to think of something very funny while he was shaving. He burst out laughing, and cut himself.'' It is oddly fitting that John dies as a result of his laughter, since Henry learns throughout the play that too much humor without action can kill a person's effectiveness.

In the second act, Henry faces another death that affects him, the death of the escaped slave, Henry Williams. Henry Thoreau tries to explain the injustice of Williams's murder, and tells Waldo that his own policy of working within the system is not effective enough to save people like Williams: ''When a man, at the border of freedom, is stopped by the rifle of a Boston policeman, he doesn't have time for Dr. Emerson's leisurely sermon on the 'slow evolving of the seasons.''' The same argument about Williams leads Henry to pressure Waldo to give a talk against slavery and the Mexican War. However, at the crucial moment, after Henry has already gathered a crowd, Waldo sends Lydian with a message, saying that ''he wants more time to meditate on these matters. . . . So that he can write a careful essay setting forth his position.'' Following this betrayal, which wounds Henry deeply, he totally denounces Waldo: ''My God, he was my god! No more! If he is the Deity, I am a doubter!''

Henry realizes that he must take matters into his own hands, but is unsure how to do that. All of these conflicting feelings manifest themselves in his nightmare, in which military members chant such things as ''Hate-two-three-four!'' and ''Learn to kill!'' underscoring the tragedy of the Mexican War that Henry wants to stop. Tragedy strikes in Henry's nightmare, too, as the little Drummer Boy (Waldo's son, Edward) is wounded, and Henry watches his brother die once again, this time as the result of the war. Henry wakes up and realizes he needs to take action. All of the gradually more serious events have hardened Henry's resolve, a fact that is manifested by the change in his language, from witty and playful, to more politically active, to silent—letting his actions speak louder than his words. Of course, readers can make many other interpretations about the play, especially since the playwrights' dreamlike, expressionistic structure inspires very different experiences in each person. In the end, as Lawrence and Lee note in their foreword to the play: "It is eminently Thoreauvian that everyone should bring to—and take from—the play something uniquely his own."

Source: Ryan D. Poquette, Critical Essay on *The Night Thoreau Spent in Jail,* in *Drama for Students,* The Gale Group, 2003.

Curt Guyette

Guyette holds a bachelor of arts degree in English writing from the University of Pittsburgh. In the following essay, Guyette examines the theme of civil disobedience in Lawrence and Lee's play.

In their play *The Night Thoreau Spent in Jail,* Jerome Lawrence and Robert E. Lee explore the issue of morality versus adherence to the law and what the conscientious course of action should be when a citizen comes into conflict with government actions he or she believes to be immoral. By dramatizing an actual event in the life of writer Henry David Thoreau, a man who personified the ideal of Americans as rugged individualists, the playwrights deliver an unambiguous message: If you believe a government's policies are wrong, then you have an ethical responsibility to oppose those acts, even if that dissent makes you a criminal in the eyes of the state.

As depicted by Lawrence and Lee, writer Henry David Thoreau was the quintessential nonconformist. A man who rejected the social conventions of his day, he gladly assumed the role of an outcast. Thoreau was, it seems, compelled to march to a drumbeat whose discordant rhythm was dictated solely by his own conscience and intellect. As portrayed in this play, a transforming moment occurred when Thoreau decided to face jail rather than support a war against Mexico he believed to be both illegal and immoral. Writing this play at the height of the U.S. war in Vietnam, Lawrence and Lee use events that occurred 125 years earlier to demonstrate that openly opposing government actions that an individual believes to be unjust is a time-honored American tradition.

"WRITING THIS PLAY AT THE HEIGHT OF THE U.S. WAR IN VIETNAM, LAWRENCE AND LEE USE EVENTS THAT OCCURRED 125 YEARS EARLIER TO DEMONSTRATE THAT OPENLY OPPOSING GOVERNMENT ACTIONS THAT AN INDIVIDUAL BELIEVES TO BE UNJUST IS A TIME-HONORED AMERICAN TRADITION."

The authors of the play certainly admire the young Thoreau, who rejected materialism and technological advancement by retreating to the unspoiled woods of Walden Pond. "He smelled the smog before we saw it," they wrote in an introduction to the play published in 1971. "It smarted his soul before it smarted our eyes." But they also saw the shortcomings of a life spent in seclusion and how a high-principled hermit may be nurturing his own soul but, by living in isolation, does nothing to help uplift his fellow man. For Thoreau to transcend that limitation and become a true hero, he had to give up the Eden-like tranquility of his beloved Walden. In production notes for the play, Lawrence and Lee explained it this way:

> Thoreau's decision to return to the human race is the shape, the parabola of the play: his evolution from withdrawal to return, the journey from hermitizing to social conscience. This is the subtext of the play.

The authors were not motivated to glorify events of the past. For them, the story of Thoreau's night in jail was a sort of parable, or lesson, that very much applied to their day and time—in fact, to any day and time. That concept is reinforced by the play's dreamlike qualities. Set in a jail cell, the story it tells knows no bounds. Characters come and go, events from the past are conjured up, abandoned, and then revisited. At its heart, this is a very political play, written in response to the events of a turbulent time in American history. As the play's authors wrote, they saw Thoreau and his writings as the embodiment of an "explosive spirit who addressed himself to the perils of our time with more power and clarity than most angry young men writing now about now." But as time has shown, like Thoreau himself, the issues this play raises are universal, and its message timeless.

The foundation of Thoreau's moral base is laid at the outset of the play. As in his real life, Thoreau is profoundly affected by the writings of Ralph Waldo Emerson, who comes to serve as the younger man's spiritual father. "Have you ever noticed, John," says the character Mother (who gets the order of things mixed up), "how much Mr. Emerson talks like our David Henry." Just as Emerson resigns from his position as church pastor when he cannot, in good conscience, perform the rites required by his congregation, Thoreau, likewise, leaves his job as a public school teacher rather than be fettered by the constraints of using only approved textbooks.

Nonconformist is the perfect word to describe Thoreau. "Henry," says Mother, "you have wits enough to know that, in order to get along, you have to go along." But that is something he will not, perhaps even cannot, do. When the law demands that a free man must turn in runaway slaves, should a person of conscience feel bound to be law abiding? For Thoreau, the answer to that question is a resounding "no." He quickly learns, though, that using principles rather than popular opinion as a personal compass comes with a price. It puts him decidedly outside the mainstream. For a man such as Thoreau, however, that price is readily paid. In his view, going along just to get along extracts a much higher toll than simple alienation from society. Henry sums up his view during a conversation with his fellow prisoner as they listen to the footsteps of a man walking outside the jail:

> I know where he's going. He's going where he's supposed to go. So he can be where he's supposed to be, at the time he's supposed to be there. Why? So he'll be liked. My God, a whole country of us who only want to be liked. But to be liked, you must never disagree. And if you never disagree, it's like only breathing *in* and never breathing *out*!

That statement, in essence, is the key to understanding the character Henry. It is as if, by his very nature, he is physically incapable of following the rest of society in lockstep. Doing so would result in intellectual and spiritual suffocation. And for Henry, that would be a much harsher fate than merely being disliked. Or, as he comes to learn, being imprisoned.

In his biography of Thoreau, Edward Wagenknecht quoted a passage from the writer's seminal essay, "Civil Disobedience": "Under a government which imprisons any unjustly the true place for a just man is also in prison." That essay is credited with influencing such leading advocates of nonviolent protest as Mohandas Gandhi and Martin Luther King Jr., both of whom endured incarceration rather than abide by laws they believed to be unjust. Likewise, Thoreau's willingness to be locked behind bars inspired Lawrence and Lee to dramatize that real-life incident, portraying it as a pivotal moment in the author's life. Until then, he was content to work as Emerson's handyman and gather huckleberries with young Edward, or tend his bean patch at Walden Pond. It is an idyllic life. Unshackled from material wants, he rejoices in the splendors of nature, living simply and freely. The fact that he is largely removed from the rest of the world troubles him not at all. While in jail, however, he has a dream that transforms him. As the playwrights noted: "His night in jail is a mystical experience for this highly sensitive man. Confined, he has the liberty to explore what he really *is.*"

Unlike his mentor Emerson, Thoreau cannot stand by silently as his nation wages an imperialistic war. In that belief, he is in good company. The playwrights quote a speech given by Abraham Lincoln who, as a young congressman from Illinois, had the political courage to swim against the tide of public opinion and condemn the Mexican War as both unnecessary and unconstitutional. Like Henry, he chose to adhere to the dictates of his conscience rather than follow the easier course of going along with the mainstream.

It is during his dream that Henry attempts to speak out but finds he has no voice. It is symbolic of his situation, and a direct result of the reclusive path he has taken to that point in his life. Unlike Waldo, who by virtue of his prominence can attract an audience and influence their thoughts, Henry, in essence, has no platform from which he can speak. He has not built the foundation for people to take him seriously and consequently is politically impotent. During times of moral crisis, dissenters need a voice that will be heard, otherwise their dissent is pointless. To emphasize the need for Henry to find his voice, Lawrence and Lee are unsparing in their depiction of war's horror. While most of the play is relentlessly stark, leaving the audience to fill in the blank spaces, the dream sequence is particularly graphic. The huckleberries may have been imaginary, but the uniforms and muskets are unmistakably realistic. There are explosions of gunfire, and the ''sky seems ripped apart by psychedelic splatterings of shrapnel.'' There is a reason Henry refuses to subsidize all this with his tax dollars: it is hell, and he will not play any part whatsoever in supporting it. However, as he stands there, holding the body of young Edward in his arms, he realizes that his quiet dissent serves no greater good. Walden, he admits to his cellmate Bailey, may indeed be heaven, but heaven is the realm of the afterlife. As he tells his new friend: ''Bailey, I tried to escape. But escape is like sleep. And when sleep is permanent, it's death.'' Which is why, at the play's end, the lights do not dim as usual and Henry does not disappear behind a closing curtain. The morning sky is ablaze with new-found glory and Henry, having grown as a result of that night's mystical experience, is ''lifted and strengthened'' by the greater challenge upon which he is ready to embark.

Like Henry, the authors of this play wanted their audience to see the light. There is no doubt Thoreau's days as a recluse are over as he leaps from the stage to be among the people. The message is clear: for one to simply follow the beat of one's own different drummer is not always good enough, like when, as Henry ultimately learns, there is a moral imperative to help others hear the same beat and then convince them to march alongside him.

Source: Curt Guyette, Critical Essay on *The Night Thoreau Spent in Jail,* in *Drama for Students,* The Gale Group, 2003.

Alan Woods

In the following essay, Woods traces the development of The Night Thoreau Spent in Jail *and the significant changes made to its first version.*

In *The Night Thoreau Spent in Jail*, Lawrence and Lee continued to explore the historic past through fiction in order to comment on the present, using Henry David Thoreau's own name and the names of his friends and fellow citizens of Concord. The play is based on Thoreau's actual incarceration when he refused to pay taxes that would go to support the Mexican-American War of 1846–48. Lawrence and Lee began work on the first draft of the play—originally titled *A Different Drummer*—in July 1966. Unlike their earlier collaborations, *A Different Drummer* initially was Lawrence's project alone. The first outline opens with the exchange that was eventually to conclude act 1:

VOICE [Emerson]: Henry, what are you doing in jail?

HENRY (*Clutching the bars and shouting back, like a whiplash*) Waldo! What are you doing out of jail???

> "THE PARALLELS BETWEEN THOREAU'S PASSIVE RESISTANCE TO THE MEXICAN-AMERICAN WAR, AND THE PROTESTS ERUPTING ACROSS THE UNITED STATES IN THE LATE 1960S TO THE VIETNAM WAR WERE OBVIOUS; AND THE PLAYWRIGHTS FULLY INTENDED THE PARALLELS TO BE SEEN."

This first version of the play employs a mock trial as the organizing focus, with figures from Thoreau's life being summoned to testify as Thoreau attempts to justify his actions. Lee's initial work on *The Night Thoreau Spent in Jail* was to serve as an editor, reacting to Lawrence's rough outline. The playwrights met to discuss the play in July 1967, but did not turn their full attention to the script until April 1969.

As a result of the playwrights' consultations, *A Different Drummer* was rethought entirely, emerging not only with a new title, but with an entirely new structure. The jail setting remained as the focal point of the play, but the trial convention was abandoned, as was any pretense at strict chronology. Rather, Lawrence and Lee embraced a fluid structure reminiscent of expressionist theatrical experimentation earlier in the twentieth century.

Once the decision was made to adopt the new format, Lawrence and Lee's work on *The Night Thoreau Spent in Jail* progressed rapidly during the summer of 1969, and the finished and revised text was completed by early October. Submitted to the American Playwrights Theatre (APT), the play was quickly accepted for production. The pilot production opened at Ohio State University on 21 April 1970—fifteen years to the day after the triumphal New York opening of *Inherit the Wind.*

The Night Thoreau Spent in Jail comments on contemporaneous events, as do most of Lawrence and Lee's plays. The parallels between Thoreau's passive resistance to the Mexican-American War, and the protests erupting across the United States in the late 1960s to the Vietnam War were obvious; and the playwrights fully intended the parallels to be seen. As early as 1967, they had noted that "the whole theme of the Thoreau piece should be the obligation to rebel non-violently. Not merely the right to rebel. But the necessity."

With Thoreau as the play's constant center, the events that shaped his political and intellectual growth swirl together as he attempts to understand what brought him to the Concord jail. Thoreau's memories climax in the phantasmagoric nightmare sequence that forms the heart of act 2. Ralph Waldo Emerson serves as an appropriate foil for Thoreau: the established intellectual leader with the moral power to provide leadership against the war who instead waffles, preferring ineffectually procrastinating discussion to direct action.

The contrast between Thoreau's activism and Emerson's failure to lead is doubled by the play's other characters, who provide different sorts of contrasts. Thoreau's cellmate, Bailey, is clearly a dramatic device, allowing Thoreau to explain his beliefs to a new person and to demonstrate his abilities as a teacher when, early in the play, he teaches Bailey to write his name. Henry's brother, John, doubles Thoreau in several ways, most significantly as Henry's surrogate in the unsuccessful wooing of Ellen.

Ellen herself is a foil for Thoreau. Not only does she articulate the comfortable bourgeois philosophy Thoreau rejects (particularly early in the play), she also displays the ability to learn and grow when she is able to articulate the key elements of Transcendentalism after John's death. Each of the minor figures reverses some element of Thoreau's character, whether it be the authoritarian pedagogical style insisted upon by Deacon Ball or Sam's unquestioning acceptance of the government's dictates.

Lawrence and Lee dramatized events in Thoreau's life that illustrated their central concerns. A brief analysis of the first act will demonstrate that it is carefully constructed to lead the audience through Thoreau's development. The play's structure appears casual and loose, although each detail carries a purpose and meaning.

Waldo's apparent age and confusion in the opening sequence establishes that the play's events will take place in fluid time; Waldo's self-centeredness, which motivates his reluctance to act, is also indicated here. Henry's exchange with his mother, which follows and overlaps the Waldo-Lydian scene, sets up immediately Thoreau's independence and self-reliance.

Thoreau's insistence upon being true to himself despite the conforming drive of society, is, of course, the central theme of the play. Henry's refusal to accept the traditional order of the alphabet, followed immediately by Waldo's "Cast Conformity behind you," reinforces his individuality. The short scene that follows with his brother, John, establishes Waldo's influence on Thoreau, as well as setting up his parallel reliance upon his brother. Both the intellectual and familial support will be wrenched away from Thoreau as the play progresses. Having Waldo's moment of self-doubt follow immediately after Henry's "I want to be as much as possible like Ralph Waldo Emerson" undercuts Henry's hero worship, letting the audience know instantly that Emerson will prove ineffective.

The play's first extended scene, Thoreau in the jail cell with Bailey, follows. Thoreau is on his own here. Although the audience does not yet know that John will be dead by the time Henry is jailed or that Waldo will have failed Thoreau as well, the first Bailey scene shows the mature Thoreau. He fuses an awareness of the world of nature heightened by the Walden experience with a rejection of the political world of "a President who went out and boomed up a war all by himself—with no help from Congress and less help from me." The scene ends with Thoreau teaching Bailey to write his name and leapfrogs into Thoreau in his Concord classroom, where Deacon Ball forces Thoreau to face another consequence of the individual's freedom: the responsibility to refuse morally unsupportable orders. Thoreau's resignation as a teacher is paralleled directly by Lawrence and Lee with Emerson's resignation of his pulpit, also on a matter of conscience.

Henry and John's own school, in the following sequence, reinforces Henry's growing awareness of the natural world and also introduces Ellen and permits Henry to explain his self-directed teaching philosophy. Henry's rejection of learning in the jail cell sounds the first note of the Thoreau school's failure, which becomes clearer in the following long scene, in which Henry explores the possibility of traditional fulfillment through marriage. The row-ing sequence with Ellen gives a further chance to explore his personal philosophy, while providing a sharp contrast between his behavior and the expected behavior of a polite middle-class suitor.

The jail cell, with Bailey's snore-response to Henry's question about marriage, provides the bridge to the next scene, the church service ultimately interrupted by Henry and his wheelbarrow working on Sunday, having taken the rest of the week off. John's recounting of Ellen's refusal is followed quickly by John's death and burial. Ellen's awareness of Transcendentalism demonstrates Henry's success as a teacher; but bereft of both John and Ellen, he turns to his second source of support, the Emersons, in the third major scene of the act. Walden is fully introduced in this scene, and the relationships between Henry and each of the Emersons are suggested. After a brief return to the cell, and Henry's mature reflection on what Walden has meant to him, the act's last major scene shows Henry's actual arrest and full explanation of why he refuses to pay his taxes. The act ends with the Henry/Waldo exchange that had opened the first version of *A Different Drummer* in Jerome Lawrence's original outline.

Although the structure of the first act of *The Night Thoreau Spent in Jail* is fluid, each of the elements dramatized has a specific purpose, culminating in Thoreau's arrest and then his challenge to Emerson, which ends the act. What appears on first viewing to be casual is, in fact, quite carefully plotted. The playwrights' success in capturing the mood of the late 1960s is clear not only in their use of the parallels between the Mexican-American and Vietnam Wars, but also in their contrast of the restrictive (and restricting) educational system represented by Deacon Ball to Thoreau's nature-centered approach. Thoreau's educational philosophy, as presented by the playwrights, is quite close to the alternative educational theories most forcefully articulated in the 1960s by A. S. Neill, Ivan Illich, and Jonathan Kozol.

The play also contributed significantly to the then-burgeoning regional theatre movement by its production through the American Playwrights Theatre, resulting in more than one hundred forty separate productions from 1970 through 1971. *The Night Thoreau Spent in Jail*'s message of individual responsibility remains current: the Hong Kong Repertory Theatre performed it in the autumn of 1989 as a memorial to the Chinese students massacred in Beijing's Tiananmen Square when the People's Army brutally crushed the freedom movement in early June 1989.

Although widely produced across North America, *The Night Thoreau Spent in Jail* was deliberately never performed either on or off Broadway, as the playwrights demonstrated that the theatre could be born and continue to live elsewhere than on a few blocks of Manhattan real estate. Even though the play is frequently produced, there has been little critical comment on the script. It many ways, *The Night Thoreau Spent in Jail* has fallen victim to the cultural dominance of the American theatre by the New York stage: scripts receive little critical attention unless they have been successfully produced in full view of the national media, centered in New York City. Although there are some indications that this bias may be lessening, it remained strongly in place when *The Night Thoreau Spent in Jail* was first produced in 1970. Lawrence and Lee's examination of individual consciousness has gone virtually unremarked other than in newspaper accounts of the (literally) hundreds of individual productions.

The Night Thoreau Spent in Jail remains in the world repertory. The play has historic significance as the greatest success of the American Playwrights Theatre, the organization founded by Lawrence and Lee in 1965 as a means of bypassing the harshly commercial conditions then beginning to dominate the Broadway stage. Headquartered at Ohio State University, where *The Night Thoreau Spent in Jail* was premiered, APT created the first truly national theatrical production mechanism seen in the United States. In significant ways, it fostered the growth of professional theatres outside New York City, helping to diminish the sole power of the Broadway stage. *The Night Thoreau Spent in Jail* was widely produced and highly successful across the country, with more than two thousand performances at APT-member theatres during its first two years alone. One scholar did note that ''more people saw that play in one season than had seen . . . *Inherit the Wind* and *Auntie Mame* in their total combined runs.'' That *The Night Thoreau Spent in Jail* still has not attracted much scholarly attention must be seen as an ironic comment on the scholarly community's lack of awareness of changes in theatrical production patterns during the past two decades, as well as on scholars ignoring evidence beneath their very noses. More than twenty years after its premiere, the Bantam edition of *The Night Thoreau Spent in Jail* has almost a half-million copies in print.

Source: Alan Woods, ''*The Night Thoreau Spent in Jail:* Introduction,'' in *Selected Plays of Jerome Lawrence and Robert E. Lee,* edited by Alan Woods, Ohio State University Press, 1995, pp. 447–506.

SOURCES

Eades, Ronald W., ''Fiction Draws Students into Culture of Law,'' in the *Law Teacher,* Spring 1997.

Lawrence, Jerome, and Robert E. Lee, Foreword to *The Night Thoreau Spent in Jail,* in *The Selected Plays of Jerome Lawrence and Robert E. Lee,* edited by Alan Woods, Ohio State University Press, 1995, p. 456.

———, *The Night Thoreau Spent in Jail,* in *The Selected Plays of Jerome Lawrence and Robert E. Lee,* edited by Alan Woods, Ohio State University Press, 1995, pp. 459–64, 467–69, 471–72, 474–75, 480–81, 483, 486–87, 489–90, 494–502, 505–06.

———, ''The Now Thoreau,'' in *The Night Thoreau Spent in Jail,* Bantam Books, 1971, p. vii.

———, ''Production Notes from the Playwrights,'' in *The Night Thoreau Spent in Jail,* Bantam Books, 1971, p. 113.

Rawson, Christopher, Review of *The Night Thoreau Spent in Jail,* in *Pittsburgh Post-Gazette,* November 5, 1998.

Wagenknecht, Edward, ''Wider Circles,'' in *Henry David Thoreau,* University of Massachusetts Press Amherst, 1981, p. 109.

Woods, Alan, ''General Introduction,'' in *The Selected Plays of Jerome Lawrence and Robert E. Lee,* edited by Alan Woods, Ohio State University Press, 1995, p. ix.

———, Introduction to *The Night Thoreau Spent in Jail,* in *The Selected Plays of Jerome Lawrence and Robert E. Lee,* edited by Alan Woods, Ohio State University Press, 1995, pp. 449, 452.

———, ''Jerome Lawrence,'' in *Dictionary of Literary Biography,* Vol. 228: *Twentieth-Century American Dramatists, Second Series,* edited by Christopher J. Wheatley, The Gale Group, 2000, pp. 161–70.

FURTHER READING

Burkett, B. G., *Stolen Valor: How the Vietnam Generation Was Robbed of Its Heroes and Its History,* Verity Press, 1998.

Burkett, a Vietnam veteran and reporter, was featured on the newsmagazine show ''20/20'' for this unflinching look at the ways in which Vietnam veterans have been misunderstood, in part due to the actions of some who have tarnished the image of this generation. Exhaustively researched, the book helps to set the record straight about a very painful time in American history.

Eisenhower, John S. D., *So Far from God: The U.S. War with Mexico, 1846–1848,* University of Oklahoma Press, 2000.

Eisenhower's in-depth history of the Mexican War offers depictions of the major military leaders from the United States, some of whom featured prominently in the Civil War two decades later. The book also views the war in its historical context, addressing the different American viewpoints of those in the North and those in the South.

Field, Ron, *Mexican-American War 1846–48,* Brasseys, Inc., 1997.

This book offers a thoroughly illustrated history of the uniforms, equipment, and weapons of both the Mexican and American armies. From the American forces, the book covers United States Regulars, Texas Rangers, and Militia members. Although information on Mexican forces is rare, this book makes good use of the available resources.

Johannsen, Robert Walter, *To the Halls of the Montezumas: The Mexican War in the American Imagination,* Oxford University Press on Demand, 1988.

Johannsen analyzes the Mexican War in view of the fact that it was the first foreign war that was heavily reported in the press. As such, it greatly affected the imagination of an America that was trying to find its identity. The book draws on a number of firsthand accounts and other original sources.

Kent, Stephen A., *From Slogans to Mantras: Social Protest and Religious Conversion in the Late Vietnam Era,* Syracuse University Press, 2001.

At the same time that young Americans were engaging in the antiwar counterculture movement, many also chose to join alternative, and sometimes radical, spiritual groups and cults. Kent, a sociologist, presents the unique view that this often overlooked trend was motivated mainly by politics, not spirituality.

Leckie, Robert, *From Sea to Shining Sea: From the War of 1812 to the Mexican War, the Saga of America's Expansion,* HarperPerennial, 1994.

Leckie examines this rich period in America's early history as an independent nation. The shape of the modern continental United States was largely determined by the end of the Mexican War, and the book offers many anecdotes that illustrate the major events during America's territorial growth, including the major people involved in the expansion.

Martin, Susan, ed., *Decade of Protest: Political Posters from the United States, Viet Nam, Cuba, 1965–1975,* Distributed Art Publishers, 1996.

The United States was not the only nation that experienced massive antiwar protests among its citizens during the Vietnam War; many people in Vietnam and Cuba also protested the war. This unique book collects samples of the various protest posters that were produced in the three countries. The images are combined with essays that give background on the posters and the historical and cultural contexts in which they were created.

The Rover

APHRA BEHN

1677

The Rover, published and first produced in 1677, was Aphra Behn's most successful play. The original full title, *The Rover; or, The Banish'd Cavaliers*, indicates that the play was a tribute to the formerly exiled cavalier and newly reinstated king, Charles II. *The Rover* is a dark comedy that mixes themes of prostitution and rape with comic buffoonery. The play expresses its author's objections to the vulnerability of women in Restoration society. Perhaps ironically, it also appeals to the prurient interests of the audience by putting women in morally compromising situations. Based loosely on her contemporary Thomas Killigrew's 1564 *Thomaso; or, The Wanderer* (1664), Behn's play is leaner, less lewd, and more profound. The plot follows the fortunes of opposing lovers, one a woman of quality masquerading as a courtesan and one a wandering rake whose philandering days end when he falls in love with her. Several near-rapes and the tragic case of a jilted courtesan, another character in the play, balance the comic treatment of sexual politics in the seventeenth century. The rover of the title is either Willmore, an exiled English sea captain on shore leave to enjoy the carnival, or Hellena, a young woman hoping to experience life and love before being committed to a convent by her brother. These two rovers meet and fall in love amid witty debates and sexual maneuvering. Willmore has many parallels to Charles II, whose exploits during his twenty-year banishment from England were well known.

Charles II enjoyed the play so much that he commissioned a private viewing of it.

AUTHOR BIOGRAPHY

Aphra Behn, a favorite of feminist literary critics, is considered to be the first woman to have made a living through her writing. There were other women writers before Behn, but few of them enjoyed financial success. Behn turned to her literary talent after the death of her husband, and she quickly proved her merit as well as her perseverance. Behn suffered from the biases of her time against women writers in general and women dramatists in particular. She was assumed by many of her contemporaries to be a prostitute; because of her connection to the theater and because at the time, women who sold their writing were seen as selling themselves. In her prefaces, Behn sometimes commented on her unique status as a woman writer and asked to be taken seriously as a writer, with equal right to freedom in what she wrote. For example, in her preface to *The Lucky Chance; or, An Alderman's Bargain* (1686), she wrote, ''All I ask, is for the privilege for my masculine part, the poet in me . . . to tread in those successful paths my predecessors have long thrived in . . . If I must not, because of my sex, have this freedom, but that you will usurp all to yourselves; I [will] lay down my Quill and you shall hear no more of me.''

Born in 1640 in Kent, England, Behn learned French and Dutch as she grew up. In 1663, she traveled with her family to Surinam, West Indies, where her father was to take an administrative post, but he died on the voyage there, and the family eventually returned. Young Behn kept a journal during her stay in Surinam, which she transformed into the novella *Oroonoko; or, The Royal Slave* (1688). By the time she was twenty-six, she had lost her husband of three years, a Dutch merchant named Behn about whom little else is known. She briefly held a position as a spy in Antwerp for King Charles II, during the war against the Dutch (1665–1667) but was not paid for her work and returned to London a pauper in the year following the Great Fire of 1666. Having unsuccessfully appealed to various friends for financial assistance, Behn served time in debtor's prison and, upon release, began her writing career. Her first play, *The Forc'd Marriage; or, The Jealous Bridegroom* (1670) established her reputation, and she continued to produce enough substantial work each year to make a living. Despite this success, Behn's reputation suffered because of the topics she chose. Many of her eighteen extant plays portray various forms of prostitution, and some of her novels and poems contain frank eroticism that shocked early audiences. Being one of the earliest female playwrights, she was seen as someone who, like an actress, displayed herself to the public. Since actresses were viewed as—and some were—prostitutes, it was assumed by many that Behn was a prostitute, too.

Like her role model, William Shakespeare, Behn often mined ideas from existing works and vastly improved upon them. She often complained that her works never attained the fame they deserved because they were ''writ by a woman.'' However, her achievement survived her, for by the nineteenth century, Virginia Woolf would exclaim in *A Room of One's Own* that a woman *could* live the writer's life, since ''Aphra Behn had done it!''

Aphra Behn died in April of 1689. Engraved on her tombstone, perhaps at the request of her lover, John Hoyle, are the words, ''Here lies a proof that wit can never be / Defence enough against mortality.'' She is buried in Westminster Abbey.

PLOT SUMMARY

Prologue

The prologue in rhyming couplets portends a play that is not just ''good conversation,'' as conventional plays present, but is full of ''wit'' and ''deboches'' [debauches], as is life.

Act 1

The scene untraditionally opens on two women. Sisters Hellena and Florinda are discussing love, which the younger sister Hellena wants to experience before her brother sends her to a nunnery, and Florinda coyly tells about her beau, an English colonel. They are interrupted by their brother Don Pedro, who announces that, to prevent Florinda from having to marry her father's choice for her, an old man, she must marry Don Pedro's friend Don Antonio the next day. The girls decide to go to the carnival that night in masks and costumed as gypsy whores, to exploit their independence before it is stifled by their prearranged futures, and Florinda hopes to encounter Belvile to tell him that she loves him. Their cousin Valeria and their governess, Callis, accompany them. Very soon they meet four English gentlemen who are also heading to the carnival.

Hellena meets and sets a date with an English sailor, Captain Willmore, who shares her goal of enjoying as many fleeting encounters with the opposite sex as he can during his two-day leave. Florinda is also successful, for she meets Colonel Belvile, the man she had fallen in love with when he protected her and her brother during the siege of Pamploma. Behind her mask, she pretends to tell Belvile his fortune, hands him a letter, and whispers to him to meet Florinda at the garden gate that night. Valeria flirts with Frederick, and the fourth Englishman, a simple country squire named Ned Blunt, wanders off with a real harlot, Lucetta. The other three joke that she will probably rob him, as they happily head off for dinner, anticipating an evening of physical pleasure.

Act 2

Blunt comes back from setting a date with what he thinks is a woman of quality, who acts as though she is in love with him. He has not bothered to learn her name. He has high hopes of paying nothing for his time with her. The others, now donning carnival masks, take their common purse of money from him, convinced that she is a common whore who will fleece him of his valuables. Walking the streets, they come across the house of the famous courtesan Angellica. Three portraits of this beauty hang outside, advertising her charms for one thousand crowns a month. Willmore falls in love with her beauty and takes one of the portraits, since he does not have the money to enjoy the original. Don Pedro and Don Antonio arrive wearing masks and vie over which of them will buy Angellica's favors. Don Pedro recognizes his friend Don Antonio, who shows no shame over betraying Florinda as he presses his case with Angellica. Pedro challenges him to a fight, but he allows Don Antonio to think it is Belvile who challenges him. After they depart, Willmore manages to get Angellica to fall in love with him so that he may enjoy her pleasures without paying. Her servant Moretta is disgusted that she would give away her charms to such a "pirate beggar." Such folly, Moretta proclaims, "is the fate of all whores."

Act 3

Hellena, Florinda, and Valeria discover that Willmore has a love interest in Angellica. Willmore then proceeds to navigate between Hellena and Angellica, professing undying love to each in turn. Angellica becomes jealous of Hellena, while Hellena takes his betrayal in stride, for she shares his trait of an inconstant heart. Meanwhile, Florinda tries Belvile's faithfulness by courting him in her mask. He proves his fidelity, so she hands him her locket as she leaves. Seeing her picture in it, he realizes it was she.

Aphra Behn

On another street, Lucetta has her servant, Sancho, lead Blunt to her bedroom, where she tricks him into removing his clothing as she slips away in the dark. Her partner and lover, Phillipo, is pleased with the haul and inflamed by the idea of her going to bed with another man. Blunt, lost and in his undergarments, realizes his folly. Meanwhile, Florinda is waiting for Belvile, but a very drunk Willmore appears instead and nearly rapes her, taking her for a common wench. Belvile and Frederick happen along just in time to save her, but the appearance of her brother causes her to retreat to her room, with a promise to meet Belvile later. In the meantime, Don Antonio has paid his thousand crowns to Angellica. Willmore, in his drunken state, fights Don Antonio and leaves him for dead, while Belvile happens on the scene in time to take the blame. Don Antonio, wounded, takes Belvile home with him to assign a punishment.

Act 4

Belvile bemoans his miserable luck, and Antonio releases him on the condition that he fight Antonio's rival (Don Pedro) in his place, masked and wearing Don Antonio's clothes. Belvile does not bother to ask the rival's identity, assuming that Don Antonio means Belvile himself as his rival for Florinda. But since Don Antonio is more concerned about his rival for Angellica, Belvile will have to duel with Don Pedro.

Florinda watches the duel, not realizing that Belvile is in Don Antonio's clothes. She thus cheers on the wrong man. At the end of the fight, Don Pedro gives in to ''Don Antonio'' (really Belvile) and agrees to let him marry his sister. Florinda gasps and tries to flee, until Belvile reveals himself to her. Don Pedro sees this and grudgingly admits that Belvile has proved himself worthy, though he takes his sister off to ponder the decision further. Meanwhile, Angellica has her servant fetch Willmore, who charms her once again despite her jealousy. Hellena appears, dressed as a boy, to plead her ''master's'' case with Angellica to release Willmore. Willmore loves the idea of a wealthy patroness, though he recognizes his ''little gypsy,'' actually Hellena, under the disguise. Once again, Angellica is ''undone'' by jealousy. However, Willmore thinks that Hellena is acting out of her own gypsy interest, so he professes his love to Angellica, thinking to gain more financially with a relationship with the rich courtesan. Willmore claims that if he ever marries, it will be to someone who ''has wit enough to manage an intrigue of love.'' The challenge thrown, Hellena departs. Willmore insults Angellica, which inflames her desire for revenge, and follows Hellena. Florinda and Valeria, in different costumes, are nearly caught by Don Pedro, but Florinda escapes into a side door, which happens to be the lodgings of the English gentlemen, where Blunt is nursing his pride and waiting for a new suit of clothes to be delivered. When Blunt sees her, he determines to seek revenge on her, as reparation for his humiliation at the hands of the harlot Lucetta. He nearly rapes Florinda, with assistance from Frederick, until the latter hears Florinda mention Belvile's name and stops the process. The other Englishmen arrive, ready to enjoy a laugh at Blunt's expense, not realizing that Florinda is being held captive in Frederick's room.

Act 5

The English gentlemen return to their quarters as they mock Blunt. Willmore, however, pities the man since Blunt did not at least enjoy the lady's favors. Blunt, desperate for a shred of respect, announces that he is holding another woman hostage. Don Pedro offers to help him discover whether she is ''of quality, or for [their] diversion.'' Willmore proposes that the man with the longest sword take her, which falls to Don Pedro and his Toledo blade. Don Pedro is about to unveil his own sister before Belvile recognizes her ring, now in Blunt's possession. However, Belvile dares not reveal her identity, for fear of her brother's wrath. At the eleventh hour, Valeria comes running in and rescues Florinda, allowing just enough time for Belvile to marry her in a hasty wedding. Valeria marries Frederick in the same ceremony.

Now Angellica arrives, wearing a mask and threatening to kill Willmore with a gun. He easily charms her out of her resolve. Don Antonio comes to her rescue and offers to take care of her. When Don Pedro returns, he graciously approves Florinda's marriage to Belvile. Finally, the two rovers negotiate a unique nuptial agreement, based on mutual mistrust, and then Willmore marries Hellena, only afterwards learning of her wealth. Don Pedro once again demurs; the nunnery is not for Hellena. A final laugh ensues when Blunt's clothes arrive, for they are the costume of one from the nation he now ''abominate[s]'': Spain.

Epilogue

A cheeky epilogue in rhymed couplets dares the audience to recognize the fact that the comic antics in the play have their basis in real sexual politics.

CHARACTERS

Don Antonio

Don Antonio, a Spanish nobleman and the wealthy son of a Viceroy of Spain, has been betrothed to Florinda, through an agreement with his good friend, Florinda's brother, Don Pedro. However, Don Antonio is intrigued with the courtesan, Angellica. It is apparent that if he marries Florinda as planned, he will keep Angellica as a mistress, too. Don Antonio fights with the English gentlemen over the right to visit Angellica and is wounded by Willmore in a brawl. Eventually, Don Antonio gives up his claim on Florinda and forms a bond with Angellica, whom he nobly undertakes to support, after her career as a courtesan is ruined.

Colonel Belvile

Belvile is an honorable and steadfast English colonel who fell in love with Florinda when he protected her from an attack during the siege of Pamplona. Belvile is one of many exiled Englishmen traveling around Europe during the Interregnum, the period after the beheading of Charles I and before the reinstatement of his son, Charles II. Unlike his English fellows, Belvile is not interested in any of the many courtesans in Naples but pines away for his true love. He hopes to find her in Naples and marry her. However, it is Belvile's bad luck to get himself into countless situations that make it difficult for him to meet Florinda and elope with her as they had planned.

Angellica Bianca

Angellica is a famous courtesan who at the time of the play's events has just lost her benefactor, Don Pedro's wealthy uncle, who had been paying her monthly expenses of 1,000 crowns. Now she is advertising for a new lover, so she has placed three portraits of herself on the outside of her palatial home, along with the price. Angellica is accustomed to a life of luxury, but she has paid for it by sacrificing her honor and virginity for the riches she extracts from the men who fall prey to her seductive beauty. For Angellica, being a courtesan is a matter of survival and independence; to fall in love would ruin her, for then she would be at the mercy of the men she uses. Unfortunately, she falls hopelessly in love with one of the worst sort of men, Captain Willmore, who wants only physical satisfaction and not a love relationship. After being ''undone'' by Willmore, Don Antonio graciously offers to be her lifelong companion, thus removing her from the need to market her body.

Ned Blunt

Blunt is a country gentleman and not as sophisticated as his friend Belvile. His favorite oath, ''adsheartlikins'' gives him away as a landed country bumpkin, a stock character. Blunt foolishly believes that a courtesan has fallen in love with his manly physique, and thus he proves an easy mark for her ruse to take him to her house and defrock him of his valuables and clothing. Blunt fears that his friends will laugh at him for his misfortune, since he had bragged overmuch of his conquest before he went with the ''wench.'' This fuels his desire for revenge, which he nearly takes upon Florinda, the next woman he meets in the street, whom he mistakes for a harlot and whom he intends to rape brutally to avenge his wounded pride. When his friends do in fact laugh at him, Blunt goes into a rage, spluttering that he is ''not an ass to be laughed at.'' He lacks their gentlemanly power of restraint and decorum. Blunt is further humiliated when, ironically, a local tailor sews him a Spanish costume, ''the mode of a nation [he] abominate[s],'' instead of a ''proper'' English one.

MEDIA ADAPTATIONS

- A 1986 Royal Shakespeare Company production of *The Rover,* produced by John Barton and starring Jeremy Irons, takes many liberties with Behn's text, replacing hundreds of lines with those of Killigrew, but the result is enjoyable.
- Another performance can be seen in a 1995 British Broadcasting Company Production for the Open University in Association with the Women's Playhouse Trust. In this production, Behn's original text is presented in full. The actors, performing on a stage filled with sand, present the characters with energy and vivacity. The video recording is available through Routledge.

Callis

Callis is governess to Florinda and Hellena. She is sympathetic to their plights, and so she willingly assists them in deceiving their brother Don Pedro so that they can enjoy the carnival in Naples. They are not so loyal to her, however, for when Florinda decides to run away from her brother's home to find and marry Belvile, Valeria pushes Callis into a chest and locks her in, to give Florinda time to escape. Neither Florinda nor Hellena shows any remorse for this subterfuge.

Florinda

Florinda is the only pure and innocent young woman in the play. Florinda is a noblewoman who has been betrothed to wizened old Don Vincentio by her father, but since she and her sister and brother are away in Naples, she has been able to put this out of her mind. In the meantime, she has fallen in love with the English Colonel Belvile, who protected her and her brother when they were besieged in Pamplona and whom she hopes to marry. Her brother, however, has different plans. Being out of the purview of their father, he hopes to confer his sister and her sizeable dowry on his friend Don Antonio. Don Pedro thinks his plan will please his sister, since Don Antonio is young and handsome. To this plan Florinda is blithely unaware, until she gets a rude awakening when her brother announces that she must marry Don Antonio the next day. Thus Florinda is willing to accompany her more adventurous sister Hellena in a final night on the town so that they each can experience a taste of love and so that Florinda can hopefully speak to Belvile of her plight. During their adventure, Florinda is twice nearly raped, first by a drunken Willmore and then by Blunt, bent on revenge against women in general and harlots in particular.

Frederick

Frederick is an English gentleman and friend to Belvile and Ned Blunt. Frederick shares Blunt's anger at the courtesans of Naples who strip Blunt of his belongings and his clothes. Thus, he is easily convinced to help Blunt rape the innocent Florinda in revenge, when they mistake her for a whore. However, he convinces Blunt to stop when Florinda mentions that she knows Belvile, and thus proves she is a ''maid of quality'' and not a harlot.

Hellena

Florinda's younger sister, lively Hellena, is destined for the nunnery, a common destination for younger sisters since the Medieval period. Before being carted off to a life of devotion devoid of men and fun, Hellena intends to spend an evening on the town in Naples, searching for ''a saint of [her] own to pray to'' so that she can experience the ''sighs'' and ''wishes'' of being in love. She and her sister don masks and colorful clothing so that they can masquerade as courtesans and flirt openly in this society that frowns on such behavior from ''women of quality.'' Hellena feels confident in her ability to play with love and not be smitten, but smitten she is, by the quintessential rover himself, Captain Willmore. Both of them espouse a policy of loving and leaving, and in this they prove a perfect match for each other. So perfect is their match that even the dour Don Pedro approves their marriage, and therefore Hellena does not have to cloister herself in a nunnery after all.

Lucetta

Lucetta is a common whore who seduces the naïve Ned Blunt into meeting her at her house to consummate their passion. He fails to recognize the harlot's trick, and she gets him to remove all of his clothes, while she steals out of the room and locks him in it. Although she enjoys stealing his belongings, she expresses some regret that he did not at least get a chance to enjoy her favors before he was stripped of his possessions. Her paramour Phillipo has no such regrets and in fact finds his passions inflamed by the thought of her being with another man.

Moretta

Moretta is Angellica's servant and is herself a courtesan to less wealthy patrons. Moretta tries to steer Angellica away from Willmore, for she sees that he does not have a noble heart. Her warnings go unwarranted and unwelcome.

Don Pedro

Don Pedro is a Spanish nobleman who has been left in charge of his two sisters in their father's absence. Don Pedro follows the European tradition of marrying off the older sister, Florinda, and committing his younger sister, Hellena, to the nunnery. Florinda's sizable dowry makes her an excellent gift for his good friend, Don Antonio. Don Pedro tries to protect his sisters' virginity by keeping them out of society.

Phillipo

Lover of the whore Lucetta, Phillipo feels fully justified in bilking an Englishman, due to the long rivalry between Spain and England. The idea that Lucetta nearly went to bed with Blunt makes Phillipo feel ''wanton,'' so he goes to bed with her himself.

Sancho

Lucetta's pimp, Sancho leads the naïve Blunt to Lucetta's house, for what Blunt thinks will be an amorous tryst but which Sancho knows will be his undoing.

Valeria

Valeria, whose name connotes the Latin-based word ''valiant'' is cousin to Florinda and Hellena.

Valeria finds the costumes and masks that the three of them wear to disguise their noblewoman's demeanor and masquerade as courtesans. Valeria falls in love with the English gentleman Frederick, and they marry at the end of the play.

Captain Willmore

Captain Willmore, the rover, is an English sailor traveling with the exiled Prince (Charles II) and who is on leave after many months at sea without any women. A man without a conscience, Willmore wants nothing more than to enjoy the pleasures of as many women as possible during his brief stay in Naples. Willmore is a smooth talker, who charms both lady and courtesan, and he repeatedly manages to earn back their love even after they catch him in another tryst. Nor does he scruple to take their money. While drunk, he attempts to rape a noblewoman. He meets his match in Hellena, who shares his appetite for adventure and love and whose streak of bold independence may inspire him to fidelity.

THEMES

Marriage and Courtship

Women in seventeenth-century Europe had few options in terms of marriage and courtship. They could not initiate relations with men, and often their parents made the final decision about whom they would marry. Families sometimes used marriages to seal business and political relationships, ignoring the daughter's interests. The practice of paying a dowry (by the bride's family to the groom's family) was also still common. Most families would invest their dowry money in the eldest daughter, vying to marry her into the best family possible. Younger daughters often were consigned to a convent, thus reducing expenses, while at the same time "contributing" to the church. In poorer families, prostitution became a viable option. Once married, often to a man she neither knew nor liked, a woman became his property, as did all of her belongings. With no means to prevent pregnancies, the wife became a baby "machine," producing heirs for the family and very often mourning their early deaths, since child mortality rates were shockingly high. Nevertheless, men expected sexual gratification from their wives (as well as from their mistresses) and required obedience and fidelity. This restrictive state of affairs inspired Mary Wollstonecraft over a hundred years later to quip that for women marriage was little more than "legalized prostitution."

In *The Rover*, Aphra Behn portrays the typical pattern of options available to women. As the eldest, Florinda is to be married to a man of her father's choosing. Hellena wryly describes the loveless marriage-bed that lies in store for Florinda if she marries the aging Don Vincentio. However, since their father is away, her brother has jurisdiction over her and has chosen his best friend as her mate. Hellena, he has dispatched to a nunnery. She has come home for a brief visit before taking her vows. Neither Florinda nor Hellena wants to obey Pedro's wishes, yet they have no recourse but to try to enjoy a day and night of freedom before their fates are sealed. That they both end up with the man they love and the freedom to marry him is nothing more than a matter of blind luck.

Prostitution

For women without a man or a family fortune to keep them, with no education and no money of their own, prostitution was a way to capitalize on their youth to try to gain a measure of independence and to avoid downright poverty. Across Europe, trade in female virtue was tolerated by the public and by the church. In England, Puritan pressure had resulted in parliamentary acts making "fornication" punishable by three-month prison sentences, even in remote villages. Cromwell's moral strictures resulted in a dramatic reduction in prostitution. However, Charles II ended this period of moral restraint by setting a personal example of licentiousness and by expressing permissiveness in his rule. Prostitution was not only reinstated, it was actually embraced as a form of "sophisticated" behavior associated with the court. For women who aspired to a wealthy clientele, the new career of the actress offered the perfect opportunity to display their "wares" and attract new clients.

The social and moral climate of Restoration England explains the centrality of the beautiful Angellica to the plot of *The Rover*. As a sought-after courtesan who can name her own price, she represents the idealized/romanticized version of prostitution that tempted women of all classes and titillated

TOPICS FOR FURTHER STUDY

- Willmore must return to his ship after a brief holiday spent to satiating his physical desires, and Hellena hopes to "love and be beloved" before joining a nunnery. Despite their initial disinclination to seek permanent relationships, they marry. What bonds will hold their marriage together?
- Faithfulness and inconstancy are persistent themes in *The Rover*, in love relationships, familial relationships, relationships among friends, and between servant and master. Trace this theme in one or more fictional or real-life relationships, and use this data to support your interpretation of the role of constancy in the play.
- Willmore is a "rake hero" whose exploits conjure laughter in some characters and admiration from others. What is his ultimate impact on the audience? Is he to be admired or mocked? Why?
- Angellica's portraits serve as advertisements to attract potential benefactors. The English travelers see the portraits and debate which is more lovely, the depictions or the woman herself, raising questions about art versus life and expectations versus reality. What other symbolic role(s) do the portraits serve in the play?
- Naples, Italy, was a thriving seaport in the seventeenth century, a place where travelers from many lands mingled together in the sunny climate. How does Behn's choice of setting affect the viewer's expectations of how the play's characters will behave? Why does she set the play during carnival time as well?
- From sword fights and robberies to the two near-rapes of Florinda, *The Rover* is full of violence, yet the main storyline revolves around love interests. What role does violence play in *The Rover*, and how does the fact that the play was written by a woman affect your assessment of the violent behavior that accompanies love interests in this play?

men's fantasies. At the same time, the moral lesson she receives after having fallen in love with a potential client would have appealed to the Puritan sympathizers in the audience. Also apparent in Behn's play is the clear distinction that was made between "ladies of quality" and "whores." Frederick, who nearly gang-rapes Florinda, along with Blunt, exclaims that he would not want to be "trussed up for a rape upon a maid of quality when we only believe we ruffle a harlot." The shift in terminology from "rape," which is an act of violence, to "ruffle," which connotes a harmless trifle, aptly represents the vast difference in social responsibility between the two classes of women. The distinction between women seeking men for marriage and women who sell themselves for money lies at the heart of Behn's play. As Elin Diamond explains in her essay "*Gestus* and the Signature in Aphra Behn's *The Rover*," this play "thematizes the marketing of women in marriage and prostitution."

STYLE

Masks

It is not surprising that, when in 1790 playwright John Kemble revised *The Rover* to remove its distasteful elements for the more prudish audiences of a later century, he renamed the piece *Love in Many Masks.* Many of the characters, but especially the roving females, wear masks in *The Rover* to hide their identity and allow them to move freely in a different environment. Characters in masks may cross social boundaries with ease and play-act different social roles from their usual ones. Thus, the character may live out a fantasy or intrude upon a scene to which he or she would otherwise be denied.

Behn's characters use their masks both for freedom of movement and to hide their identity. Hellena and Florinda, two noble ladies, want to explore the underworld of the carnival and experiment with sensuality, without being detected. Unmarried young ladies were not permitted to visit the carnival, and their brother kept them under strict control. By wearing masks, Hellena, Florinda, and their cousin Valeria attend the carnival without his knowledge. In addition, the masks allow them to behave like prostitutes and be accepted as such, even though they are not competent in the world of the courtesan. The mask frees them to experiment with the provocative language, dress, and gesture of the prostitute and to express their sexuality in a freer environment, where such behavior is not only acceptable but expected.

The mask also affects the audience's view of the character. Because the mask is rigid and therefore does not convey the nuances of facial expressions, the actor must compensate with dialogue and with clear, even exaggerated, pantomime actions. This behavior would have heightened the audience's experience of the female body on display, while the mask would free the viewers to gaze on the actresses' bodies without a sense of shame. The same dynamics were repeated in the audience, where a number of women in the disguise of the mask could be seen but not identified.

Discovery Scene

The discovery scene, often called the "screen scene," involves one or more characters eavesdropping on other characters. The construction of the Restoration theater offered several places where an eavesdropper could be visible to the audience yet seemingly undetected by the other actors on the front of the stage. The theater at Dorset Garden introduced several innovations, including archways on either side of the proscenium, with doors below and balconies above. From one of these spots, an eavesdropping actor could listen and watch, pantomiming reactions to the other characters. Before such changes were introduced to the theater, an actor might hide from the other characters behind a screen or piece of furniture, thus the alternate term "screen scene."

Discovery scenes abound in Aphra Behn's *The Rover*. From her balcony, Angellica observes Willmore's infatuation with his gypsy beauty (Hellena) as he flirts with her immediately after vowing his undying love for Angellica. This undetected observation confirms Angellica's suspicion that Willmore is an inconstant lover. It also communicates to the audience the depth of Angellica's feelings.

Audience Aside

Aphra Behn made liberal use of the "aside" to convey the fears and thoughts of her characters. In fact, there are sixty-five of them in *The Rover*. An aside is a comment directed toward the audience in a stage whisper that the other characters do not hear. Thus, there is an assumption of candor from a character who breaks the action to address a comment to the audience. Often, Behn uses the aside to chronicle the emotional reactions of an eavesdropping character to the action he or she witnesses. This way, the audience hears the character's disposition to what has happened. When Hellena discovers Willmore's interest in Angellica, the audience does not yet know she has fallen in love with him, so her jealousy, communicated in brief asides, conveys her feelings and also helps to move the plot forward. In other places, Behn's use of the aside reinforces the physical action, making sure that the audience understands them. For example, when the lovers parlay with each other from behind masks, the asides help the audience distinguish the characters from each other. At other times, the aside serves to communicate a character's intention, which may not turn out as he or she expects. For example, when Angellica remarks, "His words go to the very soul of me," the audience can tell that she is truly falling in love with him, that her seductive manner is not simply motivated by the usual goals of a courtesan with a prospective client. Behn uses the aside in the manner typical of Restoration dramatists. The technique would later evolve into one that underscored the comedic elements of the play, but throughout the seventeenth and eighteenth centuries, the aside served to inform the audience of a character's true inner feelings and intentions.

HISTORICAL CONTEXT

The Restoration

The Restoration refers to the reinstatement of a monarch as the seat of government in England, following twenty years of civil war. Charles II, who had spent eleven years in exile after the overthrow and beheading of his father, Charles I, was restored to the throne, with his rule now officially constrained by a reinstated Parliament. This Parliament had gained power from the fact that wealthy landowners had successfully toppled a king. No longer would a king of England enjoy the independence of absolute rule.

COMPARE & CONTRAST

- **Late Seventeenth Century:** After Charles II comes to the throne in the Restoration of 1660, an act of Parliament invites women to be actresses in court-sponsored theaters. Puritans brand the early actresses as prostitutes because of their willingness to be displayed on stage. Fiction merges with reality when actresses are treated as prostitutes, and eventually many actresses resort to that way of life in order to make a living. King Charles II has several mistresses who are actresses. His support of women in the theater both helps and hurts their cause.

  Today: Women hold positions as actresses, directors, playwrights, and stage managers.

- **Late Seventeenth Century:** The turmoil caused by the English civil wars of the seventeenth century has little impact on most of England. This is because England consists of a conglomerate of small villages and towns, where news travels slowly and where the populace continue their rural existence with little interest in the affairs of the big town of London. Distinct regional dialects create a language barrier and roads are difficult to travel.

  Today: National political debates in England as elsewhere in the world can be communicated instantly over the radio, television, and Internet so that England's populace can now be fairly well informed about issues of government, if they choose. Opinion polls measure popular support, and political turmoil is mild by comparison to the tumultuous seventeenth century.

- **Late Seventeenth Century:** Theaters reopen to an eager public in 1660 with the Restoration, after having been closed officially during the Interregnum (1642–1660), a time dominated by enforced Puritan values. The theaters now have ceilings and special tracks for elaborate scenery. Audiences are large, consisting of people from all social classes.

  Today: Live theater does not enjoy the popularity it once did, now that television, video, and Internet video streaming bring entertainment into the home. Ticket prices for major productions are costly so that only the well-off can afford to visit the theater regularly.

Charles I had brought this crisis of royal authority on himself when he unilaterally dismissed Parliament and attempted to run the country alone in 1629. Although he succeeded in strengthening the financial and social unity of Britain through his personal leadership during the next eleven years, his decision had grave consequences. Unfortunately, Charles I, a cold and calculating man but not an insightful one, had failed to recognize the need for a "safety valve" for contrary opinions that the Parliament had provided. Despite his obvious skill in administration, public resentment grew, fanned by the king's attempt to increase the power of the Anglican Church over the realm.

The first crack in his authority occurred when he attempted to institute Anglican practices in Scotland. This and other unwanted authoritarian measures there sparked an uprising that he could not suppress, for without funding from the wealthy landowners of the Parliament his armed forces were outnumbered by Scottish forces, and he had to back down. He needed Parliament to help him raise funds and support, but he was too proud to reconvene it. The angry Scots actually invaded England, further deteriorating his authority. Forced to call upon a new Parliament to buy them off, Charles had to bargain with an empowered group of landowners. His brittleness in doing so led to civil war between Royalists and Parliamentarians. This conflict ended with his public beheading in 1649 and the establishment of the "Commonwealth" under Oliver Cromwell, a Puritan. Cromwell wielded unprecedented power over the Parliament and ultimately declared himself "Lord Protector," granting himself almost monarchic power. During this period, Puritan values held sway. Cromwell's tyranny ended with his death in 1658, and his son's brief and ineffective rule led the Parliament to request that the exiled son of Charles I return to rule them.

Charles II came to power knowing that his regime would be unlike that of any previous monarch in England. His father had been killed by Parliament, through a "legal" process. Now an empowered Parliament, the one that had restored him to the throne, would act as a check on his rule. His power lay in his ability to negotiate with this institution. In this he succeeded, and although he secretly yearned for the absolutist rule of his forbears, he was, in many ways, too lazy to achieve it.

Restoration Theater

During his exile, Charles II had been a cavalier, roaming the continent with a band of royalist followers. When Charles II regained the throne after eighteen years of the Puritan government led by Oliver Cromwell and Cromwell's son, he restored the theater in London. During the time of Puritan rule, theaters had been burned down and stripped of their property, and those actors who dared to present informal dramas were publicly whipped for encouraging "immoral" behavior. Charles II also established two acting companies, led by Thomas Killigrew and Sir William D'Avenant. They built two royal theaters and set up a system of actors' contracts, thus creating a monopoly on acting that would last for almost two hundred years. A dozen other smaller theaters sprouted up very quickly, but the Duke's Theatre in Dorset Gardens was the largest of the new theaters and one of the best. Most of Aphra Behn's plays were produced there, including *The Rover*, her most popular play. The larger theaters probably seated about five hundred spectators.

One of the innovative attractions was a new system of scenery. Now that theaters were enclosed under a protective roof, semipermanent scenes were built and moved about on the stage by a series of tracks. A sense of depth was created by a layering of these painted scenic walls. Ropes and other devices hanging from the ceiling made it possible to lower actors and props from the "heavens," and devices mounted within the two side wings could propel items across the stage. A pit in the front of the stage contained an orchestra, for music was played before, after, and sometimes during the plays. Numerous candles were placed along the front and sides of the stage for footlights. Because of the candles, the audience was just as illuminated as the stage, and often the presence of royalty would distract from the performance. The audience enjoyed the portrayal of stock characters held up for their ridicule as much as they enjoyed watching the pretensions and antics of the audience members around them.

Either bowing to popular sentiment or due to his own fascination with the opposite sex (he had more than fifteen mistresses, some of whom were actresses), Charles II defied theatrical tradition by declaring that women not only could but should play the parts of female characters. However, to become an actress, in fact to have any association with the theater, amounted to social suicide for women. Acting was equated with prostitution, for both avocations involved portraying oneself in public. Many actresses were treated as prostitutes and in fact became them, out of financial necessity or as a result of being rejected by society. On the stage, women's roles were often treated as an opportunity to put women on display as sexual objects. For example, a female character might be caught in a state of undress or might be pushed provocatively onto a bed. In *The Rover*, Willmore expresses great delight when he learns that his "gypsy" (Hellena) is a nun, for this makes his conquest of her even more titillating, for him and for the audience.

Naples, Italy

Compared to England with its considerable Puritan influence, Naples in the seventeenth century was a den of iniquity. Having lost some of its affluence after a series of conflicts with other city-states that began a period of recession, Naples, a town of about three thousand people, was in decline. Spain took control of it, and wealthy Spanish rulers owned the finer homes and swaggered around town, bringing with them their culture of the vendetta. Bandits roamed the streets, and many women resorted to prostitution as a profitable way to earn a living. The port of Naples brought many clients to them. In general, the town-dwellers were slightly better off financially than the peasants from the surrounding area, who barely had enough to eat and who dressed in rags.

The cavaliers of *The Rover* represented the gentlemen and nobles who were exiled along with Charles II when his father was executed. Because their money went farther in towns like Naples, they were able to live out a fantasy life of adventure there with little expense.

CRITICAL OVERVIEW

Aphra Behn wrote and staged five plays before producing *The Rover* on March 24, 1677. Her reputation as a woman of letters was established enough for her to be included in a published list of playwrights called *Theatrum Poetarum,* compiled by her contemporary Edward Phillips. Despite her reputation, Behn published *The Rover* anonymously, perhaps because her play was an adaptation of another contemporary playwright, Thomas Killigrew. Behn had condensed his ten-act drama and turned it into a comedy, but as a woman writer, she was especially vulnerable to charges of plagiarism. It was not until the third issue of the printed play that she dared to include her name as its author. She did, however, append to her next anonymously published comedy the phrase "the Author of the *Rover.*"

The Rover was an immediate success and a constant favorite in major theaters for the next sixty years. Charles II loved the play and arranged for a private viewing of it. *The Rover* became so popular that in 1730 it was simultaneously being produced in three different London theaters, and leading actors played encore performances year after year. At times, audiences considered Captain Willmore to be the title character, whereas other audiences thought Hellena was the rover. The sensibilities of the age also dictated the way the roles were played and understood. Early Willmore characters were handsome and dashing, and he was seen as the hero of the play. At times, the performances emphasized the tragic victimhood (eighteenth century) of the women, whereas at other times the women were seen as plucky heroines (nineteenth century). A famous eighteenth-century actress, Elizabeth Barry, played the role of Angellica more than forty times and occasionally received equal or higher billing than her male counterparts, a rare honor for an actress. However, as the morals of the eighteenth century became more conservative, the play was produced less often, and when it was produced, the bawdier elements were edited out. John Kemble adapted *The Rover* to create a less racy version called *Love in Many Masks* (1790) that was produced in place of Behn's play. The nineteenth century continued to disparage Behn; a nineteenth-century woman writer, Julia Kavanagh (as quoted in Todd's *The Critical Fortunes of Aphra Behn*) stated in her 1863 book, *English Women of Letters: Biographical Sketches,* that Behn's plays are "so coarse as to offend even a coarse age." A reviewer for the January 1872 *Saturday Review* (as quoted in Janet Todd's *The Critical Fortunes of Aphra Behn*) marveled that anyone would bother to publish her work, exclaiming that "if Mrs. Behn is read at all, it can only be from a love of impurity for its own sake, for rank indecency of the dullest, stupidest, grossest kind, unrelieved by the faintest gleam of wit and sensibility."

Behn was rescued by nascent feminists in the early twentieth century. In 1927, Vita Sackville-West published the famous Behn biography called *Aphra Behn: The Incomparable Astrea.* Sackville-West's good friend Virginia Woolf mentions Behn in her book *A Room of One's Own,* noting with pleasure that after Aphra Behn, "shady and amorous as she was," a woman could "earn five hundred a year by [her] wits."

More recently, beginning in the 1970s, critics consider Behn an early feminist, and by 1985 Behn merited inclusion in the *Norton Anthology of Literature by Women,* edited by feminists Sandra Gilbert and Susan Gubar. A 1986 revival of the play, with Jeremy Irons as a lovable rake, inspired a reviewer in London's *Daily Mail* (as quoted in Janet Todd's *The Critical Fortunes of Aphra Behn*) to pronounce the playwright "no longer a has-Behn." Feminists generally have not admired Willmore, seeing him as a sinister villain who flourishes in what Jane Spencer describes in *Aphra Behn's Afterlife* as a "'rape culture' in which men are defined by their power over women and other men, and women are unable to escape being defined by men's views of their sexuality." At the same time, they view Hellena as a heroine; Heidi Hutner praises Behn for "rescu[ing]" Hellena—a washed-out, aging whore in Killigrew's play—and making her a strong and bold female protagonist who rebels against the patriarchal system. Feminist critics continue to debate whether Behn can be termed an early feminist or not. In fact, some contemporary critics find that Behn is overused by feminists; in her 1998 article, "Appropriating Aphra," Elizabeth Schafer accuses feminists of appropriating Behn for their own purposes, "because there is money to be made through feminism in our culture at the moment." Some of these

Hugh Quarshie, Jeremy Irons, and Peter Guinness in a scene from the 1986 production of The Rover, *performed by the Royal Shakespeare Company and directed by John Barton*

feminist critics, according to Schafer, distort Behn's original purpose as they bend her text to their own critical purposes. Aphra Behn's profound and saucy play continues to strike a responsive chord in contemporary audiences and to inspire critics to ponder her motivation and intention in writing this provocative comedy.

CRITICISM

Carole Hamilton

Hamilton is an English teacher at Cary Academy, a private college preparatory school in Cary, North Carolina. In this essay, Hamilton examines the use of the concept of a ''performative space'' in Behn's play as a means for the expression of illicit desires.

The setting of carnival time in Naples in Aphra Behn's play *The Rover* allows two sets of characters to explore their sexual desires in a ''performative space'' that grants them an unusual amount of freedom from external constraint, from public view, and from suffering the consequences of their actions. The term ''performative space'' refers to the way that characters on and off the stage respond to differing expectations that are associated with place and dress. *The Rover* explores three performative spaces: the carnival world, the theater, and London society. Carnival time is the epitome of a special performative space. Carnival goers for various reasons take advantage of the anonymity of this masked affair to engage in relationships that would otherwise be denied to them, because of their class or gender. Since the carnival represents the world turned upside down, carnival time in Naples is a time for experimenting with role reversals. In Behn's play, some of the reversals ''stick,'' generating actual changes in destiny. Just as these role reversals are enacted within the plot of Behn's *The Rover*, the theatrical space presents a performative space for audience members, too, as a place to experiment with role modification. Aphra Behn understands this function of theater, and she provides models on the stage for audience members eager to learn the seductive ways of, for example, the professional courtesan. Finally, Behn is attuned to the limited and limiting performative space occupied by women

WHAT DO I READ NEXT?

- Aphra Behn's play *The Second Part of The Rover* (1681), although it lacks the wit and vivacity of the first play, is interesting reading for its portrayal of the fate of the marriage between Willmore and Hellena. Hellena has died at sea, and Willmore once again is a rover.
- Aphra Behn's novella *Oroonoko; or, The Royal Slave* (1688) describes the fate of a captured African prince. Behn based her story on a journal she kept while visiting Surinam when she was a young girl.
- William Hogarth's 1735 engravings, *The Rake's Progress,* is a series of depictions about the consequences of immoral behavior, with each engraving portraying a different version of dissolute life. The series taken as a whole presents a cautionary moral tale.
- Daniel Defoe's *Moll Flanders* (1722) portrays a young woman who is seduced and betrayed but learns to use the power of seduction to her own advantage.

in London society. She defiantly uses her skill as a writer to create a new, public performative space for female playwrights.

During carnival time, a mood of licentiousness descends upon Naples, a city that in the seventeenth century was not known for its prudishness in the first place. Wearing costumes and masks to hide their identities, the participants are free to act on impulses they would otherwise suppress. The carnival offers a perfect opportunity for two unmarried sisters, according to critic Heidi Hutner in ''Revisioning the Female Boyd,'' to ''ramble: to leave the house, to speak their minds, to approach men of their choice.'' Going against her brother's command that she be locked up in the house until Lent, Hellena goes to the carnival to find a man and feel ''the vanity and power'' of being desirable to him. Dressed as a gypsy, she acts like one, displaying her body provocatively and pretending to read Willmore's palm, while hiding behind her mask. The freedom of carnival time lets her act upon impulses that a young lady would not normally indulge. For the male characters, too, carnival time gives people license to act out sexual desires. As Willmore exclaims to his fellow cavaliers, '''tis a kind of legal authorized fornication, where the men are not chid for't, nor the women despised, as among our dull English.'' They, too, wear masks to avoid being held accountable for the consequences of their dallying. Captain Willmore and his friends plan to take advantage of the sexual freedoms of young ladies in a carnival mood. The men drink, too, and drunkenness opens up a performative space that excuses swinish behavior. When Willmore blames his attempted rape of Florinda on the ''influence'' of the ''cursed sack'' he had been drinking, the others readily accept this excuse. But it is not just drink that influences Willmore: he responds to the influence of the performative space he occupies. The setting of the carnival is a catalyst that compels the characters to act compulsively. The mask, too, plays a role. As renowned theater director Peter Hall describes in his book *Exposed by the Mask,* even actors playing a part discover the liberating effect of the mask: ''He [the actor] can change his age, his bearing, his physique, even his sexuality. The change comes from using parts of himself that perhaps he did not know existed and from suppressing others irrelevant to this new person.'' Each of the masked characters in *The Rover* is freed by his or her mask to explore new ways of behaving. And the transformations are sudden: Valeria expresses amazement at how quickly they fell into the role of a gypsy, seeming to have ''learnt this trade of gipsies as readily as if we had been bred upon the road to Loretto.'' Hellena has so quickly found the love she sought that she is still spinning from the experience, and she asks herself, ''What the deuce should this be now that I feel?'' She has been smitten by love but also by a way of being, of taking control over her own life. She would like to occupy this performative space for longer than a day.

Hellena, like her namesake from Shakespeare's *A Midsummer Night's Dream,* awkwardly plays the role of the huntress, thus reversing the traditional roles in the amorous battle of the sexes. Behn's Hellena would prefer a permanent carnival-like performative space, a world turned upside down in terms of courtship. She says, "I don't intend that every he that likes me shall have me, but he that I like." Behn fashioned her Hellena after Shakespeare's Helena, not the Hellena from Thomas Killigrew's play *Thomaso; or, The Wanderer,* the play she adapted. Behn replaced Killigrew's Hellena, "an old decayed blind, out of fashion whore . . . that has neither teeth nor eyes," with a young miss who knows herself to be "well shaped," "clean-limbed," and "sweet-breathed." The playwright also reversed the old Hellena's fortune so that the young noblewoman could express what Behn (and the aging prostitute) knew to be true: that "a handsome woman has a great deal to do while her face is good." Therefore, Behn's Hellena dons the costume and inhabits the performative space of a prostitute, pinning advertisements to her clothing to underscore her purpose, in case anyone missed it. To all eyes, Hellena *is* a whore. From the perspective of the viewer, the "play-acting . . . and reality . . . collapse into each other, and the boundaries of performative and essential self becomes indistinct," as Derek Hughes explains in his work *The Theatre of Aphra Behn.* To Willmore, Hellena really is his "gipsie girl," and he does not comprehend that she is a titled lady until he hears it twice.

For Hellena's part, performance and reality have merged, for she continues the relationship as a hybrid of her gypsy persona with her identity of a mischievous nun-to-be. She has merged the two identities by enacting the gypsy part in the performative space of the carnival, and the resultant woman is equal to the challenge of taming the Rover's wandering habits. Although, as Heidi Hutner points out, she is "brought back into the patriarchal fold," when she requires and gets her brother's approval, she occupies her own performative space within the marriage. In *The Rover*, Behn raises significant questions about the extent to which the social/sexual self truly represents the essential self. In seventeenth-century London, the traditional performative space for marriageable women was confining; even a gypsy, common prostitute, or high-priced courtesan had more freedom. Behn also

"THE SETTING OF CARNIVAL TIME IN NAPLES IN APHRA BEHN'S PLAY *THE ROVER* ALLOWS TWO SETS OF CHARACTERS TO EXPLORE THEIR SEXUAL DESIRES IN A 'PERFORMATIVE SPACE' THAT GRANTS THEM AN UNUSUAL AMOUNT OF FREEDOM FROM EXTERNAL CONSTRAINT, FROM PUBLIC VIEW, AND FROM SUFFERING THE CONSEQUENCES OF THEIR ACTIONS."

demonstrated that in the courtship marketplace it was often difficult to distinguish one mode of performance from the other, for the lady and the prostitute had to employ similar tactics to get by in life.

As in the carnival, within the performative space of the theater itself, it was also often difficult to distinguish between prostitute and lady of quality. The theater was the other public forum where masked prostitutes masqueraded as ladies of quality. In the theater, they could rub shoulders with women of quality, some of whom wore masks to playact as prostitutes. Thus, the audience was, in some ways, another world turned upside down. Charles II had reinstated the theater after twenty years of grim Puritan suppression, and here he wanted to celebrate his triumph over them. Many of the plays he supported legitimized his own licentious behavior by staging it for the audience to celebrate with him. His interest in theater created a new performative space for women, too, one that was both liberating and problematic. He had proclaimed through an act of Parliament that women must play women's roles, thus inventing the career of the actress. However, by putting themselves on display in this fashion, they were instantly considered prostitutes, and the treatment they received at the hands of gentlemen at the back door of the theater usually succeeded in transforming them into such. Meanwhile, in the audience, prostitutes wearing masks were easily confused with ladies of quality, also wearing masks. The mask lent the woman an air of mystery and sophistication that was useful to prostitutes and ladies alike. However, as Anne Russell points out in her introduction to the Broadview edition of *The Rover*, ''the distinctions between prostitutes and 'respectable women' became blurred. The mask became a sign of the prostitute but a sign which, with its offer of anonymity, could offer some freedom from conventional roles for any woman who wore it.'' That inveterate playgoer of the seventeenth century, Samuel Pepys, frequently observed the confusion. In one diary entry, he records his reaction to a lovely woman in a mask, saying that ''one of the ladies would, and did, sit with her mask on all the play; and being exceedingly witty as ever I heard a woman, did talk most pleasantly with him; but was, I believe, a virtuous woman and of quality. . . . A more pleasant rencontre I never heard. But by that means lost the pleasure of the play wholly.'' He was more entertained by the masked audience member than he was by the play, and it would have been difficult for him to ignore her, since the Restoration theater was lit uniformly, such that the audience was as visible as the play. Sophisticated banter and sexually provocative behavior being in fashion at this time, the theater was itself a performative space for enacting, watching, and practicing the sophisticated actions of the royal court. Prostitutes could learn to be witty, like the lady Pepys observed, and ladies could learn how to display themselves, like—and not like—prostitutes.

During the Interregnum, when few theater productions were allowed, people read printed plays and imagined the scenery. The restoration of theater created cause to celebrate visual scenery again, and this time stages were more opulent than ever. Scenery went center-stage. Elaborate devices trundled across tracks inlaid in the floor so that intricately painted scenes, complete with perspective, could be rolled into place on cue. The result was an opulence never before seen, a riot and celebration of the theatrical performance space on stage, while the real-life intrigues offstage made for equally entertaining scenarios. This was just as Charles II wanted it—he actively promoted theater as a means of anti-Puritan propaganda.

To a large extent, Aphra Behn produced exactly what Charles II and his audience wanted: an erotic and sophisticated entertainment. Yet, because of the social bias against female playwrights, she could not at first take credit for her achievement. She, too, was ''masked,'' for in her prologue she refers to the playwright as an anonymous ''he,'' and she refuses to identify herself as the author of her work. Nevertheless, Behn opened up a new performative space for women writers, not just as ''the professional woman writer as a new fangled kind of whore,'' as Catherine Gallagher claims in her essay ''Who Was That Masked Woman? The Prostitute and the Playwright in the Comedies of Aphra Behn,'' but as a woman writer with, like her heroine, Hellena, the wit and power to control the theatrical performative space through establishing her own ground rules. She created this space, and by doing so, she invited other female writers to populate it.

Source: Carole Hamilton, Critical Essay on *The Rover,* in *Drama for Students,* The Gale Group, 2003.

Marion Lomax

In the following introduction excerpt, Lomax analyzes Behn's use of Carnival for her play's setting as one of escapism from the reality of the English Restoration.

Killigrew's *Thomaso,* on which *The Rover* was based, is set in Madrid in late November. There are disguises, and the Feast of St Cecilia, patron saint of music, is associated with Thomaso himself, but there is none of the pre-Lenten urgency to eat, drink, and be merry which characterises *The Rover*, and no mention of the pervading spirit of carnival which Aphra Behn introduced when she adapted and altered Killigrew's play. Behn also moved the action to Naples, where a carnival setting was associated with Roman Saturnalian revels as well as with opposition to the restrictions of the Christian tradition's Lent, which included a ban on sexual intercourse as well as the eating of meat.

If a festive spirit seems restrained in *Thomaso* this is hardly surprising. Killigrew's text was reputedly written in exile in 1654. At home, Cromwell had dissolved the Rump Parliament and set himself up as Lord Protector. It was a time of disputes and foreign wars; Royalist plots were being revived to displace Cromwell, who seemed to be taking the country back to a monarchy with himself as king. *Thomaso* was a closet drama which could not be performed at the time of writing because the theatres were closed and, even if this had not been the case, a play of its nature would have been forbidden. It was printed in 1663, after the Restoration of Charles II, when the cavaliers it celebrated were comfortably returned home—but there is no evidence that it was ever acted.

When Behn produced *The Rover* the monarchy had been reestablished for seventeen years. Mikhail Bakhtin has observed that 'Moments of death and revival, of change and renewal always led to a festive perception of the world'—but neither renewal nor change could be said to be being celebrated in 1677. If it was not pure nostalgia, on what was Aphra Behn's use of carnival based?

The play's period setting in the 1650s is very significant. Cromwell's Protectorate had suppressed pastimes and sports and, to Royalists, the period must have seemed like an indefinite extension of Lent. Joining in the festivities of carnival which were denied them at home, exiled cavaliers whiled away the time until the new order of the once-revolutionary Parliamentarians could be overthrown. Instead of being a wealthy, extravagant elite, the exiles had lost lands and money: they were now displaced and marginalised in foreign parts, and Behn's play continually stresses their 'outsider' status. Willmore is not just a rover—a pirate, one who wanders, an inconstant lover—he is a 'Tramontana rover', which, apart from signifying someone uncouth, indicates a foreigner or stranger. In fact, most of the characters are outsiders of one kind or another: Naples is under Spanish rule, Angellica Bianca is introduced as a native of Padua, even the English are divided into the impecunious cosmopolitan cavaliers and the wealthy traveller from the country, whom they befriend but constantly taunt because he never committed himself politically and kept his privileges and estate. Established incomers prey upon more recent arrivals: Lucetta exploits Blunt's ignorance of Naples and of her ways—though she does worry that her treatment of him may put paid to future dealings with foreigners if word gets around. The protagonists, then, are all away from their home ground and are vulnerable because of this. The usual social hierarchies are inverted. The Spanish, old enemies of the English, are either in power officially (Don Antonio is the viceroy's son) or unofficially (Philippo takes the spoils Lucetta tricks from Blunt and reminds us of the old quarrel about the Spanish Armada in his reference to 'old Queen Bess's' gold and the 'quarrel . . . since eighty-eight.' The English, who might have been gentlemen at home, are poor, riotous, and often despised abroad.

Although the victimisation of prostitutes was a common feature of traditional carnival, Behn does not condemn either Lucetta or Angellica Bianca but rather, at significant moments, gives them the upper hand over the English strangers, an even more disadvantaged and male social group. No matter how brave they may be, abroad they are distinguished principally by their lack of riches and often run-down appearance; even a courtesan's servant feels free to mock Willmore in his presence with 'I believe those breeches and he have been acquainted ever since he was beaten at Worcester.' Blunt has managed to retain his wealth, being no cavalier, yet he does not have the wit to keep it and escape abuse. Lucetta soon picks him out as a gullible fool:

> He's English too, and they say that's a sort of good-natured loving people, and have generally so kind an opinion of themselves that a woman with any wit may flatter 'em into any sort of fool she pleases.

"THIS IS GENDER SPECIFIC, UNLIKE THE JIBE IN *HAMLET* THAT THE ENGLISH ARE ALL MAD: BEHN'S JOKE IMPLIES THAT, AT HOME AND ABROAD, AN ENGLISH MALE IS NO MATCH FOR ANY WOMAN'S WIT."

This is gender specific, unlike the jibe in *Hamlet* that the English are all mad: Behn's joke implies that, at home and abroad, an English male is no match for any woman's wit. Both Lucetta and Angellica are victims of a male-centred society and an economy which treats them as a commodity, but each has her own methods of survival built on compromise, and they manipulate the men on whom they depend. The 'jilting wench', Lucetta, gains great wealth without giving any favours to a country gentleman, while the 'famous courtesan', who demands a ridiculously high price, eventually chooses to bestow herself for nothing on a penniless pirate and, when she cannot command his constant love, holds him at pistol-point to revenge her honour. Angellica may not win Willmore, yet she retains his admiration and the adoration and respect of someone as rich and powerful as the viceroy's son.

Behn's women are more certain of their intrinsic worth than Killigrew's female characters. They reserve the right to adjust their monetary price as it suits them, being more financially secure than many of the men in the play. Even the upright Belvile is dependent on marrying into money (the box of jewels which Florinda, his Spanish love, hides in the garden may be a metaphor for the virtue she has so much difficulty preserving, but since Jessica's flight to Lorenzo in Shakespeare's *The Merchant of Venice,* it is also a symbol of the defiant woman who breaks through family and cultural opposition to give herself and her wealth to the man of her choice). The woman-shy Frederick also has his future determined by Florinda, who tells him:

> I'll be reconciled to you on one condition—that you'll follow the example of your friend in marrying a maid that does not hate you, and whose fortune (I believe) will not be unwelcome to you.

This world, where women can take the initiative, is the world of carnival. It is a time of misrule; everything is turned upside down, prohibitions are temporarily removed, and privileges and rank suspended. Everyone, however different, can be integrated by joining in. As Bakhtin wrote:

> Carnival is not a spectacle seen by the people; they live in it, and everyone participates because its very idea embraces all the people. While carnival lasts, there is no other life outside it. During carnival time life is subject only to its laws, that is, the laws of its own freedom.

Carnival may have appealed to Restoration audiences because of its emphasis on sexual freedom, and to Aphra Behn because it extended this freedom to women as well as men. Male dramatists also created outspoken and daring women characters. Etherege's *The Man of Mode,* which was performed the year before *The Rover*, is part of a movement discernible in Restoration comedy away from a focus on the male lead and towards an awareness that 'his lady', in this case Harriet Woodvil, was the real 'centre of interest'. The fact that women were now playing women's parts, coupled with Behn's influence in contemporary theatre, probably helped to bring about this transition. Certainly one topic which was close to Behn's heart was the issue of arranged marriages and a woman's right to choose her own husband: beginning with her first play, *The Forced Marriage,* she tackled the topic at least eleven times in her dramatic works.

Unlike *Thomaso, The Rover* does not begin by focusing on the men; it opens with Hellena and Florinda discussing their lack of independence. Both women display the confidence to have opinions and desires—and to express them. Only Lucetta, of all the females in the play, seems unable to do this—perhaps because she merely exploits the carnival spirit for financial gain at the command of Philippo and is always under his control. She never manages to break free and act as she would wish. As she tells him, speaking of Blunt: 'And art thou not an unmerciful rogue, not to afford him one night for all this? I should not have been such a Jew'. But she is not allowed to follow her own desires because, as Philippo reminds her, he wants 'to keep as much of thee as I can to myself'. Lucetta, like Angellica, demonstrates how difficult it is for women—especially kept women and prostitutes—to retain their sexual freedom. Dependent on men financially for their survival, they cannot afford the luxury of dispensing favours at will. Angellica, with her greater independence and wealth, fares better than Lucetta. She also, like Hellena and Florinda, has the advantage of a female ally. Her woman, Moretta, is probably motivated more by economic considerations than emotional attachment, but we feel sure that when Angellica finally turns her back on Willmore, Moretta will be there to help her return to her old, confident state. Similarly, in I.i. Hellena fiercely takes her sister's part in criticising their father's wishes and her brother's intentions to carry them out; later, Valeria rushes to the rescue when Hellena and Florinda find themselves under threat. Supportive, energetic women are Behn's speciality.

Behn has been credited with creating more daring dialogue between the sexes than many of her male contemporaries. In *The Rover* this could be due in part to her use of Killigrew's text (which is freer than most in this respect) and particularly to her reassignment to Hellena of certain speeches which Killigrew allocated to a male character—but the freedom with which her men and women converse is also due to the way in which another aspect of carnival is allowed to flourish. Hellena has already entered fully into its spirit when the play opens, 'Nay, I'm resolved to provide myself this carnival, if there be e'er a handsome proper fellow of my humour above ground, though I ask first.' She has resolved to find her own man and initiate a relationship: her father and brother may be planning to save the cost of a dowry by placing her in a convent, but she is quite aware of what she has to offer—and to gain by making other plans. Her sister, Florinda, has already determined to defy their father and refuses to marry 'the rich old Don Vincentio', being equally sure of her worth: 'I shall let him see I understand better what's due to my beauty, birth, and fortune, and more—to my soul, than to obey those unjust commands.'

Both are set for battle when their brother, Don Pedro, enters. He apparently does not notice Hellena at first and addresses only Florinda, which suggests that he believes Hellena, the novice, to be elsewhere praying—an impression reinforced by his surprise when she cannot resist butting into the conversation to take Florinda's part. Hellena not only disobeys his command to 'Go—up to your devotion' (he leaves before she does), but she fiercely challenges everything he says, mocks Vincentio's lack of virility, and shocks Pedro with her tenacity ('Have you done yet?') and her outspoken language. Behn toned down Killigrew's description of the old prospective husband who 'farts as loud as a Musket for a jest' to 'sighs a belch or two, loud as a musket', but reserved the detail for greater impact later in Hellena's outraged, 'What then? The viceroy's son is better than that old Sir Fisty'. Pedro, shocked by his sister's disrespectful term ('old fart') for her father's choice of husband, orders her immediate incarceration for the duration of the carnival, followed at Lent by 'her everlasting penance in a monastery'.

For Hellena, the carnival has already begun: she is indulging in vigorous colloquial outspokenness—her free expression of oaths ('Now hang me if . . .') and her skills of witty mockery make her a natural sparring partner for the outspoken Willmore. Hellena looks to the carnival to provide her with experience of love and life and, as Elin Diamond aptly expresses it, 'She exercises her will only by pursuing and winning Willmore, for as it turns out he has the "more" she "would fain know"'. Unlike Lent, carnival is characterised by abundance and easy gratification. Willmore steps ashore in search of 'Love and mirth' in a 'warm climate' after having been deprived of women and good living on board ship. He may stink 'of tar and ropes' ends like a dock or pesthouse' but he has an abundance of persuasive rhetoric as well as desire: 'I have a world of love in store. Would you would . . . take some on't off my hands.' While he has been confined to male company at sea, Hellena has been pent up in a nunnery and, like him, she is eager to start making up for lost time: 'for when I begin, I fancy I shall love like anything; I never tried yet.' She has no intention of dying 'a maid, and in a captain's hands too', but the liberality of carnival does not mean that she has forgotten the realities of everyday life. Hellena's gipsy disguise *is* only a disguise: she does not really want a life of hardship and 'A cradle full of noise and mischief, with a pack of repentance at my back'. Her plain speaking and scorn of Willmore's attempts to win her persuade him into a marriage 'bargain' which, although both enter defensively, she has engineered. Perhaps marriage is as unattractive to her as it is to Willmore but, without it, the freedom to explore her sexual desires could take her back to the convent as an abandoned, unmarriageable young woman, with or without a child. Marriage may have its faults but a nunnery has few pleasures for a woman of her nature.

When Hellena first hears about Florinda's love for Belvile, she declares, 'I hope he has some mad companion or other that will spoil my devotion', and from that point on she exerts all her energies to provoke an assault on her virginity, advertising it at every opportunity, confident that she has the wit to handle the situation to her ultimate advantage. Florinda, on the other hand, is constantly fending off attempted rape from the time of her first meeting with Belvile, 'when I was exposed to such dangers as the licensed lust of common soldiers threatened when rage and conquest flew through the city.' The Englishmen like to think they are no common soldiers intent on rape and pillage, but in Willmore's drunken assault on Florinda in III.v and the mass rape planned in Act IV by Blunt with the compliance, at one point, of Frederick and the others, a modern audience may begin to doubt. While indecent behaviour towards women is part of the carnival tradition and Restoration drama frequently incorporates a physical assault on a virtuous heroine (even Nahum Tate's rewriting of *King Lear* includes an attempted rape of Cordelia), Aphra Behn's treatment of the issue raises far-reaching questions concerning sexual violence against women (particularly of different social stations) and the problems involved in the way female chastity was prized, protected, and put under siege.

The Rover's carnival setting highlights the double standards normally practised by both men and women. A society in which rich old men take young wives they cannot satisfy encourages the latter to 'ramble to supply the defects of some grave impotent husband' and allows women like Lucetta to use this as a cover for deception and robbery. When, as Belvile insists, there are wealthy 'whores' who do not fit the traditional stereotype, and wealthy wives doing much the same but without the fee, how is a man like Blunt to discern whether he is predator or prey?

> Why yes, sir, they are whores, though they'll neither entertain you with drinking, swearing, or bawdry; are whores in all those gay clothes and right jewels . . . with those great houses richly furnished . . . are whores, and arrant ones.

The men perpetuate a situation where the honour of their own women is valued and fiercely defended, but a woman without an effective protector is seen as fair game or, as Willmore puts it, 'another prize'. When circumstances temporarily remove a woman from family or marital protection, the men become victims of each other's prejudices and lusts. For all his boasting, Frederick has little experience of women; he acts according to the primitive distinctions that governed much male behaviour at the time, 'I begin to suspect something; and 'twould anger us vilely to be trussed up for a rape upon a maid of quality, when we only believe we ruffle a harlot.' The 'harlot' is, of course, Florinda: Frederick's description of her earlier as 'that damned virtuous woman' is almost realised.

The farce, which provokes both laughter and unease as the masked Florinda is physically threatened by one male after another, reaches its climax when her own brother, who has been the fiercest defender of her honour, draws the longest sword in the contest to take possession of her body. Belvile is helpless, and only the timely intervention of Valeria saves the day. The ridiculous situation was brought about by Don Pedro's insistence that Florinda should marry the man of his choosing rather than her own, and that Hellena should be denied marriage altogether. Finally, Florinda's match is a *fait accompli,* and the strain of making a stand against that of Willmore and Hellena is too great. Don Pedro consents in the face of mass resistance, relieved to 'be free from fears of her honour'. 'Guard it you now, if you can', he tells Willmore, 'I have been a slave to't long enough.' Willmore's advice that 'a woman's honour is not worth guarding when she has a mind to part with it' could be said to be the message of the play.

One freedom of carnival is the opportunity to act foolishly without regard to social position. In not opposing his sisters' marriages, Don Pedro bows to the prevailing pressures of festivity. It is a huge relief for him to relinquish the burden of patriarchal responsibility. Wickedly, Behn allows him to relish his liberation. When we first meet Pedro he is about to put on his masked costume and participate in revels he has forbidden to his sisters. By the end, in forgiving everyone, he has entered into the spirit of equality which characterises carnival life. One by one, male and female alike, the characters venture out: Florinda and Belvile to find each other, Hellena and Valeria to woo husbands, Pedro and Antonio to win Angellica, Blunt to seek an inexpensive woman, and Willmore to take any woman. Those who achieve their desires do so by complicated routes, often involving potential humiliation and risk: others are exposed to ridicule, danger, and defeat. Antonio is wounded, and Belvile, a victim of mistaken identity, is driven to participate in the equivalent of a carnivalesque mock duel. All are free to play the fool for a time, but if any person could be considered to have been elected King of Fools by his companions, that person must be Blunt.

He is victimised by Lucetta, Philippo, and Sancho in additional ways to those found in Killigrew's text, where his counterpart, Edwardo, is merely turned out of doors in his drawers in the night and is lost in the city streets by the equivalent of Sancho. Bakhtin notes that carnival hell included, amongst other things, a trap to catch fools, and Behn adds a Rabelaisian touch to Blunt's debasement by dropping him literally into excrement. On one level the foolish country fop becomes a hero of folk humour when he falls down the trapdoor into the sewer and undergoes a mock journey to the underworld, returning in the tradition of such folk heroes, to tell of the horrors he found there. At another level Blunt's fate can be seen as a veiled political comment. It is wished on him in I.ii by Frederick when, having noticed Blunt's disappearance in pursuit of Lucetta, he declares,

> I hope 'tis some common crafty sinner, one that will fit him. It may be she'll sell him for Peru: the rogue's sturdy, and would work well in a mine. At least I hope she'll dress him for our mirth, cheat him of all, then have him well-favouredly banged, and turned out naked at midnight.

The reason for Frederick's uncharacteristic vindictiveness becomes clear when Belvile catalogues details of Blunt's privileged upbringing. Never having known hardship or the sordid side of life, never having committed himself to a cause as they have done, and, therefore, never having risked life, limb, or fortune, the wealthy 'Essex calf' is a cause of deep-seated resentment—though this is usually overridden by good humour. It is as if the spirit of carnival allows Frederick's idle wish to be granted. Blunt is not sold to labour in a Peruvian mine, but he is forced underground and exposed to other nightmare experiences. He is also subjected to the carnivalesque removal of his fine clothes and their replacement with a clown-like costume—his underwear and 'an old rusty sword and buff belt'. His horrified response, 'Now, how like a morris dancer I am equipped!', and his equally disgusted view of himself in the Spanish habit he is forced to wear later signify his humiliation. Belvile's pronouncement on the new costume is telling: 'Methinks 'tis well, and makes thee look e'en cavalier'. Finally, even the Englishmen are equal—Blunt, with his possible parliamentarian leanings and fastidious fussing about his clothes, has at last to make do like one of the cavaliers.

In carnival time costume is crucial, and from the first scene of *The Rover* characters are changing their clothes and exchanging identities for a variety of purposes. When characters lose control of their state of dress, as in the case of Blunt and, later, of Florinda, who escapes to the garden 'in an undress', their vulnerability is apparent. Hellena, however, always appears to have the situation in hand and makes successful transitions from novice's garb to gipsy costume, and finally to the boy's clothes she is wearing when Willmore agrees to marry her. Female cross-dressing was popular on the Restoration stage as a means of allowing the audience to view more of the woman playing the part, so Behn may have merely been catering to audience expectations here, but Willmore's possible associations with the Earl of Rochester and John Hoyle, both of whom pursued men as well as women, probably gave her choice an additional *frisson.* Historically, there is also a link between women who adopted male attire and certain prostitutes who used such dress to signal their profession. There is no indication that Hellena's appearance would have been viewed in this way, but the ambiguous natures of costume and masquerade in the play reveal the dangers of judging by appearances.

In I.ii Belvile explains to Blunt that the 'fine pretty creatures' he is admiring 'are, or would have you think they're courtesans, who . . . are to be hired by the month'. By drawing attention in the drama to a confusion that extended from carnival into life beyond the play, Behn makes her audience question notions of respectability and notoriety in relation to women's sexuality. Nancy Copeland sees Behn's juxtapositioning of Hellena and Angellica resulting 'in a narrowing of the distance between virgin and whore that complicates the final rejection of the courtesan and her ultimate exclusion from the play's comic conclusion'. In many ways these characters are two sides of the same coin: both advertise their attractions to Willmore and pursue him in different fashions; both are willing to subsidise his poverty with money from the same source (Hellena's fortune comes from her uncle who was Angellica's 'Spanish general'); and both offer themselves to him for love. They differ mainly in the way they view that concept in relationships between men and women. Ironically, the worldly courtesan is less astute than the convent girl in assessing the nature of a rover like Willmore. In depriving Angellica of her man, Behn is not taking a moral stand: Angellica, the romantic, must give way to Hellena, the realist, who will provide her revenge. Angellica's future is left undetermined. The opportunity Behn gives her to express herself so eloquently and the sympathy this provokes on her behalf are apt reminders that love, like carnival madness, has its darker side—and that, in carnival, everyone has a voice.

Source: Marion Lomax, ''Introduction: *The Rover* and Carnival,'' in *The Rover,* edited by Marion Lomax, W. W. Norton, 1995, pp. xvii–xxvi.

Elin Diamond

In the following essay, Diamond examines the appropriation of females in The Rover *and, for Behn, in English society during her time.*

> Where the dream is at its most exalted, the commodity is closest to hand.
>
> —Theodor Adorno, *In Search of Wagner*

Near the end of act 2 of *The Rover*, after the wealthy virgins and hungry gallants have been introduced, and the reader-spectator is made aware that comic symmetry is pressing toward chase and final reward, mention is made of a beautiful courtesan whom the gallants, including the affianced ones, are trying to impress. Angellica Bianca would seem to be a supplement to the intrigue plot—a supplement since one need not intrigue to visit a whore. Yet before the virgins are rewarded with the husbands they desire, they will traverse this whore's marketplace. In ''scenes'' and ''discoveries,'' they will market themselves as she does, compete for the same male affection, suffer similar abuse. The courtesan herself enters the play not in the way the audience might expect, behind an exotic vizard, or ''discovered'' in her bedchamber after the parting of the scenes, but as a portrait, as *three* portraits, a large one hung from the balcony and two smaller ones posted on either side of the proscenium door designating her lodging. Willmore, the play's titular rover, arrives at her door, and in the absence of the courtesan he cannot afford, he appropriates her in representation—he reaches up and steals a portrait.

Willmore's gesture, I will suggest, contains information beyond the local revelation of one character's behavior. We might read Willmore's gesture as a Brechtian *Gestus* or ''gest,'' a moment in performance that makes visible the contradictory interactions of text, theater apparatus, and contemporary social struggle. In the unraveling of its intrigue plot, Aphra Behn's *The Rover* not only

> "IN A WOMAN-AUTHORED TEXT, THEN, THE GESTIC MOMENT WOULD MARK BOTH A CONVERGENCE OF SOCIAL ACTIONS AND ATTITUDES, AND THE GENDERED HISTORY OF THAT CONVERGENCE."

thematizes the marketing of women in marriage and prostitution, it ''demonstrates,'' in its gestic moments, the ideological contradictions of the apparatus Behn inherited and the society for which she wrote. Brecht's account of the *Gestus* is useful for alerting us to the vectors of historical change written into dramatic texts, but he makes no provision for gender—an unavoidable issue in Aphra Behn's own history. Educated but constantly in need of money, with court connections but no supporting family, Aphra Behn wrote plays when female authorship was a monstrous violation of the ''woman's sphere.'' Since the reopening of the theaters in 1660, Frances Boothby and the Duchess of Newcastle each had had a play produced, but no woman had challenged the Restoration theater with Behn's success and consistency. Indeed, that she could earn a living writing for the theater was precisely what condemned her. The muckraking satirist Robert Gould wrote typical slander in a short piece addressed to Behn that concluded with this couplet: ''For Punk and Poetess agree so Pat, / You cannot be This and not be That.''

In her suggestive ''Arachnologies: The Woman, The Text, and the Critic,'' Nancy Miller implicitly proposes a feminist version of the *Gestus;* texts by women writers, says Miller, encode the signs or ''emblems of a female signature'' by which the ''culture of gender [and] the inscriptions of its political structures'' might be read. In a woman-authored text, then, the gestic moment would mark both a convergence of social actions and attitudes, and the gendered history of that convergence. Robert Gould's verse, with its violent, unequivocal equation of ''poetess'' and ''punk,'' provides some evidence of the culture of gender in Restoration London. Like her male colleagues, Behn hawked her intrigue comedies and political satires in the literary and theatrical marketplace, and like them, she suffered the attacks of ''fop-corner'' and the sometimes paltry remuneration of third-day receipts. In her case, however, the status of professional writer indicated immodesty: the author, like her texts, became a commodity.

Deciphering Behn's authorial ''signature'' obliges us to read the theatrical, social, and sexual discourses that complicate and obscure its inscription. I am aiming here to open the text to what Brecht calls its ''fields of force''—those contradictory relations and ideas that signify in Behn's culture and are, as this reading will indicate, symptomatic of our own. Like Brecht, in his discussion of Shakespeare's *Coriolanus,* I am interested less in interpretative truth than in exploring a complex textual system in which author, apparatus, history, and reader-spectator each plays a signifying role. The following section will consider Behn's authorial contexts, the Restoration theater apparatus, with its proto-fetishist positioning of ''scenes'' and actresses; the next two sections focus on multivalent signs of gender in *The Rover;* and the final section, returning to the theater apparatus by way of Behn's unique obsessions, poses the question of the woman dramatist's signature: How does Aphra Behn encode the conditions of her literary and theatrical production? How does she stage the relationship between female creativity and public calumny—between what Robert Gould, in darkly humorous euphemisms, refers to as ''this'' and ''that''?

I. The Apparatus

The term ''apparatus'' draws together several related aspects in theater production: the hierarchy of economic control, the material features of machinery and properties, and, more elusively, the social and psychological interplay between stage and audience. When Aphra Behn wrote her seventeen plays (1670–1689), the theatrical hierarchy, like all cultural institutions, was patriarchal in control and participation. Charles II invested power in the first patentees, Thomas Killigrew and William D'Avenant; aristocratic or upper-class males generally wrote the plays, purchased the tickets, and formed the coteries of critics and ''witlings'' whose disruptive presence is remarked on in countless play prologues and epilogues. In its machinery and properties, the Restoration stage was not unlike Wagner's theater in Adorno's critique: dreamlike, seductive, and commodity-intensive. Though the technology was well established in Italian and French courts, and in English court masques before the Interregnum, the two new Restoration theaters gave Londoners their first view of movable painted ''scenes'' and mechanical devices or ''machines,'' installed behind the forestage and the proscenium arch. Actors posed before elaborately painted ''wings'' (stationary pieces set in receding rows) and ''shutters'' (flat painted scenes that moved in grooves and joined in the center). When the scenes parted, their characters were ''discovered'' against other painted scenes that, parting, produced further discoveries. Built in 1671, The Duke's Theater, Dorset Garden, the site of most of Behn's plays, was particularly known for its ''gawdy Scenes.''

The movement of painted flats, the discoveries of previously unseen interiors, introduced a new scopic epistemology. Seated and unruly in semicircular areas of pit, boxes, first, middle, and upper galleries, Restoration spectators, unlike their Elizabethan counterparts, were no longer compelled to imagine the features of bed-chambers, parks, or battlefields. Like Richard Flecknoe, they could rely on scenes and machines as ''excellent helps of imagination, most grateful deceptions of the sight . . . Graceful and becoming Ornaments of the Stage [transport] you easily without lassitude from one place to another, or rather by a kinde of delightful Magick, whilst you sit still, does bring the place to you.'' Assuming that Flecknoe's reaction is typical, and there is evidence that it is, Restoration stagecraft seems to have created a spectator-fetishist, one who takes pleasure in ornaments that deceive the sight, whose disavowal of material reality produces a desire for the ''delightful Magick'' of exotic and enticing representations.

I am deliberately conflating two uses of ''fetishism'' in this account of Restoration reception: one, Freud's description of the male impulse to eroticize objects or female body parts, which derives from a disavowal of a material lack (of the penis on the mother's body); and two, Marx's account of the fetishization of the commodity: at the moment of exchange, the commodity appears to be separate from the workers who produce it; the ''specific social character of private labors'' is disavowed. Nowhere are these meanings of fetishism more relevant than in discourse generated by that other ornament of the stage, the Restoration actress. In his preface to *The Tempest,* Thomas Shadwell links the new phenomenon of female performers with painted theatrical scenes, both innovative commodities for audience consumption:

> Had we not for yr pleasure found new wayes
> You still had rusty Arras had, and thredbare playes;
> Nor Scenes nor Woomen had they had their will,
> But some with grizl'd Beards had acted Woomen still.

That female fictions were to be embodied by beardless women would, Thomas Killigrew promised, be ''useful and instructive.'' What the signifying body of the actress actually meant in the culture's sexual economy is perhaps more accurately suggested by metatheatrical references in play prologues and epilogues. The actress playing Flirt in Wycherley's *The Gentleman Dancing Master* satirically invites the ''good men o' th' Exchange'' from the pit into the backstage tiring-room: ''You we would rather see between our Scenes''; and Dryden, in the Prologue to *Marriage A-la-Mode,* has the actor Hart refer to passionate tyring-room assignations.

The private writings of Samuel Pepys are even more suggestive of the sinful pleasures afforded by actresses. On October 5, 1667, he visited the Theatre Royal in Bridges Street:

> and there, going in, met with Knipp [Mrs. Knep], and she took us up into the Tireing-rooms and to the women's Shift, where Nell [Gwyn] was dressing herself and was all unready; and is very pretty, prettier than I thought; and so walked all up and down the House above, and then below into the Scene-room . . . But Lord, to see how they were both painted would make a man mad—and did make me loath them—and what base company of men comes among them, and how lewdly they talk—and how poor the men are in clothes, and yet what a show they make on the stage by candlelight, is very observable.

Candlelight has the ideological function of suturing contradictions between ''lewd'' actors and an alluring ''show,'' and even a habitual playgoer like Pepys is disturbed when the seams show. That actresses were pretty women was not surprising, but the transformation of women into painted representations beautifully exhibited by candlelight was both fascinating and disturbing. Pepys went behind the painted scenes, but the paint was still there. He hoped to separate the pretty woman from the painted actress, but it was the actress he admired—and fetishized—from his spectator's seat.

For Pepys and other Restoration commentators, the actress's sexuality tended to disavow her labor. Rather than produce a performance, she is a spectacle unto herself, a painted representation to lure the male spectator. In her professional duplicity, in her desirability, in her often public status of kept mistress, she is frequently equated with prostitutes or ''vizard-masks'' who worked the pit and galleries of Restoration theaters during and after performances. In Wycherley's *The Plain Dealer,* Mrs. Hoyden is disparaged for being "As familiar a duck . . . As an Actress in the tiring-room."

The epistemological link between the theater apparatus and illicit female signs is not of course new to the Restoration. Jonas Barish, documenting the antitheatrical prejudice, notes that Patristic condemnation of the theater, typified in tracts from the third-century Tertullian's to those of Renaissance Puritans Phillip Stubbes and William Prynne, builds on the Platonic condemnation of mimesis as the making of counterfeit copies of true originals. Actors in paint and costume contaminate their true God-given identities: "Whatever is *born,*" writes Tertullian, "is the work of God. Whatever . . . is *plastered on* is the devil's work." To the Puritan mind the presence of women on stage was an affront to feminine modesty, but more damning was the fact that the means of illusionism—use of costume, paint, masking—involved specifically female vices. The nature of theatrical representation, like the "nature" of woman, was to ensnare, deceive, and seduce.

Given this cultural legacy, and the metonymic connection between painted female performer and painted scenes, it is not surprising that the first woman to earn money circulating her own representations had a combative relationship with the theater apparatus. As we will see, Aphra Behn, more than any other Restoration playwright, exploits the fetish/commodity status of the female performer, even as her plays seek to problematize that status. She utilizes the conventional objects of Restoration satire—the marriage market, sexual intrigue, masquerade, libertine flamboyance—even as she signals, in "gestic" moments, their contradictory meanings for female fictions and historical women.

II. Virgin Commodities

The Rover (1677) and *The Second Part of The Rover* (1681), both drawn from Killigrew's *Thomaso, or The Wanderer* (1663), are Behn's only plays to label a character a courtesan; in her wholly original *The Feigned Curtezans* (1679), witty virgins impersonate famous Roman courtesans and near-debauches occur, but, as befits the romantic intrigue, marriages settle the confusion of plots and the financial stink of prostitution is hastily cleared away. If courtesans figure by name in only three plays, however, the commodification of women in the marriage market is Aphra Behn's first and most persistent theme. Beginning appropriately enough with *The Forced Marriage; or The Jealous Bridegroom* (1670), all of Behn's seventeen known plays deal to some extent with women backed by dowries or portions who are forced by their fathers into marriage in exchange for jointure, an agreed-upon income to be settled on the wife should she be widowed.

There was a lived context for this perspective. The dowry system among propertied classes had been in place since the sixteenth century, but at the end of the seventeenth century there were thirteen women to every ten men, and cash portions had to grow to attract worthy suitors. As the value of women fell by almost fifty percent, marriage for love, marriage by choice, became almost unthinkable. Women through marriage had evident exchange value; that is, the virgin became a commodity not only for her use-value as breeder of the legal heir but for her portion, which, through exchange, generated capital. If, as Marx writes, exchange converts commodities into fetishes or "social hieroglyphics," signs whose histories and qualitative differences can no longer be read, women in the seventeenth-century marriage market took on the phantasmagoric destiny of fetishized commodities; they seemed no more than objects or things. As Margaret Cavendish observed, sons bear the family name but "Daughters are to be accounted but as Movable Goods or Furnitures that wear out."

Restoration comedy, from the earliest Etherege and Sedley through Wycherley, Dryden, Vanbrugh, D'Urfey, and Congreve, mocked the marketplace values of marriage, promoting the libertine's aesthetic of "natural" love, verbal seduction, and superiority over jealous husbands and fops. But Aphra Behn concentrated on exposing the exploitation of women in the exchange economy, adding vividly to contemporary discourse on the oppressions of marriage. "Wife and servant are the same / But differ only in the name," wrote Lady Mary Chudleigh. "Who would marry," asks Behn's Ariadne (*The Second Part of the Rover*), "who wou'd be chaffer'd thus, and sold to Slavery?" The issue arises repeatedly in plays and verse of the period: not only are marriages loveless, but once married, women lose both independent identity and control of their fortunes. Ariadne again:

> You have a Mistress, Sir, that has your Heart, and all your softer Hours: I know't, and if I were so wretched as to marry thee, must see my Fortune lavisht out on her; her Coaches, Dress, and Equipage exceed mine by far: Possess she all the day thy Hours of Mirth, good Humour and Expence, thy Smiles, thy Kisses, and thy Charms of Wit.

The feminist philosopher Mary Astell would have had no sympathy for the sensuous appetites of Behn's females, but Ariadne's sentiments receive astute articulation in Astell's *Some Reflections Upon Marriage.* The money motive for marriage produces in the man contempt and ''Indifferency'' which ''proceeds to an aversion, and perhaps even the Kindness and Complaisance of the poor abused'd Wife, shall only serve to increase it.'' Ultimately, the powerless wife ends up ''mak[ing] court to [her husband] for a little sorry Alimony out of her own Estate.'' Two centuries later Engels merely restates these comments in his observation that forced marriages ''turn into the crassest prostitution—sometimes of both partners, but far more commonly of the woman, who only differs from the ordinary courtesan in that she does not [hire] out her body on piecework as a wage worker, but sells it once and for all into slavery.''

Yet in order to launch *The Rover*'s marriage plot and to provoke sympathy for her high-spirited aristocrats, Behn dissimulates the connection between virgin and prostitute. When Florinda, Hellena, and Valeria don gypsy costumes—assume the guise of marginal and exotic females—to join the carnival masquerade, they do so explicitly to evade the patriarchal arrangement of law and jointure laid down by their father and legislated by their brother Pedro: Florinda shall marry a rich ancient count and Hellena shall go into a convent, thus saving their father a second dowry and simultaneously enriching Florinda. The opening dialogue of *The Rover* is also implicitly ''gestic,'' raising questions about women's material destiny in life as well as in comic representation:

> *Florinda:* What an impertinent thing is a young girl bred in a nunnery! How full of questions! Prithee no more, Hellena; I have told thee more than thou understand'st already.
>
> *Hellena:* The more's my grief. I would fain know as much as you, which makes me so inquisitive.

Hellena dons masquerade because she desires not a particular lover but a wider knowledge. Given the conventions of Restoration comedy, this wish to know ''more than'' she already understands is troped as a wish for sexual adventure. But if we hear this dialogue dialogically—in its social register—other meanings are accessible. Women's lack of access to institutions of knowledge spurred protest from writers as diverse as Margaret Cavendish, Bathsua Makin, Mary Astell, and Judith Drake. Aphra Behn mocks a university fool in *The City Heiress* and a learned lady in *Sir Patient Fancy;* she criticizes neoclassical aesthetics in ''Epistle to the Reader,'' appended to *The Dutch Lover*, for having nothing to do with why people write or attend plays. When she translates Bernard de Fontenelle's *A Discovery of New Worlds,* however, she reveals as passionate a hunger for esoteric knowledge as these early English feminists. Unfortunately, the controlling conceit of Fontenelle's work—a mere woman is informally taught the complexities of Copernican theory—produces an untenable and revealing contradiction for Behn: ''He [Fontenelle] makes her [the Marchionness] say a great many silly things, tho' sometimes she makes observations so learned, that the greatest Philosophers in Europe could make no better.'' Insightful yet silly, wise yet a *tabula rasa,* Fontenelle's Marchionness oscillates between intellectual independence and slavish imitation. She is perhaps less a contradictory character than a projection of a male intellectual's ambivalence about female education.

Aphra Behn's Hellena seeks knowledge ''more than'' or beyond the gender script provided for her. She rejects not only her brother's decision to place her in a nunnery, but also the cultural narrative of portion, jointure, and legal dependency in which she is written not as subject but as object of exchange. Yet Hellena, too, oscillates—both departing from and reinforcing her social script. Her lines following those cited above seem, at first, to complicate and defer the romantic closure of the marriage plot. To have a lover, Hellena conjectures, means to ''sigh, and sing, and blush, and wish, and dream and wish, and long and wish to see the man.'' This thrice-reiterated wishing will result in three changes of costume, three suitors, and three marriages. As with the repetitions of ''interest,'' ''credit,'' and ''value''—commodity signifiers that circulate through the play and slip like the vizard from face to hand to face—this repetition invokes the processes underlying all wishing, to desire that will not, like a brother's spousal contract, find its ''completion.''

If we incorporate insights from feminist psychoanalytic theory, the virgins' masquerade takes on added significance, or rather this discourse helps us decode what is already implied—namely, that in an economy in which women are dependent on male keepers and traders, female desire is always already a masquerade, a play of false representations that covers over and simultaneously expresses the lack the woman exhibits—lack of the male organ and, concomitantly, lack of access to phallic privileges—to material and institutional power. Unlike the theatrical mask, which conceals a truth, the masquerade of female sexuality subverts the ''Law-of-the-Father'' that stands ''behind'' any representation. Underneath the gypsy veils and drapes of Behn's virgins, there is nothing, in a phallic sense, to see; thus no coherent female identity that can be coopted into a repressive romantic narrative. Willmore, titillated by Hellena's witty chatter, asks to see her face. Hellena responds that underneath the vizard is a ''desperate . . . lying look''—that is, she, like her vizard, may prevaricate; represented may mingle with representer—for the spectator (Willmore) there will be no validating stake.

Yet, as Behn well knew, there is means of validation, one that guarantees patriarchy's stake in portion, jointure, and the woman's body: the hymen. In Restoration comedy no witty unmarried woman was really witty unless she had property *and* a maidenhead. Behn's virgins may re-''design'' their cast of characters but they cannot change their plot. Ultimately their masquerade is dissimulation in the classic representational sense, a veil that hides a truth. Hellena's mask merely replicates the membrane behind which lies the ''true nature'' of woman: the equipment to make the requisite patrilineal heir. Thus Willmore's masterful response to Hellena's ''lying look'' is a mock-blazon of her facial features, ending in a fetishistic flourish: ''Those soft round melting cherry lips and small even white teeth! Not to be expressed, but silently adored!.'' The play in Hellena's discourse between knowing and desiring, which extends through the masquerade, completes itself in the marriage game. She exercises her will only by pursuing and winning Willmore, for as it turns out he has the ''more'' she ''would fain know.''

Willmore acts not only as the rover but as signifier for the play's phallic logic. His name metaphorizes the trajectory of desire as he roves from bed to bed ''willing more,'' making all satisfactions temporary and unsatisfying. Desire's subject, Willmore never disguises himself (he comes on stage *holding* his mask); until enriched by the courtesan Angellica Bianca, he remains in ''buff'' or leather military coat. In another sense, though, Willmore is already in disguise, or rather the entity ''Willmore'' covers a range of linguistic and social signifiers. Behn's model for Willmore (like Etherege's for Dorimont) was reputedly the womanizing courtier, the Earl of Rochester, whose name, John Wilmot, contains, like the rover's, the word (''mot'') ''will.'' Rochester was also the lover and mentor of Elizabeth Barry, the actress who first played Behn's Hellena. In Tory mythology Charles II, on the verge of fleeing England, disguised himself in buff—a leather doublet. Indeed, Willmore's first lines refer to the offstage Prince who, in exile during the Commonwealth, was also a rover. Doubled mimetically and semiotically with both Rochester and the Merry Monarch (who attended at least one performance of *The Rover* before the play was restaged at Whitehall), Willmore needs no mask to effect his ends: his libertine desire is guaranteed and upheld by patriarchal law. Hellena's playful rovings, on the other hand, and her numerous disguises, signal both ingenuity and vulnerability. Ironically, the virgins' first costume, the gypsy masquerade, represents their actual standing in the marriage market—exotic retailers of fortunes (or portions). Their masquerade defers but does not alter the structure of patriarchal exchange.

III. Painting(s), Person, Body

In contrast to the virgins' ''ramble'' are the stasis and thralldom that attend the courtesan Angellica Bianca. While the virgins are learning artful strategies of concealment, Angellica's entrance is a complicated process of theatrical unveiling. She arrives first through words, then through painted representation, then through the body of an actress who appears on a balcony behind a silk curtain. She is also the site of a different politics, one that explores desire and gender not only in the text but in the apparatus itself.

The first references to Angellica situate her beyond the market in which we expect her to function. According to Behn's gallants, she is the ''adord beauty of all the youth in Naples, who put on all their charms to appear lovely in her sight; their coaches, liveries and themselves all gay as on a monarch's birthday.'' Equated thus with sacred and secular authority, Angellica gazes on her suitors and ''has the pleasure to behold all languish for her that see her.'' This text in which desire flows from and is reflected back to a female subject is immediately followed by the grouping of the English gallants beneath the courtesan's balcony. They wait with the impatience of theater spectators for Angellica to appear—not in person but in representation, as ''the shadow of the fair substance.''

At this point the problematic connection between shadow and substance preoccupies them. Blunt, the stock country fool, is confused by the fact that signs of bourgeois and even noble status—velvet beds, fine plate, handsome attendance, and coaches—are flaunted by courtesans. Blunt is raising an epistemological issue that Behn and her colleagues often treat satirically—the neoclassical assumption regarding mimesis that imitated can be separated from imitator, nature from representation, truth from falsehood, virgin from gypsy. By suggesting that whores are indistinguishable from moral women, Behn revives the problematic of the masquerade, casting doubt on the connection/separation of sign and referent. Significantly, when Hobbes constructed his theory of sovereign authority, he employed theater metaphors to distinguish between ''*natural*'' and ''*feigned* or *artificial*'' persons. But he noted that ''person'' was itself a slippery referent:

> The word Person [persona] is Latin . . . [and] signifies the *disguise,* or *outward appearance* of a man, counterfeited on the stage; and sometimes more particularly that part of it, which disguiseth the face, as a mask or vizard: and from the stage, hath been translated to any representer of speech and action, as well in tribunals, as theatres. So that a *person* is the same that an *actor* is, both on stage and in common conversation.

Since, as Christopher Pye notes, everyone is already a ''self-impersonator, a mediated representation of himself,'' the difference between ''natural'' and ''feigned'' rests on highly unstable assumptions about identity which, both ''on stage'' and ''in common conversation'' are capable of shifting. Blunt's confusion about the true status of apparently noble women may also be read as an extratextual reference to the Restoration actress and her female spectators. As kept mistresses, actresses often displayed the fine clothing and jewels of aristocrats like the notorious Duchess of Cleveland, who regularly watched the play in vizard-mask from the king's box. Yet the respectable Mrs. Pepys also owned a vizard-mask, and on her frequent visits to the theater occasionally sat in the pit near the ''real'' vizards.

Given the theatricality of everyday Restoration life, and the ambiguity of signs representing the status and character of women, Angellica's three portraits allow Aphra Behn to comment on the pleasures and politics of theatrical signification. Though I have ignored the specifics of Behn's adaptation of her source play, it is helpful here to compare her handling of the paintings with that of Killigrew in his ten-act semiautobiographical closet drama, *Thomaso, or The Wanderer.* In both plays, one portrait is prominent and raised, and two smaller versions are posted below, one of which is snatched by the rake—Thomaso in the source play, Willmore in Behn's. But there is an important difference in the disposition of the paintings vis-à-vis the woman they represent. In *Thomaso,* 2.1, anonymous parties of men pass in front of the paintings, react scornfully to the courtesan's high price, and wander on. But in 2.2, with the arrival of Killigrew's main characters, Angellica Bianca is sitting on the balcony in full view of her prospective buyers. Her bawd challenges the men to ''compare them [the paintings and the woman] together.'' With neoclassical correctness, the men agree that the woman exceeds her representation: ''That smile, there's a grace and sweetness in it Titian could never have catch'd.'' By the time the English Thomaso and his friends arrive, the viewing of the paintings and the viewing of Angellica are almost simultaneous:

> *Harrigo:* That wonder is it I told you of; tis the picture of the famous Italian, the Angellica; See, shee's now at her Window.
>
> *Thomaso:* I see her, 'tis a lovely Woman.

Aphra Behn's Angellica Bianca never invites such explicit comparison. In fact, Behn prolongs the dialogue between titillated suitors and suggestive portraits: Angellica's simulacra, not Angellica, preoccupy her male audience. When the English cavaliers first view the paintings, Belvile, the play's fatuous moral figure, reads them as ''the fair sign[s] to the inn where a man may lodge that's fool enough to give her price.'' That is, the iconicity of the paintings, their likeness to Angellica, which so impresses Killigrew's cavaliers, is in Behn's text suppressed. Gazing on the portraits, the gallants rewrite the courtesan's monarchial description, now figuring her as a thing, a receptacle for depositing one's body. To underscore the point, Behn has Blunt ask the ontological question to which there is a ready answer in commodity discourse: ''Gentlemen, what's this?'' Belvile: ''A famous courtesan, that's to be sold.'' The infinitive phrase is curious. To be sold by whom? Released by her earlier keeper's death, Angellica and her bawd seem to be in business for themselves. At this point, however, Blunt reminds us again of the object status of the woman, as of her painted signs: ''Let's be gone; I'm sure we're no chapmen for this commodity.''

Willmore, however, monarchy's representative, succumbs to the lure of the signs, believing not only in their iconicity but in their value as pleasurable objects—for the original one must pay one thousand crowns, but on the portraits one can gaze for nothing. Penury, however, is not the real issue. Willmore seems to understand that the appeal of the paintings is precisely that they are not the original but an effective stand-in. After the two Italian aristocrats draw swords in competition for Angellica, Willmore reaches up and steals one of the small paintings, in effect cuts away a piece of the representation for his own titillation. His intentions, like his actions, are explicitly fetishistic:

> This posture's loose and negligent;
> The sight on't would beget a warm desire
> In souls whom impotence and age had chilled.
> This must along with me.

This speech and the act of appropriation occur *before* Willmore sees Angellica. Only in Behn's text do the paintings function as fetishes, as substitute objects for the female body. When challenged why he has the right to the small portrait, Willmore claims the right "of possession, which I will maintain."

At the outset of this paper I described Willmore's acquisitive gesture as a Brechtian "gest"—that moment in theatrical performance in which contradictory social attitudes in both text and society are made heuristically visible to spectators. What does this gest show? Willmore removes Angellica's portrait the way a theater manager might lift off a piece of the set—because without buying her, he already owns her. Her paintings are materially and metonymically linked to the painted scenes, which were of course owned, through the theatrical hierarchy, by patentee and king—who, in Behn's fiction, validates and empowers Willmore. This "homosocial" circuit, to use Eve Sedgwick's term, extends into the social realm. As innumerable accounts make clear, Restoration theater participated in the phallic economy that commodified women, not in the marriage market, but in the mistress market: the king and his circle came to the theater to look, covet, and buy. Nell Gwyn is the celebrated example, but Behn's biographer Angeline Goreau cites other cases. An actress in the King's Company, Elizabeth Farley, joined the royal entourage for several months, then became mistress to a Gray's Inn lawyer, then drifted into prostitution and poverty. The answer to the question, "Who is selling Angellica?" is, then, the theater itself, which, like Willmore, operates with the king's patent and authorization. When Angellica sings behind her balcony curtain for her Italian admirers, and draws the curtain to reveal a bit of beautiful flesh, then closes it while monetary arrangements are discussed, she performs the titillating masquerade required by her purchasers *and* by her spectators. This is mastery's masquerade, not to demonstrate freedom, but to flaunt the charms that guarantee and uphold male power.

If Angellica's paintings stand for the theater apparatus and its ideological complicity with a phallic economy, what happens when Angellica appears? Is illusionism betrayed? Interestingly, Aphra Behn chooses this moment to emphasize presence, not only of character but of body; Angellica emerges in the flesh and offers herself, gratis, to Willmore, finding his scornful admiration ample reason for, for the first time, falling in love. In their wooing/bargaining scene it becomes clear that Angellica wants to step out of the exchange economy symbolized by the paintings: "Canst thou believe [these yielding joys] will be entirely thine, / without considering they were mercenary?" The key word here is "entirely"; Angellica dreams of full reciprocal exchange without commerce: "The pay I mean is but thy love for mine. / Can you give that?" And Willmore responds "entirely."

A commodity, Marx writes, appears as a commodity only when it "possess[es] a double form, i.e. natural form and value form." Angellica's name contains "angel," a word whose meaning is undecidable since it refers simultaneously to the celestial figure and to the old English coin stamped with the device of Michael the archangel, minted for the last time by Charles I but still in common circulation during the Restoration. By eliminating her value-form, Angellica attempts to return her body to a state of nature, to take herself out of circulation. While the virgins of the marriage plot are talking "business" and learning the powers of deferral and unveiling, Angellica is trying to demystify and authenticate herself. She wants to step out of the paintings, to be known not by her surface but by her depth. As she "yields" to Willmore upstairs, the portraits on the balcony are removed—a sign that the courtesan is working. In this case, not only does the (offstage) "natural" body supplant its painted representation, but the courtesan, who has been in excess of, now makes up a deficiency in, the marriage plot: Angellica (with Willmore) labors for love.

Though the paintings disappear in act 3, however, the signs of commodification are still in place, or are metonymically displaced through properties and scenes to other characters in the marriage plot. We learn that Hellena's portion derives from her uncle, the old man who kept Angellica Bianca; thus the gold Willmore receives from the courtesan has the same source as that which he will earn by marrying the virgin. Like Angellica, too, the virgin Florinda uses a portrait as a calling card, and at night in the garden, "*in undress,*" carrying a little box of jewels—a double metonym for dowry and genitals—

she plans to offer herself to Belvile. Unfortunately Willmore, not Belvile, enters the garden and nearly rapes her.

Florinda's nocturnal effort at entrepreneurship takes place in the upstage scenes, where Aphra Behn, like her fellow Restoration dramatists, situated lovers' trysts and discoveries. The thematic link between commodified "Scenes" and females is particularly crucial, however, in *The Rover*. In 4.4, a disguised Florinda flees from Willmore by running in and out of the scenes until she arrives in Blunt's chamber, where another near-rape occurs. Blunt has just been cozened by a prostitute and dumped naked into the city sewer; he emerges vowing to "beat" and "kiss" and "bang" the next woman he sees, who happens to be Florinda, but now all women appear to be whores. In fact Willmore, Frederick, and even Belvile arrive soon after to break open the door and "partake" of Florinda. If Angellica Bianca makes a spectacle of herself through balcony curtains and paintings, Florinda's "undress" and her proximity to the painted scenes signify a similar reduction to commodity status.

IV. "I . . . Hang Out the Sign of Angellica"

Angellica's paintings, I have argued, are the bright links in a metonymic chain joining the text of *The Rover* to the apparatus of representation. Angellica's portraits represent the courtesan in the most radical sense. They produce an image of her and at the same time reduce her to that image. Notwithstanding her passionate address, Angellica cannot exceed her simulacra. In effect she is doubly commodified—first because she puts her body into exchange, and second because this body is equated with, indeed interchangeable with, the art object. When Willmore performs the "gest" of appropriating the painted image of Angellica, he makes visible, on the one hand, the patriarchal and homosocial economy that controls the apparatus and, on the other hand, the commodity status of paintings, of their model, and, by metonymic extension, of the painted actress and the painted scenes.

Flecknoe and Pepys, we noted earlier, testify to the intensity of visual pleasure in Restoration theater. It is a fascinating contradiction of all feminist expectation to discover that Aphra Behn, more than any of her Restoration colleagues, contributed to that visual pleasure by choosing, in play after play, to exploit the fetish/ commodity status of the female performer. The stage offered two playing spaces, the forestage used especially for comedy, where actor and audience were in intimate proximity, and the upstage or scenic stage, where wing-and-shutter settings, as much as fifty feet from the first row of spectators, produced the exotic illusionistic discoveries needed for heroic tragedy. Writing mostly comedies, Aphra Behn might be expected to follow comic convention and use the forestage area, but as Peter Holland notes, she was "positively obsessive" about discovery scenes. Holland counts thirty-one discoveries in ten comedies (consider that Sedley's *The Mulberry Garden,* 1668, uses one; Etherege's *The Man of Mode,* 1676, uses two), most of which are bedroom scenes featuring a female character "*in undress.*" Holland reasons that such scenes are placed upstage so that familiar Restoration actresses would not be distractingly exposed to the audience. We might interpret Behn's "obsession" differently: the exposed woman's (castrated) body must be obscured in order to activate scopic pleasure. Displayed in "undress" or loosely draped gowns, the actress becomes a fetish object, affording the male spectator the pleasure of being seduced by and, simultaneously, of being protected from the effects of sexual difference.

Is it also possible that this deliberate use of fetishistic display dramatizes and displaces the particular assault Behn herself endured as "Poetess/ Punk" in the theater apparatus? The contradictions in her authorial status are clear from the preface to *The Lucky Chance* (1686). Behn argues that the Woman damns the Poet, that accusations of bawdy and plagiarism are levied at her because she is a woman. On the other hand, the literary fame she desires derives from a creativity that in her mind, or rather in the social ideology she has absorbed, is also gendered: "my Masculine Part the Poet in me." In literary history, the pen, as Gilbert and Gubar have argued, is a metaphorical penis, and the strong woman writer adopts strategies of revision and disguise in order to tell her own story. In Behn's texts, the painful bisexuality of authorship, the conflict between (as she puts it) her "defenceless" woman's body and her "masculine part," is *staged* in her insistence, in play after play, on the equation between female body and fetish, fetish and commodity—the body in the "scenes." Like the actress, the woman dramatist is sexualized, circulated, denied a subject position in the theater hierarchy.

This unstable, contradictory image of authority emerges as early as Behn's first play prologue (to *The Forced Marriage, or The Jealous Bridegroom,* 1670). A male actor cautions the wits that the vizard-masks sitting near them will naturally support a woman's play and attempt to divert them from criticism. He is then interrupted by an actress who, pointing "*to the Ladies*" praises both them and, it would seem, the woman author: "Can any see that glorious sight and say / A woman shall not prove Victor today?"

The "glorious sight" is, once again, the fetishized, commodified representation of the female, standing on the forestage, sitting in the pit, and soon to be inscribed as author of a printed play. If this fascinating moment—in which a woman speaking a woman's lines summons the regard of other women—seems to put a *female* gaze into operation, it also reinforces the misogynist circuitry of the theater apparatus: that which chains actress to vizard-mask to author.

At the outset of this essay we asked how Aphra Behn encodes the literary and theatrical conditions of her production. Behn's "Postscript" to the published text of *The Rover* provides a possible answer. She complains that she has been accused of plagiarizing Killigrew simply because the play was successful and she a woman. Yet while claiming to be "vainly proud of [her] judgment" in adapting *Thomaso,* she "hang[s] out the sign of Angellica (the only stolen object) to give notice where a great part of the wit dwelt." This compliment to Killigrew may also indicate what compelled Behn to embark on this adaptation. The "sign[s] of Angellica" both constitute and represent the theater apparatus, serving as metacritical commentary on its patriarchal economy, its habits of fetishistic consumption. They may also constitute Behn's authorial signature, what Miller calls the "material . . . brutal traces of the culture of gender." As a woman writer in need of money, Behn was vulnerable to accusations of immodesty; to write meant to expose herself, to put herself into circulation; like Angellica, to sell her wares. Is it merely a coincidence that Angellica Bianca shares Aphra Behn's initials, that hers is the only name from *Thomaso* that Behn leaves unchanged?

The "signs of Angellica" not only help us specify the place of this important woman dramatist in Restoration cultural practice, they invite us to historicize the critique of fetishization that has informed so much feminist criticism in the last decade. Certainly the conditions of women writers have changed since the Restoration, but the fetishistic features of the commercial theater have remained remarkably similar. Now as then the theater apparatus is geared to profit and pleasure, and overwhelmingly controlled by males. Now as then the arrangement of audience to stage produces what Brecht calls a "culinary" or ideologically conservative spectator, intellectually passive but scopically hungry, eager for the next turn of the plot, the next scenic effect. Now as then the actor suffers the reduction of Angellica Bianca, having no existence except in the simulations produced by the exchange economy. The practice of illusionism, as Adorno points out above, converts historical performers into commodities which the spectator pays to consume.

If Restoration theater marks the historical beginning of commodity-intensive, dreamlike effects in English staging, Aphra Behn's contribution to contemporary theory may lie in her demonstration that, from the outset, dreamlike effects have depended on the fetish-commodification of the female body. When Willmore, standing in for king and court, steals Angellica's painting, Behn not only reifies the female, she genders the spectatorial economy as, specifically, a male consumption of the female image. Reading that confident gesture of appropriation as a *Gestus,* the contemporary spectator adds another viewpoint. Angellica Bianca's paintings appear to us now as both authorial "signature" and "social hieroglyphic," signs of a buried life whose careful decoding opens up new possibilities for critique and contestation.

Source: Elin Diamond, "*Gestus* and Signature in Aphra Behn's *The Rover,*" in *ELH,* Vol. 56, No. 3, 1989, pp. 519–41.

SOURCES

Behn, Aphra, *The Lucky Chance,* Methuen, 1984, p. 2.

Diamond, Elin, "*Gestus* and the Signature in Aphra Behn's *The Rover,*" in *New Casebooks: Aphra Behn,* edited by Janet Todd, St. Martin's Press, 1999, p. 33.

Gallagher, Catherine, "Who Was That Masked Woman? The Prostitute and the Playwright in the Comedies of Aphra Behn," in *New Casebooks: Aphra Behn,* edited by Janet Todd, St. Martin's Press, 1999, p. 13.

Hall, Peter, *Exposed by the Mask: Form and Language in Drama,* Theatre Communications Group, 2000, p. 35.

Hughes, Derek, *The Theatre of Aphra Behn,* Palgrave, 2001, p. 87.

Hutner, Heidi, "Revisioning the Female Body: Aphra Behn's *The Rover,* Parts I and II," in *Rereading Aphra Behn: History, Theory and Criticism,* edited by Heidi Hutner, University Press of Virginia, 1993, p. 103, 105, 107.

Killigrew, Thomas, *Thomaso; or, The Wanderer,* Part I, Henry Herringman, 1663, p. 363.

Pepys, Samuel, *The Diary of Samuel Peyps,* edited by Robert Latham and William Matthews, 11 vols., University of Berkeley Press, 1970–1983, 7:71–72.

Russell, Anne, Introduction to *The Rover* by Aphra Behn, in *The Rover,* edited by Anne Russell, Broadview Press Ltd., 1994, p. 25.

Schafer, Elizabeth, ''Appropriating Aphra,'' in *The Critical Fortunes of Aphra Behn,* edited by Janet Todd, Camden House, 1998, p. 91.

Spencer, Jane, *Aphra Behn's Afterlife,* Oxford University Press, 2000, p. 25, 192, 197.

Todd, Janet, *The Critical Fortunes of Aphra Behn,* Camden House, 1998, p. 49, 57, 87.

Woolf, Virginia, *A Room of One's Own,* Harcourt Brace, 1957, p. 67, 69.

FURTHER READING

Altaba-Artal, Dolors, *Aphra Behn's English Feminism: Wit and Satire,* Susquehanna University Press, 1999.

This is a scholarly analysis of Behn's major works, with a chapter including *The Rover.* Altaba-Artal finds significant evidence of Spanish influence in Behn's works.

Duffy, Maureen, *The Passionate Shepherdess: Aphra Behn 1640–89,* Cape, 1977.

This is an early twentieth-century biography of Aphra Behn by a feminist critic and author.

Hughes, Derek, *The Theatre of Aphra Behn,* Palgrave, 2001.

Hughes presents a chronological study of Behn's plays, putting them into historical context as well as demonstrating her development as a playwright.

Hutner, Heidi, ''Revisioning the Female Body: Aphra Behn's *The Rover,* Parts I and II,'' in *Rereading Aphra Behn: History, Theory and Criticism,* edited by Heidi Hutner, University Press of Virginia, 1993.

This essay is a feminist reading of Behn's two Rover plays.

Kreis-Schinck, Annette, *Women, Writing, and the Theater in the Early Modern Period: The Plays of Aphra Behn and Suzanne Centlivre,* Associated University Presses, 2001.

With chapters on marriage, divorce, widowhood, affairs, and abstinence, Kreis-Schinck describes how the works of these two female playwrights portray women's issues of their time.

Owens, W. R., and Lizbeth Goodman, eds., *Shakespeare, Aphra Behn and the Canon,* Routledge, 1996.

This work is actually a student text with chapters on three Shakespearean plays and one chapter on Behn's *The Rover.* This work describes various Open University (BBC) productions of these plays and their backgrounds and attempts to navigate between understanding the play in its original context and exploring its reflection of current critical interests. The book contains many black-and-white photographs of the 1995 Open University BBC production of *The Rover.*

Sackville-West, V., *Aphra Behn: The Incomparable Astrea,* Russell & Russell Publishers, 1970.

This slim volume is an early biography of Behn, containing some historical inaccuracies, written by a contemporary and friend of Virginia Woolf.

Spencer, Jane, *Aphra Behn's Afterlife,* Oxford University Press, 2000.

Spencer presents a history of the critical reception of Aphra Behn and her work, with a chapter on the reception of *The Rover* in the eighteenth century.

Todd, Janet, *The Critical Fortunes of Aphra Behn,* Camden House, 1998.

In this scholarly work, Todd traces the critical reception and influence of Aphra Behn's plays, novels, and poems.

———, *The Secret Life of Aphra Behn,* Rutgers University Press, 1997.

In this recent and very readable biography, Todd delves into the contradictions and complexities of Behn's life and work.

———, ed., *Aphra Behn,* New Casebook Series, St. Martin's Press, 1999.

Todd, a Behn specialist, edited this anthology of recent scholarly essays on the work of Aphra Behn, mostly comprised of feminist readings.

———, ed., *Aphra Behn Studies,* Cambridge University Press, 1996.

Todd presents a range of recent scholarly articles on certain of Behn's plays and poems, including one essay on *The Rover.*

The Secret Rapture

DAVID HARE

1988

In an article he wrote for the *Listener* just before *The Secret Rapture* opened in London in October 1988, David Hare revealed the source of the play's curious title. ''In Catholic theology,'' the playwright explained, ''the 'secret rapture' is the moment when the nun will become the bride of Christ: so it means death, or love of death, or death under life.'' True to its origins, the play is filled with images of death, from the opening scene, in which a young woman keeps a vigil over the body of her dead father, to the climax, in which that same young woman is murdered by her obsessed lover. In between is a family drama rich with the symbolism and topical social criticism for which Hare has become well known in more than three decades as one of Britain's most popular playwrights.

Although the play's characters and themes are rather complicated, its plot is quite simple. Isobel Glass is a humane, fairly successful small business owner. Her sister, Marion, is a self-centered, fast-rising politician in Britain's Conservative Party government in the 1980s. When their father dies, Isobel is forced to assume the responsibility for their young, reckless, alcoholic stepmother, Katherine. Because of her love and loyalty for her father, Isobel allows Katherine and the others in the play to take advantage of her, and she quickly loses her boyfriend, her business, and ultimately her life.

Hare wrote *The Secret Rapture* near the end of Prime Minister Margaret Thatcher's ten years in office. During that time, Hare suggests, the rich got much richer, while the rest suffered more and more. Still, the play is much less about politics than some of Hare's earlier work. The relationships between the characters, and Isobel's singular morality, are the real driving forces. *The Secret Rapture* is available in *The Secret Rapture and Other Plays*, by David Hare, published by Grove Press in 1998.

AUTHOR BIOGRAPHY

David Hare was born on June 5, 1947, in St. Leonard's-on-Sea in Sussex, on the southeastern coast of England. When Hare was a boy, his father was a ship's purser on a passenger liner that sailed among England, India, and Australia. The time his father spent away from home left Hare alone with his mother and sister. Surrounded by women as a child, Hare developed an appreciation for the noble qualities he found them to have. A noticeable trend in his writing from the very beginning is the presence of strong female characters, such as those found in *The Secret Rapture*. The playwright's first success, *Slag* (1970), as well as *Plenty* (1978), *Wetherby* (1985), *The Bay at Nice* (1986), *Wrecked Eggs* (1986), *Strapless* (1989), and *Skylight* (1995), all have strong, typically virtuous women characters. ''I've written about women a lot because my subject has often been goodness,'' Hare told interviewer Michael Bloom in *American Theatre* magazine. ''The idea of men being good seems to me to be slightly silly.''

Hare began his career in the alternative, or ''Fringe Theatre,'' movement of London in the late 1960s and early 1970s. The Fringe Theatre was different from the mainstream, usually government subsidized theatre of England. Fringe artists were interested in experimentation with dramatic styles; inexpensive production in nontraditional spaces, such as warehouses and apartment lofts; and the liberated, sometimes political, youth culture of the era. As a new artist on the Fringe scene, Hare earned a small salary as the literary manager for the Royal Court Theatre in 1969, where he also met some of Britain's most experimental, antiestablishment new writers and actors and launched his own career as a playwright. Some of his earliest plays were filled with political criticism and satire. *England's Ireland* (1972) is a collaborative documentary play about the political controversy and bloodshed caused by the English occupation of Northern Ireland. *The Great Exhibition* (1972) derives its name from its

David Hare

pathetic leading character, a world-weary, washed-out politician who has failed at his career and his marriage and, in a last attempt at gaining notoriety, decides to become a flasher in London. *Fanshen* (1975) is an adaptation of William Hinton's novel about the Chinese Revolution, and *Plenty* (1978) is an original work about the failure of Great Britain to live up to its post-World War II promise.

During the 1980s and 1990s, Hare became popular with a much wider audience, as his work started to premiere at the Royal National Theatre in London. He wrote a series of plays criticizing the Conservative government of Prime Minister Margaret Thatcher and the greed and self-interest he saw in British society. *The Secret Rapture* (1988) is an example of how Hare pitted virtuous figures against the destructive influence of this ''decade of greed.'' One of his best-known accomplishments during this time was a trilogy of plays about British social institutions: in *Racing Demon* (1990), Hare tackled the Church of England and won an Olivier Award for Best Play in London's West End and a Tony Award for Best Play on New York's Broadway; *Murmuring Judges* (1991) indicted Britain's legal system; and *The Absence of War* (1993) completed the series by portraying modern English politics.

Prime Minister Thatcher left office in 1990, and the Conservative government was finally voted out in 1997. As his political targets started to fall away, Hare turned his attention away from social criticism and toward more intimate, personal plays. *Skylight* (1995) and *Amy's View* (1996) portray individual relationships between a woman and her lover and a girl and her mother, respectively. *The Judas Kiss* (1998) is a biographical story about playwright Oscar Wilde, and Hare's most recent play, *Via Dolorosa* (1998), is a one-man, staged autobiography in which Hare himself performed in London and New York.

Hare has remained quite popular both in England and America. When *The Blue Room* appeared in New York in the fall of 1998, it joined *The Judas Kiss*, *Amy's View*, and *Via Dolorosa* as one of four new Hare plays to appear on Broadway within a single year.

PLOT SUMMARY

Act 1, Scene 1

The Secret Rapture begins in near darkness. Isobel Glass is seated quietly next to the deathbed of her father, Robert Glass, who died only a few hours before. Although the family has gathered together downstairs to mourn and to begin making funeral arrangements, Isobel decided she needed some peaceful time alone with her father and her thoughts.

Her calm is interrupted by her sister, Marion French, who has ventured up to Robert's bedroom to retrieve a ring she had given him just before his death. In their first exchange, the differences between the two sisters are stark and obvious. Even though Robert was married (to a woman considerably younger than he), Isobel was there nursing him in his final days and hours and even dressed him after he passed away. Marion, on the other hand, had only come to visit a few times. Instead of offering her father companionship, she sought to express her love for him by buying him an expensive ring. She wants it back now, she claims, because she is afraid that Robert's young wife, Katherine, will sell it, along with everything else in the house, to support her drinking habit.

Marion is clearly agitated—a state that defines her character. She is brusque, judgmental, and quick to anger. Isobel, on the other hand, seems all calmness and concern. She does not criticize Marion for taking the ring or for not being there when their father died. In fact, she goes out of her way to try to comfort her sister. Nevertheless, Marion thinks that Isobel must disapprove of her actions.

The two women are joined by Marion's husband, Tom French, who has come to bring them back downstairs. Initially, Tom seems to play the part of the peacekeeper. He is extremely religious. He believes that Jesus watches over him, even going so far as to help him when he has car trouble. He tries to reassure the sisters by telling them their father is now "in the hands of the Lord." As Marion's anger at both Isobel and Katherine rises, he refuses to take sides, calmly telling them, "I'm sure you both must be right." But Marion will not be calmed. Although Isobel has not raised her voice or said a single cross word against her sister, Marion insists that she makes her feel as if she is always in the wrong, and she storms out of the room.

Sensing that Tom is embarrassed by his wife's actions, Isobel points out that it is probably part of Marion's grieving process. Tom comments that Marion gets angry frequently, even though she seems to have everything she could want. She is a member of Britain's successful Conservative Party government and is probably destined for a high-level cabinet position. Since they seem to be making a meaningful personal connection, Isobel asks Tom for a favor. She explains that she cares about her sister very much and wants Tom to let her know if Marion should ever become seriously angry with her. Tom agrees, and the two leave together to join the rest of the family outside in the garden.

Scene 2

A few days later, Isobel, Marion, Tom, and Katherine are gathered on the late Robert Glass's lawn, just after his funeral. Since Robert never attended church, Isobel had located a priest for the service who did not know him. Although she provided the man considerable information about her father, apparently he used very little of it and somehow got much of the rest wrong. None of the family members is happy with the service.

While they reflect on the afternoon, a number of Robert's neighbors from the village stop by to pay their respects, but the family agrees they would prefer to be left alone. Isobel greets the mourners at the door to let them know the family's wishes and suggests that they all go down to a nearby pub.

With the service ended and the guests ushered away, Marion launches a conversation about what the future holds for Katherine. They have all been wondering what she might do with herself and with the modest estate she has inherited from her husband. Katherine admits she has led a reckless and often irresponsible life. She has faced a drug problem, is suffering from alcoholism, and has never found a proper career or even held a job for long. However, she maintains that her time with Robert changed her and that she is ready to straighten up and face the future. She announces that she will go to work with Isobel.

Isobel is as surprised as any of the others to hear about Katherine's plans. They had not discussed such an arrangement, and Isobel's small graphic arts firm only employs three people with limited business. Katherine, though, has recognized a trait in Isobel that will not allow her to say no to someone in need. It is a trait that will eventually be her downfall.

Just as the conversation is getting serious, Marion's cell phone rings, and she takes the call. Her action reveals important facets of her character: she is a borderline workaholic, more committed to her career than her family and not very sensitive to the feelings of those around her. Even Katherine complains about her rudeness. She says that she must tell everyone she meets that Marion is only her ''stepdaughter'' and that she has nothing to do with Marion's awful connection to the politics and greed of the Conservative Party. The politics of the characters in *The Secret Rapture* are another way Hare compares and contrasts them with each other. Marion and Tom are successful ''Tories,'' members of Britain's Conservative Party, which was in power throughout the 1980s under Prime Minister Margaret Thatcher. To the extent that they are political at all, the other characters in the play, including Isobel and Katherine, seem to detest the Conservatives and their greed and may be more sympathetic to Britain's Labour Party.

After Marion heads off into the house, the others discuss Katherine's bombshell announcement that she intends to go to work with Isobel. Katherine is prepared to pack up and go to stay with Isobel that very night, but Isobel is unprepared to commit to offering Katherine a job. Isobel's uncertainty brings out Katherine's vulgar side. Dying for a drink and frustrated that she is not getting her way, Katherine curses Isobel and tells her she is a fraud for pretending she is decent and caring when she is really just like all the rest. Then she storms into the house.

A moment later, Marion appears, finished with her call. She tells Tom and Isobel that Katherine is inside with a bottle of liquor she had stashed under a floorboard, complaining that Isobel won't give her a job. Tom goes inside to try to take the alcohol away, leaving the two sisters together.

Marion blames Isobel for Katherine's tantrum and her return to drinking, telling her all she really had to do to help was pretend to go along with Katherine's plans. Isobel objects that dishonesty is no way to help the situation and asks why Marion couldn't offer her a position somewhere. Of course, Marion has an easy out. ''Don't be ridiculous,'' she tells her sister. ''I'm in the Conservative Party. We can't just take on anyone at all.''

As the women argue, Katherine returns, followed quickly by Tom. She is calmer and more contained now that she has had a few drinks, and she tells everyone the story of how she and Robert Glass met. She was in a bar in another town, drunk and trying to pick up men. She had been at it, she says, for weeks. Robert showed up and took her back to his house in Gloucestershire and let her stay in the spare room. They became fond of each other, and eventually she married the much older man. ''People say I took advantage of his decency,'' Katherine admits. ''But what are good people for? They're here to help the trashy people like me.''

Again, Katherine's words are prophetic—Isobel will soon go to work where her father left off. She relents and tells Katherine that she can come to London and start to work with her the next day.

Scene 3

The third scene begins a few weeks later in Isobel's studio in London. Isobel and her partner, Irwin, are working on a new project: a book called the *Encyclopedia of Murder.* Irwin is trying to complete a graphic illustration of a gunshot wound. As they work and talk, a letter slides under the door. It is a letter of resignation from Gordon, the third employee in the firm. Irwin reveals that Gordon is resigning for a couple of reasons: he is secretly in love with Isobel and can no longer stand working so close to her, knowing he cannot have her; and he can't stand Katherine's abusive behavior in the workplace. In just a few short weeks, it seems, Katherine is already wreaking havoc in Isobel's life.

Irwin is also in love with Isobel, though it is different for him, he claims, because, unlike Gordon, ''I have you.'' Later, Irwin's possessiveness of Isobel will take on significant and serious meaning. For now, he just expresses a loyalty and a love that cause him to remain, in spite of Katherine, who may be ruining the company and their relationship.

Suddenly, Katherine appears with armfuls of flowers. Though she says she bought them from a man out front, predictably she has not paid him yet and dispatches Irwin to settle her bill. While he is gone, she announces to Isobel that she has sold Robert's house and plans to use the money to buy a flat in London, just around the corner from the studio. On top of this ''good news,'' she says she has secured an exclusive eighteen-month contract to design the book covers for one of their publishers. All she had to do, she explains, was take the older man out to dinner and flirt with him all evening.

Isobel, of course, is shocked. She is shocked that her father's house has just been suddenly sold and shocked at the tactics Katherine is using to get the business of the respectable customers she has dealt with for years. She is frustrated by the greed and the cruelty of those around her and asks why they can't all just slow down and have a decent period of mourning and grief for her lost father.

Even Irwin, though, tells her it is time to move on and let it all go. He counsels her to forget about her sense of duty to her father, leave mourning behind, and to fire Katherine before she does any more damage with their customers. Despite all the harm Katherine has already caused, though, Isobel is not prepared to let her go. Her father loved this reckless, passionate woman, and that is enough for Isobel.

Just as Isobel and Irwin are again warming up to each other, Katherine drops another bombshell. Tom, it seems, would like to invest money in their company and allow them to grow the business. Already Katherine, who doesn't even really know the business, is talking about hiring extra artists and buying a bigger place in the center of the city. The same woman who only a few weeks before was complaining about the greed in the world now laughs, ''We could be making money like hay. Everyone else is.''

Isobel finally reaches her limit and tells Katherine her behavior has been inappropriate. Katherine offers to leave if Isobel will only ask her. Irwin even tries to see her out on Isobel's behalf, but in the end Isobel again determines that Katherine must stay.

Scene 4

The fourth scene is set a few days later in the living room of Robert's house. Everyone has gathered to pack up the house before it is sold and to sign the legal documents that will turn control of Isobel's company over to Tom and a board of directors in exchange for his investment in their growth.

At the beginning of the scene, Marion and her assistant, Rhonda Milne, have just finished a meeting with a delegation from the Green Party. They had invited them out to Robert's country house to give them the impression that Marion, who is a junior minister at the Department of the Environment, actually has a country background. The Green Party delegates are interested in containing the use of nuclear power, because of its potential effects on people and the environment. Predictably, the position of Marion and the Conservative Party is that people need power and nuclear energy is a cheap and efficient way to provide it. ''Come back and see me when you're glowing in the dark,'' she tells her adversaries.

One at a time the others arrive; first Isobel, then Irwin, who complains about the way people in the country are always shooting at things, and finally Tom, who immediately presents Isobel with his business proposal and asks her to sign it. She hesitates a moment and points out that this is a big and unexpected step for her small company. She is worried about growing too quickly and especially about losing control of her work. Marion points out that Tom is the president of Christians in Business and certainly a man who can be trusted.

Echoing Katherine from the previous scene, Marion and Tom both point out that everyone is making money and that it would practically be a sin in God's eyes for them not to use their talents to make money as well. Then there is the issue of Katherine. Again, Marion calls on Isobel's overdeveloped conscience to care for their father's widow. Ironically, she asks Isobel, ''What sort of life is it if we only think about ourselves?'' She pressures Isobel to agree to giving Katherine a permanent seat on the new board of directors.

Isobel tries to enlist Irwin's aid, but in one of the most pivotal moments in the play, Irwin wavers and admits that he does like the idea of the investment and that he has great faith in Tom's word. Seeking not to lose ground, Marion quickly tells everyone that Irwin confided in her that he and Isobel were going to get married; and in recognition of the marriage and Irwin's talents, she and Tom are proposing to double Irwin's salary. The recognition that Irwin was dealing with Tom and Marion on the side and knew about the salary arrangement before coming to sign the papers is too much for Isobel. She is crushed into silence.

Marion, Tom, and Rhonda pack up and leave, telling Isobel and Irwin to think about the offer. Left alone, Irwin tries to reason with Isobel, telling her that she was the one who changed everything by bringing Katherine on board. He assures her that he loves her and would never do anything to hurt her, while off in the distance the sounds of the hunters' guns are coming closer.

Act II, Scene 5

The second act begins several months later in Isobel's new offices in London's fashionable West End. The room is filled with artists' desks and is expensively decorated. It is evening, and Irwin and Rhonda are alone, sipping champagne. Rhonda, it turns out, is a bit like a younger Katherine. She is free spirited and adventurous, and she loves to stir up trouble. The trouble she is stirring this time is with Irwin. As she tells him stories about her sexual relationships with politicians, the two draw closer and closer together. They are quite likely just about to have sex there in the office when Isobel unexpectedly returns early from a business trip.

Irwin awkwardly starts to explain that Rhonda came by to see the new offices and to use their shower, since her water had been turned off. It is an obviously awkward situation, but Isobel seems uninterested in hearing about what Irwin and Rhonda had been up to. Instead, she goes about her business in the office. While Rhonda goes off to shower, Irwin again tries to get Isobel talking about Rhonda, about his artwork, about the way Isobel has been ignoring him for weeks now. She tries to resist the conversation but finally tells Irwin that she returned from her trip because she had a call that Katherine got drunk with some important clients. One of them told her that they would not be buying their latest project, and she'd tried to kill him with a steak knife.

Isobel is obviously tired and stretched to her limits and now must again deal with Katherine's mistakes, but Irwin pushes on. He demands a conversation with Isobel about their relationship problems and her unexplainable support for Katherine, who is so clearly ruining her life. In an important moment of recognition in the play, Isobel admits that she is "being turned into a person whose only function is to suffer." Still, she can't seem to turn herself around. The one decision she has made, though, is that she no longer loves Irwin and that she will stop pretending that she does.

Interestingly, Isobel complains that Irwin makes her feel guilty and saps her strength because he demands so much of her. Katherine, and even her sister, Marion, do much the same thing with even more devastating effects, but she has not turned her back on them. This contrast is not lost on Irwin. "Tell me why you will sacrifice your whole life for Katherine?" he demands to know. To Irwin, Katherine is not just chronically dependent on other people, like Isobel and her father; she is actually evil and intentionally sets out to destroy the lives of generous people who come to her aid.

Irwin's point seems to unsettle Isobel momentarily and to cause her to think about the right thing to do. During her pause for reflection, Rhonda returns from the shower, ready to go out to the movies. In an unexpected and strange move, Isobel announces that she and Irwin would like to go along, and the scene ends.

Scene 6

Three weeks later, Marion, Tom, Irwin, and Isobel are scheduled to meet in Tom's office. Obviously, Isobel's business is struggling, losing a lot of money, and Tom and his investors have decided to pull out. They have been offered a considerable amount of money for the office space, and they are ready to sell to make a profit.

Irwin has arrived, prepared to do whatever is necessary, but he explains that Isobel will not join them as long as he is in the room. Three weeks earlier, she walked out in the middle of the movie, drove to the airport, and caught the first plane leaving the country. She came back very quickly, bought her father's house back, and has been living in Katherine's apartment, looking after her ever since. She refuses even to speak to Irwin. Painfully, Irwin admits that he is still deeply in love with Isobel, the "one certain source of good" he has known in his life.

Isobel arrives at the office building and phones Tom. Irwin leaves so Isobel can join them. Tom tells her about his proposal to sell the business, but she is unfazed. She observes that Tom will be writing the whole venture off his taxes so that instead of losing any money, he will actually be making quite a profit, but she is not angry. Even though all of her workers will be laid off and she will be losing her business, it seems she has come to expect that kind of behavior from Tom and most of the world.

Tom offers her a small, rent-free office at the base of a parking garage where she could start over again, but Isobel recognizes that it would be foolish to try, particularly without Irwin. Irwin, she realized, is obsessed with her, so she has decided to completely cut him off and make it final. Now, she has determined, she must do what her father would have wanted and take care of Katherine.

In a frightening bit of foreshadowing, Marion screams at Isobel that she should "Hide behind your father for the rest of your life. Die there!" And Isobel responds that she probably will.

Scene 7

Some time later, perhaps a few weeks, Isobel and Katherine are in her apartment late one evening having dinner. Isobel has obviously been doing all of the cooking and cleaning and shopping for the two of them, while Katherine hurls abuse at her. She complains about the meals and about the boring lives they lead now that she no longer drinks and they never go out together.

The two prepare for bed. Katherine of course takes the bedroom, leaving Isobel on the sofa. Isobel warns Katherine that she must remember to lock the door and use the deadbolt, since Irwin has somehow managed to get a key to the apartment and might come looking for her. Katherine pretends not to know anything about that, but once the lights are out, she quietly unlocks the door.

This is obviously something Katherine and Irwin have arranged. Almost immediately, he slips in through the door and confronts Isobel. She calls for Katherine, but there is no response. Irwin wants to know if he can just sleep with Isobel, but she refuses, saying it will only make him unhappier. He is obviously quite disturbed, and he pulls out a handgun, telling Isobel he plans to kill himself with it.

Isobel tells Irwin that even if he forced her to have sex with him, he would never get from her what he really wants. They will never again have the relationship they once had. As they argue, Katherine finally emerges from the bedroom to check on them. Isobel tells her to call the police or go get help from someone in the street, but Katherine refuses. Finally, Isobel herself gets up and walks out the door, closing it behind her. As soon as it closes, Irwin fires five shots through the door, killing Isobel on the other side.

Scene 8

The final scene of the play provides a sort of *denouement,* a closure of some of the loose ends of the plot and its characters. Marion, Tom, Katherine, and Rhonda are back at Robert Glass's house, uncovering the furniture and restoring it on the day of Isobel's funeral. Her death seems to have taught them some lessons, though whether their lives will completely change remains uncertain.

When she learns that all the people of the town want to walk together to the funeral, Marion realizes that everyone seems to have valued Isobel, except them. She receives a call from the Ministry and, for the first time in the play, refuses to take it. Even Tom admits that he has "slightly lost touch with the Lord Jesus." Marion cannot bring herself to go to the funeral, but before Tom leaves, they embrace, kiss, and even caress each other. It is the only moment of physical passion either of them has shown in the play, and it only seems possible after Isobel's death.

Left alone in the room after everyone has gone to the funeral, Marion laments the loss of her sister, though what she wants now is not entirely clear. "We're just beginning," she says to herself. "Isobel, why don't you come home?"

CHARACTERS

Marion French

Marion is Isobel Glass's older sister and one of the play's important antagonists. Somewhere in her late thirties, Marion has climbed the ladder of British politics and secured herself a position as a junior minister for the Department of the Environment in Britain's Conservative Party. In the 1980s, under Prime Minister Margaret Thatcher, the Conservatives (or "Tories," as they are called in Britain) earned a reputation for greed and a lack of concern for social issues such as poverty, homelessness, and the environment. Like the political party she belongs to, Marion seems interested mainly in money and power and unconcerned with the welfare of others.

While Isobel spent a great deal of time caring for their father in the weeks before his death, Marion only visited occasionally. In place of concern and affection, she tried to show him that she loved him by buying him an expensive ring. Then, just hours after his death, she returned to take it back. She is a workaholic and takes business calls even in the middle of family crises. As her husband, Tom, observes, she seems to have everything she could want, including a prominent position in a successful government; nevertheless, she is constantly angry and lashing out at others. She loses her temper with Isobel many times in the play and even scolds her husband now and then. When she is visited by members of the Green Party, a political group interested in the environment and stopping the use of nuclear energy, she viciously tells them, ''Come back and see me when you're glowing in the dark.'' As some critics pointed out, Marion's character is so one-sided that she is in danger of becoming just a walking stereotype of Thatcher's England.

As much as anyone else in the play, Marion drives Isobel toward her tragic end by taking advantage of her, playing on her conscience, and abusing her. She seems to hate Isobel for her goodness and for not being like everyone else in the world—concerned mainly with self-interest. Marion admits that she lacks the passion other people, like Isobel, seem to have for the world and does not understand what motivates them if not materialism or power. In the end, though, Marion seems changed by Isobel's death. In the final scene, she does not wear the conservative business suits she has appeared in throughout the play but a simple black mourning dress. She declines to take a business call from her department and, in her one moment of physical passion, embraces and kisses her husband before he leaves for Isobel's funeral. The final words of the play are hers: ''We're just beginning,'' she laments. ''Isobel, why don't you come home?''

Tom French

Tom is Marion's husband and acts mainly as a *foil* to the female characters in the play. In literature, a *foil* is a character that illustrates, mainly through contrast, the important traits of other characters. For example, Tom seems soft-spoken and sometimes overeager to please. When Marion and Isobel are quarreling, rather than taking sides, he tells them, ''I'm sure both of you are right.'' By contrast, Marion and Katherine are loud, brash, and highly opinionated. Tom has a head for business and makes a lot of money in investments and new ventures. Isobel, on the other hand, is afraid of risk and is more interested in doing quality work with her small graphics firm than in growing it just to make money.

Tom's most defining characteristic, however, is his religious faith. Some of his first words in the play are words of comfort spoken to Isobel just after her father's death. ''He's fine,'' Tom tells her. ''He's in the hands of the Lord.'' Tom claims his steady manner and his business success are the result of welcoming Jesus into his life. He even thinks that Jesus helped him repair his car when it was broken, and he builds a pool in his backyard just for baptisms, to convert others to his faith.

As the president of Christians in Business, Tom claims he tries to do business ''the way Jesus would have done it.'' However, his practices seem to be something less than charitable. He and Marion convince Isobel to accept investment money for her small graphics design company so that it can grow larger. They reason that the expansion will allow them all to make some of the money that everyone else is making in Britain in the 1980s, while at the same time giving Katherine a solid position and a chance to start her life again. Then, when the company starts to fail, Tom lays off all the new workers, giving them just a few weeks' worth of wages and sells off their new office space for a large profit. On top of that, it turns out that he is writing the whole investment off as a tax break. Instead of losing money, he actually makes quite a bit, while Isobel loses her business and many people lose their jobs.

Like Marion and Katherine, Tom seems to be deeply affected by Isobel's death. As he helps the two women restore Robert Glass's house on the day of Isobel's funeral, he tries to comfort his wife the way he tried to comfort Isobel in the first scene. ''The Lord Jesus . . .'' he begins to say, but his voice trails off, and he admits that he has ''slightly lost touch with the Lord Jesus.''

Isobel Glass

Isobel is by far the most complicated character in *The Secret Rapture*. She is relatively young, somewhere in her early thirties, and modestly successful. She owns her own graphic design firm, with two other employees. Unlike her sister, Marion, Isobel is not interested in making a lot of money or in the politics of the popular Conservative Party government. Instead, she is interested in living a simple life, doing what is right, and helping people in need whenever she can.

Her determined sense of morality led some critics of the play to dub her ''Saint Isobel,'' and even the other characters remark, not always kindly, on her almost other-worldly virtue. Her actions do seem to be those of a saint. She stays with her father to care for him in his final days. When he dies, she takes the abusive Katherine under her wing, providing her with a job and unlimited chances to redeem herself. She accepts mistreatment from Marion and the loss of her business through Tom's treacherous business dealings, without passing judgment on either of them. The only person she hurts in the play is Irwin, though even that action seems based on a moral decision: he has betrayed her, and she does not think it would be fair to him to continue to pretend that she loves him.

Besides her complicated morality, Isobel's character is also difficult because of her role as the play's tragic protagonist. As some critics noted, her suffering and downfall should generate sympathy, but she is often such a strong character that it is hard to believe she is the victim. Writing for the *Times Literary Supplement,* John Turner observed, ''Isobel, with her amazing and admirable verbal ferocity, is winning too much of the time to excite pity.'' Turner notes that Isobel easily dispatches Rhonda when she finds her dallying with Irwin in their office and that she boldly faces the homicidal Irwin, even hurling insults at him, just before he kills her.

Matt Wolf, another critic, suggested that Isobel suffers the fate, not just of a tragic heroine, but of a martyr. ''It's no accident that Isobel's surname is 'Glass,''' Wolf pointed out in a review of the play in the *Wall Street Journal, European Edition.* ''As the tragic outcome of the play makes clear, she holds the mirror up to the baseness of those around her, even at the cost of her own life.''

In the end, it is only Isobel's sacrifice that changes the other characters in the play. Her death causes Tom to question his relationship with Jesus and causes her sister, Marion, to finally feel some passion and connection to another person. Much like a saint who performed good deeds in life only to be killed for his actions, Isobel's love and morality begins to have an effect only after she is gone.

Katherine Glass

Katherine is the young, unstable, alcoholic widow of Robert Glass. As she admits to the other characters in the play several times, she had no direction in her life before she met Robert. She was a drug and alcohol abuser. She had never held a real job, and her relationships with men revolved around brief sexual experiences, possibly even prostitution. Ever since she was a child, Katherine has felt inferior to those around her. As a result, she tends to act out in unusual, sometimes alarming or even dangerous ways.

Robert, she claims, turned her life around and gave her a sense of purpose and dignity for the first time. As a result of Robert's death, Katherine is alone again, and she must turn to the others for support. Katherine is not a sympathetic character; there is very little to like about her. Because of her neediness and her erratic behavior, though, she becomes the play's central motivating character. She sets in motion all of the play's action.

Katherine begins by taking advantage of Isobel's loyalty to her dead father. She convinces Isobel to give her a job in her small graphic arts firm. Then she drives out one of the firm's other employees and strains the relationship between Isobel and Irwin by criticizing his work and mistreating their customers. It is largely because of Katherine that Tom and Marion decide to invest in Isobel's company, even though Isobel does not want to expand it. Then, at a crucial moment in the company's growth, she gets drunk and tries to kill an important client, dooming the company to financial failure.

Throughout the play, Isobel tries to help Katherine and to give her every opportunity to redeem herself. However, Katherine continues to abuse Isobel and to take advantage of her. At one point, Irwin even warns Isobel that Katherine is actually evil and that she is ''dreaming of ways to destroy you.'' In the end, Irwin is right. When Isobel has nothing left and is living with Katherine in her apartment, taking care of her and hiding from Irwin, it is Katherine who unlocks the door and lets Irwin in. As a result of this betrayal, Isobel, Katherine's savior, is murdered.

Rhonda Milne

Rhonda is the only minor character in *The Secret Rapture*. Somewhere in her early twenties,

Rhonda is quite attractive, highly intelligent, bold, and outspoken. She is Marion's assistant in the Department of the Environment and seems to share Marion's conservative political views. She contributes two important things to the play.

First, Rhonda is a reflection of how Marion and her Conservative Party are affecting the lives of the next generation of Britain's leaders. Rhonda has recognized the power of the Conservatives and has attached herself to that power. She is ambitious, eager to profit, and doesn't seem to mind taking advantage of other people. She helps arrange Marion's countryside meeting with the Green Party representatives and relishes the way Marion insults them and sends them back to the city.

Second, Rhonda is a temptation for Irwin and a clear sign to Isobel that their relationship is over. While Isobel is supposedly away on a business trip, Rhonda arranges to meet Irwin alone in their new offices one evening. She is supposedly there to see the new space and to use their shower, since her water has been unexpectedly turned off. However, her visit turns into a seduction as she and Irwin share a bottle of champagne and she recalls some of her sexual exploits. Sounding a little like Katherine, Rhonda admits that Marion keeps her around because she "likes the idea that I cause chaos."

Unlike the major characters in the play, Rhonda does not seem changed by Isobel's death. On the day of Isobel's funeral, when everyone is gathered at Robert's house in appropriate mourning clothes, Rhonda appears wearing a short black skirt. She is still fielding phone calls from the Ministry for Marion, though Marion now refuses to accept them. She is puzzled by the town's reaction to Isobel's death. When she learns that they all want to walk through the village as a group, she comments, "It's like everyone valued her."

Irwin Posner

When he first appears in the play, Irwin seems to be Isobel's mild-mannered and devoted sometime boyfriend. He works as the principal illustrator at Isobel's small graphic arts firm. Initially, he recognizes the problems Katherine is causing for Isobel and their company, but he continues to support Isobel and her desire to help her father's widow. When Katherine begins to criticize his work and mistreat their clients, though, Irwin urges Isobel to cut her loose. He even tries to tell Katherine to leave, but Isobel allows her to stay.

The strain Katherine places on their relationship apparently begins to affect Irwin, and he begins to act in unpredictable ways. Behind Isobel's back, he meets with Tom and Marion about their proposal to invest in her business. He tells them that he and Isobel are planning to get married, and for his help in convincing her to agree to their proposal, he accepts their offer to double his salary. Isobel sees his actions as a betrayal and decides she no longer loves him.

Frustrated at Isobel's lack of attention and affection, Irwin meets Rhonda in their offices one evening when Isobel is supposed to be out of town. Though their encounter may have begun innocently enough, by the time Isobel surprises them by returning early, they have been drinking champagne together and are on the verge of a passionate embrace. Irwin makes one last plea to Isobel to show him some affection and to get rid of Katherine before she destroys everything, but Isobel is determined and tells him that it is over between them.

When the time finally comes for Tom and Marion to close down Isobel's company, Irwin admits that Isobel, not his career or anyone else, is his "whole life." He is still in love with her, though she will not even appear in the same room with him. Irwin's obsession finally turns to violence. He stalks Isobel to Katherine's apartment, where he confronts her with a gun and demands one last time that she take him back and restore things to the way they were before. When she refuses and tries to go for help, he murders her. Her life has ended and so, apparently, has Irwin's torture. "It's over," he mutters. "Thank God."

THEMES

Sacrifice

In an interview with Anne Busby published in the program for the original production of *The Secret Rapture*, Hare revealed that the title of the play means "that moment at which a nun expects to be united with Christ. In other words, it's death." Nuns, much like saints, face their deaths after a lifetime of sacrifice. They do not live in luxury and

TOPICS FOR FURTHER STUDY

- In the play, Marion French belongs to Britain's Conservative Party, led throughout the 1980s by Britain's Prime Minister Margaret Thatcher. Known as the "Iron Lady," Thatcher was a strong and sometimes controversial leader. Research the government of Margaret Thatcher between 1979 and 1990. What were some of her accomplishments as prime minister? What were some of the strong beliefs of the Conservative Party? How were they different from the beliefs of Britain's other major political group, the Labour Party?
- There is a lot of religious imagery in *The Secret Rapture*. Isobel seems to behave like a saint. Late in the play, Irwin says she has "made some sort of vow," much like a nun or monk might. Even the title of the play, according to the playwright, means death, "that moment at which a nun expects to be united with Christ." Investigate the life of a famous saint. (You may want to check the Internet or the library for an index of well-known saints.) How are Isobel's life and experiences in the play similar to those of the saint you have chosen? How are they different? Consider such things as good deeds, patience, love for others, and sacrifice.
- The eight scenes in *The Secret Rapture* flow into each other without blackouts or curtains being drawn across the stage. This requires some creative set design and stagecraft. Pick a scene transition, such as scene 1, Robert's bedroom that changes into scene 2, the back lawn of his house; or scene 6, Tom's office that changes into scene 7, Katherine's apartment. Then, decide how you would set the stage and change the scenery right in front of the audience. You may want to draw pictures and plans illustrating your ideas or create three-dimensional models using cardboard, paper, and other craft supplies.
- One of the play's central characters, Katherine Glass, is an alcoholic. She claims to have stopped drinking several times but each time manages to start again. Her drinking binges lead to depression and to horrible behavior, such as when she attacks a business client with a steak knife in a restaurant. Research the most recent statistics and medical findings about alcoholism in the United States. How many people does this disease affect? What causes it? What have governments and physicians been doing to combat the effects of alcoholism on individuals, families, and society? What can be done to help protect yourself and others?
- Many critics have suggested that David Hare creates very strong, often virtuous, female characters in his plays. In an interview with *American Theatre* magazine, the playwright himself agreed, "I've written about women a lot because my subject has often been goodness. The idea of men being good seems to me to be slightly silly." Consider the female characters in *The Secret Rapture*. Are they strong? In what ways? Which of them is "good"? How?

collect the material possessions most people desire. Rather than enjoying some of the sensual pleasures of life favored by ordinary human beings, they spend their days tending to people in need and serving God.

There are many parallels between the life Isobel leads and the lives of nuns or saints. Like them, she has a strong, unwavering sense of morality, and she is more interested in ideas and relationships than in material wealth. Perhaps most important, she makes continual sacrifices for others, and those sacrifices eventually lead to her own death. She becomes, in essence, not a nun or a saint, but a modern martyr.

Most of the other characters in the play are materialistic. Marion and Katherine urge Isobel to go out and make money like everyone else. Tom proclaims that, "God gives us certain gifts. And he expects us to use them." Even Irwin compromises his ideals in order to double his salary and urge Isobel to expand her business. Isobel, though, is interested only in enough success to keep her happy and comfortable and in doing what is right for others. When she does finally agree to go into business with Tom, it is only because she feels outnumbered and because she feels an obligation to keep helping Katherine.

It is this urge to help others that is perhaps Isobel's single most defining feature. Isobel stayed at her father's house to care for him in his final days, while her sister Marion only appeared occasionally. She waits as long as she can before rejecting Irwin, because she would rather not hurt him. Then, when she does turn him away, she rejects him completely because she feels it is the only way for him to recover quickly. Most important, after her father's death she devotes herself entirely to caring for Katherine, even though Katherine shows herself again and again to be unworthy of Isobel's kindness and sacrifice.

By the end of the play, through her steadfast commitment to her beliefs, Isobel has lost her boyfriend, her business, and, finally, her life. The positive effect of her sacrifice is that the changes she could not achieve while she was alive seem to be accomplished by her death. Katherine, Marion, and Tom are all affected by her loss. They begin to realize that her virtue and her way of viewing the world were assets and that their own lives have been misdirected.

Dependency

Several characters in *The Secret Rapture* know or discover something about their own strengths and weaknesses as they grapple with some kind of dependency. The most obviously dependent character in the play is Katherine. As she herself admits, she has been chemically dependent, either on drugs or alcohol, for most of her life. She has always felt "mediocre." As a student in school, she struggled to keep up with her classmates academically. Then, as a young woman, she struggled with her weight and appearance and had several failed relationships. To cope with her frustrations, she turned to drugs and alcohol and eventually became dependent upon them. Though she tries to resist drinking once she starts working for Isobel, she can't help it when she is faced with a difficult situation, such as the client in the restaurant who rejects her business offer. Faced with yet another failure, she takes a drink, transforms into her wilder nature, and attempts to kill the man with a knife.

Katherine is also very dependent upon other people. She had been moving from relationship to relationship, trying to find a man who could somehow get her on her feet and give her direction. Then she met Robert Glass, Isobel and Marion's father. He took her in and became not only her husband but also her caretaker. Katherine had never held a real job, and even when she lived with Robert, she simply helped him out around his bookshop. He provided her with what she needed to survive—food, clothes, and a place to live. She, in turn, seemed to provide him with some adventure that was missing in his life. Still, as Katherine admits, "People say I took advantage of his decency. But what are good people for? They're here to help the trashy people like me."

Katherine unquestionably takes advantage of Isobel's decency. When Robert Glass dies, Isobel takes his place, and Katherine becomes dependent upon her. Katherine needs Isobel for some of the same reasons she needed Isobel's father—to give her the basic necessities of life and perhaps to serve as an object for the abuse she doles out. At the same time that Katherine moves in, Irwin Posner, Isobel's coworker and sometime boyfriend, reveals his dependency on Isobel. At one time, Isobel was interested in Irwin, but once she feels he has betrayed her, she rejects him completely. Irwin's dependency for Isobel's attention and affection becomes a dangerous obsession, which eventually leads him to murder her.

Marion and Tom display different, but not lesser, kinds of dependencies. Marion has never felt passion and has never understood other people's feelings. As a result, she has become dependent upon her personal pursuit of power, money, and prestige. Tom, on the other hand, seems naturally adept at business and making money, but at some point in his life that wasn't enough. He turned to religion and became a born-again Christian, and now he depends heavily upon his relationship with Jesus to guide him. Both Marion and Tom are affected by Isobel's death and begin to view their dependencies differently. Marion is less concerned about her career, while Tom admits that he has "slightly lost touch with the Lord Jesus."

STYLE

Symbolism

In literature, a symbol is something that represents something else. It contains both a literal meaning and an abstract meaning and is often used by the author to communicate complex ideas. In *The Secret Rapture*, the central symbol of the play is a character, Isobel Glass. She has a literal identity, or meaning, as a grieving daughter, a kindhearted business owner, and an abused caretaker for her widowed stepmother, Katherine. But she also has an abstract identity, or meaning. Through her actions and words, she resembles a saint-like figure who lives a pure life, sacrifices for others, and dies a martyr.

The first image of the play is of Isobel in a darkened room, mourning over her father in his deathbed. She was there when he passed away and tells her sister Marion, ''There's actually a moment when you see the spirit depart from the body. . . Like a bird.'' Isobel is instantly established as a pious, devoted daughter who senses things most people cannot.

Isobel is essentially a good person, committed to doing what is right and to helping other people. In ''Saint Isobel: David Hare's *The Secret Rapture* as Christian Allegory,'' Liorah Anne Golomb observed, ''Even her name, a variant of Elizabeth, has as one of its meanings 'consecrated to God.''' The basic goodness in Isobel's character, though, is both a blessing and a curse. When Marion is guilt-ridden for rushing up to her father's bedroom to retrieve a ring she had given him not long before his death, Isobel acts as a sort of confessor to her sister. She does not pass judgment on her or scold her for seeming to care only about material possessions. Still, Marion is overwhelmed by Isobel's virtue, and she complains, ''You make me feel as if I'm always in the wrong.''

Throughout the play, again and again Isobel tries to do what she feels is right in various situations, but, each time, she encounters only criticism and abuse. She hires a priest for her father's funeral, though the man never attended church, and is criticized for not simply cremating him and throwing him into the English Channel. She assumes responsibility for Katherine, her father's widow, accepting the reckless woman into her life, much as a saint might go after a sinner in order to save his or her soul. She hires Katherine into her small graphic arts firm, tends to her mental and physical needs, and is rewarded by losing her business and ruining her life.

In her relationship to Irwin, Golomb believed Isobel even begins to resemble Jesus, with Irwin playing the part of the traitor Judas. When Isobel and Irwin meet with Tom and Marion to discuss their business proposition, Golomb noted, Irwin kisses Isobel's cheek before joining the conversation. Soon afterward, it is revealed that he has sided with Tom and Marion in exchange for having his salary doubled. His kiss is like the kiss Judas offered to Jesus just before betraying him, and his salary increase is like the thirty pieces of silver Judas accepted for betraying his teacher.

Once Isobel rejects Irwin and refuses to be seen with him, her decision is absolute. Like a nun or a saint, Irwin suggests, ''My guess is she's made some sort of vow.'' Then, at the end of the play in the final moment before Irwin kills her, Isobel says on her way out the door, ''I haven't got shoes. Still you can't have everything.'' Her last words echo the popular belief that Jesus walked to his crucifixion barefoot.

Of course, it is in her death that Isobel takes on the most important symbolic significance. Just as saints who give their lives to good deeds and are killed for their beliefs become more powerful as martyrs in the minds of their followers when they are gone, Isobel's virtue begins to affect those she left behind on the day of her funeral in the final scene. Marion, Tom, and Katherine all begin to realize how important Isobel was and how their own lives can become more meaningful if they now begin to live more as she lived.

Denouement

Denouement is a French word that means ''the unknotting'' or ''unraveling.'' In literature, a denouement is a final scene that occurs after the high point, or climax, of the plot. It typically explains any unanswered questions and offers a glimpse at how the characters' world may have changed as a result of their actions.

The final scene of *The Secret Rapture* is a perfect example of a denouement. The climax of the play is past. Isobel is dead, and Irwin has even declared, ''It's over. Thank God.'' All that is left is for Tom, Marion, Katherine, and Rhonda, the other surviving characters in the play, to gather together for Isobel's funeral.

Significantly, they all meet at Robert Glass's house, where the events of the play began some months before. The house had been sold by Katherine and repurchased by Isobel, and now they are restoring it to the way it was when Isobel and Robert were both still alive. The most important function of this denouement, however, is not to show the effects of Isobel's death on the physical environment but on the souls of the characters.

Rhonda has not changed. While the others are properly dressed in dark mourning clothes, she is dressed in a short skirt and jumper and is still fielding Marion's phone calls from the Ministry. Katherine, though, is uncharacteristically quiet and subdued as she goes about the room, putting things back on their shelves where they were once before. At her husband's funeral, she was drunk and obnoxious, but she seems to have more reverence and respect for Isobel's memory. Even Tom's faith has been a little shaken. He tries to offer Marion some comforting words from Jesus but then admits, "I don't know. I've slightly lost touch with the Lord Jesus."

Marion, who may have had the furthest to go, seems to have changed the most. She now refuses to take phone calls and conduct business on the day of her sister's funeral. She also seems to have had an emotional breakthrough. She had never been able to feel or express passion, but Isobel's death seems to have sparked feeling in her. She embraces her husband warmly, even sexually. And the last words of the play are a plea from Marion. "Isobel," she asks, "why don't you come home?"

HISTORICAL CONTEXT

In a review of *The Secret Rapture* in *American Theatre* magazine, prominent London theatre critic Matt Wolf declared that the play was "directly inspired by the decade-old economic and moral climate of Margaret Thatcher's Britain." Though Hare's intimate family drama draws much of its power and appeal from its complex characters and ultimately tragic plot, Wolf's point is well made. The 1980s, both in David Hare's Britain and in the United States, are now viewed as a period of greed, conservative politics, and negligent middle-class social policies, and *The Secret Rapture* reflects this environment.

There are many similarities between the economic and social development of America and Britain during the 1980s. Both countries elected conservative leaders who believed in strong religious and national values and who opposed high taxes, high government spending, and too much control of private enterprise. In short, they believed that people would be better off if government interfered less in their lives. These are the same values expressed by Marion and Tom French and by most of the other characters in *The Secret Rapture*.

Ronald Reagan, a Republican, was elected president of the United States in 1980. Reagan believed in "supply-side" economics. This theory suggested that the economy would grow healthy if most people paid lower taxes and the government spent less money. The money people saved on taxes would be spent on products, services, or investments, which would boost the economy. Unfortunately for many, the largest tax cuts went to the wealthiest Americans, while those who earned less than the national average actually ended up paying the government more. At the same time that he was cutting taxes, Reagan was also spending less on social programs like job training, welfare assistance, child day care centers, and programs for the elderly. Reagan and the Republicans believed in strong family values, and they claimed programs like these weakened families by causing people to become dependent on the government rather than on themselves and their families.

In an attempt to promote even more economic growth, Reagan also eased government control over, or "deregulated," many industries, such as banking, communications, and energy. This actually had both positive and negative effects. Because they had fewer regulations to follow, banks could invest in riskier ventures; media corporations, such as large newspapers and radio and television stations, could merge their operations; and oil companies could search for new sources of energy in previously protected lands. Profits generated by many of these companies soared, making money for the people who worked for the companies and for investors in the companies. However, relaxed safety standards and government oversight eventually also led to more bankruptcies, investment losses, large monopolies, and environmental hazards.

In Britain, Conservative Party leader Margaret Thatcher was elected prime minister in 1979. Like Reagan in America, she believed in strong family and national values and in less government involvement in the economy and people's lives. Thatcher believed in "monetarism," which was quite similar

COMPARE & CONTRAST

- **1980s:** Margaret Thatcher is the first British prime minister in more than a century to be elected to three consecutive terms (1979–1990). Her Conservative Party is credited with Britain's economic turnaround through privatizing industries and minimizing the role of government in business and welfare. Thatcher's successses closely parallel those of President Ronald Reagan in the United States.

  Today: Tony Blair is the first Labour Party prime minister in nearly two decades. After a landslide victory in the 1997 election, Blair leads his Labour Party to an astonishing second landslide vote in 2001. Blair and the ''New Labourites'' have instituted improved health care in Britain, the national minimum wage, and careful monitoring of the country's economic stability. Blair's successes in Britain closely parallel those of President Bill Clinton in the United States.

- **1980s:** The first mass market cellular phone system appears in America in 1981. Cellular phone equipment is large and heavy. The cost of service limits its use mainly to corporations and wealthy individuals. The number of cellular telephone subscribers exceeds one million in 1987.

  Today: Advanced technology has created cell phones that fit in the palm of the hand and weigh a few ounces. Service costs are competitive with household telephones, causing many to abandon traditional phone service in favor of mobile phones. More than half of all Americans, approximately 140 million, own cell phones.

- **1980s:** In the 1950s, Britain was leader in the construction of nuclear power plants. By the 1980s, however, nuclear power is losing its appeal. The meltdown at the Three Mile Island nuclear power plant in Pennsylvania and an even more disastrous partial meltdown at the Chernobyl plant in the Ukraine in 1986 cause many environmental groups, like Britain's Green Party, to call for a ban on nuclear plants. For most of the decade, government pays little attention to environmental matters. However, by 1988, Thatcher calls the protection of the environment ''one of the great challenges of the late twentieth century.''

  Today: While early estimates predicted that nuclear power could provide up to 15 percent of the world's energy by 2000, the figure is greatly inflated. Because of public reaction to nuclear power plant problems, nuclear energy production has been scaled back significantly and now produces no more than 6 percent of the world's power.

- **1980s:** Although investing in stocks has previously been considered a pastime for the wealthy, the majority of Americans and a great many Europeans begin to discover the profits that can be made in a ''bull market.'' A ''bull market'' begins in America on August 17, 1982, when the Dow Jones Industrial Average rises 38.81 points to 831.24. This is the biggest ever one-day gain in the hundred-year history of the Dow Jones average. In Britain, millions of new investors turn to the London Stock Exchange when more flexible investing rules are introduced in 1986.

  Today: As global trade increases, more people are becoming investors. An explosion of ''dot-com'' companies (businesses related to the computer industry) in the 1990s cause the value of technology stocks to rise quite high. After climbing steadily since 1990, the American Dow Jones market passes 12,000 points in 1999. However, many start-up technology companies are unable to turn a profit, causing a downturn in stocks in 2000 that has continued to the present day.

to Reagan's "supply-side" economics. Monetarism meant carefully controlling the supply of money, lowering tax rates, and removing restrictions on how businesses could expand. Thatcher immediately began privatizing industries, like health, transportation, and education, which had been government-run in Britain for decades. She also started cutting government subsidy to welfare programs, public health, and the arts.

The economic policies of Reagan and Thatcher affected the lives of individual citizens in different ways. In America, it is generally believed that the wealthiest individuals and corporations profited the most from what became known as "Reaganomics," while middle class wages and investment income improved significantly and the poor, particularly minorities, fell behind. In Britain, the effects had quite a bit to do with geography. Thatcher's policies delivered the most benefits to the financial industry, real estate, and technology companies, which were all largely based in London and southeastern England. In those areas, wages increased and new businesses flourished. The economic boom of the time is what prompts Marion in Hare's play to tell Isobel, "There's money to be made. Everyone's making it."

At the same time, Thatcher and the Conservatives were antiunion and favored manufacturing industries less. After a yearlong coal miners' strike in 1984–1985 was defeated, labor unions faced a difficult time in Britain. Without strong unions and government subsidies, large portions of Scotland, Wales, and northern England that relied on manufacturing for survival began to face extremely high unemployment rates. Poverty and crime statistics skyrocketed together, causing a social upheaval that eventually contributed to Thatcher's defeat in the election of 1990.

Playbill cover from the 1989 theatrical production of The Secret Rapture, *written and directed by David Hare*

CRITICAL OVERVIEW

For the most part, critics in Hare's native Britain recognized *The Secret Rapture* as a clever attempt at a modern tragedy, set squarely against the social and economic impact of Prime Minister Margaret Thatcher's decade-long term of office in the 1980s. They generally praised the work for both its political commentary and its intimate, personal storytelling.

Writing for the *Sunday Times* just after the play opened in London, John Peter declared, "Hare has written one of the best English plays since the war and established himself as the finest British dramatist of his generation. *The Secret Rapture* is a family play; it is also the first major play to judge the England of the 1980s in terms that are both human and humane."

In the *Observer,* Michael Ratcliffe observed, "Hare's painful, witty, and moving new play *The Secret Rapture* is a morality of modern behavior in which the people who have all the answers face, buy out, and destroy the people who thought there were no questions to ask."

However, on the other side of the Atlantic Ocean, American critics found less to understand and like about the play. In the *New Republic,* reviewer Robert Brustein complained, "The only thing I found provocative about *The Secret Rapture*, David Hare's new play at the Ethel Barrymore, is its title." While British reviewers appreciated the way Hare infused personal tragedy with political commentary, Brustein complained that the playwright's political agenda did more harm than good. He felt that the characters lacked depth and that they "exist primarily as symbolic reflections on life and character in Margaret Thatcher's England."

Similarly, Mimi Kramer in the *New Yorker* wrote, "On the face of it, Hare's theme seems to be family relations; unfortunately, he approaches his subject so complacently as to make a mockery of character and human experience. The people who inhabit his play are more than just caricatures; they're political stereotypes."

Whether they liked or disliked the play, both British and American critics seemed particularly intrigued, and sometimes troubled, by the character, and the contradictions, of Isobel. As Hare himself declared, with Isobel he set out to create a truly virtuous heroine in the midst of societal corruption and evil. But according to some critics, Isobel's virtue did not generate the sympathy required of a central tragic character.

In *Plays International,* John Russell Taylor suggested, "Some are certain that Isobel is a saint, a wholly good woman beleaguered by a naughty world. But she would seem to lack the ruthlessness of the real saint. Most of what she does she does from cowardice and the inability to resist."

Gerald Weales, writing for *Commonweal,* noted, "However tantalizing as a character, Isobel never achieves the force, the presence of those who surround her. Her desire to withdraw, to find a quiet place . . . and the restraint which she brings to even her most assertive gestures make her a character for whom action is reaction. For this reason, a distance remains between Isobel and her family, her lover and, unfortunately, the audience."

Kramer simply found Isobel boring. "The central character of *The Secret Rapture*," she wrote, "the terminally good Isobel, seems a woman afflicted by a congenital inability to say anything interesting about anyone. She is surrounded by curious enough people. . . . But Isobel can't seem to pass judgment on any of them."

One fascinating and unique critical issue arose when the play appeared in New York for the first time. In London, *The Secret Rapture* had been directed at the National Theatre by Howard Davies, but Hare himself chose to come to America to direct the Broadway version. Frank Rich, the well-known *New York Times* critic, had seen the play in London under Davies's direction and praised it. However, his review of Hare's work in New York was scathing. "Mr. Hare, serving as his play's director for its Broadway premiere at the Barrymore, is his own worst enemy," Rich declared. He found fault with Hare's new casting, the revised set design, and the slow pace and monotonous tones of the actors. He ended his review by remarking, "I don't understand how a dramatist so deep in human stuff could allow so pallid an imitation of life to represent his play on a Broadway stage."

Ultimately, the production only ran for nineteen previews and twelve performances. Hare was so angered by Rich's review that he sent him a harsh letter, complaining that his column had closed the play and that Rich was power-hungry and irresponsible. Rich responded that his job as a reviewer was to tell the truth as he saw it to his readers. The very public debate between the artist and his critic raised some important questions about theatrical criticism in New York, where the *New York Times* reviewer, whoever he happened to be, certainly did wield a great deal of power. In a climate where fewer and fewer new plays were making it to Broadway, was it the responsibility of reviewers to criticize them in such a way that audiences would still attend? Or should they remain true to their opinions, however harsh they may be, and report only what they believe, regardless of the financial consequences? The issue has still not been resolved, and a bad review in the *Times* can still close a production within a few performances of opening night.

CRITICISM

Lane A. Glenn

Glenn has a Ph.D. and specializes in theatre history and literature. In this essay, Glenn explores David Hare's play through Aristotle's classical theory of tragedy found in the Poetics *and Arthur Miller's modern vision described in the essay "Tragedy and the Common Man."*

When David Hare's *The Secret Rapture* opened at the Royal National Theatre in London in October 1988, critics attempted to categorize the play as something familiar. Some pointed to the exaggerated portrayals of the ambitious, self-interested politician, Marion, and her almost clownishly religious businessman husband, Tom, and called the play political satire, or a contemporary comedy of manners. Others recognized the play's deeply rooted Christian symbolism and termed it a philosophical drama about contemporary life in Britain. Writing for the *Sunday Times,* John Peter remarked, "*The Secret Rapture* is a family play; it is also the first

WHAT DO I READ NEXT?

- In a career that has lasted more than thirty years, David Hare has written and adapted more than twenty stage plays and a number of screenplays, most of which combine his talents for creating intense, personal conflicts with his interest in criticizing conservative politics in Britain. Some of his best-known and most popular plays include *Plenty* (1978); *A Map of the World* (1982); his trilogy of plays about social institutions in Great Britain, *Racing Demon* (for which he earned both an Olivier Award and a Tony Award following its production in 1990), *Murmuring Judges* (1991), and *The Absence of War* (1992); and *Skylight* (1995).
- Besides writing plays and movies, David Hare has also become an accomplished director and has contributed essays to newspapers, magazines, and anthologies. One of his own collections of his work is called *Writing Left-Handed* (1991). The essays in the book describe Hare's thoughts on his plays (including *The Secret Rapture*), as well as his perspectives on theatre history in Great Britain and his opinions about a variety of contemporary political issues.
- Very early in his career, Hare was identified with other British ''political'' playwrights such as Howard Brenton, Edward Bond, Snoo Wilson, and Howard Barker. All of these writers explored the effects of politics on British society. For examples of their writing, one can read Howard Brenton's *The Romans in Britain* (1980), Edward Bond's *Saved* (1965), Snoo Wilson's *The Glad Hand* (1978), or Howard Barker's *The Loud Boy's Life* (1980).
- Margaret Thatcher served as Britain's prime minister from 1979 to 1990, longer than any other prime minister of the twentieth century. The politics of her government left a strong mark on her country and its culture, and this is reflected in the work of writers like David Hare. *Dancing with Dogma: Britain under Thatcherism* by Ian Gilmour (1992) is a critique of Thatcher's reign that describes the downside of her economic, foreign, and social policies.

major play to judge the England of the 1980s in terms both human and humane.''

For his part, the playwright himself was quite direct on the subject of style. In an interview with Robert Crew in the *Toronto Star,* Hare indicated that he was interested in writing about the psychological effect of British Prime Minister Margaret Thatcher's government on the people of Britain in the form of a *tragedy.* ''We don't have many plays with heroines or many tragedies in England at the moment,'' said Hare. ''It is commonly said that it's not possible to write a tragedy nowadays and I was interested to see whether it was.''

Hare had good reason to be uncertain. The classic definition of a *tragedy* was developed by the ancient Greeks more than 2,000 years ago. While the form was revived successfully by Shakespeare and a few of his contemporaries during the Renaissance, by the turn of the twentieth century, critics and writers alike were declaring tragedy a dead art—something that could still be read in the texts of classical writers but no longer written and performed for modern audiences. In order to determine if Hare succeeded at his task and created a modern tragedy, it is important first to understand the classical definition of the form, then to consider how it has been viewed in more recent years.

The most widespread and accepted classical definition of tragedy was described in 335 B.C.E. by the philosopher Aristotle in his *Poetics.* As it exists today, the *Poetics* is an incomplete work that has been translated from its original ancient Greek through many languages and many editions to its current twenty-six-chapter form. In it, Aristotle set out to define tragedy using the plays of classical

> "IN MANY WAYS, *THE SECRET RAPTURE* DOES SEEM TO RESEMBLE THIS CLASSICAL DEFINITION OF TRAGEDY. IT IS UNDOUBTEDLY A SERIOUS PLAY WITH UNIVERSAL THEMES."

Greek dramatists like Aeschylus, Sophocles, and Euripides as examples. Aristotle's well-known definition of tragedy appears in chapter 6 of the *Poetics:*

> Tragedy, then, is an imitation of an action that is serious, complete, and of a certain magnitude; in language embellished with each kind of artistic ornament, the several kinds being found in separate parts of the play; in the form of action, not of narrative; through pity and fear affecting the proper purgation of these emotions.

As Aristotle explains his definition and provides examples from plays of his time, such as *Oedipus the King* and *Medea,* a clearer definition of tragedy emerges that does seem to describe many of the plays of the classical Greeks and Renaissance writers like Shakespeare. A tragedy, Aristotle suggests, is a *serious* play. Its theme generally has universal interest and appeal. That is, most or all human beings can identify with the play's concerns and can therefore develop an emotional attachment to the action and characters. The central character, or *protagonist,* is typically a person of high rank or stature, often a king or nobleman. This protagonist is essentially a good person who experiences some kind of decline in fortune that usually leads to suffering and death. The decline is caused by some error or frailty, referred to as the "tragic flaw," on the part of the protagonist. Sometime before or during his suffering, the protagonist recognizes and understands his error. And, finally, the downfall of the protagonist arouses emotions such as pity and fear in the audience and effectively purges these emotions through the act of *catharsis.*

The best example of a classical tragedy, according to Aristotle, is Sophocles's *Oedipus the King.* In this work, the protagonist is a king who, as a young man, is given a prophecy that he will one day grow up to murder his father and marry his mother. Rather than face this grisly fate, he flees what he thinks is his home and settled in a new land where he inherits a throne, a fortune, and a queen. When his new kingdom is faced with a terrible plague, Oedipus asks the gods for advice, and he is told that he must find the killer of the old king. As evidence and witnesses slowly appear, Oedipus begins to realize that he has made a terrible mistake. The family he ran away from was not his family after all. A man he thought was a ruffian and whom he killed on the road was actually his father, and the queen he married turns out to be his mother. Oedipus's "tragic flaw" is his pride: he believed he could outwit the gods and escape his fate; then for a while he refuses to see the truth. He recognizes his errors, blinds himself, and then banishes himself into exile. An audience, Aristotle suggests, can easily find pity for Oedipus, particularly as he realizes his mistakes and fear that something similar could happen to them.

In many ways, *The Secret Rapture* does seem to resemble this classical definition of tragedy. It is undoubtedly a serious play with universal themes. It begins with a funeral and ends with a funeral, and in between it addresses topics such as alcoholism, family loyalty, and obsessive love. These are all concerns that most people can relate to, and they may cause audiences to develop emotional attachments to the characters involved. The central character of the play, Isobel, is not someone of high rank or stature. In fact, the highest-ranking character in the play is probably her sister, Marion, who holds a junior minister's position in Britain's government. Still, Isobel is essentially a good person who experiences terrible suffering, followed by a sudden, violent death. Her "tragic flaw" may be her goodness. She is so committed to virtue and to doing what is right that she invites the abuse of those who are not as good as she is.

Isobel does seem to experience a flash of recognition when she understands the error she is making. Just before rejecting Irwin, she tells him, "I'm being turned into a person whose only function is to suffer. And believe me, it bores me just as much as it bores you." Her insight, however, appears long before her worst suffering and doesn't seem to affect her in any significant way. Finally, when her downfall arrives and Irwin murders her, it is quite sudden, and she is strong and commanding until the very end, leaving some question as to whether the audience experiences pity and fear for her in some sort of cathartic moment.

Even with all its similarities to classical tragedy, it is clear that *The Secret Rapture* is a very different play, culturally, than Sophocles's *Oedipus the King* or Shakespeare's *Macbeth.* On the surface, it may not seem to matter that Isobel is not a queen and that the fate of a kingdom does not hang in the balance. But classical tragedy, according to many critics, does demand more from its characters and its audiences than the ordinary lives of ordinary people. That is why, as Hare observed, "it is commonly said that it is not possible to write a tragedy nowadays." We may long for the emotional catharsis offered by a well-crafted tragedy, but we are more interested in the lives of these ordinary people and the way they parallel our own than in the lives of remote kings in even remoter kingdoms.

It is this cultural contradiction that led to the belief, for much of the twentieth century, that tragedies can no longer be written. In a famous 1929 essay titled "The Tragic Fallacy," Joseph Wood Krutch declared, "Tragedies, in that only sense of the word which has any distinctive meaning, are no longer written in either the dramatic or any other form." Krutch believed that tragedies could not exist in their pure form in the twentieth century because the view most people held of themselves and the world had changed so drastically. "If the plays and the novels of today deal with littler people and less mighty emotions," Krutch maintained, "it is not because we have become interested in commonplace souls and their unglamorous adventures but because we have come, willy-nilly, to see the soul of man as commonplace and its emotions as mean."

Krutch believed that true writers of tragedy cast their plays with kings and set them in courts and on battlefields because they really believed in human greatness and that we now cast plays with common people and set them in houses and shops because we no longer believe in nobility, either its outward appearance or its inner virtue. To illustrate his point, he compared Shakespeare's *Hamlet,* in which a Danish prince seeks revenge on an uncle who murdered his father and stole his throne, to Henrik Ibsen's *Ghosts,* in which a plain young man discovers he inherited syphilis from his father, returns to his little village, and persuades his mother to poison him. Although the experiences of Ibsen's protagonist in *Ghosts* may be closer to reality for most people, Krutch insists that the play cannot be a tragedy, because it lacks the noble spirit and does not end in an uplifting or cathartic way.

Quite likely, though, Hare was less concerned with a strict, classical interpretation of tragedy when he wrote *The Secret Rapture* and more concerned with how the play would resonate with his London audiences in 1988. On a scale ranging from Sophocles to Shakespeare to Ibsen, his style is undoubtedly more similar to that of the author of *Ghosts* than to the two playwrights whose lives were more affected by the comings and goings of kings and kingdoms. Yet by a more recent definition of tragedy, he still may have succeeded at his task.

In 1949, just after his masterpiece *Death of a Salesman* opened on Broadway, American playwright Arthur Miller wrote an essay for the *New York Times* called "Tragedy and the Common Man." Miller had been taken to task, by critics who thought like Krutch, for calling *Death of a Salesman* a tragedy. In his essay, Miller defended not only his play but tragedy itself as a form of drama perfectly accessible to modern playwrights and audiences.

Miller rejected the notion that tragedies must be written about and for noblemen. "I believe that the common man is as apt a subject for tragedy in its highest sense as kings were," he stated. Far from having to exact murderous revenge or save a kingdom, Miller felt that tragic protagonists earned the title simply from struggling to find their rightful place in society. And instead of needing fate, the gods, or some catastrophic event to prompt them into action, Miller suggested, "the fateful wound from which the inevitable events spiral is the wound of indignity, and its dominant force is indignation."

The "tragic flaw" in a character, then, could simply be the character's insistence on maintaining his or her dignity, sometimes in the face of overwhelming odds. It is this struggle between the ordinary individual and the world around us, Miller suggests, that creates the pity and the fear normally connected with tragedy. Miller wrote:

> The tragic right is a condition of life, a condition in which the human personality is able to flower and realize itself. The wrong is the condition which suppresses man, perverts the flowing out of his love and creative instinct. Tragedy enlightens—and it must, in that it points the heroic finger at the enemy of man's freedom. The thrust for freedom is the quality in tragedy which exalts. The revolutionary questioning of the stable environment is what terrifies.

Miller believed that, in the end, the tragic protagonist's struggle, though doomed to failure, suggests optimism and reinforces the best qualities of human existence. Perhaps most important of all, it conveys a belief in the continual evolution and perfectibility of all humankind, kings and commoners alike.

Viewed through this critical lens, *The Secret Rapture* appears much closer to Miller's definition of tragedy for the common man than to Aristotle's noble art form. Isobel is certainly an ordinary enough person, particularly as compared to the other characters in the play. While her sister Marion is a fast-climbing politician in the national spotlight and Tom is a born-again successful and wealthy businessman, Isobel is content to operate a small graphic design company and tend to the needs of her family and friends.

Although she seems to weather most storms rather well, Isobel nevertheless suffers many indignities in the course of the play. She is initially coerced into taking care of Katherine and offering her a job, only to be betrayed by her again and again. No one seems prepared to honor the memory of Robert Glass, her father, the way she feels it should be honored. At one point she is forced to plead with Irwin, ''Are we not allowed to *mourn*? Just . . . a decent period of mourning? Can't we have that?''

Perhaps worst of all, Irwin betrays her to Marion and Tom when he deals with them behind her back and accepts a salary increase to convince Isobel to accept their business offer. The cumulative effect of all this mistreatment is a tremendous assault on Isobel's dignity, Miller's ''fateful wound, from which the inevitable events'' of the play spiral. Isobel's indignation at this treatment causes her to rebel against the world around her. She completely shuns Irwin, ignores her floundering business, and turns to the work she believes her father would appreciate: taking care of Katherine.

Whether it seems to the rest of us that Isobel has made a wise choice or not, her choice is definitely a decision to spurn the ''stable environment'' offered by Marion, Tom, and Irwin, and to thrust for the freedom she believes she will find in doing what she thinks is right. In the end, Isobel's earthly struggle does fail, but we are left with a faint sense of optimism—the impression that Isobel's sacrifice has affected the lives of those around her for the better. Marion's final words, some of the last words of the play, suggest Miller's notion of evolution and human perfectibility. ''Isobel,'' she cries. ''We're just beginning.''

With that, the tragedy is complete. Isobel, a common person, a *good* person to the very end, has wielded her virtue and fought for her dignity against a world that seems to care only for itself and its profits; and in the struggle, she has changed that world, if only a little bit.

Source: Lane A. Glenn, Critical Essay on *The Secret Rapture*, in *Drama for Students*, The Gale Group, 2003.

Liorah Anne Golomb

In the following essay, Golomb examines similarities between the characters and story in The Secret Rapture *and Christian motifs.*

> If ye were of the world, the world would love his own: but because ye are not of the world, but I have chosen you out of the world, therefore the world hateth you. (John 15:19)

In his latest play, *The Secret Rapture*, David Hare has given us a central character, Isobel, who is distinctly not of the world. Even her name, a variant of Elizabeth, has as one of its meanings ''consecrated to God.'' Dramatically, Hare took a great risk in centering his play on Isobel. She is weak, pliable and abused (a stark contrast to Hare's usual headstrong women such as Susan in *Plenty* or Peggy in *A Map of the World*), yet in order for the climax to have any impact, we must feel that something has been accomplished by her destruction, not that she has been one of life's doormats who deserves what she gets. If Isobel were merely a good woman who could not exist in a corrupt world the necessary sense of loss at her death might not be evoked, but Hare has raised her to the level of saint and martyr. Her death has a purging effect on the other characters, so that while there is loss there is also hope.

Hare begins to establish Isobel's spirituality in the first moments of the play. Isobel, sitting with the body of her recently deceased father, tells her sister Marion:

> There's actually a moment when you see the spirit depart from the body. I've always been told about it. And it's true. (*She is very quiet and still.*) Like a bird.

While Hare develops Isobel's spiritual nature, he places in contrast to her several varieties of rather earth-bound sinners, each traveling down a different path in search of salvation. Marion, the elder sister, is a Tory junior minister entirely caught up in materialism and the exhilaration of power. It is by way of this character that Hare most directly voices his familiar political dissent. Marion is so extreme in her right-wing views that she needs no opposition to make her look the fool; she is quite capable of doing it herself, as when she proudly relates her retort to members of the Green Party who opposed her standpoint on nuclear energy: "'Come back and see me when you're glowing in the dark.'"

As we meet Marion she is trying to recover a ring which she had given to her father. In justifying her actions to Isobel (who, significantly, in no way indicates that she requires justification), she explains:

> For God's sake, I mean, the ring is actually valuable. Actually no, that sounds horrid. I apologize. I'll tell you the truth. I thought when I bought it—I just walked into this very expensive shop and I thought, this is one of the few really decent things I've done in my life. And it's true. I spent, as it happens, a great deal of money, rather more . . . rather *more* than I had at the time. I went too far. I wanted something to express my love for my father. Something adequate.

Marion cannot express her feelings emotionally; instead, she equates love with a valuable object. The speech also puts Isobel in the role of confessor. Marion is driven to confess by her own guilt—guilt which she experiences because she is in the presence of such goodness. Isobel never criticizes Marion, and even agrees that she should have the ring, yet later in the scene we find that Marion is still tormented by guilt:

> MARION I'm not going to forgive you.
>
> ISOBEL What?
>
> MARION You've tried to humiliate me.
>
> ISOBEL Marion . . .
>
> MARION You've made me feel awful. It's not my fault about the ring. Or the way I feel about Katherine. You make me feel as if I'm always in the wrong.
>
> ISOBEL Not at all.
>
> MARION Oh, yes. Well, we can't all be perfect. We do try. The rest of us are trying. So will you please stop this endless criticism? Because I honestly think it's driving me mad.

It is Marion who has been seeking forgiveness, indeed, absolution, of Isobel. When she senses that her sins have not been cleansed, she turns her guilt outward and blames the confessor. Saints, it appears, can be very difficult to live with.

The second sinner in Hare's catalogue is Marion's husband Tom, a born-again Christian and Chairman of a committee which strives "to do business the way Jesus would have done it." Tom is a rather comical example of one who uses scripture to his own advantage. The Lord has indeed moved in mysterious ways when Tom, in the first scene, explains to Isobel how the Lord Jesus delivered the exact automobile parts he needed in order to repair his car so that he could give Marion the news of her father's death:

> "WHILE HARE DEVELOPS ISOBEL'S SPIRITUAL NATURE, HE PLACES IN CONTRAST TO HER SEVERAL VARIETIES OF RATHER EARTH-BOUND SINNERS, EACH TRAVELING DOWN A DIFFERENT PATH IN SEARCH OF SALVATION."

> TOM [. . .] I go to the car. Won't start. I open the bonnet. Spark-plug leads have perished. I can't believe it. I think, what on earth am I going to do? Then I think, hey, six days ago an old mate called in and left, in a shopping bag, a whole load of spare parts he'd had to buy for his car. (*He smiles in anticipation of the outcome.*) And, you know, as I go in and look for it, I tell you this, I don't have a doubt. As I move towards the bag. I've never looked inside it and yet I *know*. It's got so I know. I know that inside that bag there is going to be a set of Ford Granada leads. And *then* you have to say, well, there you are, that's it, that's the Lord Jesus. He's there when you need him. I *am* looked after.

In addition to exploiting his comic value, Hare uses Tom to highlight Isobel's authentic Christian existence, which, interestingly, does not seem to include Christ. Isobel rather rejects Christian ideology at every turn. She is politely skeptical of Tom's faith, but more significantly, she fights against being placed in the roles of saint, martyr and savior which the other characters in the play, particularly her lover Irwin, would have her take on. Her strongest denial of these roles occurs in her last scene as she rejects Irwin's desperate effort to reinstate himself into her graces:

> ISOBEL [. . .] And you have this idea that I can't accept.
>
> IRWIN What's that? (*She looks hard at him a moment.*)
>
> ISOBEL You want to be saved through another person. (*There's a silence.*)
>
> IRWIN And?
>
> ISOBEL It isn't possible.

Despite her protestations, Isobel makes one deliberate choice during the action of the play, and that is to forsake her own well-being by taking upon herself a burden, a cross to bear; specifically, a soul to save. Until she makes this choice she is an inactive character playing no part in her own destiny—indeed, a doormat. The burden which Isobel chooses to take upon herself is Katherine, her father's young widow. Katherine represents the Lost Soul and therefore the greatest challenge to those who would be saviors:

> And Levi made him a great feast in his own house: and there was a great company of publicans and of others that sat down with them.
>
> But their scribes and Pharisees murmured against his disciples, saying, Why do ye eat and drink with publicans and sinners?
>
> And Jesus, answering, said unto them, They that are whole need not a physician; but they that are sick.
>
> I came not to call the righteous, but sinners to repentance. (Luke 5:29–32)

It is not the part of Jesus that Isobel has consciously chosen to play, but that of her father Robert. Katherine sets herself up as the soul in need of salvation, naming Robert as her benefactor and personal savior, and indirectly challenges Isobel to carry on for her father:

> KATHERINE [. . .] I met your father first in the Vale of Evesham. Yeah, he stopped one night in a motel. It was appalling. I don't know how I'd ended up there. I was working the bar. Trying to pick men up—not even for money, but because I was so unhappy with myself. I wanted something to happen. I don't know how I thought these men might help me, they were travellers, small goods, that sort of thing, all with slack bellies and smelling of late-night curries. I can still smell them. I don't know why, I'd been doing it for weeks. Then Robert came in. He said 'I'll drive you to Gloucestershire. It will give you some peace.' He brought me here, to this house. He put fresh sheets in the spare room. Everything I did, before or since, he forgave. (*She sits, tears in her eyes, quite now.*) People say I took advantage of his decency. But what are good people for? They're here to help the trashy people like me.

A moment later, after a significant pause, Isobel decides to take Katherine into her home and into her graphic arts firm. That Katherine is an alcoholic, unqualified, unsocialized and irresponsible, are flaws which Isobel chooses to ignore, although she is well aware of them. Whereas Marion could only show her devotion to their father in materialistic terms, Isobel will show it through emulation of his good works. If Robert could unconditionally forgive all of Katherine's sins, then Isobel will too, even if it leads to her own destruction.

From the moment of Isobel's decision at the end of Scene 2, the action of *The Secret Rapture* roughly parallels that of the life of Jesus, with Isobel in the title role and Irwin playing the part of Judas. At the meeting in Robert's house in Scene 4 Isobel is being persuaded to sign her business over to a board of directors headed by Tom. There is a great sense that Tom, Marion and Katherine have conspired against her, but she still has one ally, Irwin—or so she thinks. As Irwin walks into the living room he greets Isobel and Hare's stage directions read: ''*He kisses her cheek before going to sit down.*'' It is the kiss of Judas, of betrayal. Irwin, it is revealed a few pages later, has sided with the others in exchange for a doubled salary, the thirty pieces of silver of the modern world.

What follows is one of the more problematic aspects of the play. Isobel can easily refuse to sign the agreement; Tom, Marion, Katherine and Rhonda (Marion's assistant) have even left the stage, thus removing the immediate pressure to sign. This is the moment when we must, in order to have compassion for Isobel, feel that when she signs the agreement she does so not because she is weak and resigned to the will of others, but because she accepts the destiny which has been written for her. Isobel here stands before an invisible Pilate and refuses to state her case and save her own life. The agreement which she will sign when the lights go down at the end of the act amounts to a renunciation of her creative and financial independence, a stripping away of both her earthly possessions and her worth as a human being. By signing, Isobel makes it convenient for the others to relegate her to the background and effect her metaphorical death.

In trying to justify his betrayal and gain Isobel's forgiveness, Irwin points out Isobel's own share of the blame, and by her silence, Isobel accepts not the blame but the futility of engaging in a struggle for self-preservation:

> IRWIN Isobel, please. Just look at me. Please. (*She doesn't turn.*) Things move on. You brought in Katherine. Be fair, it was you. It changed the nature of the firm. For better or worse. But it's changed. And you did it. Not me. (*There is silence.*) I wouldn't hurt you. You know that. I'd rather die than see you hurt. I love you. I want you. There's not a moment when I don't want you.

Irwin proceeds to suffer a fall from grace to which he will never be restored, and he undergoes an immediate character change. Suddenly he becomes obsessed with gaining love and approval from Isobel, and at the same time his sins multiply. It is as if he is competing with Katherine for Isobel's love by trying to prove himself more needy, since he knows he is not worthy. The second act opens with Irwin, immediately after having made the above pledge of devotion, flirting with a skimpily-clad Rhonda. They are unmistakably on the verge of physical intimacy when Isobel walks in. Isobel recognizes Irwin's action as a call for her attention but rather than oblige him, as she constantly obliges Katherine, she withdraws. Irwin then plays, as Hare puts it, his strong hand—he confronts Isobel with the truth about Katherine:

> IRWIN I know, you think she's just unhappy. She's maladjusted. She hates herself. Well, she does. And she is. All these things are true. But also it's true, Isobel, my dear, you must learn something else. That everyone knows except you. It's time you were told. There's such a thing as evil. You're dealing with evil. (ISOBEL *turns round, about to speak.*) That's right. And if you don't admit it, then you can't fight it. And if you don't fight it, you're going to lose.

It is my sense that Isobel knows full well that she is going to lose to the force of evil as embodied in Katherine, but her need to sacrifice herself in the attempt to save Katherine's soul overpowers any desire she might have to save her own skin. At this point in the play Katherine has already destroyed Isobel's independence, her business, and her love affair; there is not much more she can take except Isobel's life. Isobel must decide whether to give it to her or not, and in the next scene she reveals the decision she has made to Tom and Marion while on a meditative retreat to Lanzarote:

> ISOBEL [. . .] You can't get away. You think you can. You think you'll fly out. Just leave. Damn the lot of you, and go. Then you think, here I am, stark naked, sky-blue sea, miles of sand—I've done it! I'm free! Then you think, yes, just remind me, what am I meant to do now? (*She stands, a mile away in a world of her own.*) In my case there's only one answer. (*She looks absently at them, as if they were not even present.*) I must do what Dad would have wished. (*She turns, as if this were self-evident.*) That's it.

Whether or not one cares to extend the immediate meaning of "Dad" beyond Robert to God the Father, it is clear that Isobel has put herself in the same position in relation to her father that Jesus held in relation to the Holy Father: she intends to be his emissary on earth.

Irwin has sensed the sort of experience Isobel has had, and earlier in the scene he tells Marion that he believes Isobel has taken a vow. A parallel can certainly be drawn between Isobel's escape to Lanzarote and the transfiguration of Jesus which occurred on his sojourn to the mountain; Jesus, too, is instructed by his heavenly father and given a clear sense of purpose, and while "his raiment became shining, exceeding white as snow" (Mark 9:3), Hare brings Isobel into the scene with the direction "*She is also changed. She wears a long dark blue overcoat and thin glasses.*" Indeed, Isobel does seem to have taken vows, not only to continue caring for Katherine, but in the sense that a novice takes vows of poverty, chastity and obedience. The next scene finds her serving Katherine in a sparsely furnished flat and eating a simple meal of shepherd's pie. Katherine rejects the food, saying: "Your cooking is unspeakable. It's all good intentions. F— shepherd's pie. It sums you up." On one level we have Isobel compared to a bland plate of mashed potatoes and ground meat, and as a surface appraisal of Isobel's character, it is not far from the mark. Isobel lacks the volatility of Katherine, the outrageous single-mindedness of Marion, and the sensuality of Rhonda. She possesses instead a quiet strength, easily mistaken for banality. The additional comment about "good intentions," however, invites a play on the word "shepherd." Isobel, after all, has become Katherine's shepherd, her caretaker, her guardian.

Marion's reaction to the idea of a vow is both comic and revealing. That promises are things meant to be made, not kept, is evident in her response to Irwin:

> MARION I don't believe this. This is most peculiar. What is this? A *vow?* It's outrageous. People making *vows.* What are *vows?* Nobody's made vows since the nineteenth century.

Surely Marion vowed a thing or two on her rise up the political ladder, but actual integrity is a concept quite foreign to her. We have seen in her speech about the ring just how many false passes she makes before she hits upon the truth, but a trait which may be merely an amusing character flaw in others is far more devastating in an influential politician.

It is worthwhile here to take a step back to the first scene in the play. Marion has asserted that Katherine took advantage of Robert's kindness and love. Isobel responds: "Honestly, I don't think it matters much. The great thing is to love. If you're loved back then it's a bonus."

A comparison of two translations of a familiar passage from the first Epistle of Paul to the Corinthians provides some interesting insight into Isobel's statement and into her decision to sacrifice herself to Katherine. The first is from the King James Version; the second, from the New American Bible:

> Charity suffereth long, and is kind; charity envieth not; charity vaunteth not itself, is not puffed up.
>
> Doth not behave itself unseemly, seeketh not her own, is not easily provoked, thinketh no evil;
>
> Rejoiceth not in iniquity, but rejoiceth in the truth;
>
> Beareth all things, believeth all things, hopeth all things, endureth all things. [. . .]
>
> And now abideth faith, hope, charity, these three; but the greatest of these is charity. (I Cor. 13:4–7, 13)
>
> Love is patient; love is kind. Love is not jealous, it does not put on airs, it is not snobbish. Love is never rude, it is not self-seeking, it is not prone to anger; neither does it brood over injuries. Love does not rejoice in what is wrong but rejoices with the truth. There is no limit to love's forbearance, to its trust, its hope, its power to endure. [. . .]
>
> There are in the end three things that last: faith, hope, and love, and the greatest of these is love. (NAB I Cor. 13:4–7, 13)

The retranslation of the term "charity" as "love" in the second passage clearly expresses Isobel's attitude towards Katherine. Her love is unconditional and charitable and fulfills all of the conditions set forth by Paul. The more difficult Katherine makes it to be loved, the more Isobel must love her; her forbearance is truly limitless. Irwin's love for Isobel, on the other hand, is self-centered and self-serving; it lacks the quality of charity. He loves Isobel because she is good, but unless he can love that which is not good, his love is without meaning. In his last scene with Isobel, Irwin in his desperation has strayed so far from the true definition of love that he mistakes it for sex and begs Isobel to sleep with him. Isobel, however, continues to refuse him the salvation he seeks:

> ISOBEL Force me. You can force me if you like. Why not? You can take me here. On the bed. On the floor. You can f— me till the morning. You can f— me all tomorrow. Then the whole week. At the end you can shoot me and hold my heart in your hand. You still won't have what you want. (*Her gaze does not wander.*) The bit that you want I'm not giving you.

The Sacred Heart imagery in this speech is not accidental. Isobel is playing out the final moments of her drama, and as she notes with some amusement when her hour has come, "I haven't got shoes. Still you can't have everything." The belief that Jesus walked to his crucifixion without shoes, although not specified in the gospels, is common; for example, note this passage from *Waiting for Godot:*

> ESTRAGON (*turning to look at the boots.*) I'm leaving them there. (*Pause.*) Another will come, just as . . . as . . . as me, but with smaller feet, and they'll make him happy.
>
> VLADIMIR But you can't go barefoot!
>
> ESTRAGON Christ did.
>
> VLADIMIR Christ! What has Christ got to do with it? You're not going to compare yourself to Christ!
>
> ESTRAGON All my life I've compared myself to him.

Christian teaching demands that each of its followers compare himself to Christ and re-enact, throughout his life and at various times of the year, certain of the events of Jesus' life. Isobel, while never making the comparison between Christ and herself, has led a truly Christian existence. That she must be destroyed while Katherine, the sinner, goes free is an indication that spiritual goodness cannot coexist with the material world. Her death becomes sacrificial, as the crucifixion of Jesus is felt to have been: it is the blood of the lamb which whitens the robes (Rev. 7:14).

Irwin's reaction immediately after he shoots Isobel is perplexing: "It's over. Thank God." After spending the past two scenes virtually deranged because he can't have the woman he professes to love, it seems odd that he should be relieved by her death. Perhaps he has destroyed his only means of salvation, as he views Isobel to be. But he has released his burden as well. His cross—trying to live up to Isobel's standards—has been a hard one to bear. "I have no worth," he tells Isobel at his most desperate moment. "I can't feel my worth. When I was with you, it was there." Isobel in fact brought happiness to no one during her life. The pain of impossible love suffered by the offstage character Gordon is one manifestation of this. As Marion tells her:

> MARION [. . .] Everywhere you go, there are arguments. God, how I hate all this human stuff. Wherever you go, you cause misery. People crying, people not talking. It overwhelms me. Because you can't just live. Why can't you *live,* like other people?

Alternatively or perhaps additionally, Irwin's ejaculation may be an expression of relief because Isobel has been released from her trials and been made, finally, pure spirit. Gospel text of Jesus' final words on the cross vary widely. Matthew and Mark record the very human plea, "My God, my God, why hast thou forsaken me?'' (Matthew 27:46 and Mark 15:34), while that set down in Luke lacks desperation but still betrays human concerns: ''Father, into thy hands I commend my spirit'' (Luke 23:46). John, however, provides the simplest and perhaps most spiritual report of the last words spoken by Jesus before the resurrection: ''It is finished'' (John 19:30). In accordance with the dramatic motif of the Gospel of John which will be discussed below, these words end the action of Jesus' life on earth, but they signify the joy of being freed of the corporal as well. When asked about the meaning of the title of the play David Hare responded, ''It's that moment at which a nun expects to be united with Christ. In other words, it's death.'' Placed in the context of Christianity death becomes a blissful experience, the happy reward for a life of suffering, and Irwin's strange gratitude makes sense.

Although her presence on earth created division and misery, Isobel's death has ironically had a cleansing effect on the other characters. Once she is gone a certain peace does take hold of them. It seems that, despite her declaration to Irwin that one could not be saved through another person, salvation does indeed take place. In the last scene Tom, Marion and Katherine restore Robert's house as though it were a shrine to him and Isobel. In a manner reminiscent of the walk to Calvary, the villagers, we are informed, want to walk to the funeral en masse. Marion and Katherine, heretofore bitter enemies or worse, self-serving allies joined against Isobel, share a closeness which they had never before experienced, and while Tom declares, ''I've slightly lost touch with the Lord Jesus'', we know it is only Jesus the Businessman he is abandoning. Passion, too, is restored to Marion and Tom as they reaffirm a love and desire for one another that has not been evident before the final moments of the play. Overall there is a sense of health, of well-being. At last Isobel's worth is recognized, and as the play closes Marion attempts to resurrect her sister: ''Isobel. We're just beginning. Isobel, where are you? (*She waits a moment.*) Isobel, why don't you come home?''

Hare ends the text of the play here, but interestingly, in the National Theatre of Great Britain production directed by Howard Davies, Isobel is successfully resurrected. She appears upstage on a diagonal from Marion, and both sisters have their arms outstretched and are moving towards one another. Davies's addition leaves one with a very strong sense that Isobel has in fact experienced the Secret Rapture.

Thematically, *The Secret Rapture* marks something of a departure for Hare. He has seldom failed to include politics in his work, and overt references to England's economy do exist in the play; for example, the question of the ethics behind investments is raised, and Scene 6 largely concerns Isobel's realization that her business has been used as a tax write-off. A strictly political interpretation, however, yields rather unsatisfying results. One theatre monthly ironically titled its cover story preceding the New York production, ''A Kinder, Gentler David Hare,'' and we may well wonder what sort of socio-political statement the playwright intended to make. This is not to say that Hare needs to provide answers in his plays, nor has it been his practice to do so. His preferred style has been to present the problem and allow the audience to draw the conclusions. *A Map of the World* (1982) intelligently presents a dialectic on poverty in developing countries while at the same time allowing the cracks in both sides to be seen. *Fanshen* (1976) tells of both fine intentions and resultant failure during economic reform in China. But *The Secret Rapture* is politically a one-sided play, pitting Isobel's innocence and goodness against Marion as quintessential Tory capitalist, and it works thematically only until the last scene. It is one thing to destroy the last vestige of pre-Thatcher England and quite another to depict the hawk as turning vegetarian after it has had its chicken dinner. The political dimension here seems almost obligatory; Hare knows that the best arguments give some credence to the opposition, and Marion is too much of a caricature to be taken seriously. True, greed, short-sightedness and the perverse passion for ''clambering on the back [of the gravy train] and joining in the fun'' are the elements which caused the corruption of Irwin and the destruction of Isobel. But Isobel, eternally passive, might have been taken down by much weaker forces. The Good Individual is rarely suffered to exist, and Jesus is but one example from history of this phenomenon; several others come from the realm of public service. Yet Marion's remorse makes Hare's ending, if taken politically, seem naïvely optimistic. Surely we are not to conclude that the loss of an individual will shake the conscience of the oppressors, or that passive resistance will eventually win the war. Hare explains his new concerns in *The Secret Rapture* this way:

> [I]t became clear that personal character is more important to me than ideology. My anger about what's happened to English society didn't change. The difficulty of changing people became more clear. I'm bored by propaganda, either from the left or right. But

> goodness makes me weep. I see Isobel that way. So I said, Why don't I write about goodness? Why be a smartass?

Although some have suggested that Hare titled his play more for its cryptic resonance than with intent to suggest a parable, these words, taken together with the title, make it difficult to ignore the validity of the analysis given here. In choosing to write about goodness, Hare could find no parallel with which his audience would be more familiar than the drama of Jesus.

It is not inappropriate to discuss the life of Jesus in dramatic terms as I have done here. The Gospel According to John introduces the concept that Jesus' betrayal was divinely scripted:

> I speak not of you all: I know whom I have chosen: but that the scripture may be fulfilled, He that eateth bread with me hath lifted up his heel against me. [. . .] Simon Peter therefore beckoned to him, that he should ask who it should be of whom he spake.
>
> He then lying on Jesus' breast saith unto him, Lord, who is it? Jesus answered, He it is, to whom I shall give a sop, when I have dipped it. And when he had dipped the sop, he gave it to Judas Iscariot, the son of Simon.
>
> And after the sop Satan entered into him. Then said Jesus unto him, That thou doest, do quickly. [. . .]
>
> He then having received the sop went immediately out: and it was night. Therefore, when he was gone out, Jesus said, Now is the Son of man glorified, and God is glorified in him. (John 13:18, 24–27, 30–31)

John differs from the synoptic gospels in that here Jesus purposely places Satan into the body of Judas in order to fulfill the predetermined terms of the Scriptures; that is, so that the drama can unfold as written. *The Secret Rapture* is of course a drama, but in addition to the usual dictates of characters fulfilling roles, we have Isobel's choice to enact a specific part leading towards a specific and predestined end. We can question, as with Jerry in Albee's *The Zoo Story,* whether or not Isobel has knowingly moved towards her own demise. The answer in Hare's play is that it can at least be said of Isobel that she does nothing to rewrite the script. The play opens with Isobel as a figure of goodness and she remains so throughout, significantly, while everything around her changes. She comes to a crossroads where she has the option to abandon her destiny, yet she chooses to follow the path laid out for her by some Divine Playwright, ostensibly her father. It is her devotion to her role and her refusal to accommodate her own worldly needs that entitle Isobel to the status of saint.

Source: Liorah Anne Golomb, ''Saint Isobel: David Hare's *The Secret Rapture* as Christian Allegory,'' in *Modern Drama,* Vol. XXXIII, No. 4, December 1990, pp. 563–74.

SOURCES

Aristotle, *Poetics* (c. 335 B.C.), translated by S. H. Butcher, in *Dramatic Theory and Criticism: Greeks to Gratowski,* edited by Bernard F. Dukore, Holt, Rinehart and Winston, pp. 31–55, originally published by Hill and Wang, 1961.

Bloom, Michael, Interview with David Hare, in *American Theatre,* November 1989, p. 33.

Brustein, Robert, Review of *The Secret Rapture,* in *New Republic,* November 20, 1989, pp. 29–30.

Busby, Anne, Interview with David Hare, in the original program for *The Secret Rapture,* Royal National Theatre of Great Britain, 1988.

Crew, Robert, ''Interview with David Hare,'' in *File on Hare,* compiled by Malcolm Page, Methuen Drama, 1990, p. 75, originally published in the *Toronto Star,* February 11, 1989, Sec. F, p. 3.

Golomb, Liorah Anne, ''Saint Isobel: David Hare's *The Secret Rapture* as Christian Allegory,'' in *Modern Drama,* Vol. 33, No. 4, December 1990, pp. 563–74.

Hare, David, ''Love, Death and Edwina,'' in *File on Hare,* compiled by Malcom Page, Methuen Drama, 1990, p. 75, originally published in *Listener,* September 15, 1988, p. 38.

Kramer, Mimi, Review of *The Secret Rapture,* in *New Yorker,* November 13, 1989, p. 111.

Krutch, Joseph Wood, ''The Tragic Fallacy,'' in *Dramatic Theory and Criticism: Greeks to Gratowski,* edited by Bernard F. Dukore, Holt, Rinehart and Winston, Inc., pp. 868–80, originally published in *The Modern Temper,* Harcourt Brace Jovanovich, 1929.

Miller, Arthur, ''Tragedy and the Common Man,'' in *Dramatic Theory and Criticism: Greeks to Gratowski,* edited by Bernard F. Dukore, Holt, Rinehart and Winston, Inc., pp. 894–97, originally published in *New York Times,* February 27, 1949.

Peter, John, Review of *The Secret Rapture,* in *File on Hare,* compiled by Malcom Page, Methuen Drama, 1990, p. 77, originally published in *Sunday Times,* October 9, 1988, sec. C, p. 8.

Ratcliffe, Michael, Review of *The Secret Rapture,* in *File on Hare,* compiled by Malcom Page, Methuen Drama, 1990, p. 77, originally published in *Observer,* October 9, 1988, p. 43.

Rich, Frank, Review of *The Secret Rapture,* in *New York Times,* October 27, 1989, p. C-3.

Taylor, John Russell, Review of *The Secret Rapture,* in *File on Hare,* compiled by Malcom Page, Methuen Drama, 1990, p. 75, originally published in *Plays International,* November 1988, p. 23–24.

A scene from a 1988 production of The Secret Rapture, *performed at Lyttelton Theatre in London*

Turner, John, Review of *The Secret Rapture,* in *Times Literary Supplement,* October 14, 1988, p. 1148.

Weales, Gerald, Review of *The Secret Rapture,* in *Commonweal,* December 1989, pp. 671–72.

Wolf, Matt, Review of *The Secret Rapture,* in *Wall Street Journal, European Edition,* October 21–22, 1988, p. 12.

———, "Thanks a Lot, Mrs. Thatcher," in *American Theatre,* January 1989, p. 50.

FURTHER READING

Eyre, Richard, *Utopia and Other Places,* Bloomsbury Publishing Ltd., 1993.

Richard Eyre was the artistic director of Britain's Royal National Theatre from 1988 to 1997. He directed several of Hare's plays at the National during that time. This autobiographical collection of essays includes Eyre's thoughts on actors and the theatre, British politics, and the importance of social class in England.

Homden, Carol, *The Plays of David Hare,* Cambridge University Press, 1995.

This analysis of selected plays and films by David Hare, including his trilogy *Racing Demon* (1990), *Murmuring Judges* (1991), and *The Absence of War* (1992), suggests that Hare is one of the leading playwrights of Britain's post-World War II generation.

Kerensky, Oleg, *The New British Drama: Fourteen Playwrights since Osborne and Pinter,* Taplinger Publishing Company, 1977.

This book is a survey of Britain's emerging new playwrights in the late 1960s and 1970s, including David Hare, Howard Barker, Edward Bond, Howard Brenton, Peter Shaffer, Tom Stoppard, and others.

Oliva, Judy Lee, *David Hare: Theatricalizing Politics,* ProQuest UMI, 1990.

This comprehensive analysis of more than twenty of Hare's plays, television scripts, and films pays special attention to how the playwright's selection of content and style create a critique of politics and British society.

Page, Malcolm, comp., *File on Hare,* Methuen Drama, 1990.

This collection of excerpted criticism of Hare's plays, taken largely from theatre reviews in London and New York newspapers and magazines, also includes a chronology of Hare's work.

Zeifman, Hersh, ed., *David Hare: A Casebook,* Garland Publishing, 1994.

This collection of essays about Hare's most important plays is accompanied by a chronology of his work and a bibliography of Hare interviews and criticism.

Glossary of Literary Terms

A

Abstract: Used as a noun, the term refers to a short summary or outline of a longer work. As an adjective applied to writing or literary works, abstract refers to words or phrases that name things not knowable through the five senses. Examples of abstracts include the *Cliffs Notes* summaries of major literary works. Examples of abstract terms or concepts include ''idea,'' ''guilt'' ''honesty,'' and ''loyalty.''

Absurd, Theater of the: See *Theater of the Absurd*

Absurdism: See *Theater of the Absurd*

Act: A major section of a play. Acts are divided into varying numbers of shorter scenes. From ancient times to the nineteenth century plays were generally constructed of five acts, but modern works typically consist of one, two, or three acts. Examples of five-act plays include the works of Sophocles and Shakespeare, while the plays of Arthur Miller commonly have a three-act structure.

Acto: A one-act Chicano theater piece developed out of collective improvisation. *Actos* were performed by members of Luis Valdez's Teatro Campesino in California during the mid-1960s.

Aestheticism: A literary and artistic movement of the nineteenth century. Followers of the movement believed that art should not be mixed with social, political, or moral teaching. The statement ''art for art's sake'' is a good summary of aestheticism. The movement had its roots in France, but it gained widespread importance in England in the last half of the nineteenth century, where it helped change the Victorian practice of including moral lessons in literature. Oscar Wilde is one of the best-known ''aesthetes'' of the late nineteenth century.

Age of Johnson: The period in English literature between 1750 and 1798, named after the most prominent literary figure of the age, Samuel Johnson. Works written during this time are noted for their emphasis on ''sensibility,'' or emotional quality. These works formed a transition between the rational works of the Age of Reason, or Neoclassical period, and the emphasis on individual feelings and responses of the Romantic period. Significant writers during the Age of Johnson included the novelists Ann Radcliffe and Henry Mackenzie, dramatists Richard Sheridan and Oliver Goldsmith, and poets William Collins and Thomas Gray. Also known as Age of Sensibility

Age of Reason: See *Neoclassicism*

Age of Sensibility: See *Age of Johnson*

Alexandrine Meter: See *Meter*

Allegory: A narrative technique in which characters representing things or abstract ideas are used to convey a message or teach a lesson. Allegory is typically used to teach moral, ethical, or religious lessons but is sometimes used for satiric or political purposes. Examples of allegorical works include Edmund Spenser's *The Faerie Queene* and John Bunyan's *The Pilgrim's Progress.*

Allusion: A reference to a familiar literary or historical person or event, used to make an idea more easily understood. For example, describing someone as a ''Romeo'' makes an allusion to William Shakespeare's famous young lover in *Romeo and Juliet.*

Amerind Literature: The writing and oral traditions of Native Americans. Native American literature was originally passed on by word of mouth, so it consisted largely of stories and events that were easily memorized. Amerind prose is often rhythmic like poetry because it was recited to the beat of a ceremonial drum. Examples of Amerind literature include the autobiographical *Black Elk Speaks,* the works of N. Scott Momaday, James Welch, and Craig Lee Strete, and the poetry of Luci Tapahonso.

Analogy: A comparison of two things made to explain something unfamiliar through its similarities to something familiar, or to prove one point based on the acceptedness of another. Similes and metaphors are types of analogies. Analogies often take the form of an extended simile, as in William Blake's aphorism: ''As the caterpillar chooses the fairest leaves to lay her eggs on, so the priest lays his curse on the fairest joys.''

Angry Young Men: A group of British writers of the 1950s whose work expressed bitterness and disillusionment with society. Common to their work is an anti-hero who rebels against a corrupt social order and strives for personal integrity. The term has been used to describe Kingsley Amis, John Osborne, Colin Wilson, John Wain, and others.

Antagonist: The major character in a narrative or drama who works against the hero or protagonist. An example of an evil antagonist is Richard Lovelace in Samuel Richardson's *Clarissa,* while a virtuous antagonist is Macduff in William Shakespeare's *Macbeth.*

Anthropomorphism: The presentation of animals or objects in human shape or with human characteristics. The term is derived from the Greek word for ''human form.'' The fables of Aesop, the animated films of Walt Disney, and Richard Adams's *Watership Down* feature anthropomorphic characters.

Anti-hero: A central character in a work of literature who lacks traditional heroic qualities such as courage, physical prowess, and fortitude. Anti-heros typically distrust conventional values and are unable to commit themselves to any ideals. They generally feel helpless in a world over which they have no control. Anti-heroes usually accept, and often celebrate, their positions as social outcasts. A well-known anti-hero is Yossarian in Joseph Heller's novel *Catch-22.*

Antimasque: See *Masque*

Antithesis: The antithesis of something is its direct opposite. In literature, the use of antithesis as a figure of speech results in two statements that show a contrast through the balancing of two opposite ideas. Technically, it is the second portion of the statement that is defined as the ''antithesis''; the first portion is the ''thesis.'' An example of antithesis is found in the following portion of Abraham Lincoln's ''Gettysburg Address''; notice the opposition between the verbs ''remember'' and ''forget'' and the phrases ''what we say'' and ''what they did'': ''The world will little note nor long remember what we say here, but it can never forget what they did here.''

Apocrypha: Writings tentatively attributed to an author but not proven or universally accepted to be their works. The term was originally applied to certain books of the Bible that were not considered inspired and so were not included in the ''sacred canon.'' Geoffrey Chaucer, William Shakespeare, Thomas Kyd, Thomas Middleton, and John Marston all have apocrypha. Apocryphal books of the Bible include the Old Testament's Book of Enoch and New Testament's Gospel of Peter.

Apollonian and Dionysian: The two impulses believed to guide authors of dramatic tragedy. The Apollonian impulse is named after Apollo, the Greek god of light and beauty and the symbol of intellectual order. The Dionysian impulse is named after Dionysus, the Greek god of wine and the symbol of the unrestrained forces of nature. The Apollonian impulse is to create a rational, harmonious world, while the Dionysian is to express the irrational forces of personality. Friedrich Nietzche uses these terms in *The Birth of Tragedy* to designate contrasting elements in Greek tragedy.

Apostrophe: A statement, question, or request addressed to an inanimate object or concept or to a nonexistent or absent person. Requests for inspiration from the muses in poetry are examples of apostrophe, as is Marc Antony's address to Caesar's corpse in William Shakespeare's *Julius Caesar*: ''O, pardon me, thou bleeding piece of earth, That I am meek and gentle with these butchers!. . . Woe to the hand that shed this costly blood!. . . ''

Archetype: The word archetype is commonly used to describe an original pattern or model from which all other things of the same kind are made. This term was introduced to literary criticism from the psychology of Carl Jung. It expresses Jung's theory that behind every person's ''unconscious,'' or repressed memories of the past, lies the ''collective unconscious'' of the human race: memories of the countless typical experiences of our ancestors. These memories are said to prompt illogical associations that trigger powerful emotions in the reader. Often, the emotional process is primitive, even primordial. Archetypes are the literary images that grow out of the ''collective unconscious.'' They appear in literature as incidents and plots that repeat basic patterns of life. They may also appear as stereotyped characters. Examples of literary archetypes include themes such as birth and death and characters such as the Earth Mother.

Argument: The argument of a work is the author's subject matter or principal idea. Examples of defined ''argument'' portions of works include John Milton's *Arguments* to each of the books of *Paradise Lost* and the ''Argument'' to Robert Herrick's *Hesperides.*

Aristotelian Criticism: Specifically, the method of evaluating and analyzing tragedy formulated by the Greek philosopher Aristotle in his *Poetics.* More generally, the term indicates any form of criticism that follows Aristotle's views. Aristotelian criticism focuses on the form and logical structure of a work, apart from its historical or social context, in contrast to ''Platonic Criticism,'' which stresses the usefulness of art. Adherents of New Criticism including John Crowe Ransom and Cleanth Brooks utilize and value the basic ideas of Aristotelian criticism for textual analysis.

Art for Art's Sake: See *Aestheticism*

Aside: A comment made by a stage performer that is intended to be heard by the audience but supposedly not by other characters. Eugene O'Neill's *Strange Interlude* is an extended use of the aside in modern theater.

Audience: The people for whom a piece of literature is written. Authors usually write with a certain audience in mind, for example, children, members of a religious or ethnic group, or colleagues in a professional field. The term ''audience'' also applies to the people who gather to see or hear any performance, including plays, poetry readings, speeches, and concerts. Jane Austen's parody of the gothic novel, *Northanger Abbey,* was originally intended for (and also pokes fun at) an audience of young and avid female gothic novel readers.

Avant-garde: A French term meaning ''vanguard.'' It is used in literary criticism to describe new writing that rejects traditional approaches to literature in favor of innovations in style or content. Twentieth-century examples of the literary *avant-garde* include the Black Mountain School of poets, the Bloomsbury Group, and the Beat Movement.

B

Ballad: A short poem that tells a simple story and has a repeated refrain. Ballads were originally intended to be sung. Early ballads, known as folk ballads, were passed down through generations, so their authors are often unknown. Later ballads composed by known authors are called literary ballads. An example of an anonymous folk ballad is ''Edward,'' which dates from the Middle Ages. Samuel Taylor Coleridge's ''The Rime of the Ancient Mariner'' and John Keats's ''La Belle Dame sans Merci'' are examples of literary ballads.

Baroque: A term used in literary criticism to describe literature that is complex or ornate in style or diction. Baroque works typically express tension, anxiety, and violent emotion. The term ''Baroque Age'' designates a period in Western European literature beginning in the late sixteenth century and ending about one hundred years later. Works of this period often mirror the qualities of works more generally associated with the label ''baroque'' and sometimes feature elaborate conceits. Examples of Baroque works include John Lyly's *Euphues: The Anatomy of Wit,* Luis de Gongora's *Soledads,* and William Shakespeare's *As You Like It.*

Baroque Age: See *Baroque*

Baroque Period: See *Baroque*

Beat Generation: See *Beat Movement*

Beat Movement: A period featuring a group of American poets and novelists of the 1950s and 1960s—including Jack Kerouac, Allen Ginsberg, Gregory Corso, William S. Burroughs, and Lawrence Ferlinghetti—who rejected established social and literary values. Using such techniques as stream of consciousness writing and jazz-influenced free verse and focusing on unusual or abnormal states of mind—generated by religious ecstasy or the use of drugs—the Beat writers aimed to create works that were unconventional in both form and subject matter. Kerouac's *On the Road* is perhaps the best-known example of a Beat Generation novel, and Ginsberg's *Howl* is a famous collection of Beat poetry.

Black Aesthetic Movement: A period of artistic and literary development among African Americans in the 1960s and early 1970s. This was the first major African-American artistic movement since the Harlem Renaissance and was closely paralleled by the civil rights and black power movements. The black aesthetic writers attempted to produce works of art that would be meaningful to the black masses. Key figures in black aesthetics included one of its founders, poet and playwright Amiri Baraka, formerly known as LeRoi Jones; poet and essayist Haki R. Madhubuti, formerly Don L. Lee; poet and playwright Sonia Sanchez; and dramatist Ed Bullins. Works representative of the Black Aesthetic Movement include Amiri Baraka's play *Dutchman,* a 1964 Obie award-winner; *Black Fire: An Anthology of Afro-American Writing,* edited by Baraka and playwright Larry Neal and published in 1968; and Sonia Sanchez's poetry collection *We a BaddDDD People,* published in 1970. Also known as Black Arts Movement.

Black Arts Movement: See *Black Aesthetic Movement*

Black Comedy: See *Black Humor*

Black Humor: Writing that places grotesque elements side by side with humorous ones in an attempt to shock the reader, forcing him or her to laugh at the horrifying reality of a disordered world. Joseph Heller's novel *Catch-22* is considered a superb example of the use of black humor. Other well-known authors who use black humor include Kurt Vonnegut, Edward Albee, Eugene Ionesco, and Harold Pinter. Also known as Black Comedy.

Blank Verse: Loosely, any unrhymed poetry, but more generally, unrhymed iambic pentameter verse (composed of lines of five two-syllable feet with the first syllable accented, the second unaccented). Blank verse has been used by poets since the Renaissance for its flexibility and its graceful, dignified tone. John Milton's *Paradise Lost* is in blank verse, as are most of William Shakespeare's plays.

Bloomsbury Group: A group of English writers, artists, and intellectuals who held informal artistic and philosophical discussions in Bloomsbury, a district of London, from around 1907 to the early 1930s. The Bloomsbury Group held no uniform philosophical beliefs but did commonly express an aversion to moral prudery and a desire for greater social tolerance. At various times the circle included Virginia Woolf, E. M. Forster, Clive Bell, Lytton Strachey, and John Maynard Keynes.

Bon Mot: A French term meaning ''good word.'' A *bon mot* is a witty remark or clever observation. Charles Lamb and Oscar Wilde are celebrated for their witty *bon mots.* Two examples by Oscar Wilde stand out: (1) ''All women become their mothers. That is their tragedy. No man does. That's his.'' (2) ''A man cannot be too careful in the choice of his enemies.''

Breath Verse: See *Projective Verse*

Burlesque: Any literary work that uses exaggeration to make its subject appear ridiculous, either by treating a trivial subject with profound seriousness or by treating a dignified subject frivolously. The word ''burlesque'' may also be used as an adjective, as in ''burlesque show,'' to mean ''striptease act.'' Examples of literary burlesque include the comedies of Aristophanes, Miguel de Cervantes's *Don Quixote,*, Samuel Butler's poem ''Hudibras,'' and John Gay's play *The Beggar's Opera.*

C

Cadence: The natural rhythm of language caused by the alternation of accented and unaccented syllables. Much modern poetry—notably free verse—deliberately manipulates cadence to create complex rhythmic effects. James Macpherson's ''Ossian poems'' are richly cadenced, as is the poetry of the Symbolists, Walt Whitman, and Amy Lowell.

Caesura: A pause in a line of poetry, usually occurring near the middle. It typically corresponds to a break in the natural rhythm or sense of the line but is sometimes shifted to create special meanings or rhythmic effects. The opening line of Edgar Allan Poe's ''The Raven'' contains a caesura following ''dreary'': ''Once upon a midnight dreary, while I pondered weak and weary. . . . ''

Canzone: A short Italian or Provencal lyric poem, commonly about love and often set to music. The *canzone* has no set form but typically contains five or six stanzas made up of seven to twenty lines of eleven syllables each. A shorter, five- to ten-line ''envoy,'' or concluding stanza, completes the poem.

Masters of the *canzone* form include Petrarch, Dante Alighieri, Torquato Tasso, and Guido Cavalcanti.

Carpe Diem: A Latin term meaning "seize the day." This is a traditional theme of poetry, especially lyrics. A *carpe diem* poem advises the reader or the person it addresses to live for today and enjoy the pleasures of the moment. Two celebrated *carpe diem* poems are Andrew Marvell's "To His Coy Mistress" and Robert Herrick's poem beginning "Gather ye rosebuds while ye may. . . . "

Catharsis: The release or purging of unwanted emotions— specifically fear and pity—brought about by exposure to art. The term was first used by the Greek philosopher Aristotle in his *Poetics* to refer to the desired effect of tragedy on spectators. A famous example of catharsis is realized in Sophocles' *Oedipus Rex,* when Oedipus discovers that his wife, Jacosta, is his own mother and that the stranger he killed on the road was his own father.

Celtic Renaissance: A period of Irish literary and cultural history at the end of the nineteenth century. Followers of the movement aimed to create a romantic vision of Celtic myth and legend. The most significant works of the Celtic Renaissance typically present a dreamy, unreal world, usually in reaction against the reality of contemporary problems. William Butler Yeats's *The Wanderings of Oisin* is among the most significant works of the Celtic Renaissance. Also known as Celtic Twilight.

Celtic Twilight: See *Celtic Renaissance*

Character: Broadly speaking, a person in a literary work. The actions of characters are what constitute the plot of a story, novel, or poem. There are numerous types of characters, ranging from simple, stereotypical figures to intricate, multifaceted ones. In the techniques of anthropomorphism and personification, animals—and even places or things—can assume aspects of character. "Characterization" is the process by which an author creates vivid, believable characters in a work of art. This may be done in a variety of ways, including (1) direct description of the character by the narrator; (2) the direct presentation of the speech, thoughts, or actions of the character; and (3) the responses of other characters to the character. The term "character" also refers to a form originated by the ancient Greek writer Theophrastus that later became popular in the seventeenth and eighteenth centuries. It is a short essay or sketch of a person who prominently displays a specific attribute or quality, such as miserliness or ambition. Notable characters in literature include Oedipus Rex, Don Quixote de la Mancha, Macbeth, Candide, Hester Prynne, Ebenezer Scrooge, Huckleberry Finn, Jay Gatsby, Scarlett O'Hara, James Bond, and Kunta Kinte.

Characterization: See *Character*

Chorus: In ancient Greek drama, a group of actors who commented on and interpreted the unfolding action on the stage. Initially the chorus was a major component of the presentation, but over time it became less significant, with its numbers reduced and its role eventually limited to commentary between acts. By the sixteenth century the chorus—if employed at all—was typically a single person who provided a prologue and an epilogue and occasionally appeared between acts to introduce or underscore an important event. The chorus in William Shakespeare's *Henry V* functions in this way. Modern dramas rarely feature a chorus, but T. S. Eliot's *Murder in the Cathedral* and Arthur Miller's *A View from the Bridge* are notable exceptions. The Stage Manager in Thornton Wilder's *Our Town* performs a role similar to that of the chorus.

Chronicle: A record of events presented in chronological order. Although the scope and level of detail provided varies greatly among the chronicles surviving from ancient times, some, such as the *Anglo-Saxon Chronicle,* feature vivid descriptions and a lively recounting of events. During the Elizabethan Age, many dramas— appropriately called "chronicle plays"—were based on material from chronicles. Many of William Shakespeare's dramas of English history as well as Christopher Marlowe's *Edward II* are based in part on Raphael Holinshead's *Chronicles of England, Scotland, and Ireland.*

Classical: In its strictest definition in literary criticism, classicism refers to works of ancient Greek or Roman literature. The term may also be used to describe a literary work of recognized importance (a "classic") from any time period or literature that exhibits the traits of classicism. Classical authors from ancient Greek and Roman times include Juvenal and Homer. Examples of later works and authors now described as classical include French literature of the seventeenth century, Western novels of the nineteenth century, and American fiction of the mid-nineteenth century such as that written by James Fenimore Cooper and Mark Twain.

Classicism: A term used in literary criticism to describe critical doctrines that have their roots in ancient Greek and Roman literature, philosophy, and art. Works associated with classicism typically exhibit restraint on the part of the author, unity of design and purpose, clarity, simplicity, logical organization, and respect for tradition. Examples of literary classicism include Cicero's prose, the dramas of Pierre Corneille and Jean Racine, the poetry of John Dryden and Alexander Pope, and the writings of J. W. von Goethe, G. E. Lessing, and T. S. Eliot.

Climax: The turning point in a narrative, the moment when the conflict is at its most intense. Typically, the structure of stories, novels, and plays is one of rising action, in which tension builds to the climax, followed by falling action, in which tension lessens as the story moves to its conclusion. The climax in James Fenimore Cooper's *The Last of the Mohicans* occurs when Magua and his captive Cora are pursued to the edge of a cliff by Uncas. Magua kills Uncas but is subsequently killed by Hawkeye.

Colloquialism: A word, phrase, or form of pronunciation that is acceptable in casual conversation but not in formal, written communication. It is considered more acceptable than slang. An example of colloquialism can be found in Rudyard Kipling's *Barrack-room Ballads:* When 'Omer smote 'is bloomin' lyre He'd 'eard men sing by land and sea; An' what he thought 'e might require 'E went an' took—the same as me!

Comedy: One of two major types of drama, the other being tragedy. Its aim is to amuse, and it typically ends happily. Comedy assumes many forms, such as farce and burlesque, and uses a variety of techniques, from parody to satire. In a restricted sense the term comedy refers only to dramatic presentations, but in general usage it is commonly applied to nondramatic works as well. Examples of comedies range from the plays of Aristophanes, Terrence, and Plautus, Dante Alighieri's *The Divine Comedy,* Francois Rabelais's *Pantagruel* and *Gargantua,* and some of Geoffrey Chaucer's tales and William Shakespeare's plays to Noel Coward's play *Private Lives* and James Thurber's short story "The Secret Life of Walter Mitty."

Comedy of Manners: A play about the manners and conventions of an aristocratic, highly sophisticated society. The characters are usually types rather than individualized personalities, and plot is less important than atmosphere. Such plays were an important aspect of late seventeenth-century English comedy. The comedy of manners was revived in the eighteenth century by Oliver Goldsmith and Richard Brinsley Sheridan, enjoyed a second revival in the late nineteenth century, and has endured into the twentieth century. Examples of comedies of manners include William Congreve's *The Way of the World* in the late seventeenth century, Oliver Goldsmith's *She Stoops to Conquer* and Richard Brinsley Sheridan's *The School for Scandal* in the eighteenth century, Oscar Wilde's *The Importance of Being Earnest* in the nineteenth century, and W. Somerset Maugham's *The Circle* in the twentieth century.

Comic Relief: The use of humor to lighten the mood of a serious or tragic story, especially in plays. The technique is very common in Elizabethan works, and can be an integral part of the plot or simply a brief event designed to break the tension of the scene. The Gravediggers' scene in William Shakespeare's *Hamlet* is a frequently cited example of comic relief.

Commedia dell'arte: An Italian term meaning "the comedy of guilds" or "the comedy of professional actors." This form of dramatic comedy was popular in Italy during the sixteenth century. Actors were assigned stock roles (such as Pulcinella, the stupid servant, or Pantalone, the old merchant) and given a basic plot to follow, but all dialogue was improvised. The roles were rigidly typed and the plots were formulaic, usually revolving around young lovers who thwarted their elders and attained wealth and happiness. A rigid convention of the *commedia dell'arte* is the periodic intrusion of Harlequin, who interrupts the play with low buffoonery. Peppino de Filippo's *Metamorphoses of a Wandering Minstrel* gave modern audiences an idea of what *commedia dell'arte* may have been like. Various scenarios for *commedia dell'arte* were compiled in Petraccone's *La commedia dell'arte, storia, technica, scenari,* published in 1927.

Complaint: A lyric poem, popular in the Renaissance, in which the speaker expresses sorrow about his or her condition. Typically, the speaker's sadness is caused by an unresponsive lover, but some complaints cite other sources of unhappiness, such as poverty or fate. A commonly cited example is "A Complaint by Night of the Lover Not Beloved" by Henry Howard, Earl of Surrey. Thomas Sackville's "Complaint of Henry, Duke of Buckingham" traces the duke's unhappiness to his ruthless ambition.

Conceit: A clever and fanciful metaphor, usually expressed through elaborate and extended comparison, that presents a striking parallel between two seemingly dissimilar things—for example, elaborately comparing a beautiful woman to an object like a garden or the sun. The conceit was a popular device throughout the Elizabethan Age and Baroque Age and was the principal technique of the seventeenth-century English metaphysical poets. This usage of the word conceit is unrelated to the best-known definition of conceit as an arrogant attitude or behavior. The conceit figures prominently in the works of John Donne, Emily Dickinson, and T. S. Eliot.

Concrete: Concrete is the opposite of abstract, and refers to a thing that actually exists or a description that allows the reader to experience an object or concept with the senses. Henry David Thoreau's *Walden* contains much concrete description of nature and wildlife.

Concrete Poetry: Poetry in which visual elements play a large part in the poetic effect. Punctuation marks, letters, or words are arranged on a page to form a visual design: a cross, for example, or a bumblebee. Max Bill and Eugene Gomringer were among the early practitioners of concrete poetry; Haroldo de Campos and Augusto de Campos are among contemporary authors of concrete poetry.

Confessional Poetry: A form of poetry in which the poet reveals very personal, intimate, sometimes shocking information about himself or herself. Anne Sexton, Sylvia Plath, Robert Lowell, and John Berryman wrote poetry in the confessional vein.

Conflict: The conflict in a work of fiction is the issue to be resolved in the story. It usually occurs between two characters, the protagonist and the antagonist, or between the protagonist and society or the protagonist and himself or herself. Conflict in Theodore Dreiser's novel *Sister Carrie* comes as a result of urban society, while Jack London's short story ''To Build a Fire'' concerns the protagonist's battle against the cold and himself.

Connotation: The impression that a word gives beyond its defined meaning. Connotations may be universally understood or may be significant only to a certain group. Both ''horse'' and ''steed'' denote the same animal, but ''steed'' has a different connotation, deriving from the chivalrous or romantic narratives in which the word was once often used.

Consonance: Consonance occurs in poetry when words appearing at the ends of two or more verses have similar final consonant sounds but have final vowel sounds that differ, as with ''stuff'' and ''off.'' Consonance is found in ''The curfew tolls the knells of parting day'' from Thomas Grey's ''An Elegy Written in a Country Church Yard.'' Also known as Half Rhyme or Slant Rhyme.

Convention: Any widely accepted literary device, style, or form. A soliloquy, in which a character reveals to the audience his or her private thoughts, is an example of a dramatic convention.

Corrido: A Mexican ballad. Examples of *corridos* include ''Muerte del afamado Bilito,'' ''La voz de mi conciencia,'' ''Lucio Perez,'' ''La juida,'' and ''Los presos.''

Couplet: Two lines of poetry with the same rhyme and meter, often expressing a complete and self-contained thought. The following couplet is from Alexander Pope's ''Elegy to the Memory of an Unfortunate Lady'': 'Tis Use alone that sanctifies Expense, And Splendour borrows all her rays from Sense.

Criticism: The systematic study and evaluation of literary works, usually based on a specific method or set of principles. An important part of literary studies since ancient times, the practice of criticism has given rise to numerous theories, methods, and ''schools,'' sometimes producing conflicting, even contradictory, interpretations of literature in general as well as of individual works. Even such basic issues as what constitutes a poem or a novel have been the subject of much criticism over the centuries. Seminal texts of literary criticism include Plato's *Republic,* Aristotle's *Poetics,* Sir Philip Sidney's *The Defence of Poesie,* John Dryden's *Of Dramatic Poesie,* and William Wordsworth's ''Preface'' to the second edition of his *Lyrical Ballads.* Contemporary schools of criticism include deconstruction, feminist, psychoanalytic, poststructuralist, new historicist, postcolonialist, and reader-response.

D

Dactyl: See *Foot*

Dadaism: A protest movement in art and literature founded by Tristan Tzara in 1916. Followers of the movement expressed their outrage at the destruction brought about by World War I by revolting against numerous forms of social convention. The Dadaists presented works marked by calculated madness and flamboyant nonsense. They stressed total freedom of expression, commonly through primitive displays of emotion and illogical, often senseless, poetry. The movement ended shortly after the war, when it was replaced by surrealism. Proponents of Dadaism include Andre Breton, Louis Aragon, Philippe Soupault, and Paul Eluard.

Decadent: See *Decadents*

Decadents: The followers of a nineteenth-century literary movement that had its beginnings in French aestheticism. Decadent literature displays a fascination with perverse and morbid states; a search for novelty and sensation—the "new thrill"; a preoccupation with mysticism; and a belief in the senselessness of human existence. The movement is closely associated with the doctrine Art for Art's Sake. The term "decadence" is sometimes used to denote a decline in the quality of art or literature following a period of greatness. Major French decadents are Charles Baudelaire and Arthur Rimbaud. English decadents include Oscar Wilde, Ernest Dowson, and Frank Harris.

Deconstruction: A method of literary criticism developed by Jacques Derrida and characterized by multiple conflicting interpretations of a given work. Deconstructionists consider the impact of the language of a work and suggest that the true meaning of the work is not necessarily the meaning that the author intended. Jacques Derrida's *De la grammatologie* is the seminal text on deconstructive strategies; among American practitioners of this method of criticism are Paul de Man and J. Hillis Miller.

Deduction: The process of reaching a conclusion through reasoning from general premises to a specific premise. An example of deduction is present in the following syllogism: Premise: All mammals are animals. Premise: All whales are mammals. Conclusion: Therefore, all whales are animals.

Denotation: The definition of a word, apart from the impressions or feelings it creates in the reader. The word "apartheid" denotes a political and economic policy of segregation by race, but its connotations— oppression, slavery, inequality—are numerous.

Denouement: A French word meaning "the unknotting." In literary criticism, it denotes the resolution of conflict in fiction or drama. The *denouement* follows the climax and provides an outcome to the primary plot situation as well as an explanation of secondary plot complications. The *denouement* often involves a character's recognition of his or her state of mind or moral condition. A well-known example of *denouement* is the last scene of the play *As You Like It* by William Shakespeare, in which couples are married, an evildoer repents, the identities of two disguised characters are revealed, and a ruler is restored to power. Also known as Falling Action.

Description: Descriptive writing is intended to allow a reader to picture the scene or setting in which the action of a story takes place. The form this description takes often evokes an intended emotional response—a dark, spooky graveyard will evoke fear, and a peaceful, sunny meadow will evoke calmness. An example of a descriptive story is Edgar Allan Poe's *Landor's Cottage,* which offers a detailed depiction of a New York country estate.

Detective Story: A narrative about the solution of a mystery or the identification of a criminal. The conventions of the detective story include the detective's scrupulous use of logic in solving the mystery; incompetent or ineffectual police; a suspect who appears guilty at first but is later proved innocent; and the detective's friend or confidant—often the narrator—whose slowness in interpreting clues emphasizes by contrast the detective's brilliance. Edgar Allan Poe's "Murders in the Rue Morgue" is commonly regarded as the earliest example of this type of story. With this work, Poe established many of the conventions of the detective story genre, which are still in practice. Other practitioners of this vast and extremely popular genre include Arthur Conan Doyle, Dashiell Hammett, and Agatha Christie.

Deus ex machina: A Latin term meaning "god out of a machine." In Greek drama, a god was often lowered onto the stage by a mechanism of some kind to rescue the hero or untangle the plot. By extension, the term refers to any artificial device or coincidence used to bring about a convenient and simple solution to a plot. This is a common device in melodramas and includes such fortunate circumstances as the sudden receipt of a legacy to save the family farm or a last-minute stay of execution. The *deus ex machina* invariably rewards the virtuous and punishes evildoers. Examples of *deus ex machina* include King Louis XIV in Jean-Baptiste Moliere's *Tartuffe* and Queen Victoria in *The Pirates of Penzance* by William Gilbert and Arthur Sullivan. Bertolt Brecht parodies the abuse of such devices in the conclusion of his *Threepenny Opera.*

Dialogue: In its widest sense, dialogue is simply conversation between people in a literary work; in its most restricted sense, it refers specifically to the speech of characters in a drama. As a specific literary genre, a "dialogue" is a composition in which characters debate an issue or idea. The Greek philosopher Plato frequently expounded his theories in the form of dialogues.

Diction: The selection and arrangement of words in a literary work. Either or both may vary depending on the desired effect. There are four general types of diction: ''formal,'' used in scholarly or lofty writing; ''informal,'' used in relaxed but educated conversation; ''colloquial,'' used in everyday speech; and ''slang,'' containing newly coined words and other terms not accepted in formal usage.

Didactic: A term used to describe works of literature that aim to teach some moral, religious, political, or practical lesson. Although didactic elements are often found in artistically pleasing works, the term ''didactic'' usually refers to literature in which the message is more important than the form. The term may also be used to criticize a work that the critic finds ''overly didactic,'' that is, heavy-handed in its delivery of a lesson. Examples of didactic literature include John Bunyan's *Pilgrim's Progress,* Alexander Pope's *Essay on Criticism,* Jean-Jacques Rousseau's *Emile,* and Elizabeth Inchbald's *Simple Story.*

Dimeter: See *Meter*

Dionysian: See *Apollonian and Dionysian*

Discordia concours: A Latin phrase meaning ''discord in harmony.'' The term was coined by the eighteenth-century English writer Samuel Johnson to describe ''a combination of dissimilar images or discovery of occult resemblances in things apparently unlike.'' Johnson created the expression by reversing a phrase by the Latin poet Horace. The metaphysical poetry of John Donne, Richard Crashaw, Abraham Cowley, George Herbert, and Edward Taylor among others, contains many examples of *discordia concours.* In Donne's ''A Valediction: Forbidding Mourning,'' the poet compares the union of himself with his lover to a draftsman's compass: If they be two, they are two so, As stiff twin compasses are two: Thy soul, the fixed foot, makes no show To move, but doth, if the other do; And though it in the center sit, Yet when the other far doth roam, It leans, and hearkens after it, And grows erect, as that comes home.

Dissonance: A combination of harsh or jarring sounds, especially in poetry. Although such combinations may be accidental, poets sometimes intentionally make them to achieve particular effects. Dissonance is also sometimes used to refer to close but not identical rhymes. When this is the case, the word functions as a synonym for consonance. Robert Browning, Gerard Manley Hopkins, and many other poets have made deliberate use of dissonance.

Doppelganger: A literary technique by which a character is duplicated (usually in the form of an alter ego, though sometimes as a ghostly counterpart) or divided into two distinct, usually opposite personalities. The use of this character device is widespread in nineteenth- and twentieth-century literature, and indicates a growing awareness among authors that the ''self'' is really a composite of many ''selves.'' A well-known story containing a *doppelganger* character is Robert Louis Stevenson's *Dr. Jekyll and Mr. Hyde,* which dramatizes an internal struggle between good and evil. Also known as The Double.

Double Entendre: A corruption of a French phrase meaning ''double meaning.'' The term is used to indicate a word or phrase that is deliberately ambiguous, especially when one of the meanings is risque or improper. An example of a *double entendre* is the Elizabethan usage of the verb ''die,'' which refers both to death and to orgasm.

Double, The: See *Doppelganger*

Draft: Any preliminary version of a written work. An author may write dozens of drafts which are revised to form the final work, or he or she may write only one, with few or no revisions. Dorothy Parker's observation that ''I can't write five words but that I change seven'' humorously indicates the purpose of the draft.

Drama: In its widest sense, a drama is any work designed to be presented by actors on a stage. Similarly, ''drama'' denotes a broad literary genre that includes a variety of forms, from pageant and spectacle to tragedy and comedy, as well as countless types and subtypes. More commonly in modern usage, however, a drama is a work that treats serious subjects and themes but does not aim at the grandeur of tragedy. This use of the term originated with the eighteenth-century French writer Denis Diderot, who used the word *drame* to designate his plays about middle-class life; thus ''drama'' typically features characters of a less exalted stature than those of tragedy. Examples of classical dramas include Menander's comedy *Dyscolus* and Sophocles' tragedy *Oedipus Rex.* Contemporary dramas include Eugene O'Neill's *The Iceman Cometh,* Lillian Hellman's *Little Foxes,* and August Wilson's *Ma Rainey's Black Bottom.*

Dramatic Irony: Occurs when the audience of a play or the reader of a work of literature knows something that a character in the work itself does not know. The irony is in the contrast between the intended meaning of the statements or actions of a character and the additional information understood by the audience. A celebrated example of dramatic irony is in Act V of William Shakespeare's *Romeo and Juliet,* where two young lovers meet their end as a result of a tragic misunderstanding. Here, the audience has full knowledge that Juliet's apparent ''death'' is merely temporary; she will regain her senses when the mysterious ''sleeping potion'' she has taken wears off. But Romeo, mistaking Juliet's drug-induced trance for true death, kills himself in grief. Upon awakening, Juliet discovers Romeo's corpse and, in despair, slays herself.

Dramatic Monologue: See *Monologue*

Dramatic Poetry: Any lyric work that employs elements of drama such as dialogue, conflict, or characterization, but excluding works that are intended for stage presentation. A monologue is a form of dramatic poetry.

Dramatis Personae: The characters in a work of literature, particularly a drama. The list of characters printed before the main text of a play or in the program is the *dramatis personae.*

Dream Allegory: See *Dream Vision*

Dream Vision: A literary convention, chiefly of the Middle Ages. In a dream vision a story is presented as a literal dream of the narrator. This device was commonly used to teach moral and religious lessons. Important works of this type are *The Divine Comedy* by Dante Alighieri, *Piers Plowman* by William Langland, and *The Pilgrim's Progress* by John Bunyan. Also known as Dream Allegory.

Dystopia: An imaginary place in a work of fiction where the characters lead dehumanized, fearful lives. Jack London's *The Iron Heel,* Yevgeny Zamyatin's *My,* Aldous Huxley's *Brave New World,* George Orwell's *Nineteen Eighty-four,* and Margaret Atwood's *Handmaid's Tale* portray versions of dystopia.

E

Eclogue: In classical literature, a poem featuring rural themes and structured as a dialogue among shepherds. Eclogues often took specific poetic forms, such as elegies or love poems. Some were written as the soliloquy of a shepherd. In later centuries, ''eclogue'' came to refer to any poem that was in the pastoral tradition or that had a dialogue or monologue structure. A classical example of an eclogue is Virgil's *Eclogues,* also known as *Bucolics.* Giovanni Boccaccio, Edmund Spenser, Andrew Marvell, Jonathan Swift, and Louis MacNeice also wrote eclogues.

Edwardian: Describes cultural conventions identified with the period of the reign of Edward VII of England (1901–1910). Writers of the Edwardian Age typically displayed a strong reaction against the propriety and conservatism of the Victorian Age. Their work often exhibits distrust of authority in religion, politics, and art and expresses strong doubts about the soundness of conventional values. Writers of this era include George Bernard Shaw, H. G. Wells, and Joseph Conrad.

Edwardian Age: See *Edwardian*

Electra Complex: A daughter's amorous obsession with her father. The term Electra complex comes from the plays of Euripides and Sophocles entitled *Electra,* in which the character Electra drives her brother Orestes to kill their mother and her lover in revenge for the murder of their father.

Elegy: A lyric poem that laments the death of a person or the eventual death of all people. In a conventional elegy, set in a classical world, the poet and subject are spoken of as shepherds. In modern criticism, the word elegy is often used to refer to a poem that is melancholy or mournfully contemplative. John Milton's ''Lycidas'' and Percy Bysshe Shelley's ''Adonais'' are two examples of this form.

Elizabethan Age: A period of great economic growth, religious controversy, and nationalism closely associated with the reign of Elizabeth I of England (1558–1603). The Elizabethan Age is considered a part of the general renaissance—that is, the flowering of arts and literature—that took place in Europe during the fourteenth through sixteenth centuries. The era is considered the golden age of English literature. The most important dramas in English and a great deal of lyric poetry were produced during this period, and modern English criticism began around this time. The notable authors of the period—Philip Sidney, Edmund Spenser, Christopher Marlowe, William Shakespeare, Ben Jonson, Francis Bacon, and John Donne—are among the best in all of English literature.

Elizabethan Drama: English comic and tragic plays produced during the Renaissance, or more narrowly, those plays written during the last years of and few years after Queen Elizabeth's reign. William Shakespeare is considered an Elizabethan dramatist in the broader sense, although most of his work was produced during the reign of James I. Examples of Elizabethan comedies include John

Lyly's *The Woman in the Moone,* Thomas Dekker's *The Roaring Girl, or, Moll Cut Purse,* and William Shakespeare's *Twelfth Night.* Examples of Elizabethan tragedies include William Shakespeare's *Antony and Cleopatra,* Thomas Kyd's *The Spanish Tragedy,* and John Webster's *The Tragedy of the Duchess of Malfi.*

Empathy: A sense of shared experience, including emotional and physical feelings, with someone or something other than oneself. Empathy is often used to describe the response of a reader to a literary character. An example of an empathic passage is William Shakespeare's description in his narrative poem *Venus and Adonis* of: the snail, whose tender horns being hit, Shrinks backward in his shelly cave with pain. Readers of Gerard Manley Hopkins's *The Windhover* may experience some of the physical sensations evoked in the description of the movement of the falcon.

English Sonnet: See *Sonnet*

Enjambment: The running over of the sense and structure of a line of verse or a couplet into the following verse or couplet. Andrew Marvell's "To His Coy Mistress" is structured as a series of enjambments, as in lines 11–12: "My vegetable love should grow/Vaster than empires and more slow."

Enlightenment, The: An eighteenth-century philosophical movement. It began in France but had a wide impact throughout Europe and America. Thinkers of the Enlightenment valued reason and believed that both the individual and society could achieve a state of perfection. Corresponding to this essentially humanist vision was a resistance to religious authority. Important figures of the Enlightenment were Denis Diderot and Voltaire in France, Edward Gibbon and David Hume in England, and Thomas Paine and Thomas Jefferson in the United States.

Epic: A long narrative poem about the adventures of a hero of great historic or legendary importance. The setting is vast and the action is often given cosmic significance through the intervention of supernatural forces such as gods, angels, or demons. Epics are typically written in a classical style of grand simplicity with elaborate metaphors and allusions that enhance the symbolic importance of a hero's adventures. Some well-known epics are Homer's *Iliad* and *Odyssey,* Virgil's *Aeneid,* and John Milton's *Paradise Lost.*

Epic Simile: See *Homeric Simile*

Epic Theater: A theory of theatrical presentation developed by twentieth-century German playwright Bertolt Brecht. Brecht created a type of drama that the audience could view with complete detachment. He used what he termed "alienation effects" to create an emotional distance between the audience and the action on stage. Among these effects are: short, self-contained scenes that keep the play from building to a cathartic climax; songs that comment on the action; and techniques of acting that prevent the actor from developing an emotional identity with his role. Besides the plays of Bertolt Brecht, other plays that utilize epic theater conventions include those of Georg Buchner, Frank Wedekind, Erwin Piscator, and Leopold Jessner.

Epigram: A saying that makes the speaker's point quickly and concisely. Samuel Taylor Coleridge wrote an epigram that neatly sums up the form: What is an Epigram? A Dwarfish whole, Its body brevity, and wit its soul.

Epilogue: A concluding statement or section of a literary work. In dramas, particularly those of the seventeenth and eighteenth centuries, the epilogue is a closing speech, often in verse, delivered by an actor at the end of a play and spoken directly to the audience. A famous epilogue is Puck's speech at the end of William Shakespeare's *A Midsummer Night's Dream.*

Epiphany: A sudden revelation of truth inspired by a seemingly trivial incident. The term was widely used by James Joyce in his critical writings, and the stories in Joyce's *Dubliners* are commonly called "epiphanies."

Episode: An incident that forms part of a story and is significantly related to it. Episodes may be either self-contained narratives or events that depend on a larger context for their sense and importance. Examples of episodes include the founding of Wilmington, Delaware in Charles Reade's *The Disinherited Heir* and the individual events comprising the picaresque novels and medieval romances.

Episodic Plot: See *Plot*

Epitaph: An inscription on a tomb or tombstone, or a verse written on the occasion of a person's death. Epitaphs may be serious or humorous. Dorothy Parker's epitaph reads, "I told you I was sick."

Epithalamion: A song or poem written to honor and commemorate a marriage ceremony. Famous examples include Edmund Spenser's

''Epithalamion'' and e. e. cummings's ''Epithalamion.'' Also spelled Epithalamium.

Epithalamium: See *Epithalamion*

Epithet: A word or phrase, often disparaging or abusive, that expresses a character trait of someone or something. ''The Napoleon of crime'' is an epithet applied to Professor Moriarty, arch-rival of Sherlock Holmes in Arthur Conan Doyle's series of detective stories.

Exempla: See *Exemplum*

Exemplum: A tale with a moral message. This form of literary sermonizing flourished during the Middle Ages, when *exempla* appeared in collections known as ''example-books.'' The works of Geoffrey Chaucer are full of *exempla.*

Existentialism: A predominantly twentieth-century philosophy concerned with the nature and perception of human existence. There are two major strains of existentialist thought: atheistic and Christian. Followers of atheistic existentialism believe that the individual is alone in a godless universe and that the basic human condition is one of suffering and loneliness. Nevertheless, because there are no fixed values, individuals can create their own characters—indeed, they can shape themselves—through the exercise of free will. The atheistic strain culminates in and is popularly associated with the works of Jean-Paul Sartre. The Christian existentialists, on the other hand, believe that only in God may people find freedom from life's anguish. The two strains hold certain beliefs in common: that existence cannot be fully understood or described through empirical effort; that anguish is a universal element of life; that individuals must bear responsibility for their actions; and that there is no common standard of behavior or perception for religious and ethical matters. Existentialist thought figures prominently in the works of such authors as Eugene Ionesco, Franz Kafka, Fyodor Dostoyevsky, Simone de Beauvoir, Samuel Beckett, and Albert Camus.

Expatriates: See *Expatriatism*

Expatriatism: The practice of leaving one's country to live for an extended period in another country. Literary expatriates include English poets Percy Bysshe Shelley and John Keats in Italy, Polish novelist Joseph Conrad in England, American writers Richard Wright, James Baldwin, Gertrude Stein, and Ernest Hemingway in France, and Trinidadian author Neil Bissondath in Canada.

Exposition: Writing intended to explain the nature of an idea, thing, or theme. Expository writing is often combined with description, narration, or argument. In dramatic writing, the exposition is the introductory material which presents the characters, setting, and tone of the play. An example of dramatic exposition occurs in many nineteenth-century drawing-room comedies in which the butler and the maid open the play with relevant talk about their master and mistress; in composition, exposition relays factual information, as in encyclopedia entries.

Expressionism: An indistinct literary term, originally used to describe an early twentieth-century school of German painting. The term applies to almost any mode of unconventional, highly subjective writing that distorts reality in some way. Advocates of Expressionism include dramatists George Kaiser, Ernst Toller, Luigi Pirandello, Federico Garcia Lorca, Eugene O'Neill, and Elmer Rice; poets George Heym, Ernst Stadler, August Stramm, Gottfried Benn, and Georg Trakl; and novelists Franz Kafka and James Joyce.

Extended Monologue: See *Monologue*

F

Fable: A prose or verse narrative intended to convey a moral. Animals or inanimate objects with human characteristics often serve as characters in fables. A famous fable is Aesop's ''The Tortoise and the Hare.''

Fairy Tales: Short narratives featuring mythical beings such as fairies, elves, and sprites. These tales originally belonged to the folklore of a particular nation or region, such as those collected in Germany by Jacob and Wilhelm Grimm. Two other celebrated writers of fairy tales are Hans Christian Andersen and Rudyard Kipling.

Falling Action: See *Denouement*

Fantasy: A literary form related to mythology and folklore. Fantasy literature is typically set in nonexistent realms and features supernatural beings. Notable examples of fantasy literature are *The Lord of the Rings* by J. R. R. Tolkien and the Gormenghast trilogy by Mervyn Peake.

Farce: A type of comedy characterized by broad humor, outlandish incidents, and often vulgar subject matter. Much of the ''comedy'' in film and television could more accurately be described as farce.

Feet: See *Foot*

Feminine Rhyme: See *Rhyme*

Femme fatale: A French phrase with the literal translation "fatal woman." A *femme fatale* is a sensuous, alluring woman who often leads men into danger or trouble. A classic example of the *femme fatale* is the nameless character in Billy Wilder's *The Seven Year Itch,* portrayed by Marilyn Monroe in the film adaptation.

Fiction: Any story that is the product of imagination rather than a documentation of fact. characters and events in such narratives may be based in real life but their ultimate form and configuration is a creation of the author. Geoffrey Chaucer's *The Canterbury Tales,* Laurence Sterne's *Tristram Shandy,* and Margaret Mitchell's *Gone with the Wind* are examples of fiction.

Figurative Language: A technique in writing in which the author temporarily interrupts the order, construction, or meaning of the writing for a particular effect. This interruption takes the form of one or more figures of speech such as hyperbole, irony, or simile. Figurative language is the opposite of literal language, in which every word is truthful, accurate, and free of exaggeration or embellishment. Examples of figurative language are tropes such as metaphor and rhetorical figures such as apostrophe.

Figures of Speech: Writing that differs from customary conventions for construction, meaning, order, or significance for the purpose of a special meaning or effect. There are two major types of figures of speech: rhetorical figures, which do not make changes in the meaning of the words, and tropes, which do. Types of figures of speech include simile, hyperbole, alliteration, and pun, among many others.

Fin de siecle: A French term meaning "end of the century." The term is used to denote the last decade of the nineteenth century, a transition period when writers and other artists abandoned old conventions and looked for new techniques and objectives. Two writers commonly associated with the *fin de siecle* mindset are Oscar Wilde and George Bernard Shaw.

First Person: See *Point of View*

Flashback: A device used in literature to present action that occurred before the beginning of the story. Flashbacks are often introduced as the dreams or recollections of one or more characters. Flashback techniques are often used in films, where they are typically set off by a gradual changing of one picture to another.

Foil: A character in a work of literature whose physical or psychological qualities contrast strongly with, and therefore highlight, the corresponding qualities of another character. In his Sherlock Holmes stories, Arthur Conan Doyle portrayed Dr. Watson as a man of normal habits and intelligence, making him a foil for the eccentric and wonderfully perceptive Sherlock Holmes.

Folk Ballad: See *Ballad*

Folklore: Traditions and myths preserved in a culture or group of people. Typically, these are passed on by word of mouth in various forms—such as legends, songs, and proverbs— or preserved in customs and ceremonies. This term was first used by W. J. Thoms in 1846. Sir James Frazer's *The Golden Bough* is the record of English folklore; myths about the frontier and the Old South exemplify American folklore.

Folktale: A story originating in oral tradition. Folktales fall into a variety of categories, including legends, ghost stories, fairy tales, fables, and anecdotes based on historical figures and events. Examples of folktales include Giambattista Basile's *The Pentamerone,* which contains the tales of Puss in Boots, Rapunzel, Cinderella, and Beauty and the Beast, and Joel Chandler Harris's Uncle Remus stories, which represent transplanted African folktales and American tales about the characters Mike Fink, Johnny Appleseed, Paul Bunyan, and Pecos Bill.

Foot: The smallest unit of rhythm in a line of poetry. In English-language poetry, a foot is typically one accented syllable combined with one or two unaccented syllables. There are many different types of feet. When the accent is on the second syllable of a two syllable word (con-*tort*), the foot is an "iamb"; the reverse accentual pattern (*tor* -ture) is a "trochee." Other feet that commonly occur in poetry in English are "anapest", two unaccented syllables followed by an accented syllable as in inter-*cept*, and "dactyl", an accented syllable followed by two unaccented syllables as in *su*-i-cide.

Foreshadowing: A device used in literature to create expectation or to set up an explanation of later developments. In Charles Dickens's *Great Expectations,* the graveyard encounter at the beginning of the novel between Pip and the escaped convict Magwitch foreshadows the baleful atmosphere and events that comprise much of the narrative.

Form: The pattern or construction of a work which identifies its genre and distinguishes it from other genres. Examples of forms include the different genres, such as the lyric form or the short story form, and various patterns for poetry, such as the verse form or the stanza form.

Formalism: In literary criticism, the belief that literature should follow prescribed rules of construction, such as those that govern the sonnet form. Examples of formalism are found in the work of the New Critics and structuralists.

Fourteener Meter: See *Meter*

Free Verse: Poetry that lacks regular metrical and rhyme patterns but that tries to capture the cadences of everyday speech. The form allows a poet to exploit a variety of rhythmical effects within a single poem. Free-verse techniques have been widely used in the twentieth century by such writers as Ezra Pound, T. S. Eliot, Carl Sandburg, and William Carlos Williams. Also known as *Vers libre.*

Futurism: A flamboyant literary and artistic movement that developed in France, Italy, and Russia from 1908 through the 1920s. Futurist theater and poetry abandoned traditional literary forms. In their place, followers of the movement attempted to achieve total freedom of expression through bizarre imagery and deformed or newly invented words. The Futurists were self-consciously modern artists who attempted to incorporate the appearances and sounds of modern life into their work. Futurist writers include Filippo Tommaso Marinetti, Wyndham Lewis, Guillaume Apollinaire, Velimir Khlebnikov, and Vladimir Mayakovsky.

G

Genre: A category of literary work. In critical theory, genre may refer to both the content of a given work—tragedy, comedy, pastoral—and to its form, such as poetry, novel, or drama. This term also refers to types of popular literature, as in the genres of science fiction or the detective story.

Genteel Tradition: A term coined by critic George Santayana to describe the literary practice of certain late nineteenth-century American writers, especially New Englanders. Followers of the Genteel Tradition emphasized conventionality in social, religious, moral, and literary standards. Some of the best-known writers of the Genteel Tradition are R. H. Stoddard and Bayard Taylor.

Gilded Age: A period in American history during the 1870s characterized by political corruption and materialism. A number of important novels of social and political criticism were written during this time. Examples of Gilded Age literature include Henry Adams's *Democracy* and F. Marion Crawford's *An American Politician.*

Gothic: See *Gothicism*

Gothicism: In literary criticism, works characterized by a taste for the medieval or morbidly attractive. A gothic novel prominently features elements of horror, the supernatural, gloom, and violence: clanking chains, terror, charnel houses, ghosts, medieval castles, and mysteriously slamming doors. The term ''gothic novel'' is also applied to novels that lack elements of the traditional Gothic setting but that create a similar atmosphere of terror or dread. Mary Shelley's *Frankenstein* is perhaps the best-known English work of this kind.

Gothic Novel: See *Gothicism*

Great Chain of Being: The belief that all things and creatures in nature are organized in a hierarchy from inanimate objects at the bottom to God at the top. This system of belief was popular in the seventeenth and eighteenth centuries. A summary of the concept of the great chain of being can be found in the first epistle of Alexander Pope's *An Essay on Man,* and more recently in Arthur O. Lovejoy's *The Great Chain of Being: A Study of the History of an Idea.*

Grotesque: In literary criticism, the subject matter of a work or a style of expression characterized by exaggeration, deformity, freakishness, and disorder. The grotesque often includes an element of comic absurdity. Early examples of literary grotesque include Francois Rabelais's *Pantagruel* and *Gargantua* and Thomas Nashe's *The Unfortunate Traveller,* while more recent examples can be found in the works of Edgar Allan Poe, Evelyn Waugh, Eudora Welty, Flannery O'Connor, Eugene Ionesco, Gunter Grass, Thomas Mann, Mervyn Peake, and Joseph Heller, among many others.

H

Haiku: The shortest form of Japanese poetry, constructed in three lines of five, seven, and five syllables respectively. The message of a *haiku* poem usually centers on some aspect of spirituality and provokes an emotional response in the reader. Early masters of *haiku* include Basho, Buson, Kobayashi

Issa, and Masaoka Shiki. English writers of *haiku* include the Imagists, notably Ezra Pound, H. D., Amy Lowell, Carl Sandburg, and William Carlos Williams. Also known as *Hokku.*

Half Rhyme: See *Consonance*

Hamartia: In tragedy, the event or act that leads to the hero's or heroine's downfall. This term is often incorrectly used as a synonym for tragic flaw. In Richard Wright's *Native Son,* the act that seals Bigger Thomas's fate is his first impulsive murder.

Harlem Renaissance: The Harlem Renaissance of the 1920s is generally considered the first significant movement of black writers and artists in the United States. During this period, new and established black writers published more fiction and poetry than ever before, the first influential black literary journals were established, and black authors and artists received their first widespread recognition and serious critical appraisal. Among the major writers associated with this period are Claude McKay, Jean Toomer, Countee Cullen, Langston Hughes, Arna Bontemps, Nella Larsen, and Zora Neale Hurston. Works representative of the Harlem Renaissance include Arna Bontemps's poems ''The Return'' and ''Golgotha Is a Mountain,'' Claude McKay's novel *Home to Harlem,* Nella Larsen's novel *Passing,* Langston Hughes's poem ''The Negro Speaks of Rivers,'' and the journals *Crisis* and *Opportunity,* both founded during this period. Also known as Negro Renaissance and New Negro Movement.

Harlequin: A stock character of the *commedia dell'arte* who occasionally interrupted the action with silly antics. Harlequin first appeared on the English stage in John Day's *The Travailes of the Three English Brothers.* The San Francisco Mime Troupe is one of the few modern groups to adapt Harlequin to the needs of contemporary satire.

Hellenism: Imitation of ancient Greek thought or styles. Also, an approach to life that focuses on the growth and development of the intellect. ''Hellenism'' is sometimes used to refer to the belief that reason can be applied to examine all human experience. A cogent discussion of Hellenism can be found in Matthew Arnold's *Culture and Anarchy.*

Heptameter: See *Meter*

Hero/Heroine: The principal sympathetic character (male or female) in a literary work. Heroes and heroines typically exhibit admirable traits: idealism, courage, and integrity, for example. Famous heroes and heroines include Pip in Charles Dickens's *Great Expectations,* the anonymous narrator in Ralph Ellison's *Invisible Man,* and Sethe in Toni Morrison's *Beloved.*

Heroic Couplet: A rhyming couplet written in iambic pentameter (a verse with five iambic feet). The following lines by Alexander Pope are an example: ''Truth guards the Poet, sanctifies the line,/ And makes Immortal, Verse as mean as mine.''

Heroic Line: The meter and length of a line of verse in epic or heroic poetry. This varies by language and time period. For example, in English poetry, the heroic line is iambic pentameter (a verse with five iambic feet); in French, the alexandrine (a verse with six iambic feet); in classical literature, dactylic hexameter (a verse with six dactylic feet).

Heroine: See *Hero/Heroine*

Hexameter: See *Meter*

Historical Criticism: The study of a work based on its impact on the world of the time period in which it was written. Examples of postmodern historical criticism can be found in the work of Michel Foucault, Hayden White, Stephen Greenblatt, and Jonathan Goldberg.

Hokku: See *Haiku*

Holocaust: See *Holocaust Literature*

Holocaust Literature: Literature influenced by or written about the Holocaust of World War II. Such literature includes true stories of survival in concentration camps, escape, and life after the war, as well as fictional works and poetry. Representative works of Holocaust literature include Saul Bellow's *Mr. Sammler's Planet,* Anne Frank's *The Diary of a Young Girl,* Jerzy Kosinski's *The Painted Bird,* Arthur Miller's *Incident at Vichy,* Czeslaw Milosz's *Collected Poems,* William Styron's *Sophie's Choice,* and Art Spiegelman's *Maus.*

Homeric Simile: An elaborate, detailed comparison written as a simile many lines in length. An example of an epic simile from John Milton's *Paradise Lost* follows: Angel Forms, who lay entranced Thick as autumnal leaves that strow the brooks In Vallombrosa, where the Etrurian shades High over-arched embower; or scattered sedge Afloat, when with fierce winds Orion armed Hath vexed the Red-Sea coast, whose waves o'erthrew Busiris and his Memphian chivalry, While with perfidious hatred they pursued The sojourners of

Goshen, who beheld From the safe shore their floating carcasses And broken chariot-wheels. Also known as Epic Simile.

Horatian Satire: See *Satire*

Humanism: A philosophy that places faith in the dignity of humankind and rejects the medieval perception of the individual as a weak, fallen creature. ''Humanists'' typically believe in the perfectibility of human nature and view reason and education as the means to that end. Humanist thought is represented in the works of Marsilio Ficino, Ludovico Castelvetro, Edmund Spenser, John Milton, Dean John Colet, Desiderius Erasmus, John Dryden, Alexander Pope, Matthew Arnold, and Irving Babbitt.

Humors: Mentions of the humors refer to the ancient Greek theory that a person's health and personality were determined by the balance of four basic fluids in the body: blood, phlegm, yellow bile, and black bile. A dominance of any fluid would cause extremes in behavior. An excess of blood created a sanguine person who was joyful, aggressive, and passionate; a phlegmatic person was shy, fearful, and sluggish; too much yellow bile led to a choleric temperament characterized by impatience, anger, bitterness, and stubbornness; and excessive black bile created melancholy, a state of laziness, gluttony, and lack of motivation. Literary treatment of the humors is exemplified by several characters in Ben Jonson's plays *Every Man in His Humour* and *Every Man out of His Humour.* Also spelled Humours.

Humours: See *Humors*

Hyperbole: In literary criticism, deliberate exaggeration used to achieve an effect. In William Shakespeare's *Macbeth,* Lady Macbeth hyperbolizes when she says, ''All the perfumes of Arabia could not sweeten this little hand.''

I

Iamb: See *Foot*

Idiom: A word construction or verbal expression closely associated with a given language. For example, in colloquial English the construction ''how come'' can be used instead of ''why'' to introduce a question. Similarly, ''a piece of cake'' is sometimes used to describe a task that is easily done.

Image: A concrete representation of an object or sensory experience. Typically, such a representation helps evoke the feelings associated with the object or experience itself. Images are either ''literal'' or ''figurative.'' Literal images are especially concrete and involve little or no extension of the obvious meaning of the words used to express them. Figurative images do not follow the literal meaning of the words exactly. Images in literature are usually visual, but the term ''image'' can also refer to the representation of any sensory experience. In his poem ''The Shepherd's Hour,'' Paul Verlaine presents the following image: ''The Moon is red through horizon's fog;/ In a dancing mist the hazy meadow sleeps.'' The first line is broadly literal, while the second line involves turns of meaning associated with dancing and sleeping.

Imagery: The array of images in a literary work. Also, figurative language. William Butler Yeats's ''The Second Coming'' offers a powerful image of encroaching anarchy: Turning and turning in the widening gyre The falcon cannot hear the falconer; Things fall apart. . . .

Imagism: An English and American poetry movement that flourished between 1908 and 1917. The Imagists used precise, clearly presented images in their works. They also used common, everyday speech and aimed for conciseness, concrete imagery, and the creation of new rhythms. Participants in the Imagist movement included Ezra Pound, H. D. (Hilda Doolittle), and Amy Lowell, among others.

In medias res: A Latin term meaning ''in the middle of things.'' It refers to the technique of beginning a story at its midpoint and then using various flashback devices to reveal previous action. This technique originated in such epics as Virgil's *Aeneid.*

Induction: The process of reaching a conclusion by reasoning from specific premises to form a general premise. Also, an introductory portion of a work of literature, especially a play. Geoffrey Chaucer's ''Prologue'' to the *Canterbury Tales,* Thomas Sackville's ''Induction'' to *The Mirror of Magistrates,* and the opening scene in William Shakespeare's *The Taming of the Shrew* are examples of inductions to literary works.

Intentional Fallacy: The belief that judgments of a literary work based solely on an author's stated or implied intentions are false and misleading. Critics who believe in the concept of the intentional fallacy typically argue that the work itself is sufficient matter for interpretation, even though they may concede that an author's statement of purpose can be useful. Analysis of William Wordsworth's *Lyrical Ballads* based on the observations about poetry he makes in his "Preface" to the second edition of that work is an example of the intentional fallacy.

Interior Monologue: A narrative technique in which characters' thoughts are revealed in a way that appears to be uncontrolled by the author. The interior monologue typically aims to reveal the inner self of a character. It portrays emotional experiences as they occur at both a conscious and unconscious level. images are often used to represent sensations or emotions. One of the best-known interior monologues in English is the Molly Bloom section at the close of James Joyce's *Ulysses.* The interior monologue is also common in the works of Virginia Woolf.

Internal Rhyme: Rhyme that occurs within a single line of verse. An example is in the opening line of Edgar Allan Poe's "The Raven": "Once upon a midnight dreary, while I pondered weak and weary." Here, "dreary" and "weary" make an internal rhyme.

Irish Literary Renaissance: A late nineteenth- and early twentieth-century movement in Irish literature. Members of the movement aimed to reduce the influence of British culture in Ireland and create an Irish national literature. William Butler Yeats, George Moore, and Sean O'Casey are three of the best-known figures of the movement.

Irony: In literary criticism, the effect of language in which the intended meaning is the opposite of what is stated. The title of Jonathan Swift's "A Modest Proposal" is ironic because what Swift proposes in this essay is cannibalism—hardly "modest."

Italian Sonnet: See *Sonnet*

J

Jacobean Age: The period of the reign of James I of England (1603–1625). The early literature of this period reflected the worldview of the Elizabethan Age, but a darker, more cynical attitude steadily grew in the art and literature of the Jacobean Age. This was an important time for English drama and poetry. Milestones include William Shakespeare's tragedies, tragi-comedies, and sonnets; Ben Jonson's various dramas; and John Donne's metaphysical poetry.

Jargon: Language that is used or understood only by a select group of people. Jargon may refer to terminology used in a certain profession, such as computer jargon, or it may refer to any nonsensical language that is not understood by most people. Literary examples of jargon are Francois Villon's *Ballades en jargon,* which is composed in the secret language of the *coquillards,* and Anthony Burgess's *A Clockwork Orange,* narrated in the fictional characters' language of "Nadsat."

Juvenalian Satire: See *Satire*

K

Knickerbocker Group: A somewhat indistinct group of New York writers of the first half of the nineteenth century. Members of the group were linked only by location and a common theme: New York life. Two famous members of the Knickerbocker Group were Washington Irving and William Cullen Bryant. The group's name derives from Irving's *Knickerbocker's History of New York.*

L

Lais: See *Lay*

Lay: A song or simple narrative poem. The form originated in medieval France. Early French *lais* were often based on the Celtic legends and other tales sung by Breton minstrels—thus the name of the "Breton lay." In fourteenth-century England, the term "lay" was used to describe short narratives written in imitation of the Breton lays. The most notable of these is Geoffrey Chaucer's "The Minstrel's Tale."

Leitmotiv: See *Motif*

Literal Language: An author uses literal language when he or she writes without exaggerating or embellishing the subject matter and without any tools of figurative language. To say "He ran very quickly down the street" is to use literal language, whereas to say "He ran like a hare down the street" would be using figurative language.

Literary Ballad: See *Ballad*

Literature: Literature is broadly defined as any written or spoken material, but the term most often refers to creative works. Literature includes poetry, drama, fiction, and many kinds of nonfiction writing, as well as oral, dramatic, and broadcast compositions not necessarily preserved in a written format, such as films and television programs.

Lost Generation: A term first used by Gertrude Stein to describe the post-World War I generation of

American writers: men and women haunted by a sense of betrayal and emptiness brought about by the destructiveness of the war. The term is commonly applied to Hart Crane, Ernest Hemingway, F. Scott Fitzgerald, and others.

Lyric Poetry: A poem expressing the subjective feelings and personal emotions of the poet. Such poetry is melodic, since it was originally accompanied by a lyre in recitals. Most Western poetry in the twentieth century may be classified as lyrical. Examples of lyric poetry include A. E. Housman's elegy ''To an Athlete Dying Young,'' the odes of Pindar and Horace, Thomas Gray and William Collins, the sonnets of Sir Thomas Wyatt and Sir Philip Sidney, Elizabeth Barrett Browning and Rainer Maria Rilke, and a host of other forms in the poetry of William Blake and Christina Rossetti, among many others.

M

Mannerism: Exaggerated, artificial adherence to a literary manner or style. Also, a popular style of the visual arts of late sixteenth-century Europe that was marked by elongation of the human form and by intentional spatial distortion. Literary works that are self-consciously high-toned and artistic are often said to be ''mannered.'' Authors of such works include Henry James and Gertrude Stein.

Masculine Rhyme: See *Rhyme*

Masque: A lavish and elaborate form of entertainment, often performed in royal courts, that emphasizes song, dance, and costumery. The Renaissance form of the masque grew out of the spectacles of masked figures common in medieval England and Europe. The masque reached its peak of popularity and development in seventeenth-century England, during the reigns of James I and, especially, of Charles I. Ben Jonson, the most significant masque writer, also created the ''antimasque,'' which incorporates elements of humor and the grotesque into the traditional masque and achieved greater dramatic quality. Masque-like interludes appear in Edmund Spenser's *The Faerie Queene* and in William Shakespeare's *The Tempest.* One of the best-known English masques is John Milton's *Comus.*

Measure: The foot, verse, or time sequence used in a literary work, especially a poem. Measure is often used somewhat incorrectly as a synonym for meter.

Melodrama: A play in which the typical plot is a conflict between characters who personify extreme good and evil. Melodramas usually end happily and emphasize sensationalism. Other literary forms that use the same techniques are often labeled ''melodramatic.'' The term was formerly used to describe a combination of drama and music; as such, it was synonymous with ''opera.'' Augustin Daly's *Under the Gaslight* and Dion Boucicault's *The Octoroon, The Colleen Bawn,* and *The Poor of New York* are examples of melodramas. The most popular media for twentieth-century melodramas are motion pictures and television.

Metaphor: A figure of speech that expresses an idea through the image of another object. Metaphors suggest the essence of the first object by identifying it with certain qualities of the second object. An example is ''But soft, what light through yonder window breaks?/ It is the east, and Juliet is the sun'' in William Shakespeare's *Romeo and Juliet.* Here, Juliet, the first object, is identified with qualities of the second object, the sun.

Metaphysical Conceit: See *Conceit*

Metaphysical Poetry: The body of poetry produced by a group of seventeenth-century English writers called the ''Metaphysical Poets.'' The group includes John Donne and Andrew Marvell. The Metaphysical Poets made use of everyday speech, intellectual analysis, and unique imagery. They aimed to portray the ordinary conflicts and contradictions of life. Their poems often took the form of an argument, and many of them emphasize physical and religious love as well as the fleeting nature of life. Elaborate conceits are typical in metaphysical poetry. Marvell's ''To His Coy Mistress'' is a well-known example of a metaphysical poem.

Metaphysical Poets: See *Metaphysical Poetry*

Meter: In literary criticism, the repetition of sound patterns that creates a rhythm in poetry. The patterns are based on the number of syllables and the presence and absence of accents. The unit of rhythm in a line is called a foot. Types of meter are classified according to the number of feet in a line. These are the standard English lines: Monometer, one foot; Dimeter, two feet; Trimeter, three feet; Tetrameter, four feet; Pentameter, five feet; Hexameter, six feet (also called the Alexandrine); Heptameter, seven feet (also called the ''Fourteener'' when the feet are iambic). The most common English meter is the iambic pentameter, in which each line contains ten syllables, or five iambic feet, which individually are composed of an unstressed syllable followed by an accented syllable. Both of the following lines from Alfred, Lord Tennyson's

''Ulysses'' are written in iambic pentameter: Made weak by time and fate, but strong in will To strive, to seek, to find, and not to yield.

Mise en scene: The costumes, scenery, and other properties of a drama. Herbert Beerbohm Tree was renowned for the elaborate *mises en scene* of his lavish Shakespearean productions at His Majesty's Theatre between 1897 and 1915.

Modernism: Modern literary practices. Also, the principles of a literary school that lasted from roughly the beginning of the twentieth century until the end of World War II. Modernism is defined by its rejection of the literary conventions of the nineteenth century and by its opposition to conventional morality, taste, traditions, and economic values. Many writers are associated with the concepts of Modernism, including Albert Camus, Marcel Proust, D. H. Lawrence, W. H. Auden, Ernest Hemingway, William Faulkner, William Butler Yeats, Thomas Mann, Tennessee Williams, Eugene O'Neill, and James Joyce.

Monologue: A composition, written or oral, by a single individual. More specifically, a speech given by a single individual in a drama or other public entertainment. It has no set length, although it is usually several or more lines long. An example of an ''extended monologue''—that is, a monologue of great length and seriousness—occurs in the one-act, one-character play *The Stronger* by August Strindberg.

Monometer: See *Meter*

Mood: The prevailing emotions of a work or of the author in his or her creation of the work. The mood of a work is not always what might be expected based on its subject matter. The poem ''Dover Beach'' by Matthew Arnold offers examples of two different moods originating from the same experience: watching the ocean at night. The mood of the first three lines— The sea is calm tonight The tide is full, the moon lies fair Upon the straights. . . . is in sharp contrast to the mood of the last three lines— And we are here as on a darkling plain Swept with confused alarms of struggle and flight, Where ignorant armies clash by night.

Motif: A theme, character type, image, metaphor, or other verbal element that recurs throughout a single work of literature or occurs in a number of different works over a period of time. For example, the various manifestations of the color white in Herman Melville's *Moby Dick* is a ''specific'' *motif,* while the trials of star-crossed lovers is a ''conventional'' *motif* from the literature of all periods. Also known as *Motiv* or *Leitmotiv.*

Motiv: See *Motif*

Muckrakers: An early twentieth-century group of American writers. Typically, their works exposed the wrongdoings of big business and government in the United States. Upton Sinclair's *The Jungle* exemplifies the muckraking novel.

Muses: Nine Greek mythological goddesses, the daughters of Zeus and Mnemosyne (Memory). Each muse patronized a specific area of the liberal arts and sciences. Calliope presided over epic poetry, Clio over history, Erato over love poetry, Euterpe over music or lyric poetry, Melpomene over tragedy, Polyhymnia over hymns to the gods, Terpsichore over dance, Thalia over comedy, and Urania over astronomy. Poets and writers traditionally made appeals to the Muses for inspiration in their work. John Milton invokes the aid of a muse at the beginning of the first book of his *Paradise Lost:* Of Man's First disobedience, and the Fruit of the Forbidden Tree, whose mortal taste Brought Death into the World, and all our woe, With loss of Eden, till one greater Man Restore us, and regain the blissful Seat, Sing Heav'nly Muse, that on the secret top of Oreb, or of Sinai, didst inspire That Shepherd, who first taught the chosen Seed, In the Beginning how the Heav'ns and Earth Rose out of Chaos. . . .

Mystery: See *Suspense*

Myth: An anonymous tale emerging from the traditional beliefs of a culture or social unit. Myths use supernatural explanations for natural phenomena. They may also explain cosmic issues like creation and death. Collections of myths, known as mythologies, are common to all cultures and nations, but the best-known myths belong to the Norse, Roman, and Greek mythologies. A famous myth is the story of Arachne, an arrogant young girl who challenged a goddess, Athena, to a weaving contest; when the girl won, Athena was enraged and turned Arachne into a spider, thus explaining the existence of spiders.

N

Narration: The telling of a series of events, real or invented. A narration may be either a simple narrative, in which the events are recounted chronologically, or a narrative with a plot, in which the account is given in a style reflecting the author's artistic concept of the story. Narration is sometimes used as a synonym for "storyline." The recounting of scary stories around a campfire is a form of narration.

Narrative: A verse or prose accounting of an event or sequence of events, real or invented. The term is also used as an adjective in the sense "method of narration." For example, in literary criticism, the expression "narrative technique" usually refers to the way the author structures and presents his or her story. Narratives range from the shortest accounts of events, as in Julius Caesar's remark, "I came, I saw, I conquered," to the longest historical or biographical works, as in Edward Gibbon's *The Decline and Fall of the Roman Empire,* as well as diaries, travelogues, novels, ballads, epics, short stories, and other fictional forms.

Narrative Poetry: A nondramatic poem in which the author tells a story. Such poems may be of any length or level of complexity. Epics such as *Beowulf* and ballads are forms of narrative poetry.

Narrator: The teller of a story. The narrator may be the author or a character in the story through whom the author speaks. Huckleberry Finn is the narrator of Mark Twain's *The Adventures of Huckleberry Finn.*

Naturalism: A literary movement of the late nineteenth and early twentieth centuries. The movement's major theorist, French novelist Emile Zola, envisioned a type of fiction that would examine human life with the objectivity of scientific inquiry. The Naturalists typically viewed human beings as either the products of "biological determinism," ruled by hereditary instincts and engaged in an endless struggle for survival, or as the products of "socioeconomic determinism," ruled by social and economic forces beyond their control. In their works, the Naturalists generally ignored the highest levels of society and focused on degradation: poverty, alcoholism, prostitution, insanity, and disease. Naturalism influenced authors throughout the world, including Henrik Ibsen and Thomas Hardy. In the United States, in particular, Naturalism had a profound impact. Among the authors who embraced its principles are Theodore Dreiser, Eugene O'Neill, Stephen Crane, Jack London, and Frank Norris.

Negritude: A literary movement based on the concept of a shared cultural bond on the part of black Africans, wherever they may be in the world. It traces its origins to the former French colonies of Africa and the Caribbean. Negritude poets, novelists, and essayists generally stress four points in their writings: One, black alienation from traditional African culture can lead to feelings of inferiority. Two, European colonialism and Western education should be resisted. Three, black Africans should seek to affirm and define their own identity. Four, African culture can and should be reclaimed. Many Negritude writers also claim that blacks can make unique contributions to the world, based on a heightened appreciation of nature, rhythm, and human emotions—aspects of life they say are not so highly valued in the materialistic and rationalistic West. Examples of Negritude literature include the poetry of both Senegalese Leopold Senghor in *Hosties noires* and Martiniquais Aime-Fernand Cesaire in *Return to My Native Land.*

Negro Renaissance: See *Harlem Renaissance*

Neoclassical Period: See *Neoclassicism*

Neoclassicism: In literary criticism, this term refers to the revival of the attitudes and styles of expression of classical literature. It is generally used to describe a period in European history beginning in the late seventeenth century and lasting until about 1800. In its purest form, Neoclassicism marked a return to order, proportion, restraint, logic, accuracy, and decorum. In England, where Neoclassicism perhaps was most popular, it reflected the influence of seventeenth-century French writers, especially dramatists. Neoclassical writers typically reacted against the intensity and enthusiasm of the Renaissance period. They wrote works that appealed to the intellect, using elevated language and classical literary forms such as satire and the ode. Neoclassical works were often governed by the classical goal of instruction. English neoclassicists included Alexander Pope, Jonathan Swift, Joseph Addison, Sir Richard Steele, John Gay, and Matthew Prior; French neoclassicists included Pierre Corneille and Jean-Baptiste Moliere. Also known as Age of Reason.

Neoclassicists: See *Neoclassicism*

New Criticism: A movement in literary criticism, dating from the late 1920s, that stressed close textual analysis in the interpretation of works of literature. The New Critics saw little merit in historical and biographical analysis. Rather, they aimed to examine the text alone, free from the question of how external events—biographical or otherwise—may have helped shape it. This predominantly American school was named "New Criticism" by one of its practitioners, John Crowe Ransom. Other important New Critics included Allen Tate, R. P. Blackmur, Robert Penn Warren, and Cleanth Brooks.

New Negro Movement: See *Harlem Renaissance*

Noble Savage: The idea that primitive man is noble and good but becomes evil and corrupted as he becomes civilized. The concept of the noble savage originated in the Renaissance period but is more closely identified with such later writers as Jean-Jacques Rousseau and Aphra Behn. First described in John Dryden's play *The Conquest of Granada,* the noble savage is portrayed by the various Native Americans in James Fenimore Cooper's ''Leatherstocking Tales,'' by Queequeg, Daggoo, and Tashtego in Herman Melville's *Moby Dick,* and by John the Savage in Aldous Huxley's *Brave New World.*

O

Objective Correlative: An outward set of objects, a situation, or a chain of events corresponding to an inward experience and evoking this experience in the reader. The term frequently appears in modern criticism in discussions of authors' intended effects on the emotional responses of readers. This term was originally used by T. S. Eliot in his 1919 essay ''Hamlet.''

Objectivity: A quality in writing characterized by the absence of the author's opinion or feeling about the subject matter. Objectivity is an important factor in criticism. The novels of Henry James and, to a certain extent, the poems of John Larkin demonstrate objectivity, and it is central to John Keats's concept of ''negative capability.'' Critical and journalistic writing usually are or attempt to be objective.

Occasional Verse: poetry written on the occasion of a significant historical or personal event. *Vers de societe* is sometimes called occasional verse although it is of a less serious nature. Famous examples of occasional verse include Andrew Marvell's ''Horatian Ode upon Cromwell's Return from England,'' Walt Whitman's ''When Lilacs Last in the Dooryard Bloom'd''— written upon the death of Abraham Lincoln—and Edmund Spenser's commemoration of his wedding, ''Epithalamion.''

Octave: A poem or stanza composed of eight lines. The term octave most often represents the first eight lines of a Petrarchan sonnet. An example of an octave is taken from a translation of a Petrarchan sonnet by Sir Thomas Wyatt: The pillar perisht is whereto I leant, The strongest stay of mine unquiet mind; The like of it no man again can find, From East to West Still seeking though he went. To mind unhap! for hap away hath rent Of all my joy the very bark and rind; And I, alas, by chance am thus assigned Daily to mourn till death do it relent.

Ode: Name given to an extended lyric poem characterized by exalted emotion and dignified style. An ode usually concerns a single, serious theme. Most odes, but not all, are addressed to an object or individual. Odes are distinguished from other lyric poetic forms by their complex rhythmic and stanzaic patterns. An example of this form is John Keats's ''Ode to a Nightingale.''

Oedipus Complex: A son's amorous obsession with his mother. The phrase is derived from the story of the ancient Theban hero Oedipus, who unknowingly killed his father and married his mother. Literary occurrences of the Oedipus complex include Andre Gide's *Oedipe* and Jean Cocteau's *La Machine infernale,* as well as the most famous, Sophocles' *Oedipus Rex.*

Omniscience: See *Point of View*

Onomatopoeia: The use of words whose sounds express or suggest their meaning. In its simplest sense, onomatopoeia may be represented by words that mimic the sounds they denote such as ''hiss'' or ''meow.'' At a more subtle level, the pattern and rhythm of sounds and rhymes of a line or poem may be onomatopoeic. A celebrated example of onomatopoeia is the repetition of the word ''bells'' in Edgar Allan Poe's poem ''The Bells.''

Opera: A type of stage performance, usually a drama, in which the dialogue is sung. Classic examples of opera include Giuseppi Verdi's *La traviata,* Giacomo Puccini's *La Boheme,* and Richard Wagner's *Tristan und Isolde.* Major twentieth-century contributors to the form include Richard Strauss and Alban Berg.

Operetta: A usually romantic comic opera. John Gay's *The Beggar's Opera,* Richard Sheridan's *The Duenna,* and numerous works by William Gilbert and Arthur Sullivan are examples of operettas.

Oral Tradition: See *Oral Transmission*

Oral Transmission: A process by which songs, ballads, folklore, and other material are transmitted by word of mouth. The tradition of oral transmission predates the written record systems of literate society. Oral transmission preserves material sometimes over generations, although often with variations. Memory plays a large part in the recitation and preservation of orally transmitted material. Breton lays, French *fabliaux,* national epics (including the Anglo-Saxon *Beowulf,* the Spanish *El Cid,* and the Finnish *Kalevala*), Native American myths and legends, and African folktales told by plantation slaves are examples of orally transmitted literature.

Oration: Formal speaking intended to motivate the listeners to some action or feeling. Such public speaking was much more common before the development of timely printed communication such as newspapers. Famous examples of oration include Abraham Lincoln's ''Gettysburg Address'' and Dr. Martin Luther King Jr.'s ''I Have a Dream'' speech.

Ottava Rima: An eight-line stanza of poetry composed in iambic pentameter (a five-foot line in which each foot consists of an unaccented syllable followed by an accented syllable), following the abababcc rhyme scheme. This form has been prominently used by such important English writers as Lord Byron, Henry Wadsworth Longfellow, and W. B. Yeats.

Oxymoron: A phrase combining two contradictory terms. Oxymorons may be intentional or unintentional. The following speech from William Shakespeare's *Romeo and Juliet* uses several oxymorons: Why, then, O brawling love! O loving hate! O anything, of nothing first create! O heavy lightness! serious vanity! Mis-shapen chaos of well-seeming forms! Feather of lead, bright smoke, cold fire, sick health! This love feel I, that feel no love in this.

P

Pantheism: The idea that all things are both a manifestation or revelation of God and a part of God at the same time. Pantheism was a common attitude in the early societies of Egypt, India, and Greece—the term derives from the Greek *pan* meaning ''all'' and *theos* meaning ''deity.'' It later became a significant part of the Christian faith. William Wordsworth and Ralph Waldo Emerson are among the many writers who have expressed the pantheistic attitude in their works.

Parable: A story intended to teach a moral lesson or answer an ethical question. In the West, the best examples of parables are those of Jesus Christ in the New Testament, notably ''The Prodigal Son,'' but parables also are used in Sufism, rabbinic literature, Hasidism, and Zen Buddhism.

Paradox: A statement that appears illogical or contradictory at first, but may actually point to an underlying truth. ''Less is more'' is an example of a paradox. Literary examples include Francis Bacon's statement, ''The most corrected copies are commonly the least correct,'' and ''All animals are equal, but some animals are more equal than others'' from George Orwell's *Animal Farm.*

Parallelism: A method of comparison of two ideas in which each is developed in the same grammatical structure. Ralph Waldo Emerson's ''Civilization'' contains this example of parallelism: Raphael paints wisdom; Handel sings it, Phidias carves it, Shakespeare writes it, Wren builds it, Columbus sails it, Luther preaches it, Washington arms it, Watt mechanizes it.

Parnassianism: A mid nineteenth-century movement in French literature. Followers of the movement stressed adherence to well-defined artistic forms as a reaction against the often chaotic expression of the artist's ego that dominated the work of the Romantics. The Parnassians also rejected the moral, ethical, and social themes exhibited in the works of French Romantics such as Victor Hugo. The aesthetic doctrines of the Parnassians strongly influenced the later symbolist and decadent movements. Members of the Parnassian school include Leconte de Lisle, Sully Prudhomme, Albert Glatigny, Francois Coppee, and Theodore de Banville.

Parody: In literary criticism, this term refers to an imitation of a serious literary work or the signature style of a particular author in a ridiculous manner. A typical parody adopts the style of the original and applies it to an inappropriate subject for humorous effect. Parody is a form of satire and could be considered the literary equivalent of a caricature or cartoon. Henry Fielding's *Shamela* is a parody of Samuel Richardson's *Pamela.*

Pastoral: A term derived from the Latin word ''pastor,'' meaning shepherd. A pastoral is a literary composition on a rural theme. The conventions of the pastoral were originated by the third-century Greek poet Theocritus, who wrote about the experiences, love affairs, and pastimes of Sicilian shepherds. In a pastoral, characters and language of a courtly nature are often placed in a simple setting. The term pastoral is also used to classify dramas, elegies, and lyrics that exhibit the use of country settings and shepherd characters. Percy Bysshe Shelley's ''Adonais'' and John Milton's ''Lycidas'' are two famous examples of pastorals.

Pastorela: The Spanish name for the shepherds play, a folk drama reenacted during the Christmas season. Examples of *pastorelas* include Gomez

Manrique's *Representacion del nacimiento* and the dramas of Lucas Fernandez and Juan del Encina.

Pathetic Fallacy: A term coined by English critic John Ruskin to identify writing that falsely endows nonhuman things with human intentions and feelings, such as ''angry clouds'' and ''sad trees.'' The pathetic fallacy is a required convention in the classical poetic form of the pastoral elegy, and it is used in the modern poetry of T. S. Eliot, Ezra Pound, and the Imagists. Also known as Poetic Fallacy.

Pelado: Literally the ''skinned one'' or shirtless one, he was the stock underdog, sharp-witted picaresque character of Mexican vaudeville and tent shows. The *pelado* is found in such works as Don Catarino's *Los effectos de la crisis* and *Regreso a mi tierra.*

Pen Name: See *Pseudonym*

Pentameter: See *Meter*

Persona: A Latin term meaning ''mask.'' *Personae* are the characters in a fictional work of literature. The *persona* generally functions as a mask through which the author tells a story in a voice other than his or her own. A *persona* is usually either a character in a story who acts as a narrator or an ''implied author,'' a voice created by the author to act as the narrator for himself or herself. *Personae* include the narrator of Geoffrey Chaucer's *Canterbury Tales* and Marlow in Joseph Conrad's *Heart of Darkness.*

Personae: See *Persona*

Personal Point of View: See *Point of View*

Personification: A figure of speech that gives human qualities to abstract ideas, animals, and inanimate objects. William Shakespeare used personification in *Romeo and Juliet* in the lines ''Arise, fair sun, and kill the envious moon,/ Who is already sick and pale with grief.'' Here, the moon is portrayed as being envious, sick, and pale with grief—all markedly human qualities. Also known as *Prosopopoeia.*

Petrarchan Sonnet: See *Sonnet*

Phenomenology: A method of literary criticism based on the belief that things have no existence outside of human consciousness or awareness. Proponents of this theory believe that art is a process that takes place in the mind of the observer as he or she contemplates an object rather than a quality of the object itself. Among phenomenological critics are Edmund Husserl, George Poulet, Marcel Raymond, and Roman Ingarden.

Picaresque Novel: Episodic fiction depicting the adventures of a roguish central character (''picaro'' is Spanish for ''rogue''). The picaresque hero is commonly a low-born but clever individual who wanders into and out of various affairs of love, danger, and farcical intrigue. These involvements may take place at all social levels and typically present a humorous and wide-ranging satire of a given society. Prominent examples of the picaresque novel are *Don Quixote* by Miguel de Cervantes, *Tom Jones* by Henry Fielding, and *Moll Flanders* by Daniel Defoe.

Plagiarism: Claiming another person's written material as one's own. Plagiarism can take the form of direct, word-for-word copying or the theft of the substance or idea of the work. A student who copies an encyclopedia entry and turns it in as a report for school is guilty of plagiarism.

Platonic Criticism: A form of criticism that stresses an artistic work's usefulness as an agent of social engineering rather than any quality or value of the work itself. Platonic criticism takes as its starting point the ancient Greek philosopher Plato's comments on art in his *Republic.*

Platonism: The embracing of the doctrines of the philosopher Plato, popular among the poets of the Renaissance and the Romantic period. Platonism is more flexible than Aristotelian Criticism and places more emphasis on the supernatural and unknown aspects of life. Platonism is expressed in the love poetry of the Renaissance, the fourth book of Baldassare Castiglione's *The Book of the Courtier,* and the poetry of William Blake, William Wordsworth, Percy Bysshe Shelley, Friedrich Holderlin, William Butler Yeats, and Wallace Stevens.

Play: See *Drama*

Plot: In literary criticism, this term refers to the pattern of events in a narrative or drama. In its simplest sense, the plot guides the author in composing the work and helps the reader follow the work. Typically, plots exhibit causality and unity and have a beginning, a middle, and an end. Sometimes, however, a plot may consist of a series of disconnected events, in which case it is known as an ''episodic plot.'' In his *Aspects of the Novel,* E. M. Forster distinguishes between a story, defined as a ''narrative of events arranged in their time-sequence,'' and plot, which organizes the events to a ''sense of causality.'' This definition closely mirrors Aristotle's discussion of plot in his *Poetics.*

Poem: In its broadest sense, a composition utilizing rhyme, meter, concrete detail, and expressive language to create a literary experience with emotional and aesthetic appeal. Typical poems include sonnets, odes, elegies, *haiku,* ballads, and free verse.

Poet: An author who writes poetry or verse. The term is also used to refer to an artist or writer who has an exceptional gift for expression, imagination, and energy in the making of art in any form. Well-known poets include Horace, Basho, Sir Philip Sidney, Sir Edmund Spenser, John Donne, Andrew Marvell, Alexander Pope, Jonathan Swift, George Gordon, Lord Byron, John Keats, Christina Rossetti, W. H. Auden, Stevie Smith, and Sylvia Plath.

Poetic Fallacy: See *Pathetic Fallacy*

Poetic Justice: An outcome in a literary work, not necessarily a poem, in which the good are rewarded and the evil are punished, especially in ways that particularly fit their virtues or crimes. For example, a murderer may himself be murdered, or a thief will find himself penniless.

Poetic License: Distortions of fact and literary convention made by a writer—not always a poet—for the sake of the effect gained. Poetic license is closely related to the concept of ''artistic freedom.'' An author exercises poetic license by saying that a pile of money ''reaches as high as a mountain'' when the pile is actually only a foot or two high.

Poetics: This term has two closely related meanings. It denotes (1) an aesthetic theory in literary criticism about the essence of poetry or (2) rules prescribing the proper methods, content, style, or diction of poetry. The term poetics may also refer to theories about literature in general, not just poetry.

Poetry: In its broadest sense, writing that aims to present ideas and evoke an emotional experience in the reader through the use of meter, imagery, connotative and concrete words, and a carefully constructed structure based on rhythmic patterns. Poetry typically relies on words and expressions that have several layers of meaning. It also makes use of the effects of regular rhythm on the ear and may make a strong appeal to the senses through the use of imagery. Edgar Allan Poe's ''Annabel Lee'' and Walt Whitman's *Leaves of Grass* are famous examples of poetry.

Point of View: The narrative perspective from which a literary work is presented to the reader. There are four traditional points of view. The ''third person omniscient'' gives the reader a ''godlike'' perspective, unrestricted by time or place, from which to see actions and look into the minds of characters. This allows the author to comment openly on characters and events in the work. The ''third person'' point of view presents the events of the story from outside of any single character's perception, much like the omniscient point of view, but the reader must understand the action as it takes place and without any special insight into characters' minds or motivations. The ''first person'' or ''personal'' point of view relates events as they are perceived by a single character. The main character ''tells'' the story and may offer opinions about the action and characters which differ from those of the author. Much less common than omniscient, third person, and first person is the ''second person'' point of view, wherein the author tells the story as if it is happening to the reader. James Thurber employs the omniscient point of view in his short story ''The Secret Life of Walter Mitty.'' Ernest Hemingway's ''A Clean, Well-Lighted Place'' is a short story told from the third person point of view. Mark Twain's novel *Huck Finn* is presented from the first person viewpoint. Jay McInerney's *Bright Lights, Big City* is an example of a novel which uses the second person point of view.

Polemic: A work in which the author takes a stand on a controversial subject, such as abortion or religion. Such works are often extremely argumentative or provocative. Classic examples of polemics include John Milton's *Aeropagitica* and Thomas Paine's *The American Crisis.*

Pornography: Writing intended to provoke feelings of lust in the reader. Such works are often condemned by critics and teachers, but those which can be shown to have literary value are viewed less harshly. Literary works that have been described as pornographic include Ovid's *The Art of Love,* Margaret of Angouleme's *Heptameron,* John Cleland's *Memoirs of a Woman of Pleasure; or, the Life of Fanny Hill,* the anonymous *My Secret Life,* D. H. Lawrence's *Lady Chatterley's Lover,* and Vladimir Nabokov's *Lolita.*

Post-Aesthetic Movement: An artistic response made by African Americans to the black aesthetic movement of the 1960s and early '70s. Writers since that time have adopted a somewhat different tone in their work, with less emphasis placed on the disparity between black and white in the United States. In the words of post-aesthetic authors such as Toni Morrison, John Edgar Wideman, and Kristin Hunter, African Americans are portrayed as looking inward for answers to their own questions, rather than always looking to the outside world. Two well-known examples of works produced as part of the post-aesthetic movement are the Pulitzer Prize-winning novels *The Color Purple* by Alice Walker and *Beloved* by Toni Morrison.

Postmodernism: Writing from the 1960s forward characterized by experimentation and continuing to apply some of the fundamentals of modernism, which included existentialism and alienation. Postmodernists have gone a step further in the rejection of tradition begun with the modernists by also rejecting traditional forms, preferring the anti-novel over the novel and the anti-hero over the hero. Postmodern writers include Alain Robbe-Grillet, Thomas Pynchon, Margaret Drabble, John Fowles, Adolfo Bioy-Casares, and Gabriel Garcia Marquez.

Pre-Raphaelites: A circle of writers and artists in mid nineteenth-century England. Valuing the pre-Renaissance artistic qualities of religious symbolism, lavish pictorialism, and natural sensuousness, the Pre-Raphaelites cultivated a sense of mystery and melancholy that influenced later writers associated with the Symbolist and Decadent movements. The major members of the group include Dante Gabriel Rossetti, Christina Rossetti, Algernon Swinburne, and Walter Pater.

Primitivism: The belief that primitive peoples were nobler and less flawed than civilized peoples because they had not been subjected to the tainting influence of society. Examples of literature espousing primitivism include Aphra Behn's *Oroonoko: Or, The History of the Royal Slave,* Jean-Jacques Rousseau's *Julie ou la Nouvelle Heloise,* Oliver Goldsmith's *The Deserted Village,* the poems of Robert Burns, Herman Melville's stories *Typee, Omoo,* and *Mardi,* many poems of William Butler Yeats and Robert Frost, and William Golding's novel *Lord of the Flies.*

Projective Verse: A form of free verse in which the poet's breathing pattern determines the lines of the poem. Poets who advocate projective verse are against all formal structures in writing, including meter and form. Besides its creators, Robert Creeley, Robert Duncan, and Charles Olson, two other well-known projective verse poets are Denise Levertov and LeRoi Jones (Amiri Baraka). Also known as Breath Verse.

Prologue: An introductory section of a literary work. It often contains information establishing the situation of the characters or presents information about the setting, time period, or action. In drama, the prologue is spoken by a chorus or by one of the principal characters. In the "General Prologue" of *The Canterbury Tales,* Geoffrey Chaucer describes the main characters and establishes the setting and purpose of the work.

Prose: A literary medium that attempts to mirror the language of everyday speech. It is distinguished from poetry by its use of unmetered, unrhymed language consisting of logically related sentences. Prose is usually grouped into paragraphs that form a cohesive whole such as an essay or a novel. Recognized masters of English prose writing include Sir Thomas Malory, William Caxton, Raphael Holinshed, Joseph Addison, Mark Twain, and Ernest Hemingway.

Prosopopoeia: See *Personification*

Protagonist: The central character of a story who serves as a focus for its themes and incidents and as the principal rationale for its development. The protagonist is sometimes referred to in discussions of modern literature as the hero or anti-hero. Well-known protagonists are Hamlet in William Shakespeare's *Hamlet* and Jay Gatsby in F. Scott Fitzgerald's *The Great Gatsby.*

Protest Fiction: Protest fiction has as its primary purpose the protesting of some social injustice, such as racism or discrimination. One example of protest fiction is a series of five novels by Chester Himes, beginning in 1945 with *If He Hollers Let Him Go* and ending in 1955 with *The Primitive.* These works depict the destructive effects of race and gender stereotyping in the context of interracial relationships. Another African American author whose works often revolve around themes of social protest is John Oliver Killens. James Baldwin's essay "Everybody's Protest Novel" generated controversy by attacking the authors of protest fiction.

Proverb: A brief, sage saying that expresses a truth about life in a striking manner. "They are not all cooks who carry long knives" is an example of a proverb.

Pseudonym: A name assumed by a writer, most often intended to prevent his or her identification as the author of a work. Two or more authors may work together under one pseudonym, or an author may use a different name for each genre he or she publishes in. Some publishing companies maintain ''house pseudonyms,'' under which any number of authors may write installations in a series. Some authors also choose a pseudonym over their real names the way an actor may use a stage name. Examples of pseudonyms (with the author's real name in parentheses) include Voltaire (Francois-Marie Arouet), Novalis (Friedrich von Hardenberg), Currer Bell (Charlotte Bronte), Ellis Bell (Emily Bronte), George Eliot (Maryann Evans), Honorio Bustos Donmecq (Adolfo Bioy-Casares and Jorge Luis Borges), and Richard Bachman (Stephen King).

Pun: A play on words that have similar sounds but different meanings. A serious example of the pun is from John Donne's ''A Hymne to God the Father'': Sweare by thyself, that at my death thy sonne Shall shine as he shines now, and hereto fore; And, having done that, Thou haste done; I fear no more.

Pure Poetry: poetry written without instructional intent or moral purpose that aims only to please a reader by its imagery or musical flow. The term pure poetry is used as the antonym of the term ''didacticism.'' The poetry of Edgar Allan Poe, Stephane Mallarme, Paul Verlaine, Paul Valery, Juan Ramoz Jimenez, and Jorge Guillen offer examples of pure poetry.

Q

Quatrain: A four-line stanza of a poem or an entire poem consisting of four lines. The following quatrain is from Robert Herrick's ''To Live Merrily, and to Trust to Good Verses'': Round, round, the root do's run; And being ravisht thus, Come, I will drink a Tun To my *Propertius.*

R

Raisonneur: A character in a drama who functions as a spokesperson for the dramatist's views. The *raisonneur* typically observes the play without becoming central to its action. *Raisonneurs* were very common in plays of the nineteenth century.

Realism: A nineteenth-century European literary movement that sought to portray familiar characters, situations, and settings in a realistic manner. This was done primarily by using an objective narrative point of view and through the buildup of accurate detail. The standard for success of any realistic work depends on how faithfully it transfers common experience into fictional forms. The realistic method may be altered or extended, as in stream of consciousness writing, to record highly subjective experience. Seminal authors in the tradition of Realism include Honore de Balzac, Gustave Flaubert, and Henry James.

Refrain: A phrase repeated at intervals throughout a poem. A refrain may appear at the end of each stanza or at less regular intervals. It may be altered slightly at each appearance. Some refrains are nonsense expressions—as with ''Nevermore'' in Edgar Allan Poe's ''The Raven''—that seem to take on a different significance with each use.

Renaissance: The period in European history that marked the end of the Middle Ages. It began in Italy in the late fourteenth century. In broad terms, it is usually seen as spanning the fourteenth, fifteenth, and sixteenth centuries, although it did not reach Great Britain, for example, until the 1480s or so. The Renaissance saw an awakening in almost every sphere of human activity, especially science, philosophy, and the arts. The period is best defined by the emergence of a general philosophy that emphasized the importance of the intellect, the individual, and world affairs. It contrasts strongly with the medieval worldview, characterized by the dominant concerns of faith, the social collective, and spiritual salvation. Prominent writers during the Renaissance include Niccolo Machiavelli and Baldassare Castiglione in Italy, Miguel de Cervantes and Lope de Vega in Spain, Jean Froissart and Francois Rabelais in France, Sir Thomas More and Sir Philip Sidney in England, and Desiderius Erasmus in Holland.

Repartee: Conversation featuring snappy retorts and witticisms. Masters of *repartee* include Sydney Smith, Charles Lamb, and Oscar Wilde. An example is recorded in the meeting of ''Beau'' Nash and John Wesley: Nash said, ''I never make way for a fool,'' to which Wesley responded, ''Don't you? I always do,'' and stepped aside.

Resolution: The portion of a story following the climax, in which the conflict is resolved. The resolution of Jane Austen's *Northanger Abbey* is neatly summed up in the following sentence: ''Henry and Catherine were married, the bells rang and every body smiled.''

Restoration: See *Restoration Age*

Restoration Age: A period in English literature beginning with the crowning of Charles II in 1660 and running to about 1700. The era, which was characterized by a reaction against Puritanism, was the first great age of the comedy of manners. The finest literature of the era is typically witty and urbane, and often lewd. Prominent Restoration Age writers include William Congreve, Samuel Pepys, John Dryden, and John Milton.

Revenge Tragedy: A dramatic form popular during the Elizabethan Age, in which the protagonist, directed by the ghost of his murdered father or son, inflicts retaliation upon a powerful villain. Notable features of the revenge tragedy include violence, bizarre criminal acts, intrigue, insanity, a hesitant protagonist, and the use of soliloquy. Thomas Kyd's *Spanish Tragedy* is the first example of revenge tragedy in English, and William Shakespeare's *Hamlet* is perhaps the best. Extreme examples of revenge tragedy, such as John Webster's *The Duchess of Malfi,* are labeled "tragedies of blood." Also known as Tragedy of Blood.

Revista: The Spanish term for a vaudeville musical revue. Examples of *revistas* include Antonio Guzman Aguilera's *Mexico para los mexicanos,* Daniel Vanegas's *Maldito jazz,* and Don Catarino's *Whiskey, morfina y marihuana* and *El desterrado.*

Rhetoric: In literary criticism, this term denotes the art of ethical persuasion. In its strictest sense, rhetoric adheres to various principles developed since classical times for arranging facts and ideas in a clear, persuasive, appealing manner. The term is also used to refer to effective prose in general and theories of or methods for composing effective prose. Classical examples of rhetorics include *The Rhetoric of Aristotle,* Quintillian's *Institutio Oratoria,* and Cicero's *Ad Herennium.*

Rhetorical Question: A question intended to provoke thought, but not an expressed answer, in the reader. It is most commonly used in oratory and other persuasive genres. The following lines from Thomas Gray's "Elegy Written in a Country Churchyard" ask rhetorical questions: Can storied urn or animated bust Back to its mansion call the fleeting breath? Can Honour's voice provoke the silent dust, Or Flattery soothe the dull cold ear of Death?

Rhyme: When used as a noun in literary criticism, this term generally refers to a poem in which words sound identical or very similar and appear in parallel positions in two or more lines. Rhymes are classified into different types according to where they fall in a line or stanza or according to the degree of similarity they exhibit in their spellings and sounds. Some major types of rhyme are "masculine" rhyme, "feminine" rhyme, and "triple" rhyme. In a masculine rhyme, the rhyming sound falls in a single accented syllable, as with "heat" and "eat." Feminine rhyme is a rhyme of two syllables, one stressed and one unstressed, as with "merry" and "tarry." Triple rhyme matches the sound of the accented syllable and the two unaccented syllables that follow: "narrative" and "declarative." Robert Browning alternates feminine and masculine rhymes in his "Soliloquy of the Spanish Cloister": Gr-r-r—there go, my heart's abhorrence! Water your damned flower-pots, do! If hate killed men, Brother Lawrence, God's blood, would not mine kill you! What? Your myrtle-bush wants trimming? Oh, that rose has prior claims— Needs its leaden vase filled brimming? Hell dry you up with flames! Triple rhymes can be found in Thomas Hood's "Bridge of Sighs," George Gordon Byron's satirical verse, and Ogden Nash's comic poems.

Rhyme Royal: A stanza of seven lines composed in iambic pentameter and rhymed *ababbcc.* The name is said to be a tribute to King James I of Scotland, who made much use of the form in his poetry. Examples of rhyme royal include Geoffrey Chaucer's *The Parlement of Foules,* William Shakespeare's *The Rape of Lucrece,* William Morris's *The Early Paradise,* and John Masefield's *The Widow in the Bye Street.*

Rhyme Scheme: See *Rhyme*

Rhythm: A regular pattern of sound, time intervals, or events occurring in writing, most often and most discernably in poetry. Regular, reliable rhythm is known to be soothing to humans, while interrupted, unpredictable, or rapidly changing rhythm is disturbing. These effects are known to authors, who use them to produce a desired reaction in the reader. An example of a form of irregular rhythm is sprung rhythm poetry; quantitative verse, on the other hand, is very regular in its rhythm.

Rising Action: The part of a drama where the plot becomes increasingly complicated. Rising action leads up to the climax, or turning point, of a drama. The final "chase scene" of an action film is generally the rising action which culminates in the film's climax.

Rococo: A style of European architecture that flourished in the eighteenth century, especially in France. The most notable features of *rococo* are its extensive use of ornamentation and its themes of lightness, gaiety, and intimacy. In literary criticism, the term is often used disparagingly to refer to a decadent or over-ornamental style. Alexander Pope's "The Rape of the Lock" is an example of literary *rococo.*

Roman a clef: A French phrase meaning ''novel with a key.'' It refers to a narrative in which real persons are portrayed under fictitious names. Jack Kerouac, for example, portrayed various real-life beat generation figures under fictitious names in his *On the Road.*

Romance: A broad term, usually denoting a narrative with exotic, exaggerated, often idealized characters, scenes, and themes. Nathaniel Hawthorne called his *The House of the Seven Gables* and *The Marble Faun* romances in order to distinguish them from clearly realistic works.

Romantic Age: See *Romanticism*

Romanticism: This term has two widely accepted meanings. In historical criticism, it refers to a European intellectual and artistic movement of the late eighteenth and early nineteenth centuries that sought greater freedom of personal expression than that allowed by the strict rules of literary form and logic of the eighteenth-century neoclassicists. The Romantics preferred emotional and imaginative expression to rational analysis. They considered the individual to be at the center of all experience and so placed him or her at the center of their art. The Romantics believed that the creative imagination reveals nobler truths—unique feelings and attitudes—than those that could be discovered by logic or by scientific examination. Both the natural world and the state of childhood were important sources for revelations of ''eternal truths.'' ''Romanticism'' is also used as a general term to refer to a type of sensibility found in all periods of literary history and usually considered to be in opposition to the principles of classicism. In this sense, Romanticism signifies any work or philosophy in which the exotic or dreamlike figure strongly, or that is devoted to individualistic expression, self-analysis, or a pursuit of a higher realm of knowledge than can be discovered by human reason. Prominent Romantics include Jean-Jacques Rousseau, William Wordsworth, John Keats, Lord Byron, and Johann Wolfgang von Goethe.

Romantics: See *Romanticism*

Russian Symbolism: A Russian poetic movement, derived from French symbolism, that flourished between 1894 and 1910. While some Russian Symbolists continued in the French tradition, stressing aestheticism and the importance of suggestion above didactic intent, others saw their craft as a form of mystical worship, and themselves as mediators between the supernatural and the mundane. Russian symbolists include Aleksandr Blok, Vyacheslav Ivanovich Ivanov, Fyodor Sologub, Andrey Bely, Nikolay Gumilyov, and Vladimir Sergeyevich Solovyov.

S

Satire: A work that uses ridicule, humor, and wit to criticize and provoke change in human nature and institutions. There are two major types of satire: ''formal'' or ''direct'' satire speaks directly to the reader or to a character in the work; ''indirect'' satire relies upon the ridiculous behavior of its characters to make its point. Formal satire is further divided into two manners: the ''Horatian,'' which ridicules gently, and the ''Juvenalian,'' which derides its subjects harshly and bitterly. Voltaire's novella *Candide* is an indirect satire. Jonathan Swift's essay ''A Modest Proposal'' is a Juvenalian satire.

Scansion: The analysis or ''scanning'' of a poem to determine its meter and often its rhyme scheme. The most common system of scansion uses accents (slanted lines drawn above syllables) to show stressed syllables, breves (curved lines drawn above syllables) to show unstressed syllables, and vertical lines to separate each foot. In the first line of John Keats's *Endymion,* ''A thing of beauty is a joy forever:'' the word ''thing,'' the first syllable of ''beauty,'' the word ''joy,'' and the second syllable of ''forever'' are stressed, while the words ''A'' and ''of,'' the second syllable of ''beauty,'' the word ''a,'' and the first and third syllables of ''forever'' are unstressed. In the second line: ''Its loveliness increases; it will never'' a pair of vertical lines separate the foot ending with ''increases'' and the one beginning with ''it.''

Scene: A subdivision of an act of a drama, consisting of continuous action taking place at a single time and in a single location. The beginnings and endings of scenes may be indicated by clearing the stage of actors and props or by the entrances and exits of important characters. The first act of William Shakespeare's *Winter's Tale* is comprised of two scenes.

Science Fiction: A type of narrative about or based upon real or imagined scientific theories and technology. Science fiction is often peopled with alien creatures and set on other planets or in different dimensions. Karel Capek's *R.U.R.* is a major work of science fiction.

Second Person: See *Point of View*

Semiotics: The study of how literary forms and conventions affect the meaning of language. Semioticians include Ferdinand de Saussure, Charles Sanders Pierce, Claude Levi-Strauss, Jacques Lacan, Michel Foucault, Jacques Derrida, Roland Barthes, and Julia Kristeva.

Sestet: Any six-line poem or stanza. Examples of the sestet include the last six lines of the Petrarchan sonnet form, the stanza form of Robert Burns's "A Poet's Welcome to his love-begotten Daughter," and the sestina form in W. H. Auden's "Paysage Moralise."

Setting: The time, place, and culture in which the action of a narrative takes place. The elements of setting may include geographic location, characters' physical and mental environments, prevailing cultural attitudes, or the historical time in which the action takes place. Examples of settings include the romanticized Scotland in Sir Walter Scott's "Waverley" novels, the French provincial setting in Gustave Flaubert's *Madame Bovary,* the fictional Wessex country of Thomas Hardy's novels, and the small towns of southern Ontario in Alice Munro's short stories.

Shakespearean Sonnet: See *Sonnet*

Signifying Monkey: A popular trickster figure in black folklore, with hundreds of tales about this character documented since the 19th century. Henry Louis Gates Jr. examines the history of the signifying monkey in *The Signifying Monkey: Towards a Theory of Afro-American Literary Criticism,* published in 1988.

Simile: A comparison, usually using "like" or "as", of two essentially dissimilar things, as in "coffee as cold as ice" or "He sounded like a broken record." The title of Ernest Hemingway's "Hills Like White Elephants" contains a simile.

Slang: A type of informal verbal communication that is generally unacceptable for formal writing. Slang words and phrases are often colorful exaggerations used to emphasize the speaker's point; they may also be shortened versions of an often-used word or phrase. Examples of American slang from the 1990s include "yuppie" (an acronym for Young Urban Professional), "awesome" (for "excellent"), wired (for "nervous" or "excited"), and "chill out" (for relax).

Slant Rhyme: See *Consonance*

Slave Narrative: Autobiographical accounts of American slave life as told by escaped slaves. These works first appeared during the abolition movement of the 1830s through the 1850s. Olaudah Equiano's *The Interesting Narrative of Olaudah Equiano, or Gustavus Vassa, The African* and Harriet Ann Jacobs's *Incidents in the Life of a Slave Girl* are examples of the slave narrative.

Social Realism: See *Socialist Realism*

Socialist Realism: The Socialist Realism school of literary theory was proposed by Maxim Gorky and established as a dogma by the first Soviet Congress of Writers. It demanded adherence to a communist worldview in works of literature. Its doctrines required an objective viewpoint comprehensible to the working classes and themes of social struggle featuring strong proletarian heroes. A successful work of socialist realism is Nikolay Ostrovsky's *Kak zakalyalas stal* (*How the Steel Was Tempered*). Also known as Social Realism.

Soliloquy: A monologue in a drama used to give the audience information and to develop the speaker's character. It is typically a projection of the speaker's innermost thoughts. Usually delivered while the speaker is alone on stage, a soliloquy is intended to present an illusion of unspoken reflection. A celebrated soliloquy is Hamlet's "To be or not to be" speech in William Shakespeare's *Hamlet.*

Sonnet: A fourteen-line poem, usually composed in iambic pentameter, employing one of several rhyme schemes. There are three major types of sonnets, upon which all other variations of the form are based: the "Petrarchan" or "Italian" sonnet, the "Shakespearean" or "English" sonnet, and the "Spenserian" sonnet. A Petrarchan sonnet consists of an octave rhymed *abbaabba* and a "sestet" rhymed either *cdecde, cdccdc,* or *cdedce.* The octave poses a question or problem, relates a narrative, or puts forth a proposition; the sestet presents a solution to the problem, comments upon the narrative, or applies the proposition put forth in the octave. The Shakespearean sonnet is divided into three quatrains and a couplet rhymed *abab cdcd efef gg.* The couplet provides an epigrammatic comment on the narrative or problem put forth in the quatrains. The Spenserian sonnet uses three quatrains and a couplet like the Shakespearean, but links their three rhyme schemes in this way: *abab bcbc cdcd ee.* The Spenserian sonnet develops its theme in two parts like the Petrarchan, its final six lines resolving a problem, analyzing a narrative, or applying a proposition put forth in its first eight lines. Examples of sonnets can be found in Petrarch's *Canzoniere,* Edmund Spenser's *Amoretti,* Elizabeth Barrett

Browning's *Sonnets from the Portuguese,* Rainer Maria Rilke's *Sonnets to Orpheus,* and Adrienne Rich's poem ''The Insusceptibles.''

Spenserian Sonnet: See *Sonnet*

Spenserian Stanza: A nine-line stanza having eight verses in iambic pentameter, its ninth verse in iambic hexameter, and the rhyme scheme ababbcbcc. This stanza form was first used by Edmund Spenser in his allegorical poem *The Faerie Queene.*

Spondee: In poetry meter, a foot consisting of two long or stressed syllables occurring together. This form is quite rare in English verse, and is usually composed of two monosyllabic words. The first foot in the following line from Robert Burns's ''Green Grow the Rashes'' is an example of a spondee: Green grow the rashes, O

Sprung Rhythm: Versification using a specific number of accented syllables per line but disregarding the number of unaccented syllables that fall in each line, producing an irregular rhythm in the poem. Gerard Manley Hopkins, who coined the term ''sprung rhythm,'' is the most notable practitioner of this technique.

Stanza: A subdivision of a poem consisting of lines grouped together, often in recurring patterns of rhyme, line length, and meter. Stanzas may also serve as units of thought in a poem much like paragraphs in prose. Examples of stanza forms include the quatrain, *terza rima, ottava rima,* Spenserian, and the so-called *In Memoriam* stanza from Alfred, Lord Tennyson's poem by that title. The following is an example of the latter form: Love is and was my lord and king, And in his presence I attend To hear the tidings of my friend, Which every hour his couriers bring.

Stereotype: A stereotype was originally the name for a duplication made during the printing process; this led to its modern definition as a person or thing that is (or is assumed to be) the same as all others of its type. Common stereotypical characters include the absent-minded professor, the nagging wife, the troublemaking teenager, and the kind-hearted grandmother.

Stream of Consciousness: A narrative technique for rendering the inward experience of a character. This technique is designed to give the impression of an ever-changing series of thoughts, emotions, images, and memories in the spontaneous and seemingly illogical order that they occur in life. The textbook example of stream of consciousness is the last section of James Joyce's *Ulysses.*

Structuralism: A twentieth-century movement in literary criticism that examines how literary texts arrive at their meanings, rather than the meanings themselves. There are two major types of structuralist analysis: one examines the way patterns of linguistic structures unify a specific text and emphasize certain elements of that text, and the other interprets the way literary forms and conventions affect the meaning of language itself. Prominent structuralists include Michel Foucault, Roman Jakobson, and Roland Barthes.

Structure: The form taken by a piece of literature. The structure may be made obvious for ease of understanding, as in nonfiction works, or may obscured for artistic purposes, as in some poetry or seemingly ''unstructured'' prose. Examples of common literary structures include the plot of a narrative, the acts and scenes of a drama, and such poetic forms as the Shakespearean sonnet and the Pindaric ode.

Sturm und Drang: A German term meaning ''storm and stress.'' It refers to a German literary movement of the 1770s and 1780s that reacted against the order and rationalism of the enlightenment, focusing instead on the intense experience of extraordinary individuals. Highly romantic, works of this movement, such as Johann Wolfgang von Goethe's *Gotz von Berlichingen,* are typified by realism, rebelliousness, and intense emotionalism.

Style: A writer's distinctive manner of arranging words to suit his or her ideas and purpose in writing. The unique imprint of the author's personality upon his or her writing, style is the product of an author's way of arranging ideas and his or her use of diction, different sentence structures, rhythm, figures of speech, rhetorical principles, and other elements of composition. Styles may be classified according to period (Metaphysical, Augustan, Georgian), individual authors (Chaucerian, Miltonic, Jamesian), level (grand, middle, low, plain), or language (scientific, expository, poetic, journalistic).

Subject: The person, event, or theme at the center of a work of literature. A work may have one or more subjects of each type, with shorter works tending to have fewer and longer works tending to have more. The subjects of James Baldwin's novel *Go Tell It on the Mountain* include the themes of father-son relationships, religious conversion, black life, and sexuality. The subjects of Anne Frank's

Diary of a Young Girl include Anne and her family members as well as World War II, the Holocaust, and the themes of war, isolation, injustice, and racism.

Subjectivity: Writing that expresses the author's personal feelings about his subject, and which may or may not include factual information about the subject. Subjectivity is demonstrated in James Joyce's *Portrait of the Artist as a Young Man,* Samuel Butler's *The Way of All Flesh,* and Thomas Wolfe's *Look Homeward, Angel.*

Subplot: A secondary story in a narrative. A subplot may serve as a motivating or complicating force for the main plot of the work, or it may provide emphasis for, or relief from, the main plot. The conflict between the Capulets and the Montagues in William Shakespeare's *Romeo and Juliet* is an example of a subplot.

Surrealism: A term introduced to criticism by Guillaume Apollinaire and later adopted by Andre Breton. It refers to a French literary and artistic movement founded in the 1920s. The Surrealists sought to express unconscious thoughts and feelings in their works. The best-known technique used for achieving this aim was automatic writing—transcriptions of spontaneous outpourings from the unconscious. The Surrealists proposed to unify the contrary levels of conscious and unconscious, dream and reality, objectivity and subjectivity into a new level of "super-realism." Surrealism can be found in the poetry of Paul Eluard, Pierre Reverdy, and Louis Aragon, among others.

Suspense: A literary device in which the author maintains the audience's attention through the buildup of events, the outcome of which will soon be revealed. Suspense in William Shakespeare's *Hamlet* is sustained throughout by the question of whether or not the Prince will achieve what he has been instructed to do and of what he intends to do.

Syllogism: A method of presenting a logical argument. In its most basic form, the syllogism consists of a major premise, a minor premise, and a conclusion. An example of a syllogism is: Major premise: When it snows, the streets get wet. Minor premise: It is snowing. Conclusion: The streets are wet.

Symbol: Something that suggests or stands for something else without losing its original identity. In literature, symbols combine their literal meaning with the suggestion of an abstract concept. Literary symbols are of two types: those that carry complex associations of meaning no matter what their contexts, and those that derive their suggestive meaning from their functions in specific literary works. Examples of symbols are sunshine suggesting happiness, rain suggesting sorrow, and storm clouds suggesting despair.

Symbolism: This term has two widely accepted meanings. In historical criticism, it denotes an early modernist literary movement initiated in France during the nineteenth century that reacted against the prevailing standards of realism. Writers in this movement aimed to evoke, indirectly and symbolically, an order of being beyond the material world of the five senses. Poetic expression of personal emotion figured strongly in the movement, typically by means of a private set of symbols uniquely identifiable with the individual poet. The principal aim of the Symbolists was to express in words the highly complex feelings that grew out of everyday contact with the world. In a broader sense, the term "symbolism" refers to the use of one object to represent another. Early members of the Symbolist movement included the French authors Charles Baudelaire and Arthur Rimbaud; William Butler Yeats, James Joyce, and T. S. Eliot were influenced as the movement moved to Ireland, England, and the United States. Examples of the concept of symbolism include a flag that stands for a nation or movement, or an empty cupboard used to suggest hopelessness, poverty, and despair.

Symbolist: See *Symbolism*

Symbolist Movement: See *Symbolism*

Sympathetic Fallacy: See *Affective Fallacy*

T

Tale: A story told by a narrator with a simple plot and little character development. Tales are usually relatively short and often carry a simple message. Examples of tales can be found in the work of Rudyard Kipling, Somerset Maugham, Saki, Anton Chekhov, Guy de Maupassant, and Armistead Maupin.

Tall Tale: A humorous tale told in a straightforward, credible tone but relating absolutely impossible events or feats of the characters. Such tales were commonly told of frontier adventures during the settlement of the west in the United States. Tall tales have been spun around such legendary heroes as Mike Fink, Paul Bunyan, Davy Crockett, Johnny Appleseed, and Captain Stormalong as well as the real-life William F. Cody and Annie Oakley. Literary use of tall tales can be found in Washington Irving's *History of New York,* Mark Twain's *Life on the Mississippi,* and in the German R. F. Raspe's *Baron Munchausen's Narratives of His Marvellous Travels and Campaigns in Russia.*

Tanka: A form of Japanese poetry similar to *haiku.* A *tanka* is five lines long, with the lines containing five, seven, five, seven, and seven syllables respectively. Skilled *tanka* authors include Ishikawa Takuboku, Masaoka Shiki, Amy Lowell, and Adelaide Crapsey.

Teatro Grottesco: See *Theater of the Grotesque*

Terza Rima: A three-line stanza form in poetry in which the rhymes are made on the last word of each line in the following manner: the first and third lines of the first stanza, then the second line of the first stanza and the first and third lines of the second stanza, and so on with the middle line of any stanza rhyming with the first and third lines of the following stanza. An example of *terza rima* is Percy Bysshe Shelley's ''The Triumph of Love'': As in that trance of wondrous thought I lay This was the tenour of my waking dream. Methought I sate beside a public way Thick strewn with summer dust, and a great stream Of people there was hurrying to and fro Numerous as gnats upon the evening gleam,. . .

Tetrameter: See *Meter*

Textual Criticism: A branch of literary criticism that seeks to establish the authoritative text of a literary work. Textual critics typically compare all known manuscripts or printings of a single work in order to assess the meanings of differences and revisions. This procedure allows them to arrive at a definitive version that (supposedly) corresponds to the author's original intention. Textual criticism was applied during the Renaissance to salvage the classical texts of Greece and Rome, and modern works have been studied, for instance, to undo deliberate correction or censorship, as in the case of novels by Stephen Crane and Theodore Dreiser.

Theater of Cruelty: Term used to denote a group of theatrical techniques designed to eliminate the psychological and emotional distance between actors and audience. This concept, introduced in the 1930s in France, was intended to inspire a more intense theatrical experience than conventional theater allowed. The ''cruelty'' of this dramatic theory signified not sadism but heightened actor/audience involvement in the dramatic event. The theater of cruelty was theorized by Antonin Artaud in his *Le Theatre et son double* (*The Theatre and Its Double*), and also appears in the work of Jerzy Grotowski, Jean Genet, Jean Vilar, and Arthur Adamov, among others.

Theater of the Absurd: A post-World War II dramatic trend characterized by radical theatrical innovations. In works influenced by the Theater of the absurd, nontraditional, sometimes grotesque characterizations, plots, and stage sets reveal a meaningless universe in which human values are irrelevant. Existentialist themes of estrangement, absurdity, and futility link many of the works of this movement. The principal writers of the Theater of the Absurd are Samuel Beckett, Eugene Ionesco, Jean Genet, and Harold Pinter.

Theater of the Grotesque: An Italian theatrical movement characterized by plays written around the ironic and macabre aspects of daily life in the World War I era. Theater of the Grotesque was named after the play *The Mask and the Face* by Luigi Chiarelli, which was described as ''a grotesque in three acts.'' The movement influenced the work of Italian dramatist Luigi Pirandello, author of *Right You Are, If You Think You Are.* Also known as *Teatro Grottesco.*

Theme: The main point of a work of literature. The term is used interchangeably with thesis. The theme of William Shakespeare's *Othello*—jealousy—is a common one.

Thesis: A thesis is both an essay and the point argued in the essay. Thesis novels and thesis plays share the quality of containing a thesis which is supported through the action of the story. A master's thesis and a doctoral dissertation are two theses required of graduate students.

Thesis Play: See *Thesis*

Three Unities: See *Unities*

Tone: The author's attitude toward his or her audience may be deduced from the tone of the work. A formal tone may create distance or convey politeness, while an informal tone may encourage a friendly, intimate, or intrusive feeling in the reader. The author's attitude toward his or her subject matter may also be deduced from the tone of the words he or she uses in discussing it. The tone of John F. Kennedy's speech which included the appeal to ''ask not what your country can do for you'' was intended to instill feelings of camaraderie and national pride in listeners.

Tragedy: A drama in prose or poetry about a noble, courageous hero of excellent character who, because of some tragic character flaw or *hamartia*, brings ruin upon him- or herself. Tragedy treats its subjects in a dignified and serious manner, using poetic language to help evoke pity and fear and bring about catharsis, a purging of these emotions. The tragic form was practiced extensively by the ancient Greeks. In the Middle Ages, when classical works were virtually unknown, tragedy came to denote any works about the fall of persons from exalted to low conditions due to any reason: fate, vice, weakness, etc. According to the classical definition of tragedy, such works present the "pathetic"—that which evokes pity—rather than the tragic. The classical form of tragedy was revived in the sixteenth century; it flourished especially on the Elizabethan stage. In modern times, dramatists have attempted to adapt the form to the needs of modern society by drawing their heroes from the ranks of ordinary men and women and defining the nobility of these heroes in terms of spirit rather than exalted social standing. The greatest classical example of tragedy is Sophocles' *Oedipus Rex.* The "pathetic" derivation is exemplified in "The Monk's Tale" in Geoffrey Chaucer's *Canterbury Tales.* Notable works produced during the sixteenth century revival include William Shakespeare's *Hamlet, Othello,* and *King Lear.* Modern dramatists working in the tragic tradition include Henrik Ibsen, Arthur Miller, and Eugene O'Neill.

Tragedy of Blood: See *Revenge Tragedy*

Tragic Flaw: In a tragedy, the quality within the hero or heroine which leads to his or her downfall. Examples of the tragic flaw include Othello's jealousy and Hamlet's indecisiveness, although most great tragedies defy such simple interpretation.

Transcendentalism: An American philosophical and religious movement, based in New England from around 1835 until the Civil War. Transcendentalism was a form of American romanticism that had its roots abroad in the works of Thomas Carlyle, Samuel Coleridge, and Johann Wolfgang von Goethe. The Transcendentalists stressed the importance of intuition and subjective experience in communication with God. They rejected religious dogma and texts in favor of mysticism and scientific naturalism. They pursued truths that lie beyond the "colorless" realms perceived by reason and the senses and were active social reformers in public education, women's rights, and the abolition of slavery. Prominent members of the group include Ralph Waldo Emerson and Henry David Thoreau.

Trickster: A character or figure common in Native American and African literature who uses his ingenuity to defeat enemies and escape difficult situations. Tricksters are most often animals, such as the spider, hare, or coyote, although they may take the form of humans as well. Examples of trickster tales include Thomas King's *A Coyote Columbus Story,* Ashley F. Bryan's *The Dancing Granny* and Ishmael Reed's *The Last Days of Louisiana Red.*

Trimeter: See *Meter*

Triple Rhyme: See *Rhyme*

Trochee: See *Foot*

U

Understatement: See *Irony*

Unities: Strict rules of dramatic structure, formulated by Italian and French critics of the Renaissance and based loosely on the principles of drama discussed by Aristotle in his *Poetics.* Foremost among these rules were the three unities of action, time, and place that compelled a dramatist to: (1) construct a single plot with a beginning, middle, and end that details the causal relationships of action and character; (2) restrict the action to the events of a single day; and (3) limit the scene to a single place or city. The unities were observed faithfully by continental European writers until the Romantic Age, but they were never regularly observed in English drama. Modern dramatists are typically more concerned with a unity of impression or emotional effect than with any of the classical unities. The unities are observed in Pierre Corneille's tragedy *Polyeuctes* and Jean-Baptiste Racine's *Phedre.* Also known as Three Unities.

Urban Realism: A branch of realist writing that attempts to accurately reflect the often harsh facts of modern urban existence. Some works by Stephen Crane, Theodore Dreiser, Charles Dickens, Fyodor Dostoyevsky, Emile Zola, Abraham Cahan, and Henry Fuller feature urban realism. Modern examples include Claude Brown's *Manchild in the Promised Land* and Ron Milner's *What the Wine Sellers Buy.*

Utopia: A fictional perfect place, such as "paradise" or "heaven." Early literary utopias were included in Plato's *Republic* and Sir Thomas More's *Utopia,* while more modern utopias can be found in

Samuel Butler's *Erewhon,* Theodor Herzka's *A Visit to Freeland,* and H. G. Wells' *A Modern Utopia.*

Utopian: See *Utopia*

Utopianism: See *Utopia*

V

Verisimilitude: Literally, the appearance of truth. In literary criticism, the term refers to aspects of a work of literature that seem true to the reader. Verisimilitude is achieved in the work of Honore de Balzac, Gustave Flaubert, and Henry James, among other late nineteenth-century realist writers.

Vers de societe: See *Occasional Verse*

Vers libre: See *Free Verse*

Verse: A line of metered language, a line of a poem, or any work written in verse. The following line of verse is from the epic poem *Don Juan* by Lord Byron: ''My way is to begin with the beginning.''

Versification: The writing of verse. Versification may also refer to the meter, rhyme, and other mechanical components of a poem. Composition of a ''Roses are red, violets are blue'' poem to suit an occasion is a common form of versification practiced by students.

Victorian: Refers broadly to the reign of Queen Victoria of England (1837–1901) and to anything with qualities typical of that era. For example, the qualities of smug narrowmindedness, bourgeois materialism, faith in social progress, and priggish morality are often considered Victorian. This stereotype is contradicted by such dramatic intellectual developments as the theories of Charles Darwin, Karl Marx, and Sigmund Freud (which stirred strong debates in England) and the critical attitudes of serious Victorian writers like Charles Dickens and George Eliot. In literature, the Victorian Period was the great age of the English novel, and the latter part of the era saw the rise of movements such as decadence and symbolism. Works of Victorian literature include the poetry of Robert Browning and Alfred, Lord Tennyson, the criticism of Matthew Arnold and John Ruskin, and the novels of Emily Bronte, William Makepeace Thackeray, and Thomas Hardy. Also known as Victorian Age and Victorian Period.

Victorian Age: See *Victorian*

Victorian Period: See *Victorian*

W

Weltanschauung: A German term referring to a person's worldview or philosophy. Examples of *weltanschauung* include Thomas Hardy's view of the human being as the victim of fate, destiny, or impersonal forces and circumstances, and the disillusioned and laconic cynicism expressed by such poets of the 1930s as W. H. Auden, Sir Stephen Spender, and Sir William Empson.

Weltschmerz: A German term meaning ''world pain.'' It describes a sense of anguish about the nature of existence, usually associated with a melancholy, pessimistic attitude. *Weltschmerz* was expressed in England by George Gordon, Lord Byron in his *Manfred* and *Childe Harold's Pilgrimage,* in France by Viscount de Chateaubriand, Alfred de Vigny, and Alfred de Musset, in Russia by Aleksandr Pushkin and Mikhail Lermontov, in Poland by Juliusz Slowacki, and in America by Nathaniel Hawthorne.

Z

Zarzuela: A type of Spanish operetta. Writers of *zarzuelas* include Lope de Vega and Pedro Calderon.

Zeitgeist: A German term meaning ''spirit of the time.'' It refers to the moral and intellectual trends of a given era. Examples of *zeitgeist* include the preoccupation with the more morbid aspects of dying and death in some Jacobean literature, especially in the works of dramatists Cyril Tourneur and John Webster, and the decadence of the French Symbolists.

Cumulative Author/Title Index

N

O

P

R

S

Nationality/Ethnicity Index

Argentinian

Austrian

Bohemian (Czechoslovakian)

Canadian

Chilean

Subject/Theme Index

*Boldface terms appear as subheads in Themes section.